Legal Aspects of Privatisation:
A Comparative Study of European Implementations

Bulent Seven

ISBN: 1-58112-174-1

DISSERTATION.COM

USA • 2002

Legal Aspects of Privatisation: A Comparative Study of European Implementations

Copyright © 2001 Bulent Seven
All rights reserved.

Dissertation.com
USA • 2002

ISBN: 1-58112-174-1

www.dissertation.com/library/1121741a.htm

INTRODUCTION 1
I. General Remarks.. 1
II. Aims of the Study.. 4
III. Structure and Scope of the Thesis 5
Chapter 1: The Concept and its Origins 6
Chapter 2: The Limits of Privatisation: How far Can Privatisation Go? 6
Chapter-3: Legal and Institutional Framework for Privatisation.................. 7
Chapter-4: Legal Issues Arising during the Privatisation Transactions 7
General Conclusions... 7

CHAPTER I 8

THE CONCEPT AND ITS ORIGINS 8

I. IDEA and MEANING of PRIVATISATION 8
A. The Concept of Privatisation... 8
1. Idea 8
2. Definitions... 18
a. Different Names for Privatisation.. 19
b. Different Definitions of Privatisation 23
c. Analysis on non-divestiture measures.. 30
d. Definitions in Different Privatisation Laws 32
i. General.. 32
ii. Approaches... 34
e. Analysis.. 34
i. General.. 34
ii. Range and Structure of Privatisation 36
iii. Full Privatisation-Partial Privatisation.................................. 36
i. General.. 36
ii. Why Partial Privatisation?.. 37
f. Our Approach to Privatisation in this study 38
B. The scale of privatisation 40
C. Historical Background 43
1. Reasons for Nationalisation 46
2. Rethinking Nationalisation.. 47
3. The Emergence of Privatisation 48
4. Assessment... 50
D. Structure of the Process of Privatisation 53

II. WHY PRIVATISATION: THE FACTORS 54
A. Disappointing Performance of SOEs 55
B. Budget deficits and public finance crises 57
C. International obligations or aspirations 58
D. Changes in the international economy 60
E. Ideological debate on economic management 61
F. Important roles of certain SOEs... 61

III. PERFORMANCE and OWNERSHIP 62
   A. Introduction 62
   B. The Performance of Privatised Companies 64
      1. General 64
      2. Economic Literature and Empirical Studies 67
      3. Does Ownership Really Matter? 72
         a. General 72
         b. Difficulties 73
         c. Consumer aspects 75
   C. Conclusions 76

IV. The AIMS and OBJECTIVES of PRIVATISATION 78
   A. Introduction 78
      1. Some government's approaches to privatisation 82
      2. Conflicts among Privatisation Objectives and Policies 87
         a. Conflict among objectives 87
         b. Conflict in Privatisation Policies 88
      3. The Main Objective: Budgetary and Financial Improvements 88
      4. Political Considerations 89
   B. Analysis of the Goals of Privatisation 91

V. PRIVATISATION in the FORMER SOCIALIST COUNTRIES 92
   A. General View 92
      1. Establishing Market Economy 92
      2. Collapse of Communism 93
      3. Progress 94
   B. Differences between Eastern European and Western European Countries in the Privatisation Issue 95
      1. General 95
      2. Main Purpose 95
      3. Scope 96
      4. Weak Economy and Newly-Established Democracy 96
      5. Technical and Practical Facts 98
      6. Political facts 99
      7. Complex process 100
      8. Costs 100
      9. Slow trend 101
      10. Different methods and techniques 102
      11. Difference in Institutional Structure 102
   C. Similarities among Eastern European Privatisation Programmes 103
   D. Differences among Former Socialist Countries 105
   E. Analysis 107

VI. CONCLUSIONS 109

CHAPTER II 114

THE LIMITS OF PRIVATISATION: How Far Can Privatisation Go? 114

I. The NATURE of PUBLIC ENTERPRISES 114
A. General 114
B. Change the Role of the State 116
  1. Multiplication of SOEs 116
  2. Change of the role 117

II. CAN ALL SECTORS and ACTIVITIES be PRIVATISED? 117
A. General 117
B. Strategic sectors 118
  1. General 118
  2. Definition of the strategic industries 119
    a. General 119
    b. Golden (special) Shares 119
      i. General 119
      ii. Some other characteristics of this method 123
      iii. Analysis 124
C. Racial, Ethnic and Other Considerations 127
  1. General 127
  2. Domestic Groups 128
D. National sovereignty and economic security 128
E. Privatisation Laws and Some Government's Approaches 129
F. Analysis: What Services Should a Government Finance? 133
  1. General 133
  2. Possible Areas 134
  3. Conclusions 135
G. Constitutional Protection for SOEs 139
  1. The constitutional dimension 139
  2. Constitutional issues 141
    a. General 141
    b. Issues 141

III. POSSIBLE REACTIONS to PRIVATISATION: Criticism on Privatisation 143
A. General 143
B. Analysis 144

IV. REGULATION in the PRIVATISATION PROCESS 145
A. Introduction 145
B. Any Model for Regulation? 146
C. Why Regulation is Needed in Privatisation Process 148
  1. General Remarks 148
  2. Protection of Universal Service Obligations 149
D. Monitoring 153
E. Analysis on regulation 154

V. CONCLUSIONS 156

CHAPTER III 166

LEGAL AND INSTITUTIONAL FRAMEWORK FOR PRIVATISATION 166

I. OVERVIEW 166
- A. General 166
  - 1. Basic Requirements 166
  - 2. Structure of the Approach 167
    - a. General 167
    - b. Impediments 168
- B. Defining the Privatisation Policy 169
  - 1. General 169
  - 2. Transparency 170

II. INSTITUTIONAL MEASURES for PRIVATISATION 172
- A. General 172
- B. Different approaches and institutions 173
  - 1. General 173
  - 2. Institutional structure in former socialist countries 175
- C. Analysis 178

III. LEGAL FRAMEWORK for PRIVATISATION 180
- A. Market Friendly Legal Environment 180
- B. Property Law 181
- C. Future Expropriations 183
- D. Intellectual Property 183
- E. Price Liberalisation 184
- F. Business Legislation 184
  - 1. General 184
  - 2. Contract Law 185
  - 3. Company law 186
  - 4. Accounting and Auditing Legislation 187
  - 5. Liquidation and bankruptcy 187
  - 6. Transfer of Liabilities 188
- G. Environmental Legislation 189
- H. Tax Law and taxation 190
- I. Currency and Foreign Exchange 192
- J. Dispute Settlement 192

IV. PRIVATISATION LAW 193
- A. General 193
- B. Scope and Structure of the Privatisation Law 195
  - 1. General 195
  - 2. Main Factors in the Privatisation Law 197
  - 3. Analysis 200
- C. Case of Former Socialist Countries 201
- D. Functions of Privatisation Law 204
  - 1. General 204

2. Advantages and Disadvantages	204
a. Advantages	204
b. Disadvantages	205
3. Analysis	205
E. General or Specific Privatisation Law	206
1. General	206
2. General Legislation	206
a. General	206
b. Options in general legislation	207
3. Specific Legislation	208
V. LEGAL STAGES in the PRIVATISATION PROCESS	**209**
A. General	209
1. Deciding the Stages in Privatisation	209
2. Getting Ready for Privatisation	210
a. Initial Requirements and Considerations	210
b. Legal Changes in the Company	211
B. Stages	213
1. Decision to Privatise	213
a. General	213
b. Period between privatisation decision and actual privatisation	214
i. General	214
ii. Transitional and Interim Provisions	215
2. Identifying privatisation candidates	215
3. Feasibility study	216
a. General	216
b. Valuation of enterprises	216
i. General	216
ii. Principles in Valuation	219
c. Options for privatisation and timing	220
d. Minimising the risk of choosing poor candidates for privatisation	220
4. Privatisation Plan	221
a. General	221
b. Restructuring Discussions	222
i. General	222
ii. Debate on restructuring	222
iii. Different Restructuring Implementations	224
i. Former Socialist Countries	224
ii. Western Economies	224
iv. Analysis	224
c. Privatisation Technique	225
d. Selecting Buyers	225
i. General	225
ii. Legal Restrictions on Buyer Selection	226
i. Restitution of Nationalised Enterprises	226
ii. Exclusion of or Limitation on Public-Sector Participation	226
iii. Restrictions on Foreign Participation in the Privatisation Process	227
iv. Restrictions on certain individuals	227
v. Preferential Schemes	228
vi. Retaining Shares	229
5. Costs (Expenses) in the Privatisation Process	229

VI. LEGAL METHODS of PRIVATISATION 231
A. Appropriate Method 231
   1. General 231
   2. Legal Techniques 233
      a. General 233
      b. Scope of the Study 234
B. Restitution 234
   1. General 234
   2. Issues to be addressed in the restitution process 235
   3. Debate on restitution 237
      a. Advocates' Points: Justifying the past 237
      b. Opponents' Points: Detrimental to privatisation process 237
   4. Approaches 238
   5. Analysis 239
C. Public Offering 241
   1. General 241
   2. Certain objectives in Public Offering 242
   3. Legal and organisational procedure 243
      a. General 243
      b. Financial advisers and sales agents 244
      c. Internal steps in public offerings 244
      d. Prospectus, share instrument, and timing 245
   4. Conclusions 246
D. Trade Sale 248
   1. General 248
   2. Certain Goals in Trade Sale Method 248
   3. Procedure for Auction (Open Bidding) 249
      a. General 249
      b. Two-Part Open Bidding Procedure 250
   4. Negotiated sales 251
      a. General 251
      b. Direct negotiation 252
E. Management-Employee Buyout 253
   1. General 253
   2. Criticisms on this method 254
   3. Analysis on Management-Employee Buyouts 255
F. Free Distribution of Shares-Mass Privatisation (Voucher System) 256
   1. General 256
      a. Concept and structure 256
      b. Unique implementation 257
   2. Why Mass Privatisation? 258
   3. Designing the voucher scheme 260
   4. Debate and Discussion on Voucher system 262
      a. Criticisms 262
      b. Advantages 263
   5. Analysis on Voucher System 263
G. Liquidation 265
H. Financing 265
I. Allocation of privatisation proceeds 266

VII. CONCLUSIONS 268

CHAPTER IV 274

LEGAL ISSUES ARISING DURING THE PRIVATISATION TRANSACTIONS 274

I. COMPETITION LAW ISSUES 274
A. Competition in the Context of Privatisation 274
B. Privatisation and Monopolies 276
1. General 276
2. Breaking up Monopolies 276
   a. General 276
   b. Some measures 277
   c. Anti-trust provisions and regulations 278
      i. General 278
      ii. Appropriate Legislation 280
      iii. The Importance of Appropriate Legislation 281
      iv. Structure of Legislation 281
      v. Alternative and Interim Approaches and Provisions 283
      vi. Implementation bodies 284
   d. Non-discrimination against the Private Sector 285
      i. General 285
      ii. An essential policy 285
3. Is privatisation vital for competition? 286
4. Analysis 286
C. The Consumer Dimension 289
1. General 289
2. Impact of privatisation on consumers 289
   a. General 289
   b. Price Control 290
3. Consumers in the former socialist countries 291
4. Analysis 292
D. Conclusions 296

II. LABOUR LAW ISSUES DURING in PRIVATISATION 301
A. Impact of Privatisation on Labour 301
B. Privatisation and Labour Relations: Labour Market Consequences of Privatisation 303
1. Initial remarks 303
   a. Our approach 303
   b. A key issue: Restructuring the labour force 303
2. Labour Legislation 304
C. Opposition and Reaction of Employees 305
1. Public Sector Employees 305
2. Impact of Privatisation on Levels of Employment: Lay offs 305
   a. Expectations: Fear of Job Losses 305
   b. Practice 306
3. Other points 308
   a. General 308
   b. Pay and Social Conditions 309

D. Legal Measures and Approaches to Labour Issues 310
   1. Delaying and freezing employment reduction 310
      a. General 310
      b. Analysis 311
   2. Severance payment regulations and a system of early warning for mass lay-offs 311
      a. General 311
      b. Analysis 312
   3. Reintegration of laid-off workers 313
      a. General 313
      b. Analysis 313
   4. Restrictions in the privatisation legislation 314
      a. General 314
      b. Analysis 315
   5. Working with the Attrition Rate/Transfer of Employees to Other SOEs 315
      a. General 315
      b. Analysis 316
   6. Employee Participation in the Privatisation Process 316
      a. General 316
      b. Analysis 318
   7. Transfer of Employees to the new Company: The Acquire Rights Directive 77/187/EEC
....319
      a. General 319
      b. Analysis 320
   8. Overall Analysis on Legal Approaches 321
      a. General 321
      b. Special Provisions for Disabled Employees 324
E. Conclusions 325

III. FOREIGN INVESTMENT LEGISLATION ISSUES: LEGAL RESTRICTIONS ON FOREIGN INVESTMENT in the PRIVATISATION TRANSACTIONS 330
A. Foreign Investment in the Privatisation Process 330
   1. General 330
   2. Debate on Foreign Investment 331
      a. General 331
      b. Benefits of Foreign Investment in the Privatisation Process: Advantages 332
      c. Disadvantages 332
      d. A case: Turkish Dilemma 333
         i. General 333
         ii. Constitutional Court's Decisions 333
         iii. Amendment to the constitution 335
         iv. Provisions Governing Foreign Participation in the Privatisation Process 335
   3. Other issues: Certain demands from investors 337
      a. General 337
      b. Some examples 337
      c. Analysis 338
B. Types of Legal Restrictions on Foreign, Ownership in the Privatisation Process 338
   1. Requiring special permission or approval 338
   2. Prohibition of Participation in Certain Sectors 341
   3. Requiring Extra or Additional Conditions 341
   4. Creating Special Rights (Special Arrangements) 341
C. Conclusions 343

IV. PRIVATISATION and the EUROPEAN UNION 349
A. Introduction 349
B. Privatisation and the EU 350
1. Privatisation Transactions in EU: The Scale 350
2. Policy of European Union on Privatisation 351
a. General 351
b. The Treaty of Rome: "Neutral Policy" on the Type of Ownership 351
c. Certain documents and reports 351
d. Analysis 352
3. Privatisation and State Aid 354
a. General 354
b. European Commission's Approach 355
i. General 355
ii. Decisions of the commission 357
c. Services of general economic interest 360
C. Certain Factors and Developments Encouraging Member States to Privatise in the EU ... 361
1. General 361
2. Single European Act (SEA) 362
3. The Maastricht Treaty and European Monetary Union (EMU) 363
a. General 363
b. European Monetary Union (EMU) 364
D. EU Privatisation Policies and Candidate Countries 365
E. Conclusions 368

GENERAL CONCLUSION FOR THE THESIS 370

Future of Privatisation 377

Will Public Administration Disappear? 378

BIBLIOGRAPHY 379

Abbreviations

BiH: *Federation of Bosnia and Herzegovina*

BOO: *Build-Own-Operate*

BOT: *Build-Operate-Transfer*

BTO: *Build-Transfer-Operate*

EBRD: *International Monetary Fund European Bank for Reconstruction and Development*

EMU: *European Monetary Union*

EU: *European Union*

FID: *General Directorate of Foreign Investment (of Turkey)*

GAO: *United States General Accounting Office*

IMF: *International Monetary Fund*

NBER: *National Bureau of Economic Research (of the United States)*

OECD: *Organisation for Economic Co-operation and Development*

PSBR: *Public sector borrowing requirement*

SEA: *Single European Act*

SOE: *State Owned Enterprise*

USAID: *United States Agency for International Development*

USO: *Universal Service Obligations*

INTRODUCTION

I. General Remarks

Over the last decade there has been a widespread change of opinion about the role of state and private enterprises in promoting economic growth.[1] A strong consensus has emerged that the achievement of more dynamic economic growth requires a greater role for the private sector. Underlying this consensus is the belief that resources will be used more productively if they are transferred to the private sector. A key element of this new market orthodoxy has been the privatisation of state-owned enterprises (SOEs).[2]

The privatisation trend is widely thought to have started in the United Kingdom when the Conservative government came into the office after the elections of 1979. While the Thatcher government may not have been the first to launch a privatisation program, it is without question the most important historically. Since the launch of the United Kingdom privatisation program in the early 1980s, the privatisation wave has swept over the world, touching every continent, every political system, and every sector. Its emphasis has moved gradually from industrial, commercial, and financial sectors to the infrastructure sectors and then to municipal services; it has only recently started to reach education, health, and administrative activities like custom administration.[3] Apparently, privatisation trend has reached many areas like public

---

[1] A great deal of interest has been directed towards the degree of influence that public authorities should be allowed to exercise on industry. The role and influence of the state has changed in this respect over the time. (Maria Bengtsson, Agneta Marell and Andrew Baldwin, "Business-Induced Barriers in Explaining the Effects of Deregulation-Two Swedish Case Studies", Who Benefits from Privatisation?, Edited by: Moazzem Hossain, Justin Malbon, Routledge Studies in the Modern World Economy, London and New York, 1998, p.157)

[2] Lawrence Bouton, Mariusz A. Sumlinski, " IFC Discussion Paper Number 31-Trends in Private Investment in Developing Countries, Statistics for 1970-95," December 1996, February 1997 (revised)

[3] Pierre Guislain, *The Privatization Challenge: A Strategic, Legal, and Institutional Analysis of International Experience, (The Privatization Challenge)*, The World Bank, Washington DC, 1997, p.287; Michael Moran and Tony Prosser, "Introduction: Politics, Privatisation and Constitutions", Privatisation and Regulatory

transportation, public schools, national parks, waterworks, fire departments, infrastructure (including airports, bridges, and turnpikes), social security pensions, medical-care, the post office, public hospitals, and social services.[4]

Privatisation represents a reversal of the process of nationalisation begun early in this century.[5] And it is considered as one of the most effective means to both reduce state spending and to enforce market discipline in the provision of key services, thereby securing a more efficient allocation and use of resources.[6]

The trend of privatisation is now a worldwide phenomenon affecting both the traditional capitalist countries and the former socialist countries.[7] It is hard to find a country without a privatisation program, Malaysia has sold its National Lottery[8], Buenos Aires its zoo, the Czech Republic the guest house of the Communist Party;[9] Indonesia have hired a foreign firm to undertake their customs inspection.[10] In the US, in San Francisco, privatisation has been taking

---

Change in Europe, Edited by: Michael Moran and Tony Prosser, Open University Press, Buckingham & Philadelphia, 1994, p.9

[4] See: p. 40-42 about the scale of privatisation

[5] "The Evolution of Privatisation", Privatisation: Motives and Methods, US Energy Information Administration, URL: http://www.eia.doe.gov

[6] Derek Braddon and Deborah Foster, "An Inter-disciplinary Approach to the Analysis of Privatization and Marketization" Privatization: Social Science Themes and Perspectives, Edited By: Derek Braddon and Deborah Foster, Centre for Social and Economic Research, Faculty of Economics and Social Science, University of West England, Ashgate Publishing Limited, England & USA, 1996, p.292

In one comment (former) president of Chile stated that: " We seek today to resolve the age-old dilemmas of the state and the market, the private and public sectors. Both seek to be more effective and to offer higher quality services in their respective spheres". (Eduardo Frei, "The Chilean Perspective", President of Chile, web page of Center for International Private Enterprise, URL: http://www.cipe.org/)

[7] David Parker, "Nationalisation, Privatisation, and Agency Status within Government: Testing for the Importance of Ownership", (Nationalisation, Privatisation, and Agency), Privatisation and Regulation-A Review of the Issues, Edited by: Peter M. Jackson and Catherine Price, Longman Group Limited, 1994, p.149

[8] For the privatisation of Sports Toto Malaysia see: Ahmed Galal, Leroy Jones, Pankaj Tandon, Ingo Vogelsang, *Welfare Consequences of Selling Public Enterprises-An Empirical Analysis*, The International Bank for Reconstruction and Development, The World Bank, Published for the World Bank, Oxford University Press, New York, 1994, p.371-392; Winnie Goh and Jomo Sundram, "Privatisation in Malaysia-A Social and Economic Paradox", Who Benefits from Privatisation?, Edited by: Moazzem Hossain, Justin Malbon, Routledge Studies in the Modern World Economy, London and New York, 1998, p.186

[9] Sunita Kikeri, John Nellis, Mary Shirley, Outreach Nr. 3, Policy Views from the Country Economics Department, The World Bank, July 1992

[10] Anne O. Krueger, "Comment on Wiliam A. Niskanen, Guidelines Delineating the Private and the Government Sector", Privatisation-Symposium in Honor of Herbert Giersch, Edited By: Horst Siebert, Institut fur Weltwirtschaft an der Universitat Kiel, J.C.B. Mohr (Paul Siebeck), Tubingen, 1992, p.227

place in the case of golf courses;[11] privatisation of nuclear power plants is being discussed in some countries like Argentina.[12] Today there are even discussions to privatise the privatisation.[13]

Although a considerable amount of privatisation has now taken place, we are still in the early post-privatisation period. In other words, despite the widespread adoption of privatisation measures in recent years, the body of knowledge on the impact of privatisation is, generally, limited.[14] Therefore, in many cases, it is still too early to draw definitive lessons[15]; the process itself is going on.

It is also an extremely broad and diversified process embracing widely differing scenarios, concerning a huge range of enterprises operating in every sector of activity and of every possible size; moreover, it is implemented in countries with very different political, legal, economic and social systems, conditions, and objectives. This precludes a single approach applicable to all countries and all privatisation operations.[16]

As we will examine in the following pages[17] the weight of academic research is now decidedly in favour of the proposition that privately-owned firms are more efficient and more profitable than otherwise-comparable state-owned firms. Furthermore, the empirical evidence

---

[11] Lisa Snell, "Getting Greens in the Black: Golf-course Privatization Trends and Practices", Policy Study No. 260, Reason Public Policy Institute, URL: http://www.rppi.org/
[12] "Privatization Update", web page of Center for International Private Enterprise, URL: http://www.cipe.org/
[13] Roman Fryman and Andrzej Rapaczynski, "Evolution and Design in Eastern European Transition", Privatisation Process in Eastern Europe-Theoretical Foundations and Empirical Results, Edited by: Maria Baldassarri, Luigi Paganetto, Edmund S. Phelps, St. Martin's Press, 1993, p.91
[14] Paul Cook, "Privatisation in the United Kingdom-Policy and Performance", Privatisation in the European Union-Theory and Policy Perspectives, Edited by: David Parker, Routledge, London and New York, 1988, p. 236
Particularly in some former socialist countries like Russia, only limited information has been available concerning the results of the privatisation process. (John S. Earle, "Privatization in Russia Offers Lessons for Others", web page of Center for International Private Enterprise, URL: http://www.cipe.org/)
[15] "Is Privatization Succeeding in Central and Eastern Europe?", An Interview with Roman Frydman, by the Center for International Private Enterprise, Center for International Private Enterprise, web page of the World Bank, URL: http:/www.worldbank.org; Oleh Havrylyshyn, Donald McGettigan, "Privatization in Transition Countries: Lessons of the First Decade", IMF, Economic Issues No.18, Washington DC, August, 1999, p.4; Demetra Smith Nightingale, Nancy Pindus, "Privatization of Public Social Services: A Background Paper", October 15, 1997, Urban Institute, URL:http://www.urban.org/; Eytan Sheshinski and Luis Felipe López-Calva Privatisation and its Benefits: Theory and Practice, development Discussion Paper No: 698, Harvard Institute for International Development, Harvard University, April 1999, p.6, 29
[16] Guislain, (The Privatization Challenge), p.146, 147

that exists suggests that non-privatising reform measures, such as price deregulation and market liberalisation, can improve the efficiency of state owned enterprises (SOEs), but it also seems likely that these reforms would be even more effective if coupled with privatisation.

II. Aims of the Study

The main aims of this dissertation are as follows:

(a) To present a comprehensive analysis of the concept of privatisation its origins and limits,

(b) To identify the legal and institutional framework for privatisation in different European countries from a comparative perspective,

(c) To define and analyse particularly legal issues which arise during the privatisation transactions: e.g. labour law, competition law etc.

(d) To evaluate which features of the successful legal and organisational framework of privatisation have been successful so as to provide guidelines for those individuals and organisations participating in the privatisation exercises.

---

[17] See: p.62-78

III. Structure and Scope of the Thesis

A. Definition Issues

This study focuses upon the legal aspects of the privatisation. Since privatisation is a multi-faced concept[18], its legal aspects can only be understood after a detailed analysis of the wider concept of privatisation.

In our study, privatisation is defined as the divestiture and transfer of state owned enterprises (SOEs) or their assets from government or its agencies to private bodies which results in a private party or parties controlling the company, this is the definition.

Following this definition, in order to call an activity privatisation both ownership and control must be transferred to the private body. In principle, therefore; build-own-operate (BOO) or build-operate-transfer (BOT), build-transfer-operate (BTO) contracts, and other such private management arrangements, fall outside the scope of this study. Since privatisation has been defined in terms of the transfer of enterprise ownership from the public to private sector. Privatisation could be defined strictly to include only cases of the transfer of 100 per cent or at least a majority share of a public enterprise, or its assets, to private shareholders.

However, this thesis will examine private management arrangements (non-divestiture measures of privatisation) while we are dealing with the performance of privatised firms when the issue comes to the reforms and different measures taken by some countries for state owned enterprises (SOEs). Also in the second chapter we will deal with the non-divestiture measures of privatisation.

We should point out at the outset that in most cases, it is difficult to draw clear border line between legal and economical aspects of privatisation.[19]

---

[18] Paul Starr, "The Meaning of Privatisation", web page of University of Princeton, URL: http://princeton.edu/#starr/meaning.html

B. Structure of the Thesis

This dissertation is divided into four chapters and ends with a section of general conclusions.

Chapter 1: The Concept and its Origins

The first chapter presents a comprehensive analysis of the concept of privatisation and its origins. The analysis will include the definition, origin, scope, structure, reasons and goals of privatisation.

Differences in the privatisation pattern between former socialist countries and western economies will also be examined, as well some differences among former socialist countries as well. We will also look out the performance of the privatised firms.

Chapter 2: The Limits of Privatisation: How far Can Privatisation Go?

The limit of privatisation is a highly controversial issue. In the second chapter this thesis examines whether there are activities or enterprises which are quintessentially state activities and cannot under any circumstances be entrusted to private bodies. This examination will discuss the concept of *strategic* or *vital* sectors. In relation to this issue, we will deal with a basic question: What services or products should government produce?

It has even a feminist aspect, for this see: Susan H. Williams, "Globalization, Privatization, and a Feminist Public", web page of Indiana University, USA, URL: http://www.law.indiana.edu/glsj/vol4/no1/wilpgp.html

[19] For the economical aspects of privatisation see: John Vickers and George Yarrow, *Privatization: An Economic Analysis, (An Economic Analysis)* The Mit Press, England, 1988; Ray Rees, "Economic Aspects of Privatization in Britain", Privatization in Western Europe-Pressures, Problems and Paradoxes, Edited By: Vincent Wright, Pinter Publishers, Great Britain, 1994, p.44-56; Fuat M. Andic, "The Case for Privatisation: Some Methodological Issues", Privatisation and Deregulation in Global Perspective, Edited By: Dennis J. Gayle, and Jonathan N. Goodrich, Pinter Publishers, USA, 1990, p.35-48. For the theoretical perspectives on privatisation see: Dieter Bös, *Privatization-A Theoretical Treatment*, Clarendon Press, Oxford, 1991; Dieter Bös, Theoretical Perspectives on Privatisation: Some Outstanding Issues, Privatisation in the European Union, Theory and Policy Perspectives, Edited By: David Parker, London and New York, 1998, p.49-69. For the industrial perspectives of privatisation see: Jacques de Brandt, "Privatisation in an Industrial Policy Perspective-The Case of France", Privatisation in the European Union, Theory and Policy Perspectives, London and New York, 1998, p.88-100

Chapter-3: Legal and Institutional Framework for Privatisation

The third chapter provides a comparative study of the legal institutional framework for the privatisations. In this chapter, we deal with four main issues:

(i) What is the structure of the privatisation legislation in the country in question? Is there a general privatisation law or a specific law? (ii) What institutions are put in charge of privatisation process? (iii) What are the legal procedures in privatisation transactions? (iv) Is there any ideal legal institutional framework for the privatisation process?

Chapter-4: Legal Issues Arising during the Privatisation Transactions

In the fourth chapter we deal with some legal issues arising in the course of the privatisation process. This analysis begins with a study of the competition law issues related to privatisation also covers labour law issues, international law issues, and foreign investment legislation issues. In each subtitle we will set out the issue and in our analysis, we will seek to provide the possible legal solutions to each issue.

General Conclusions

In this part of the thesis, we will draw together the conclusions which have emerged from the thesis as a whole.

This section not only provides a summary of the work; it also raises points which need to be emphasised at this stage even if they have not figured prominently in the individual chapters.

CHAPTER I

THE CONCEPT and its ORIGINS

In this chapter we deal with the concept of privatisation and its origins. The analyses will include the definition, origin, scope, structure, reasons and goals of privatisation.

The differences in the privatisation trend between former socialist countries and western economies will also be examined. We will also look out the performance of the privatised firms.

I. IDEA and MEANING of PRIVATISATION

A. The Concept of Privatisation

1. Idea

Privatisation is a new concept. However we believe that the origin of the idea of privatisation is old as the origin of the debate on private versus public ownership. Therefore it can be traced back to ancient Greece.

Thus, Plato thought private ownership and private property[20] were evil and favoured communal ownership. In the Republic Plato states that:

"*...Once they [guardians] start acquiring their own lands, houses, and money, they will have become householders and farmers instead of guardians. From being the allies of the other citizens they will turn into hostile masters.*[21]*...I think, that if they are going to be true guardians*

---

[20] Private property means that individuals' rights to the use of (and income from) the resource they own are exclusive and transferable to others at whatever prices are mutually agreeable. [Louis de Alessi, "Property Rights and Privatization", Prospects for Privatization, Edited by: Steve H. Hanke, APS (Proceedings of The Academy of Political Science), Volume 36, Number 3, New York, 1987, p.26]

[21] Plato, *The Republic*, Edited by: G. R. F Ferrari, Translated by: Tom Griffith, Cambridge University Press, Cambridge, UK, 2000, p.110. Also see: p.262

they should not have private houses, or land, or property of any kind, but that they should receive their livelihood from other citizens as payment for their guardianship, and all make use of these resources jointly[22]*...It will stop them introducing private pleasures and pains along private property...since they have no private property apart from their own bodies, everything else being jointly owned..."*[23]

His student Aristotle, however, thought communal ownership was inefficient; that it allowed the lazy to take advantage of the industrious. According to Aristotle:

"...It is universal truth that men find difficulty in living together...especially when it comes to hold a property in common.[24]*...it is evidently better, therefore, that property should be subject to private ownership...and it is special business of the legislator to make the necessary arrangements to that end..."*[25] *And yet by reason of goodness, and in respect of use we must take account not only of the disadvantages from which those who hold property in common will be saved, but also the benefits they will lose*[26]*...No legislator could hope to build a state unless he distributed and divided its constituent parts into associations for common meals on the one hand, and on the other into clans and tribes; and it is therefore obvious that Plato's suggested legislation does nothing more original that forbid the guardians to cultivate the soil..."*[27]

From the ideological point of view, privatisation is considered to lead to smaller government, lower taxes, and less government intervention in public affairs.[28] In that context, we believe that among economic and social theories, liberal theory seems to be the closest system to

---

[22] Plato, p.163. Also see: p.252
[23] Plato, p.164
[24] Aristotle, *Aristotle's Politics and Athenian Constitution*, Edited and Translated by: John Warrington, J. M. Dent & Sons Ltd., London, 1959, p.34
[25] Aristotle, p.35
[26] Aristotle, p.36
[27] Aristotle, p.36, 37
[28] Carl E.Van Horn, "The Myths and Realities of Privatisation", Privatisation and Its Alternatives, Edited By: William T. Gormley, The University of Wisconsin Press, Wisconsin, USA, 1991, p.261, 262. For this also see: Ira W. Lieberman, "Privatisation: The Theme of the 1990s-An Overview", Columbia Journal of World Business,

the idea of privatisation; classical liberalism is often represented as a purely privatising ideology.[29]

Liberalism refers to the following concepts: (a) limited government, in order to protect human liberty and avoid totalitarian regimes; (b) the virtues of free-market economics, the preservation of economic liberty and initiative in conjunction with the right to private ownership; and, (c) a civil rather than a political society, in which the mediating institutions of the civil order are vibrant and provide the necessary constraints for the market and public morality.[30] Therefore in the classical liberal constitutional order[31], the activities of government, no matter how the

---

Focus Issue: Privatisation, Spring 1993, Volume XXVIII, No.1, p.13, 14; Paul, Starr "The New Life of the Liberal State: Privatisation and the Restructuring of State-Society Relations", http://www.princeton.edu/~starr/newstate.html

[29] Paul Starr, "The Meaning of Privatization", web page of University of Princeton, URL: http://www.princeton.edu/~starr/meaning.html; Elizabeth Martinez and Arnoldo Garcia, "What is "Neo-Liberalism"?, web page of Corporate Watch, URL: http://www.corpwatch.org/trac/corner/glob/neolib.html
Also see: Steve M. Hanke, "Privatization versus Nationalization", Prospects for Privatization, Edited by: Steve H. Hanke, APS (Proceedings of The Academy of Political Science), Volume 36, Number 3, New York, 1987, p.2; James Mitchell, "Britain: Privatisation as Myth", Privatisation and Deregulation in Canada and Britain-Proceedings of a Canada/United Kingdom Colloquium, Gleneagles, Scotland, Edited By: Jeremy Richardson, The Institute for Research on Public Policy, Dartmouth Publishing Company Limited, England, Canada, 1990, p.19; Janice A. Beecher, Twenty Myths About Privatisation, Alliance for Redesigning Government, National Academy of Public Administration, URL: http://www.alliance.napawash.org/; Demetra Smith Nightingale, Nancy Pindus, "Privatization of Public Social Services: A Background Paper", October 15, 1997, Urban Institute, URL: http://www.urban.org/; Jozef M. van Brabant, "Industrial Policy in Eastern Europe-Governing the Transition", (Industrial Policy in Eastern Europe), International Studies in Economics and Econometrics, Volume 31, Kluwer Academic Publishers, Dordrecht, The Netherlands, 1993, p.142-170; Ann Bernstein, "The State and the Market in Developing Countries", web page of Center for International Private Enterprise, URL: http://www.cipe.org/; Richard L. Lesher, "Democracy's Promise: Building a Modern Economy", web page of Center for International Private Enterprise, URL: http://www.cipe.org/; Jeremy J. Richardson, "The Politics and Practice of Privatisation in Britain", Privatization in Western Europe-Pressures, Problems and Paradoxes, Edited By: Vincent Wright, Pinter Publishers, Great Britain, 1994, p.64, 65; "The Privatisation Revolution, Adapted from Remarks by Lawrence W. Reed", Mackinac Center for Public Policy for The Future of American Business, A Shavano Institute for National Leadership Seminar, Indianapolis, Indiana, May 21, 1997, URL: http://www.privatisation.org

[30] Gregory M. A. Gronbacher, "The Philosophy of Classical Liberalism", web page of Acton Institute, URL: http://www.acton.org/cep/papers/classicallib.html; Amy H. Sturgis, "The Rise, Decline, and Reemergence of Classical Liberalism", The Locke Smith Institute, 1994, web page of Belmont University, URL: http://www.belmont.edu/lockesmith/essay.html

[31] Classical liberalism is a term used to describe a political philosophy commonly held in nineteenth-century England and France. Classical liberal political thought has its beginnings in John Locke. Classical liberalism can be divided into several schools or branches, but the common strain throughout revolves around a strident defence of liberty in all its dimensions–social, political, and economic. At the heart of liberalism is a passionate commitment to the pursuit of liberty. Liberty as a political theory translates into a wider social vision. Classical liberals advocate free markets, a vibrant array of non-governmental institutions (such as civic groups, schools, churches, the free press, etc.), and a minimum of tax-financed government services. Classical liberals firmly believe that government's first duty is to protect both persons and property from physical harm. They also emphasize the strict enforcement of contracts. Classical liberals, consider liberty to be the highest political value. Some examples of classical liberal thinkers include: John Locke, Frederic Bastiat, Adam Smith, David Hume, Francois de Voltaire, Adam Ferguson, Lord John Acton, Thomas Jefferson, John Stuart Mill, John Stuart Mill, Herbert Spencer, Henry David Thoreau, Frederic Bastiat, Alexis de Tocqueville and Friedrich Hayek [Gregory M. A. Gronbacher, "The

agents are selected, are functionally restricted to the parameters for social interaction. Governments, ideally, were to be constitutionally prohibited from direct action aimed at "carrying out" any of the several basic economic functions: (i) setting the scale of values, (ii) organizing production, and (iii) distributing the product. These functions were to be carried out beyond the conscious intent of any person or agency; they were performed through the operation of the decentralised actions of the many participants in the economic nexus, as coordinated by markets, and within a framework of "laws and institutions" that were appropriately maintained and enforced by government.[32]

One of the principles of the liberal theory of the state is that the state is not superior to other institutions and power of the state ought to be fragmented and distributed amongst many centres.[33] According to this theory, government produces more regulation and services than it should. Individual, families, and private organisations should provide regulation and services according to the demands of the private market. Publicly held assets should be sold to the highest

---

Philosophy of Classical Liberalism", web page of Acton Institute, URL: http://www.acton.org/cep/papers/classicallib.html; "Historical Roots of Libertarianism", web page of Libertarian Organisation, URL: http://www.libertarian.org/history.html; Yusuf Prögler, "Economic Neo-Liberalism: The Target of Popular Protests against Global Capitalism", web page of Muslimedia International, URL: http://www.muslimedia.com/archives/features00/capitalism.htm; Dean Russell, "Who is a Libertarian?", URL: http://www.daft.com/~rab/liberty/history/whois-1955.html; "A History of Libertarian", URL: http://www.daft.com/~rab/liberty/history/; John Ahrens, "The Classical Liberal Tradition in Contemporary US Politics", University of Hartford, September 1990, web page of John Ahrens, URL: http://ahrens.hanover.edu/ahrens/vita_mss/lib-con.html; "Introduction", URL: http://www.libertyguide.com/guide/guideintro.html; Elizabeth Martinez and Arnoldo Garcia, "What is "Neo-Liberalism"?, web page of Corporate Watch, URL: http://www.corpwatch.org/trac/corner/glob/neolib.html; "Theoretical Roots of Libertarianism", web page of Libertarian Organisation, URL: http://www.sbe.csuhayward.edu/~sbesc/frlect.html; Amy H. Sturgis, "The Rise, Decline and Reemergence of Classical Liberalism", web page of LockeSmith Institute, URL: http://www.belmont.edu/lockesmith/]
[32] James M. Buchanan, "Notes on the Liberal Constitution", the Cato Journal, Vol.14, No1, web page of Cato Institute, URL: http://www.cato.org/pubs/journal/cj14n1-1.html
This framework-maintenance role, properly assigned to government in the classical liberal order, included the protection of property and the enforcement of voluntary contracts, the effective guarantee of entry and exit into industries, trades, and professions, the insured openness of markets, internal and external, and the prevention of fraud in exchange. This framework role for government also was considered to include the establishment of a monetary standard, and in such fashion as to insure predictability in the value of the designated monetary unit. (James M. Buchanan, "Notes on the Liberal Constitution", the Cato Journal, Vol.14, No1, web page of Cato Institute, URL: http://www.cato.org/pubs/journal/cj14n1-1.html)
[33] L.J.M. Cooray, "The Australian Achievement: From Bondage To Freedom", URL: http://www.ourcivilisation.com/cooray/btof/chap162.htm

bidder. Once state owned enterprises are privatised potentially profit-making enterprises would then be managed more effectively and the public would pay less for the services received.[34]

Among liberal philosophers and economist Adam Smith developed the idea of privatising the King's assets in The Wealth of Nations.[35] Smith involved some paragraphs on the subject of privatisation. In the Wealth of Nations he first argued that argued that:

"In every great monarchy of Europe the sale of crown lands would produce a very large sum of money, which, if applied to the payment of public debts, would deliver from mortgage a much greater revenue than any which lands ever afforded to the crown...When the crown lands had become private property, they would, in the course of a few years, become well-improved and well-cultivated...the revenue which the crown derives from the duties and customs and excise, would necessarily increase with the revenue and consumption of the people..."[36]

Smith went on that:

"Princes have frequently engaged in many other mercantile projects...They have scarcely ever succeeded. The profusion with which the affairs of princes are always managed renders it almost impossible that they should. The agents of a prince regard the wealth of their master as inexhaustible; all are careless at what expense they transport his goods from one place to another...No two characters seem more inconsistent than those of a trader and sovereign."[37]

---

[34] E.Van Horn, p.13, 14
[35] Adam Smith, *An Inquiry into the Nature and Causes of the The Wealth of Nations*, John Lubbock's Hundred Books, Gorge Routledge and Sons Limited, London and New York, (no date), Book V, Chapter-II, Part-I, p. 650, Book V, Chapter-II, Part-I, p. 644, Book I, Chapter VI, p.38
[36] Smith, Book V, Chapter-II, Part-I, p. 650; web page of Adam Smith Institute, URL: http://www.adamsmith.org.uk/; Sheshinski and López-Calva, p.4
[37] Smith, Book V, Chapter-II, Part-I, p. 644

According to him:

"...As soon as the land of any country has all become private property, the landlords, like all other men, love to reap where they never sowed, and demand a rent even for its natural produce..."[38]

Other liberal economist and philosophers have involved in privatisation ideas. A more recent example is Hayek. In the "Constitutions of Liberty" Hayek argues that it would be necessary that any special advantages, including subsidies, which government gives to its own enterprises in any field, should also be made available to competing private agencies. Although Hayek does not support the idea of excluding all state owned enterprises from the system, he thinks that they ought to be kept in narrow limits. Hayek, however, more importantly states that:

"...it may become a real danger to liberty if too large a section of economic activity comes to the subject to the direct control of the state."[39]

Another relatively recent example is Milton Friedman. He strongly promoted the idea of privatisation. He states that: *"...I tell the people in Eastern Europe when I see them that I can tell them what to do in three words: privatise, privatise, privatise..."*[40]

Although liberal theory seems to be the closest system to the idea of privatisation; the connection between liberalism and privatisation should be made with caution and the following points need to be taken into account in evaluating this link:

(a) As we will examine in the following pages, privatisation and liberalisation are two different concepts. Liberalisation refers to the opening up of any industry to competitive

---

[38] Smith, Book I Chapter VI, p.38
[39] F.A. Hayek, *The Constitution of Liberty*, Routledge & Kegan Paul, London, 1960, p.224
Hayek provides a liberal approach to economic issues. He stresses that he is not conservative but liberal. (Hayek, *The Constitution of Liberty*, p.397-411)

pressures.[41] In other words, liberalisation refers to the abolition or relaxation of the monopoly powers of nationalised industries.[42] The opening up of public monopolies to private firms is a form of privatisation (in terms of broader understanding of privatisation)[43] that is also liberalising. However, it is entirely possible to privatise without liberalising, by selling shares of monopolies without significantly subjecting them to competitive forces. Conversely, it is also possible to liberalise without privatising-that is to introduce competition into public sector without transferring ownership.[44] Governments can also privatise and liberalise together by both selling state enterprises and deregulating entry into their markets.[45] Finally it is even possible to nationalise and liberalise at the same time, as the French socialists demonstrated in the early 1980s when they first nationalised banks and later liberalised financial markets.[46]

(b) Secondly the trend toward privatisation might be explained in straightforward political and ideological terms if these developments had been limited to liberal governments. However, privatisation have been adopted by Labour governments in Britain, New Zealand and Australia, by socialists in Spain, and by a variety of countries with more mixed regimes as

---

[40] Milton Friedman, "Economic Freedom, Human Freedom, Political Freedom", Delivered November 1, 1991, web page of The California State University, Hayward, School of Business & Economics, URL: http://www.sbe.csuhayward.edu/~sbesc/frlect.html

[41] Paul Starr, "The Limits of Privatization", (Limits of Privatization), Privatization and Deregulation in Global Perspective, Edited by: Dennis J. Gayle and Jonathan N. Goodrich, Pinter Publishers, London, 1990, p.110
Liberals favour competition. For example, Hayek states that: "...competition (is) superior... not only because it is in most circumstances the most efficient method known, but even more because it is the only method by which our activities can be adjusted to each other without coercive or arbitrary intervention of authority. (F.A. Hayek, *The Road to Serfdom*, George Routledge & Sons Ltd., Frome and London, 1944, p.27). "...competition operates as a discovery procedure not only by giving anyone who has the opportunity to exploit special circumstances the possibility to do so profitability, but also by conveying to the other parties the information that there is some such opportunity. It is by this conveying of information in coded form that the competitive efforts of the market game secure the utilisation of widely dispersed knowledge..." (F.A. Hayek, *Law, Legislation, and Liberty-Volume-2-The Mirage of Social Justice*, Routledge & Kegan Paul, London and Henley, 1976, p.117)

[42] Kate Ascher, *The Politics of Privatisation-Contracting out Public Services*, Macmillian Education Limited, Hong Kong, 1987, p.7

[43] See: p. 24-32

[44] Starr, (Limits of Privatization), p.110

[45] Paul Starr, "The New Life of the Liberal State: Privatisation and the Restructuring of State-Society Relations", URL: http://www.princeton.edu/~starr/newstate.html

[46] Paul Starr, "The Meaning of Privatization", web page of University of Princeton, URL: http://www.princeton.edu/~starr/meaning.html

different as those of Japan and Mexico.[47] Countries that not long ago were nationalising multinationals have been inviting new foreign investment and selling off pieces of the public sector. For example in France, any of the companies that the socialists nationalised were privatised by Chirac half a decade later; and perhaps more important, the French socialists on their return to power did not seek to renationalise the firms the conservatives sold. Socialists throughout Western Europe now seem more keen on liberalising markets than on seizing control of the means of production.[48]

Even communist countries have been taking some steps to reform their state owned enterprises. For example Cuba is also experimenting with privatisation. A law passed by the Cuban national assembly privatised most public housing in 1986.[49] In China in a case of a partial privatisation, workers in three state-owned factories in southern China have invested \$2.9 million to buy 30 percent of the enterprises. Some state owned homes are also being sold. There has been an explosion of private enterprises. Since 1978, privately owned restaurants and shops have been opening at four times the arte of their state counterparts.[50]

(c) Privatisation may ultimately result in less state control, but it first requires states to develop capacities they may not previously have had, such as the capacity to maintain the rule of law, instill confidence among investors, supervise contracts, and provide expedient

---

[47] See: p. 40-42
For example according to United Kingdom government one of the objectives of the Treasury is to promote privatisation. (Web page of UK Treasury, URL: http://www.hm-treasury.gov.uk/pub/html/econbf/eb09/4hmt.html; http://www.hm-treasury.gov.uk/drep/1996/s12.html; HM Treasury Departmental Report for 1995, web page of UK Treasury, URL: http://www.hm-treasury.gov.uk/drep/1995/index.html)

[48] Paul Starr, "The New Life of the Liberal State: Privatisation and the Restructuring of State-Society Relations", URL: http://www.princeton.edu/~starr/newstate.html

[49] Peter Young, "Privatization Around the World", (Privatization Around the World), Prospects for Privatization, Edited by: Steve H. Hanke, APS (Proceedings of The Academy of Political Science), Volume 36, Number 3, New York, 1987, p.194; María C. Werlau, "Update on Foreign Investment in Cuba: 1996-97", web page of University of Texas, URL: http://lanic.utexas.edu/

[50] Young, (Privatization Around the World), p.193
According to Young "...Throughout the world, socialism has been revealed as a failed ideology. It neither delivers the goods nor provides the motivation..."(p.205)
Also see: "Cautious Privatisation in China", web page of Le Monde Diplomatique, URL: http://www.monde-diplomatique.fr/en/1997/11/china; Justin Yifu Lin, Fang Cai and Zhou Li, "The Lessons of

administration of official rules and regulations.[51] Government will still need to regulate a delivered service even though it has been privatised, since privatising a service does not leave government without responsibilities. Issues of public safety, public health, and quality of service will arise.[52] Therefore privatisation does not mean public administration will disappear.[53]

2. Assessment

The origin of the idea of privatisation lies in the debate between private and public ownership. While Plato was describing private ownership "evil", Aristotle thought private ownership is superior to public ownership.

Worldwide privatisation has drawn support on both ideological and pragmatic grounds. Ideologically, privatisation has been associated with liberalism. Liberals favour privatisation because it reassigns decisions from government employees to private individuals, buttressing individual liberties and fostering a more democratic society.[54]

We believe that in the privatisation movement ideological factors and considerations have been important; the underlying impetus for privatisation however, has been practical[55]: For example one pragmatic approach was that the fact that SOEs were losing money and many of

---

China's Transition to a Market Economy", The Cato Journal, Volume 16, No: 2, web page of Cato Institute, URL: http://www.cato.org/pubs/journal/cj16n2-3.html

[51] Starr, Paul, "The New Life of the Liberal State: Privatisation and the Restructuring of State-Society Relations", URL: http://www.princeton.edu/~starr/newstate.html

[52] Robert W. Bailey, "Uses and Misuses of Privatization", Prospects for Privatization, Edited by: Steve H. Hanke, APS (Proceedings of The Academy of Political Science), Volume 36, Number 3, New York, 1987, p.148
Even liberals believe that regulation is needed. Thus according to Hayek; "...special regulations for the use of facilities provided by government for the public are undoubtedly necessary..."(F. A. Hayek, *Law Legislation and Liberty-Volume-3-the Political Order of a Free People*, Routledge & Kegan Paul, 1979, 48)

[53] See: p. 378

[54] de Alessi, p.24

[55] Therefore in many countries both liberal and socialist governments have adopted privatisation programmes. For example in Austria all major parties implemented privatisation programmes. (Delia Meth-Cohn and Wolfgang C. Müller, "Looking Reality in the Eye: The Politics of Privatization in Austria", Privatization in Western Europe-Pressures, Problems and Paradoxes, Edited By: Vincent Wright, Pinter Publishers, Great Britain, 1994, p.160-179)
Similarly, privatisation has not been an ideological issue in the Netherlands. [Rudy B. Andeweg, "Privatization in the Netherlands: The Results of a Decade", Privatization in Western Europe-Pressures, Problems and Paradoxes, Edited By: Vincent Wright, Pinter Publishers, Great Britain, 1994, p.199. Andeweg states that: "...Dutch privatisation (is) neo-corporatist/bureaucratic, not party political..."(p.199)]

them were in deep financial crisis; politicians found it easy to sell and get rid of SOEs instead of raising taxes.[56] In other words, it was realised that the political benefits of privatisation might exceed the economic benefits. Raising money from the sale of public assets was less politically damaging than raising taxes or cutting public spending and was regarded as a more acceptable means of reducing the public sector borrowing requirements.[57]

Similarly privatisation diverts claims away from the state. Just as employment is privatised, so too are consumer dissatisfactions privatised.[58] Furthermore worldwide both liberal and socialist governments have been implementing privatisation processes. Therefore privatisation represented a pragmatic solution to specific administrative, financial and economic problems.[59]

Finally the collapse of socialism in the 1980s and 1990s left liberalism the only player in the field. According to Fukuyama: "…liberal democracy may constitute the *end point of mankind's ideological evolution* and *the final form of human government*, and as such constituted the *end of history*".[60] It is arguable whether the liberal democracy is the end of the history but our analysis revealed that, since the launch of first privatisation efforts, the concept of privatisation has lost its ideological character and turned into a pragmatic economic and social instrument that almost all governments have adopted around the world. In other words privatisation can be considered as a "pragmatic" approach instead of an ideological approach, it cannot be attached purely to one ideology or system.

---

[56] Thus for example in the United Kingdom it became politic to regard privatisation receipts as a means by which tax cuts could be financed without the need to cut public expenditure. [Privatization in the United Kingdom, The Facts and Figures, (Compiled by Peter Curwen), [Privatization in the United Kingdom, Ernst & Young], Ernst & Young, 1994, p.19]
[57] Peter M. Jackson and Catherine Price, "Privatisation and Regulation: A Review of the Issues", Privatisation and Regulation-A Review of the Issues, Edited by: Peter M. Jackson and Catherine Price, Longman Group Limited, 1994, p.14
[58] Starr, Paul, "The New Life of the Liberal State: Privatisation and the Restructuring of State-Society Relations", URL: http://www.princeton.edu/~starr/newstate.html
[59] de Alessi, p.24
[60] Francis Fukuyama, *The End of History and the Last Man*, Penguin Books, England, 1992, p.xi

2. Definitions

Although privatisation programmes and policies are currently in progress the world over- in Europe, North America, Japan, and numerous developing and newly industrialised countries[61]- there is currently no widespread agreement on the nature of privatisation.[62]

The term "privatisation" can have different meanings depending on the starting point and approach in the definition. The starting point will vary depending upon the scope, range or structure of privatisation. Because each country has different social, political and economic differences and circumstances, the definition and even the understanding of the concept of privatisation may vary.[63]

Furthermore different governments and authors have different approaches therefore the definition and understanding from the concept of privatisation is not always the same.[64]

Finally since privatisation as a trend is an ongoing process, we can say that there is a "continuing evolution of the meaning of privatisation". In other words, since 1979 the meaning of the term privatisation has itself undergone a process of evolution.[65]

---

[61] Vickers and Yarrow, (An Economic Analysis), p.1

[62] Demetrius S. Iatridis, "A Global Approach to Privatization", Privatization in Central and Eastern Europe- Perspectives and Approaches, Edited by: Demetrius S. Iatridis and June Gary Hopps, Praeger Publishers, USA, 1998, p.4; "What is Privatisation", Privatisation Database, URL: http://privatisation.org

[63] Jonathan Bradley, "Privatisation in Central and Eastern Europe: Models and Ideologies", Privatisation: Social Science Themes and Perspectives, Edited By: Derek Braddon and Deborah Foster, Centre for Social and Economic Research, Faculty of Economics and Social Science, University of West England, Ashgate Publishing Limited, England & USA, 1996, p.262

[64] For one approach see: Charles Stampford, "Cautionary Reflections on the Privatisation Push", Edited by: Moazzem Hossain, Justin Malbon, Routledge Studies in the Modern World Economy, London and New York, 1998, p.250. Also see: Terence C. Daintith, "Legal Forms and Techniques of Privatisation, Legal Aspects of Privatisation, XXIst Colloquy on European Law, Budapest, 15-17 October 1991, Council of Europe Press, the Netherlands, 1993, p.60; Jozef M.van Brabant, "On the Economics of Property Rights and Privatisation in Transitional Economies", (Property Rights, Privatisation, Transitional Economies), Privatisation Policy and Performance-International Perspective, Edited By: Paul Cook, Colin Kirkpatrick, Prentice Hall, Harvester Wheatsheaf, Great Britain, 1995, p.70; Richard E. Ericson, "The Concept and Objectives of Privatisation", Privatisation in Eastern Europe: Legal, Economic, and Social Aspects, Parker School of Foreign and Comparative Law, Edited By: Hans Smit and Vratislav Pechota, the Netherlands, 1993, p.22

[65] Privatisation in the United Kingdom, Ernst & Young, 1994, p.xi

19

a. Different Names for Privatisation

Privatisation often goes by different names in different countries, often because privatisation has been deemed to be politically too contreversial term. Thus, for example, "capitalisation" in Bolivia[66], "peopleisation" in Sri Lanka and "equitisation" in Vietnam, all refer to "privatisation". Similarly, the terms "commercialisation" of Canadian National (the railway company) and "strategic consolidation" of Belgacom (the Belgian Telecommunications Company) were used to refer to the recent privatisation of these companies. In the Netherlands, on the other hand, the term privatisation has been used not only to designate what is classified here as such but also to describe the process of corporatisation an SOE that continues, however, to be owned by the state.[67]

Finally, in Slovenia[68] and Macedonia[69], the parliament and government seem to prefer the term "transformation" instead of "privatisation". The law on privatisation does not mention the term privatisation.[70]

---

[66] There are two main reasons for Bolivian government to choose the term "capitalisation" instead of the concept "privatisation".
(a) One reason, as mentioned above, is political and historical. In Bolivia privatisation is seen a continuation of imperialism and colonialism in a different form. According to some authors: " But Bolivians were suspicious of privatisation. They feared it meant a loss of jobs, a loss of the nation's patrimony, and a return to (probably Yankee) imperialism."(Andrew Ewing and Susan Goldmark, "Privatization by Capitalization The Case of Bolivia: A Popular Participation Recipe for Cash-Starved SOEs", Public Policy for Private Sector, The World Bank, FPD Note No.31, November 1994, p.1)
(b) On the other hand in Bolivia, the title of the law covers privatisation activities is "Capitalisation Law". The official body in charge of privatisation process is Ministry of Capitalisation. Finally in this country privatisation is carried out in an unusual way that involves a capital injection to the enterprise. (Ewing and Goldmark, p.1, 2, 3). The key elements capitalisation are as follows: (a) The government does not sell off the state-owned company but sets up "mixed capital corporations" to which a private partner contributes a 50% capital investment. (b) The private partner's contribution stays in that mixed capital corporations, increasing its value substantially. (c) The mixed capital corporations are transformed into a fully private company during this process, while the government's holding in the mixed capital corporations is contributed to a pension program that provides annuity income to Bolivian citizens over the age of 65. (José A. Valdez, Capitalization: Privatizing Bolivian Style", web page of the Center for International Enterprise", URL: http//www.cipe.org/; Henry Gibbon, Privatization in 1995 and Beyond, web page of Center for International Private Enterprise, URL: http//www.cipe.org/)
[67] Guislain, (The Privatization Challenge), p.12
[68] The Law on Transformation of the Ownership of Enterprises, 11 November 1992. (For the full text of this law see: URL: http://www.privatizationlink.com/
[69] Law on Transformation of Socially Owned Enterprises of Macedonia, (For the full text of Macedonian Privatisation law see the web page of Macedonian Privatisation Agency, URL: http//www.mpa.org.mk)

Some of the different names reflect real differences in processes.

To understand privatisation both in its narrow sense and as a broader regulatory issue, we point to some other terms[71]:

-*Corporatisation* relates to the shifting of enterprises and activities away from the generality of government to special incorporated (though still public) bodies, usually in the form of the public or statutory corporation or state-owned company.[72] In that case the government would own all the shares.[73] Particularly in former socialist countries corporatisation is one of the first steps of privatisation.[74]

-*Commercialisation* relates to the changes within the public agencies (departments of government or existing corporate bodies) that introduce commercial (market place) disciplines as

---

For Macedonian case one reason might be the fact that the Privatisation law (Law on Transformation of Socially Owned Enterprises) also designs non-divestiture options like leasing (Article 73-75). In that context the term "transformation" covers both divestiture and non-divestiture measures of privatisation.

[70] According to one author "privatisation" is unpopular in Eastern European countries because, it cynically referred to as privatizatsiya (in Russian), or "grabification" the giving away of government wealth to a few well-connected and unscrupulous businesspersons and bankers. (Iatridis, p.23)

In the case of Thailand, the term "privatisation" is used to denote all the methods used to develop the role of the private sector, including deregulation or facilitating market access with a view to increasing competition between enterprises in the public sector and those in the private sector. (Privatisation in Europe, Asia and Latin America, What Lessons can be Drawn?, Summary of the Presentations at the International Workshop on Privatisation Organised by the OECD in April 1994, Sao Paulo, URL: http://oecd.org)

[71] But even these terms are sometimes being used to refer privatisation. [David Donaldson and Dileep Wagle, Privatization: Principles and Practice (Executive Summary), International Finance Corporation, 1995, footnote: 1, p.6; Keith Hartley, "Contracting-out in Britain- Achievements and Problems", Privatisation and Deregulation in Canada and Britain-Proceedings of a Canada/United Kingdom Colloquium, Gleneagles, Scotland, Edited by: Jeremy Richardson, The Institute for Research on Public Policy, Dartmouth Publishing Company Limited, England, Canada, 1990, p.180; András Inotai, "Experience with Privatisation in East Central Europe", Privatisation-Symposium in Honor of Herbert Giersch, Edited By: Horst Siebert, Institut fur Weltwirtschaft an der Universitat Kiel, J.C.B. Mohr (Paul Siebeck), Tubingen, 1992, p.177, 180; Tony Prosser, *Nationalised Industries and Public Control-Legal, Constitutional and Political Issues, (Nationalised Industries)*, Basil Blackwell Ltd., 1986, UK & USA, p.76

For the relation between privatisation and the concepts of "freedom", "democracy", and "justice" see: Nicholas Buttle, "Privatisation and Ethichs", Privatization: Social Science Themes and Perspectives, Edited By: Derek Braddon and Deborah Foster, Centre for Social and Economic Research, Faculty of Economics and Social Science, University of West England, Ashgate Publishing Limited, England & USA, 1996, p.17-39

[72] Hendrik J. de Ru and Roger Wettenhall, " Progress, Benefits and Costs of Privatisation: An Introduction", National Review of Administrative Sciences, Volume 56, Number 1, March 1990, Symposium on the Progress, Benefits and Costs of Privatisation, p.9

[73] Bryan Carsberg, *Competition and Private Ownership: The New Orthodoxy, (Competition and Private Ownership)*, The Stamp Memorial Lecture, University of London, 29 November 1993, p.7

[74] For example in Albania, according to Law No.7926, dated 20.4.1995 " On Transformation of State-Owned Enterprises in Commercial Companies" every enterprise should be transformed in one or several anonymous

primary behavioural guidelines.[75] Furthermore, commercialisation of SOEs means their transformation into state-owned.[76]

Liberalisation: Two related processes, privatisation and liberalisation, need to be more carefully distinguished than they are in much discussion. In that context, liberalisation refers to the opening up of any industry to competitive pressures.[77] In other words, liberalisation refers to the abolition or relaxation of the monopoly powers of nationalised industries.[78] The opening up of public monopolies to private firms is a form of privatisation (in terms of broader understanding of privatisation) that is also liberalising. However, it is entirely possible to privatise without liberalising, as the Thatcher government has demonstrated by selling shares of monopolies like British Telecom and British Gas, without significantly subjecting them to competitive forces. Conversely, it is also possible to liberalise without privatising-that is to introduce competition into public sector without transferring ownership.[79]

In other words, privatisation and liberalisation-the opening up of competitive forces-are logically quite distinct concepts. Public ownership does not imply state monopoly, and private

---

or limited companies. (Web page of Economic Development Agency of Albanian Government, URL: http://www.aeda.gov.al/)

[75] de Ru and Wettenhall, p.9; Ted Kolderie, "The Two Different Concepts of Privatisation", Privatisation and Deregulation in Global Perspective, Edited By: Dennis J. Gayle and Jonathan N.Goodrich, Pinter Publishers, London, 1990, p.32, 33, 34; Bradley, p.263

However, incorrectly, some authors see commercialisation as a form of privatisation. (See: The Privatization Revolution, Adapted from Remarks by Lawrence W. Reed, Mackinac Center for Public Policy for The Future of American Business, A Shavano Institute for National Leadership Seminar, Indianapolis, Indiana, May 21, 1997, URL: http//www.privatisation.org

On the other hand some authors consider commercialisation as "the preliminary stage before privatisation". (Barbara Blaszczyk, Moving Ahead: Privatization in Poland", web page of Center for International Private Enterprise, URL: http://www.cipe.org/)

[76] Andrej Juris, "Economic Reform in Slovakia", web page of Center for International Private Enterprise, URL: http//www.cipe.org/

[77] Paul Starr, "The Limits of Privatization", (Limits of Privatization), Privatization and Deregulation in Global Perspective, Edited by: Dennis J. Gayle and Jonathan N. Goodrich, Pinter Publishers, London, 1990, p.110

[78] Kate Ascher, *The Politics of Privatisation-Contracting out Public Services*, Macmillian Education Limited, Hong Kong, 1987, p.7

[79] Starr, (Limits of Privatization), p.110

ownership does not entail competition. Nevertheless, privatisation and liberalisation are frequently intertwined in policy debate and public perception.[80]

Finally, we must point out that privatisation has been frequently part of a broader attempt to liberalise economies characterised by stagnation.[81]

Decentralisation: The concept of decentralisation is often used to describe the privatisation measures. However, decentralisation covers all kinds of activities aiming to reduce the size and power of the central government. The main goal of the decentralisation activities and measures is to spread the central government jurisdictions and responsibilities to the local authorities.

Decentralisation is particularly a current issue in countries that are governed by federal systems.[82]

Deregulation: the term deregulation is used in a great variety of ways, and is often confused with both privatisation and liberalisation.[83] The central issue in deregulation is whether the role of government should be reduced, with market forces replacing government regulation.[84] Deregulation is the removal of statutory restrictions on competition. It can take the form of encouraging or requiring public or private sector companies to compete with each other, or of

---

[80] Vickers and Yarrow, (An Economic Analysis), p.45; Peter Young, "The Lessons of Privatisation", web page of Center for International Private Enterprise, URL: http://www.cipe.org/; Joshua Aizenman, "Privatisation in Emerging Markets", Working Paper Series, National Bureau of Economic Research (NBER), Working Paper 6524, Cambridge, April 1998, URL: http://www.nber.org/papers/w6524. [According to Aizenman privatisation and liberalisation are complementary steps, reinforcing each other through the political process. (p.16)]

[81] Joshua Aizenman, "Privatisation in Emerging Markets", National Bureau of Economic Research, NBER Working Paper Series 6524, Cambridge, USA, p.1

[82] Teresa Ter-Minassian, "Decentralization and Macroeconomic Management", Western Hemisphere Department, International Monetary Fund (IMF) Working Paper, IMF, November 1997

[83] For example in one study deregulation and liberalisation have been used to refer the same meaning. [Privatization in the United Kingdom, Ernst & Young, 1994, p.39. "...Deregulation or liberalisation, simply means..."(p.39)]

[84] Tom Weyman-Jones, "Deregulation", Privatisation and Regulation-A Review of the Issues, Edited by: Peter M. Jackson and Catherine Price, Longman Group Limited, 1994, p.99

allowing new entrants to the markets of established nationalised industries and regulated monopolies.[85]

Denationalisation: This term refers to both the selling off of nationalised industries to the private sector and the gradual withdrawal from comprehensive public provision in the areas like education, health and social services.[86]

Restructuring: This concept is different from privatisation. Restructuring of an economy can be done in several ways: de-politicising management by giving managers more autonomy, increasing competition, improving financial discipline (including through bankruptcy and liquidation of loss-making firms), revamping state asset management systems, and privatising firms.[87] However it is possible to privatise a SOE without restructuring or it is possible to implement a restructuring programme in a SOE without privatising it. Therefore these two concepts are different and they should be clearly distinguished.

From the above survey we can see that privatisation can be defined as a wide variety processes.

b. Different Definitions of Privatisation

First privatisation can de defined very narrowly as a *permanent transfer of control*, as a consequence of a transfer of ownership right from a public to one or more private parties.[88] In

---

[85] Matthew Bishop and John Kay, *Does Privatisation Work?-Lessons from the United Kingdom, (Does Privatisation Work?),* Centre for Business Strategy Report Series, Centre for Business Strategy, London Business School, Hobbs the Printers of Southampton, 1988, p.9
[86] Ascher, p.6, 7
[87] Stijn Claessens, Simeon Djankov, and Gerhard Pohl, Ownership and Corporate Governance—Evidence from the Czech Republic", Public Policy for the Private Sector, The World Bank Group, Note No: 111, May 1997, p.1
[88] Iatridis, p.5, Guislain, (The Privatization Challenge), p.10; "Privatizing State-Owned Companies", The Prosperity Papers Series, Prosperity Paper Three, web page of Center for International Private Enterprise, URL: http://www.cipe.org/
The first definition of privatisation can, however, be qualified, in so far as the transfer may be total or merely partial. Holding all the shares in a firm is not the same as merely holding a majority or even a minority large enough to put a stop to certain decisions. Privatisation is thus partial if full ownership is not transferred. We will deal with this issue in the following pages. (For this also see: Stuart Butler, "Privatisation for Public Purposes",

this definition, the concept of privatisation refers to the transfer of shares of public assets to private buyers or takers, which tends to equate a change in the distribution of the enterprise's capital to a change in management.[89]

Secondly, a broader definition of privatisation include any measure that results in temporary transfer to the private sector of activities exercised until then by a public agency. Such definition therefore also covers the following non-divestiture concepts:[90]

-*Subcontracting (contracting out)*[91], whereby the public agency that previously conducted the activity now subcontracts its execution to a private party; this subcontracting can cover an entire public service, such a rubbish collection, or only part of the activity, such as water or electricity meter reading and billing, ambulance and other emergency services, health care, education, transport, road construction and maintenance, equipment repair, food services (catering), laundry, cleaning of streets, schools, and offices; etc.[92]

Privatisation and Its Alternatives, Edited By: William T. Gormley, The University of Wisconsin Press, USA, 1991, p.18)
Finally, it doesn't matter whether the assignment or transfer takes place by payment (sale) or some other means (free distribution of shares, for example). It also matters little whether the public agency is the state, the government, a ministry, a government department, a local authority, public sector, or any other public entity. The term divestiture is sometimes used restrictively to refer to a transfer of securities (SOE shares) or assets from the public sector to the private sector; a capital increase by an SOE may thus qualify as a privatisation though a divestiture.

[89] Olivier Bouin, "The Privatisation in Developing Countries: Reflections on a Panacea", Policy Brief No. 3, OECD Development Centre, OECD 1992

[90] Attila Harmany, "The Methods of Privatisation", (Methods), Privatisation in Eastern Europe: Legal, Economic, and Social Aspects, Parker School of Foreign and Comparative Law, Edited By: Hans Smith and Vratislav Pechota, the Netherlands, 1993, p.39; Privatisation in Europe, Asia and Latin America, What Lessons Can be Drawn?, Summary of the Presentations at the International Workshop on Privatisation Organised by the OECD in April 1994, Sao Paulo, URL: http://oecd.org; Guislain, (The Privatization Challenge), p.10; Morris Bornstein, "Privatisation in Central and Eastern Europe: Techniques, Policy Options and Economic Consequences", Privatisation Liberalisation and Destruction-Recreating the Market in Central and Eastern Europe, Edited By: Lasló Csaba, Dartmouth Publishing Company Limited, England & USA, 1994, p.234

[91] Sometimes it is referred to as "outsourcing". Outsourcing is, however, different from contracting out. Under outsourcing, a government entity remains fully responsible for the provision of affected services and maintains control over management decisions, while another entity operates the function or performs the service. This approach includes contracting out, the granting of franchises to private firms, and the use of volunteers to deliver public services. ["Terms Related to Privatization Activities and Processes", July 1997 GAO (General Accounting Office of USA), URL: http://www.privatisation.org/]

[92] In other words contracting out is the process by which activities, although remaining publicly organised and financed, are carried out by private sector companies. As mentioned above various services, generally within the local government and health authority sector, are put out to competitive tender. [Bishop and Kay, (Does Privatisation Work?), p.9]

25

Furthermore, contracting out can take many forms, including the relatively straightforward award of a contract for services, long-term arrangements that involve innovative private project financing, lease-back of capital equipment, or long-term per-unit fees for service. [93] The public agency or authority may contract with a private firm or individual, but it may also contract out to voluntary or co-operative organisations, or in some cases to other public sector agencies.[94]

Under contracting out arrangements, public authorities continue to bear direct responsibility both for the provision arrangements and for the quality of service provided although the work is actually carried out by the employees of private firms.[95]

In Britain contracting-out have been used in some areas, sectors and government departments like National Health Service (catering, cleaning, laundry etc.) area and defence sector (catering, cleaning, ground maintenance, re-fitting of warships, ferry services and even

---

According to the definition of General Accounting Office of USA: "Contracting out is the hiring of private-sector firms or non-profit organisations to provide goods or services for the government. Under this approach, the government remains the financier and has management and policy control over the type and quality of goods or services to be provided. Thus, the government can replace contractors that do not perform well." [Privatisation: Lessons Learned by State and Local Governments United States General Accounting Office (GAO) Report to the Chairman, [General Accounting Office], House Republican Task Force on Privatisation, March 1997, United States General Accounting Office Washington, D.C. 20548 General Government Division, March 14, 1997, p.1, 44, URL: http://www.privatisation.org/]

Also see: Guislain, (The Privatization Challenge), p.10; Philip Keefer, "Contracting out-An Opportunity for Public Sector Reform and Private Sector Development in Transition Economies", The World Bank, July 1998, p.2

There are some other activities that can be added to the list: Accountancy and architectural services, careers advice, computer and data processing services, housing valuation and sales, fire protection, and social welfare services such as child care, military procurement. (Hartley, p.178). Also contracting out of prison management (and construction) has become widespread in the United States. (Keefer, p.9) Contracting out has been used in many countries in Europe. For example this method was used in Sweden. (Jan-Erik Lane, "Sweden-Privatization and Deregulation", Privatization in Western Europe-Pressures, Problems and Paradoxes, Edited By: Vincent Wright, Pinter Publishers, Great Britain, 1994, p.195)

Finally we must point out that in some cases, particularly in order to reduce the costs of bidding, a certain number of public agencies may create a pool and a single arrangement or contract can be auctioned. (For this see: Michael Klein, "Infrastructure Concessions-To Auction or Not to Auction?", Public Policy for the Private Sector, Note No: 159, The World Bank, November 1998, p.1)

[93] "Harnessing the Market: The Opportunities and Challenges of Privatisation", Department of Energy of USA-Privatisation Home Page, URL: http://www.osti.gov

In the U.S., the term has often been broadly applied to the contracting out of the management of public schools, prisons, airports, sanitation services, and a variety of other government-owned institutions, especially at the state and local levels. (Demetra Smith Nightingale, Nancy Pindus, "Privatization of Public Social Services: A Background Paper", October 15, 1997, Urban Institute, URL: http://www.urban.org/. Also see: URL: http://www.encyclopedia.com)

[94] Ascher, p.8

security guarding), home office (prison escort services, security services in the Treasury), Inland Revenue (cleaning), Metropolitan Police (vehicle wheel-clamping and the removal and storage of illegally parked vehicles).[96]

Management contracts: These contracts are agreements between government and a private company, in which, government pays a fee to the private company for managing the SOE. These contracts are common in hotels, airlines, and agriculture. Management contracts are usually less politically contentious than sales. They avoid the risk of asset concentration, and can enhance productivity. Governments nonetheless tend to prefer sales for a number of reasons. Typically, contractors do not assume risk; operating losses must be borne by the owner (the state) even though it has relinquished day-to-day control of the operation. Many standard management contracts are flat fee for service arrangements, payable regardless of profits, which provide little incentive to improve efficiency. Further, management contracts are time-consuming to develop and can be expensive to implement. Unless proper legal safeguards are developed, and enforced by monitoring, there is a risk that the contractor may run down the assets. Another drawback is that few management contractors provide adequate training for local counterparts. These risks can be reduced with properly drawn-up contracts, but that requires strengthening government's capacity to negotiate, monitor and enforce contractual obligations.[97]

Under the *franchising* contract, the government grants a concession or privilege to a private sector entity to conduct business in a particular market or geographical area--for example, operating concession stands, hotels, and other services provided in certain national

---

[95] Ascher, p.7
[96] Hartley, p.178, 179
For the implementation of contracting out in the United Kingdom see: Ceri Thomas, "Contracting-Out: Managerial Strategy or Political Dogma", Privatisation in the United Kingdom, Edited By: V.V. Ramanadham, Routledge, London and New York, 1988, p.153-170.
[97] *Privatization: The Lessons of Experience, (The Lessons of Experience)*, Country Economics Department, The World Bank, (no date), p.25-26

parks. The government may regulate the service level or price, but users of the service pay the provider directly.[98]

With the recently increasing interest in private participation in infrastructure, franchising has taken root in power, solid waste, telecommunications, and water enterprises in developing countries as diverse as China, Guinea, Hungary, and Mexico.[99] In the United Kingdom franchise schemes have been applied to passenger rail.[100]

Leases (or affermage) overcome some of the drawbacks to management contracts. In leases, the private party, which pays the government a fee to use the assets, assumes the commercial risk of operation and maintenance, and thus has greater incentives (and obligations) to reduce costs and maintain the long-term value of the assets. And fees are usually linked to performance and revenues.[101] In other words in the lease-and- operate contract private contractor is responsible at its own risk for provision of the service, including operating and maintaining the infrastructure, typically against payment of a lease fee.[102] Furthermore, if the lease includes an option to buy, however the operation could be regarded as a divestiture.[103]

Concessions: In that group there are some arrangements. In BOT contracts (build-operate-transfer) the private contractor is also responsible for building and financing new investments. At the end of the concession term, the sector assets are returned to the state (or

---

[98] "Terms Related to Privatization Activities and Processes", July 1997 GAO (General Accounting Office of USA), URL: http://www.privatisation.org/

[99] Antony W. Dnes, "Franchising and Privatisation", Public Policy for the Private sector, The World Bank, Note No: 40, March 1995, p.1; "Types and Techniques of Privatization", Privatization Database, URL: http://www.privatization.org

[100] Dnes, p.3, 4

[101] The Lessons of Experience, p.25-26
Lease arrangements have been widely used in Africa, particularly in sectors where it is difficult to attract private investors. (p.26) [Privatizing State-Owned Companies", The Prosperity Papers Series, Prosperity Paper Three, web page of Center for International Private Enterprise, URL: http//www.cipe.org/]

[102] Pierre Guislain and Michel Kerf, "Concessions-The Way to Privatise Infrastructure Sector Monopolies", Public Policy for the Private Sector, The World Bank, Note no 59, October 1995, p.1

[103] Guislain, (Privatization Challenge), p.10

municipality).[104] In other words, with *Build-Operate-Transfer* (BOT) arrangements, the private sector designs, finances, builds, and operates the facility over the life of the contract. At the end of this period, ownership reverts to the government.[105]

BOO *(build-own-operate)* is a similar scheme but does not involve transfer of the assets. [106] With Build-Own-Operate (BOO) arrangements, the private sector retains permanent ownership and operates the facility on contract. [107]

A variation of BOO and BOT, is the *Build-Transfer-Operate* (BTO) model, under which title transfers to the government at the time construction is completed. [108]

Finally in *"universal service obligations"* (USO) contracts, require the private company in charge of providing the service to give access to all groups in the area of the concession, regardless the level of income. In the case of USO, the contract must also specify pricing schemes (possibility of cross-subsidies) and mechanisms for public subsidies when they are necessary.[109]

Concessions often used for the privatisation of infrastructure sectors with monopolistic characteristics[110]. Concession*s* is different from leases[111], in these kinds of contracts, the holder has responsibility for capital expenditures and investments. Although concessions are more desirable, they are less feasible then leases. This is so because private financing tends to be weak in comparison to the size of the investment, particularly in sectors or countries where the political and economical risks are seen to be high. In such instances, the government might have

---

[104] Guislain and Kerf, p.1
[105] "Types and Techniques of Privatization", Privatization Database, URL: http://www.privatization.org
In the case of BOT schemes, conditions under which the assets will be transferred either to the public entity of to another private investor once the concessions is over have to be spelled out in the contract. (Sheshinski and López-Calva, p.23)
[106] Guislain and Kerf, p.1
[107] "Types and Techniques of Privatization", Privatization Database, URL: http://www.privatization.org
[108] "Types and Techniques of Privatization", Privatization Database, URL: http://www.privatization.org
[109] Sheshinski and López-Calva, p.23, 24. Also see: p.149-153
[110] Guislain, (Privatization Challenge), p.10

to assume responsibility for planning and investment.[112] However leases, BOTs, and BOOs are generally granted for fixed periods.[113]

Although the responsibility of the private sector under a concession always includes the operation and maintenance of the system or facilities and the supply of the infrastructure service, it may or may not include the design, construction, and financing of the new infrastructure.[114] The legal status of assets built and financed by the private operator may also vary.[115]

---

[111] However some authors consider leases as a "concession-type arrangement". (Guislain and Kerf, 1-4)
[112]: Guislain and Kerf, p. 1-4
[113] Guislain and Kerf, p.1
[114] Guislain, and Michel, p.2
[115] Guislain, and Michel, p.2

Table 1

Supply and civil works contracts
Technical Assistance Contracts
Sub-contracting
Management Contracts (MC)
Performance Based MCs
Leasing (affermage)
BOT and concessions
BOO
Divestiture
Source: [Guislain & Kerf, (Concessions, p.1) & (Privatisation, p.12]

c. Analysis on non-divestiture measures

Contracting out, private management arrangements which includes, concessions, management contracts, leases and concession arrangements (BOTs, BOOs etc.) are particularly useful and can help facilitate later sale in activities where it is difficult to attract private investors and in low income countries where: (i) capital markets and domestic private sectors are weak; (ii) an unfavourable policy framework makes private investors reluctant to take on ownership of large assets in need of modernisation (railways, water, power); (iii) where capacity to regulate is poor;[116] or (iv) it is very difficult to introduce competition.[117]

Because concession-type agreements can be made as specific as required, they are well suited to situations in which more general and vaguely defined regulatory approaches would deter investors. And they can be tailored to allocate risks in a variety of ways to give investors the comfort they need to venture their capital in specific countries and markets.[118]

The flexibility of concession-type agreements is clearly one of its main strengths, but it can also be perplexing. Designing a scheme that strikes the right balance between the interests of the investors, the consumers, and the public authorities and that fits the conditions of the sector and the country concerned is pivotal. It requires a clear identification of the objectives and of the tradeoffs that must be taken into account to achieve them. Blueprints and model contracts can rarely be transposed from one country and sector to another.[119]

In conclusion non-divestiture options are likely to work best when they are a step toward full privatisation.[120] Furthermore, privatising management usually does not bring the increased investment that can be a major accomplishment of ownership change.[121]

---

[116] The Lessons of Experience, p.25-26
We must also point out that, when the specific period ends or if special circumstances exist (for example if the private contractor breaches the agreement) government or the public agency may re-auction the private management arrangements. (Michael Klein, "Rebidding for Concessions", Public Policy for the Private Sector, Note No: 161, The World Bank, November 1998)
[117] Guislain and Kerf, p.4, footnote, 1
[118] Guislain and Kerf, p.4
[119] Guislain and Kerf, p.4
[120] Macedonian Privatisation law states that the enterprise may conclude an agreement for leasing of a part of the assets of the enterprise. However according to the article this can be applied only "for a limited time exceeding 7 years " (Article 73/1, 74/2). Furthermore Macedonian Privatisation law provides two important principles:
(a) After the appraisal of the value of the assets which are being leased has been completed, the enterprise shall carry out the procedure for collecting offers, through public auction. (Article 73/2)
(b) The Leasing Agreement shall include a buying arrangement (buy-out clause) for the assets being leased, where besides the payment for leasing, purchase of the assets shall be included. (Article 74/1)
As a conclusion, Macedonian privatisation Law designed "leasing" as a step toward and lead to full privatisation [See also article 75 which designs the buying out arrangement and other details in the leasing contracts. (For the full text of Macedonian Privatisation law see the web page of Macedonian Privatisation Agency, URL: http//www.mpa.org.mk)]

Finally, the term privatisation can have an even wider connotation, to include the privatisation not just of enterprises and sectors but also of an entire economy. [122] In other words, in the broadest sense, it is often applied as a cover-all term to refer to whole range of actions designed to subject administrative activity to the disciplines.[123]

In that context the wider connotation includes all other definitions and some other activities such as: (a) the cessation of state controls over the private provision of goods and services, generally referred to as a process of deregulation, (b) the imposition of user charges and fees (for example on prescriptions) in respect of services previously supplied at zero cost to their consumers.[124]

d. Definitions in Different Privatisation Laws

i. General

If a privatisation law exists, in most cases the law provides a definition. And, from the legal point of view, privatisation also means what the privatisation law states.

Similarly, Lithuanian Privatisation law states that one of the methods of privatisation is "lease with the option to purchase" [Article 13/-5, Law on the Privatisation of State-Owned and Municipal Property, 4 November 1997 No. VIII-480, Vilnius, web page of Lithuanian State Property Fund, URL: http://www. http://www.vtf.lt/en/frame22.html]

[121] If the circumstances we mentioned above exist, non-divestiture options may bring significance positive changes to the economy. For example, according to an author a growing volume of evidence showing that contacting out with, a competitive tendering, results in substantial cost savings with estimates usually ranging from 20 percent to 30 percent. (The British government has claimed that privatisation has resulted in higher productivity and profitability. (Hartley, p.190). However, Hartley points out the difficulties and different methods of measuring these kinds of results. (p.190).

Finally we must point out that, non-divestiture measures can also be applied in some areas. For example BOT can be used in the privatisation of roads. Since state cannot always afford to build new roads, private investors may build and operate some roads under the BOT contracts. However, regulation is needed in order to protect consumers. In some countries like Turkey, motorists pay a fee when they use specific motorways or routes. [For privatisation of roads see: Martin Ball, "Liberate the Roads-The Benefits That Will Come from Road Privatisation", URL: http://www.libertarian.org/]

[122] Guislain, (The Privatization Challenge), p.11

[123] de Ru and Wettenhall, p.6; "The Privatization Revolution", Adapted from Remarks by Lawrence W. Reed, Mackinac Center for Public Policy for The Future of American Business, A Shavano Institute for National Leadership Seminar, Indianapolis, Indiana, May 21, 1997, URL: http://www.privatisation.org

[124] Privatisation in the United Kingdom, Ernst & Young, 1994, p.xi

For example, according to the Lithuanian Privatisation Law, privatisation means "...transfer of state-owned and municipal property (shares and other property) to the ownership of potential buyers under privatisation transactions concluded in accordance with the procedure established by this Law, also transfer of state or municipality control in state or municipality controlled enterprises by floating a new issue of shares financed with additional contributions."[125]

On the other hand, Latvian Privatisation Law states that privatisation means "... a set of uniform activities, as a result of which a state or municipal asset unit changes ownership."[126] And, according to Russian Federation Federal Law on Privatisation, "...privatisation of state and municipal property shall be understood to mean the paid alienation of the property (objects of privatisation) owned by the Russian Federation, the subjects of the Russian Federation or municipal entities in favour of private and legal persons. [127]

Furthermore, article 1/3 of the Law of the Republic of Belarus on "Denationalisation and Privatisation of the State property in the Republic of Belarus" states that privatisation is "the acquisition by natural or juridical persons of the property right for objects belonging to the state."[128]

---

[125] Article 1/1, Republic of Lithuania, "Law on the Privatisation of State-Owned and Municipal Property" (Official translation), 4 November 1997, No. VIII-480, Vilnius, web page of Lithuanian State Privatisation Agency and State Property Fund, URL: http://www.vtf.lb/
[126] Part I, The Republic of Latvia Saeima Law on Privatization of State and Municipal Asset Units, passed on 17.02. 1994, web page of Latvian Privatisation Agency, URL: http://www.lpa.bkc.lv/
[127] Chapter I, Article 1, "Russian Federation Federal Law, On Privatisation of State Property and the Basic Principles of Privatisation of Municipal Property in the Russian Federation", Adopted by the State Duma on June 24, 1997, Approved by the Federation Council on July 3, 1997
[128] Law No. 2103 of January 19, 1993

Armenian Privatisation Law defines privatisation as "...alienation of the right of ownership or other property rights of state property in favour of physical and legal persons and enterprises not possessing the statues of legal persons..." [129]

Georgian Privatisation Law provides another definition. The Law stipulates that: "Privatisation means the purchase of property right on the state-owned property by physical or legal persons or their unions, as a result of which the state losses the right to own, use and dispose the privatised property, and state bodies–the right to manage it." [130]

Finally, according to Albanian privatisation legislation: "By privatisation is meant the total or partial transfer of the right to ownership, use and development to the juridical or physical person." [131]

ii. Approaches

Different countries pursue different objectives in their privatisation programmes. On the other hand each privatisation law is tailored according the social, political and economic needs and circumstances of each country. Therefore definition and understanding of privatisation may vary in different privatisation laws.

e. Analysis

i. General

As we discussed above, there is no single definition of privatisation; it covers a broad range of methods and models.[132] The term privatisation although popularly associated with the

---

[129] Article 3/1, The Law of the Republic of Armenia on Privatisation of State Property, Enacted by the Supreme Council of RA, December 17, 1997, we page of Ministry of State Property Management Republic of Armenia, URL: http://www.privatisation.am/

[130] Article 1/b, Law of Georgia on State Property Privatisation, web page of Ministry of State Property Management of Georgia, URL: http://web.sanet.ge/mospm/

[131] Article 3/2, Law No. 8306, dated 14.3.1998, On the Strategy for the privatisation of Strategic Sectors. Web page of Economic Development Agency of Albanian Government, URL: http://www.aeda.gov.al/

sale of nationalised industries to the private sector, has been used to describe several government microeconomic policies. Frequently, privatisation is used as an umbrella term for a variety of policies such as deregulation, contracting out, and the transfer of state assets other than by the sale of nationalised industries.[133] In other words, the term privatisation has generally been defined and understood as any process aimed at shifting functions and responsibilities, in whole or in part, from the government to the private sector.[134]

As it can be seen, in most cases, the word "privatisation" itself is considered an umbrella term that has come to describe a multitude of government initiatives designed to increase the role of the private sector.[135]

Although each is separate and distinct, these tiers and definitions of privatisation are by no means sealed off from one another. On the contrary, there is a close interaction among them. First of all, the strategy adopted for the upper levels will largely determine that applied at the lover levels. A privatisation strategy for an SOE (state owned enterprise) must be consistent with the country's sectoral and macroeconomic strategies. Often, the privatisation of an enterprise will make sense only as a component of a sectoral and macroeconomic program.[136]

The degree of privatisation of a given economy will depend on the extent of prior state ownership and control and the scope of the reform program undertaken. Transition economies have by necessity embarked on the broadest programs of this kind, of which enterprise and sector privatisations form an integral part.[137]

---

[132] Demetra Smith Nightingale and Nancy Pindus, "Privatization of Public Social Services: A Background Paper", October 15, 1997, Urban Institute, URL: http//www.urban.org/
According to one definition privatisation is "the transfer to private ownership and control of assets or enterprises which were previously under public ownership". (John Black, *A Dictionary of Economics*, Oxford Paperback Reference, Oxford University Press, New York, 1997, p.369)

[133] Bishop and Kay, (Does Privatisation Work?), p.9

[134] General Accounting Office, p.1, 46

[135] Ascher, p.4

[136] Guislain, (The Privatization Challenge), p11

[137] Guislain, (The Privatization Challenge), p11

Under these explanations we can conclude that full and pure privatisation involves of transferring both all the assets and the control of the SOE.

ii. Range and Structure of Privatisation

Privatisation can also be classified according to the privatisation techniques that consider the level of investment responsibility and the degree of the risk transferred to the private sector, and to the relative irreversibility of the privatisation transaction. (See table 1)[138]

iii. Full Privatisation-Partial Privatisation

i. General

Finally privatisation simply can be full privatisation or partial privatisation.[139] Full privatisation is the transfer of 100% of ownership and control to the private buyer or buyers; partial divestiture is anything less. Partial divestiture in turn reflects a continuum of choice on the ownership scale but a discontinuity on the control scale, depending on whether or not a controlling interest is sold.[140]

The decision to relinquish control should be separated from that of how much of the ownership to sell. At the first blush it might be thought that there is a simple correlation: selling a majority of shares relinquishes control. In fact, holding a majority of shares is neither necessary nor sufficient to retain control. It is not necessary for the reason that a 20% stake or less is sufficient to control a company if the remaining shares are widely dispersed. It is not sufficient

---

[138] Guislain, (The Privatization Challenge), p11
[139] Robert W. Poole, "Privatization: Providing Better Services with Lower Taxes", web page of Reason Magazine, URL: http://www.reason.com
[140] Galal, Jones, Tandon and Vogelsang, p.583
There is also a variation of partial sale in the case of fragmentation, or breaking-up and/or restructuring the SOE into component parts and selling them separately. The profitable parts of the company are then sold as separate firms. Many of the former socialist economies featured large holding companies consisting of many different kinds of enterprises. These holding companies will have to be broken up and recombined before any other type of privatisation takes place. ("Privatizing State-Owned Companies", The Prosperity Papers Series, Prosperity Paper Three, web page of Center for International Private Enterprise, URL: http://www.cipe.org/)

because the government can retain nonvoting stock and thus receive the financial benefits of ownership while ceding control.[141]

Opposite measure is also possible. The majority of assets may remain in government's hand but private body that is holding the minority shares may take the control of the enterprise. In that case there are two possibilities. Government may keep only the non-voting shares or golden shares can be issued on behalf of the private investor.

As a summary, the counter-argument is that it is entirely possible for the government to transfer effective control without selling a majority of its shares; conversely; it may retain effective control even after it has sold a majority of its stake; and it may exercise control differently even if it has only sold a minority of its holding to the private sector. Therefore there is no one-to-one relationship between ownership and control.[142]

ii. Why Partial Privatisation?

The first economic argument for partial privatisation follows from the difficulty of determining a fair price for the enterprise in an uncertain environment. The second economic argument follows from the difficulty of actually obtaining a fair price for the enterprise, even if it can be determined, when the offering is large relative to the existing capital market. Selling part of the shares initially, letting the market set a price over time, and later selling the rest can thus increase government revenues.[143]

The political argument for partial privatisation is that, in the presence of contending political forces, the alternative to the compromise of partial privatisation may be no privatisation, at least for the time being.[144]

---

[141] Galal, Jones, Tandon and Vogelsang, p.583, 584
[142] Galal, Jones, Tandon and Vogelsang, p.564
[143] Galal, Jones, Tandon and Vogelsang, p.585
[144] Galal, Jones, Tandon and Vogelsang, p.585

For example, in many countries, partial privatisation has been undertaken as a strategy of gradual introduction of a company in the stock market, for reasons related to the perceived absorption capacity of the latter. That has been the case in many British (BT, British Gas), Spanish (Telefonica, Argentaria) and Italian companies (ENI, Telecom Italia). In other cases, however, partial privatisation has been the final objective: Deutsche Telecom, France Telecom and Royal KPN of the Netherlands have been only partially floated with the state intending to remain a controlling shareholder; some of the smaller economies have kept large stakes of their utilities (telecoms in Czech Republic and electricity in Belgium), after having sold important minority stakes to strategic foreign investors.[145]

Partial privatisation, in some circumstances that were mentioned above, may improve both the country's economic welfare and the government's political well being.

f. Our Approach to Privatisation in this study

For the sake of clarify of analysis, it is necessary to be clear about the specific type of privatisation being analysed.

First of all, various definitions of privatisation and various forms of privatisation should be distinguished clearly.

This thesis will concentrate on the type of privatisation that refers to permanent divestiture and transfer of state owned enterprises (SOEs) or their assets from government or its agencies to private bodies which results in private body control over the company. This contstitutent elements of this narrower form of privatisation will consist of the following:

(a) Government or one of its agencies (for example, local government, enterprise itself etc.) must transfer the state owned enterprise or its assets,

---

[145] Stilpon Nestor and Ladan Mahboobi, Privatisation of Public Utilities; The OECD Experience, Rio, 23

(b) This transfer should be permanent,

(c) The transfer should be done to a private body (If the opposite side of the privatisation contract is another state owned enterprise or government agency the contract cannot be considered "privatisation")[146]

(d) After the divestiture of SOE's assets, the private body(ies) should get the control of the privatised company.[147]

One consequence of this definition is that build-own-operate (BOO) or build-operate-transfer (BOT), build-transfer-operate (BTO) contracts, and other such private management arrangements, in principle, fall outside the scope of this study.[148] In other words, in our approach

---

April 1999, footnote 13, p.27

[146] Some privatisation laws provide restrictions on state owned enterprise to participate in the privatisation of other state owned enterprises. For example according to article 3/1 of the Estonian Privatisation Law: "Entity entitled to participate in privatisation may be any natural person or legal person with the exception of a commercial undertaking where the State of Estonia or a local authority owns directly or through other persons more than a third of voting power as nominated by stocks or shares." [Estonian Law on Privatisation, (unofficial translation), web page of Estonian Privatisation Agency, URL: http//www.eea.ee/]

However, some privatisation laws do not specify the buyer in the privatisation transactions (privatisation subject) clearly. Thus Latvian Privatisation Law defines privatisation subject (buyer): "...a specified person or a legal entity, eligible to obtain state or municipal property during privatisation process". [Part I (Terms and Concepts Used in this Law), The Republic of Latvia Law on Privatisation of State and Municipal Asset Units, passed on 17.02. 1994, web page of Latvian Privatisation Agency, URL: http://www.lpa.bkc.lv/]

[147] Furthermore after the divestiture the government generally has no role concerning financial support, management, regulation, or oversight. [General Accounting Office, p.1, 44]

Different countries have adopted different approaches. For example, according to Lithuanian Privatisation Law "transfer of control at the enterprise controlled by the state" is one of the methods of privatisation. However, the law states that an enterprise controlled by the state or municipality may be privatised by the transfer of control only in the event of failure to sell the shares in the enterprise or when no less than 1/2 of shares owned by the state or municipality in the enterprise under the state or municipality control have been privatised by the methods prescribed by privatisation Law and specified in the privatisation programme. (Article 18, Law on the Privatisation of State-Owned and Municipal Property, 4 November 1997 No. VIII-480, Vilnius, web page of Lithuanian State Property Fund, URL: http://www.vtf.lt/en/frame22.html)

[148] For similar approaches see: V. Bhaskar, Privatisation and Developing Countries: The Issues and the Evidence", United Nations Publications, No.47, August 1992, p.1; Hendrik J. de Ru and Roger Wettenhall, " Progress, Benefits and Costs of Privatisation: An Introduction", National Review of Administrative Sciences, Volume 56, Number 1, March 1990, Symposium on the Progress, Benefits and Costs of Privatisation, p.9; Bishop and Kay, (Does Privatisation Work?), p. 9, 10; Joze Mencinger, "Privatization Dilemmas in Slovenia", Privatization, Liberalization and Destruction-Recreating the Market in Central and Eastern Europe, Edited By: László Csaba, Dartmouth Publishing Company Limited, England & USA, 1994, p.156

Examples for other approaches see: Robert E. Anderson, Simeon Djankov, Gerhard Pohl, "Privatization and Restructuring in Central and Eastern Europe", Public Policy for the Private Sector, The World Bank, July 1997, Note no. 123. This study defines a "privatised" firm as one that has had more than a third of its shares transferred to private investors. (p.2)

Also see: David Gillen and Douglas Cooper, "Public Versus Private Ownership and Operation of Airports and Seaports in Canada", The Fraser Institute, URL: http://www.fraserinstitute.ca; Cosmo Graham and Tony

privatisation has been defined in terms of the transfer of enterprise ownership from the public to private sector. It can be strictly defined to include only cases of the sale of 100 per cent or at least a majority share of a public enterprise, or its assets, to private shareholders. Full or complete privatisation would mean the complete transfer of ownership and control of a government enterprise or asset to the private sector.

We will, however, discuss private management arrangements (non-divestiture measures of privatisation) while we are dealing with the performance of privatised firms when the issue comes to the reforms and different measures taken by some countries for the state owned enterprises (SOEs). We will also deal with regulation issues in non-divestiture arrangements.

As we pointed out above, some countries may chose pre-privatisation models or "soft privatisation" measures (non-divestiture options),[149] instead of transferring existing enterprises or assets from the public to the private sector (divestiture, asset transfer). Such approaches which are often motivated by ideological, economic and social reasons are likely to work best when they are a step toward and lead to full privatisation.[150]

B. The scale of privatisation

The majority of both developed and developing countries, and more recently the countries of Eastern and Central Europe, have launched programmes for transferring public sector property to the private sector. In the developing countries, these programmes have been actively promoted by international organisations, notably the United States Agency for International Development (USAID) and the World Bank, the latter making some of its structural adjustment loans conditional upon the implementation of privatisation operations.

Prosser, "Privatising Nationalised Industries: Constitutional Issues and New Legal Techniques", (Privatising Nationalised Industries), Modern Law Review, Volume: 50, January 1987, p.16, 17. [In this study Graham and Prosser limits privatisation "to the sale of state enterprises, in whole or in part". (p.16)]

[149] Alternatively non-divestiture measures can be considered as "semi-privatisations" or "soft privatisation measures".

Privatisation therefore rapidly became a priority task for the governments of many developing countries.[151]

The global wave of privatisation started in the United Kingdom in 1979 and since then,[152] it has become one of the most important questions discussed in Western and Eastern European countries as well as in many other countries in the world.[153] Various businesses have been privatised; the largest privatisation to date has been the sale of Japanese Telecom for $73 billion.[154] According to some estimation, total world privatisation proceeds reached $600 billions in 2000.[155]

---

[150] See: p.30-32
[151] Bouin, p.1
[152] Paul Cook and Colin Kirkpatrick, "Privatisation Policy and Performance", Privatisation Policy and Performance-International Perspective, Edited By: Paul Cook, Colin Kirkpatrick, Prentice Hall, Harvester Wheatsheaf, Great Britain, 1995, p.3. See also: Cento Veljanovski, "Privatisation: Progress, Issues, and Problems, "Privatisation and Deregulation in Global Perspective", Edited By: Dennis J. Gayle and Jonathan N.Goodrich, Pinter Publishers, USA, 1990, p.63; Janet Rothenberg Pack, "The Opportunities and Constraints of Privatisation," Privatisation and Its Alternatives, Edited By: William T. Gormley, The University of Wisconsin Press, Wisconsin, USA, 1991, p.281; Madsen Pirie, Privatisation, (Privatisation), Wildwood House Limited, England, 1988, p.3; Attila Harmathy, "General Report", (General Report), Legal Aspects of Privatisation, XXIst Colloquy on European Law, Budapest, 15-17 October 1991, Council of Europe Press, 1993, p.197; Graham and Prosser, (Privatising Nationalised Industries), p.17, 18 [Graham and Prosser divides British privatisation programme into three stages (p.17, 18)]

According to some authors privatisation is a "revolution". (For this idea see: Euromoney, Privatisation Special Issue, 15 February 1996, Month 2, p.75-78)
[153] Stephen Martin and David Parker, *The Impact of Privatisation-Ownership and Corporate Performance in the UK*, London and New York 1997, p.1; Jacques Frederic Robert, "Law and Privatisations-A General Presentation of Issues, Legal Aspects of Privatisation, XXIst Colloquy on European Law, Budapest, 15-17 October 1991, Council of Europe Press, 1993, p.17, 18; de Ru and Wettenhall, p.10; Michael Klein and Neil Roger, Back to the Future, "The Potential in Infrastructure Privatisation", Public Policy for the Private Sector, The World Bank, FPD Note No: 30, November 1994; Donaldson and Wagle, p.1; Iatridis, p.3; Narendar V. Rao, Northeastern, C. Bhaktavatsala Rao, Steve Dunphy, "International Perspectives on Privatisation of State Owned Enterprises", Small Business Advancement National Center, University of Central Arkansas, URL: http://www.sbaer.uca.edu/; Samuel, S. Brian, "A New Look at African Privatization", IFC Corporate Finance Services Department, The World Bank, 1999, URL: http://www.ifc.org/ifc/publications/pubs/impact/impsm99/privatization/privatization.html

One study indicates that Latin America and the Caribbean was the leading privatising region. East Asia was next followed by Europe and Central Asia (which includes the formerly planned economies of Central and Eastern Europe and the former Soviet Union). [Mary M. Shirley, "Getting Bureaucrats Out of Business: Obstacles to State Enterprise Reform", web page of Center for International Private Enterprise, URL: http//www.cipe.org/]

Finally we must point out that privatisation is a current topic in the United States as well. [For privatisation in USA see: Florencio López-de-Silanes, Andrei Shleifer, Robert W. Vishny, "Privatisation in the United States", National Bureau of Economic Research (NBER), Working Paper #5113, May 1995]. However, privatisation in the US falls outside the scope of this study.
[154] "The Evolution of Privatisation", Privatisation: Motives and Methods, US Energy Information Administration, URL: http//www.eia.doe.gov
[155] *Privatisation in the UK and Turkey with Particular Reference to the Coal Sector, (Privatisation in the UK and Turkey)*, University of Marmara, European Community Institute, Istanbul, 1996, p.1

For the scale of the privatisation process see: http/www.privatizationlink.com. Also see: Cook, p.222; Vincent Wright, "Industrial Privatization in Western Europe: Pressures, Problems and Paradoxes", Privatization in

42

When the privatisation trend started in the United Kingdom, the programme began cautiously, however, and was extended to the public utilities, namely telecommunications (1984)[156], gas (1986), water (1989), electricity (1990-1991), coal (1995) and the railways (1995-7). By 1997 the total value of United Kingdom privatisation sales had risen to around £100 billion and the share of nationalised industries in GDP had fallen to fewer than 2 per cent[157] The U.K. program is still under way, even the current Labour government has embraced privatisation.[158]

Western Europe-Pressures, Problems and Paradoxes, Edited By: Vincent Wright, Social Change in Western Europe Series, Pinter Publishers, Great Britain, 1994, p.1; 1998 Privatisation Trends, "Introduction and Summary", http://www.oecd.org//daf/peru/no_frames/privatisation/priv_trends98.html

For the database of the privatisation transactions around the world see: URL: http://www.privatizationlink.com

In 1990–98, 154 developing countries had some private activity in one infrastructure sector, and 14 had private activity in three or four sectors. Middle-income countries have attracted most private activity; among low-income countries only China and India have attracted substantial private investment. (Neil Roger, "Recent Trends in Private Participation in Infrastructure", Public Policy for the Private Sector, The World Bank, Note No: 196, September 1999)

In the OECD by 1997, global privatisation proceeds increased dramatically to reach $153.8 billion, which compared to the 1996 figure of $97.2 billion, represents a 58 per cent increase. Preliminary data from 1998 indicate a drop from the 1997 record number: global privatisation proceeds reached $114.5 billion, or 25% less than the year before. Nevertheless, within OECD the strong trend for further offerings seems to have largely survived the difficult market conditions of 1998, as privatisation proceeds only fell by about 10 per cent. (Stilpon Nestor and Ladan Mahboobi, Privatisation of Public Utilities; The OECD Experience, Rio, 23 April 1999)

[156] The efforts for privatisation have begun first in telecommunication sector in 1981. [Bishop and Kay, (Does Privatisation Work?), p.47]. The stock market flotation of British Telecom was the first sale of a major public utility in the United Kingdom, and in its sale and chosen method of regulation it represented something of a model for later privatisations (p.51).

[157] "The Evolution of Privatisation", Privatisation: Motives and Methods, US Energy Information Administration, URL: http://www.eia.doe.gov; "The United Kingdom", Chapter V, General Accounting Office of USA, URL: http://eia.doe.gov; Henry Gibbon, "Guide for Divesting Government-Owned Enterprises", (Guide), How-To Guide No: 15, Reason Public Policy Institute, URL: http://www.privatization.org, p.2; Wright, p.10; Bishop and Kay, (Does Privatisation Work, p.4; Prosser, (Nationalised Industries), p.77

[158] Dick Welch and Olivier Frémond, The Case-by-Case Approach to Privatisation-Techniques and Examples, World Bank Technical Paper No. 403, The World Bank, Washington, D.C. Also see: *Her Majesty's Treasury Guide to the United Kingdom Privatisation Programme*, December 1993; Implementing Privatisation: The UK Experience, web page of UK Treasury, URL: http://www.hm-treasury.gov.uk

According to United Kingdom government one of the objectives of the Treasury is to promote privatisation. (Web page of UK Treasury, URL: http://www.hm-treasury.gov.uk/pub/html/econbf/eb09/4hmt.html; http://www.hm-treasury.gov.uk/drep/1996/s12.html; HM Treasury Departmental Report for 1995, web page of UK Treasury, URL: http://www.hm-treasury.gov.uk/drep/1995/index.html)

"...Overall, privatisation had beneficial effects, with productivity improved and the economy better able to respond to change... (Public Private Partnerships-The Government's Approach, London: The Stationery Office, Published with the permission of HM Treasury on behalf of the Controller of Her Majesty 's Stationery Office, 2000, p.23)... The Government is learning the lessons of past attempts to involve the private sector in public services and businesses, in particular from the privatisation policies of the 1980s and early 1990s..."(p.12)

In the UK total 119 enterprises fully or partially privatised. (Web page of UK Treasury, URL: http://www.hm-treasury.gov.uk)

C. Historical Background

The current wave of privatisation follows a long period characterised by nationalisation and growth of the size of the public sector in the economy.[159] Like today's privatisations, these nationalisations took place in practically every area of economic activity and in a great majority of countries.[160]

In the nineteenth century, railways, canals, roads, and gas, power, and water systems were initially privately owned, operated, and funded in most countries.[161] However, in Western Europe, the nationalisation trend took hold in the 1930s[162] and in the years immediately preceding the Second World War and continued after the war ended. At the time, European governments of divergent political viewpoints were largely in agreement over the benefits of a strong state role in their domestic economies.[163] For example, in the 1930's and 1940's in Spain, the Franco government nationalised the state petroleum resources, which later emerged as Repsol--Spain's state oil company.[164] The Mussolini government in Italy did the same and formed what was to become ENI, Italy's state petroleum company. Energy resources were nationalised at about the same time elsewhere in Europe--although in other nations often by more freely elected governments.[165] In other regions, nationalisation often involved the

---

[159] In other words, privatisation represents a reversal of the process of nationalisation begun early in this century. ("The Evolution of Privatisation", Privatisation: Motives and Methods, US Energy Information Administration, URL: http//www.eia.doe.gov)

[160] Guislain, (The Privatization Challenge), p.3. The United States is among the few countries that was only marginally effected by this trend. [Guislain, (The Privatization Challenge), p.3]

[161] Michael Klein, Neil Roger, Back to the Future, "The Potential in Infrastructure Privatisation", Public Policy for the Private Sector, The World Bank, FPD Note No: 30, November 1994

[162] "The Evolution of Privatisation", Privatisation: Motives and Methods, US Energy Information Administration, URL: http//www.eia.doe.gov

[163] "The Evolution of Privatisation", Privatisation: Motives and Methods, US Energy Information Administration, URL: http//www.eia.doe.gov

[164] Oscar Fanjul and Luis Mañas "Privatization in Spain: The Absence of a Policy", Privatization in Western Europe-Pressures, Problems and Paradoxes, Edited By: Vincent Wright, Pinter Publishers, Great Britain, 1994, p.140; "The Evolution of Privatisation", Privatisation: Motives and Methods, US Energy Information Administration, URL: http//www.eia.doe.gov

[165] "The Evolution of Privatisation", Privatisation: Motives and Methods, US Energy Information Administration, URL: http//www.eia.doe.gov; Iberto Martinelli, "The Italian Eperience: A Historical Perspective",

expropriation of foreign-owned domestic petroleum properties. Russia was the first to nationalise its petroleum industry following the Bolshevik Revolution in 1918.[166]

In France from 1930 to 1953, controls on state owned enterprises in France gradually increased.[167] Hence, the first nationalisations took place under the Front Populaire governments of 1936-37 (armaments, aviation, railways); the movement resumed immediately after liberation (after the Second World War) with the nationalisation of coal mining, air transport, electricity, gas, banks, and insurance companies.[168] The nationalisation trend in France continued when Mitterrand government came to the office in 1981.[169]

In Portugal during the revolutionary period (1974-6) a large number of companies came either directly or indirectly under state control.[170]

In Britain, between 1945 and 1951 a wide range of industries, including coal (1946), gas (1948), electricity (1947), steel (1949), inland waterways and long distance road haulage (1947) and railways, (1947) were nationalised; many hundreds of thousands of workers became

---

State-Owned Enterprise in the Western Economies, Edited By: Raymond Vernon and Yair Aharoni, Croom Helm Ltd., 1981, p.88
[166] "The Evolution of Privatisation", Privatisation: Motives and Methods, US Energy Information Administration, URL: http://www.eia.doe.gov
[167] Sabino Cassese, "Public Control and Corporate Efficiency", State-Owned Enterprise in the Western Economies, Edited By: Raymond Vernon and Yair Aharoni, Croom Helm Ltd., 1981, p.146
[168] Matthew Bishop and John Kay, "Privatisation in Western Economies", (Western Economies), Privatisation-Symposium in Honor of Herbert Giersch, Edited By: Horst Siebert, Institut fur Weltwirtschaft an der Universitat Kiel, J.C.B. Mohr (Paul Siebeck), Tubingen, 1992, p.193; Guislain, (The Privatization Challenge), p.3, 6; Michael Klein and Neil Roger, Back to the Future, "The Potential in Infrastructure Privatisation", Public Policy for the Private Sector, The World Bank, FPD Note No: 30, November 1994; Hervé Dumez and Alain Jeunemaitre, "Privatization in France: 1983-1993", "Industrial Privatization in Western Europe: Pressures, Problems and Paradoxes", Privatization in Western Europe-Pressures, Problems and Paradoxes, Edited By: Vincent Wright, Pinter Publishers, Great Britain, 1994, p.84; E. Leslie Normanton, "Accountability and Audit", State-Owned Enterprise in the Western Economies, Edited By: Raymond Vernon and Yair Aharoni, Croom Helm Ltd., 1981, p.64
In this respect, the United States, which has never nationalised industry in the first place, stands in a position fundamentally different from the Western European countries with extensive public enterprise sectors. (Paul Starr, "The Meaning of Privatisation", web page of University of Princeton, http://princeton.edu/~starr/meaning.html)
[169] Thomas D. Lancaster, "Deregulating the French Banking System", Privatization and Deregulation in Global Perspective, Edited by: Dennis J. Gayle and Jonathan N. Goodrich, Pinter Publishers, London, 1990, p.377, 378. Privatisation in France, started after the right (Chirac government) won the parliamentary elections of March 1986 (p.378, 379, 380).
[170] David Corkill, "Privatisation in Portugal", Privatization in Western Europe-Pressures, Problems and Paradoxes, Edited By: Vincent Wright, Pinter Publishers, Great Britain, 1994, p.215, 216

employees of state owned enterprises.[171] The motivation was political, economic and philosophical.[172] However, much of the post-war nationalisation in Britain was motivated, at least in part, by the belief that competitive solutions were unsuitable in the markets in question, and there were particular concerns about natural monopoly in industries such as gas, electricity, railways, water, and telecommunications.[173]

The 1970s were characterised by the multiplication of the number of public enterprises in the majority of developing countries.[174]

In Central and Eastern Europe, nationalisations were imposed under Soviet influence after the Second World War. [175] For example in Czechoslovakia[176] almost all the large enterprises had been nationalised between 1948 and 1955.[177]

In Turkey the origins of the state economic enterprises can be traced back to the 1930s early years of the Republic. State economic enterprises (SOEs) provided the initial impetus for industrialisation in Turkey, which involved import substitution in basic consumer-goods industries, and they compensated for the lack of an indigenous business elite at the time. While private business became increasingly important in the post-1950 period, the SOEs that were established in the 1930s continued to perform a central, if modified, role in industrialisation.

---

[171] Bishop and Kay, (Western Economies), p.195; Richardson, p.58-62; Normanton, p.159
For example the Gas industry was nationalised in 1948. [Bishop and Kay, (Does Privatisation Work?), p.57]
[172] Gerry Grimstone, "The British Privatisation Programme", (British Privatisation), Privatisation and Deregulation in Britain and Canada, Edited by: J.J. Richardson, The Institute for Research on Public Policy, 1990, England & Canada, p.4
[173] Vickers and Yarrow, (An Economic Analysis), p.45
[174] Olivier Bouin, "The Privatisation in Developing Countries: Reflections on a Panacea", Policy Brief No. 3, OECD Development Centre, OECD 1992; Grimstone, (British Privatisation), p.3, 4.
[175] Guislain, (The Privatization Challenge), p.6
[176] Today's Czech Republic and Slovakia
[177] Carlo Boffito, "Privatisation in Central Europe and the Soviet Union", Privatisation Process in Eastern Europe- Theoretical Foundations and Empirical Results, Edited by: Maria Baldassarri, Luigi Paganetto, Edmund S. Phelps, St. Martin's Press, 1993, p.52

Between 1963 and 1978, when the import-substitution strategy was implemented under successive five-years plans, the SOEs were still dominant[178]

1. Reasons for Nationalisation

The purposes of state ownership and state owned enterprises have been various: to change the distribution of power between the public and the private sector, to improve the country's bargaining power with foreign enterprises, to help create industries that seemed necessary for future growth, to insulate the country from the military and political pressures of other governments, to contribute stability and employment.[179] In other words, close control of infrastructures was dictated by reasons of national security, social peace and economic equality between citizens of most countries.[180]

In the wake of the Second World War and with the cold war in full swing, these considerations were of utmost importance. Making sure that utilities were run in a way that kept the enemies of the nation at bay and these vital industries under clear national control was essential, in view of the imminence of the communist threat. At the same time, the political threat that communism represented made the pursuit of re-distributional objectives necessary in the provision of utilities.[181]

Some of these state objectives of control were pursued by statutorily limiting ownership by foreigners. Other countries imposed strict limits to the control of utilities, for example by prohibiting individual investors from acquiring substantial blocks of shares in utilities. But in

---

[178] Ziya Öniş, "The Evolution of Privatisation in Turkey: The Institutional Context of Public-Enterprise Reform", Int. J. Middle East Studies 23, 1991, USA, p.163
[179] Raymond Vernon, "Introduction", State-Owned Enterprise in the Western Economies, Edited By: Raymond Vernon and Yair Aharoni, Croom Helm Ltd., 1981, p.9
[180] Nestor and Mahboobi, p.2, 3.
For example, public ownership of basic industries such as iron and steel, chemicals, heavy engineering, and petrochemicals was justified in terms of their strategic importance in providing essential inputs to the emerging manufacturing sector. (Ramesh Adhikari and Colin Kirkpatrick, "Public Enterprise in Less Developed Countries: An Empirical Review", Public Enterprise at the Crossroads-Essays in Honour of V.V. Ramanadham, Edited By: John Heath, London and New York, Routledge, 1990, p.41)

most countries, these objectives were served by making the provision of utilities a state function, often by constitutional means.

Viewed as natural monopolies, and regarded as strategic and sensitive from a national security perspective, SOEs (state owned enterprises) were afforded a statutory monopoly status.[182] However, during all these periods, public enterprises played an important role, the main reason was because many developing countries had only limited traditions of domestic capitalist development, and state ownership seemed necessary in the absence of a developed class of industrialists.[183]

2. Rethinking Nationalisation

The end of the cold war was a powerful catalyst in rethinking and narrowing the boundaries of national security. Suspicion between neighbours was further attenuated through regional economic integration, as in the case of the EU and, more recently NAFTA.[184] Direct ownership and control of "sensitive" firms has been increasingly viewed as a grossly disproportionate response to a rather narrow problem. As a result, regulation and golden shares, were seen as more appropriate tools.[185]

Over the past twenty years, a sharp reversal of the nationalisation trend has been going on, spurred by a new international economic and political environment and by other factors. The average number of annual nationalisation operations, which peaked in the first half of the 1970`s, has fallen steadily since then and now extremely small. Over the same period, the volume of

---

[181] Nestor and Mahboobi, p.2, 3
[182] Nestor and Mahboobi, p.2
[183] V. Bhaskar, Privatisation and Developing Countries: The Issues and the Evidence", United Nations Publications, No.47, August 1992, p.3
[184] The NAFTA which grew out of the Canada-US Free Trade Agreement (1988) went beyond a classical free trade agreement. In addition to provisions on free trade, it included provisions on services, international investment and binding arbitration concerning trade remedy laws. (Brigid Laffan, "The European Union: A Distinctive Model of Internationalisation?", European Integration Online Papers (EIoP) Vol. 1 (1997) N° 18, URL: http://eiop.or.at/eiop/texte/1997-018a.htm
[185] Nestor and Mahboobi, p.3

privatisation operations has accelerated, surpassing the volume of nationalisations around 1980 and growing exponentially in the past few years.[186]

Countries started making use of international financial and know-how resources without many scruples. Many of the formerly state-owned utilities are now buying utilities in other countries. From the United Kingdom to Hungary, industries such as telecommunications, water distribution and electricity, hitherto considered extremely sensitive, are today run by foreign firms or owned by foreign institutional investors.[187]

3. The Emergence of Privatisation

There is no consensus on the beginning of privatisation trend. In fact, it is difficult to put a certain and a sharp date for a social and economic development.

Some studies conclude that privatisation debate and subsequent implementation of privatisation policies began in the UK in the early 1980s.[188]

According to some authors this trend began in the 1970's in Chile[189] and gained international prominence with the Thatcher government's privatisation programme in the UK.

---

[186] Guislain, (The Privatization Challenge), p.6
In 1990s the following trends have emerged in private participation in infrastructure in developing countries in?
-Private activity has grown rapidly, but the public sector still dominates.
-Private activity declined in 1998 from a high in 1997, falling most in East Asia and in energy.
-Telecommunications and energy have been the leading sectors in private participation, and
-Latin America and East Asia the leading regions.
-Almost all developing countries have some private activity in infrastructure (Neil Roger, "Recent Trends in Private Participation in Infrastructure", Public Policy for the Private Sector, The World Bank, Note No: 196, September 1999)

[187] Nestor and Mahboobi, p.3; Joseph E. Stiglitz, "Some Theoretical Aspects of the Privatization: Applications to Eastern Europe", (Some Theoretical Aspects), Privatization Process in Eastern Europe-Theoretical Foundations and Empirical Results, Edited by: Maria Baldassarri, Luigi Paganetto, Edmund S. Phelps, St. Martin's Press, 1993, p.179, 180; Bruno Jossa, "Is There an Option to the Denationalization of Eastern European Enterprises", Privatization Process in Eastern Europe-Theoretical Foundations and Empirical Results, Edited by: Maria Baldassarri, Luigi Paganetto, Edmund S. Phelps, St. Martin's Press, 1993, p.205; Dominick Salvatore, "Foreign Trade, Foreign Direct Investments and Privatisation in Eastern Europe", Privatization Process in Eastern Europe-Theoretical Foundations and Empirical Results, Edited by: Maria Baldassarri, Luigi Paganetto, Edmund S. Phelps, St. Martin's Press, 1993, p.223

The first wave of privatizations under the Pinochet regime in Chile, in 1974 and 1975, consisted mostly of re-privatisation of about 250 firms nationalized without legal transfer during the socialist regime of Salvador Allende.[190] However Bartell and Sullivan point out that in Chile, the lack of supervision of the financial system led to the failure of the initial privatisation process with the result that the government re-nationalised many of the companies and banks and had to redo the entire process at a later date.[191]

Some other studies state that, although most people associate modern privatisation programs with Margaret Thatcher's conservative government which came to power in Great Britain in 1979, the first large-scale, ideologically-motivated "denationalisation" program of the post-war era was launched by the Christian Democrat government of Konrad Adenauer in the Federal Republic of Germany.[192]

---

[188] Justin Malbon, "Gaining Balance on the Regulatory Tightrope", who Benefits from Privatisation, Edited by: Moazzem Hossain, Justin Malbon, Routledge Studies in the Modern World Economy, London and New York, 1998, p.9

[189] Bhaskar, p.1
Also see: Guislain, (The Privatization Challenge), p.2. Guislain does not give a specific date; he provides a short chronology of the trend (p.1, 2). And according to him: "The first privatisation program of the Chilean government was an economic failure. Owing to the economic crisis of the early 1980s, the government had to take back many enterprises that had been privatised just a few years earlier, between 1974-1979. This was due in large part to the excessive concentration of shareholders within a few large conglomerates that were deeply in debt as a consequence of; in particular, the acquisition carried out under the privatisation program. These enterprises taken back by the government were later reprivatised, beginning in 1985." (p.1, 2)
For this issue also see: William L. Megginson, Jeffry M. Netter, "From State to Market: A Survey of Empirical Studies on Privatization", for presentation at: Global Equity Markets, A joint conference of the SBF Bourse de Paris and the New York Stock Exchange, Paris, France, December 10- 11, 1998, Current Draft, February 9, 1999, footnote 3; William P. Glade, "Privatisation in Chile", Public Enterprise at the Crossroads-Essays in Honour of V.V. Ramanadham, Edited By: John Heath, London and New York, Routledge, 1990, p.157-173

[190] Ernest Bartell, Privatization: The Role of Domestic Business, The Helen Kellogg Institute for International Studies, University of Notre Dame, Working Paper Series, Number 198, June 1993, p.8

[191] John D. Sullivan, "Privatization and Economic Reforms", web page of Center for International Private Enterprise, URL: http://www.cipe.org/; Bartell, p.8
According to Bartell:"...(privatisation in Chile in 1974 and 1975) was the rapid privatization itself that was intended to be a principal policy instrument in the achievement of macroeconomic stabilization, presumably by bringing government budgets into balance through divestiture of subsidized, inefficient, and loss-making public firms....In fact, this wave of privatizations was a failure on several counts..." (Ernest Bartell, Privatization: The Role of Domestic Business, The Helen Kellogg Institute for International Studies, University of Notre Dame, Working Paper Series, Number 198, June 1993, p.8)

[192] William L. Megginson and Jeffry M. Netter, "From State to Market: A Survey of Empirical Studies on Privatization", for presentation at: Global Equity Markets, A Joint Conference of the SBF Bourse de Paris and the New York Stock Exchange, Paris, France, December 10- 11, 1998, Current Draft, February 9, 1999

These authors point out that, in 1961, West Germany sold some shares in a nationally owned electricity and mining company in 1959.[193] The German government also sold a majority stake in Volkswagen in a public share offering heavily weighted in favour of small investors. In 1964, the government launched an even larger offering for shares in another SOE (state owned enterprise) called VEBA (a heavy industrial and communications conglomerate) and Preussag. Both offerings were initially received very favourably, but the appeal of share ownership did not survive the first cyclical downturn in stock prices, and the government was forced to bailout many small shareholders.[194] In 1965 and 1966 there had been more privatisations in VEBA and in Lufthansa.[195]

On the other hand some authors do believe that, privatisation began in the United Kingdom following the election in 1979 of a Conservative government.[196]

Finally, some studies follow a mixed approach. They do not give any specific date and they consider the process started in a number of countries.[197]

4. Assessment

First of all we should point out that, there are examples of earlier sales of state assets, such as West Germany after 1950 and 1960s, Ireland in the 1960s and 1970s, and Italy in the

---

[193] C. Foster, "Privatisation, Public Ownership and the Regulation of Natural Monopolies", Blackwell Publishers, Oxford (UK) & Cambridge, (USA), 1992, p.108

[194] William L. Megginson, Jeffry M. Netter, "From State to Market: A Survey of Empirical Studies on Privatization", for presentation at: Global Equity Markets, A Joint Conference of the SBF Bourse de Paris and the New York Stock Exchange, Paris, France, December 10-11, 1998, Current Draft, February 9, 1999

[195] Foster, p.108

[196] Colin Kirkpatrick, "The United Kingdom Privatisation Model: Is it Transferable to Developing Countries", Privatisation in the United Kingdom, Edited By: V.V. Ramanadham, Routledge, London and New York, 1988, p. 235, 236; Privatisation in the UK and Turkey, p.1; Malbon, p.11; Pirie, (Privatisation), p.3

Some international organisations like ILO (International Labour Organisation) also states that the privatisation process started in the United Kingdom, in the early 1980s. (For this see: World Labour report 1995-Privatisation-the Human Impact, URL: http://www.ilo.org)

[197] For example General Accounting Office (GAO) of USA does not mention a specific date, in a report it states that: ".... Countries as different as the United Kingdom and Chile have led the way in privatization..." ("Privatisation as a Global Phenomenon", Chapter I, URL: http://www.eia.doe.gov)

1950s and 1960s, France in 1970s, Chile in 1970s[198] and even in the United Kingdom in the early 1950s.[199] However, these early sales, mentioned above, were not part of a systematic programme aimed at slimming down the state sector. For example, one of the main objectives in West Germany was to curtail the power of the trade unions coupled with a wish to spread share ownership more widely.[200]

While the Thatcher government may not have been the first to launch a privatisation program, it is without question the most important historically. Therefore, although there are some early sales, it was the British Conservative government of 1979 that started and launched a privatisation programme which later on developed into a comprehensive measure of systematic economic activities and aims that cover many state owned enterprises (SOEs) in many sectors, including major areas like transportation, communications, energy and steel.[201]

---

[198] In Chile relatively few assets are still in state hands. However, the process is still moving apace. (Henry Gibbon, Privatization in 1995 and Beyond, web page of Center for International Private Enterprise, URL: http//www.cipe.org/)

[199] Wright, p.1
In Britain in 1951 the incoming Conservative government had undone few of their own earlier nationalisation measures of the Attlee government's. They had denationalised only some road haulage, and iron and steel. However, these enterprises were renationalised by the Wilson government in 1967. [Foster, p.108]
Furthermore in the UK in the early years of the Health government of 1970-74 an initial attempt at mounting a "denationalisation programme" was made, however the programme did not last long. (Rees, p.44).

[200] David Parker, "Privatisation in the European Union-An Overview", (Privatisation in the European Union), Privatisation in the European Union, Theory and Policy Perspectives, Edited By: David Parker, London, 1998, p.12; Josef Esser, "Germany: Symbolic Privatizations in a Social Market Economy", Privatization in Western Europe-Pressures, Problems and Paradoxes, Edited By: Vincent Wright, Pinter Publishers, Great Britain, 1994, p.111. [According to Esser these privatisations were failure (p.111)].

[201] According to some authors nowhere privatisation policies are being carried out as vigorously and extensively as in Britain. [Vickers and Yarrow, (An Economic Analysis), p.1]
However, it is difficult to say that the British privatisation programme started out with a coherent set of clearly specified aims and objectives. (Julia O'Connell Davidson, "Metamorphosis? Privatisation and the Restructuring of Management and Labour", (Metamorphosis), Privatisation and Regulation-A Review of the Issues, Edited by: Peter M. Jackson and Catherine Price, Longman Group Limited, 1994, p.170). The first official statement of the objectives for privatisation was not made until November 1983. (Mitchell, p.19)
Furthermore in the British privatisation programme, although the government did not mention explicitly, one of the main objectives of the government was to reduce the power of the unions. Because the Conservative government which held power from 1970-74 had been defeated in an election which took place during, and had been provoked by, a strike in the state owned coal industry which had led to a substantial reductions in output in the electricity industry-also state owned. A preoccupation of the Conservative Party in opposition was to ensure that this never happened again and an influential, but still unpublished, report advocated private ownership as the best means of reducing what was perceived as the excessive power of public sector trade unions. [Bishop and Kay, (Western Economies), p.195, 196; Bishop and Kay, (Does Privatisation Work?), p.1, 3; Privatization in the United Kingdom, p.20; Jackson and Price, p.14]

Finally, privatisation as a concept did not appear in the dictionaries in 1979 yet it dominated the economic and political arena couple of years later.[202]

Britain's former Conservative government under Margaret Thatcher, who took office in 1979, is widely credited with pioneering and legitimising privatisation as an official state policy.[203] The British privatisation programme has been more far reaching than in any other comparable country.[204] It is a source of astonishment for three reasons: its scale[205], its scope, and the fact that it was achieved in a democratic political system.[206]

The British privatisation programme has been on a heroic scale; almost all of the industrial public sector is now in private hands, and one of the important outcomes from the British privatisation programme is that there is almost no field of activity that cannot be privatised.[207]

Finally, the British case is important not only because of the scale of the programme, but also because of its international impact. Britain has become a pioneer in privatisation. The

---

Some authors argue that the change in ownership involved in privatisation has had a limited effect on trade unions. (Jackson and Price, p.19). Privatisation was, however, not the major means of tackling public sector trade unions. Through three major Employment Acts passed in 1980, 1982, and 1984 the government reformed trade unions. (Mitchell, p.27)

[202] Mitchell, p.15; Parker, (Nationalisation, Privatisation, and Agency), p.149; Mike Wright and Steve Thompson, "Divestiture of Public Sector Assets", Privatisation and Regulation-A Review of the Issues, Edited by: Peter M. Jackson and Catherine Price, Longman Group Limited, 1994, p.35

[203] William L. Megginson, "The Impact of Privatisation", web page of Center for International Private Enterprise, URL: http//www.cipe.org/

Discussion of privatisation in the United Kingdom began in the 1970s with the policy analysis by the Conservative opposition. [Bishop and Kay, (Does Privatisation Work?), p.3]

[204] Privatization in the United Kingdom, Ernst & Young, 1994, p.xi. According to this study: "The Thatcher government failed to be re-elected in 1983, it is unlikely that any other country would have taken over the mantle in promoting the virtues of privatisation..."(p.59)

[205] Among developed economies, the United Kingdom's electric utility industry privatisation efforts have been the first, largest, and most ambitious thus far. ("The United Kingdom", Chapter V, General Accounting Office of USA, URL: http://eia.doe.gov)

[206] In 1979, the proportion of British industry owned and controlled by the state was at its highest-ever level. [Grimstone, (British Privatisation), p.3]

The fact that, British privatisation programme has been implemented under a democratic system is an important difference between English and Chilean privatisation processes. It is true that, Chile has been very successful country in stimulating its economy and downsizing its state sector, but that policy was initially carried out under the highly repressive dictatorship of Augusto Pinochet, and it is doubtful the same, often draconian policies could have been implemented under a democratic government. (Howard J. Wiarda, "Modernizing the State in Latin America", web page of Center for International Private Enterprise, URL: http://www.cipe.org/)

achievements of British governments since 1979 are widely admired in the developing countries.[208]

D. Structure of the Process of Privatisation

The process of transferring public enterprises to private ownership began more slowly in the developing countries, but the pace appears to have accelerated in the later years of the decade, and has continued during the 1990's. Prominent in the former category were the United Kingdom, Canada, France, Spain and Italy; in the latter group, the main countries were Chile, Jamaica, Argentina, Brazil, Malaysia, Mexico, Turkey and Sri Lanka. In the terms of the number as opposed to value of sales, the African economies of Cote d'Ivoire, Guinea and Togo were also actively pursuing privatisation programmes and governments all around the world have adopted privatisation programmes.[209]

---

[207] Tony Prosser and Michael Moran, *Privatization and Regulatory Change in Europe*, Edited By: Michael Moran and Tony Prosser, Open University Press, Buckingham-Philadelphia, 1994, p. 48

[208] Moran and Prosser, (Introduction), p.5
"I would like to nail my flag to the mast straight away and claim credit for the United Kingdom for a policy which has swept the globe. Privatisation has now been adopted by governments on all continents. I am proud that the vision and innovation of UK firms in delivering the UK's programme over the last fifteen years is now helping other Governments in their own privatisation programmes..." [George Young, the (former) Financial Secretary's speech to the World Privatisation Conference, 6 March 1995, web page of the Treasury, URL: http://www.hm-treasury.gov.uk/pub/html/speech95/fst/sp060395.html]
In another speech financial secretary of United Kingdom states that: "...the approach developed for the UK Government's electricity industry privatisation has been closely analysed by Governments in Argentina, Italy, Portugal, the Philippines and several Asian countries. Several of these have now adopted our approach of separating supply, generation, and distribution functions in order to foster competition to the benefit of the consumer. [George Young, the (former) Financial Secretary's speech to the World Privatisation Conference, 6 March 1995, web page of the Treasury, URL: http://www.hm-treasury.gov.uk/pub/html/speech95/fst/sp060395.html]
However, as we will discuss later on, since Britain has special circumstances we do not think that it can, always, be an example to other countries. For example, Canada has adopted some aspects of British privatisation programme; however, its privatisation programme is a unique reflection of the country's economic, social, political, legal and historical circumstances. (Janet Smith, "Canada's Privatisation Programme", Privatisation and Deregulation in Canada and Britain-Proceedings of a Canada/United Kingdom Colloquium, Gleneagles, Scotland, Edited by: Jeremy Richardson, The Institute for Research on Public Policy, Dartmouth Publishing Company Limited, England, Canada, 1990, p.37, 44)
Also see: Gibbon, (Guide), p.2

[209] Cook-Kirkpatrick, p.5; Robert, p.17, 18; Moazzem Hossain, Justin Malbon, "Introduction", Who Benefits from Privatisation?, Edited by: Moazzem Hossain, Justin Malbon, Routledge Studies in the Modern World Economy, London and New York, 1998, p.1
Privatisation in the United States has been quite different because so much of the economy was in private hands. The process there changed its venue from the federal government to state and local governments, which have adopted privatisation as a way to balance their budgets while maintaining tolerable levels of services. While asset sales were uncommon in the US, the contracting out of services to private providers has been the dominant method.

Privatisation is also spreading to countries with socialist governments or those governed by socialist majorities.[210] In Spain, for example, sales of government interests in bus manufacturing, sherry, construction, high technology, food manufacturing, banking and other sectors are all under way.[211] The other group of countries that has contributed significantly to privatisation has been the previously socialist countries, now in transition, with the largest share accounted for by the Eastern European countries. In that group, the most significance successful example was East Germany.

II. WHY PRIVATISATION: THE FACTORS

Each country has different social, political and economical circumstances. Therefore, the reasons for privatisation and the decline of nationalisation activity vary from country to country and even one enterprise to another. For example in the United Kingdom, the privatisation programme has been driven by both political ideology and pragmatism. Although there are many considerations, when the programme began in 1979, it was largely a reaction to the shortcomings of the public enterprise sector's performance and the failure of previous attempts to exercise effective parliamentary control of their management and operations. Privatisation was expected to result in increased efficiency and better management. In addition, the proceeds from privatisation met a rising share of the government's revenue needs, and helped to finance tax cuts.[212]

(Ewa Baginska, "Legal Aspects of the Privatization Process in Poland", web page of Civic Education Project, URL: http://www.cep.org.hu/)

[210] Robert, p.17

[211] Oliver Letwin, "Privatising the World-A Study of International Privatisation in Theory and Practice", London, 1988, p.21

[212] Kirkpatrick, p.236

In other words, in the United Kingdom, as in many other countries, the political pressure for privatisation came from a combination of disillusionment with the result of state ownership and from a belief that private ownership would bring substantial economic benefits. State-owned industries were viewed as highly inefficient, slow at developing and introducing new technologies, subject to over-frequent and damaging political intervention and dominated by powerful trade unions. Privatisation seemed to offer a means of ridding the state of the financial burden of loss-making activities, while at the same time spreading share ownership and curtailing union power. Moreover, privatisation sales offered a tempting source of state funding at a time when economic policy was geared to reducing the public sector-borrowing requirement. (Martin and Parker, p.1)

However, the following reasons can be considered the most common facts of the privatisation trend in the international arena.

A. Disappointing Performance of SOEs

SOEs have generally posted disappointing performances; although some of the SOEs function well[213], many others are considered notoriously inefficient.[214] Most SOEs in most developing countries have suffered severe, sustained losses.[215] They manage to survive through tariff protection against competing imports, preferences in public procurement, exclusive rights, and preferential access to credit, governmental guarantees, tax exemptions, and public subsidies.[216] The chronic losses incurred by state-owned firms often force governments to borrow or print

---

According to Graham background factors in British privatisation programme are as follows:
(a) The neo-liberal ideas of Conservative Party and Margaret Thatcher, (b) The aim of cutting back the public expenditure and in that context cutting back the public sector borrowing requirement (PSBR), (c) The financial difficulties of nationalised industries. (Cosmo Graham, "Privatization-The United Kingdom Experience", Brooklyn Journal of International Law, Volume XXI, 1995, Number 1, p.190, 191)

[213] The performance of some state-owned enterprises--for example, in Malaysia and France--has been excellent. (Paul Starr, "The Meaning of Privatisation", web page of University of Princeton, http://princeton.edu/~starr/meaning.html). In France, in Renault and EDF (an electrical heating company) the performance was very good. (Jean-Pierre C. Anastassopoulos, "The French Experience: Conflicts with Government", State-Owned Enterprise in the Western Economies, Edited By: Raymond Vernon and Yair Aharoni, Croom Helm Ltd., 1981, p.111)
Finally the most efficient steel company in the world, is the Korean Posco (Pohang Steel Company) which is state owned. (Jackson and Price, p.20)

[214] For example, British nationalised industries, like others elsewhere in the world, were generally disappointing. Criticisms were continually voiced about their low return on capital employed, their record on prices, productivity and manpower costs, and about the low level of customer satisfaction that they provided. [Grimstone, (British Privatisation), p.4]
Gerd Schwartz and Paulo Silva Lopes, "Privatization and Reform of Public Enterprises: An Overview of Policy Trade-offs, Experiences, and Outcomes", Privatization in Central and Eastern Europe-Perspectives and Approaches, Edited by: Demetrius S. Iatridis and June Gary Hopps, Praeger Publishers, USA, 1998, p.38, 39; Guislain, (The Privatization Challenge), p.6; Nestor and Mahboobi; Privatisation Trends in OECD Countries-June 1996, http://www.oecd.org; Robert Poole, "Privatization: Providing Better Services with Lower Taxes", the web page of Reason Magazine, URL: http://www.reason.com; Olivier Bouin, "The Privatisation in Developing Countries: Reflections on a Panacea", Policy Brief No. 3, OECD Development Centre, OECD 1992

[215] "Privatizing State-Owned Companies", The Prosperity Papers Series, Prosperity Paper Three, web page of Center for International Private Enterprise, URL: http://www.cipe.org/

[216] Paul Starr, "The New Life of the Liberal State: Privatisation and the Restructuring of State-Society Relations", URL: http://www.princeton.edu/~starr/newstate.html; Guislain, (The Privatization Challenge), p.6; Nestor and Mahboobi, p.4

money to cover them. These measures lead to high inflation, which discourages investment and causes capital flight.[217]

SOEs are also thought to serve political objectives or purposes and consequently suffer frequent interference by government and bureaucrats.[218] In some countries they have also contributed to income redistribution in favour of the relatively well-off over the poor, who generally lack access to both the jobs the SOEs provide and their products. Almost everywhere, the burden SOEs impose on state finances has become untenable.[219]

As a summary, SOE's are generally characterised by: Poor financial performance, overstaffing, dependence on subsidies and unilateral budget transfers, highly centralised and politicised organisations, exclusion of domestic competitors, poor export performance, corrupt practices, and being vehicles for capital flight.[220]

---

[217] "Privatizing State-Owned Companies", The Prosperity Papers Series, Prosperity Paper Three, web page of Center for International Private Enterprise, URL: http://www.cipe.org/

[218] For example, in one study it has bee pointed out that in Italy, politicians have asked managers of public enterprises to respond to four main areas of concern: creating new jobs and avoiding fires, responding to labour needs in specific geographic areas, filling positions for political patronage and financing political campaigns. (Franco A. Grassini, "The Italian Enterprises: The Political Constraints", State-Owned Enterprise in the Western Economies, Edited By: Raymond Vernon and Yair Aharoni, Croom Helm Ltd., 1981, p.72)

[219] Guislain, (The Privatization Challenge), p.6, 7; Bhaskar, p.1

[220] W. Lieberman, p.10; Anibal Santos, "Privatisation and State Intervention-(An Economic Approach)", Deregulation or Re-regulation-Regulatory Reform in Europe and the United States, Edited by: Giandomenico Majone, Pinter Publishers, London, 1990, p.140

B. Budget deficits and public finance crises

Another important reason for the move to privatisation is that most governments find themselves facing deep budget deficits and public finance crises. The state no longer has the financial resources either to offset the losses of SOEs or to provide the capital increases necessary for their development.[221] For example, in the U.K., the borrowing and losses of SOEs were running at about £ 3 billion a year.[222]

The incompatibility between the structural nature of public sector expansion, and the instability of government financial resources made the system increasingly fragile. At the beginning of the 1980s, the drying up of external financing sources (deterioration of the terms of trade, debt crisis), together with the reduced tax take caused by the recessions induced by these external shocks, suddenly triggered a public finance crisis in the majority of developing countries. Loss-making enterprises were accused of being an unbearable burden on the budget and of using the resources made available to them in an unproductive fashion. The increasing financial burden caused by the virtually systematic salvage of ailing private enterprises reinforced the criticisms concerning budget transfers to public enterprises. The impossibility of financing the haphazard expansion of the public sector led governments to consider reforms and to accept the prospect of privatisation as a miracle cure for their difficulties.[223]

---

[221] Guislain, (The Privatization Challenge), p.7; Timothy Ash, Paul Hare and Anna Canning, "Privatisation in the Former Centrally Planned Economies", Privatisation and Regulation-A Review of the Issues, Edited By: Peter M Jackson and Catherine M Price, Longman Group Limited, London & New York, 1994, p.215; "The Evolution of Privatisation", Privatisation: Motives and Methods, US Energy Information Administration, URL: http//www.eia.doe.gov; John Heath, "Survey of Contributions", Public Enterprise at the Crossroads-Essays in Honour of V.V. Ramanadham, Edited By: John Heath, London and New York, Routledge, 1990, p.4

[222] "International Perspectives on Privatisation of State Owned Enterprises", Narendar V. Rao, Northeastern, C. Bhaktavatsala Rao and Steve Dunphy, Small Business Advancement National Center, University of Central Arkansas, URL: http://www.sbaer.uca.edu/

[223] Olivier Bouin, "The Privatisation in Developing Countries: Reflections on a Panacea", Policy Brief No. 3, OECD Development Centre, OECD 1992

In other words, the decision to privatise was thus to a large extent dictated by the limitation of states' financial resources. For this reason, one of the prime objectives set for privatisation was to help reduce current budget deficits through the revenue obtained from transfer operations.

Finally we must point out that, in the United Kingdom one of the important reasons for privatisation was to cut nationalised industry cash requirements. Thus, as soon as the Thatcher government began, there was intense pressure from within the Treasury to achieve the maximum possible public asset sales in order to reduce the public sector-borrowing requirement. The Thatcher government in 1979 was frustrated in its desire to cut current public expenditure by the need to pay out more in social security benefits because of rising unemployment.[224]

C. International obligations or aspirations

Appearance of privatisation on the development agenda is also due to external pressures from international aid donors and banking agencies, such as the World Bank, OECD and the International Monetary Fund.[225] The US Agency for International Development (USAID) promotes denationalisation for avowedly ideological reasons.[226] For USAID, greater supply of supply-side economics is an end itself.

International bodies such as the World Bank are more sensitive to the diversity of economic culture worldwide and adopt a more pragmatic approach to privatisation. The World

---

[224] Foster, p.113, 116

[225] Moazzem Hossain, "Liberalisation and Privatisation-India's Telecommunications Reforms", Who Benefits from Privatisation?, Edited by: Moazzem Hossain, Justin Malbon, Routledge Studies in the Modern World Economy, London and New York, 1998, p.214

In that context, for example both Romania and Bulgaria have received financial support from IMF. (Daniel Daianu, "The Changing Mix of Disequilibra during Transition: A Romanian Perspective"", Privatisation, Liberalization and Destruction-Recreating the Market in Central and Eastern Europe, Edited By: László Csaba, Dartmouth Publishing Company Limited, England & USA, 1994, p.198, Tatiana Houbenova-Dellisivkova, "Liberalisation and Transformation in Bulgaria", Privatisation, Liberalization and Destruction-Recreating the Market in Central and Eastern Europe, Edited by: László Csaba, Dartmouth Publishing Company Limited, England & USA, 1994, p.218)

These international financial organisations, particularly, IMF has been playing an important role in developing countries, especially in former socialist countries.

Emil Constantinescu, President of Romania states that: "The restructuring of the Romanian economy as well as the whole program ... pursues the well-known directions of the International Monetary Fund and of the World Bank." (Emil Constantinescu President of Romania, on May 5, 1997, the President of Romania, Emil Constantinescu, delivered this speech at CIPE's Regional Conference, "Generating Investment through Economic Reform," in Bucharest, Romania, web page of Center for International Private Enterprise, URL: http://www.cipe.org/)

[226] According to U.S. Agency for International Development (USAID): "Privatisation offers a clear means to limit the authority of government. By removing the government from economic activities, it eliminates opportunities for recurrent corrupt dealing in sales, employment, procurement, and financing contracts."

Bank points to growing debts of many state-owned enterprises swallowing public spending which could otherwise go on health or education. The Bank illustrates the impact of even modest improvements in efficiency of state firms.[227] On the other hand, G-10 considers privatisation "crucial" particularly for former socialist countries.[228]

Finally, a radical reform of public finances, involving an overhaul of the public sector, may also be needed to satisfy international obligations or aspirations. This applies in particular to member states of the European Union (EU), who are constrained by EU rules in their ability to subsidise state enterprises and most comply with strict fiscal requirements imposed by the Maastricht Treaty to qualify for membership in the Monetary Union. It also applies to countries that have committed to structural adjustment programs with the World Bank, OECD[229] or the International Monetary Fund.[230] It is also not by accident that the most intensive privatisation

---

("Institutional Reforms: Privatization", U.S. Agency for International Development, URL: http://www.info.usaid.gov/)

[227] Michael Beesley and Stephen Littlechild, *Privatisation: Principles, Problems and Priorities*, Lloyds Bank Annual Review, Volume I, Edited By: Christopher Johnson, Pinter Publishers, London and New York, 1988, p.124; Olivier Bouin, "The Privatisation in Developing Countries: Reflections on a Panacea", Policy Brief No. 3, OECD Development Centre, OECD 1992; Hossain, and Malbon, (Introduction), p.1; Attila Chikán, "The Revolution in Ownership", Reconnecting Europe, p.25, URL: http://www.ac.com

The World Bank provides financial support and credits for the privatisation programs in some countries. For example, The World Bank approved a US$759.6 million Economic Reform Loan for Turkey to support the government's reforms in public expenditure management, social security, agriculture, and infrastructure (telecommunications and energy). The loan also supports the disinflation program and acceleration of privatisation. (22nd May 2000, URL: http://www.cnn.com, http://www.presswire.net). The World Bank provides financial support and loans for privatisation and restructuring programs in former socialist countries; one example is the Former Yugoslav Republic of Macedonia. (Joseph Pernia and S. Ramachandran, "The Macedonian Gambit— Enterprise cum Bank Restructuring", Public Policy for the Private Sector, The World Bank, Note No. 62, November 1995, p.1)

For the World Bank Contribution to Private Participation in Infrastructure see: Ömer Karasapan, "The World Bank Contribution to Private Participation in Infrastructure", Public Policy for the Private Sector, The World Bank, Note No: 55, October 1995

Finally according to Bulgarian government the privatisation programme is complied with commitments shouldered by the government in the agreements with the International Monetary Fund and the World Bank. (Bulgarian Foreign Investment Agency, URL: http://www.bfia.org/privat.htm; Official web page of Bulgarian Privatisation Agency, URL: http://www.privatisation.online.bg)

[228] Lamberto Dini, "Privatisation Processes in Eastern Europe: Theoretical Foundations and Empirical Results", Privatisation Process in Eastern Europe- Theoretical Foundations and Empirical Results, Edited by: Maria Baldassarri, Luigi Paganetto, Edmund S. Phelps, St. Martin`s Press, 1993, p.9

[229] For OECD activities in Privatisation see: "Background Information on the OECD`s Privatisation Activities", URL: http://www.oecd.org:80/daf/peru/CONTENT/backpriv.htm#The RAGP

[230] Paul Starr, "The Meaning of Privatisation", web page of University of Princeton, URL: http://princeton.edu/~starr/meaning.html; also see: Guislain, (The Privatization Challenge), p.7, 8

For example in Portugal Cavaco government embraced privatisation for a variety of motives. First, the sell-offs were seen as a means of raising much needed cash that could be channelled directly into reducing the level of public debt, thereby meeting one of the Maastricht convergence criteria. (Corkill, p. 217, 220)

programs of recent years have materialised among EU countries in the run up to the EMU.[231] Although in the Treaty of Rome European Union has adopted a neutral policy towards privatisation, in practice, the EU encourages and in some cases requires member countries to implement privatisation in certain sectors. For example, EC competition policy directives that aims to limit state aid to industry states and signal that inefficient industries can no longer rely on state subsidies for their survival.[232]

D. Changes in the international economy

Rapid changes in the international economy have also helped hasten the decline of the typical SOE. Globalisation of the economy,[233] accelerated technological innovation, and growing integration of markets compel businesses to adopt highly flexible strategies and continuously adjust them to changing circumstances. That may, among other things, require the formation of alliances with foreign partners in the area of technology, procurement, or trade, or even through cross-shareholdings or integration in international groups. SOEs are notoriously ill placed to function so flexibility and to forge such alliances.[234]

One of the main reasons for utilities and infrastructures to come under the government's purview in the 1950s and 1960s was the perceived lack of resources in the private sector to finance their rapid and wide expansion. Financial markets were fragmented into closed national areas with low liquidity and insufficient savings. International capital flows were not only a

---

[231] Nestor and Mahboobi, p.6
See: p. 349-369 on Privatisation and European Union
[232] This was the case in Portugal's accession to the EC. (Corkill, p.217)
[233] "Privatisation as a Global Phenomenon", Chapter I, URL: http://www.eia.doe.gov
[234] For example, technological developments in telecommunications and electricity generation industries have reduced capital intensity, and the lead times involved in the provision of services, and thus expanded the potential for competition in activities that were once dominated by monopolies.(Nestor and Mahboobi, p.5, 6; Privatisation Trends in OECD Countries-June 1996, URL: http://www.oecd.org; Privatisation in Europe, Asia and Latin America, What Lessons can be Drawn?, Summary of the Presentations at the International Workshop on Privatisation Organised by the OECD in April 1994, Sao Paulo, URL: http://www.oecd.org; Guislain, (The Privatization Challenge), p.8

small fragment of what they are today; they were also largely dominated by direct sovereign lending (or aid) and other debt flows explicitly or implicitly guaranteed by governments.[235]

E. Ideological debate on economic management

Furthermore, the ideological debate on economic management and privatisation has evolved substantially in response to the growing globalisation of the economy and to the end of the cold war and confrontation between socialist and capitalist models of development. The narrowing of ideological schisms has produced a more pragmatic approach to economic reform, of which privatisation forms part.[236]

In some economic sectors the reasons evoked to justify state intervention no longer exist. In infrastructure sectors (telecommunications and electricity generation, for example), technological and other developments have made it possible to introduce competition into activities formerly thought to be natural monopolies, thus obviating the justification for the survival of large monopolies.[237]

F. Important roles of certain SOEs

Some SOEs employee considerable number of employees or they provide essential products for defence industry etc. In other words, in each country some SOEs are very important for the economy and whole society. States simply cannot let those enterprises go bankrupt. Thus in the United Kingdom, for example the rescue of Rolls Royce under previous Conservative

---

[235] Nestor and Mahboobi, p.6
For example, the state owned oil companies of Western Europe were created to achieve national goals that existing market mechanism and private enterprises could not achieve alone. (Øystein Noreng, "State-Owned Oil Companies: Western Europe", State-Owned Enterprise in the Western Economies", Edited By: Raymond Vernon and Yair Aharoni, Croom Helm Ltd., 1981, p.117). Lack of capital and high risks were the main obstacles for private enterprises to make investment in the oil sector.
[236] Robinson, Neil, "Corporate Interests and the Politics of Transition in Russia: 1991-1994", Privatization in Central and Eastern Europe-Perspectives and Approaches, Edited by: Demetrius S. Iatridis and June Gary Hopps, Praeger Publishers, USA, 1998, p.170-173; Guislain, (The Privatization Challenge), p.8
[237] Guislain, (The Privatization Challenge), p.8

government suggests that the strategic role of an industry in the economy, and possible defence commitments, will be more important in privatisation decision.[238]

III. PERFORMANCE and OWNERSHIP[239]

A. Introduction

Neo-classical economic theory suggests that the relationship between ownership and performance is tenuous; efficiency is seen mainly as a function of market and incentive structures. In theory, it makes little difference whether a firm is privately or publicly owned as long as:

(a) It operates in a competitive or contestable market without barriers to entry or, just as important, barriers to exit.

(b) The owner instructs management to follow the signals provided by the market and gives it the autonomy to do so.

(c) Management is rewarded and sanctioned on the basis of performance[240].

Evidence shows that the theory does indeed apply in practice--with two crucial qualifications. First, the full set of necessary conditions is only rarely met. And second, even when it is met, it tends to stay met for only a while; the necessary conditions cannot be made to endure.[241]

---

[238] Graham and Prosser, (Privatising Nationalised Industries), p. 19, 31; Prosser, (Nationalised Industries), p.50, 78, 79
According to Prosser: "...It is highly unlikely that a de-nationalised British telecom, or British Aerospace with its major defence role, would be allowed to go bankrupt by the government..." (p.78, 79)
[239] John Nellis, "Is Privatisation Necessary", Public Policy for the Private Sector, The World Bank, FPD Note No. 7, May 1994
[240] Inotai, p.167; Adhikari and Kirkpatrick, p.25, 43
[241] Inotai, p.167

There are a number of modern amendments to neo-classical reasoning that attempt to establish a clearer relationship between ownership and efficiency. These come mainly from public choice theory and the literature on principal and agents.[242]

The theoretically applicable solutions, rather than privatisation have indeed been tried, or are presently being tried, around the world--with some highly positive responses. New Zealand's "corporatisation" efforts of the mid-1980s achieved efficiency and financial gains in ten of eleven enterprises.[243]

The most powerful recent empirical evidence to support the thesis that reform can work without ownership change comes from China. There are now about 1.3 million township and village enterprises employing 90 million people. They account for more than 20 percent of China's industrial production and are growing far more rapidly than the traditional state-owned enterprise (SOE) sector. Their financial and economic performance surpasses that of the traditional SOEs by two or even three times. They are a stunning example of how positive performance can be achieved by firms that are not privately owned--but that are made to act as if they were.[244]

All these solutions are based on the idea that perceived deficiencies of public enterprise performance can be corrected by changes in policy, incentives, and institutions, and that ownership change is not necessary.[245]

---

[242] John Nellis, "Is Privatisation Necessary", Public Policy for the Private Sector, The World Bank, FPD Note No. 7, May 1994
[243] John Nellis, "Is Privatisation Necessary", Public Policy for the Private Sector, The World Bank, FPD Note No. 7, May 1994
[244] John Nellis, "Is Privatisation Necessary", Public Policy for the Private Sector, The World Bank, FPD Note No. 7, May 1994; State-Owned Enterprise (SOE) Reform in China, Senior Experts Meeting organised by the OECD and the Development Research Centre (DRC) of the State Council of the People's Republic of China, Synthesis Note, by the OECD Secretariat Beijing (China), 20-21 July 1998, URL: http://www.oecd.org//
[245] John Nellis, "Is Privatisation Necessary", Public Policy for the Private Sector, The World Bank, FPD Note No. 7, May 1994

Finally in Poland early progress showed that state enterprises could raise efficiency quite quickly, and this encouraged the idea that efficiency could be achieved by state industries without privatisation. Upon closer investigation it appeared that Polish managers of state firms performed well because they expected privatisation and hoped their achievements would assure their survival when it came.[246]

B. The Performance of Privatised Companies

1. General

The public currently suffers from a poor image owing to what is seen as an unduly rigid structure and undue protection from the authorities and to what is presumed to be a systematic failure adapt to technical progress and innovation[247]. In the privatisation literature state enterprises are considered inefficient and private ownership will produce superior efficiency outcomes because of the following factors:

(a) State-owned industries suffer from excessive political intervention[248] Politicians interfere less in the affairs of private than public firms. Political interference is a major cause of efficiency-reducing conditions in public enterprises; it manifests itself in overstaffing, under-capitalisation, inappropriate plant location, wrong use of inputs, and many other costly acts;[249]

---

[246] Havrylyshyn and McGettigan, p.4

[247] Robert, p.25; Maurice R. Garner, "Has Public Enterprise Failed?" Privatisation in the United Kingdom, Edited by: V.V. Ramanadham, Routledge, London and New York, 1988, p.26-38.
There is even discussion whether state owned enterprises can be considered in public ownership. According to some authors: "state owned firms are often described as being in 'public ownership,' but this is a fiction. The public has none of the rights implied by ownership; they do not control such industries, and cannot alienate their alleged share of them. Privatisation can be used to transfer state industries into the real ownership of large numbers of the public." (Madsen Pirie, "Privatisation: 10 Lessons of Experience", President of the Adam Smith Institute, URL: http://privatizationlink.com)

[248] Carsberg, (Competition and Private Ownership), p.8; Kirkpatrick, p. 239; "International Perspectives on Privatisation of State Owned Enterprises", Narendar V. Rao, Northeastern, C. Bhaktavatsala Rao, Steve Dunphy, Small Business Advancement National Center, University of Central Arkansas, URL: http://www.sbaer.uca.edu/

[249] Howard Raiffa, "Decision Making in the State-Owned Enterprise"", State-Owned Enterprise in the Western Economies, Edited By: Raymond Vernon and Yair Aharoni, Croom Helm Ltd., 1981, p.54-62

(b) Management in the state industries has vague, fluctuating and often conflicting objectives. Political time frames are often incompatible with the longer time cycles that successful investment needs[250];

(c) Politicians and civil servants fail to monitor managerial behaviour as effectively as the private capital market and, amongst other things, this leads to over-investment and the trading of more output for lower profits;

(d) Trade unions in the public sector are able to succeed in obtaining above market wages, employment levels and conditions of work at the expense of consumers;

(e) Private firms are subject to exit much more often than public enterprises. Private firms are more subject to bankruptcy, liquidation, hostile take-over, and closure than public corporations. When exit is a real possibility, there is a greater likelihood that owners and managers will take active, efficiency enhancing measures to avoid it. Also bankruptcy is not a credible threat when there are seemingly unlimited taxpayers funds to call upon[251];

(f) Managerial salaries in the public sector are politically determined and rarely compare well with the pay of equivalent jobs in the private sector. Consequently, the quality of management suffers. Private ownership establishes a market for managers, leading to higher-quality management;

(g) There is a lack of performance related rewards in the public sector;

(h) Public sector firms are insufficiently consumer orientated when operating in monopoly markets;

---

[250] Yair Aharoni, "Managerial Discretion", State-Owned Enterprise in the Western Economies", Edited By: Raymond Vernon and Yair Aharoni, Croom Helm Ltd., 1981, p.184
[251] In that context, unlike private firms, SOEs could borrow from public funds without in effect ever needing to repay the loans since the government would be obliged to cancel any debt which became too large to be serviced. (Privatization in the United Kingdom, Ernst & Young, 1994, p. 24)

(i) State ownership confuses the regulation of the activities of industry with the role of ownership so that state regulation is less effective;[252]

(j) Capital markets subject privately owned firms to greater scrutiny and discipline than they do public enterprises. Public enterprises often operate on "soft budget constraint", because of explicit or implicit guarantees from the state, public enterprises can borrow capital at less-than-market interest rates, and they often enjoy outright subsidies and other concessions from the state;[253]

(k) Private firms are supervised by self-interested board members and shareholders, rather than by disinterested bureaucrats, and are thus more likely than public firms to use capital efficiently and to maintain it;[254]

(l) Public enterprises are not profitable.[255]

In sum it has been argued that public enterprises suffer from an array of institutional problems. Their objectives are often numerous and ill defined, ranging from profit maximisation to regional development and employment. Frequently they report to several levels of management including both politicians and bureaucrats. Management incentives are seldom linked to performance, and performance itself is seldom evaluated.[256]

In the literature it is often noted that government owned monopolies charge lower prices than they might under private ownership. The reasoning is that governments tend to use pricing

---

[252] Martin and Parker, p.5
[253] In other words public enterprises don't pay their taxes, their utility bills, their accounts payable to other public enterprises, customs duties etc.
[254] In other words it is commonly argued that under large-scale state ownership little interest was shown, either by management or workers, in improving the efficiency of production. (Ash, Hare and Canning, p.214)
[255] Aizenman, p.15
It is argued that, taxes are used to cover SOE losses. (Kenneth J. Arrow, "On Finance and Decision Making", State-Owned Enterprise in the Western Economies, Edited By: Raymond Vernon and Yair Aharoni, Croom Helm Ltd., 1981, p.64, 65)
[256] Galal, Jones, Tandon and Vogelsang, p.543. According to these authors: "...a public enterprise operates much like a soccer game in which no score is kept and there is neither goal nor referee..."(p.551).

of utilities to attempt to control inflation, redistribute income and buy votes.[257] It is also argued that, in many developing countries, SOEs absorb large amounts of funds that could be better spent on basic social services.[258]

Finally, it has been argued that, these adverse reasons emerge in much sharper focus in countries with communist command economy models where systems have been grossly deficient in fundamental corporate, legal and financial practices that normally enable benchmarking of firms with regard to their objectives, performance and integrity of management.[259]

2. Economic Literature and Empirical Studies

In the economic literature there are different approaches to the issue of ownership and efficiency. A number of empirical studies have compared the performance of public and private enterprises, but the results vary.[260]

(a) One group of studies including those done by Vickers and Yarrow and Sheshinski and López-Calva argue that ownership matters in the sense that changes in the structure of property rights are likely to have significant effects upon firm behaviour.[261] In other words, they assert

---

[257] Galal, Jones, Tandon and Vogelsang, p.543

[258] Mary M. Shirley, "Getting Bureaucrats Out of Business: Obstacles to State Enterprise Reform", web page of Center for International Private Enterprise, URL: http//www.cipe.org/

[259] Under the communist regime inefficiently run firms did not face the threat of bankruptcy. They simply received fiscal transfers to cover the difference between their revenues and costs. The existence of soft budget constraints meant firms were able to induce the government to finance their deficits. [Aaron Tornell, "Privatizing the Privatised", NBER (National Bureau of Economic Research) Working Paper Series, Working Paper 7206, URL: http://www.nber.org/papers/w7206, Cambridge, July 1999, p.14]. Furthermore, a socialist enterprise never faced the problem of losing demand for its products because its "customers" were its captives within the plan. (Fryman and Rapaczynski, p.67)

Also see: "International Perspectives on Privatisation of State Owned Enterprises", Narendar V. Rao, Northeastern, C. Bhaktavatsala Rao, Steve Dunphy, Small Business Advancement National Center, University of Central Arkansas, URL: http://www.sbaer.uca.edu/

[260] John Nellis, "Is Privatisation Necessary", Public Policy for the Private Sector, The World Bank, FPD Note No. 7, May 1994; Galal, Jones, Tandon, Vogelsang, p.11, 12, 16

[261] Vickers and Yarrow, (An Economic Analysis), p.44; Sheshinski and López-Calva, p.28. [Furthermore this study points out that privatisation reduces the net transfer to SOE's in the aggregate. These transfers become positive if the government actually starts collecting taxes from privatised firms. (p.28)]

According to one study, three quarters of executives interviewed in a survey said the quality of decision-making in their company had improved. Eight out of ten think staff now have greater responsibility and a bigger role in decision-making, while 82 percent say staff are now more committed to making the business successful. ("Central

68

that state ownership produces poor performance[262]; private enterprises outperform state owned enterprises[263] and the private sector is superior to the public sector particularly where competition is effective.[264]

These studies also maintain that evidence on the privatisation experience to date has consistently shown that a change in ownership has improved performance considerably at the firm level, both in terms of productive efficiency and profitability. In terms of financial objectives, such as fostering the development or further expansion of equity markets, privatisation has been a great success. In terms of economic objectives, privatisation has generally had a positive effect on consumer welfare as the separation of commercial from the non-commercial functions has allowed for a more transparent allocation of resources, thereby diminishing rents. The degree of success, however, has depended on the post- privatisation market structure, and the introduction of competition; or the existence of effective regulatory regimes, where introduction of competition was not possible and natural monopolies persisted.[265]

---

and Eastern European Businesses Poised to Challenge Western Competitors", Recent Headlines, Andersen Consulting Study, URL: http://www.ac.com).
[262] "International Perspectives on Privatisation of State Owned Enterprises", Narendar V. Rao, Northeastern, C. Bhaktavatsala Rao, Steve Dunphy, Small Business Advancement National Center, University of Central Arkansas, URL: http://www.sbaer.uca.edu/
[263] Havrylyshyn and McGettigan, p.10. According to these authors: "... any privatisation is better than none..."(p.10)
[264] "Privatization Policy", The Fraser Institute, URL: http://www.fraserinstitute.ca/, p.2, 3. However, the Fraser Institute believes that competition is also a very important factor in the economy. (p.3).
The British government has claimed that privatisation has resulted in higher productivity and profitability. (Hartley, p.181). Some authors argue that most privatised industries in the United Kingdom have grown since privatisation, and in general, profits have risen across most of the 1979 public sector. [Bishop and Kay, (Does Privatisation Work?), p.40]
The following reasons are considered some factors for using the private sector:
(a) To obtain special skills or supplement staff for short periods of time, (b) To meet demands beyond current government capacity, (c) To reduce costs, (d) To improve service quality, (e) To provide clients with more choice of providers and levels of service, (f) Ideology: less government is better. (Demetra Smith Nightingale, Nancy Pindus, "Privatization of Public Social Services: A Background Paper", October 15, 1997, Urban Institute, URL: http//www.urban.org/)
[265] Nestor and Mahboobi, p.2, 19; John Redwood, "Privatisation: A Consultant's Perspective", (Consultant's Perspective), Privatisation and Deregulation in Global Perspective, Edited By: Dennis J. Gayle and Jonathan N.Goodrich, Pinter Publishers, USA, 1990, 61; Vickers and Yarrow, (An Economic Analysis), p.2; Peter Young, "The Lessons of Privatisation", web page of Center for International Private Enterprise, URL: http//www.cipe.org/; Aizenman, p.15 [According to Aizenman privatisation in developing countries may entail positive effects by changing the menu of taxes.(p.15)]

(b) Other authors have argued that privatisation is not a necessary condition for improved productive efficiency of state owned enterprises. The dual effect of corporatisation of SOEs and introduction of increased competition to the markets in which they operate is mainly responsible for their improved economic performance. [266]

Bishop and Kay have suggested that there is no direct relation between privatisation and the improvements in performance of the privatised firms.[267] Furthermore Woodward has asserted that, there is no close and direct relation between ownership and efficiency.[268]

(c) Some authors argue that the costs of privatisation in Third World countries have been much higher and benefits much less than in the centre nations. According to this view, third world countries have experienced increased malnutrition, poverty, and political unrest in the 1980s since privatisation.[269]

(d) Numerous methodological and technical difficulties are involved in comparing the relative efficiency of public and private enterprises; the economics literature now contains a large number of such studies. In one study, ninety-five studies have been examined and analysed. Of these, sixty-eight produced results showing that private corporations were more efficient than public corporations, seven concluded that public corporations were more efficient, and remaining twenty found that there to be no difference between public and private firms. A study by

---

[266] Allan Brown, "The Economics of Privatisation-Case Study of Australian Telecommunications", Edited by: Moazzem Hossain, Justin Malbon, Routledge Studies in the Modern World Economy, London and New York, 1998, p.72; Kirkpatrick, p. 239. According to Kirkpatrick: "...it is difficult to believe that existing public enterprises are not capable of achieving significant improvements in efficiency...internal restructuring of public enterprise organisation and management and public sector reforms are likely to make a more significant...contribution to improving public enterprise performance..."(p.242)

[267] Bishop and Kay, (Western Economies), p.206, 207

[268] Nick Woodward, "Public Enterprise, Privatization, and Cultural Adoption", Public Enterprise at the Crossroads-Essays in Honour of V.V. Ramanadham, Edited By: John Heath, London and New York, Routledge, 1990, p.270

[269] Melvin Burke, "Private versus Public Construction in Honduras: Issues of Economics and Ideology", Privatization and Deregulation in Global Perspective, Edited by: Dennis J. Gayle and Jonathan N. Goodrich, Pinter Publishers, London, 1990, p.214.

According to Burke: "...In...Third World countries the private foreign sectors have benefited most from the sale of public enterprises. Debt, depression, devaluation, and dependency have all been enhanced by

Industry Commission of Australia concluded that the weight of empirical evidence view that under competitive conditions private firms were generally more efficient than public firms. [270]

(i) A study compared the pre- and post-privatisation performance of sixty-one companies in eighteen countries (six developing and twelve industrial) and thirty-two industries. It constructed a timeline of the operating results from the last few years of public ownership through the first years after privatisation. And it tested for the results most governments expect: increased profitability, increased operating efficiency, increased capital investment spending, and increased output. It also tested for a result that governments hope for but generally do not expect to achieve: privatisation without lowering employment levels. The study tested for these results both for the full sample and for several subsamples: Privatisations of firms in competitive and non-competitive industries, full and partial privatisations; privatisations involving firms headquartered in OECD countries and in developing countries, and "control" and "revenue" privatisations. [271]

The study showed significant increases among newly private firms in profitability, output per employee, capital spending, and employment. It also found that the financial policies of these firms start to resemble those typically associated with private entrepreneurial companies—with lower leverage and higher dividend pay out ratios. [272]

---

privatisation through periphery. These countries have also experienced increased malnutrition, poverty, and political unrest in the 1980s since privatisation"(p.214)

[270] Brown, p.72

[271] William L. Megginson, Robert C. Nash, and Matthias van Randenborgh, "The Privatization Dividend", A Worldwide Analysis of the Financial and Operating Performance of Newly Privatized Firms, Public Policy for the Private Sector, The World Bank, February 1996, Note No. 68

[272] William L. Megginson, Robert C. Nash, and Matthias van Randenborgh, The Privatization Dividend, A Worldwide Analysis of the Financial and Operating Performance of Newly Privatized Firms, Public Policy for the Private Sector, The World Bank, February 1996, Note No. 68

71

(ii) Another study compares the extent of restructuring by firms in seven Central and Eastern European countries: Bulgaria, the Czech Republic, Hungary, Poland, Romania, the Slovak Republic also found out that privatisation promotes efficiency.[273]

(iii) The World Bank, IMF, OECD and some other international financial institutions studies also found out that privatisation was good for the economy as a whole and led to higher productivity and faster growth in all but one case.[274]

(iv) Studies investigating the relative technical efficiency and profitability of SOEs and private enterprises generally support the proposition that private sector performance is superior.[275] Therefore the empirical literature, in majority supports private ownership and privatisation.

(v) Another World Bank study concludes that the output, profitability, and operating efficiency of newly-privatised companies increases significantly in the years after they are sold off.[276]

(vi) Finally another study found out that privatisation leads to welfare and gains are possible across countries at different level of development.[277]

---

[273] Robert E. Anderson, Simeon Djankov, Gerhard Pohl, "Privatization and Restruction in Central and Eastern Europe", Public Policy for the Private Sector, The World Bank, July 1997, Note no. 123

[274] Sunita Kikeri, John Nellis and Mary Shirley, Outreach Nr. 3, "Policy Views from the Country Economics Department", The World Bank, July 1992; David Donaldson and Dileep Wagle, Privatization: Principles and Practice (Executive Summary), International Finance Corporation, 1995, footnote: 1; Privatisation Trends in OECD Countries-June 1996, http://www.oecd.org; Havrylyshyn and McGettigan, p.4. [(According to Havrylyshyn and McGettigan: "... several thousand privatised firms in seven Eastern European countries shows that they average annual productivity growth of 4-5 percent, five times the rate for state-owned enterprises."(p.4)]

Another World Bank study on Mexico finds significance improvements in the performance of the newly privatised firms, with profits rising by 40 per cent. (Rafael La Porta and Florencio López-de-Silanes, "The Benefits of Privatisation: Evidence from Mexico", Public Policy for the Private Sector, The World Bank Group, Note No: 117, June 1997,p.1). According to the study: Empirical analysis of the raw data shows that the profitability of firms in the sample increased significantly after privatisation according to four indicators, all ratios-operating income to sales, net income to sales, operating income to fixed assets, and net income to fixed assets. (p.2)

[275] Lawrence Bouton, Mariusz A. Sumlinski, " IFC Discussion Paper Number 31-Trends in Private Investment in Developing Countries, Statistics for 1970-95," December 1996, February 1997 (revised)

[276] William L. Megginson & Jeffry M. Netter, "Equity to the People: The Record on Share Issue Privatization Programs", p.3, The World Bank, URL: http://www.worldbank.org

However, when a public enterprise monopoly is privatised and is granted continued protection from market competition, an improvement in financial performance may simply be a reflection of greater exploitation of market power.[278]

3. Does Ownership Really Matter?

a. General

In many countries, there is a critical debate on the performance of state owned enterprises, and the criticisms on state owned enterprises are more or less the same in all over the world.[279] Policy makers and academics have slowly become convinced that state ownership tends to lower internal efficiency of companies in product markets. While it had generally been recognised that privately owned companies were more efficient than publicly owned enterprises, academic studies from the 1970s and early 1980s tended to conclude that it was the lack of competition and the sectoral concentration of public companies, and not so much the ownership structure, which explained the differences in efficiency between private and public owned companies. However, most of these studies were based on a comparison of cost between different companies in public and private ownership, and more recent studies, which have looked at the same company before and after privatisation have demonstrated the emergence of significant efficiency gains.[280]

---

[277] Galal, Jones, Tandon and Vogelsang, p.563. The study focuses on different firms in England, Mexico, Chile and Malaysia before and after privatisation. According to this study:" ...the most important conclusion (of the study) is that ownership matters..." (p.570). However, the authors also point out that success was caused, not by the simple act of privatisation alone, but by privatisation in combination with a set of accompanying measures and policies. (p.570). The authors named these policies as "regulation" and "sale conditions"(p.570). However, as we will discuss later on we think these policies are very comprehensive. In that context, according to us the most important measures are the high level of competition, rule of law, other institutional factors with an appropriate regulation which creates and protects the general market environment.
[278] Kirkpatrick, p. 241; Inotai, p.167
[279] For example in Greece, like in many countries, criticism is usually levelled at: (a) the low productivity of public enterprises, in particular that of their employees, (b) the lack of innovation and management initiative, (c) the deficits in problem firms and in some utilities. (Spyros K. Lioukas and Demetrios B. Papoulias, "The Effectiveness of Public Enterprises in Greece", Public Enterprise at the Crossroads-Essays in Honour of V.V. Ramanadham, Edited By: John Heath, London and New York, Routledge, 1990, p.174)
[280] Web page of the World Bank, URL: http://www.oecd.org/

However in a large body of economics literature it is argued that, what is wrong with public enterprise is not its public ownership but the fact that it usually operates in monopoly markets, and in such markets all enterprises-whether public or private-tend to be inefficient.[281]

Indeed it has been argued that particularly in less developed countries an internal restructuring of public service organisation and management and public sector reform is likely to make a more significant contribution to improving public enterprise performance.[282]

Moreover, in recent years some studies have shown that it is not always the case that privatisation means efficiency and development in the economy as it has seen in the examples of Associated British Ports and British Aerospace. On balance, however, privatisation does seem to have been generally associated with higher profitability.[283]

b. Difficulties

Most governments find it difficult if not impossible to apply the entire package of qualifying conditions that are essential for reforms short of ownership change to work. The landscape, particularly in developing countries, and now in ex-socialist countries as well, is littered with partial attempts to impose reform where the government owners hadn't the will or the fortitude or the knowledge or the capacity or the luck to impose the whole of the reform package--and the results were minimal, modest, or non-existent.[284]

There are innumerable examples in which government owners kept prices for the products of supposedly reformed public enterprises too low to cover costs, out of fear of the political consequences of price increases. Governments may shut off direct budget flows to public enterprises, but few then go on to block concessionary transfers from the banking system.

---

[281] Galal, Jones, Tandon and Vogelsang, p.541
[282] Kirkpatrick, p.242. According to Kirkpatrick: "...it is difficult to believe that existing public enterprises are not capable of achieving significant improvements in efficiency..."(p.242)
[283] Martin and Parker, p.155, 168

Governments grant operational autonomy to managers, but not with regard to hiring and firing, or plant location, or from whom to obtain inputs. Technically innocuous board of director reforms have been halted in Kenya, Morocco, and elsewhere because board membership is a lucrative core part of the patronage system. Most governments have non-economic objectives for their public enterprise systems. While they want them to be profitable and productive, they are most often unwilling or incapable of allowing these commercial aims to take clear precedence over the non-commercial. Thus, their reform efforts tend to be partial. [285]

While many countries have struggled to rationalise the operations of their SOEs, only a few have succeeded in staunching the waste and inefficiency that too often prevail under state ownership.[286] However, in the few cases in which governments do establish and maintain the precedence of commercial over non-commercial aims, the results are, as we have seen in China, very good. But they tend not to last. The common case is that bad times make for good policies-- in crises governments do establish the precedence of commercial objectives, they do impose a harder budget constraint, and they do give autonomy to public enterprise managers to achieve commercial aims. But again and again, when the crisis fades, or when the regime changes, or when some major political claim arises, commitment to the priority of commercial aims and to non-interference in day-to-day management of the firm fades with it. Examples of backsliding include the New Zealand Post Office, the Japanese National Railway, Pakistan public industrial enterprises, and some of the Korean government invested enterprises. [287]

---

[284] John Nellis, "Is Privatisation Necessary", Public Policy for the Private Sector, The World Bank, FPD Note No. 7, May 1994

[285] John Nellis, "Is Privatisation Necessary", Public Policy for the Private Sector, The World Bank, FPD Note No. 7, May 1994

[286] "Gauging the Results of State Enterprise Reform", web page of Center for International Private Enterprise, URL: http://www.cipe.org/

[287] John Nellis, "Is Privatisation Necessary", Public Policy for the Private Sector, The World Bank, FPD Note No. 7, May 1994; Dennis J. Gayle and Bruce Seaton, "New Zealand: A Welfare State through Corporatization?", Privatization and Deregulation in Global Perspective, Edited by: Dennis J. Gayle and Jonathan N. Goodrich, Pinter Publishers, London, 1990, p.329-346. Also see: "International Perspectives on Privatisation of State Owned Enterprises", Narendar V. Rao, Northeastern, C. Bhaktavatsala Rao, Steve Dunphy, Small Business Advancement National Center, University of Central Arkansas, URL: http://www.sbaer.uca.edu/; Mary M. Shirley,

c. Consumer aspects

The success of privatisation should not be judged in terms of improvements in performance indicators such as productivity and profitability. In that context, particularly the consumers need to be considered. Consumers can benefit from privatisation by paying less for their service, by facing more stable prices, or by receiving an improvement in the quality of the service.[288]

Finally privatisation is not costless. There are important transaction costs that need to be offset against any gains. For example there are the agency costs of floating new shares on the stock market.[289] There are also advertising costs. Thus in the UK, very large privatisations, especially British Telecom, British Gas, and water authorities and the electricity industry have required massive marketing campaigns to ensure that the government's objectives of a successful transition to the private sector and wide spread of share ownership are met.[290]

"Getting Bureaucrats Out of Business: Obstacles to State Enterprise Reform", web page of Center for International Private Enterprise, URL: http://www.cipe.org/
    Finally we must point out that even in China it is argued that privatisation would be a solution to inefficient state owned enterprises (SOEs). In that context, it seems that privatising small SOEs would not encounter great difficulties in terms of country's economic realities as well as ideological flexibility. The problem occurs in privatisation of large sized enterprises. However, the idea of privatising large SOEs is controversial not only because of its economic practicability, but also because of its political and ideological sensitivity. (Hua Sheng and Du Haiyan, "State-Owned Enterprise Reform in China", Public Enterprise at the Crossroads-Essays in Honour of V.V. Ramanadham, Edited By: John Heath, London and New York, Routledge, 1990, p.82; Will Martin, "China's Economic Policies and World Trade Reforming China's Trading System, web page of Center for International Private Enterprise, URL: http//www.cipe.org/). As we discussed, socialist ideology has unquestionably been one reason for the protracted delay of privatisation. But another is of a more practical nature: China's more than 300,000 state enterprises provide jobs and a wide range of social welfare benefits to approximately 120 million workers. Any privatisation measure in the economy may result of closure of some unprofitable SOEs. And closing unprofitable factories would bring significant hardship and severe social dislocation to China's labour force that is already experiencing rising unemployment rates. (John J. Callebaut, "Reforms are Key to China's Global Integration", web page of Center for International Private Enterprise, URL: http://www.cipe.org/)

[288] Jackson and Price, p.17
[289] Khalid Khan, *Privatisation and its Legal Aspects in Developing Countries with Special Reference to Pakistan*, Lahore, February 1998, p.31-32
[290] Wright and Thompson, p.60
See: p.229-231 for the costs in the privatisation process

C. Conclusions

We can conclude that in the privatisation literature, the overwhelming consensus is that private ownership is more efficient in providing private goods in competitive markets.[291] Thus some late comprehensive studies show that, privatisation, with appropriate measures and policies, provides positive outcomes for the economy and private sector is more efficient to public sector.[292] Technically, however, it is not always possible to measure and compare the performance of the firms before and after privatisation.[293] The only valid comparison would be to evaluate the performance of the privatised enterprise with what it would have been had the enterprise remained public, "all other things being equal". But privatisation operations generally take place in a rapidly changing environment whose impact on the performance has to be assessed. In the developing countries, this assessment is all the more difficult because of the multiple impacts of the implementation of economic and financial liberalisation programmes.[294]

---

[291] Paul Starr, "The Meaning of Privatization", URL: http://www.princeton.edu./~starr/meaning.html; Vickers and Yarrow, (An Economic Analysis), p.426; "Privatizing State-Owned Companies", The Prosperity Papers Series, Prosperity Paper Three, web page of Center for International Private Enterprise, URL: http//www.cipe.org/

[292] Galal, Jones, Tandon and Vogelsang, p.527. The study finds out that, in eleven of twelve cases the outcome was positive. (p.527)

[293] In other words it is very difficult to measure efficiency and the gains of privatisation. (Jackson and Price, p.16). There are problems in finding suitable test beds-sectors where both public and private enterprises operate. [Bishop and Kay, (Does Privatisation Work?), p.12, 37]

According to one approach financial performance is best judged using such indicators as pre-tax profitability. ("Gauging the Results of State Enterprise Reform", web page of Center for International Private Enterprise, URL: http://www.cipe.org/)

However, the results in different studies on performance of privatised firms are mixed and often varied depending on the precise performance measure used. [Parker, (Nationalisation, Privatisation, and Agency), p.154, 164]

Also see: Nicholas Barberis, Maxim Boycko, Andrei Shleifer, Natalia Tsukanova, How Does Privatization Work? Evidence from the Russian Shops, National Bureau of Economic Research, NBER Working Paper Series, Working Paper No: 5136, Cambridge, MA, May 1995, p.2; Spyros K. Lioukas and Demetrios B. Papoulias, "The Effectiveness of Public Enterprises in Greece", Public Enterprise at the Crossroads-Essays in Honour of V.V. Ramanadham, Edited By: John Heath, London and New York, Routledge, 1990. (In this study authors provide some methods of measuring the effectiveness of state owned enterprises, p.175-177; Privatization in the United Kingdom, Ernst & Young, 1994, p.xi)

[294] Cook and Kirkpatrick, p.18, 19; Olivier Bouin, "The Privatisation in Developing Countries: Reflections on a Panacea", Policy Brief No. 3, OECD Development Centre, OECD 1992

In other words the impact of privatisation on enterprise needs to be seen against the general background of buoyant economic conditions, and generally improving performance, thus, making it difficult disentangle cause-and-effect relations.[295]

Although in Western economies a number of measures have been adapted to measure and analyse the ownership-performance relation; applying such performance indicators to former socialist countries, is problematical. Because, the structure of the economy is very different. For example, in ex-socialist countries since stock markets are just beginning to operate, no reliable measures of firm value are available.[296]

The little empirical analysis comparing the effectiveness of public versus private service ownership shows no clear evidence that private service delivery is inherently more effective or less effective than public service delivery.[297] Furthermore, in measuring performance of the firms, there has been a tendency in the empirical literature towards reliance upon variables that are easily observable.[298] However, customers and some social objectives of state owned enterprises (SOEs) should also be taken into account.

The success of privatisation and the performance of privatised enterprises vary in each country and even in different sectors. In many countries, the results of privatisation and the reform of public enterprises have, so far, fallen short of expectations, particularly with respect to generating the proceeds of privatisation and improving economic efficiency.[299] However, although there are some unsuccessful examples and attempts in the privatisation programs, it is

---

[295] Kirkpatrick, p.237
[296] Peter Young, "The Lessons of Privatisation", web page of Center for International Private Enterprise, URL: http//www.cipe.org/; John S. Earle, "Privatization in Russia Offers Lessons for Others", web page of Center for International Private Enterprise, URL: http//www.cipe.org/. (However, in his study Earle concludes that on average, privatised firms in Russia appear to perform somewhat better than do state firms).
[297] Demetra Smith Nightingale, Nancy Pindus, "Privatization of Public Social Services: A Background Paper", October 15, 1997, Urban Institute, URL: http//www.urban.org/
[298] Vickers and Yarrow, (An Economic Analysis), p.39
[299] Schwartz and Silva Lopes, p.38

still early to draw some definitive conclusions. It is only in the medium and long term that one can see the effect of ownership on enterprise decisions.[300]

Within the microeconomic literature, it has been theoretically established that, under conditions of perfect competition, absence of information problems, and complete contracts, ownership does not matter, i.e., you would observe the same performance of the firms regardless their ownership structure.[301]

IV. The AIMS and OBJECTIVES of PRIVATISATION

A. Introduction

Every strategy must start by clearly stating the objectives that are being pursued[302], because these determine the approach taken and choices made. As the reasons for privatisation are varied as styles of sale and the countries undertaking them, there are several, political and economic aims for privatisation.[303] Some of them are general-such as "to improve productivity in the economy and to reduce public expenditures[304], to raise the efficiency of the economy, and to enhance its social orientation, improving the payments balance of the state[305];-others are specific-e.g. limiting the power of the trade unions, gaining votes of people who could buy publicly owned houses at discount prices.[306]

---

[300] "Is Privatization Succeeding in Central and Eastern Europe?", An Interview with Roman Frydman, by the Centre for International Private Enterprise, Centre for International Private Enterprise, web page of the World Bank, URL: http:/www.worldbank.org
[301] Sheshinski and López-Calva, p.4
[302] Letwin, p.xi; Madsen Pirie, "Privatisation: 10 Lessons of Experience", President of the Adam Smith Institute, http://www.privatizationlink.com
[303] Stilpon Nestor and Ladan Mahboobi, Privatisation of Public Utilities; The OECD Experience, Rio, 23 April 1999
[304] Article 1, Law No. 4046, Adopted on 27 November 1994, Concerning Arrangements For The Implementation Of Privatization And Amending Certain Laws And Decrees With The Force of Law
[305] The beginning (preface) of Russian Federation Federal Law, On Privatisation of State Property and the Basic Principles of Privatisation of Municipal Property in the Russian Federation, Adopted by the State Duma on June 24, 1997, Approved by the Federation Council on July 3, 1997
[306] Harmathy, General Report, p.210

All too often the objectives of a privatisation program are not clearly spelled out. Lack of transparency in government policymaking or disagreements over the objectives to be pursued are among the causes. Defining and agreeing on objectives is an essential stage in the process, however; to omit it is to court failure or, at the very least, to risk poor policy choices and sub-optimal outcomes. Privatisation objectives should form an integral part of the broader objectives of the economic reform program.[307]

Governments privatise SOEs for many reasons and every government or author has his own list of objectives[308] (see table 2). The most often cited reasons are: to raise new revenue for the state; to promote economic efficiency; to reduce government interference in the economy (to cut back the participation of the government in the economy); to promote wider share-ownership[309]; to provide the opportunity to introduce competition[310], to develop the nation's capital markets[311], to promote development of the local equity market, to reduce the influence of the unions,[312] to provide greater incentives for employees, to reduce government interference in management, to substitute market finance for capital projects in place of government funding, to reduce taxation by reducing public sector borrowing, to reduce the government's operating

---

[307] Guislain, (The Privatization Challenge), p.291
Once the government's objectives have been defined a broad range of legal instruments will need to be analysed to determine whether they allow privatisation and fit with its objectives or whether they need to be amended, suspended, or repealed to allow or facilitate privatisation. As we will mention in the second chapter broadly, public enterprise laws and the legal status of the SOEs to be privatised must, for instance, be conducive to privatisation or be amended. The rules governing the creation and operation of public agencies (which may apply to the privatisation agency), civil service regulations, public finance legislation, legislation on state or public property, and other aspects of public and administrative law also must be considered. [Guislain, (The Privatization Challenge), p.291]

[308] For example for a list of the main objectives see: Nestor and Mahboobi, p. 9-12; Hossain and Malbon, (Introduction), p.1; Justin Malbon, "Gaining Balance on the Regulatory Tightrope", Edited by: Moazzem Hossain, Malbon, p.9; Kirkpatrick, p. 240; Melvin Burke, "Private versus Public Construction in Honduras: Issues of Economics and Ideology", Privatization and Deregulation in Global Perspective, Edited by: Dennis J. Gayle and Jonathan N. Goodrich, Pinter Publishers, London, 1990, p.213; "Privatizing State-Owned Companies", The Prosperity Papers Series, Prosperity Paper Three, web page of Center for International Private Enterprise, URL: http//www.cipe.org/

[309] In that issue, for British case see: Vickers and Yarrow, (An Economic Analysis), p.1; Prosser, (Nationalised Industries), p.80

[310] John Vickers and George Yarrow, *Privatisation and Natural Monopolies, (Natural Monopolies)*, Public Policy Center, 1985, p.xiii; David Donaldson and Dileep Wagle, Privatization: Principles and Practice (Executive Summary), International Finance Corporation, 1995, p.3

deficit, to raise cash through SOE sales, to generate new sources of tax revenue, to reduce external dept[313], to deepen domestic capital markets and broaden domestic equity ownership[314], to strengthen capital markets[315], to encourage the return of flight capital, to promote domestic investment, attract direct foreign investment and new technology[316], to increase domestic and international business confidence, to create opportunities for employment through real growth, to increase productive and operating efficiency, to turn around or restructure sick SOEs, to increase exports, to improve the quality of services, to reduce the role of the state in the economy, to allow firms to raise capital in commercial markets, to reduce the grip of a particular party or group on the economy (such as trade unions, the Communist Party and the nomenclature), to reduce costs in the public sector, to bring more flexibility to market, widen participation in the stock exchange, to modernise the economy, [317] to remove the public agencies from those

---

[311] William L. Megginson, "The Impact of Privatisation", web page of Center for International Private Enterprise, URL: http://www.cipe.org/
[312] Prosser, (Nationalised Industries), p.81
[313] Carsberg, (Competition and Private Ownership), p.8
[314] Stuart Bell, "Privatisation Through Broad-Based Ownership Strategies-A More Popular Option", Public Policy for the Private Sector, The World Bank, FPD note No. 33, January 1995
Also see: Gibbon, (Guide), p.14-16. Gibbon suggests a list of measures can be taken by governments to maximise participation in the privatisation transactions. Some of them are as follows:
(a) Giving the smallest investor priority in allocation of shares instead of following the traditional private sector practice of scaling back to the benefit of the largest applicant; (b) Making purchases more generally affordable through instalment payments (typically three payments over 12-15 months), which also gives the investor a higher initial return on investment; (c) Using public relations and other marketing advisors to develop a major advertising campaign to attract the small investor; and (d) Offering incentives to encourage individual applications in the offering and retention of shares in the longer term.
[315] Peter Young, "The Lessons of Privatisation", web page of Center for International Private Enterprise, URL: http://www.cipe.org/
[316] "Privatizing State-Owned Companies", The Prosperity Papers Series, Prosperity Paper Three, web page of Center for International Private Enterprise, URL: http://www.cipe.org/
[317] Gerd Schwartz, "Privatisation in Eastern Europe, Experience and Preliminary Policy Lessons", Privatisation Policy and Performance-International Perspective, Edited By: Paul Cook, Colin Kirkpatrick, Prentice Hall, Harvester Wheatsheaf, Great Britain, 1995, p.31. See also: Khan, p.10-20; Grzegorz E. Domanski, "Legal Concepts of Privatisation: Privatisation of State-Owned Enterprises Through Transformation into Corporate Entities, Privatisation in Eastern Europe: Legal, Economic, and Social Aspects, Edited By: Hans Smit, Vratislav Pechota, Parker School of Foreign and Comparative Law Columbia University, New York, 1993, p.31; Lieberman, p.11; Martin and Parker, p.6; Privatisation in Europe, Asia and Latin America, What Lessons can be Drawn?, Summary of the Presentations at the International Workshop on Privatisation Organised by the OECD in April 1994, Sao Paulo, URL: http://www.oecd.org; Andeweg, p.198; Iatridis, p.22; Olivier Bouin, "The Privatisation in Developing Countries: Reflections on a Panacea", Policy Brief No. 3, OECD Development Centre, OECD 1992; The Lessons of Experience, p.21; William T. Gormley, "The Privatisation Controversy", Privatisation and Its Alternatives, Edited By: William T. Gormley, The University of Wisconsin Press, USA, 1991, p.3; Wright, p.13-18; van Brabant, (Property Rights, Privatisation, Transitional Economies), p.59; Starr, (The Limits of Privatization), p.117; Ash, Hare and Canning, p.215; URL: http://www.portugal.org; Bradley, p.264. [Bradley provides a particular and spare list of objectives of former socialist countries. (p.268)]; Gibbon, (Guide), p.2, 3; van Brabant, (Industrial Policy in Eastern

activities that are not inherently governmental functions or core business lines, to improve the management of remaining activities, to reduce the costs of doing business; and to shift greater performance and financial risk to the private sector,[318] to strengthen the role of the private sector in the economy; to improve the public sector's financial health; and to free resources for allocation in other important areas of government activity,[319] to increase consumer choice upon up nationalised industries to the discipline of the capital and products markets, to reduce inflation,[320] to redress past justice when private property was expropriated by the state without proper compensation (restitution or financial compensation), to redistribute wealth and income by the repartition of some state property equally among all citizens (free transfer of shares), and weaken the old power structure of communist elites.[321]

Depending on the social, political, legal and economic differences and circumstances some goals or objectives may have a dominant and pioneer position in the privatisation progress. For example, in communist countries characterised by systemic collapse of economies and

---

Europe), p.91-95. [According to van Brabant the main purpose of privatisation is "to engineer a fundamental transformation of state economic activity"(p.91)]; Demetra Smith Nightingale, Nancy Pindus, "Privatization of Public Social Services: A Background Paper", October 15, 1997, Urban Institute, URL: http://www.urban.org/; Grimstone, (British Privatisation), p.6, [Grimstone provides a list of objectives of British privatisation programme]; William L. Megginson & Jeffry M. Netter, "Equity to the People: The Record on Share Issue Privatization Programs", p.2, Web page of the World Bank, URL: http://www.worldbank.org; Mitchell, p.19. [According to Mitchell combining these sets of objectives it is possible to identify three general types: free market objectives, revenue raising, and changing attitudes and values. (p.19)]; López-de-Silanes, p.3, 4. (López-de-Silanes states that all privatisation goals can be summarised in two basic objectives: (a) Efficiency enhancement, in terms of depolitisation of state owned enterprises (SOEs) and improvement of corporate governance, (b) Revenue generation, either to get out fiscal crises or to achieve redistributive purposes. However, we must point out that, it is questionable whether this approach covers some other privatisation goals like: reduce taxation, attract foreign investment, increase exports etc.)

As a specific case, according to US Energy Information Administration the objectives of governments in energy privatisations are as follows: (a) raising revenue for the state; (b) raising investment capital for the industry or company being privatised; (c) reducing government's role in the economy; (d) promoting wider share ownership; (e) increasing efficiency; (f) introducing greater competition; and (g) exposing firms to market discipline ("The Evolution of Privatisation", Privatisation: Motives and Methods, US Energy Information Administration, URL: http://www.eia.doe.gov)

[318] "The Opportunities and Challenges of Privatisation", Chapter I, US Department of Energy, URL: http://home.osti.gov/
[319] Sheshinski and López-Calva, p.7
[320] Foster, p.116
[321] Bornstein, p.235

political framework, privatisation of SOEs has emerged as an almost mandatory requirement of the transition to free market economy.[322]

It is also argued that, in countries characterised by mounting foreign debts and budget deficits such as Argentina, Mexico and Brazil, privatisation of SOEs has emerged as a major revenue earner and macro-economic stabiliser. In countries such as the U.K. and France that have over the years lost their global, competitive edge, privatisation has emerged as a major stimulus to improve industrial efficiency.[323]

1. Some government's approaches to privatisation

As we mentioned above in each country governments state different privatisation objectives. The aims and objectives can be stated by certain government institutions (privatisation agencies, ministry in charge of privatisation process, council of ministers etc.)

For example, Turkish Privatisation Administration states that the reasons of privatisation are: To allow market forces to stimulate the economy; to increase productivity and efficiency; to increase quality, and diversity of the goods and services, to promote widespread share ownership and to speed up the development of the capital markets.[324]

On the other hand according to Privatisation Agency Federation of Bosnia and Herzegovina the primary goals that the federation privatisation program are to achieve or support during the economy and social transformation process include: post war reconstruction; fast

---

[322] "International Perspectives on Privatisation of State Owned Enterprises", Narendar V. Rao, Northeastern, C. Bhaktavatsala Rao and Steve Dunphy, Small Business Advancement National Center, University of Central Arkansas, URL: http://www.sbaer.uca.edu/

[323] "International Perspectives on Privatisation of State Owned Enterprises", Narendar V. Rao, Northeastern, C. Bhaktavatsala Rao, Steve Dunphy, Small Business Advancement National Center, University of Central Arkansas, URL: http://www.sbaer.uca.edu/; Galal, Jones, Tandon and Vogelsang, p.560, 561; John D. Sullivan, "Privatization and Economic Reforms", web page of Center for International Private Enterprise, URL: http://www.cipe.org/; Peter Young, "The Lessons of Privatisation", web page of Center for International Private Enterprise, URL: http//www.cipe.org/

[324] Web page of Privatisation Administration of Turkey, URL: http://www.oib.gov.tr/
In addition, article 2 of the Turkish Privatisation Law provides the principles in the privatisation implementations.

economic revival; increased employment; and liquidation of domestic and foreign debts accumulated by enterprises, banks and the state.[325]

In the UK in 1977, the Conservative government published a document outlining their plans to reduce state ownership, and in 1978, the Ridley Report proposed detailed strategies for doing so. By 1979, specific firms had been identified. "Monopoly nationalised industries" and "monopoly trade unions" were blamed by Mrs Thatcher as the principal evils of the UK economy. Mrs Thatcher's other objectives were: "strong defence, more resources for law and order, lower taxation, more private enterprise, and less government control".[326]

The main objectives and goals of the privatisation programme in Britain can be summarised as follows: to reduce government involvement in industry, to improve efficiency, to reduce the public sector borrowing requirement (PSBR), to ease problems in public sector wage bargaining by weakening the unions;[327] to widen share ownership, to encourage employee share

---

Also see: Letwin, p.26.
[325] According to the government of Bosnia and Herzegovina privatisation benefits can be classified as short-term and long-term:
Short-term: Citizens have an opportunity to become private owners; the banking sector is restructured; the Federation settles its internal debt; monopolies are broken up leading to an increase in goods and services; conditions for greater competition are created, oftentimes providing citizens with lower prices; and, creates the conditions for the development of a capital markets.
Long-term: Privatisation provides the basis for the improvement of efficiencies in production; provides access to international markets and "know-how", or new technology and improved management techniques; and, access to new investment opportunities. (Web page of Privatisation Agency of Federation of Bosnia and Herzegovina; URL: http://www.zpf.com.ba/)
[326] Graham, p.189; Privatisation in the UK and Turkey, p.5
"The Ridley report referred only to the sale of shares in the National Freight Corporation, sale of the recently nationalised aerospace and shipbuilding industries and of the National Enterprise Board's holdings, a complete review of the British National Oil Corporation's activities and relaxation of bus licensing." (Graham, p.189)
As we mentioned above (p.42) according to United Kingdom government one of the objectives of the Treasury is to promote privatisation. (Web page of UK Treasury, URL: http://www.hm-treasury.gov.uk/pub/html/econbf/eb09/4hmt.html; http://www.hm-treasury.gov.uk/drep/1996/s12.html; HM Treasury Departmental Report for 1995, web page of UK Treasury, URL: http://www.hm-treasury.gov.uk/drep/1995/index.html)
In the UK particularly following objectives were mentioned: (a) The achievement of wider share ownership among the British public, (b) Reducing the public sector borrowing requirement. (Rees, p.50)
[327] In other words, as far as public sector unions were concerned, privatisation was seen as a means of reducing their size, bargaining power and influence over policy.

ownership, to provide the opportunity to introduce competition, to expose SOEs to market discipline, to develop the national capital market, to gain political advantage[328]

The UK privatisation programme has developed in the pursuit of various objectives[329], and different objectives have had a priority at particular times. Financial arguments have at times been central, but less important at others, depending on the government's perception of its fiscal position.[330]

Moreover, in some countries privatisation laws can provide certain aims as privatisation objectives. Different governments around the world have been stating different lists for the goals of the privatisation programmes in their privatisation laws. For example, Moldavian Privatisation Law states that "The main objectives of the Privatisation Program are completing privatisation of public property, restructuring of privatised enterprises, revitalising the economy and improving the living condition of population, modifying the Government role to fit the market requirements, cutting down the Government expenditures on managing the economy and termination of subsidies to the loss-making companies".[331]

According to Law on the Privatisation of State-owned Companies Engaged in Retail Trade, Catering and Consumer Services of Hungary [332] "The aim of the Act is to improve economic efficiency, to encourage, for the sake of the development of market conditions and competition, private enterprise to play a determinative role in retail trade, the catering industry and in consumer services. " Similarly, Act XXXIX of 1995 on the Sale of State-Owned

---

[328] *Her Majesty's Treasury Guide to the United Kingdom Privatisation Programme*, December 1993, p.4; Richardson, p.62-64; Privatisation in the UK and Turkey, p.61-80, 251-256; William L. Megginson, Jeffry M. Netter, "From State to Market: A Survey of Empirical Studies on Privatization", for presentation at: Global Equity Markets, A joint conference of the SBF Bourse de Paris and the New York Stock Exchange, Paris, France, December 10-11, 1998, Current Draft, February 9, 1999; Brabant, p.59; Vickers and Yarrow, (An Economic Analysis), p.4
[329] See: Graham and Prosser, (Privatising Nationalised Industries), p.16, 17-20
[330] Bishop and Kay, (Does Privatisation Work?), p.10; Tony Prosser, "Social Limits to Privatization", (Social Limits), Brooklyn Journal of International Law, Volume XXI, 1995, Number 1, p.215
[331] Article 1, Law on Privatization Program 1997-1998
[332] ACT No. LXXIV of 1990

Entrepreneurial Assets, states that "Parliament passes the following Act for the purpose of strengthening economic relations built on private ownership, reasonably accelerating the diminution of state ownership, allocation of state-owned entrepreneurial assets to private ownership based on market conditions and reducing the economic role played by the state"

Finally, according to Latvian Privatisation Law: "The goal of privatisation is the creation of favourable environment for private capital activities in Latvia, by changing a state or a municipal asset unit ownership in the interests of the economic development of Latvia, and the reduction of entrepreneurial activity performed by the state and municipality."[333]

---

[333] Article 2/1, The Republic of Latvia Saeima Law On Privatization of State and Municipal Asset Units, (Web page of Latvian Privatisation Agency, URL: http://www.lpa.bkc.lv/PrivatLawGB.htm#B001_)

Table 2	Goals and Objectives of Privatisation

a. Efficiency and Development of the Enterprise
-Foster the enterprise's efficiency and its domestic and international competitiveness
-Introduce new technologies and promote innovation
-Upgrade plant and equipment
-Increase productivity, including utilisation of industrial plant
-Improve the quality of the goods and services produced
-Introduce new management methods and teams
-Allow the enterprise to enter into domestic and international alliances essential to its survival

b. Efficiency and Development of the Economy
-Create a market economy, this is the key objective in economies in transition
-Encourage private enterprise and expansion of the private sector in general
-Promote macroeconomic or sectoral efficiency and competitiveness
-Foster economic flexibility and eliminate rigidities
-Promote competition, particularly by abolishing the monopolies
-Establish or develop efficient capital markets, allowing better capture and mobilisation of domestic savings
-Improve access to foreign markets for domestic products
-Promote domestic investment
-Promote integration of the domestic economy into the world economy
-Maintain or create employment

c. Budgetary and Financial Goals
As a summary the objectives aiming budgetary and financial improvements can be summarised as follows:
-Maximise net privatisation receipts in order to fund government expenditures, reduce taxation, trim the public sector deficit, or pay off public dept
-Reduce financial drain of the SOEs on the state (in the form of subsidies, unpaid taxes, loan arrears, guarantees given, and so on)
-Mobilise private sources to finance investments that can no longer be founded from public finances
-Generate new sources and tax revenues
-Limit the future risk of demands on the budget inherent in state ownership of businesses, including the need to provide capital for their expansion or to rescue them if they are in financial trouble
-Reduce capital flight abroad and repatriate capital already transferred

d. Income Distribution or Redistribution
-Foster broader capital ownership and promote popular and mass capitalism
-Develop a national middle class
-Foster the economic development of a particular group (ethnic or other) in society
-Encourage employee ownership (also important for efficiency reasons)
-Restore full rights to former owners of property expropriated by previous regimes
-Enrich those managing or implementing privatisation projects (rarely an admitted objective)

e. Political considerations
Reduce the size and scope of the public sector or its share in economic activity
Redefine the field of activity of the public sector, abandoning production tasks and focusing on the core of governmental functions, including the creation of an environment favourable to private economic activity
Reduce or eliminate the ability of a future government to reverse the measures taken by the incumbent government to alter the role of the state in the economy
Reduce the opportunities for corruption and misuse of public property by government officials and SOE managers
Reduce the grip of a particular party or group on the economy
Raise the government's popularity and its likelihood of being returned to power in the next election are seem to be the political objectives and considerations beyond privatisation

Source: Guislain (Privatization Challenge), p.18, 19; Guislain (The World Bank), p.4

2. Conflicts among Privatisation Objectives and Policies

a. Conflict among objectives

Privatisation objectives can sometimes conflict[334], or appear to conflict, thus complicating the implementation of a privatisation programme. For instance, the sale of a public monopoly without provision for price regulation could achieve a higher sale price. This policy could further the objective of raising revenue to reduce public sector debt, but would conflict with the objective of creating a competitive industry and promoting economic efficiency. Similarly, the objective of promoting wide ownership may conflict with the objective of fostering good performance governance.[335] In some cases apparent conflicts among objectives can be resolved by careful analysis and policy design. For instance, some of the conflicts between the objectives of promoting wide share ownership and fostering good corporate governance can be resolved by appropriate use of voting and non-voting shares, combined with careful design of corporate management structures.[336] On the other hand the best way to achieve wider share ownership is the model of mass (voucher) privatisation that involves the free or virtually free distribution of privatised assets. However, in this model, the potentially negative point is that, it fails to raise revenues for the state, it risks excessive dispersal of ownership leading to weak control.[337]

Finally it is difficult to achieve some objectives of privatisation. For example it is argued that privatisation would lead to wider share ownership. However, it is unlikely that the poorer sections of society in the former socialist countries will participate even in schemes involving the

---

[334] Privatisation in Europe, Asia and Latin America, What Lessons can be Drawn?, Summary of the Presentations at the International Workshop on Privatisation Organised by the OECD in April 1994, Sao Paulo, URL: http://www.oecd.org; Hartley, p.180

[335] *Comparative Experiences with Privatization-Policy Insights and Lessons Learned*, United Nations Conference on Trade and Development, United Nations, New York and Geneva, 1995, p.8, 9; Stilpon Nestor and Ladan Mahboobi, Privatisation of Public Utilities; The OECD Experience, Rio, 23 April 1999; Graham, p.192

[336] Comparative Experiences with Privatization-Policy Insights and Lessons Learned, United Nations Conference on Trade and Development, United Nations, New York and Geneva, 1995, p.8, 9

[337] Bradley, p.2681

free distribution of shares. One reason for this is that the poor are less well educated, and may simply be confused by the complexity of privatisation process; [338] also there is no habit or culture of investing in ordinary shares.[339]

b. Conflict in Privatisation Policies

Sometimes privatisation objectives and the actual acts of governments can be in conflict. For example in Portugal it was expected that the involvement of foreign capital would bring new investments, transfer technology and improve productivity. However, privatisation legislation put significance type and amount of restriction in the foreign participation in privatisation transaction and these prevented foreign investors becoming involved in the privatisation programme.[340]

Finally we must point out that in most cases, as in the UK, at different times, one or other of the objectives have been sacrificed for others. There has been no consistent rationale for the policy of privatisation; rather it has appeared to meet particular political needs at particular moments in time.[341]

3. The Main Objective: Budgetary and Financial Improvements

Among the many objectives assigned to privatisation, reduction of the budget deficit is those most frequently aimed at.[342] This is particularly true for the ex-socialist countries where the

---

[338] Ash, Hare and Canning, p.223
[339] Bradley, p.268
When some of these goals are conflicting, governments need to be prepared to sacrifice some in order to get others. (S. Brian Samuel, "The Ten Commandments of African Privatization", International Finance Corporation (IFC), The World Bank, URL: http://www.ifc.org/ifc/publications/pubs/impact/impsm99/commandm/commandm.html)
[340] Corkill, p.213-227
[341] Bishop and Kay, (Does Privatisation Work?), p.12
[342] Olivier Bouin, "The Privatisation in Developing Countries: Reflections on a Panacea", Policy Brief No. 3, OECD Development Centre, OECD 1992; Galal, Jones, Tandon and Vogelsang, p.560; Jack M. Mintz, Duanjie Chen and Evangelia Zorotheos, Taxing Issues with Privatisation: A Checklist, International Tax Program, Institute of International Business, University of Toronto, p.2, URL: http://www.worldbank.org/; Redwood, p.54, 55; Paul Starr, "The Meaning of Privatisation", web page of University of Princeton, URL: http://princeton.edu/#starr/meaning.html; Jean-Jacques Rosa, " Comment on Jan Winiecki (The Political Economy

previous fiscal structures of command economies exposed state budgets to the special risk of deficit because sharply falling revenues from state company profits and increased spending on social benefits.[343]

Perhaps the most important practical advantage of privatisation is that the state can raise money when selling assets. As many governments are facing financial crises, budgetary matters and short-term revenue maximisation tend to be high on the list of governmental objectives.[344]

Germany is the exception that proves the rule, for budgetary considerations have, all in all, been of very little importance in the Federal Republic of Germany, where privatisation has, more than elsewhere, been based on ideological motives that transcended the purely pragmatic considerations referred to above.[345]

4. Political Considerations[346]

Privatisation is also a political process.[347] Political arguments, in summary, are: the encouragement of pluralist systems, the reduction of bureaucratic influence, and gathering

---

of Privatization), Privatisation-Symposium in Honor of Herbert Giersch, Edited By: Horst Siebert, Institut fur Weltwirtschaft an der Universitat Kiel, J.C.B. Mohr (Paul Siebeck), Tubingen, 1992, p.95; Inotai, p.166; Robert, p.25, 26; Brabant, p.49

This is true even if advantage is, not always mentioned as the first aim of privatisation. Instead, reference is made to the struggle against inflation. [Harmathy, (General Report), p.211]

In that context, it is argued that, for example, in Turkey, a mere 5% reduction in SOE operating costs would reduce the fiscal deficit by about one-third. (Mary M. Shirley, "Getting Bureaucrats Out of Business: Obstacles to State Enterprise Reform", web page of Center for International Private Enterprise, URL: http://www.cipe.org/)

However, in some countries like Sweden efficiency was not a direct issue in the privatisation programme, the main goal of the process was "promoting the competition". The government also wanted a clear division between politics and business; government argued that public ownership distorts competition. (Johan Willner, "Privatisation in Finland, Sweden and Denmark-Fashion or Necessity", Privatisation in the European Union-Theory and Policy Perspectives, Edited By: David Parker, London and New York, 1988, p.177)

[343] Bradley, p.268

[344] Guislain, (The Privatization Challenge), p.17

However, in some countries, such as in Turkey, the Privatisation Law provides that "using the proceeds of privatisation for general budget expenditure and/or investments" is one of the principles in the privatisation implementations. (Article 2/c, Law No: 4046).

[345] Robert, p.26

[346] Richardson, p.57-82; Enrico C. Perotti and Pieter van Oijen, "Privatization, Political Risk and Stock Market Development in Emerging Economies", July 1999, web page of oecd, URL: http://www.oecd.org; Brown, p.96; Jan Winiecki, "The Political Economy of Privatization", Privatisation-Symposium in Honor of Herbert Giersch, Edited By: Horst Siebert, Institut fur Weltwirtschaft an der Universitat Kiel, J.C.B. Mohr (Paul Siebeck), Tubingen, 1992, p.71-96

popular support through widespread asset ownership.[348] In practice the design of privatisation programs in transition economies is largely dictated by political rather than economic conditions.[349]

Privatisation can only be implemented within supportive domestic policy environments[350]; in other words the main requirements for a successful privatisation is political agreement commitment, and willpower.[351]

Strong political commitment is essential for a legislative package including privatisation, it also ensures its effective implementation. Reforming the macro-legal environment implies not only new laws and regulations fostering private initiatives and activities, but also institutions and administrative personnel to support, implement and enforce such laws and regulations.[352]

Finally, as we examined above[353], it was realised that the political benefits of privatisation might exceed the economic benefits. Raising money from the sale of public assets was less politically damaging than raising taxes or cutting public spending and was regarded as a more acceptable means of reducing the public sector borrowing requirements.[354]

---

[347] Donaldson and Wagle, p.6; "Political and Organizational Strategies for Streamlining", Privatisation Database, URL: http://www.privatisation.org/
[348] Bradley, p.265
[349] Havrylyshyn and McGettigan, p.5
[350] Dennis J. Gayle and Jonathan N.Goodrich, Exploring the Implications of Privatisation and Deregulation, Privatisation and Deregulation in Global Perspective, Edited By: Dennis J. Gayle and Jonathan N.Goodrich, Pinter Publishers, London, 1990, p.14
[351] "Mass Privatisation: An Initial Assessment", web page of oecd, URL: http://www.oecd.org; "Report on Privatisation and Lessons Learned", GAO (General Accounting Office of USA), URL: http//www.privatisation.org/Collection/P...egies/GaoPrivReport--lessons-learned.html; "International Perspectives on Privatisation of State Owned Enterprises", Narendar V. Rao, Northeastern, C. Bhaktavatsala Rao, Steve Dunphy, Small Business Advancement National Center, University of Central Arkansas, URL: http://www.sbaer.uca.edu/
Therefore, depending on the specific situation, political constraints can also be analysed as negative objectives. [Pierre Guislain, *Divestiture of State Enterprises-An Overview of the Legal Framework, (The World Bank)*, The World Bank Technical Paper, Number 186, The World Bank, Washington, D.C., 1992, p.5]
[352] Guislain, (The World Bank), p.10
[353] See: p.16, 17
[354] Jackson and Price, p.14

B. Analysis of the Goals of Privatisation

Among the many objectives assigned to privatisation, it is well known that reduction of the budget deficit and increased economic efficiency are those most frequently aimed at.[355] It seems that, although it is not explicitly being mentioned in the legal drafts and official documents the current wave of privatisations is largely a response to the financial crisis facing many governments.[356] In other words, privatisation operations were decided upon in a context of public finance crisis and governments generally expected them not only to provide additional revenue resulting from the transfer of public shares or assets, but also to help reduce budget transfers to the enterprises concerned.[357]

Privatisation should be viewed against the backdrop of the internationalisation of the economy, which further restricts the options for resolving the chronic difficulties of SOEs. This globalisation, which is reflected in new forms of international law, is broadening the very definition of the relevant market for goods and services. It increasingly renders the subsidies and tariff protection enjoyed by many SOEs, and it fosters the development of flexible enterprises able to adjust quickly to constantly evolving international markets.[358]

Many privatisation programs appear to focus more on revenue generation; however, the primary objective should be to provide the consumers and the economy with more competitive services, whether in terms of quality, range of services, price or volume.[359]

In theory, the reasons of each department in a government should be fairly predictable: a treasury or finance ministry should be wanting to reduce fiscal deficits and decrease the national

---

[355] Olivier Bouin, "The Privatisation in Developing Countries: Reflections on a Panacea", Policy Brief No. 3, OECD Development Centre, OECD 1992
[356] Guislain, (The Privatization Challenge), p.17
[357] Olivier Bouin, "The Privatisation in Developing Countries: Reflections on a Panacea", Policy Brief No. 3, OECD Development Centre, OECD 1992
[358] Guislain, (The Privatization Challenge), p.288, 289
[359] Guislain, (The Privatization Challenge), p.291

debt; the department of industry should be wanting to increase the operational efficiency of the businesses; the department of trade should be wanting to increase competition and reduce economic distortions; the department of employment should be wanting to spread employee involvement.[360]

V. PRIVATISATION in the FORMER SOCIALIST COUNTRIES

A. General View

1. Establishing Market Economy

A programme of privatisation in a developing country is really a programme for reform[361], this consideration is valid particularly in Central and Eastern European countries hence privatisation in these countries is a prominent key element and landmark for to establish the market economy.[362]

Historically, in former socialist countries, industrial development had been characterised by inefficient allocation of resources; while governments spent heavily on defence, production of consumer goods was neglected. Heavy industry was favoured and economies of scale were consistently emphasised, leading to the creation of mega-firms with little or no competition in the domestic market. Facing chronic input shortages and poor distribution, many of these firms

---

[360] Letwin, p.26
[361] Beesley and Littlechild, p.137
[362] Cook and Kirkpatrick, p.4; Lamberto Dini, "Privatisation Processes in Eastern Europe: Theoretical Foundations and Empirical Results", Privatisation Process in Eastern Europe-Theoretical Foundations and Empirical Results, Edited by: Maria Baldassarri, Luigi Paganetto, Edmund S. Phelps, St. Martin's Press, 1993, p.15; Olivier Bouin, "The Privatisation in Developing Countries: Reflections on a Panacea", Policy Brief No. 3, OECD Development Centre, OECD 1992; Holger Schmieding, "Alternative Approaches to Privatisation: Some Notes on the Debate", Privatisation-Symposium in Honor of Herbert Giersch, Edited By: Horst Siebert, Institut fur Weltwirtschaft an der Universitat Kiel, J.C.B. Mohr (Paul Siebeck), Tubingen, 1992, p.97; Inotai, p.163; Bradley, p.267; Wright and Thompson, p.65; "International Perspectives on Privatisation of State Owned Enterprises", Narendar V. Rao, Northeastern, C. Bhaktavatsala Rao, Steve Dunphy, Small Business Advancement National Center, University of Central Arkansas, URL: http://www.sbaer.uca.edu/; Luigi Paganetto, Pasquale Lucio Scandizzo, "Privatisation and Competitive Behaviour: Endogenous Objectives, Efficiency and Growth-(Comment)", Privatisation Process in Eastern Europe-Theoretical Foundations and Empirical Results, Edited by: Maria Baldassarri, Luigi Paganetto, Edmund S. Phelps, St. Martin's Press, 1993, p.151; Ivan Mikloš, "Privatization in

sought to produce as many of their own manufacturing components as possible. SOEs were therefore highly integrated, both vertically and horizontally, and a small and medium sized business sector was prevented from developing.[363]

2. Collapse of Communism

As we mentioned above, after the collapse of communism in 1989-91, all of the newly elected governments of the region faced the imperative need to create something resembling a market economy as quickly as possible.[364] In these countries it is hoped that privatisation will provide the basis for the rapid transformation of these economies from highly inefficient economies into developed market economies.[365]

Privatisation has been viewed as an integral element in the process of transition from a centrally planned to a market-oriented economy, although the contribution of privatisation to the move towards a market economy has varied.[366]

1996", Centre for Economic and Social Analysis of Slovak Republic, URL: http//www.mesa10.sk/. (According to Mikloš privatisation is one of the key pillars of economic transformation).

[363] Chikán, p.23, 24

[364] William L. Megginson, Jeffry M. Netter, "From State to Market: A Survey of Empirical Studies on Privatization", for Presentation at: Global Equity Markets, A Joint Conference of the SBF Bourse de Paris and the New York Stock Exchange, Paris, France, December 10- 11, 1998, Current Draft, February 9, 1999; Domanski, p.31; Mary M. Shirley, "Getting Bureaucrats Out of Business: Obstacles to State Enterprise Reform", web page of Center for International Private Enterprise, URL: http//www.cipe.org/; Iván Major, *Privatization in Eastern Europe-A Critical Approach*, Edward Elgar Publishing Limited, England & USA, 1993, p.1

While political developments in the Former Soviet Union connected with perestroika and glasnost probably did most to bring about the collapse of the former communist regimes it was the very poor state of their economies that first pushed Gorbachev into contemplating reform. (Ash, Hare and Canning, p.214)

[365] Ash, Hare and Canning, p.213

[366] In other words privatisation is being used to transform communism into capitalism. (Iatridis, p.3, 9, 12; Holger Schmieding, "Alternative Approaches to Privatisation: Some Notes on the Debate", Privatisation-Symposium in Honor of Herbert Giersch, Edited By: Horst Siebert, Institut fur Weltwirtschaft an der Universitat Kiel, J.C.B. Mohr (Paul Siebeck), Tubingen, 1992, p.99

The basic institutions of socialism in a Soviet-type economy are: (a) state ownership in productive assets, (b) central planning of resources, (c) one-party political monopoly. (Major, p.7)

Eastern European countries are dealing with three main issues: (a) What forms of ownership should supersede state ownership? (b) What is the optimal sequence of reforms? (c) What is the optimal speed of the reforms? (Martin C. Spechler, "Privatization, Competition, and Structural Change in Eastern Europe", Edited by: Demetrius S. Iatridis and June Gary Hopps, Praeger Publishers, USA, 1998, p.34. Also see: Cook and Kirkpatrick, p.4)

One of the bases of the Communist Party's strength was not only its monopoly in the political sphere, but its monopoly in the economic. [Stiglitz, (Some Theoretical Aspects), p.186, 187; Ericson, p.22]

3. Progress

Therefore, in each of former Soviet-type economies, after one to two years of struggling to build working market economies, privatisation has generally come to be considered the key or cornerstone to successful economic transformation. Massive privatisation has moved to the front of the agenda in all of the transforming economies of Eastern Europe.[367]

Hungary was the first country in the region that started privatisation of state owned enterprises (SOEs).[368] In Russia 100,000 small-scale businesses have been auctioned; 14,000 medium and large-scale firms sold; and, 30-40 million new shareholders created.[369] However, political considerations required these governments to significantly limit foreign purchases of divested assets. Since the region had very little financial savings, these twin imperatives compelled governments throughout the region to launch "mass privatisation"[370] programs that generally involved distributing vouchers *free* to the population that citizens could then use to bid for shares in companies being privatised.[371]

---

[367] E. Ericson, p.21; Ira W.Lieberman, Andrew Ewing, Michael Mejstrik, Joyita Mukherjee and Peter Fidler, *Mass Privatisation in Central and Eastern Europe and the Former Soviet Union, A Comparative Analysis*, Studies of Economies in Transformation, The World Bank, Washington, D.C., 1995, p.2; Attila Harmathy, (General Report), p.211; Stanley Fischer, Ratna Sahay, "The Transition Economies After Ten Years", IMF (International Monetary Fund), Working Paper 7664, Cambridge, February 2000, p.19, URL: http://www.nber.org/papers/w7664; Stanley Fischer, "Privatisation in East European Transformation", National Bureau of Economic Research (NBER), Working Paper Series, No:3703, Cambridge, May 1991, p.1; Mencinger, p.154

[368] Andrej Juris, "Economic Reform in Slovakia" web page of Center for International Private Enterprise, URL: http//www.cipe.org/

[369] Donaldson and Wagle, p.3; Sunita Kikeri, John Nellis, Mary Shirley, Outreach Nr. 3, Policy Views from the Country Economics Department, The World Bank, July 1992; Lieberman, Ewing, Mejstrik, Mukherjee and Fidler, p.1

In Russia after these privatisations, private sector accounted for about 62 per cent of GDP. (Bradley, p.271)

[370] See: p. 256-265

[371] William L. Megginson, Jeffry M. Netter, "From State to Market: A Survey of Empirical Studies on Privatization", for Presentation at: Global Equity Markets, A Joint Conference of the SBF Bourse de Paris and the New York Stock Exchange, Paris, France, December 10- 11, 1998, Current Draft, February 9, 1999

B. Differences between Eastern European and Western European Countries in the Privatisation Issue

1. **General**

There are important distinctions between privatisation in West European countries and in the former socialist states[372]; therefore, as we will discuss later on, privatisation in Central and Eastern Europe is unlikely to follow the well-known path and techniques of privatisation in industrialised countries.[373] In other words Western models in privatisation are not appropriate for former socialist countries.[374]

2. **Main Purpose**

The first difference is brought by the main purpose of privatisation. Thus, while the West European countries choose the privatisation of the public enterprises with the purpose to increase efficiency and reduce the public budget costs, in the East European countries, the privatisation is a way of reorganising the entire economy, in fact the only way to establish a market economy out of the centralised economy structures.[375]

---

[372] Cook and Kirkpatrick, p.4; Harmathy, (Methods), p.39; van Brabant, (Property Rights, Privatisation and Transitional Economies), p.49

Also see: Moran and Prosser, (Introduction), p.10, 11, 12. According to these authors Britain, as a Western economy and democracy, has many advantages in the privatisation programme when it is compared to the former socialist countries. The advantages of Britain in that context are: A highly developed capital market, an elaborate jurisprudence provided by company law and labour law, a particular constitutional tradition that allowed rapid solutions to technical problems like the valuation of assets, and that conferred freedom to offer assets for sale unhindered by claims for restitution; and a unitary constitutional structure. (p.11)

[373] According to some authors, the difference between United Kingdom and former socialist countries is huge and therefore United Kingdom cannot be a model for privatisation; these countries should follow the model provided by their far more successful allies in Central Europe. (For this opinion see: Stampford, p.262, 263)

[373] Inotai, p.163

[374] For similar opinion see: Bradley, p.261, 268, 278, 282

[375] Simona Iliescu Nastase, "La protection juridique de la propriété privée dans le nouveau contexte social et économique de la Roumanie", (Juridical Protection of Private Property in the New Social and Economic Context of Romania), Chapter 4, Individual Democratic Institutions Research Fellowships 1994-1996, web page of NATO, URL: http://www.nato.int/acad/fellow/94-96/iliescu/index.htm

3. Scope

The fundamental difference resides in the scope of the privatisation process. In the Eastern and Central European countries an overwhelming majority of industry was in possession of the state, while in West European countries private undertakings and private property have always predominated.[376]

In other words, the state owned virtually all of the instruments and means of production: Banks, communications, mass media, land and other natural resources, most housing and transport, enterprises, state farms, and the like. What was not state-owned usually was in the ownership of collectives or co-operatives of various types. [377]

The scale of privatisation is huge and the process is often perceived as to be completed in a very short time.[378] In other words, in the former socialist economies it is not a few state owned enterprises that have to privatised, but practically the economy as such.[379]

4. Weak Economy and Newly-Established Democracy

A democratic system requires appropriate institutional, political, social and legal framework. In most former socialist countries democratic reforms are still on the way.[380]

---

[376] Under the system of central planning, the state completely controls all economic activity, which, by definition, means that there is no formal private sector. ("Privatizing State-Owned Companies", The Prosperity Papers series, Prosperity Paper Three, web page of Center for International Private Enterprise, URL: http://www.cipe.org/)

[377] W.E. Butler and Maryann E.Gashi-Butler, Foreign Investment in Russia: The New Legal Environment, Privatisation and Economic Development in Eastern Europe and the CIS, Investment, Acquisition and Managerial Issues, Edited By: Haydn Shaughnessy, John and Wiley & Sons, England, 1994, p.14, 22, 23, 25

[378] Rosario Bonavoglia, " Evolution and Design in Eastern European Transition; Comment", Privatisation Process in Eastern Europe-Theoretical Foundations and Empirical Results, Edited by: Maria Baldassarri, Luigi Paganetto, Edmund S. Phelps, St. Martin's Press, 1993, p.105

[379] Inotai, p.163; Moran and Prosser, (Introduction), p.4; Saul Estrin, "Economic Transition and Privatisation: The Issues", Privatisation in Central and Eastern Europe, Edited By: Saul Estrin, Longman Group Limited, 1994, London and New York, p.4; Bornstein, p.253

The magnitude of privatisation already achieved is unprecedented, with hundreds of thousands of small firms and service establishments, and perhaps 60,000 medium- and large-scale operations, privatised in less than a decade. That is nearly 10 times the number of privatisations in the rest of the world in the previous 10 years or so. [Havrylyshyn and McGettigan, p.3]

The ex-socialist countries are economically much weaker than the industrialised countries that embarked on privatisation; high inflation, high unemployment and increasing social inequality are some main economic problems.[381]

An important difference is the lack of capital and the rather large number of possible buyers in the former socialist countries. This is the partly a result of the previous system, but it is also a consequence of the historically under-developed position of these countries.[382] East

---

In some cases the size of the state owned enterprises is also huge. For example, one company, Gazprom, dominates the Russian natural gas industry and is the world's largest gas company. ("Russia", US Energy Information Administration, URL: http//www.eia.doe.gov)
[380] Fryman and Rapaczynski, p.91
[381] Inotai, p.164, 177; Miroslav Hrncír, "Financial Intermediation in ex-Czechoslovakia: An Assessment", Privatisation, Liberalization and Destruction-Recreating the Market in Central and Eastern Europe, Edited By: László Csaba, Dartmouth Publishing Company Limited, England & USA, 1994, p.170. [According to Hrncír: "...Underdevelopment of financial intermediation proved to be a major constraint on Czechoslovak transition..." (p.181)]
   The control of inflation and the introduction of currency convertibility are generally regarded as being among fundamental requirements for successful economic transformation. However, inflation in many of the former socialist countries is high. For example in the first year of its stabilisation programme, 1990, inflation in Poland was running at a rate of 584.7. (Ash, Hare and Canning, p.215; Hrncír, p.171). Hyperinflation delayed some structural reforms including privatisation. (Boffito, p.55). Also in Bulgaria, high inflation was one of the obstacles in the privatisation programme. (Maria Prohaska, "Privatization in Bulgaria: Pushing Forward", web page of Center for International Private Enterprise, URL: http//www.cipe.org/)
   In that context, for Hungarian case see: Eva Voszka, "Privatization in Hungary: Results and Open Issues", web page of Center for International Private Enterprise, URL: http//www.cipe.org/
   Bulgarian government considered the restricted free financial resources as a "negative factor". (Bulgarian Foreign Investment Agency, URL: http://www.bfia.org/privat.htm; web page of Bulgarian Privatisation Agency, URL: http:// www.privatisation.online.bg)
   Another important economic and social issue in former socialist countries is the high level of black (untaxed) economy. For example in Ukraine, the informal economy is estimated at one-third to one-half of the total economy. (State Property Fund of Ukraine, URL: http//www.ukrmassp.kiev.ua/Prgrm98-1.htm)
   Furthermore, in some other aspects the structure of the economy in former socialist countries is different than western economies. For example, in Russia, 70 percent of industry worked in the area of heavy machine building and the defence industry and only 30 percent in the area of consumer goods. (Alexander Chesnokov, "A business View of Russia's Economy", an address given by Alexander Chesnokov to the Center for International Private Enterprise Board of Directors at the U.S. Chamber of Commerce in Washington, DC, on April 6, 1999, web page of Center for International Private Enterprise, URL: http//www.cipe.org/)
   Finally, we must point out that, in some countries the origins economic and social problems lie also in the internal and civil wars. For example, in the past, Bosnia and Herzegovina had a well-developed industrial economy. It was one of the leaders of the former Soviet economies and a reliable supplier of export goods and services. The war and several years' lack of growth in the domestic economy have added important factors for consideration in the privatisation program of the country. These factors are characterised by enormous destruction of property, human loss and displacement of citizens, market loss, obsolete technology, decrease in consumer purchasing power and the accumulation of debts of enterprises, banks and the state. (Web page of Agency of Privatisation of Federation of Bosnia and Herzegovina, URL: http://www.zpf.com.ba/)
[382] Guislain, (The World Bank), p.6. According to Guislain: "...Eastern Europe provides a good illustration of the difficulty of privatising SOEs in the absence of a market-based legal and institutional framework..."(p.6)
   The Eastern European countries require a massive injection of western capital, technology, modern managerial skills, as well as access to western markets for Eastern European manufactured products.(Salvatore, p.241); Kirkpatrick, p. 241; Bradley, p.268; Kirkpatrick, p.236, 240; Niels Mygind, "Privatisation, Governance and

Germany is an exception, as this country found buyers within its new western borders when it was unified with West Germany.[383]

One of the many obstacles to further development is the absence of a genuine banking system.[384]

In these countries lack of well-developed markets prevents or at least limits privatisation transactions.[385] Because certain methods of privatisation like public offering requires well-developed financial market.

As a summary in other regions, privatisation occurred in nations with an appropriate legal system, a significant private sector, and markets for goods and factors of production. These features facilitated the transformation of state enterprises into private firms. In former socialist countries privatisation is expected to help create a market economy.[386]

5. Technical and Practical Facts

Other difference between the two experiences resides in establishing the value of the firm or of the assets that are being privatised. Such a value, in the absence of a stock market and of a market record of the factors within and outside the firm, is clearly almost impossible to estimate

---

Restructuring of Enterprises in the Baltics, Baltic Regional Programme," Organisation for Economic Co-operation and Development (OECD), Paris, April/May 2000, p.43

[383] On the other hand according to some authors there is even serious doubt that the East European bureaucracies could be trusted to achieve successful results in the privatisation process. It is now common to hear complaints that economic reform in the Eastern Europe is being slowed by the spoiling tactics of the "old guard" of bureaucrats and state enterprise managers who see privatisation as a direct threat to their own privileged position in society. (Ash, Hare and Canning, p.216; Frydman and Rapaczynski, p.74; Privatisation in Europe, Asia and Latin America, What Lessons Can be Drawn?, Summary of the Presentations at the International Workshop on Privatisation Organised by the OECD in April 1994, Sao Paulo, URL: http://oecd.org). However, some authors argue that in Western economies privatisation implementations have also met some problems because of the resistance bureaucracies. For example in Britain managers of Britain's nationalised industries have successfully resisted the advent of effective competition in the privatisation process by their influence on the government and the support of employees. [Vickers and Yarrow, (An Economic Analysis), p.46]

[384] Fryman and Rapaczynski, p.73

[385] Maciej Grabowski, Economic Reform in Poland, Economic Reform Today Working Papers, Number 4, web page of Center for International Private Enterprise, URL: http//www.cipe.org/

[386] Bornstein, p.254

the value of the firm. Another difference concerns the lack of a record of market performance of the firms in former socialist countries. [387]

6. Political facts

Privatisation has political reasons in the former socialist countries as well. The centrally directed economy was a part of a political system admitting only one power and liquidating every possible sources of independence. As a result of the privatisation not only the economic monopoly is broken down but the political system is changing as well.[388]

Decentralisation and privatisation have been leading to market economy and liberalisation in the ex-socialist countries. Here the privatisation campaign means more than in other countries of Europe; it is part of the process of democratisation.[389] These changes and activities amount to more than a new economic settlement, though they are indeed that; they also involve a new constitutional and political settlement.[390]

---

[387] Luigi Paganetto, Pasquale Lucio Scandizzo, "Privatisation and Competitive Behaviour: Endogenous Objectives, Efficiency and Growth"; Comment", Privatisation Process in Eastern Europe-Theoretical Foundations and Empirical Results, Edited by: Maria Baldassarri, Luigi Paganetto, Edmund S. Phelps, St. Martin's Press, 1993, p.152; Inotai, p.172; *Legal Aspects of Privatization in Industry, (Legal Aspects of Privatization)*, United Nations Publications, Geneva, January 1992, p.7

To assess the overall performance of activities targeted for privatization, to support informed privatization decisions, and to make these decisions easier to implement and justify to potential critics, policy makers need reliable and complete cost data on government activities. (Report on Privatisation and Lessons Learned, GAO (General Accounting Office of USA), URL: htpp//www.privatisation.org/Collection/P...egies/GaoPrivReport--lessons-learned.html)

[388] Joze Mencinger, "Privatization Dilemmas in Slovenia", Privatization, Liberalization and Destruction-Recreating the Market in Central and Eastern Europe, Edited By: László Csaba, Dartmouth Publishing Company Limited, England & USA, 1994, p.155

[389] One study states that: "...Communism has left a legacy of corrupt business practices in the former (socialist countries)..."(Inna Pidluska, Corruption Versus Clean Business in Ukraine, web page of the Center for International Enterprise", URL: http://www.cipe.org/)

According to some authors in order to prevent corruption in Eastern European privatisation programmes, these countries should start privatisation as soon as possible after the collapse of communism and proceed as fast as possible, relying extensively on non-standard methods. (Ivan Miklos, Corruption Risks in the Privatisation Process- A Study of Privatisation Developments in the Slovak Republic, Focusing on the Causes and Implications of Corruption Risks, Bratislava, May 1995); Bradley, p.265, 266; Davidson, (Metamorphosis), p.171

[390] Moran and Prosser, (Introduction), p.2, 9

7. Complex process

At the same time, privatisation is more complex and more complicated in these countries.[391] The communist regimes seized large amounts of private property and restitution is one of the important issues.[392] Therefore, one of the preconditions of privatisation is answering the question whether factories, land houses, etc., should be given back to previous owners or to their heirs as they were deprived from their property without compensation.[393] However, private claims can often be complicated and drawn out, and may delay the privatisation transactions.[394]

As a summary, privatisation in Central and Eastern Europe faces considerably more difficulty than occasional privatisation programs in developed market economies. In the latter, ownership rights are simply transferred from the state to the private sector; the rights themselves are already well established and supported by a number of institutions that safeguard their clarity, enforceability, and transferability.[395] However, in former socialist countries property rights and relevant safeguards and institutions are still being created.

8. Costs

One other difference is that, the costs and uncertainties of privatisation can be substantially reduced when privatisation takes place in a predominantly private economic environment. In the reforming countries, this framework has still to be created, or, in the best

---

[391] Mencinger, p.153
[392] See: p.234-241
[393] For the Estonian case see: "Finding Real Owners-Lessons from Estonia's Privatisation Program", Public Policy for the Private Sector, The World Bank, Note no: 66, January, 1996; Mait Miljan and Kuino Turk, "Privatization in Estonia", Privatization in Central and Eastern Europe-Perspectives and Approaches, Edited by: Demetrius S. Iatridis and June Gary Hopps, Praeger Publishers, USA, 1998, p.55, 56; Boffito, p.53
[394] It is far from easy to deal with the smaller property holders, for in most cases at least 40 years have passed since confiscation. Establishing claims to property is therefore frequently difficult as many of the ownership records have been destroyed or are missing. In the case of the land many of the relevant boundaries have since been changed and it is physically very difficult to establish the precise location of parcels of land now incorporated into large state and collective farms. (Ash, Hare and Canning, p.221)
[395] Marek Hessel, "How Corporate Governance Makes Privatisation Succeed", web page of Center for International Private Enterprise, URL: http://www.cipe.org/

case, it is in the process of implementation.[396] Therefore, predominance of state ownership makes privatisation very difficult and expensive.[397]

Furthermore in most of the Eastern and Central European economies it is generally recognised that former owners of land and property should receive compensation. This is an additional cost.[398]

9. Slow trend

Since in these countries the basic conditions for the development of the private sector, a legal and regulatory framework, basic physical and human infrastructure, a conducive economic environment are still lacking[399]; the privatisation process, in some cases[400], is slow compared to some industrialised western countries. [401]

---

[396] Inotai, p.164
[397] Marek Dabrowski, "The Role of the Government in Postcommunist Countries", Privatization, Liberalization and Destruction-Recreating the Market in Central and Eastern Europe, Edited By László Csaba, Dartmouth Publishing Company Limited, England & USA, 1994, p28
[398] Ash, Hare and Canning, p.221
[399] "...The Russian economy faces several key obstacles. First is a lack of expertise among Russian managers...["Safeguarding Russian Investors: Securities Chief Speaks Out", interview with Dmitry Vasiliyev, (former) Chairman of the Federal Commission for the Securities Market in Russia], web page of Center for International Private Enterprise, URL: http://www.cipe.org/]
One study concludes that: "[In former socialist countries] the insufficient quality of state administration seems to be an important barrier to the active role of government (in the privatisation process)...[Dabrowski, p.31]
Finally according to one study: "...A comparative analysis of the economic policy of the Russian Federation, the Ukraine and Belarus reveals that in all these countries the political decision-makers still hesitate to enter the long and painful road to a market economy. (Klaus Schrader, "In Search of the Market: a Comparison of Post-Soviet Reform Policies", Privatization, Liberalization and Destruction-Recreating the Market in Central and Eastern Europe, Edited By: László Csaba, Dartmouth Publishing Company Limited, England & USA, 1994, p.268)
[400] The small enterprises, mostly retail stores and enterprises in trade and services, has proceeded with rapid pace across Eastern Europe, while privatisation of large enterprises, such as mines, steel mills, shipyards, petrochemical complexes and textile mills, has been proceeding with much slower speed. This has been due two main reasons: (i) large enterprises usually have an obsolete capital stock and employ obsolete production technologies, and may therefore be unlikely to attract interested buyers at positive prices; and (ii) large enterprises account for a big share of employment and production in the economy, and privatisation or shut-down may be politically difficult for various reasons ranging from nationalism to the potentially strong averse impact on output and employment. (Schwartz, p.43)
[401] Fryman and Rapaczynski", p.74; Rosario Bonavoglia, "Evolution and Design in Eastern European Transition; Comment", Privatisation Process in Eastern Europe-Theoretical Foundations and Empirical Results, Edited by: Maria Baldassarri, Luigi Paganetto, Edmund S. Phelps, St. Martin's Press, 1993, p.107; Ash, Hare and Canning, p.213, 217, 221, 222
According to some authors: "Private ownership is not the major difference between a Soviet-type and a capitalist economy. Rather, it is one of the ways in which the major difference between two economic systems manifests itself, namely the difference in the devices and procedures for the co-ordination of a complex division of labour in time and space. (Schmieding, p.98)

102

The lack of suitable legal framework, the claims of dispossessed previous owners, the present practice of self-management, the lack of capital market institutions, the lack of an efficient institutional framework and the points mentioned above are the reasons for the slow process.[402]

10. Different methods and techniques

The privatisation process in the ex-socialist countries has lent itself to the use of specialised techniques, which reflect the special circumstances faced by the countries of Central and Eastern Europe and the former Soviet Union.[403]

In other words, the privatisation techniques that have been used in former socialist countries differ from the methods that have been applied in Western European countries. For example because of its character, one of the methods, restitution, has not been used in Western countries. On the other hand although there are some efforts to privatise SOEs via public offering, this method is not a common method for divestiture (privatisation) in the former socialist countries.[404]

11. Difference in Institutional Structure

Almost all former socialist countries have established special agencies, offices or ministries to implement their privatisation programme. However, the institutional approach for privatisation is different in Western European countries. In Western economies, mainly the

---

[402] Schmieding, p.99; Inotai, p.171, 173. According to Inotai legal barriers are most serious in the selling of land and in the restrictions on managing private savings in the foreign exchange. (p.173)

[403] "Privatizing State-Owned Companies", The Prosperity Papers Series, Prosperity Paper Three, web page of Center for International Private Enterprise, URL: http://www.cipe.org/; Bornstein, p.253, 254

[404] It is difficult for former socialist countries to use public offerings, there are several obstacles, two important reasons are following: (a) To be successful, public offerings require a well-functioning and absorptive domestic capital market. However, domestic capital markets post-socialist countries are not well developed. [Stuart Bell, "Privatisation Through Broad-Based Ownership Strategies-A More Popular Option", Public Policy for the Private Sector, The World Bank, FPD note No. 33, January 1995, p.3]. (b) Public share offerings on stock markets can be used for large, profitable, relatively well-known state enter-prises. In the ex-socialist countries the majority of SOEs do not carry these criteria. [Welch and Frémond, p.10]
See p. 241-247

existing ministries (and in most cases Ministry of Finance and/or Ministry of economy) are in charge of the privatisation transactions. For example in France, in principle, Ministry of Economy and Finance is responsible for carrying out privatisation.[405] Similarly, in the Netherlands and Portugal Ministry of Finance is responsible for the sale of the state shares. Furthermore, in Spain it is the council of ministries who is responsible for divestiture process.[406]

C. Similarities among Eastern European Privatisation Programmes

All Eastern European privatisation programmes have a number of important commonalities. One element common to all Eastern European privatisation programmes, for example, is special rules for the privatisation of small enterprises, such as retail stores, hotels, restaurants, gasoline stations, small service enterprises and accordingly, they have faced a strong domestic demand in all Eastern European countries.[407]

---

[405] A law of 1986 established a Privatisation Commission. However, the commission responsibility is mainly is about the valuation of the enterprise. [Comparative Overview of Privatisation Policies and Institutions in Member OECD Countries, OECD Privatization and Enterprise Reform Unit (September 1998), p.13; web page of OECD, URL: http://www.oecd.org]

[406] Comparative Overview of Privatisation Policies and Institutions in Member OECD Countries, OECD Privatization and Enterprise Reform Unit (September 1998), p.12-16; the web page of OECD, URL: http://www.OECD.com; Kolderie, p.26; Cook and Kirkpatrick, p.11; Web page of Canadian Department of Foreign Affairs and International Trade, http://www.dfait-maeci.gc.ca/english/geo/europe/84679-e.htm

The only exemption among the Western economies is Turkey. Law No: 4046 (Law Concerning Privatisation and Regulation of Implementations of Privatisation and Amendment to Certain Laws and Statutory Decrees) has established Privatisation Administration and Privatisation High Council. According to the article 4 of Law No: 4046 the Privatisation Administration is the executive body for privatisation and the Privatisation High Council is the ultimate decision-making body for privatisation in Turkey. (Article 3). [For this and for the full text of Turkish Privatisation Law see: web page of Turkish Privatisation Administration, URL: http://www.oib.gov.tr/]

[407] In other words, in former socialist procedure of privatisation varies depending on the size of the state owned enterprises. These countries adapted different provisions for (a) small and medium scale enterprises and (b) large-scale enterprises. In most cases, privatisation law provides different rules on these two groups of enterprises. For example Czech privatisation has proceeded on several fronts. In this country, according to the size of the enterprises (small, medium, large) different measures have been taken. In the early years of the transition the small or medium scale enterprises have been privatised. (Jan Hanousek and Eugene A. Kroch, "A Model of Learning in Sequential Bidding: Voucher Privatization in the Czech Republic: Wave I", January 1995, URL: http//www.ssc.upenn.edu/~alexv/cast/february/jan.html)

Similarly, from the size of the enterprise point of view, privatisation in Latvia, Estonia and Lithuania may be divided in the two stages: Small privatisation and large privatisation. [For the case of these Baltic countries see: Niels Mygind, "Privatisation, Governance and Restructuring of Enterprises in the Baltics, Baltic Regional Programme," Organisation for Economic Co-operation and Development (OECD), Paris, April/May 2000]

Finally, in Albania, privatisation started with the privatisation of small and medium sized enterprises, and eventually the massive privatisation program for large enterprises was launched. (Web page of Economic Development Agency of Albanian Government, URL: http://www.aeda.gov.al/)

The other common point was that, all ex-socialist countries adopted laws, including privatisation laws to implement the privatisation programmes. In the former socialist countries the constitution and related laws have been altered, amended and modified to establish basic and fundamental rules for privatisation.

Almost all Eastern European privatisation programmes contain an element of restitution. In East Germany, large parts of industrial property and land are subject to restitution claims.[408] There are other elements that are common to Eastern European privatisation programmes, such as the largely demand-determined early privatisations of companies in good financial conditions.

On the other hand, almost all Eastern European countries have established special departments, units and agencies to implement their privatisation programmes.[409]

Furthermore, more or less, all Eastern European countries have amended their private investment laws to allow foreign investors to participate in the privatisation transation.[410]

Finally, in most transition economies (ex-socialist countries), although a wide range of privatisation activities are happening, a high proportion of economic activity remains in state

---

[408] Schwartz, p.37, 38. For the Estonian case see: "Finding Real Owners-Lessons from Estonia's Privatisation Program", Public Policy for the Private Sector, The World Bank, Note no: 66, January 1996

[409] Some examples are as follows:
- Belarus: Ministry of State Property,
- Bosnia-Herzegovina: Agency for Privatisation,
- Bulgaria: Privatisation Agency,
- Croatia: Privatisation Fund,
- Estonia: Privatisation Agency,
- Georgia: Ministry of State Property Management,
- Hungary: Privatisation and State Holding Co.,
- Latvia: Privatisation Agency,
- Lithuania: State Privatisation Agency,
- Macedonia: Privatisation Agency,
- Moldova: Ministry of Privatisation,
- Poland: Privatisation Ministry,
- Romania: State Ownership Fund,
- Russia: Federal Property Fund, Privatisation Centre and Russian Federal Stock Corporation
- Slovak Republic: National Property Fund,
- Ukraine: State Property Agency. (For this list see: URL: http://www.privatizationlink.com, a web page which has been prepared by the World Bank.)

hands. For example, one of the most advanced countries in private sector development, the Czech Republic, still holds all or a majority stake in the major utilities.[411]

D. Differences among Former Socialist Countries

Although there are similarities in Eastern European countries in their privatisation strategies and programmes, there are some important differences and distinctions.[412] For example, although private-sector activity has proved notoriously difficult to measure in former socialist countries, Czech Republic, Hungary and Poland both had significant private sectors compared with other ex socialist countries in 1989.[413]

There are also market differences among Eastern European countries, particularly with respect to the acceptance of mass privatisation and the acceptance of foreign investment. In general, domestic credit in Eastern Europe is severely constrained, particularly in relation to that available to potential Western buyers. Hence, in the absence of mass privatisation schemes, domestic credit constraints would make sales to foreign investors almost unavoidable. In Hungary, for example, the rejection of mass privatisation has necessarily meant a strong openness to foreign investment. Other countries, particularly those in which mass privatisation is

---

[410] See: p.330-348
[411] Havrylyshyn and McGettigan, p.4
[412] Schwartz, p.39
[413] Chikán, p.23

About Poland, Chikán states that: "Largely due to the fact that the agricultural sector in Poland had never been organised into state-owned co-operatives, in 1989 the private sector accounted for around 30 per cent of Polish GDP".(p.23)

Czechoslovakia started with the best macroeconomic conditions, with Hungary also in a relatively good position. Bulgaria, Croatia, Hungary, and Poland had inherited large external debts, while others had accumulated virtually no debt. [Stanley Fischer, Ratna Sahay, "The Transition Economies After Ten Years", IMF (International Monetary Fund), Working Paper 7664, Cambridge, February 2000, p.10, URL: http://www.nber.org/papers/w7664]

The Czech Republic has the most privatised economy, the lowest unemployment rate, one of the lowest inflation rates, and the highest share of gross foreign investment in GDP in Eastern Europe. (The World Bank, URL: http://www.worldbank.org/ecspf/final/html/czech_republic.htm). Therefore the former Czechoslovakia started transition with some comparative advantages: relative macroeconomic stability, low foreign debt. (Hrncir, p.167) On the other hand, under socialism, Albania was a country with the highest proportion of the economy in state hands and with the least reform to its enterprise-management methods. (Konstandin Kristo, "Economic Reform in Albania", web page of Center for International Private Enterprise, URL: http//www.cipe.org/)

expected to play an important role, have sometimes placed more restrictions on foreign investment.[414]

The slow trend which we have discussed above was not the case for (East) Germany, with the financial and technical support of (West) Germany, privatisation process was implemented very smoothly and painlessly.[415]

Finally, Russia has a special and spare part in the ex-socialist countries. The Russian transition experience stands out as unique.[416] Given the size and power of Russia, that was inevitable.[417] Compared to other former socialist countries, in most cases, the social, political, economical and financial conditions and circumstances of Russia are different. These factors, for example, create less favourable atmosphere for investors who wish to involve and make investment in privatisation transactions. [418] The political system is not yet sufficiently institutionalised.[419] Because of economic and political instability with other unique

---

[414] Schwartz, p.39
[415] Richard L. Lesher, "Democracy's Promise: Building a Modern Economy", web page of Center for International Private Enterprise, URL: http://www.cipe.org/
[416] Malle, p.72-74
[417] Stanley Fischer and Ratna Sahay, "The Transition Economies After Ten Years", IMF (International Monetary Fund), Working Paper 7664, Cambridge, February 2000, p.21, URL: http://www.nber.org/papers/w7664
[418] In one interview (former) chairman of the Federal Commission for the Securities Market in Russia states that: "...The Russian economy faces serious consequences unless it can offer adequate safeguards. Not only are foreigners reluctant to invest in Russia, but Russians do not trust it either. ["Safeguarding Russian Investors: Securities Chief Speaks Out", interview with Dmitry Vasiliyev, (former) Chairman of the Federal Commission for the Securities Market in Russia, web page of Center for International Private Enterprise, URL: http://www.cipe.org/]
However, the adoption of the first democratic constitution in Russian history on 12 December 1993 is a landmark for the foreign investor and Russian citizens. (Butler and Gashi-Butler, p.14)
Also see: Matthew A. Piasecki, "Looking for Fresh Investment Opportunities in Central Europe and Russia: A Path Finding Guide", Privatisation and Economic Development an Eastern Europe and the CIS-Investment, Acquisition and Managerial Issues, Edited By: Haydn Shaughnessy: John Wiley & Sons, England, 1994, p.42; Boffito, p.283
Finally, although no systematic programme for widespread privatisation of state owned enterprises was adopted in the Soviet Union before its collapse, the USSR did witness some degree of privatisation of both small and large enterprises in the last year or so before its collapse. (Thomas E. Weisskopf, "Economic Perspectives on Privatization in Russia: 1990-1994", Privatization in Central and Eastern Europe-Perspectives and Approaches, Edited by: Demetrius S. Iatridis and June Gary Hopps, Praeger Publishers, USA, 1998, p.105)
[419] Boffito, p.57

circumstances the privatisation process is also slower and harder than the rest of Eastern Europe.[420]

E. Analysis

Because of the reasons we discussed above, privatisation in Central and Eastern Europe faces considerably more difficulty than occasional privatisation programs in developed market economies. In the latter, ownership rights are simply transferred from the state to the private sector; the rights themselves are already well established and supported by a number of institutions that safeguard their clarity, enforceability, and transferability.[421]

In the ex-socialist countries, different economic and political circumstances have dictated unique privatisation methods-such as mass privatisation through vouchers or investment funds, large-scale privatisation through state holding agencies and small-scale privatisation through auctions-in addition to the approaches commonly employed in developing countries.[422] As a result, different levels of private economic activities, diverging macroeconomic conditions, different degrees of pre-transformation economic reforms, and different socio-political climates characterised these countries as they began initiating major privatisation programs.[423]

---

[420] Ash, Hare and Canning, p.213
A possibility that a Communist led government might regain power has been another factor causing foreign investors to be apprehensive about their investment commitments in Russia. ("The Legal and Political Environment of Privatisation", URL: http//www.eia.doe.gov)
Kenneth J. Arrow and Edmund S. Phelps, "Proposed Reforms of the Economic System of Information and Decision in the USSR: Commentary and Advice", Privatisation Process in Eastern Europe- Theoretical Foundations and Empirical Results, Edited by: Maria Baldassarri, Luigi Paganetto, Edmund S. Phelps, St. Martin's Press, 1993, p.46
Russia needs to undergo large amount of deconstruction in the military industrial complex while carrying out privatisation. According to some authors, this distinctive element explains the resistance to privatisation of powerful groups and their nationalistic overtones. (Malle, p.96)
[421] Marek Hessel, "How Corporate Governance Makes Privatization Succeed", web page of Center for International Private Enterprise, URL: http//www.cipe.org/
[422] "Privatizing State-Owned Companies", The Prosperity Papers Series, Prosperity Paper Three, web page of Center for International Private Enterprise, URL: http//www.cipe.org/
[423] Inotai, p.164

Therefore we believe that developed countries cannot be model in privatisation for former socialist countries[424]; however, ex-socialist countries may benefit from some experiences of western economies.[425] According to us, privatisation in Eastern Europe should be designed along simple, basic lines, avoiding the high-tech instruments of financial markets that are appropriate to advanced stages of capitalism.[426]

---

[424] In that context, the United Kingdom cannot be a model for former socialist countries. Thus the privatisation programme in UK was accomplished so easily because of the peculiar freedom given to the government with a parliamentary majority to implement policy free from constitutional and other legal constraints, whilst existence of a developed system of financial markets made the technical achievement of the rapid disposal of large enterprises possible. The regulatory style characteristic of Britain also permits government to create regulatory systems easily and in a form that retains the power to determine the degree of competition and the initial operating environment for the privatised utilities in its own hands. (Prosser, and Moran, Privatization and Regulatory Change, p. 48)

[425] Fischer, p.4

[426] For the same opinion and approach see: Martin L. Weitzman, "How Not to Privatize", Privatization Process in Eastern Europe-Theoretical Foundations and Empirical Results, Edited by: Maria Baldassarri, Luigi Paganetto, Edmund S. Phelps, St. Martin's Press, 1993, p.251. According to Weitzman "If you are planning to fly an airplane, your first lesson should be on a simple, basic, no-frills model, not a supersonic, state-of-the-art, extraordinarily sophisticated version, because there are too many things that can too easily go wrong with high technology in a low technology environment"(p.251).
Simplicity was one of the main concerns in the Lithuanian privatisation laws and in the privatisation programme. (Lithuanian Business Information Centre, URL: http//www.lbic.lt/)
There is also a discussion on whether privatisation should be implemented fast or slow. There is a fear that speedy privatisation risks incorrect implementation, with inadequate development of supporting institutions and the danger that the whole process is taken over by anti-reform interests primarily seeking government favours. (Havrylyshyn and McGettigan, p.5). However, it can be argued that speedy progress would prevent corruption and uncertainty.
Furthermore, proponents of slow privatisation put forward three basic arguments (i) macroeconomic stabilisation, domestic price liberalisation, and current account convertibility have to precede privatisation because efficient decisions can only be made on the basis of correct relative prices. (ii) introduction of competition policies and current account convertibility has to precede privatisation to prevent monopoly profits; and (iii) introduction of modern tax systems and accounting procedures, and financial market and capital market reforms, have to precede privatisation to allow for proper enterprise valuation. Proponents of fast privatisation basically pointed toward the broader macroeconomic consequences of continuing to burden the economy with a large and inefficient state enterprise sector for decades to come. (Schwartz, p.36, 37)
Although former socialist countries have common points, they have very different elements. Therefore, according to us, each country should decide and develop its own adequate privatisation policy. There are some factors determine the speed of the privatisation progress:
(a) One important factor that determines the speed of the privatisation program is the of the financial and legal structure of the country concern. For example, in East Germany direct-sale privatisation took place at remarkable speed, an approach that has proved to be both a painful and an expensive basis for economic revival. At the start of transition less than 5 per cent of property was in private hands; the rest was either state- or co-operatively-owned (80 per cent and 15 per cent respectively). In just four years, the state privatisation agency, the Treuhandanstalt, had privatised the entire economy (Chikán, p.26; Grimstone, (British Privatisation), p.10). This success is largely due to the highly develop financial and legal infrastructure of (West) Germany.
(b) Another factor is the privatisation method used. In that context, voucher privatisation where each citizen receives a certain number of privatisation vouchers free or with a very little fee, is the fastest way and method in privatisation. This method has been used in some former socialist countries including Czech Republic, Romania and Slovenia. For example, Czech voucher privatisation included the majority of state enterprises and achieved the ownership transformation of hundreds, if not thousands, of enterprises in a very short time. (Chikán, p.26)

VI. CONCLUSIONS

We believe that the origin of the idea of privatisation is old as the origin of the debate on private versus public ownership. Therefore it can be traced back to the ancient Greece. For the past decade, a major process of redefinition of the role of the state has been under way in many countries. Privatisation is a central component of this process. However, since privatisation is a new concept there is no consensus on the definition and structure of this phenomenon.

As we discussed, technically it is not always possible to measure and compare the performance of the firms before and after privatisation. Furthermore there are important economic differences between western countries and former socialist economies. Therefore applying same performance indicators to former socialist countries can be problematical.[427]

The empirical analysis or economic literature show no clear evidence that private service delivery is inherently more effective or less effective than public service delivery.[428] However, it seems that, private firms can be more efficient than public entities to the extent that they are better able to resist nefarious political interference.[429] We can conclude that in the privatisation

---

We must point out that because of political, social and financial instability, a speedy progress would have better outcome for ex socialist countries. Because delays to privatisation can increase the risk, as was the case for many Slovak SOEs. Having slated a large number of enterprises for privatisation, a change in government brought new policies that stressed slower privatisation. Many companies were left without a clear direction. While they awaited new owners, corporate control was weak and short-term decision-making prevailed. (Chikán, p.29)

Finally, different countries persuade different approaches. For example, according to Estonian government the structure of the Estonian Privatisation Agency was developed to facilitate more rapid privatisation. [Estonian Privatisation Agency, URL: http//www.eea.ee/). Similarly, government of Bosnia and Herzegovina Federation states that one of the basic principles of this privatisation is the speed and privatisation is scheduled to be conducted in a short time-period. (Web page of Agency of Privatisation of Federation of Bosnia and Herzegovina, URL: http://www.zpf.com.ba/). Similarly, Croatian government believes that privatisation programme should be implemented speedy. (Web page of Croatian Government, URL: http://www.hfp.hr/privatization/privat.htm)

Also see: Maria Prohaska, "Privatization in Bulgaria: Pushing Forward", web page of Center for International Private Enterprise, URL: http//www.cipe.org/)

[427] See: p. 76-78

[428] Demetra Smith Nightingale, Nancy Pindus, "Privatization of Public Social Services: A Background Paper", October 15, 1997, Urban Institute, URL: http//www.urban.org/

[429] Michael Klein, Neil Roger, Back to the Future, "The Potential in Infrastructure Privatisation", Public Policy for the Private Sector, The World Bank, FPD Note No: 30, November 1994

literature, the overwhelming consensus is that private ownership is more efficient in providing private goods in competitive markets.[430]

In general, increases in profitability are not equivalent to increases in efficiency. This will only be true in a competitive environment. It is observed in cross-country studies that profitability increases more and productivity less in regulated or less competitive sectors.[431]

The success of privatisation and the performance of privatised enterprises vary in each country and even in different sectors. In many countries, the results of privatisation have, so far, fallen short of expectations.[432] It is, however still early to draw some definitive conclusions. It is only in the medium and long term that one can see the effect of ownership on enterprise decisions.[433] If, in the majority of developing countries, privatisation programmes have not so far really achieved their economic and financial objectives, this seems to be due to three factors: the existence of many constraints (legal, social, or technical) preventing the satisfactory development of these programmes; the ambiguous attitude of governments towards privatisation operations; and insufficient awareness of their close links with other structural reforms.[434]

Among the many objectives assigned to privatisation, it is well known that reduction of the budget deficit and increased economic efficiency is those most frequently aimed at.[435] It seems that, although it is not explicitly being mentioned in the legal drafts and official

---

[430] Paul Starr, "The Meaning of Privatization", URL: http://www.princeton.edu./~starr/meaning.html; Vickers and Yarrow, (An Economic Analysis), p.426; "Privatizing State-Owned Companies", The Prosperity Papers Series, Prosperity Paper Three, web page of Center for International Private Enterprise, URL: http//www.cipe.org/
[431] Sheshinski and López-Calva, p.27
[432] Schwartz and Silva Lopes, p.38
[433] "Is Privatization Succeeding in Central and Eastern Europe?", An Interview with Roman Frydman, by the Centre for International Private Enterprise, Centre for International Private Enterprise, web page of the World Bank, URL: http:/www.worldbank.org
[434] Olivier Bouin, "The Privatisation in Developing Countries: Reflections on a Panacea", Policy Brief No. 3, OECD Development Centre, OECD 1992
[435] Olivier Bouin, "The Privatisation in Developing Countries: Reflections on a Panacea", Policy Brief No. 3, OECD Development Centre, OECD 1992

documents the current wave of privatisations is largely a response to the financial crisis facing many governments.[436]

The other solutions rather than privatisation, regulatory systems, are costly and often fail to achieve their goals.[437]

The aging paradigm of public enterprise monopolies will have to discarded and replaced by a sector structure that is more dynamic, competitive, and open to the private sector. Rapid changes are taking places in the infrastructure sectors. Ports, airports, railways, and power companies can no longer be seen as monolithic, monopolistic entities; rather than they represent a range of separable activities.[438]

Particularly, in the ex-socialist countries, there is a wide gap between expectations and reality; reality is much behind the schedule.[439] It seems that particularly in these countries, learning processes will take time and mistakes will be made.[440] And in former socialist countries, experience has shown that the transition from a planned to a market economy is neither simply nor easy. In the short run, the costs are much higher than the benefits, but in the long run, it is

---

[436] Guislain, (The Privatization Challenge), p.17

[437] Michael Klein, Neil Roger, Back to the Future, "The Potential in Infrastructure Privatisation", Public Policy for the Private Sector, The World Bank, FPD Note No: 30, November 1994; "Is Privatization Succeeding in Central and Eastern Europe?", An Interview with Roman Frydman, by the Centre for International Private Enterprise, Centre for International Private Enterprise, web page of the World Bank, URL: http:/www.worldbank.org

[438] Guislain, (The Privatization Challenge), p.288

[439] Inotai, p.170, 171; Fischer, p.4, 5. [Fischer states that: "...the experience of privatisation in almost all developing countries has been disappointing..."(p.4, 5)]

The public opinion in the region generally shows a high degree of scepticism about privatisation. (Ash, Hare and Canning, p.219)

However, there are some successful cases like Skoda in Czech Republic. (Skoda's Receipe for Success, web page of Center for International Private Enterprise, URL: http//www.cipe.org/)

We must point that the analysis above is valid for the large-scale enterprises. In general privatisation for small-scale enterprises were successful. [Stanley Fischer and Ratna Sahay, "The Transition Economies After Ten Years", IMF (International Monetary Fund), Working Paper 7664, Cambridge, February 2000, p.19, URL: http://www.nber.org/papers/w7664]

Finally see: Sheshinski and López-Calva, p.24. [According to this study failures in privatisation of infrastructure can be explained fundamentally by two types of policy mistakes: first, poorly design of concessions -- mainly in the area of distribution of risks and public guarantees, and second, inappropriate regulatory structure and/or weak enforcement by regulatory institutions.(p.24)]

hoped that the benefits will exceed the costs.[441] However, it is important to stress that while privatisation raises particular problems and dilemmas, it is merely one element, though a very important one, in the process of transition from a socialist to a market economy.[442] Nevertheless, fundamental economic reform is essential for the whole region, and well-designed privatisation plans that involve rather than isolate the majority of population could well act as an important catalyst for bringing about the economic and political transformation of these societies.[443]

In former socialist countries, the success of transition depends heavily on the development of stable political conditions and strong institutions guided by democratic principles and rules.[444] The formerly socialist economies should privatise in all possible ways that encourage competition, and they should experiment with all available methods.[445]

There are important distinctions between privatisation in West European countries and in the former socialist states due to specific economic circumstances and the privatisation methods chosen.[446] Therefore, privatisation in Central and Eastern Europe is unlikely to follow the well-known path and techniques of privatisation in industrialised countries. In other words Western models in privatisation are not appropriate for former socialist countries; these countries should develop their own pragmatic solutions.[447] Particularly, in Eastern European countries for a

---

[440] Rudiger Soltwedel, "Comment on Holger Schmieding, (Alternative approaches to Privatisation: Some Notes on the Debate)", Privatisation-Symposium in Honor of Herbert Giersch, Edited By: Horst Siebert, Institut fur Weltwirtschaft an der Universitat Kiel, J.C.B. Mohr (Paul Siebeck), Tubingen, 1992, p.110; Hrncir, p.167

[441] Mate Babic, "Privatization and Restructuring in Croatia", Privatization in Central and Eastern Europe-Perspectives and Approaches, Edited by: Demetrius S. Iatridis and June Gary Hopps, Praeger Publishers, USA, 1998, p.150

[442] Saul Estrin, "Economic Transition and Privatisation: The Issues", Privatisation in Central and Eastern Europe, Edited By: Saul Estrin, Longman Group Limited, 1994, London and New York, p.3

[443] Ash, Hare and Canning, p.214

[444] "Conclusions", Privatization in Central and Eastern Europe-Perspectives and Approaches, Edited by: Demetrius S. Iatridis and June Gary Hopps, Praeger Publishers, USA, 1998, p.197

[445] Sunita Kikeri, John Nellis, Mary Shirley, Outreach Nr. 3, Policy Views from the Country Economics Department, The World Bank, July 1992

[446] Peter Young, "The Lessons of Privatisation", web page of Center for International Private Enterprise, URL: http//www.cipe.org/

[447] In one interview (former) chairman of the Federal Commission for the Securities Market in Russia states that: "...The first lesson is that emerging markets cannot borrow the experience of Western countries. You cannot just transfer their legislation to other countries. We are at a different stage of development". ["Safeguarding Russian Investors: Securities Chief Speaks Out", interview with Dmitry Vasiliyev, (former) Chairman of the Federal

privatisation program to gain momentum, early sales have to succeed. This suggests privatising the easy candidates first.[448] According to us, particularly in former socialist countries, privatisation process should be designed on the following principles:

- *Broad participation:* All citizens should be encouraged to participate in the process.

- *Transparency:* Rules for privatisation will be known to all who wish to participate, thus providing public transparency (scrutiny) for privatisation process.

- *Speed:* Privatisation should scheduled to be conducted in a short period of time.[449]

- *Simplicity:* Rules, methods and procedure and other details should be simple and provisions for citizen's participation in the process should not require any particular skills or knowledge.[450]

Commission for the Securities Market in Russia], web page of Center for International Private Enterprise, URL: http//www.cipe.org/]

[448] Donaldson and Wagle, p.3

[449] Particularly small-scale enterprises should be privatised as quickly as possible. [Tornell, p.3]

[450] For the same approach see: Web page of agency of Privatisation of Federation of Bosnia and Herzegovina; URL: http://www.zpf.com.ba/

Simplicity was one of the main concerns in the Lithuanian privatisation laws and in the privatisation programme. (Web page of Lithuanian Business Information Centre, URL: http//www.lbic.lt/)

CHAPTER II

THE LIMITS OF PRIVATISATION: How Far Can Privatisation Go?

This chapter examines whether there are activities or enterprises which cannot be privatised. This examination will discuss the concept of strategic or vital sectors and will deal with a basic question: What services or products should government produce?

I. The NATURE of PUBLIC ENTERPRISES

A. General

In the privatisation literature little analysis has been made on the limits of privatisation. It is a highly controversial issue.

Limits of privatisation may derive from a number of factors: (a) legal sources (constitutions, acts, international treaties, contracts etc.) (b) natural factors. (For example it is not possible to privatise common goods, such as the use of air) or (c) economic factors (it is not economic to privatise unemployment agencies, services and benefits, in other words it is almost impossible to find a investor willing to buy an unemployment agency providing benefits for free of charge), (d) social factors (If privatisation of a certain SOE will cause massive lay offs government may keep this SOE in its hands), (e) other factors (For example monuments and historical places cannot be privatised).

According to some authors, public ownership is a response to the failure of private markets to achieve efficient and equitable outcomes. It is argued that, unlike private enterprises, whose key objective is to maximise profits, public enterprises have to contend with multiple objectives-including general economic objectives, such as the control of strategic resources, delivery of essential goods and services[1], employment policies, and price controls, and non-economic objectives, ranging from social obligations[2] to political patronage-that often conflict with the maximisation of profits.[3]

It is universally agreed that state owned enterprises should operate to serve public interest and general welfare.[4] Furthermore, public sector organisations are seen as having to pursue a range of social and economic goals (creating employment, maintaining a national presence in the key industries, sustaining local businesses, developing domestic technology, providing vocational training in high-technology industries, decentralising industry).[5] In that context, utilities have two characteristics: They supply essential goods or services and their core business is a natural monopoly. The essential nature of the goods or services provided introduces an obligation to provide consumers access to them on a non-discriminatory basis at a fair price.[6] By

---

[1] Vickers and Yarrow, (An Economic Analysis), p.7, 9, 27; Anibal Santos, "Privatisation and State Intervention-(An Economic Approach)", Deregulation or Re-regulation-Regulatory Reform in Europe and the United States, Edited by: Giandomenico Majone, Pinter Publishers, London, 1990, p.139; Aharoni, p.184

The economic literature is more precise and useful in the definition of the concept of public good, which applies to only a few public services. To qualify as a public good, an asset or service must possess certain features. For example it must be impossible, at least in practice, to exclude specific people from using it (non-excludability), and there must be non-rivalry in consumption, which implies that its consumption by one person in no way prevents its consumption by others (no crowding-out effect). Few infrastructure activities can be regarded as public goods: examples are traffic signalling, street lighting, and traffic control. However, the fact that a service is indeed a public good in no way implies that it should be provided by a public agency. [For this see: Guislain, (The Privatization Challenge), p.25, footnote 6; Niskanen, p.220; Braddon and Foster, p.293].

[2] For example, in former socialist countries, companies were not merely employers; they were the providers of housing, pensions, holidays, childcare and other services. (Chikán, p.24)

[3] Schwartz and Silva Lopes, p.38; Bishop and Kay, (Western Economies), p.194, 195, 196; Wright and Thompson, p.10

Finally we must point out that, in some cases government socio-economic objectives for public enterprises are often defined ambiguously; usually the goals are stated in general terms like "maximisation of society's well being" or "increase of living standards". Furthermore, in some cases the objectives may be inconsistent with each other. (Adhikari and Kirkpatrick, p.41)

[4] John Lintner, "Economic Theory and Financial Management", State-Owned Enterprise in the Western Economies, Edited By: Raymond Vernon and Yair Aharoni, Croom Helm Ltd., 1981, p.24

[5] According to some Beesley and Avans in Britain, allocative efficiency was seen as the major objective and the major principle for organising public enterprises. (Michael Beesley and Tom Avans, "The British Experience: The Case of British Rail", State-Owned Enterprise in the Western Economies, Edited By: Raymond Vernon and Yair Aharoni, Croom Helm Ltd., 1981, p.117)

[6] Justin Malbon, "Gaining Balance on the Regulatory Tightrope", Edited by: Moazzem Hossain, Justin Malbon, Routledge Studies in the Modern World Economy, London and New York, 1998, p.11

contrast corporations are seen as single-minded profit maximisers, simplifying both management and accountability.[7]

B. Change the Role of the State

1. Multiplication of SOEs

The 1970s were characterised by the multiplication of the number of public enterprises in the majority of developing countries; mainly because of the thought that they cover the strategic sectors.[8] During the 1970s, however, public enterprises proliferated in sectors that could scarcely be called strategic: service activities (marketing and exporting offices, tourism, hotels and catering, financial services, etc.) and to a lesser extent small and medium industrial enterprises. This expansion of the public sector in all directions is evidence of the growing role of the state within the different types of mixed economy in the developing countries and resulted in the most heterogeneous public appropriations in the late 1970s. It made a reaction in favour of the private sphere in the form of privatisation virtually inevitable.[9]

Moreover, public enterprises often need to kept afloat at the taxpayer's expense, either through explicit governmental subsidies, such as direct cash grants, or through implicit subsidies,

---

[7] Stampford, p.251; Maurice R. Garner, "Has Public Enterprise Failed?" Privatisation in the United Kingdom, Edited by: V.V. Ramanadham, Routledge, London and New York, 1988, p.30, 31
[8] State owned enterprises were widely promoted during the 1960s and 1970s on the basis of following principal premises:
-Such enterprises encouraged broad social responsibility and responsiveness to the public interest,
-SOEs helped to create stable investment and employment partners,
-SOEs provided models for improved industrial relations,
-SOEs were essentials for production in sectors characterised by extended time horizons and great perceived risk, as in nuclear power generation,
-SOEs could beneficially replace private natural monopolies, producing higher output at lower prices, with the utilities as a favourite example,
-SOEs provided irreplaceable means of direction and control in defence-related industry,
-SOEs could successfully stimulate sectoral competition, as shown by the cases of Renault and Crédit Lyonnais in France,
-SOEs were potent instruments of decolonisation, given the desire of nationalist political elites to radically reduce foreign corporate ownership within the private sector. (Gayle, p.9)
[9] Olivier Bouin, "The Privatisation in Developing Countries: Reflections on a Panacea", Policy Brief No. 3, OECD Development Centre, OECD 1992

such as subsidised credit, guaranteed sales to the government at the fixed prices, reductions of tax liabilities, governmental injections of equity, or preferential exchange rates.[10]

Finally because of the burden of the SOEs, some authors argue that, the state has failed to implement appropriate economic and social policies.[11]

2. Change of the role

In the first place, governments find themselves in the paradoxical situation of having to reduce their own power of intervention in the economy by transferring public enterprises to the private sector. With this in mind, many governments considered privatisation as making it possible simultaneously to resolve certain contradictions in the functioning of mixed economies and to satisfy the international financial institutions (such as the World Bank, IMF, OECD) requirements.[12]

II. CAN ALL SECTORS and ACTIVITIES be PRIVATISED?

A. General

Different terms are used to refer to sectors or activities that are deemed to be ineligible for privatisation. In some countries, reference is made to *strategic, vital or sensitive* economic sectors or activities. In some other countries, the view is that natural monopolies or public services should not be privatised.

---

[10] Schwartz and Silva Lopes, p.38; Bishop and Kay, (Western Economies), p.194, 195, 196
According to Shirley: "The economic problems that arise when bureaucrats are in business; that is, when governments own and operate enterprises that could be run as private firms... bureaucrats typically perform poorly in business, not because they are incompetent ... but because they face contradictory goals and perverse incentives that can distract and discourage even very able and dedicated public servants. (Mary M. Shirley, "Getting Bureaucrats Out of Business: Obstacles to State Enterprise Reform", web page of Center for International Private Enterprise, URL: http//www.cipe.org/)

[11] In economic terms, state failure means supplying a country with public goods that are too highly priced and too low in quality-in both cases for structural reasons. In political terms, state failure means a chronic inability to take decisions widely agreed to be necessary-again for deep-seated reasons. (Martin Jänicke, *State Failure-The Impotence of Politics in Industrial Society*, Translated by: Alan Braley, Polity Press, Cambridge & Oxford, 1990, p.1)

B. Strategic sectors

1. General

As mentioned above, the concept of strategic or vital sectors are often used to describe the areas that cannot be privatised.

Throughout the world, the privatisation of enterprises with strategic military or economic significance raises especially sensitive questions of sovereignty and security. In most oil-producing countries, for example, no government is likely to try to privatise the state oil companies because of the likely domestic political reaction. Even in Great Britain, the prospective sale of a helicopter company to an American company caused a political stir.[13]

In Ukraine more than 5,000 strategic industries have been excluded from privatisation in the transportation, defence, energy, communications, and agricultural sectors.[14]

The conflict between privatisation and national interests depends on the relative power of a given state in the world system--the weaker the state, the more likely the conflict. Economically strong nations, knowing that they can privatise without jeopardising their sovereignty, lecture the weak on the perils of state enterprise and restrictions on investment.[15]

---

[12] Olivier Bouin, "The Privatisation in Developing Countries: Reflections on a Panacea", Policy Brief No. 3, OECD Development Centre, OECD 1992

[13] Paul Starr, "The Meaning of Privatisation", web page of University of Princeton, URL: http://princeton.edu/~starr/meaning.html; Iatridis, p.23; Inotai, p.174

The concept strategic sector is an important reason to impose restriction on foreign investors. However this approach may be detrimental to the privatisation process, particularly in the former socialist countries where the lack of capital is a common fact. Therefore if foreign participation remains limited in the ex-socialist countries, privatisation can only be fuelled by free-of-charge distribution of part of the state assets. In this case, ideological and national security reasons may collide with efficiency criteria. (Inotai, p.174)

[14] Web page of State Property Fund of Ukraine, URL: http//www.ukrmassp.kiev.ua/Prgrm98-1.htm

[15] Paul Starr, "The Meaning of Privatisation", web page of University of Princeton, URL: http://princeton.edu/~starr/meaning.html.

According to Starr: "Despite its commitment to free market, the Reagan Administration intervened in 1987 to prevent the sale to a Japanese corporation of a private American semiconductor company with important defence contracts. On the other hand, the Reagan administration has sought to privatise some of NASA's satellite launch operations partly in the hope of strengthening the private American space industry in its competition with the Europeans."

2. Definition of the strategic industries

a. General

The definition of strategic industries has always been uncertain and there is no consensus on the definition of strategic sectors or areas.[16] On the other hand, rapid technological evolution and the widespread dissemination of innovation have rendered a great deal of ownership restrictions obsolete, in what used to be either "natural" monopolies or national security related sectors.

b. Golden (special) Shares

i. General

Governments often attach special conditions to privatisation sales, demanding a special or "golden share" to protect the enterprise from an unwelcome take over (usually aimed at preventing a foreign take over) or to give the government influence on company matters it considers of national importance.[17] Generally speaking, a golden share gives the government the right to intervene to block changes in corporate control, take-overs, or foreign participations;[18]

---

[16] However, some privatisation laws provide definition of strategic sectors. Thus, according to Albanian privatisation legislation: "By strategic sectors of economy are meant: the industry of energy and mining, oil and gas, post, telecommunications, forests and water reserves, roadways and railroads, sea ports, airports, air and rail transport, as well as the sector of second level banks and insurance companies with total state capital." (Article 4, Law No. 8306, dated 14.3.1998, On the Strategy for the Privatisation of Strategic Sectors, web page of Economic Development Agency of Albanian Government, URL: http://www.aeda.gov.al/). Furthermore according to the law, strategic enterprises can be privatised, but the in no case privatisation can be higher than 20% of the capital of the enterprise. (Article 8)

[17] Cosmo Graham and Tony Prosser, "Golden Shares: Industrial Policy by Stealth", (Golden Shares), Public Law, Autumn, 1988, p.413; Paolo Saba, Privatizing Network Industries, The Competition Policy Perspective, OECD, Competition Law and Policy Division, Helsinki, September 17-18, 1998

[18] Madsen Pirie, "Privatisation: 10 Lessons of Experience", President of the Adam Smith Institute, http://privatizationlink.com; Privatisation Trends in OECD Countries-June 1996, http://oecd.org; Guislain, p.256, 257

Some privatisation laws provide a definition for golden shares. Thus, in Albanian privatisation legislation golden share is defined "a share of special characteristics which the state holds for a definite period of time in order to exercise exclusive rights on decision-making for special decisive society issues, but not for its daily work." (Article 1, Law No. 8306, dated 14.3.1998, On the Strategy for the privatisation of Strategic Sectors. Web page of Economic Development Agency of Albanian Government, URL: http//www.aeda.gov.al/)

Also see: William L. Megginson & Jeffry M. Netter, "Equity to the People: The Record on Share Issue Privatization Programs", p.8, web page of the World Bank, URL: http://www.worldbank.org

they are designed to allow government to prevent undesirable take-overs and changes in control.[19] Golden shares are special shares created by law or by the company's articles of agreement for the specific purpose of according their holder (the state or government) special rights that go well beyond those attached to ordinary shares. The rights attached to them are often described in the sale prospectus for the state owned enterprises.[20]

Golden shares normally involve the government's right to approve major corporate actions such as the sale of the majority of shares to a third party, sale of major assets, and liquidation or reorganisation.[21] In most cases the special share requires that certain provisions in the articles of incorporation of a company may not be changed without the specific consent of the special shareholder. The details of those provisions vary according to the circumstances of each company, but they typically include a prohibition on any one person, or group of persons acting in concert, from controlling more than say 15 percent of the equity of a company.[22]

The "golden share" technique has been used by many countries, including France[23], Hungary[24] Turkey[25], the Netherlands[26] and the United Kingdom,[27] to privatise enterprises that are

---

[19] Graham and Prosser, (Privatising Nationalised Industries), p.36
[20] Guislain, (The Privatization Challenge), p.130, 131; Guislain, (The World Bank), p.57
[21] Welch and Frémond, p.17
[22] Gibbon, (Guide), p.8
The rights conferred by golden shares are not, however, necessarily limited to controlling shareholder composition; they can extend to other decisions of the company. [Guislain, (The Privatization Challenge), p. 131, 132]

[23] Golden shares have also been employed in the French privatisation programme. The golden share schemes provide a much weaker form of intervention after privatisation in France than Britain. However, in France another scheme has been used: creation of "hard cores" of investors to whom a proportion of the capital on privatisation is allocated by the government, restrictions being imposed on disposal for a period of five years. And such hard cores have been created in almost all the French privatisations. [Graham and Prosser, (Golden Shares), p.421, 422]. Therefore in France there has been little reliance on the golden share, but rather on the creation of hard cores of investors. (p.430).
In France the government can hold a golden share giving it the right to approve any participation exceeding 10 percent of a privatised company's shares. (Welch and Frémond, p.17)

[24] In Hungary, the state has golden shares in 20 of the largest businesses, and retains minority ownership in some of the largest banks. (URL: http://www.worldbank.org)

[25] Turkish Privatisation Law, Article 13

[26] In this country parliament stipulates that the government should retain at least a majority or priority shareholding in a privatised company, as it was the case in the Netherlands. [Andeweg, p.202]
In the Netherlands even the Conservative-Liberal Party, which is closest to a free market ideology, has supported continued government involvement. (p.202)]

considered *strategic* and that provide *essential* services, as a way to keep some degree of government control over a privatised company, mainly with respect to future transfers of shares. [28]

In the UK special or golden shares, entitling government to retain some kind of interest in a privatised concern, have been introduced in many transactions. In other words, in the United Kingdom privatisations have as a rule, used the "golden share" technique, as it did in the cases of Britoil, Jaguar, Enterprise Oil, Sealink, Amersham International, Cable & Wireless, British Telecom, British Gas, British Airways.[29] In the UK the first special share was created in 1982 when 100 per cent of the equity in Amersham International was sold. There are currently 21 outstanding special shares, these are primarily in the electricity generating and transmission industries and certain defence companies.[30]

In the United Kingdom different types of restrictions have been imposed by golden shares. The most commonly used among these have been a restriction on the issue of new voting shares and a restriction on the proportion of the total shares which could be held by a single shareholder (other than Treasury). This was normally set at 15 per cent and, if exceed, the

---

[27] Privatization in the United Kingdom, Ernst & Young, p.6. This study indicated that golden shares have been introduced in 23 privatisations. (p.6,7, 8, 9). Alse see: Prosser, p.99-101
In the UK special shares are held by the Secretary of State with policy responsibility for the privatised industry. The rights attached to a Special Share cannot be varied without the Government's consent. ("Special Rights Shares", p. 2, web page of UK Treasury, URL: http://www.hmtreasury.gov.uk/pep/specialg.pdf)
In the United Kingdom, however, in addition to golden shares similar powers are available to government under ordinary law (a) If competition authority considers that a merger situation has been created and operates, or may be expected to operate, against the public interest, the Secretary of State may take and order to prevent the adverse effects, (b) Industry Act 1975 empowers the Secretary of State to take action where an important manufacturing undertaking passes under foreign control. [Graham and Prosser, (Golden Shares), p.417-419]

[28] Paolo Saba, Privatizing Network Industries, The Competition Policy Perspective, OECD, Competition Law and Policy Division, Helsinki, September 17-18, 1998

[29] Privatization in the United Kingdom, Ernst & Young, p.6. This study indicated that golden shares have been introduced in 23 privatisations. (p.6,7, 8,9); Prosser, p.99-101

[30] "Special Rights Shares", p. 2, web page of UK Treasury, URL: http://www.hmtreasury.gov.uk/pep/specialg.pdf
In the UK special shares were not, however, used in all cases; indeed a wide range of privatisations have been effected without Special Shares; these include Associated British Ports, some British Rail subsidiaries, Railtrack, the National freight consortium, major Rover Group subsidiaries. Civil Service businesses, such as ECGD, PSA Projects and PSA Building Management were also sold without Special Shares. ("Special Rights Shares", p. 2, web page of UK Treasury, URL: http://www.hmtreasury.gov.uk/pep/specialg.pdf)

acquirer was obliged to sell off the surplus holding.[31] Other frequently used restrictions were in relation to special voting rights or provisions, disposal of assets, winding up or dissolution, appointment of a British chief executive, and government appointed directors.[32]

In one document UK government states that: "…(in the UK) typical special share powers include:

(i) a clause providing that the holder of the Special Share may redeem the Share at any time for its face value (usually £1);

(ii) a clause limiting shareholdings by any one person, or group of persons acting in concert, to 15 per cent, with powers for the board of Directors to disenfranchise any shareholder in breach of this limit to the extent of the excess;

(iii) a clause entrenching itself, and the two clauses above, against amendment unless there is both a resolution passed by the ordinary shareholders at general meeting in the usual way and the holder of the special share has given written consent."[33]

While creating golden shares UK government states different reasons for different enterprises. For example according to the government in British Aerospace and Rolls-Royce golden shares have been created for "national security", in Jaguar they have been created for "the national interest", in BT the reason has been "national interest and stability for UK citizens", while in Royal Ordnance it has been "strategic importance", in Belfast International Airport

---

[31] Privatization in the United Kingdom, Ernst & Young, 1994, p.8; Tony Prosser, "Constitutions and Political Economy: The Privatisation of Public Enterprises in France and Great Britain", (Constitutions and Political Economy), Modern Law Review, Volume 53, May 1990, p.316; Graham and Prosser, (Privatising Nationalised Industries), p.36; Graham, p.196-202

[32] Privatization in the United Kingdom, Ernst & Young, 1994, p.9

[33] "Special Rights Shares", p. 3, 4, web page of UK Treasury, URL: http://www.hmtreasury.gov.uk/pep/specialg.pdf

The 15 per cent limit on shareholding is a widely used feature of Special Shares created for a utility sale but it was decided in 1988 that provisions relating to the right to appoint Chief Executives should be confined to privatised industries with a defence or security dimension. ("Special Rights Shares", p. 4, web page of UK Treasury, URL: http://www.hmtreasury.gov.uk/pep/specialg.pdf)

123

"military operations", in Scottish Nuclear "unwelcome takeovers", and finally in Rosyth Royal Dockyard and Devonport Royal Dockyard the reason for golden shares has been "to protect British interest".[34]

ii. Some other characteristics of this method

Governments may create golden shares for a limited time, in this case, golden shares will be valid in a specific period and when the period ends, golden shares would expire.[35] In some case golden shares can be created for a unlimited time. For example, in the United Kingdom in the majority of cases the golden shares were of indefinite duration with the government reserving the right to terminate them at a time of its choosing. Thus, in Cable & Wireless, Sealink Stena Line, VSEL Consortium, BG, Rolls-Royce, National Grid Group, National Power, PowerGen, Scottish Power, Belfast International Airport golden shares are "non-time limited".[36] Less commonly, as with Enterprise Oil, British Steel, Water Companies, Regional Electricity Companies, and Jaguar, a termination date [alone] was specified.[37]

---

[34] Web page of UK Treasury, URL: http://www.hm-treasury.gov.uk/pep/specials.html
According to UK government the key aims of the restrictions imposed by Special Shares has been to preserve the independence of companies:
-because of their strategic importance or,
-in order to give newly privatised industries time to adjust to the private sector and to establish a track record. ("Special Rights Shares", p. 3, web page of UK Treasury, URL: http://www.hmtreasury.gov.uk/pep/specialg.pdf)
Furthermore According UK government states that "...Special shares have been used in...circumstances in a number of privatisations where there has been a need to protect a business from takeover, for example on national security grounds or, as a temporary measure, to allow the management time to adjust to the private sector..." ("Special Rights Shares", p. 1, web page of UK Treasury, URL: http://www.hmtreasury.gov.uk/pep/specialg.pdf)

[35] As in the case of Regional Electricity Company in Britain. (For this see: Stephen C. Littlechild, Privatisation, Competition and Regulation, The Institute of Economic Affairs, Occasional Paper 10, London, 2000, p.38)
Also see: Madsen Pirie, "Privatisation: 10 Lessons of Experience", President of the Adam Smith Institute, http://privatizationlink.com; Privatisation Trends in OECD Countries-June 1996, URL: http://www.oecd.org; Guislain, (The Privatization Challenge), p.256, 257

[36] Web page of UK Treasury, URL: http://www.hm-treasury.gov.uk/
According to UK government where there is a security dimension, the Special Share is likely to be long-term ("timeless"), unless security priorities change. Where there is no security dimension the Share is likely to be a temporary arrangement ("time-limited"). ["Special Rights Shares", p. 3, web page of UK Treasury, URL: http://www.hmtreasury.gov.uk/pep/specialg.pdf]

[37] Privatization in the United Kingdom, Ernst & Young, p.9
In other words, in UK privatisation transactions, there is generally no fixed time period for the ending of a golden share scheme. In some cases, there is a specific date in the articles before which the government will not

In the case of defence-related industries, it is common to place a (lower) limit on the proportion of the company that may be held by overseas investors. In the U.K. this ruling has applied to Rolls Royce and British Aerospace.[38] Furthermore in the UK it has been the practice for special shares in companies with a defence or security dimension to include provisions to appoint or nominate directors.[39]

iii. Analysis

When the state has the right to decide on issues concerning public and strategic interests or when a certain level of control is required to be preserved, the state holds "the golden share" or a defined packet of shares under ownership.[40] In that context even the enterprises considered as "strategic" can be privatised if the government uses the *golden share* technique.[41]

By allowing the government to veto some corporate decisions or share transfers, for example, this technique prolongs state control, beyond privatisation, even though the state is now only a minority shareholder (sometimes with a single share). Therefore this method is also a type of legal restriction on selecting of buyers in the privatisation transactions.[42]

A golden share would be appropriate in certain limited circumstances where there is a clear need to protect a newly privatised business from unwelcome take-over on national security

---

redeem the share; in other cases, the share may be redeemed on request. [Graham and Prosser, (Golden Shares), p.414].

[38] Gibbon, (Guide), p.8
[39] "Special Rights Shares", p. 4, web page of UK Treasury, URL: http://www.hmtreasury.gov.uk/pep/specialg.pdf
[40] Article 10, Law No. 8306, dated 14.3.1998, On the Strategy for the Privatisation of Strategic Sectors of Albania, Web page of Economic Development Agency of Albanian Government, URL: http://www.aeda.gov.al/
[41] Madsen Pirie, "Privatisation: 10 Lessons of Experience", President of the Adam Smith Institute, URL: http://privatizationlink.com; Privatisation Trends in OECD Countries-June 1996, URL: http://www.oecd.org; Guislain, p.256, 257.
Also see: William L. Megginson & Jeffry M. Netter, "Equity to the People: The Record on Share Issue Privatization Programs", p.8, The World Bank, URL: http://www.worldbank.org
[42] Guislain, (The Privatization Challenge), p.130, 131; Guislain, (The World Bank), p.57

grounds or, as a temporary measure, to provide an opportunity for management to adjust to the private sector.[43]

Although they may be necessary in some cases, (particularly in defence related industries) golden shares are by no means an essential feature of privatisation policies. On the contrary, by interfering with the normal functioning of the market and blocking certain types of take-overs, golden shares can diminish incentives for management performance and adversely affect the operating results of the privatised company.[44]

As a rule, conditions attached to privatisations and in that context particularly golden shares by government detract from an enterprise's value because they increase uncertainty or restrain privatised firms' commercial freedom of action.[45]

Golden shares might be a much more flexible tool of retaining some form of control over such companies, as long as they are narrowly defined in terms of both scope and time.[46]

The golden share technique has been frequently used to enable governments to control future transfers of blocks of shares of privatised airlines, so that any future changes in shareholders do not bring the enterprise under foreign control, thereby causing it to lose the right to operate certain international routes.[47]

The use of special shares should be the exception, not the rule.[48] Thus, the British government made a clear statement that it would not use the power of the golden share except in "extreme" circumstances, having the nature of a national emergency.[49]

---

[43] Gibbon, (Guide), p.8
[44] Guislain, (The Privatization Challenge), p.132
[45] Welch and Frémond, p.17
[46] "Management and Sale of Residual State Shareholdings", web page of OECD, http://www.oecd.org:80/daf/peru/CONTENT/agpresi.htm
[47] Guislain, (The Privatization Challenge), p. 131, 132
[48] "…The use of special shares should be the exception, not the rule Their use should be confined to those companies where the Government judges that it needs to retain specific limited powers over the future ownership, control, or conduct of a privatised company. Given the objective of establishing as clean a break as possible when

It is important that special shares be time-limited wherever possible and should in any case have their continued existence subject to review.[50] Where special shares are agreed to be necessary it is important that they should avoid provisions enabling the government to interfere in the general conduct of the privatised business.[51]

Finally restrictions on foreign ownership of shares affecting nationals of other EC member states are prohibited under EC law (for example 43 of the Treaty of Rome - right of establishment, 294-equal treatment as regards participation in the capital of companies, and article 56-free movement of capital). There are only some justifications for such restrictions:[52]

(a) article 296.1(b) permits measures considered necessary for the protection of the essential interests of a member state's security, which are connected with the protection of, or trading in, arms, ammunition and war material. Even where justified, the restriction has to be proportionate and not distort competition in non-military products.[53]

---

transferring a company to the private sector the creation of Special Shares should be avoided wherever possible…" ("Special Rights Shares", p. 2, 3, web page of UK Treasury, URL: http://www.hmtreasury.gov.uk/pep/specialg.pdf)

[49] Carsberg, (Competition and Private Ownership), p.7. However, Carsberg believes that that the holding of the golden share had no perceptible effect on practice. (p.7)

However as mentioned above, in the UK on contrary to these statements golden share technique has been introduced in many privatisation transactions and in most cases they have been created for a non-limited time.

According to Prosser: "The golden share provisions have been of very little effect in the UK, partly because of their limited nature, partly because of bad drafting, but perhaps more fundamentally because of their existence contradicts an important justification for privatisation in a UK context; that the market for corporate control, largely implemented through hostile takeovers, is a key mechanism for increasing enterprise efficiency"[Prosser, (Social Limits p.219, 220)].

[50] "Special Rights Shares", p. 3, web page of UK Treasury, URL: http://www.hmtreasury.gov.uk/pep/specialg.pdf

[51] "Special Rights Shares", p. 3, web page of UK Treasury, URL: http://www.hmtreasury.gov.uk/pep/specialg.pdf

[52] "Special Rights Shares", p. 5, web page of UK Treasury, URL: http://www.hmtreasury.gov.uk/pep/specialg.pdf

[53] "Special Rights Shares", p. 5, web page of UK Treasury, URL: http://www.hmtreasury.gov.uk/pep/specialg.pdf

(b) under article 86(2) where the privatised company is an undertaking entrusted with the operation of services of general economic interest or a revenue-producing monopoly where the application of the Treaty would obstruct the performance of a task entrusted to it.[54]

Requirements that the chairman, chief executive and other senior management should be British nationals are prohibited under Article 39 and 294 of the Treaty of Rome. They can only be justified under article 296.1(b) on security or public policy grounds. These latter exemptions are narrowly interpreted and would have to be proportionate.[55]

C. Racial, Ethnic and Other Considerations

1. General

Like national interests, the more parochial concerns of politically dominant racial and ethnic groups may also confound privatisation plans. In many countries, ethnic minorities, such as Indians in East Africa, make up disproportionate numbers of the potential domestic buyers of public assets. When a country's bureaucratic and entrepreneurial classes differ in ethnic composition, privatisation may be understood as a transfer of wealth and power from one group to another and be politically resisted for that reason. Even if privatisation is adopted, the field of potential buyers may be so restricted that potential gains from more efficient management evaporate.[56]

In former socialist countries, in order to prevent Russian influence, some governments have taken some legal and political approaches and measures to prevent Russian investors to take control of the enterprises. For example in Estonia, the course of privatisation was strongly linked to the fight for independence from Moscow and the transfer of productive assets to

---

[54] "Special Rights Shares", p. 5, web page of UK Treasury, URL: http://www.hmtreasury.gov.uk/pep/specialg.pdf
[55] "Special Rights Shares", p. 6, web page of UK Treasury, URL: http://www.hmtreasury.gov.uk/pep/specialg.pdf

indigenous Estonians. In order to prevent Russian influence, the country introduced its own currency, the Kroon, in 1992 that functioned as a shield against a massive inflow of Russian currency. [57]

2. Domestic Groups

Particularly, in countries where there was no mass privatisation, the sale of state assets could not generate political support because few people benefited from it. For example, in Russia, the perception has been that certain groups, namely nomenclature (political class) rather than the population as a whole, have benefited from privatisation; therefore the process has contributed to a split in the society. On the other hand in Slovakia, privatisation also clearly benefited specific groups. Once that happens, there is no question about whether privatisation generates consensus because there are no grounds for the consensus. [58]

D. National sovereignty and economic security

Another serious, yet less tangible, barrier to privatisation is directly related to the question of national sovereignty and its relation to economic security. In the developing and ex-socialist countries, domestic investors often lack sufficient capital to invest in privatising firms, thereby arousing concern that privatisation will mean handing over the "national patrimony" to

---

[56] Paul Starr, "The Meaning of Privatisation", web page of University of Princeton, URL: http://princeton.edu/~starr/meaning.html
[57] Chikán, p.26
[58] "Is Privatization Succeeding in Central and Eastern Europe?", An Interview with Roman Frydman, by the Centre for International Private Enterprise, Centre for International Private Enterprise, web page of the World Bank, URL: http:/www.worldbank.org; David Satter, "Russia's Deepening Crisis", web Page of Huston Institute, URL: http://www.hudson.org

In related with this issue, some companies of certain origin may become more prominent among investors in a particular industry/geography. This can often be explained by:
-A country of origin's pre-eminence in a particular industry (e.g., large US/British involvement in oil and gas throughout the region, or almost totally Anglo-Saxon dominated accounting/audit and consulting market)
-Historic ties (e.g., pre-war German economies ties with the Czech lands and Russia),
-Geographic proximity (e.g.; significant Scandinavian participation in Poland and the Baltic Republics),
-Size of emigrant community from the region (e.g., special US focus on Russia and Poland),
-Commercial/trade links during the post-war period (e.g., French connection with the TV industry, Italian automotive links through Fiat, German links in electrical, machine and component industries) [Matthew A. Piasecki, Looking for Fresh Investment Opportunities in Central Europe and Russia: A Path Finding Guide, Privatisation and

foreign investors. The foreign control of SOEs, a common outcome in privatisation, evokes fears of political manipulation and/or economic sabotage that have been commonly associated with multinationals in the past. The repatriation of profits feeds these fears, as funds obtained from local operations, rather than being reinvested to support the local economy, are often taken out of the country.[59]

E. Privatisation Laws and Some Government's Approaches

Privatisation laws can provide some provisions defining some sectors, industries or enterprises as "strategic". Following examples show that in different countries different enterprises, sectors or activities are considered *vital, sensitive* or *strategic*.

For example, Turkish Privatisation Law does not provide a clear definition of the strategic sectors, although this concept has been used in the law. However, article 13 of the Turkish Privatisation Law concerning, "Determination of strategic fields and organisations and of the preference shares" states that:

"In relation to organisations under the scope of privatisation program, the Privatisation High Council is authorised:

(a) To determine strategic subjects and organisations;

(b) In the event that the state's shareholdings in organisations determined to be strategic... falls below 50%, and for the purposes of preventing monopolisation and of protecting national economic and security interests, to determine the number of preference shares granting special management and approval rights in the management bodies of the organisations and the rights attaching to those shares which the state shall enjoy; to change the quantity

---

Economic Development an Eastern Europe and the CIS-Investment, Acquisition and Managerial Issues, Edited By: Haydn Shaughnessy: John Wiley & Sons, England, 1994, p.43]
[59] "Privatizing State-Owned Companies", The Prosperity Papers Series, Prosperity Paper Three, web page of Center for International Private Enterprise, URL: http://www.cipe.org/

of these shares and the rights attaching there to; and to remove such sectors and organisations determined to be strategic from the scope of this program.

....however...if and when more than 49% of the capital shares of the organisations listed below are decided to be privatised, preference shares must be established in them:

- Turkish Airlines (THY)

- Turkish Ziraat Bank

- Turkish Halk Bank

- TMO (Soil Products Office) Alcoholid Factory

- Turkish Petroleum (TPAO refineries)"

As it can be seen, the article 13 states two basic provisions:

(a) It does not specify the strategic sectors or enterprises but it gives authorisation to the Privatisation High Council to decide and determine the strategic sectors. However, the article considers Turkish Airlines (THY), Turkish Ziraat Bank, Turkish Halk Bank, TMO (Soil Products Office) Alcoholid Factory, Turkish Petroleum (TPAO refineries) as strategic. (b) In case the Privatisation High Council determines and considers some enterprises as strategic, it has also authorisation to create some "golden shares".

On the other hand Slovak Privatisation Law defines some sectors or areas as strategic. According to Slovak Privatisation Law, following enterprises cannot be privatised: (a) railroads and Transport Depots of Eastern Slovakia; (b) forests, constructions and facilities used in forest industry and shares of companies owned by the state, if these do not constitute an object of settlement pursuant a special legal norm; (c) ground and underground waters and property used for water flows and underground water management and protection, and shares of companies; (d) shares of companies or property used for postal service, which are determined by the state.[60]

Furthermore according to Bulgarian Privatisation Agency, the privatisation of the following companies is not allowed:

-power production, coal mining, production of electric power in the Atomic Power Plant, power transfer and distribution, transfer and storing of natural gas;

-the national transport infrastructure;

-post services;

-territorial cadastre [land], geodesy and geoprotection;

-water supply and sewerage;

-duty-free zones;

-forests within the framework of the state forest fund.[61]

However, the agency states that the companies fulfilling specific state functions or in a process of restructuring will be offered for privatisation after co-ordination between the sector ministries and the bodies as described in the the Privatisation Law.[62]

---

[60] Article 10/3, The Act No.92/1991, dated February 26, 1991 on the Conditions of Transfer of State Property to Other Persons, (Web page of Ministry for Administration and Privatisation of National Property of the Slovak Republic, URL: http//www.privatiz.gov.sk/anglicky/act92.htm)

Furthermore, in Slovakia, in accordance with the 1995 law, privatisation did not include enterprises in some sectors and areas assets such as gas, telecommunications, armaments, pharmaceuticals, agriculture, or electricity since they were considered "strategic". (National Property Fund of Slovakia, URL: http://www.privatiz.gov.sk/; web page of the World Bank, URL: http://www.worldbank.org; Peter Bisák, "Goals and Policies of the Privatisation Process", Minister of Privatisation & Administration of National Property, Slovak Republic, http://www.kenpubs.co.uk/investguide/slovakia/bisak.html)

[61] Web page of Bulgarian Privatisation Agency, URL: http:// www.privatisation.online.bg

[62] Bulgarian government also points out that privatisation will not lead to a decrease of the commitments of the privatised companies concerning defence-mobilisation readiness, the civil defence of the country, and the state reserve in 1998. Some special laws and legal acts will continue to play a very important role, namely the Defence and Armed Forces Act, Council of Ministers' Regulation No 150/1992, No 19/1993 and No 409/1993 which require fulfilment of the respective tasks concerning the defence of the country by the respective company irrespective of the fact that the company capital shares (stocks) have changed their owner. [Bulgarian Foreign Investment Agency, URL: http://www.bfia.org/privat.htm; web page of Bulgarian Privatisation Agency, URL: http://www.privatisation.online.bg; World Bank, URL: http://www.worldbank.org]

Finally Georgian Privatisation Law provides a long of list enterprises that cannot be privatised. According to article 4 of the Georgian Privatisation Law the following state property is not liable to privatisation:

"a) Natural resources, water resources, territorial waters, continental shelf, special economic and frontier zones, forest reserve, air space, protected or specially used natural territories;

b) Historic and art monuments approved under established order, state archives of historic and cultural importance, state collection of film, photo and phono materials, state museums, theatres, archives and collections of ministries, departments, scientific-research institutes;

c) Mobilization stores, state reserves, stores of precious metals;

d) Transmission and control systems of the electric power sector;

e) Institutions of the Academy of Sciences of Georgia working in fundamental sciences, state institutes of higher education and affiliated scientific-research institutes financed by the state;

f) Ports and landing piers of national importance, hydraulic engineering constructions, lighthouses and signal lights, water area;

g) Railways of national importance, gas mains, roads (in the case of non-existence of parallel state road), aircraft flight management systems and take-off and landing strips;

h) Main and reserve property of the Ministries of Security, Internal Affairs and Defence, Procurator's Office and the court system;

i) Frequency spectrum, state postal communications, TV-radio broadcasting, trunk-line and international telephone communications, means of governmental communications and position of Georgia on the geo-stationary orbit;

j) Enterprises producing radioactive materials and materials for military purposes, property of affiliated

---

However, government announces that from the year 1999 work will start on the privatisation of companies in some sectors, which have not been included so far in the process - companies of the mining and processing industries, the defence industry. (Web page of Bulgarian Foreign Investment Agency, URL: http://www.bfia.org/privat.htm; Web page of Bulgarian Privatisation Agency, URL: http://www.privatisation.online.bg)

test-experimental and scientific institutions;

k) State cemeteries and pantheons;

l) Unified state system of water supply and wastewater disposal facilities;

m) State medical institutions of vital importance included in the lists approved according to the established order;

n) Premises of state bodies."[63]

F. Analysis: What Services Should a Government Finance?

1. General

We should point out that, there is no consensus in the privatisation literature on the concept of public services and strategic enterprises.

The concept, public services, may embrace the large infrastructure sectors, as well as commercial services like the postal service and such functions as education, health, social security, justice and national defence.[64]

The term public service itself is ambiguous and it has never been precisely defined and often used subjectively.[65] There seems to be a confusion between the concept of services rendered to the public and accessible on a non-discriminatory basis, and that of services provided by the government or a public enterprise. This issue complicates the debate about how certain services should be provided to the public. This is particularly the case in countries with an administrative tradition influenced by the French and in formerly socialist countries.[66]

---

[63] Article 4, Law of Georgia on State Property Privatisation, web page of Ministry of State Property Management of Georgia, URL; http://web.sanet.ge/mospm/
[64] Guislain, (The Privatization Challenge), p. 24, 25
[65] The term "public service" has been used to describe, among other things, services provided by public entities; services provided under the control, regulation, jurisdiction of the government or a public agency; services paid for, financed, or guaranteed by the government or a public agency; and services provided to the public or in the public interest. [Guislain, (The Privatization Challenge), footnote 5, p.24]
[66] Guislain, (The Privatization Challenge), p.24, 25

The analysis about what services should a government finance and what services should a government produce should not be concluded that the government should produce all services financed primarily by taxation. Similarly, there is no strong case that all services produced by the government should be financed primarily by taxation.

First of all we should point out that there is no general answer to this question; the set of services a government should finance may differ both among nations and over time and will depend importantly on the features of the constitution.

A constitutional consensus on the set of services that government is authorised to finance is important. However the rules prescribed by the constitution are the only normative basis for judging whether the government has made the correct choice. [67]

Economic theory provides little guidance about what services should be produced by government or, more generally, by non-profit organisations. The overwhelming empirical evidence, however, suggests that there should be a presumption, but not an exclusive presumption, in favour of production by profit-seeking private firms.[68]

Keynes argued, government spending on any service would increase total spending and output, whatever the direct value of the service financed. This assertion was an important part of the rationalisation of increased government spending for the next 40 years, but finally fell victim to inflation. [69]

2. Possible Areas

Governments may adopt privatisation programmes for almost all sectors. There are eleven areas in which the privatisation may mainly take place: a. air transport and navigation b.

---

[67] Niskanen, p.217. According to Niskanen a government should finance a specific service only if authorised by the constitution; this restrains in inherent in the general rule that no government should be allowed to define its own powers. (p.217)
[68] A. Niskanen, p.217

railways and local transport c. post service and telecommunication[70] d. maritime transport[71] e. radio and television f. energy g. financial institutions, like banks[72] h. social security i. education, j. defence sector k. housing.[73]

3. Conclusions

First of all, as we mentioned above, there is no general answer to this question; the set of services a government should finance may differ both among nations and over time and will depend importantly on the features of the constitution.[74]

Administration of justice would seem to be the perfect example of a pure state function, but even here private provisions is a viable and often used option, as evidenced by for example, the frequent recourse to private arbitration and other alternative dispute resolution mechanisms. In France, the United Kingdom, the United States, and other countries, privatisation has spread also to the management of prisons,[75] and private security companies and growing at a rapid pace all over the world, often substituting for or complementing the state's police force[76]. Supporters of privatisation in justice argue that, in the public-sector production of crime control, ignorance abounds, costs are high and rising, and both the quality and the quantity of the effective output of

---

[69] A. Niskanen, p.220
[70] Paul Starr, "The Limits of Privatization", (Limits of Privatization); Privatization and Deregulation in Global Perspective, Edited by: Dennis J. Gayle and Jonathan N. Goodrich, Pinter Publishers, London, 1990, p.121, 122
[71] Lourdes Trujillo and Gustavo Nombele, "Multiservice Infrastructure: Privatizing Port Services", Public Policy for the Private Sector, September 2000, The World Bank, p.43-46
[72] Robert, p.38
For banks and privatisation see: Kalman Mizsei, Eleventh Plenary Session of the OECD Advisory Group on Privatisation (AGP) on Banks and Privatisation, Privatisation of Individual Banks or of the Banking system?, Rome, 18 and 19 September 1997; "Banks and Privatisation," OECD Advisory Group on Privatization - Synthesis Note (September 1998), URL: http://www.privatizationlink.com; Hans-Joachim Beyer, Claudia Dziobek, and John R. Garrett, Economic and Legal Considerations of Optimal Privatisation: Case Studies of Mortgage Firms (DePfa Group and Fannie Mae), IMF, Monetary and Exchange Affairs, Working Papers 99/69, May 1999
[73] Ewoud Hondius, "Privatisation and Consumer Protection", Legal Aspects of Privatisation, XXIst Colloquy on European Law, Budapest, 15-17 October 1991, Council of Europe Press, the Netherlands, 1993, p.149
The companies that have secondary functions in the defence sector may be subject to privatisation
[74] Niskanen, p.220
[75] For privatisation of prisons see: Oliver Hart, Andrei Shleifer, Robert W. Vishny, "The Proper Scope of Government: Theory and an Application to Prisons, National Bureau of Economic Research (NBER), Working Paper Series, No; 5744, Cambridge, September 1996
[76] Guislain, (The Privatization Challenge), p.26

the criminal justice system clearly have room for improvement.[77] For example in the case of prisons, it is argued that, there is a great need for upgrading of prison conditions and building new prisons. The public sector does not have very many resources to do this. The model of private enterprise is providing a total package of financing, building, owning and operating. [78]

On the other hand, there are many firms provide private investigation and employ such services. Insurance companies' employees investigate many crimes (i.e., if their losses are large enough to warrant investigation costs), and private firms provide similar services to some of these companies. Many other private organisations and businesses also employ private criminal investigators.[79]

Publication of a country's official gazette is another example of an activity that can be privatised. [80]

Private sector participation in air navigation and is also at an early stage. Several countries, including Germany, New Zealand, and Switzerland, recently corporatised their air navigation services through the creation of corporations with independent financial and legal status, as a step toward eventual privatisation through public offerings. [81]

---

[77] Bruce L. Benson, "Crime Control Through Private Enterprise", The Independent Review, Volume: II, Number: 3, Winter 1998, p.341

[78] Robert W. Poole, "The Limits of Privatization", (Limits), National Review of Administrative Sciences, Volume 56, Number 1, March 1990, Symposium on the Progress, Benefits and Costs of Privatisation, p.88
For privatisation discussions in the case of prisons see: The web page of Connecticut University, URL: http//www.uconn.edu/

[79] Bruce L. Benson, "Crime Control Through Private Enterprise", The Independent Review, Volume: II, Number: 3, Winter 1998, p.347
There is a fear and criticism that providers of private security and justice are likely to abuse their power. However, according to Lenson: "... at least two to three times as many private security officers as public police in (USA) and even so public police kill many more people than private security employees do. The truth is, private security personnel commit relatively little violence, which is not surprising. After all, less than 10 percent of the total private security force is armed." (Bruce L. Benson, "Crime Control Through Private Enterprise", The Independent Review, Volume: II, Number: 3, Winter 1998, p.350, 351)

[80] Guislain, (The Privatization Challenge), p.26

[81] British Airports Authority (BAA) was privatised in 1987 and since then British government privatised many airports including Heathrow, Gatwick, Aberdeen and Stansted airports. (Ellis J. Juan, "Privatising Airports-Options and Case Studies", Public Policy for The Private Sector, The World Bank, Note No. 82, June 1996, "The Privatization Revolution", Adapted from Remarks by Lawrence W. Reed, Mackinac Center for Public Policy for

Social security[82] provides another illustration, as does tax or customs administration. Customs administration was privatised in Indonesia and Latvia. Customs warehouses are also managed by private operators in an increasing number of countries. Withholding of income taxes by employers or of taxes on interest or dividends by financial institutions are examples of partial privatisation of the tax function. Even tax collection can be privatised in some cases, with public authorities selling their tax claims to private collectors.[83]

Privatisation could well be extended to other areas of state and local authority. Privatisation of public housing projects that is being done now in the United Kingdom through sale to tenants via co-operative or condominium ownership would lead to improved housing. Tenant owners would take more care of their apartments and common areas than do tenants in public housing.[84]

Privatisation also could be extended to public higher education. Privatisation of public systems of higher education could take various forms. Public colleges could be converted into institutions like independent private colleges that tend to be more cost effective and less subject

---

The Future of American Business, A Shavano Institute for National Leadership Seminar, Indianapolis, Indiana, May 21, 1997, URL: http://www.privatisation.com)

[82] "Privatizing State-Owned Companies", The Prosperity Papers Series, Prosperity Paper Three, web page of Center for International Private Enterprise, URL: http://www.cipe.org/; Joshua Aizenman, "Privatisation in Emerging Markets", National Bureau of Economic Research, NBER Working Paper Series 6524, Cambridge, USA. (The paper deals with the theoretical aspect of social security privatisation)

If social security is privatised, the government would still require people to put aside funds for retirement but would allow them to choose their own retirement investments. [Starr, (Limits of Privatization), p.117]. Starr argues that, blacks and other disadvantaged minorities depend especially on the components of social security, such as disability, health insurance, and survivors' benefits. Because of their higher costs in these areas, many of them could not purchase privately the full package of social security benefits. (p.119, 120). However, in that case government should enact provisions to protect disadvantages minorities from the negative effects of privatisation, such as some subsidies to private insurance companies. Finally, privatisation in social security does not always mean that the state social security will disappear. People will have choice between private and state social security schemes.

(For privatisation in social security see the papers of Cato Institute on social security privatisation project: Web page of Cato Institute, URL: http://www.cato.org)

[83] Guislain, (The Privatization Challenge), p.25, 26

[84] Donald Grunewald, "Privatization at the State and Local Level", URL: http://www.self-gov.org; Starr, (The Limits of Privatization), p.122.

Thatcher government sold a million units of public housing by offering them to the tenants at well below market value. (The Privatization Revolution, Adapted from Remarks by Lawrence W. Reed, Mackinac Center for Public Policy for The Future of American Business, A Shavano Institute for National Leadership Seminar,

to improper political influences than public institutions of a similar kind. Also school districts may hire alternative providers, groups of teachers organised as small companies.[85]

Privatisation of some other institutions, such as hospitals, is already taking place in some areas of the country.[86] However, it is argued that, the difficulty of privatising some public goods is that public administration is essential to their character. In that context, when functions of the where the state exercises its peculiar prerogatives of sovereignty like the administration of justice, foreign policy, military defence and the collection of taxes concerned[87], state exercises of coercive power. Therefore in these areas the state's authority, supported by its monopoly of legitimate violence, rests on the claim to be acting impartially on behalf of the entire community. It is argued that particularly dangerous for the state to put coercive power over persons in the hands of employees accountable, in the first instance, to a private firm.[88]

There is a debate on in the case of prisons. As we mentioned above, under the appropriate regulation and strict supervision of state administration, privatisation can be implemented in the case of prisons.[89]

We must point out that, it is not "acceptable" to privatise[90] cultural and historical monuments because of moral considerations. However, it is possible to use non-divestiture

---

Indianapolis, Indiana, May 21, 1997, URL: http://www.privatisation.org; Privatization in the United Kingdom, Ernst & Young, p. 28)

[85] W. Poole, (Limits) p.88, 89

[86] Donald Grunewald, "Privatization at the State and Local Level", URL: http://www.self-gov.org; Ray Robinson, "Markets in Health Care", Privatisation and Regulation-A Review of the Issues, Edited by: Peter M. Jackson and Catherine Price, Longman Group Limited, 1994, p.198-212

[87] However, tax collection can be privatised in some cases, with public authorities selling their tax claims to private collectors.

[88] Starr, (The Limits of Privatization), p.119, 121

[89] For opposite opinion see: Starr, (The Limits of Privatization), p.119. According to Starr, private prisons are not acceptable, since in the case of prisons, state exercises one of its coercive powers. (p.119)

According to Starr: "When the government prosecutes a tax evader or a court sentences someone convicted of a crime, it sends a message to the entire community about public values and rules that the community lives by. Privatisation of... prisons confuses the message that the rendering of justice ought to communicate". (p.120, 121)

We must point out that, contracting out of prison management (and construction) has become widespread in the United States. (Keefer, p.9)

[90] As we pointed out in the first chapter for the scope of this study privatisation, unless otherwise specified, refers to "divestiture".

options in tourism sector. For example, a state owned hotel may be leased by a private investor. Similarly management of a museum may be given to a private investor or certain services (cleaning, catering) may be carried out under contracting out arrangements and contracts.[91]

Finally, saying that something can be privatised does not mean that it should be privatised. In each case one should analyse the costs and benefits of public versus private provision of a given service, including the associated transaction costs, as well as economic, financial, political, social, and other aspects.[92]

G. Constitutional Protection for SOEs

1. The constitutional dimension

The proper functioning of a market economy and the success of privatisation depends on the adequate protection of private property rights. The right to engage in business is part of the individual freedoms enshrined in most constitutions. Freedom of trade and industry, contractual freedom, the right to freely choose a professional activity, the right of association, the principle of equality before the law and non-discrimination between the various economic actors, are fundamental rules. Moreover, there is the right to appeal against unlawful state action. Finally, the procedures related to the control of constitutionality of laws are also a part this panoply.[93]

---

[91] Some privatisation laws have provisions on cultural heritage. For example according to article 4 of Law on Transformation of Socially Owned Enterprises of Macedonia: "In the transformation procedure, the physical and legal entities can not acquire ownership rights over... the cultural and historical monuments which by Law are of public interest for the Republic, and are under special protection. (For the full text of Macedonian Privatisation law see the web page of Macedonian Privatisation Agency, URL: http://www.mpa.org.mk/)
Similarly Privatisation Law of Federation of Bosnia and Herzegovina (BiH) states that "objects of cultural and historical importance" cannot be privatised. (Article 8/2). ["Official Gazette of Federation BiH", No 27/97, Nov 28th, 1997. [For the full text of the Law on Privatisation of Enterprises, Federation of Bosnia and Herzegovina (BiH) in word format see: Web page of Agency for Privatisation of Federation of Bosnia and Herzegovina, URL: http//www. http://www.apf.com.ba/zakonie/index.htm/]

[92] Guislain, (The Privatization Challenge), p.26

[93] Privatisation in Europe, Asia and Latin America, What Lessons can be Drawn?, Summary of the Presentations at the International Workshop on Privatisation Organised by the OECD in April 1994, Sao Paulo, URL: http://www.oecd.org

140

A country's constitution or fundamental law, where such a document exists, may contain provisions that affect privatisation operations either directly or indirectly. In the absence of written constitution, provisions of a constitutional nature may well have the same effect. Provisions of this kind may limit the scope of the privatisation program, determine to whom decision-making authority belongs, or impose certain controls on privatisation authorities, or address all three.[94]

Therefore a first mandatory step in evaluating the legal requirements for privatisation is the country's constitution or fundamental law, where such legal document exists. In many socialist countries, all productive assets (including enterprises) were state or "all people's" property by virtue of the constitution, and the state sector received special protection and privileges.[95]

National constitutions often contain specific provisions concerning the infrastructure sectors, notably railways, telecommunications, and electric power. Such provisions fall mainly into five categories. Some constitutions preclude any private ownership or operation of infrastructure sectors. Others enable the legislator to reserve certain activities to the public sector but do not spell out which ones. A third class of provisions does not allow the transfer of control over specific infrastructure sectors or enterprises to the private sector, while permitting non-controlling private shareholdings. In a fourth group of countries, the constitution reserves certain sectors to the state; but does not prohibit the government from granting concessions to the private sector. A fifth type limits or excludes foreign participation in infrastructure sectors.[96]

---

[94] Daintith, p.58; Guislain, (The World Bank), p.33, 34
Therefore a constitution exists, the following points should be considered as well:
-the principles set by the constitution on the privatisation itself and/or economic activities,
-the structure of the constitution (whether it is flexible or non-flexible or whether it is written or unwritten)
[95] Guislain, (The World Bank), p.33
[96] Guislain, (The Privatization Challenge), p.246
In France, the Preamble to the 1946 constitution provides that: "Any resource or enterprise whose operation has acquired or is in the process of acquiring the character of a public service or of a monopoly of fact, must become public property". However: (a) The meaning of a national public service and of a monopoly is by no means clear,

2. Constitutional issues

a. General

Privatisation, irrespective of its scale and methods used, alters radically the role of the state in the economy. It is for this reason that most constitutions require governments to pass legislation defining the scope and main thrust of privatisation programmes.[97]

Although the constitutional order in most market economies does not lay down precise rules for delimiting the public and private sectors, the state can retain a monopoly over certain activities. As mentioned above, these are usually some areas, activities or services that are natural monopolies or activities considered to be of strategic importance such as the arms industry or natural resources. If privatisations are envisaged in these sectors, the constitutions may have to be amended.[98]

b. Issues

Some countries like Spain, Portugal, France, Germany and Turkey and without exception all ex-socialist countries faced constitutional law issues in implementing their privatisation programme. Because constitutions were providing a protection system for the SOEs.

In Germany the constitution provides constitutional protection for the public monopolies. Privatisation of the railways and the postal services (including telecommunications) requires a two-thirds majority in the Bundestag and the Bundesrat to pass the necessary constitutional

---

(b) Secondly Conseil Constitutionnel has been flexible on that matter [Prosser, (Constitutions and Political Economy), p.310, 311; Prosser, (Social Limits), p.215]

[97] Privatisation in Europe, Asia and Latin America, What Lessons can be Drawn?, Summary of the Presentations at the International Workshop on Privatisation Organised by the OECD in April 1994, Sao Paulo, URL: http://www.oecd.org

[98] Privatisation in Europe, Asia and Latin America, What Lessons can be Drawn?, Summary of the Presentations at the International Workshop on Privatisation Organised by the OECD in April 1994, Sao Paulo, URL: http://www.oecd.org

amendment.[99] Article 87 of the constitution that concerns the areas of direct federal administration, provided that post and telecommunications were federal government undertakings. This provision was amended on August 30, 1994, and a new article 143b was added; the separation of the postal services from the telecommunications company and their privatisation were authorised.[100]

In Turkey, many privatisation transactions were cancelled by the Constitutional Court and other high courts because of the uncertainty in the Turkish Constitution on privatisation. For example, in 1994, the Turkish Constitutional Court drew the line between legislative and executive competencies with regard to privatisation, and quashed the privatisation decree in question on the grounds that the government had exceeded its powers.[101]

In September 1999, the Turkish constitution was amended, and the concept of the privatisation for the first time was mentioned. Article 47 of the Turkish Constitution concerning nationalisation and privatisation is as follows:

"...The rules and regulations concerning privatisation of the assets and enterprises that are owned by the state, state economic enterprises or other public corporations are prescribed by law. Which of the investments or services that are carried out bye the state, state economic enterprises or other public corporations may be performed by or delegated to real or corporate body through private law contracts are prescribed by law."[102]

Furthermore, in Portugal, the 1976 constitution prohibited the state from selling off more than 49 per cent of nationalised undertakings. It was only in June 1989 that the government,

---

[99] Wright, p.24
[100] Guislain, (The Privatization Challenge), p.248
[101] Privatisation in Europe, Asia and Latin America, What Lessons can be Drawn?, Summary of the Presentations at the International Workshop on Privatisation Organised by the OECD in April 1994, Sao Paulo, URL: http://www.oecd.org; Guislain, (The Privatization Challenge), footnote 69, p.244; Privatization Update, web page of Center for International Private Enterprise, URL: http//www.cipe.org
[102] For the full text of Turkish Constitution in English see the web page of the Turkish Parliament, URL: http://www.tbmm.gov.tr/

backed by a large parliamentary majority, managed to obtain a constitutional amendment allowing it to launch its privatisation programme. [103]

Finally, in Slovakia the Constitutional Court cancelled some privatisation laws and decrees.[104]

III. POSSIBLE REACTIONS to PRIVATISATION: Criticism on Privatisation

A. General

In every social, political, and economic change there will be different reactions. Privatisation effects wide range of sectors, people and organisations; therefore, there are strong criticisms on the process. When government decides the feasible areas or activities for privatisation, political factors including reactions from different groups may play an important role.

The opposition may come from the labour force employed in the public enterprises that fear job losses, and from government officials whose area of authority and opportunity for patronage will be reduced. Where liberalisation is accompanied with privatisation process further resistance may come from those groups who currently enjoy the protected economic rents created by the system of regulation and controls. Certain political groups of a nationalist or populist bent may also oppose privatisation.[105]

---

[103] Corkill, p.219, 220; Privatisation in Europe, Asia and Latin America, What Lessons can be Drawn?, Summary of the Presentations at the International Workshop on Privatisation Organised by the OECD in April 1994, Sao Paulo, URL: http://www.oecd.org; Guislain, (The World Bank), p.33; Wright, p.24

[104] Constitutional Court of Slovakia ruled that certain privatisation laws and decrees from 1994–1996 was unconstitutional (Ivan Mikloš, "Privatization in 1996", Centre for Economic and Social Analysis of Slovak Republic, URL: http://www.mesa10.sk/)

Finally, Brazil and Mexico had to revise their constitutions several times before they could privatise activities that were reserved to the public sector. [Privatisation in Europe, Asia and Latin America, What Lessons can be Drawn?, Summary of the Presentations at the International Workshop on Privatisation Organised by the OECD in April 1994, Sao Paulo, URL: http://www.oecd.org; Guislain, (The World Bank), p.33]

[105] Kirkpatrick, p.241; Letwin, p.x; Olivier Bouin, "The Privatisation in Developing Countries: Reflections on a Panacea", Policy Brief No. 3, OECD Development Centre, OECD 1992

"Privatizing State-Owned Companies", The Prosperity Papers Series, Prosperity Paper Three, web page of Center for International Private Enterprise, URL: http//www.cipe.org/

Furthermore in terms of service delivery, there are concerns that the profit motive of private companies will result in a reduction in services and a propensity to "cream," or serve those who are most easily served and most likely to succeed.[106] In other words, opponents charge that privatisation would lead to monopolies, loss of service, reduced flexibility, and unfairness among users as well as between modes.[107]

Finally we should point out that criticisms can come from the government or parliament itself. For example the economic policy committee of the Russian State Duma concluded that privatisation in Russia, in the words of the committee's chairman, Vladimir Lisichkin, "was equivalent to economic sabotage which almost completely destroyed the Russian economy."[108]

B. Analysis

The strongest opposition to privatisation comes from public employees and unions representing public employees, stemming essentially from a fear that public sector jobs will be

---

For example in Poland, influential industrial groups, especially in parts of heavy industry, together with some political parties and trade union leaders effectively lobbied against privatisation. Instead of fast privatisation and radical restructuring, they were interested in keeping the state-owned sector unchanged and obtaining preferential government treatment for chosen enterprises or sectors. (Barbara Blaszczyk, Moving Ahead: Privatization in Poland ", web page of Center for International Private Enterprise, URL: http//www.cipe.org/). In Bulgaria, SOE managers, government officials, and large banks resisted against privatisation. (Maria Prohaska, "Privatization in Bulgaria: Pushing Forward", web page of Center for International Private Enterprise, URL: http//www.cipe.org/); American Federation of State, County and Municipal Employees, URL: http//www.afscme.org/]

It is argued that privatisation was not popular in Russia because Russians actually refer to the process as "prikhvatizatsiia"-"grabisation"-rather than privatizatsiia. ("Putting Privatisation Online", web page of Center for International Private Enterprise, URL: http://www.cipe.org/)

[106] Smith and Pindus, (Privatization of Public Social Services), URL: http://www.urban.org/

[107] Gillen, David and Cooper, Douglas, "Public Versus Private Ownership and Operation of Airports and Seaports in Canada", The Fraser Institute, URL: http://www.fraserinstitute.ca

Sometimes the level of the criticism is very strong. [For example according to one author: "... We sell our children and grandchildren into poverty and slavery tomorrow for cash in our pockets today. The national debt rises, jails expand, jobs vanish - but profits are soaring... Now we want to turn our back on everything we have created. We want to sell off our schools, and parks and playgrounds...Think about it... (R. Campbell, Carol, Privatization, Profits and Publicity-The New Trinity, M. David Lewis Enterprises Web Page, URL: http://www.mdle.com/WrittenWord/ccampbell/carol9.htm]

[108] Satter, David, "Russia's Deepening Crisis", Web Page of Houston Institute, URL: http://www.hudson.org

lost.[109] Governments need to take appropriate measures to solve labour law issues in privatisation programmes.[110]

As we will examine in the following pages[111] some services (for example gas, electricity, telecommunication, transportation) provided by certain SOEs are essential. Certain obligations, called "universal service obligations" derive from those services. In that context, after privatisation private investors should be obliged to provide the services on a basis of a uniform charge not directly linked in every case to the actual costs incurred, to all customers reasonably requesting it.[112] Regulation, in that context universal service obligations, will protect certain social groups (low-income groups) from the possible negative effects (i.e. price increases) of privatisation.

Finally, reliable and complete cost data on government activities are needed to assess the overall performance of activities targeted for privatisation, to support informed privatisation decisions, and to make these decisions easier to implement and justify to potential critics.[113]

IV. REGULATION in the PRIVATISATION PROCESS[114]

A. Introduction

Transferring certain functional responsibilities to the private sector does not divest public agencies of accountability for public safety and health, environmental protection, and oversight of monopolistic enterprises. Inherently public functions must be maintained at the governmental

---

[109] Demetra Smith Nightingale and Nancy Pindus, "Privatization of Public Social Services: A Background Paper", (Privatization of Public Social Services), October 15, 1997, Urban Institute, URL: http://www.urban.org/
[110] See: p.301-329
[111] See: p.149-153
[112] Sheshinski, and López-Calva, p.25
[113] General Accounting Office, p.5
[114] In the broader sense regulation is not an activity of an undifferentiated state; the activity of regulation can be undertaken at various levels, ranging from international organisations to private bodies. (Laura MacGregor, Tony Prosser and Charlotte Villiers, "Regulation and Markets Beyond 2000: Conclusion", Regulation and Markets Beyond 2000, Edited By: Laura MacGregor, Tony Prosser and Charlotte Villiers, Dartmouth and Ashgate Publishing Companies, UK & USA, 2000, p.341. Also see: Laura MacGregor, Tony Prosser and Charlotte Villiers

level in order to preserve the public trust.[115] Furthermore governments cannot stand aloof from certain strategic decisions of industry.[116]

When a government reduces its direct role in the delivery of services, it creates a need to enhance monitoring and oversight that evaluates compliance with the terms of the contract and evaluates performance in delivering services to ensure that the government's interests are fully protected.[117] It is easy to understand the government's point of view. It wants to ensure that the privatised enterprise continues to behave in the national interest, instead of simply pursuing greater efficiency and higher profits. If privatised enterprises are working efficiently, this means they are providing real and stable jobs and enhancing national wealth. However, there are, legitimate concerns which government has about protecting customers.[118]

B. Any Model for Regulation?

There is no single model for regulation of privatised companies.[119] In that context, regulators have two primary legal duties. First to ensure that all reasonable demands for the product are satisfied. Whether private suppliers carry out their activities properly. Whether private investors fulfil the health, security, and environmental etc. requirements properly. For example in the case of water sector, whether water companies provide healthy and quality drinking water. Second, that companies are able to finance the carrying out of their activities. Subject to these duties, they have a duty to promote the interests of consumers, as well as having duties to protect the interests of the elderly and disabled.[120]

"Introduction", Regulation and Markets Beyond 2000, Edited By: Laura MacGregor, Tony Prosser and Charlotte Villiers, Dartmouth and Ashgate Publishing Companies, UK & USA, 2000, p.1-18)
[115] A. Beecher, Janice, "Twenty Myths About Privatisation", Alliance for Redesigning Government, National Academy of Public Administration, URL: http://www.alliance.napawash.org/
[116] Graham and Prosser, (Privatising Nationalised Industries), p.49; Prosser, (Nationalised Industries), p.98
[117] Report on Privatisation and Lessons Learned, GAO (General Accounting Office of USA), URL: http://www.privatisation.org/Collection/P...egies/GaoPrivReport--lessons-learned.html
[118] Hondius, p.153, 154
[119] Tony Prosser, *Law and Regulators*, (*Law and Regulators*), Clarendon Press, Oxford, 1997, p.30
[120] Graham, p.209

Finally institutional model for regulation may vary country to country. For example in Turkey Competition Authority together with Ministry of Trade and sectorial ministers are in charge of regulation of privatised SOEs. [121] On the other hand in Britain, since the utilities were privatised at different times and have distinctive regulatory requirements, a separate regulatory office has been established for each industry-telecoms, gas, water and power.[122] In the British model each office is headed by a regulator appointed for a fixed term, normally five years. There is also a separate body with regulatory duties in relation to airports and air traffic control. Broadly the aim of a regulatory regime is to put in place a framework of regulation that is explicit and transparent in nature and which operates through incentives on managers of the business rather than through the complex administrative arrangements which has characterised control under government ownership.[123]

"...With the privatisation of our utilities, we have addressed this dilemma by establishing an independent regulatory system. This ensures a framework of control which is explicit and transparent in nature, and which operates on incentives on business managers. For example, prices are controlled through explicit formulae, giving incentives to raise profits through efficiency. The system separates the management of the industries from their regulation, protecting consumers from the abuse of monopoly power; but also separating the politician from the industries, giving the industries a secure framework within which they can plan their future..." [George Young, the (former) Financial Secretary's speech to the World Privatisation Conference, 6 March 1995, web page of the Treasury, URL: http://www.hm-treasury.gov.uk/pub/html/speech95/fst/sp060395.html]

[121] Web page of Turkish Competition Authority, URL: http://www.rekabet.gov.tr/; Web page of Turkish Ministry of Trade, URL: http://www.sanayi.gov.tr/, Web page of Turkish Embassy in Washington, URL: http://turkey.org

[122] Gibbon, (Guide), p.6
On the other hand, different firms operate in different environments and under different circumstances. ("Privatizing State-Owned Companies", The Prosperity Papers series, Prosperity Paper Three, web page of Center for International Private Enterprise, URL: http://www.cipe.org/)

[123] Gibbon, (Guide), p.7
In Britain the structure of regulation is as follows: The utility company is given a license in the first instance by the Secretary of State. The license contains terms and conditions that the utility is obliged to follow. A regulatory office is also set up, at arms length from the relevant government department, headed by the director general. The regulator's function is to make sure that the license terms and conditions are followed and that they are appropriate for current conditions. If the regulator wishes to change the license this can be done by agreement or, failing that, the regulator must take a reference to the Competition Commission will decide whether or not the regulator's proposal is in the public interest. [Graham, p.208] "Regulatory references under the privatisation statutes usually arise from proposals for licence changes by a regulator which are disputed by the licensee. They often involve price controls. Licence modification references are made by the regulator concerned. The issue referred to the Commission is whether a particular matter operates or may be expected to operate against the public interest. If the Commission finds that there is an adverse effect on the public interest which could be remedied or prevented by a licence modification, the regulator is required to make a licence modification". ["Consultation on Reporting Side Procedures and Practices", 5 July 1999, web page of UK Competition Commission, URL: http://www.competition-commission.org.uk/trancon.htm; Consultation on Steps to Increase Openness and Transparency, web page of UK Competition Commission, URL: http://www.competition-commission.org.uk/trancon.htm)]

C. Why Regulation is Needed in Privatisation Process

1. General Remarks

Privatisation may make the existing regulations obsolete; therefore a process of re-regulation is often necessary to preserve the conditions for reaching an economic optimum. Governments that have introduced major privatisation programmes cannot ignore this factor.[124]

There are examples showing the need to adopt the regulatory framework after privatisation. In the privatisation process, where it is impossible to introduce effective competition, or to introduce immediately, regulation can act as a surrogate to protect consumers. In this case regulation is intended to prevent the application of private rationale from being solely for the benefit of the purchaser and to the detriment of all other economic agents.[125] Furthermore in that context, price regulation is needed to prevent excessive profits of the privatised firm. The price regulation will particularly protect low-income groups.[126]

Even effective competition can be introduced; regulation can support competition by limiting the conditions in which monopoly power can arise.[127] Furthermore regulation is needed to address other issues like environmental requirements, safety measures, and quality standards in privatised industries.[128] Finally regulation is needed for the continuation of certain essential

---

[124] In the United Kingdom case we have witnessed an increase in regulatory activity and the introduction of legislation by central government into public service areas in an effort to create, sustain and control new markets. (Braddon and Foster, p.290)

[125] Bouin, Olivier, "The Privatisation in Developing Countries: Reflections on a Panacea", Policy Brief No. 3, OECD Development Centre, OECD 1992; Bill Baker and Sophie Trémolet, Utility Reform, "Regulating Quality Standards to Improve Access for the Poor", Public Policy for the Private Sector, September 2000, The World Bank, p.17-21

Also see: Penelope Brook, Cowen and Nicola Tynan, "Reaching the Urban Poor with Private Infrastructure" Public Policy for the Private Sector, Note No: 188, The World Bank, June 1999

[126] Prosser, *(Law and Regulators)*, p.11; Gibbon, (Guide), p.6

In the United Kingdom at the core of this regulatory mechanism is the periodic review of price controls. (Green, Richard, "Utility Regulation-A Critical Path for Revising Price Controls", Public Policy for the Private Sector, Note No; 185, The World Bank, May 1999, p.1)

For the customer dimension and price regulation in the privatisation see competition section: p.289-295

[127] Prosser, *(Law and Regulators)*, p.11

[128] Prosser, *(Law and Regulators)*, p.11

services to all citizens on a non-discriminatory basis. For example privatisation of transport and telecommunications enterprises gives rise to the problem of access to these services for disadvantaged social categories and of the territorial coverage of remote regions. Certain transport routes, certain telecommunications networks, certain water or electricity distribution networks could be abandoned because deemed unprofitable by the new private operators. When such public services are privatised, it appears essential to have clauses concerning public service obligations for the private purchaser or contractor. [129]

2. Protection of Universal Service Obligations

Some services (for example gas, electricity, telecommunication, transportation) provided by certain SOEs are essential. They are necessary for participation in social life consisting basic human services. Those services create an obligation called "universal service obligations" to its suppliers. In that context, after privatisation private investors should be under obligation to provide the services on a basis of a uniform charge not directly linked in every case to the actual costs incurred, to all customers reasonably requesting it.

The concept of universal service obligations was also recognised in the European Union in Council Resolution 93/C213/01[130] and 94/C48/01[131] on the review of the situation of the telecommunications sector and the need for further development in that market, which established as a major goal for Community telecommunications policy the liberalisation of all public voice telephony services, whilst maintaining universal service. The main elements of

---

[129] Bouin, Olivier, "The Privatisation in Developing Countries: Reflections on a Panacea", Policy Brief No. 3, OECD Development Centre, OECD 1992
[130] Council Resolution of 22 July 1993 on the review of the situation in the telecommunications sector and the need for further development in that market (93/C 213/01), web page of the European Union, URL: http://europa.eu.int/ISPO/infosoc/legreg/docs/93c21301.html
[131] Council Resolution of 7 February 1994 on universal service principles in the telecommunications sector (94/C 48/01), web page of the European Union, URL: http://europa.eu.int/ISPO/infosoc/legreg/docs/94c4801.html

universal service have been developed, in Council Directives 90/387/EEC[132] and 92/44/EEC,[133] and Council Recommendations 92/382/EEC[134] and 92/383/EEC.[135]

The European Commission had produced a definition of universal service defining it as ""a defined minimum set of services of specified quality which is available to all users independent of their geographical location and, in the light of specific national conditions, at an affordable price".[136] The concept of universal service is based on the principles of universality, equality, continuity and affordability.[137] Finally, the Commission stressed in that Communication that universal service was a dynamic and evolving concept and that it would be kept under regular review, particularly, with regard to its scope, level, quality and affordability within the European Union.[138]

In this context the Communication on Universal Service of 13 March 1996 it was recognised that "affordability is at the heart of the framework for universal service in the Community". That Communication also indicated that "Member States should ensure that appropriate measures are taken, (e.g. price caps, targeted tariff schemes) necessary to maintain

---

[132] Council Resolution of 28 June 1990 on the establishment of the internal market for telecommunications services through the implementation of open network provision (90/387/EEC), web page of the European Union, URL: http://europa.eu.int/ISPO/infosoc/legreg/docs/90387eec.html

[133] Council Resolution of 5 June 1992 on the application of open network provision to leased lines, web page of the European Union, URL: http://europa.eu.int/ISPO/infosoc/legreg/docs/9244eec.html

[134] Council Resolution of 5 June 1992 on the harmonized provision of a minimum set of packet-switched data services (PSDS) in accordance with open network provision (ONP) principles (92/382/EEC), web page of the European Union, URL: http://europa.eu.int/ISPO/infosoc/legreg/docs/92382eec.html

[135] Council Resolution of 5 June 1992 on the provision of harmonized integrated services digital network (ISDN) access arrangements and a minimum set of ISDN offerings in accordance with open network provision (ONP) principles (92/383/EEC), web page of the European Union, URL: http://europa.eu.int/ISPO/infosoc/legreg/docs/92383eec.html

[136] Council Resolution of 7 February 1994 on universal service principles in the telecommunications sector (94/C 48/01), web page of the European Union, URL: http://europa.eu.int/ISPO/infosoc/legreg/docs/94c4801.html; Green Paper on the Liberalisation of Telecommunications Infrastructure and Cable Television Networks, web page of the European Union, web page of the European Union, URL: http://europa.eu.int

[137] Commission Communication on Assessment Criteria for National Schemes for the Costing and Financing of Universal Service in telecommunications and Guidelines for the Member States on Operation of such Schemes, Brussels, 27.11.96 COM(96) 608, web page of the European Union, URL: http://europa.eu.int; Green Paper on the Liberalisation of Telecommunications Infrastructure and Cable Television Networks, web page of the European Union, web page of the European Union, URL: http://europa.eu.int

[138] Commission Communication on Assessment Criteria for National Schemes for the Costing and Financing of Universal Service in telecommunications and Guidelines for the Member States on Operation of such Schemes, Brussels, 27.11.96 COM(96) 608, web page of the European Union, URL: http://europa.eu.int

the affordability of services for all users, particularly in the run up to full competition". [139] At the same time the Commission made clear that "greater [tariff] flexibility must be conditional upon the regulatory framework (i) including adequate measures to ensure affordability; ensuring that price increases for users in remote and rural areas, other than adjustments to achieve cost-orientation, are not used to compensate operators for losses in revenue resulting from price decreases elsewhere and (iii) ensuring that any differences in pricing between high cost areas and low cost areas do not endanger the affordability of universal service".[140]

Universal service obligations do represent a burden, but the state chooses to finance it directly or indirectly.[141] The Council Resolution and Commission statement 94/C 48 of 7 February 1994 recognised that universal service might be financed through internal transfers, access fees or other mechanisms, which take due account of the principles of transparency, non-discrimination and proportionality, while ensuring compliance with competition rules in order to make a fair contribution to any burden which the provision of universal service represents. In addition, it noted the particular circumstances associated with the provision of universal service in peripheral regions with less developed networks and that the concept of universal service needed to evolve to keep pace with advances in technology, market development and changes in user demand.[142]

---

[139] Commission Communication on Assessment Criteria for National Schemes for the Costing and Financing of Universal Service in telecommunications and Guidelines for the Member States on Operation of such Schemes, Brussels, 27.11.96 COM(96) 608, web page of the European Union, URL: http://europa.eu.int

[140] Commission Communication on Assessment Criteria for National Schemes for the Costing and Financing of Universal Service in telecommunications and Guidelines for the Member States on Operation of such Schemes, Brussels, 27.11.96 COM(96) 608, web page of the European Union, URL: http://europa.eu.int

[141] Web page of the European Union, URL: http://europa.eu.int

[142] Green Paper on the Liberalisation of Telecommunications Infrastructure and Cable Television Networks, web page of the European Union, web page of the European Union, URL: http://europa.eu.int

According to the EU "The dual aim, therefore, should be to provide consumers and business with a diverse offering of quality telecommunications services at competitive prices whilst guaranteeing universal access to basic telecommunications services for all citizens. The goal of providing affordable access to basic telecommunications services for all citizens emphasises the need to provide service as cost effectively as possible and implies that access should be provided at prices below cost for some, if the process of rebalancing pricing structures leads to some customers leaving the network, being dissuaded from joining or facing unreasonably high prices for basic telecommunications services. This is not an argument for maintaining inefficient, across the board subsidies for access but for developing targeted schemes for needy citizens and uneconomic customers." (Green Paper on the

152

Universal service obligations can be put either in specific codes [privatisation law, sectoral acts (Gas Act, Electricity Act etc.)] or they can be attached to licenses or privatisation contracts. Once universal service provisions are added in legislation, private investor (supplier) must provide these services to all customers. However according to the European Commission obligations should be imposed in relation to universal service only where there is a risk that the goal of ensuring affordable access to a defined level of universal service throughout a given area cannot be achieved in a competitive environment without the creation of specific mechanisms to share fairly amongst market players any identified costs attributable to those obligations which the universal service provider(s) has (have) incurred. [143]

For example in Britain, the Telecommunications Act 1984 imposes two primary duties on the director of telecommunications:

(a) to secure that they are provided throughout the UK, save in so far as the provision thereof is impracticable or not reasonably practicable, such telecommunications services as satisfy all reasonable demands for them including, in particular, emergency services, public call box services, directory information services, maritime services and services in rural areas. [144]

(b) without prejudice to the generality of paragraph (a) above, to secure that any person by whom any such services fall to be provided is able to finance the provision of those services. [145]

Furthermore in Britain the standard license conditions require that all domestic customers in the license area must be supplied with service without undue preference or undue discrimination in the processing of applications; a dominant supplier is also prohibited from

---

Liberalisation of Telecommunications Infrastructure and Cable Television Networks, web page of the European Union, web page of the European Union, URL: http://europa.eu.int)
[143] Commission Statement to the Minutes of the 1910th Meeting of Council (Telecommunications) on 27th March 1996 on who Contributes to Universal Service The need for specific obligations to be imposed to guarantee universal service, web page of the European Union, URL: http://europa.eu.int

undue preference or undue discrimination in charges. It also require all suppliers to comply with other social obligations, including services for pensioners and the disabled and disconnection procedures[146]

Finally the key elements of the regulatory framework, including tariffs, degree of competition, interconnection regime, and performance targets, are defined in the concession contract or operating license. Because of the element of monopoly, public service obligations tend to include detailed specifications on the service to be provided, the obligation to supply, equal treatment of users, continuity of service, and so on. In consideration of these obligations, concessions often grant certain exclusive rights to the private operator. These terms need to be monitored and enforced and may need to be revised from time to time to reflect changing conditions. Thus, concessions (or the legal framework that governs them) may grant the public authority or a regulator a certain amount of discretion and, at the same time, provide recourse against the decisions of the authority or regulator.[147]

D. Monitoring

When a government's direct role in the delivery of services is reduced through privatisation, a need is created for enhanced monitoring and oversight that evaluates compliance with the terms of the privatisation agreement and evaluates performance in delivering services to ensure that the government's interests are fully protected.[148] For example, in Latvia, privatisation

---

[144] Telecommunications Act 1984, s.3(1)(a)
[145] Telecommunications Act 1984, s.3 (1)(b)
[146] Prosser, (*Law and Regulators*), p.109
Thus in Britain at the time of privatisation of BT strong fears were expressed that it would lead to a loss of call boxes, especially in rural and low-income areas. To avoid this complex provisions were included in the BT license. [Prosser, (*Law and Regulators*), p.78, 79] Also there was a fear that in a competitive market new suppliers could "cherry-pick" the most profitable customers. When gas sector was privatised such cherry picking prevented by provisions inserted in the licenses from discriminating unfairly between customers There is also a fear that customers such as the elderly, the disabled, and those on low incomes would be avoided by new suppliers. This can be prevented by imposing universal service obligation into licenses or privatisation contracts. [Prosser, (*Law and Regulators*), p.108].
[147] Guislain and Michel, p.3
[148] General Accounting Office, p.6

agency monitors the implementation of the concluded agreements to ensure compliance with these agreements, and can break agreements, if the privatisation subject does not comply with the terms of these agreements.[149]

Parliament need to be regularly informed of privatisation developments if circumstances require (for example if it will ensure the transparency) and play an active role in determining the general policy framework; it should be consulted on the appointment of top privatisation officials. However, its active involvement in policy implementation might render the process excessively vulnerable to short-term political consideration.[150]

E. Analysis on regulation

An adequate regulatory framework is the key determinant of success in the privatisation process.[151] Regulation is necessary.[152] However, regulation of economic activities is very controversial. What should the structure of the regulation be? Can government regulate all the details? What is the limit in regulation? Which points or factors should be taken account in the regulation? These and similar issues and questions will arise in different countries and in different sectors.

In most cases it is difficult to give a clear answer or provide an accurate solution to these issues. However we believe that, privatisation will not work unless governments put their industry into private ownership and subject to the incentives and pressures which bear upon private owners. If the new owners still have to be subject to the detailed rule of the planners, none of the economic gains of privatisation will be yielded. Privatisation works by making

---

[149] Article 8/11, The Republic of Latvia Law on Privatisation of State and Municipal Asset Units, passed on 17.02. 1994, web page of Latvian Privatisation Agency, URL: http://www.lpa.bkc.lv/
[150] Web page of the OECD, URL: http://www.oecd.org/
[151] Edwards, Sebastian, "Public Sector Deficits and Macroeconomic Stability in Developing Countries", Working Paper Series, National Bureau of Economic Research (NBER), Working Paper 5407, Cambridge, January 1996, p.32
[152] Prosser, (Nationalised Industries), p.90

industries respond to commercial signals. They have to attract investment on the basis of their predicted performance. They have to set prices that take into account the demand and the competition. They have to pay wages that attract sufficient labour without making their products too expensive. They have to locate where it is efficient for them to be, given their supplies and their markets. If all of these are controlled by a government reluctant to release its controls, then the enterprise is private in name only, with none of the benefits that this status normally brings.

Finally we must point out that many developing countries are burdened by an unreasonably high level of government regulation of economic activity that may have to be reduced in order to attract investors. The streamlining of licensing and other government regulations and permits required to conduct business should be a priority in such countries. [153]

---

[153] Guislain, (The World Bank), p.16

V. CONCLUSIONS

There is no theory that bears on how far a nation should go down the road to privatisation and what remaining services should a government produce.[154] The decision to privatise and how to privatise is political.[155] The issue "how far the privatisation might go" is highly controversial.

Although, government employees operate a casino in Ghana, bake cookies in Egypt, assemble watches in India, mine salt in Mexico, make matches in Mali, and bottle cooking oil in Senegal;[156] it is now widely held view that the government should generally not be the owner of companies in competitive sectors, such as industry or financial services.

The opinion is more divided when it comes to the supply of public services, such as energy and transport. Some would argue that these sectors are natural monopolies which should be government owned in order to avoid the abuse of the monopoly power. Others would maintain that, given a right regulatory framework, there is no reason why these sectors should not be privately owned.[157]

The changing structure of the economy and technological changes have created new situations and there is no more ground for state monopoly in telecommunication, the coal and steel industry and road transport, each of them being in a deep crisis.[158] In other words, privatisation affects practically all sectors. Even activities traditionally reserved for the public sector are increasingly being entrusted to private operators. Almost all large transactions have occurred in "strategic" sectors that traditionally used to be publicly controlled: utilities, such as

---

[154] Niskanen, p.224
[155] Letwin, p.29; Privatisation in Europe, Asia and Latin America, What Lessons can be Drawn?, Summary of the Presentations at the International Workshop on Privatisation Organised by the OECD in April 1994, Sao Paulo, URL: http://www.oecd.org
[156] Mary M. Shirley, "Getting Bureaucrats Out of Business: Obstacles to State Enterprise Reform", web page of Center for International Private Enterprise, URL: http://www.cipe.org/
[157] Privatisation Trends in OECD Countries-June 1996, URL: http://www.oecd.org
[158] Harmathy, General Report, p.211

telecommunications, power, or gas; natural resources, including mines, railways, steel and financial services, including banking and insurance.[159]

The role of the government in the economy seems to be one of the most controversial questions both in economic theory and in practice.[160] According to us, the government should finance only those public goods for which the total value is higher than the cost and non-paying beneficiaries may not be efficiently excluded.[161] Also the public sector should provide or continue to provide services that a citizen may reasonably expect to be offered by the state.[162] In that context, international relations, diplomacy, national defence, police work, immigration and border control, central banking, financial markets regulation are the areas that cannot be privatised.[163] Furthermore providing provision of law and order cannot be privatised. In other words, these functions and areas constitute "core government" that only a government can perform and should continue to perform.[164]

However, we should point out that private sector may co-operate in some aspects of these functions. For example, government may hire a private consulting firm to create policies and provide alternative solutions in foreign or immigration policy. Similarly, a private security firm may involve in the education or training of police force.

---

[159] Guislain, (The Privatization Challenge), p.3
[160] Dabrowski, p.21
[161] Niskanen, p.220, 221
[162] Braddon and Foster, p.293
[163] Robert, p.35, 36, 37
However, we must point out that in two African countries, private organisations have played major role in the peace process in the international arena. In Mozambique the initial contacts between the rebels of Mozambique National Resistance and the government took place in Rome, and were facilitated by the Santo Egidio Community, a lay Catholic organisation, with the support of the Mozambican Catholic Church. In South Africa, the business community, foreign and private organisations, and a broad spectrum of churches promoted the informal talks between leading representatives of the African National Congress and of the white establishment that initiated the transitional process, while business and the churches created the framework for the National Peace Accord. (Jaime Nogueira Pinto, "The Crisis of the Sovereign State and the Privatisation of Defence and Foreign Affairs", Heritage Foundation Lecture, No 649, Lectures and Educational Programs, The Heritage Foundation, URL: http//www.heritage.org/, November 19, 1999, p.7)
[164] David R. Hunter, Putting Government Reform on a Firmer Foundation, Andersen Consulting Company, URL: http://www.ac.com

It is now widely acknowledged that the private sector can perform these activities more efficiently and at lower cost to the consumer. But the state has an increasingly important role to play in promoting macroeconomic stability and in adopting and enforcing rules of the game in a complex economic and social environment.[165]

The fundamental issue revolves around the prospective role of the state in the economy. Eventually, the state will become a central co-ordinator, rather than a detailed prescriber of production, distribution and consumption patterns. These tasks should be increasingly devolved to financially autonomous firms that operate within the guidelines set by the newly emerging institutions and by the framework of macroeconomic policies that aim at co-ordinating decisions indirectly.[166]

In several countries there is still large-scale state intervention is some sectors, with artificially maintained subsidies and barriers to market entry.[167]

---

[165] Privatisation in Europe, Asia and Latin America, What Lessons can be Drawn?, Summary of the Presentations at the International Workshop on Privatisation Organised by the OECD in April 1994, Sao Paulo, URL: http://www.oecd.org; Iatridis, p.5; "Conclusions", Privatization in Central and Eastern Europe-Perspectives and Approaches, Edited by: Demetrius S. Iatridis and June Gary Hopps, Praeger Publishers, USA, 1998, p.195, 196
[166] Brabant, p.49; Santos, p.141
[167] Privatisation in Europe, Asia and Latin America, What Lessons can be Drawn?, Summary of the Presentations at the International Workshop on Privatisation Organised by the OECD in April 1994, Sao Paulo, URL: http://www.oecd.org; Systemic Change and Privatisation Law, (Summary), The Hungarian Academy of Sciences, URL: http://www.mta.hu/strat/angol/kot4.html

In Portugal, although major companies have been returned to the private sector, a significant number have still to be privatised. And there is even an opinion that Portugal had missed the boat and optimum time for disposing of the more problematic companies had passed. (Corkill, p.226). Revenues have been raised by privatisation in Portugal also supports this approach (p.227)

In some former socialist countries like Poland, largest enterprises have not begun privatisation, such as heavy industry, mining or natural monopolies. (Maciej Grabowski, Economic Reform in Poland, Economic Reform Today Working Papers, Number 4, web page of Center for International Private Enterprise, URL: http//www.cipe.org/). In this country, a large group (some 2,000) of state-owned enterprises has never been included in the process. (Barbara Blaszczyk, Moving Ahead: Privatization in Poland ", web page of Center for International Private Enterprise, URL: http://www.cipe.org/; Ewa Baginska, "Legal Aspects of the Privatization Process in Poland", Web page of Civic Education Project, URL: http//www.cep.org.hu/) As a conclusion, in Poland, although privatisation has reduced the size of the public sector, state ownership is still quite prominent across the economy, with a strong presence in mining, fuels, power generation, defence, heavy chemicals, telecommunications, air and rail transport, sugar, spirits and insurance. (Vincent Koen, "Poland-Privatisation as the Key to Efficiency", web page of OECD, URL: http://www.oecd.org/publications/observer/213/spotlight.htm)

Finally we must point out that in Scandinavian countries, such as in Sweden, many large-scale enterprises have not been privatised. (Lane, p.195)

Revenue maximisation should not be the primary goal of privatisation. Privatisation works best when it's part of a larger program of reforms promoting efficiency.[168]

In successful countries privatisation programmes were accompanied by reforms to open markets, remove price and exchange rate distortions, and encourage the development of the private sector through free entry.

In some extents, countries can benefit from privatising management without privatising the ownership of assets. Management contracts, leases, and concessions have been successfully used the world over, particularly in sectors where it is difficult to attract private investors. But because a change in ownership is usually needed to lock in performance gains, private management arrangements are likely to work best when they are a step toward full privatisation.

Transparency is critical for economic and political success. In that context, regulation should provide appropriate measures to minimise corruption. Transparency and anti-corruption legislation is particularly important in former socialist countries where black economy is a common problem.[169]

Golden shares are in no way essential features of privatisation laws. To the contrary, by barring the normal operation of the market and blocking some types of take-overs (the most

---

[168] John Nellis, "Time to Rethink Privatisation in Transition Economies", IFC-International Finance Corporation, Discussion Paper Number 38, The World Bank, Washington, D.C., p.29

[169] However some studies point out that, particularly in ex socialist countries corruption is a common problem in the privatisation process. (Chikán, p.32) Russia today is classified in some international surveys as the most corrupt country in the world, after Nigeria. (David Satter, "Russia's Deepening Crisis", Web Page of Huston Institute, URL: http://www.hudson.org). According to Satter: "... bribery became an inevitable and accepted part of nearly all business dealings in Russia... Approximately twenty-thousand crimes connected with official corruption are recorded in Russia every year, but this is probably less than 1 percent of the real total. A recent poll of Moscow businessmen revealed that several-thousand bribes are given and taken in the capital every day. Russian businessmen use bribes to gain access to low-interest credits, licenses to export raw materials, and lucrative tax exemptions, some of which are worth billions of dollars... commercial organisations spend between 30 and 50 percent of their profits on ensuring "co-operative" relationships with government officials, instead of investing in the real economy. (David Satter, "Russia's Deepening Crisis", web Page of Houston Institute, URL: http://www.hudson.org).

In former socialist countries, currently those participating in the process are increasingly viewed as having earned their income from either illegal means in the "grey" or "black" economies or from having been prominent among the nomenclature of the former communist system. (Ash, Hare and Canning, p.220)

frequent purpose of golden shares), they may reduce management incentives and performance in the privatised companies.[170]

Where golden shares are needed, they should be defined in the narrowest sense possible by limiting the scope the extraordinary rights they confer to the government to what is strictly necessary, and by restricting the duration of those rights. Golden shares-especially where they are held by governments without solid, credible track records-otherwise unduly restrict privatisation and reduce privatisation benefits, whether in the form of lower proceeds or less-efficient service providers.[171]

In other words, in order to develop a free market in shares, special shares should be, as far as possible, time limited. For example, in Britain special shares in 10 water companies and 12 electricity distribution companies expired five years to the day after privatisation. Also the provisions attached to a special share may be amended or waived where the government deems the circumstances to warrant it.[172]

Regulation is critical to the successful privatisation of monopolies; and in some cases the regulation might be strong.[173] Governments should prepare the framework to protect consumers from the privatisation activities. Similarly, governments need to pay special attention to developing a social safety net. If the social cost of privatisation of a specific enterprise is high (i.e. if privatisation will cost large-scale redundancies) the process for this specific enterprise can be suspended until all social problems are solved.

---

[170] Guislain, (The World Bank), p.57
[171] Guislain, (The Privatization Challenge), p.257; Privatization in the United Kingdom, Ernst & Young, p.24
[172] Gibbon, (Guide), p.8
[173] Galal, Jones, Tandon and Vogelsang, p.544

In adjusting the public-private balance, no single remedy is appropriate.[174] And in that context, privatisation is not the solution to every economic and administrative problem. Selling an enterprise to the private sector does not mean an end to questions about public control and accountability. Most of the privatised industries are major concerns whose operations have significant social and economic impact.[175]

Furthermore, the experiences have revealed that, the success of the privatisation is also up to the relevant economic conditions and reforms.[176] It is argued that privatisation cannot proceed without the implementation of a whole series of other inter-related reforms, including enterprise restructuring, price liberalisation and the development of the institutions of the market.[177]

In other words, privatisation can be only partially successful unless it is accompanied by a whole series of comprehensive supporting reforms such as the reform of banking and legal systems, tax reform and development of competition policy.[178]

To give companies the incentive to improve efficiency, banks must be independent of the state, so that their decisions are commercially driven and well-connected SOEs are prevented from simply replacing government transfers with soft credits.[179]

Economists are now generally agreed that simply changing the ownership of assets is not sufficient.[180] They also point out that the real problem with public enterprise is not its ownership

---

[174] Starr, (The Limits of Privatisation), p.122, 123
[175] Moran and Prosser, (Introduction), p.7
[176] Andic, p.35
[177] Ash, Hare and Canning, p.218; Janice A. Beecher, Twenty Myths About Privatisation, Alliance for Redesigning Government, National Academy of Public Administration, URL: http://www.alliance.napawash.org/; John D. Sullivan, "Privatization and Economic Reforms", web page of Center for International Private Enterprise, URL: http://www.cipe.org/; Tornell, p.350, 362
[178] Ash, Hare and Canning, p.232; Bradley, p.282; Lieberman, Ewing, Mejstrik, Mukherjee and Fidler, p.43; Aizenman, p.16
[179] Chikán, p.30
[180] Jackson and Price, p.14; Moran and Prosser, (Introduction), p.7; Woodward, p.279; Tornell, p.36

Some governments also emphasise the importance of competition. For example, according to Bosnia and Herzegovina government:" Experience in central and eastern Europe has shown that progress requires simultaneous

but the non-competitive markets in which it operates.[181] In other words the real issue is not so much public versus private ownership; it is monopoly versus competition.[182]

According to us the most important is the high level of competition[183], rule of law, other institutional factors with an appropriate regulation that creates and protects the general market environment.[184]

Unless effective competition and regulation are introduced, the privatisation of firms with market power brings about private ownership in precisely the circumstances where it has least to offer.[185]

It would be wrong to judge the success or the performance of the privatisation programme purely in terms of cost efficiency. Society has other goals and these were in large measure reflected in the objectives of the public enterprises. In addition to serving customer needs, public enterprises were used as instruments of government policy to assist with the achievement of employment generation, the development of under-develop regions, earning foreign exchange, and distributional equity. Where the market infrastructure is under-developed,

---

effort in three critical, inter-related areas: developing a business environment that promotes competition and supports private sector development, privatising socially- and state-owned assets, and developing a disciplined and competitive financial sector." (Web page of Agency of Privatisation of Federation of Bosnia and Herzegovina, URL: http://www.zpf.com.ba)

[181] Galal, Jones, Tandon, and Vogelsang, p.579
[182] Nightingale and Pindus, "Privatization of Public Social Services" URL: http://www.urban.org/
[183] Hartley, p.193, 194; Kirkpatrick, p.240; Bishop and Kay, (Does Privatisation Work), p.15
[184] Competition provides choices, and choice is one of the strongest points in the case for privatisation. [Starr, (The Limits of Privatization), p.117; Ash, Hare and Canning, p.232]

In that context according to economists four elements are essential: (a) Macroeconomic stability, (b) Hard budget constraints, (c) Competitive markets, and (d) Adequate property rights. [Havrylyshyn and McGettigan, p.8, 9, 10; Chang K. Lee, "Privatization and Cooperative Labor-Management Relations", Cornell University, Department of City and Planning, May 1998, URL: http://www.cce.cornell.edu/; Fryman and Rapaczynski, p.99]

We can add (i) opening the economy to foreign trade and (ii) legal and institutional reforms to this list. (See also: Saul Estrin, "Economic Transition and Privatisation: The Issues", Privatisation in Central and Eastern Europe, Edited By: Saul Estrin, Longman Group Limited, 1994, London and New York, p.3)

[185] Vickers and Yarrow, (An Economic Analysis), p.3. The authors also point out that it can be argued that the degree of competition and the effectiveness of regulatory policy have rather larger effects on performance than ownership. (p.3)

as in developing countries, public enterprises play an important role in meeting these objectives.[186]

It was argued that privatisation will discipline management by cutting off government subsidies. It is true that, privatisation has reduced many governments' need to continue large subsidies to state owned enterprises (SOEs).[187] However, privatisation is no guarantee that subsidies will stop. Private companies are not bashful about asking for help, usually in the form of tax benefits. And if privatisation occurs without liberalisation, privatised monopolies can obtain subsidies through regulatory protection.[188]

Privatisation is not an overnight process; it will be a lengthy process. Therefore for some time yet the majority of large industrial enterprises may remain in the state sector.[189] Privatisation should be seen as a longer-term process and as but one part of a wider market reform strategy.[190]

In the privatisation process, an initial step that should be taken is the removal of the "soft budget constraint" for enterprises. Thus, enterprises, be they in the state or private sector, must realise that if they are unable to operate profitability they will face the prospect of bankruptcy. The threat of closure must therefore act to stimulate improved performance.[191]

---

[186] Jackson and Price, p.25
[187] Peter Young, "The Lessons of Privatisation", web page of Center for International Private Enterprise, URL: http//www.cipe.org/
[188] Starr, (The Limits of Privatization), p.116
[189] Ash, Hare and Canning, p.232
For example, in the United Kingdom several years have gone by between the time government committed itself to privatising industries and the full transfer of ownership to the public. ("Dimensions of Privatisation", US Energy Information Administration, URL: http://www.eia.doe.gov); Havrylyshyn, McGettigan, p.4)
Also see: William L. Megginson & Jeffry M. Netter, "Equity to the People: The Record on Share Issue Privatization Programs", p.12, The World Bank, URL: http://www.worldbank.org
[190] Ash, Hare and Canning, p.233
[191] In that context, SOEs should be denied access to access to subsidies, tax exemptions, procurement set-asides or soft loans. (Mary M. Shirley, "Getting Bureaucrats Out of Business: Obstacles to State Enterprise Reform", web page of Center for International Private Enterprise, URL: http://www.cipe.org/). However, some SOEs, like the ones carrying social services for elderly people, abandoned kids or unemployed people, should function on soft-budget system.
Ash, Hare and Canning, p.232. [According to these authors: "...The state has to learn how to say no to inefficient enterprises (and workers) requesting financial support to prevent bankruptcy". (p.232)]

Privatisation has made some significance changes in the economy and society. For example, in Britain this privatisation resulted in the number of shareholders roughly tripling since 1979. There are now 10 million individual shareholders compared to 3 million in 1979.[192] Similarly in France privatisation transactions have quadrupled the number of shareholders, from 1.5 million before 1986 when the process began to 6 million.[193]

We should point out that although in former socialist countries, there is a wide gap between expectations and reality; privatisation made significant changes. These countries have been taking important steps towards market economy. Thus, the state sector today represents less than half of the economies of Eastern Europe.[194]

---

[192] "...The number of share-owners in the UK has risen to some 10 million, three times the number in 1979... We could have secured our primary objective of privatisation without extending to ordinary people the opportunity of acquiring a stake in the country's future. But we believe in a plural society, where wealth should be distributed more widely into private ownership, when it is released from public ownership. Hence the opportunity, built into privatisation, for the man in the street to taste share ownership. Amongst those who seized this opportunity were the employees of the businesses concerned, who for the first time could see a direct link between their efforts and their capital..." [George Young, the (former) Financial Secretary's speech to the World Privatisation Conference, 6 March 1995, web page of the Treasury, URL: http://www.hm-treasury.gov.uk/pub/html/speech95/fst/sp060395.html]. The flotations of British Telecom and British Gas were of particular significance; each created the world's largest shareholder register when sold. [Bishop and Kay, (Does Privatisation Work), p.33, 87; Privatization in the United Kingdom, Ernst & Young, p.21. However we must point out that most shareholders have shares in only a few companies. Indeed, the Stock exchange-treasury survey found that 78 percent of all shareholders owned shares in two or fewer companies. (p.33)]

According to one study privatisation accomplished three significance achievements in the UK: (a) It created large revenues, (b) It did widen share ownership in the UK, (c) It has produced a dramatic reduction in the size of the publicly owned sector of industry. (Richardson, p.72, 73)

[193] Gibbon, (Guide), p.3

The British government has claimed that privatisation has resulted in higher productivity and profitability. (Hartley, p.181)

It is important to note that the various components and mechanisms of the different privatisation programs have fundamentally important effects, not only in facilitating the transformation of ownership, but also in terms of their post-privatisation implications for the larger prospect of economic restructuring. (Lieberman, Ewing, Mejstrik, Mukherjee and Fidler, p.48)

As we discussed above privatisation had very important effects on former socialist countries' economies. For example in Bulgaria the number of the private enterprises in the last couple of years has increased from 24,550 to 400,000. (Alexander Stoyanov, "Economic Reform in Bulgaria", web page of Center for International Private Enterprise, URL: http://www.cipe.org/)

However some authors believe from developing countries and less develop countries, that significance of privatisation as a policy option has been exaggerated. (Kirkpatrick, p.242). According to Kirkpatrick: "...[privatisation] is likely to be difficult to achieve, its potential benefits often appear to be limited, and its adoption may involve significant political costs..."(p.242)

Also see: V.V. Ramanadham, "A Concluding Review", Privatisation in the United Kingdom, Edited By: V.V. Ramanadham, Routledge, London and New York, 1988, p.293

[194] William L. Megginson, "The Impact of Privatisation", web page of Center for International Private Enterprise, URL: http//www.cipe.org/)

Finally privatisation is not the answer; it is one of the answers. It is not a panacea. Privatisation is but one manifestation of the underlying philosophy of introducing private sector capital, skill, techniques and expertise into the business of government at every level.[195]

For example, in Hungary he bigger proportion of the competitive sector is already in private ownership. (Eva Várhegyi, Hungary, News and Views, web page of Center for International Private Enterprise, URL: http://www.cipe.org/)

Furthermore, in Russia more than one million small businesses were created. (Alexander Chesnokov, "A Business view of Russia's Economy", an address given by Alexander Chesnokov to the Center for International Private Enterprise Board of Directors at the U.S. Chamber of Commerce in Washington, DC, on April 6, 1999, web page of Center for International Private Enterprise, URL: http://www.cipe.org/)

[195] George Young, the (former) Financial Secretary's speech to the World Privatisation Conference, 6 March 1995, web page of the Treasury, URL: http://www.hmtreasury.gov.uk/pub/html/speech95/fst/sp060395.html

CHAPTER III

LEGAL and INSTITUTIONAL FRAMEWORK for PRIVATISATION

The third chapter provides a comparative study of the legal framework for the privatisations. This chapter deals with the following issues:
(a) What is the structure of the privatisation legislation in the country in question? (b) What institutions are put in charge of privatisation process? (b) What methods are introduced in privatisation transactions? (c) Is there any ideal legal framework for the privatisation process?

I. OVERVIEW

A. General

1. Basic Requirements

The concept of legal and institutional framework for privatisation covers legislation, institutions and systems needed for the successful design and implementation of a privatisation program.

Ideally, a legal, institutional and regulatory framework fostering private sector activity in general and privatisation in particular will be ready in place. In most developing and transition countries, however, this will not be the case. Governments need to establish an organisational and analytical structure to implement the privatisation effort. This structure can include commissions, staff offices, and analytical frameworks for privatisation decision-making.[1]

---

[1] General Accounting Office, p.5

Therefore, before implementing the privatisation, the activities should focus on those legal instruments that absolutely have to be in place if privatisation is to succeed.[2]

2. Structure of the Approach

a. General

Privatisation requires a comprehensive legal framework. Legislation is a vital fact in the privatisation process. Therefore an appropriate legal framework should be ready in place. To implement the legislation requires a whole range of new institutions, together with trained personnel. Also, it requires an independent judicial system of courts, judges, lawyers, procedures and regulations. Without this fabric a market economy cannot function, and privatisation will not be effective.[3]

The structure of the legal and institutional framework for privatisation will depend on the specific situation of each country, including the legal framework in place, the scope and nature of the privatisation program, the administrative and other capabilities to implement the program, and the political context.[4] In some cases, new institutions are set up to monitor and implement privatisation; in others, existing institutions are remodelled. Although there is no consensus on an ideal institutional structure for privatisation, it is essential for every country to clearly define the respective roles and powers of the main decision-makers involved. The allocation of responsibility will need to take place in advance, whether in general regulation governing public

---

[2] Guislain, (The Privatization Challenge), p.292, 293
[3] Colin, Jones, *Privatisation in East Europe and the Former Soviet Union, A Financial Times Management Report,* Published and Distributed, London, 1986, p.13
For example, billions of dollars of planned investment activity in Russia has for a long time been put on hold awaiting passage of a property rights law. ("The Legal and Political Environment of Privatisation", US Energy Information Administration, URL: http://www.eia.doe.gov)
[4] Guislain, (The Privatization Challenge), p.293
Country characteristics are wholly beyond the control of divestiture decision-makers, and market structure partly so, but the way the sale is structured can be varied to cope with the exogenous circumstances. (Galal, Jones, Tandon and Vogelsang, p.537)

sector operations; or new provisions contained in a privatisation law; or special laws, such as for the creation of privatisation agencies; or applicable provisions of company or SOE legislation.[5]

b. Impediments

Legal experts advising governments on privatisation need to determine which laws or legal institutions create the most severe bottlenecks for successful privatisation in the concerned country. These will differ from country to country and will depend on the specific privatisation programs. Once identified, the removal of these obstacles should become priorities in a larger legislative reform package fostering privatisation.[6]

Imprecise property rights, arbitrary application of the law, and weak financial markets, to take only few examples, can hinder the smooth execution of privatisation operations. The elimination of these constraints should therefore be part of the package of basic reforms. Where they cannot be eliminated, the government may need to find creative ways to achieve its objectives despite these legal obstacles.[7]

Finally privatisation almost always involves some changes in a nation's legal system. In several regions, legal reform has been an important key to the successful privatisation of state-owned industries, especially with regard to the protection of property rights and the reliable enforcement of contracts. The equal treatment of foreign investors and domestic investors by the judicial system has also been important.[8]

---

[5] Comparative Overview of Privatisation Policies and Institutions in Member OECD Countries, (Comparative Overview of Privatisation), OECD Privatization and Enterprise Reform Unit (September 1998), p.4, web page of OECD, URL: http://www.oecd.org
[6] Guislain, (The World Bank), p.32
[7] Schwartz, p.36, 37
[8] "The Legal and Political Environment of Privatisation", US Energy Information Administration, URL: http://www.eia.doe.gov
See: p. 330-348

B. Defining the Privatisation Policy

1. General

Each country embarking on a privatisation program faces the choice of which of its SOEs to privatise, how to divest the assets, and the parties to whom the assets will be sold. On a broad level, the strategy will reflect the objectives of the country's privatisation program, which will be unique to the political and economic circumstances of each country.[9]

One of the most important steps in implementing the privatisation programme is to set a clear timetable at the beginning of process, examining where the critical decision points are going to be and deciding and contemplating a rigorous legislative time-table in cases where legislation is needed. So that government can be sure that the necessary legal measures should be put in place before privatisation. The government should also co-operate with the relevant associations to solve the legal and economical problems or provide adequate solutions during the privatisation implementations.

As part of the overall strategy, the critical path of reforms needed for successful implementation of the privatisation program should be outlined. The sequencing and prioritisation of such reforms need to be thought through from the beginning, they are intimately linked with the choice of privatisation techniques. If the government wishes to privatise SOEs as corporate entities, for example, prior corporatisation of the SOE may be necessary. If a public flotation is envisaged, a reform of capital markets may be in order.[10]

---

[9] "Privatizing State-Owned Companies", The Prosperity Papers Series, Prosperity Paper Three, web page of Center for International Private Enterprise, URL: http//www.cipe.org/

[10] Guislain, (The World Bank), p.8

2. Transparency

One of the essential and vital points in the political acceptability for the privatisation process is full transparency.[11] Hence, a non-transparent economy establishes best conditions for stable or even gradually increasing corruption and abuse of power.[12] Transparency is a concern in many governments, particularly in Eastern Europe.[13]

In the privatisation process there are several reasons why a corrupt firm may pay off officials. A corrupt firm may pay to be included in the list of qualified bidders, to have officials

---

[11] Donaldson and Wagle, p.3. Also see: Ivan Miklos, "Corruption Risks in the Privatisation Process-A Study of Privatisation Developments in the Slovak Republic, Focusing on the Causes and Implications of Corruption Risks", Bratislava, May 1995, URL: http://privatizationlink.com. According to this study: " Corruption cannot be avoided in the privatisation process. However, the degree of corruption is primarily determined by privatisation forms and methods that are employed pace of privatisation and respect for the equal opportunities principle."
Also see: Susan Rose-Ackerman, "Redesigning the State to Fight Corruption-Transparency, Competition, and Privatization", Public Policy for the Private Sector, The World Bank, Note No.75, April 1996. (In the conclusion part of the study Rose-Ackerman states that: "...Corruption can never be entirely eliminated. Under many realistic conditions, it is simply too expensive to reduce corruption to zero...")
For this issue furthermore see: "State Owned Enterprises, Privatisation, and Corporate Governance in OECD Countries," web page of OECD, URL: http://www.oecd.org:80/daf/peru?CONTENT/agpsoes.htm; Holger, p.100; Petter Langseth, "How to Fight Corruption on the Ground"," web page of the Center for International Enterprise", URL: http://www.cipe.org/; Alexander Stoyanov, "Economic Reform in Bulgaria", web page of Center for International Private Enterprise, URL: http://www.cipe.org/
Finally we must point out that, there are several attempts (including some agreements) in the international arena to fights against corruption. (For this see: Nancy Zucker Boswell, "New Tools to Fight Corruption", web page of the Center for International Enterprise", URL: http//www.cipe.org/)

[12] Eugen Jurzyca, "Transparency in the Slovak Economy", web page of Center for International Private Enterprise, URL: http//www.cipe.org/; Tibor Vidos, "The Role Of Transparency In Political Decision Making and Its Effect on The Economy" web page of Center for International Private Enterprise, URL: http//www.cipe.org/

[13] For example according to Bulgarian government: "...(in order to secure) transparency (of the privatisation process) is the flexible use of various privatisation techniques -auctions, competitions, negotiations with potential buyers, especially in cases of strictly simplified and reduced privatisation procedures. The Privatisation Agency and the sector ministries and committees will use mainly competitions and auctions as procedures for privatisation, due to the fact that they are the shortest and the most clearly legally regulated ones." (Web page of Bulgarian Bulgarian Foreign Investment Agency, URL: http://www.bfia.org/privat.htm; web page of Bulgarian Privatisation Agency, URL: http:// www.privatisation.online.bg; Maria Prohaska, "Privatization in Bulgaria: Pushing Forward", web page of Center for International Private Enterprise, URL: http//www.cipe.org/).
On the other hand one survey found out that 57% of adult Bulgarians believe that their politicians are primarily interested in securing special privileges for themselves and their friends. (Corruption in Bulgaria Threatens Social Stability, web page of Center for International Private Enterprise, URL: http//www.cipe.org/)
For transparency issues in Ukraine see: Web page of State Property Fund of Ukraine, URL: http://www.ukrmassp.kiev.ua/Prgrm98-1.htm
Furthermore see: Maciej Grabowski, Economic Reform in Poland, Economic Reform Today Working Papers, Number 4, web page of Center for International Private Enterprise, URL: http://www.cipe.org/

171

structure the bidding specifications so that it is the only qualified supplier, or to be selected as the winning contractor.[14]

In that context, conflict of interest provisions for government officials, state owned enterprises insiders and private agents, clear rules for auctions, specific criteria for the evaluation process in the context of competitive bidding, open procedures in the selection of private advisors[15], and rigorous publicity requirements for individual transactions are measures that might enhance transparency and significantly reduce public criticism of the process. The privatisation legislation should provide this transparency in the legal bases.[16]

As a summary, transparency should be obtained in every privatisation transaction.[17] This can be ensured by having clear and simple selection criteria for evaluating bids, clearly defined

---

[14] Susan Rose-Ackerman, "The Political Economy of Corruption-Causes and Consequences", Public Policy for the Private Sector, The World Bank, Note No: 74, April 1996

[15] In tenders for selection of advisors, the (Privatisation) Administration conducts a pre-qualification study in line with the nature of the subject matter of the tender and characteristics of the sector and based on experience and competence factor, at least three consultants are invited to bid in writing and the bargaining method is adopted. [Article 18/C-g, "Law Concerning Privatisation and Regulation of Implementations of Privatisation and Amendment to Certain Laws and Statutory decrees, Law Nr.4046, Date of Passage: 24 November 1994, Official Gazette Nr. 22124, Date of official Gazette: 27. 11. 1994 9 (Privatisation Law), web page of Turkish Privatisation Administration, URL: http://www.oib.gov.tr]

[16] Web page of the OECD, URL: http://www.oecd.org/
In other words, whether a law or other subordinate legal instruments comprise legislation, transparency is essential for building political support. Clear rules and guidelines should be adopted as regards specific categories of privatisation transaction, especially sales through auctions, competitive bids, and the selection of private consultants
In some former socialist countries like Albania, the privatisation of state-owned property has witnessed significant levels of corruption. Privatizations are usually conducted through administrative acts rather than auctions, rendering the process less transparent and more conducive to insider deals. (Konstandin Kristo, "Economic Reform in Albania", web page of Center for International Private Enterprise, URL: http//www.cipe.org/)
According to one study, the main components of a transparent tender process are: (a) competitive bidding, (b) equal access to information, (c) clear evaluation criteria and documented procedures, (d) disclosure of the purchase price, (e) adequate monitoring, (f) compliance with the law ("Building Transparency into the Privatization Process", Adam Smith Institute, web page of Center for International Private Enterprise, URL: http://www.cipe.org)

[17] Some Privatisation Law emphasises the importance of transparency in the privatisation process For example, article 19 Law on Privatisation of Enterprises, Federation of Bosnia and Herzegovina states that: "... In the procedure of enterprise privatisation through any of the methods, and in accordance with ...(Privatisation) Law, the ...Agency for Privatisation is required to ensure fairness, competitiveness and transparency." [For the full text of the Law on Privatisation of Enterprises, Federation of Bosnia and Herzegovina (BiH) in word format see: Web page of Agency for Privatisation of Federation of Bosnia and Herzegovina, URL: http://www.apf.com.ba/zakonie/index.htm/]

competitive bidding procedures, disclosure of purchase price and buyer, well-defined institutional responsibilities, and adequate monitoring and supervision program.[18]

II. INSTITUTIONAL MEASURES for PRIVATISATION

A. General

One of the first questions to be considered by any government contemplating a programme of privatisation is whether it should set up any specialised agency for this purpose, and if so, what the remit of agency (or agencies) should be.[19]

Most privatisation laws clarify the respective roles and powers of the key actors in the privatisation program, such as the legislature (parliament), the government, the privatisation minister, the minister of finance, the agency(ies) responsible for privatisation.[20]

It is essential that the law define in clear terms the respective spheres of responsibility of the various authorities that play a role in the privatisation process, such as the parliament, and the government, the privatisation minister or agency, the management of the SOEs or other institutions involved. Mechanisms need to be set up that make these authorities accountable for their actions and create appropriate incentives and penalties ensure proper execution of the privatisation program.[21]

---

[18] Guislain, (The World Bank), p.39
[19] Comparative Overview of Privatisation Policies and Institutions in Member OECD Countries, OECD Privatization and Enterprise Reform Unit (September 1998), p.4, the web page of OECD, URL: http://www.oecd.org
[20] Furthermore general SOE legislation, enterprise specific legislation and SOE by-laws need to be checked to ascertain the powers of the SOE's board and management in the privatisation process. One critical dimension would be restrictions on the power to sell SOE assets, including financial participations. In many instances, the SOE legislation or by-laws will define the powers of SOE bodies, including shareholders meeting (if any), board or directors and the general manager, and set financial thresholds to demarcate their respective powers as well as the powers of the state. [Guislain, (The World Bank), p.40]
[21] Guislain, (The Privatization Challenge), p.111, 112

B. Different approaches and institutions

1. General

In most economies the decision to privatise a SOE lies with the parliament. The overall responsibility for the implementation of the privatisation programme lies with the Treasury, the Ministry of Finance and/or the Ministry of Economy or the Privatisation Agency. Other institutions carrying oversight responsibility are parliamentary committees, the council of ministers and especially created privatisation commissions. Furthermore the use of private advisers is a characteristic of most privatisation programmes. [22]

2. Institutional Models for Privatisation

Institutional structures of the privatisation institutions vary from country to country. There are two main models for the institutional structure of privatisation:

(a) *Existing ministries system*: In some countries existing ministries, individually or together (in most cases Ministry of Economy and/or Finance) are in charge of privatisation

---

[22] Comparative Overview of Privatisation Policies and Institutions in Member OECD Countries, OECD Privatization and Enterprise Reform Unit (September 1998), p.4, the web page of OECD, URL: http://www.oecd.org; Frederic C. Rich and William A. Plapinger, "Getting It Right in Privatisation", International Financial Law Review, Special Issue on Privatisation, Volume 13, p.11; Comparative Overview of Privatisation Policies and Institutions in Member OECD Countries, OECD Privatization and Enterprise Reform Unit (September 1998), p.4, web page of OECD, URL: http://www.oecd.org

In some countries privatisation bodies vary according to the areas that are going to be privatised. Furthermore, the jurisdiction in the privatisation progress is divided between central government, local governments and privatisation agency. For example, in the Federation of Bosnia and Herzegovina (BiH) approval and implementation of privatisation, according to Privatisation Law, will be carried out by the Agency for Privatisation of Federation BiH and Cantonal Privatisation Agencies. (Article 2, Law on Privatisation of Enterprises, web page of Agency for Privatisation of Federation of Bosnia and Herzegovina, URL: http//www.http://www.apf.com.ba/zakonie/index.htm/)

However, Bosnian Privatisation Law provides an exemption from the provisions of Article 2 of the Privatisation Law. Thus, the law states that: "As an exemption from the provisions of Article 2 of this Law, the decision on methods, deadlines and authorised Agency for the privatisation of enterprises from the sector of electric power production and distribution, transport and communications except for road transportation, water supply, mining and forestry, public media, gambling and arms and military equipment industry will be made by the Government of Federation BiH based on proposals made by the Federal Agency. The list of enterprises from Paragraph 1 of this Article will be determined by the Parliament of Federation BiH (Article 3) [For the full text of the Law on Privatisation of Enterprises, Federation of Bosnia and Herzegovina (BiH) in word format see: Web page

process. For example in the Netherlands and Portugal Ministry of Finance is responsible for the privatisation of SOEs. Furthermore, in Spain it is the council of ministries who is responsible for divestiture process. On the other hand, in Sweden, the procedure is handled by the ministry in charge of the administration of the enterprise in question. In France, in principle, Ministry of Economy and Finance is responsible for carrying out privatisation.[23] In the United Kingdom the Treasury has general responsibility for the privatisation policy and is consulted on key decisions in each transaction. Any necessary operational or financial restructuring or regulation of the industry is performed by the department having the most detailed knowledge of the industry to be sold. This department is also responsible for its privatisation. In cases where subsidiaries of public enterprises are being sold, the enterprise in question is usually the actual vendor, whereas the relevant Minister is monitoring the process to ensure that best value is achieved.[24]

(b) *Special unit system:* In this institutional model governments establish special agencies, offices or ministries to implement their privatisation programmes. They are new institutions that have been created to handle the privatisation process. Almost all former socialist countries adopted this institutional model.[25] Furthermore in Turkey, according to article 3 of the Privatisation Law, the Privatisation High Council is the ultimate decision-making body for

---

of Agency for Privatisation of Federation of Bosnia and Herzegovina, URL: http://www.apf.com.ba/zakonie/index.htm/]

[23] A law of 1986 established a Privatisation Commission. However, the commission responsibility is mainly is about the valuation of the enterprise. [Comparative Overview of Privatisation Policies and Institutions in Member OECD Countries, OECD Privatization and Enterprise Reform Unit (September 1998), p.13; the web page of OECD, URL: http://www.oecd.org]

[24] Comparative Overview of Privatisation Policies and Institutions in Member OECD Countries, OECD Privatization and Enterprise Reform Unit (September 1998), 12-16; the web page of OECD, URL: http://www.oecd.org; Kolderie, p.26; Cook and Kirkpatrick, p.11; Web page of Canadian Department of Foreign Affairs and International Trade, http://www.dfait-maeci.gc.ca/english/geo/europe/84679-e.htm

In other words the United Kingdom, have set up no specialised machinery. There, the ministry responsible for the enterprise has carried through each privatisation in question. [This issue will be set out in the following chapters; for this see: Daintith, p.71-72]

The only exemption among the Western economies is Turkey. Law No: 4046 (Law Concerning Privatisation and Regulation of Implementations of Privatisation and Amendment to Certain Laws and Statutory Decrees) has established Privatisation Administration and Privatisation High Council. According to the article 4 of Law No: 4046 the Privatisation Administration is the executive body for privatisation. On the other hand, the Privatisation High Council is the ultimate decision-making body for privatisation in Turkey. (Article 3). [For this and for the full text of Turkish Privatisation Law see the web page of Turkish Privatisation Administration, URL: http//www.oib.gov.tr/]

privatisation in Turkey. The law states the Privatisation Administration is the executive body for privatisation.[26]

2. Institutional structure in former socialist countries

The institutional structure of privatisation in ex-socialist countries is different from western economies. As we examined above, in western economies, mainly the existing ministries (and in most cases Ministry of Finance and/or Ministry of Economy) are in charge of the privatisation transactions.[27] However, almost all-former socialist countries have established special agencies, offices or ministries to implement their privatisation programme.

The list below shows the countries that have privatisation agencies[28]:

(a) *Armenia:* The Ministry of State Property Management,[29]

(b) *Albania:* Ministry of Public Economy and Privatisation[30] and Ministry of Finance[31],

(c) *Belarus:* Ministry of State Property,

(d) *Federation of Bosnia-Herzegovina:* Agency for Privatisation,[32]

---

[25] Institutional structure in former socialist countries will be examined under a separate subtitle below.
[26] Law No: 4046: Law Concerning Privatisation and Regulation of Implementations of Privatisation and Amendment to Certain Laws and Statutory Decrees, Web page of Turkish Privatisation Administration, URL: http://www.oib.gov.tr/
[27] Turkey is the only exemption. Although it is not a former socialist country Turkey has created a special institution (Privatisation Administration and Privatisation High Council) to implement its privatisation programme. (See p. 163, 164)
[28] For the internet links of the mentioned privatisation agencies see: URL: http://www.privatizationlink.com; URL: http://www.worldbank.org/
[29] "...The Ministry of State Property Management is responsible for all privatisation activity within Armenia...(Web page of Ministry of State Property Management Republic of Armenia, URL: http://www.privatisation.am/)
[30] "The Ministry of Public Economy and Privatisation ... is in charge of carrying out the implementation of the privatisation strategy ... except for banking and insurance sectors conform to all relevant procedures in line with the approved legal framework. (Article 13, Law No. 8306, dated 14.3.1998, On the Strategy for the Privatisation of Strategic Sectors of Albania, Web page of Economic Development Agency of Albanian Government, URL: http//www.aeda.gov.al/)
[31] "The Ministry of Finance is in charge of carrying out the implementation of the privatisation strategy in the sector of the second level banks with total state capital and of insurance companies with total state capital..." (Article 14, Law No. 8306, dated 14.3.1998, On the Strategy for the Privatisation of Strategic Sectors of Albania, Web page of Economic Development Agency of Albanian Government, URL: http//www.aeda.gov.al/)

(e) *Bulgaria:* Privatisation Agency,[33]

(f) *Croatia:* Privatisation Fund and Ministry of Privatisation,[34]

(g) *The Czech Republic:* National Property Fund,

(h) *Estonia:* Privatisation Agency,[35]

(i) *Georgia:* Ministry of State Property Management,[36]

(j) *(East) Germany:* Treuhandanstalt[37],

(k) *Hungary:* Privatisation and State Holding Co.,[38]

---

[32] The Law on Privatization Agency, "Official Gazette of the Federation of Bosnia and Herzegovina", No 18/96, URL: http//www.apf.com.ba/zakonie/la1.zip

[33] Web page of Bulgarian Privatisation Agency, URL: http/www.privatisation.online.bg/

[34] Web page of Croatian Government: URL: http://www.hfp.hr/privatization/privat.htm

[35] "Privatisation of property owned by the State is carried out by the Estonian Privatisation Agency, who is authorised to hold the state property in accordance with the present Law. (Article 4/1, Estonian Law on Privatisation, web page of Estonian Privatisation Agency, URL: http// http://www.eea.ee/english/indexe.htm)

Article 6/1 of Estonian Privatisation Law states that: "The Agency is a government institution established on the basis of the present Law, subordinated to the Minister of Economics the statutes whereof are approved by the Government." Estonian Law on Privatisation, (unofficial translation), web page of Estonian Privatisation Agency, URL: http//www.eea.ee/

Article 7. Main tasks of the Agency

The main task of the Agency shall be to organise privatisation of state property and carry out other tasks resulting from Property Reform. In order to fulfil the main task the Agency: (a) compiles privatisation programmes and lists of privatisation; (b) holds, uses and disposes the property entered in the privatisation list on behalf of the State until actual privatisation of the property; (c) determines and organises transformation, merger, division, restructuring, stabilisation and liquidation of enterprises and state commercial undertakings the stocks or shares of which have been confirmed in the privatisation list; (d) holds negotiations with legally designated subjects of Property Reform; (e) organises municipalisation and re-nationalisation of state property; (f) organises disposition of state property on the list of privatisation into the economic activities, including making contributions into the stock capital or share capital of a commercial undertaking and, also leasing or usage of state property; (g) concludes contracts of sale of state property to be privatised and effects control over the fulfilment of these contracts on behalf of the State. [Estonian Law on Privatisation, (unofficial translation), web page of Estonian Privatisation Agency, URL: http//www.eea.ee/]

Also see: Mygind, p.7, 8

[36] "Management and privatisation of state property is carried out by the Ministry of State Property Management of Georgia". (Article 3/1, Law of Georgia on State Property Privatisation, web page of Ministry of State Property Management of Georgia, URL: http://web.sanet.ge/mospm/).

The Ministry of State Property Management is the sole governmental agency responsible for carrying out the privatisation of state property and for controlling the related organisational issues (Web page of Ministry of State Property Management of Georgia, URL: http://web.sanet.ge/mospm/)

[37] Thomas Raiser, "The Challenge of Privatization in the Former East Germany: Reconciling the Conflict Between Individual Rights and Social Needs", A Fourth Way?-Privatization, Property, and the Emergence of New Market Economies, Edited By; Gregory S. Alexander and Grazyna Skapska, Routledge, 1994, p.4

[38] The Hungarian Privatization and State Holding Company (ÁPV Rt.) is the main proprietor of the entrepreneurial assets of the Hungarian State. (Web page of Hungarian Privatization and State Holding Company, URL: http://www.apvrt.hu/english/m1.html)

177

(l) *Latvia:* Privatisation Agency,[39]

(m) *Lithuania:* State Privatisation Fund,[40]

(n) *Macedonia:* Privatisation Agency,[41]

(o) *Moldova:* Ministry of Privatisation and State Property Administration[42],

(p) *Poland:* Privatisation Ministry,[43]

(q) *Romania:* State Ownership Fund,[44]

(r) *Russia:* Federal Property Fund and Russian Federal Stock Corporation,[45]

In Hungary, the aim was to speed the process after the obvious failure of the centralised, bureaucratic approach. Under this program, initiated in 1991, the government identified nearly 500 small and medium- sized companies for a special self-privatisation project. Accordingly, the State Property Agency reserved for itself only controlling functions, such as legal control and delegated rights and responsibilities of selling the state assets to private consulting firms. (Eva Voszka, "Privatization in Hungary: Results and Open Issues", web page of Center for International Private Enterprise, URL: http//www.cipe.org/)

[39] "The Privatisation Agency is a state joint stock company, non-profit organisation operating in compliance with this Law... Pursuant to this Law, the state in the person of the Cabinet of Ministers establishes the Privatisation Agency... The Privatisation Agency is a legal entity, has its own bank accounts and a seal." (Section I, Article 7, The Republic of Latvia Saeima Law On Privatization of State and Municipal Asset Units (Web page of Latvian Privatisation Agency, URL: http://www.lpa.bkc.lv/PrivatLawGB.htm#B001_)

[40] "Privatisation institutions shall be as follows: The State Property Fund...(and) property funds of municipalities, or other departments of municipality administration ... Municipal councils shall have the right to refrain from setting up said municipal property privatisation institution and to authorise the mayor to conclude an agreement with the Property Fund concerning privatisation of objects owned by the municipality. (Article 3/1, Law on the Privatisation of State-Owned and Municipal Property, 4 November 1997 No. VIII-480, Vilnius, web page of Lithuanian State Property Fund, URL: http//www. http://www.vtf.lt/en/frame22.html)

[41] "For the purpose of organising, control and carrying out transformation, Agency of the Republic of Macedonia for Privatisation...shall be founded. (Article 8). [For the full text of Macedonian Privatisation law see the web page of Macedonian Privatisation Agency, URL: http//www.mpa.org.mk]

[42] "The Ministry of Privatisation and State Property Administration shall be the only body which conducts the Government policy in privatisation sphere and co-ordinates along with the central specialised state authorities and local public administration the privatisation activities". (Article 5, Law on Privatisation Program 1997-1998, web page of Ministry of Privatisation and State Property Administration, URL: http//www.privatization.md/

[43] The Privatisation Agency is legal state entity established by virtue of the Law on the Office of the Treasury and the statue granted by one order of the Chairman of the Council of Ministers. The Minister of the Treasury supervises the Agency. The Agency is specialised body established to privatise Treasury companies, companies in which the Treasury has its share and also state and communal enterprises. The Agency sells corporate shares and stakes and it also disposes of the assets of state enterprises on the basis of the Treasury minister's authorisation determining the range and conditions of privatisation. (Web page of Ministry of Treasury, URL: http://www.mst.gov.pl/

[44] "State Ownership Fund is a public institution, legal entity, subordinated to the Romanian Government (According to Law no. 99 of May 26, 1999). Its main task is to sell the shares it holds in state owned companies. SOF was initially established by Law no.58/1991 but its status has recently been updated by the Emergency Ordinance no. 88/1997 and Law 99 of May 26, 1999" (Web page of Romanian State Ownership Fund, URL: http://www.sof.ro/fps/English/dfps.htm)

(s) *Slovak Republic:* National Property Fund,[46]

(t) *Slovenia:* Restructuring and Privatisation Agency,

(u) *Ukraine:* State Property Fund.[47]

C. Analysis

The smooth progress of privatisation requires that decision-making authority in the area is not be spread over a vast number of different institutions; such a wide spread could result both in institutional infighting and in increased transaction costs for the potential investor. Privatisation institutions should be accountable both to the executive branch and the parliament. Even where more than one privatisation institution exists, a clear-cut definition of their respective competencies is needed, in order to avoid unnecessary bottlenecks[48].

---

[45] The Russian Federal Property Fund operates under the Council of Ministers of the Russian Federation in the capacity of a specialised financial institution, carrying out legislation stipulated by the Russian Federation, with the functions of privatisation given to the Council as regulated by federal objectives. ("Regulations of the Russian Federal Property Fund," approved by Presidential Decree of the Russian Federation 2173 from December 17, 1993, web page of Russian Federal Property Fund, URL: http://www2.akm.ru/eng/rffi/rffi.htm). The Federal Stock Corporation was founded on the initiative of the Russian Federal Property Fund in December 1994. The Federal Stock Corporation is a general agent of the Russian Federal Property Fund, which, as the seller of property shares remaining in the state ownership..." (Web page of Federal Stock Corporation, URL: http://www.fe.msk.ru/infomarket/ffk/levnew1.html)

[46] The Fund is a legal entity established in 1991 pursuant to the Act of the National Council, No. 253/1991 Coll. on The Scope of Activities of the Bodies in the Slovak Republic in Terms of State Property transfer to Other Persons and on the National Property Fund of the Slovak Republic. The purpose of its existence and its main activity is to transfer the State property identified for privatisation to non-State entities. (Web page of National Property Fund, URL: http://www.natfund.gov.sk/english/)

In Slovakia, in November 1996, Slovakia's Supreme Court transferred responsibility for direct sales of state enterprises to the government, though previous sales remained valid. (National property Fund of Slovakia, URL: http//www.privatiz.gov.sk/; Web page of the World Bank, URL: http://www.worldbank.org)

[47] Ukrainian State Property Fund, URL: http://www.spfukraine.com/eng/strategic/index.htm

[48] Web page of the OECD, URL: http://www.oecd.org/

However, a highly fragmented decision-making structure could create institutional bottlenecks and confuse investors. Where more that one institution exists, an effective mechanism for policy co-ordination and conflict resolution need to be put in place

On the other hand according to some authors privatisation in Eastern Europe should be designed along simple, basic lines, avoiding the high-tech instruments of financial markets that are appropriate to advanced stages of capitalism since they have special circumstances. (Weitzman, p. 251)

A degree of independence in managing resources (including human) and the possibility of their rapid redeployment according to the actual policy implementation needs are essential factors of institutional efficiency in the context of a rapidly changing economic environment. [49]

Investors in a sector that is being privatised via a contract with the government are keenly interested in the enforcement aspects of their arrangement with the state. They will favour a neutral agency that has the human resources capacity to process the necessary information and the power to enforce without interference from a bureaucracy that may be politically motivated. The agency will need sufficient financial resources to attract skilled employees to evaluate and verify information from the regulated entity[50]

Finally, we must point out some privatisation laws provide rules on the supervision of the activities of the privatisation agencies. Regardless of the structure of the privatisation institution, law should provide some mechanisms to supervise its activities.[51]

---

[49] Web page of the OECD, URL: http://www.oecd.org/
[50] Gayle P. W. Jackson, "Government for Modern Markets", web page of Center for International Private Enterprise, URL: http://www.cipe.org/
[51] According to Latvian Privatisation Law: "Activities of the Privatisation Agency are supervised by the Supervisory Board appointed by the Cabinet of Ministers ...It includes also representatives recommended by the Parliament factions. The Minister supervising the privatisation of the state property is the state authorised representative in the Privatisation Agency, he performs functions assigned to the general meeting of the Privatisation Agency and he is the Chairman of the Supervisory Board. The Cabinet of Ministers appoints the director general of the Privatisation Agency on the recommendation of the Minister supervising the privatisation of the state property. Other state institutions also supervise the Privatisation Agency activities in compliance with the procedure stipulated by the law. (Article 9, The Republic of Latvia Saeima Law On Privatization of State and Municipal Asset Units, passed on 17.02. 1994 effective from 18 March 1994), [Web page of Latvian Privatisation Agency, URL: http://www.lpa.bkc.lv/PrivatLawGB.htm#B001_]

Similarly, Lithuanian Privatisation Law states that privatisation operation will be monitored and supervised by a committee. According to the law: "The Privatisation Commission is a government institution set up for the purpose of privatisation supervision and operating in accordance with this Law and the statutes approved by the Government". (Article 5/1, Law on the Privatisation of State-Owned and Municipal Property, 4 November 1997 No. VIII-480, Vilnius, web page of Lithuanian State Property Fund, URL: http://www.vtf.lt/en/frame22.html).

However, if there is a dispute between State Property Fund and Privatisation Committee, government shall take the final decision. ["If the Privatisation Commission decides to decline the draft programme or project...the Property Fund shall have the right to submit the draft decision for consideration to the Government which shall take the final decision..." (Article5/6)]

III. LEGAL FRAMEWORK for PRIVATISATION

A. Market Friendly Legal Environment[52]

When deciding on the location of their production activities investors first of all expect a country's legal system to provide certain qualities. These entail a guarantee of the market order itself, protection against political arbitrariness and enforceability of claims resulting from private contracts. In a market economy the state offers a legal system as a public good which is a prerequisite to the production of public goods. A market system can only work, if engaging in economic activities are guaranteed by law without any discrimination.[53]

A macro-legal environment conducive to private sector development must be clearly be in place for successful divestiture (privatisation). For example, if exists, discrimination against the private sector should be abolished.[54]

The existing legislation should be assessed in order to determine whether it enables and fosters the privatisation (divestiture) process under consideration. Such assessment would indicate whether the implementation of the proposed divestiture program can be done within the existing legal framework, or whether it should be modified to allow or facilitate privatisation.[55]

---

[52] In a market economy: (a) Economic arrangements arise out of voluntary and free exchange of value between individuals and/or firms. Values associated with exchanges of goods and services are set by supply and demand as registered in an uncontrolled price system. The claim to legitimacy is that both parties to transactions perceive benefit from the exchange. (b) Freedom of association for economic activity is established and guaranteed by law to individuals to form firms, co-operatives, unions and other forms of economic activity. (c) Freedom to own and exchange both personal property and the means of the production is guaranteed by law for all individuals regardless of socio-economic background. (d) Freedom of movement and information is guaranteed by law, (e) Free entry into and out of markets is guaranteed by law for individuals and firms. (f) Competition is maintained in markets as a function of a legal and regulatory system that prevents monopoly and/or collusion through restraint of trade, price fixing, government charters and other barriers. (g) The role of government is to regulate the creation and maintenance of the market system through establishment of objective laws (rules) that protect individuals and firms from corrupt practices. (John D. Sullivan, "Market Institutions and Democracy", web page of Center for International Private Enterprise, URL: http//www.cipe.org/)

[53] Schrader, p.260

[54] Mary M. Shirley, "Getting Bureaucrats Out of Business: Obstacles to State Enterprise Reform", web page of Center for International Private Enterprise, URL: http//www.cipe.org/; Guislain, (The World Bank), p.10
For Romanian case: Daianu, p.189-215

[55] Marek Hessel, "How Corporate Governance Makes Privatization Succeed", web page of Center for International Private Enterprise, URL: http//www.cipe.org/; Guislain, (The World Bank), p.10; Khan, p.32-37

Thus the development of legislation and enforcement of company code, rules on trade of ownership rights, bankruptcy legislation etc. often play important roles in influencing for the distribution of rights and thus for the development of corporate governance.[56]

As a summary, governments often take the appropriate legal measures to ensure that the legal system provides appropriate and sufficient measures for a market friendly environment. In other words legislation should provide the legal basis for the market friendly environment.

B. Property Law

Property rights are at the heart of the privatisation of state assets[57] and property laws are the cornerstone of any market economy and are normally protected by the country's constitution or constitutional tradition. Some constitutions or legal systems, the communist ones in particular, do not recognise the right to private property. Where this is the case, amendments to the constitution should be made to enable the whole privatisation (divestiture) process.[58]

The state can reduce uncertainties about the value of goods and services being exchanged by:
(a) Having a clear system of property rights; (b) Imposing standard measurements; (c) Devoting resources to sorting and grading; (d) Gathering and disseminating timely price data and encouraging competition to reduce asymmetries of information among parties to an exchange; and (e) Clarifying the laws. (Gayle P. W. Jackson, "Government for Modern Markets", web page of Center for International Private Enterprise, URL: http//www.cipe.org/)
For the steps taken in former socialist countries to create a market friendly environment see: Eva Voszka, "Privatization in Hungary: Results and Open Issues", web page of Center for International Private Enterprise, URL: http://www.cipe.org/; Tornell, p.18
One of the important issues to be addressed is the right of shareholders or investors in the privatised company. Each country should develop and provide its own approach by considering its economic, social circumstances and legal traditions. (Rafael La Porta, Florencio López-de-Silanes, Andrei Shleifer, and Robert Vishny, "Which Countries Give Investors the Best Protection?, Public Policy for the Private Sector, the Worldbank Group, Note No: 109, April 1997)
[56] Mygind, p.5
In that context, the most important institutions are as follows: (a) Competition on the product market, (b) Bankruptcy procedures, securing the take-over by creditors in case of default, (c) Legislation on registration, transfer, and enforcement of ownership rights, (d) The development of the financial system for supply of loans to enterprises, (e) The development of the stock exchange and a market for ownership of firms. [Mygind, p.27]
[57] Bruce A. Reznik, "Property Rights in a Market Economy", web page of Center for International Private Enterprise, URL: http://www.cipe.org/; Bornstein, p.237; Schrader, p.261
[58] Guislain, (The World Bank), p.11
In Poland provisions on property rights in the constitution were amended in 1989. (Ewa Baginska, "Legal Aspects of the Privatization Process in Poland", web page of Civic Education Project, URL: http//www.cep.org.hu/). Similarly, in Slovenia constitutional conditions for the property reform were created by a set of amendments to the constitution adopted in November 1988. (Mencinger, p.157)

Property legislation is important in all types of privatisation. Successful privatisation requires the ability to transfer free and clear property titles. In the preparation of a privatisation program, the legal analyst need to investigate how ownership and property rights are defined in the country concerned; how private ownership rights are recognised and protected[59]; what limits, if any, are placed on the transferability of such rights; how titling, registration mechanism function; what enforcement mechanisms exists to protect one's rights, including how effective the court system is; what limitations may apply to foreign ownership of certain types of property, such as land etc. Also to be investigated is the availability of proper mortgaging procedures or other collateral mechanisms, and related foreclosure systems.[60]

When the property regime in a country is not clear and property rights are not adequately protected, or where acquisition of property by foreigners or other groups is subject to restrictions, the divestiture legislation should attempt to remove these barriers.[61]

As we discussed above, privatisation requires well-defined ownership rights. However, ownership rights are not well defined in former socialist countries. For example, a particular problem is that land in many former socialist countries was not property of the firms, but

---

In some former socialist countries the property rights in some areas is highly controversial. For example, in Russia rights to private land ownership continue to be at the core of differences between Russia's reformers and conservative political parties. Reformers wish to unlock potential land wealth by constructing a private regime for control and use, while conservative forces argue that land resources must be kept under the tight control of the state. However, On March 7, 1996, Russian (former) president Boris Yeltsin issued a decree strengthening the rights of individuals to control and use agricultural land. (Leonard J. Rolfes, "The Struggle for Private Land Rights in Russia", web page of the Center for International Enterprise", URL: http://www.cipe.org/)

For state ownership and property rights in former socialist countries see: Major, p.8-15

Furthermore see: Richard L. Lesher, "Democracy's Promise: Building a Modern Economy", web page of Center for International Private Enterprise, URL: http//www.cipe.org/; Fischer, p.2; Alexander Stoyanov, "Economic Reform in Bulgaria", web page of Center for International Private Enterprise, URL: http://www.cipe.org/. [Stoyanov states that: "... To date experience of Bulgaria with the economic reform process supports the conclusions made in the other ex-socialist countries--the establishment of private property ownership has to be enhanced with an efficient institutional, (legal) and market arrangements."]

[59] Laws must be enforced to be effective. For this reason, a government should have institutions and mechanisms to protect private property. (Bruce A. Reznik, "Property Rights in a Market Economy", web page of Center for International Private Enterprise, URL: http://www.cipe.org/)

[60] Guislain, (The World Bank), p.11; Legal Aspects of Privatization, p.15-17

For example, in the case of mass privatisation, in the absence of transparent and enforceable property rights, the role of the various shareholders in future ownership decisions will remain uncertain for some time to time. (Lieberman, Ewing, Mejstrik, Mukherjee and Fidler, p.39)

183

remained property of the state, so that as a first step the Treasury must sell or somehow transfer the land on which the factory or firm is operating.[62]

C. Future Expropriations

Entrepreneurs are less likely to invest in countries where their assets may be subject to expropriation or where contracts are not enforced. Businesses' perceptions of the risk of government expropriation and contract repudiation are strongly correlated with economic growth.[63] Therefore, investors may require guarantees against re-nationalisation before committing themselves financially.[64]

D. Intellectual Property

In our increasingly global economy, intellectual property --patents, trademarks and copyrights--has become a valuable and increasingly prominent asset.[65]

Investment decisions, whether by foreigners or nationals, are conditioned by the existence and effective enforcement of intellectual property laws protecting the owners' property rights. The legal framework for intellectual property protection typically includes international agreements to which the country has adhered as well as national laws dealing with patents, trademarks, copyright, trade secrets, know -how and licensing.[66]

---

[61] Guislain, (The World Bank), p.11
See also p. 330-348
[62] Paul J.J., "Privatization and Foreign Direct Investment in the East European Transformation: Theory, Options and Strategies", Privatization, Liberalization and Destruction-Recreating the Market in Central and Eastern Europe, Edited By: László Csaba, Dartmouth Publishing Company Limited, England & USA, 1994, p. 38
[63] Deborah Bräutigam, "Managing Economic Reform in New Democracies", web page of Center for International Private Enterprise, URL: http//www.cipe.org/
[64] Guislain, (The World Bank), p.14
In some countries, for example in Bulgaria, legislation provides that foreign investments are protected against expropriation. (Daniela Bobeva and Aexander Bozhkov, "Privatisation and Foreign Investments in Bulgaria", Privatisation and Foreign Investments in Eastern Europe, Edited By: Iliana Zloch-Christy, USA, 1995, p.151)
[65] Bruce A. Reznik, "Property Rights in a Market Economy", web page of Center for International Private Enterprise, URL: http//www.cipe.org/
[66] Guislain, (The World Bank), p.14

E. Price Liberalisation

Free and autonomous price setting by firms is essential for the functioning of a competitive market economy. In addition regulations may be needed to prevent or sanction abuses. Price liberalisation legislation should precede privatisation, in particular in countries with heavy government controls on prices. Without the freedom to set prices, few investors would be interested in buying SOEs.[67]

F. Business Legislation

1. General

General business legislation is highly relevant to divestiture (privatisation). First, the applicability of ordinary corporate laws to the privatisation transactions envisaged needs to be checked. In this context, liquidation, insolvency, bankruptcy, and capital market legislation are particularly relevant. Second, some of the laws reviewed may need to be amended, suspended or abrogated in order to enable or facilitate privatisation. Third, the nature and investor-friendliness of a country's business law is a determinant of investment, foreign as well as domestic. A sound legal framework for business activity is bound to facilitate the divestiture process and increase its changes for success.[68]

---

[67] Hossain, p.214; Guislain, (The World Bank), p.15
See: p. 145-155 on regulation and privatisation
In the case of former socialist countries, most countries entered the transition process with a monetary overhang and the need for price liberalisation. [Stanley Fischer and Ratna Sahay, "The Transition Economies After Ten Years", IMF (International Monetary Fund), Working Paper 7664, Cambridge, February 2000, p.6, URL: http://www.nber.org/papers/w7664]
In Slovakia, since 1989, significant changes have taken place in the Slovak economy. Price liberalisation and the elimination of barriers to international trade imposed market values on goods and services and exposed market participants to external competition. (Andrej Juris, "Economic Reform in Slovakia" web page of Center for International Private Enterprise, URL: http://www.cipe.org/; Alexander Stoyanov, "Economic Reform in Bulgaria", web page of Center for International Private Enterprise, URL: http://www.cipe.org/)
Furthermore see: Tatiana Houbenova-Dellisivkova, "Liberalisation and Transformation in Bulgaria", Privatisation, Liberalization and Destruction-Recreating the Market in Central and Eastern Europe, Edited By: László Csaba, Dartmouth Publishing Company Limited, England & USA, 1994, p.218

[68] Guislain, (The World Bank), p.19

2. Contract Law

Contract law and enforcement mechanisms for private contracts are a cornerstone of the legal framework for a market economy regulating the way in which property rights are transferred.[69]

The legal system must also guarantee the liberty of private contracting which constitutes the essence of a market order. A sanction mechanism is necessary to enforce contractual fidelity.[70]

A contract law is therefore is essential to deal with the following: (a) When has a contract come into existence? (b) What are the terms of contract? (c) When has a breach occurred? (d) What remedies are available to the innocent party? (e) What measure of damages should be given?, (f) Does the innocent party have a duty to mitigate his loss? (g) Will the courts uphold penalty clauses in contracts which provide for a specific sum to be paid in damages for breach?[71]

Some former socialist countries have been taking steps to modify their business legislations. (For Bulgarian case see: Alexander Stoyanov, "Economic Reform in Bulgaria", web page of Center for International Private Enterprise, URL: http//www.cipe.org/)

For example, in Estonia, after enacting the Privatisation Law, another important step was the passing of the legal acts regulating the Estonian securities market in the years 1993 and 1994 (Law on Securities Market, the procedural rules of the public selling of shares, Law on Commercial Trade of Vouchers, etc.). These legal acts made starting the public selling of shares for vouchers possible during the last quarter of 1994. (Estonian Privatisation Agency, URL: http://www.eea.ee/)

A properly functioning autonomous commercial banking system is critical to private sector development. Effective banking systems are needed to allow domestic investors to leverage their purchases and enable local and foreign investors to finance future working capital requirements domestically. In addition, a broad range of financial sector laws, including sureties, credit, leasing and insurance, may also affect the success of the privatisation program. [Guislain, (The World Bank), p.27; Alexander Stoyanov, "Economic Reform in Bulgaria", web page of Center for International Private Enterprise, URL: http//www.cipe.org/]

[69] Guislain, (The World Bank), p.19
[70] Schrader, p.260
[71] Legal Aspects of Privatization, p.23

3. Company law

Company laws typically set the basic rules for the establishment, incorporation, management, operation and liquidation of companies. Many company laws are overly cumbersome, and may need to be amended to allow the expedient setting up of a company.[72]

In the case of the privatisation by the state of its holdings in a joint venture company with private shareholders, company law and company bylaws would often grant the other shareholders the right to approve any transfer of shares to non-shareholders or even a right of first refusal (pre-emptive rights). Where this is the case, the government may first wish to consult with other shareholders to explore various alternatives for restructuring and/or privatisation. Alternatively, where the risk exists that minority shareholders could block the implementation of the privatisations, some privatisation laws have included a special derogation from normal company law. Such provisions should normally be avoided, however, as they amount to a unilateral modification by the state of a commercial agreement it had entered into with other parties.[73]

Attention should also be paid to rules pertaining to the creation, operation and sale of subsidiaries, affiliates and branches. This is important for a number of reasons, including (i) the proliferation in many countries of subsidiaries of SOEs, which are most often subject to ordinary company law; (i) the existence in a large number of countries of state holding companies which are the legal owners of many SOEs; and (iii) the fact that many private buyers of SOEs are existing corporations that may want to organise the acquired company as a subsidiary.[74]

---

[72] Guislain, (The World Bank), p.20; Legal Aspects of Privatization, p.20-22
[73] Guislain, (The World Bank), p.20
[74] Guislain, (The World Bank), p.20

4. Accounting and Auditing Legislation

For privatisation potential buyers may not be overly concerned with the SOE's financial accounts, but more with a precise status of its assets and liabilities. Where buyers are to take a large stake in the company, they will want to have the opportunity to carry out a through audit of the company's financial situation and would typically place little faith in the SOE's official accounts, either because of poor accounting regulations in the country, lack of familiarity with the accounting standards of the country or poor records and accounting within the SOE.[75]

Legally, enforceable accounting rules generally accepted international accounting principles often greatly improve the prospects for a successful divestiture program by creating greater transparency and certainty, hence reducing risk.[76]

5. Liquidation and bankruptcy

Liquidation and bankruptcy are critical exit mechanisms, which allow under-performing enterprises to be wound up, hence freeing resources up for more productive uses. They are also often used as privatisation mechanisms.[77]

One should check whether commercial liquidation, bankruptcy and insolvency laws apply to SOEs or not. Where such laws do apply, one would have to ascertain whether the

---

[75] In the case of a public flotation, however, individual investors would not have the opportunity or resources to personally investigate company operations, including accounts. Such investors need to rely on financial statements audited and certified by reputable and independent auditors. Furthermore, such audits should be a prerequisite for listing the company's shares on a stock exchange. [Guislain, (The World Bank), p.21]
In that context, former socialist countries have taken steps to enact new laws on auditing. In Lithuania, a law on investment companies was passed on July 1995, strengthening the regulation on auditing. [Niels Mygind, "Privatisation, Governance and Restructuring of Enterprises in the Baltics, Baltic Regional Programme," Organisation for Economic Co-operation and Development (OECD), Paris, April/May 2000, p.21]

[76] Guislain, (The World Bank), p.22

[77] Guislain, (The World Bank), p.22, Tornell p.19
Bankruptcy regulations are important because they bear directly on issues of firm management, shareholder monitoring, and employment. (John Waterbury, "Deregulating the Economy: A Key Second Generation Reform", web page of Center for International Private Enterprise, URL: http//www.cipe.org/)

existing legal provisions are adequate to deal with the expected SOE liquidations, particularly with respect to the protection of SOE creditors. [78]

6. Transfer of Liabilities

As in many instances, SOEs would not be attractive take-over targets with their existing debts and liabilities, many governments have released them from such obligations either at the stage of prior corporatisation of the SOE, or of negotiation of the divestiture transaction with the interested bidders. [79]

Most legal systems have specific rules regarding transfer of debts and obligations (including contingent liabilities, such as those resulting from on-going or potential litigation). In civil law countries, a transfer of liability would be subject to the creditors' approval. Without such approval, the original debtor would remain liable.[80]

Some privatisation law provides that the privatised company is the legal successor of the previous state owned enterprise (SOE). For example final paragraph of article 7 of Law on Transformation of Socially Owned Enterprises of Macedonia states that: "… The company(ies) [that has been transformed into joint stock or limited liability companies under privatisation scheme]… shall be the legal successor of the transformed enterprise."[81]

---

[78] Guislain, (The World Bank), p.22; Legal Aspects of Privatization, p.24
Former socialist countries have been taking steps to enact new laws. For example, the legislation on bankruptcy procedures was developed quite early in Estonia, September 1992. The law was strictly enforced so already by 1995 more than 1000 bankruptcy procedures had been implemented. However, this is not the case in Latvia and Lithuania. In these two countries, bankruptcy laws were passed in 1992, but the implementation was relatively weak. The legislation has been strengthened in Latvia in 1996 and in Lithuania in 1997 and the implementation has been tightened in the latest years. [Mygind, p.27]
For Russian case see: Malle, p.75
[79] Guislain, (The World Bank), p.24
[80] Guislain, (The World Bank), p.24
[81] For the full text of Macedonian Privatisation law see the web page of Macedonian Privatisation Agency, URL: http://www.mpa.org.mk
Furthermore according to Latvian Privatisation Law provides that: "…the purchase agreement and deed of transfer, the new owner of the unit undertakes all liabilities of the unit in privatisation to the amount prescribed by the Privatisation Agency or municipality, and he shall comply with them pursuant to the procedure prescribed by the Law and the agreement. (Article 53/3, The Republic of Latvia Law on Privatisation of State and Municipal Asset Units, passed on 17.02. 1994, web page of Latvian Privatisation Agency, URL: http//www.lpa.bkc.lv/)

G. Environmental Legislation[82]

One of the important aspects of privatisation legislation is environmental legislation. Thus investors are particularly concerned about the environmental obligations of the state-owned company they are acquiring, because in most cases the transformed company assumes all the rights and duties of the state-owned enterprise from which it was formed.[83]

Therefore in general, interested buyers need to know the extent of their liability for environmental damage or violations of environmental legislation due to the former SOE. If liable, they may want to negotiate of ceiling of liability above which they would be compensated by the state. If the new owners are not liable, will the state assume responsibility? If SOE facilities do not conform to environmental regulations, will exemptions be granted or will the buyer be given a certain time period to comply? Who bears the cleaning up costs incurred in bringing a factory or land up to environmental standards?[84] Governments need to establish clear policies on assignment of environmental risk.[85]

All these questions may find an answer in the country's environmental or privatisation laws, or upon which the parties to a divestiture transaction may agree in their contractual

---

Finally Turkish Privatisation Law states that: "With respect to organisations in the scope of the privatisation program: All kinds of rights, benefit and obligations belonging to and/or at the disposition of organisations prior to their inclusion in the scope of the privatisation program shall survive after their inclusion into the program and even after their privatisation. If an enterprise, operations or operational units are independently transformed to a joint-stock company, the Administration shall decide which rights and obligations of their parent will be transferred to the new joint-stock company..." [Article 20/B, "Law Concerning Privatisation and Regulation of Implementations of Privatisation and Amendment to Certain Laws and Statutory decrees, Law Nr.4046, Date of Passage: 24 November 1994, Official Gazette Nr. 22124, Date of official Gazette: 27. 11. 1994 (Privatisation Law), web page of Turkish Privatisation Administration, URL: http://www.oib.gov.tr]

[82] One of the issues in the privatisation transactions is the environmental law problems. Many SOEs have significant potential liabilities that need to be addressed prior to sale, this issue particularly common in Eastern Europe. (The Lessons of Experience, p.35; Malbon, p.29-31)

[83] Susan S. Cummings "Privatisation and the Environment in Poland: The Impact of Environmental Contamination and Potential Obligations on Polish Privatisation Transactions", URL: http://www.feem.it/feem/notifeem/294/5.html

[84] Guislain, (The World Bank), p.25

[85] Susan L. Rutledge, Selling State Companies to Strategic Investors-Trade Sale Privatizations in Poland, Hungary, the Czech Republic, and the Slovak Republic, Volume One, Analysis of Issues, The World Bank, January 1995, p.3; Legal Aspects of Privatization, p.17, 18

documents. Also potential buyers will be interested in new environmental regulations that could effect their future obligations.[86]

H. Tax Law and taxation

Prior to a privatisation, it is quite common that tax policies evolve in such a way to offset the advantage that untaxed state-owned companies have in competition with taxable investor-owned companies. If a company is to be privatised, how would tax policy be applied on the new entity compared to its competitors? Will the tax policies affecting the industry need to be revised in light of the privatisation?[87]

Amongst many factors that influence the price at which the company is sold, an important variable to determine is the tax burden of the company. If sellers and buyers overestimate the amount of taxes to be paid after the privatisation, the price of the company will be too low. The converse will hold when the taxes are underestimated. Thus, it is very important for governments and investors to know the prevailing tax regime affecting the company after privatisation.[88]

Usually, a state-owned company is not responsible to pay company taxes and certain indirect taxes, such as capital and property taxes. When the company is privatised, the company must then be subject to new forms of taxes that were previously not levied on the state-owned

---

[86] Bruce D. Cowen and Kathryn R. Braithwaite, "Economy vs. Environment: Striving for Equilibrium", web page of Center for International Private Enterprise, URL: http://www.cipe.org/; Bruce D. Cowen and Kathryn R. Braithwaite, "Economy vs. Environment: Striving for Equilibrium", web page of Center for International Private Enterprise, URL: http://www.cipe.org/; Guislain, (The World Bank), p.25; John Waterbury, Deregulating the Economy: A Key Second Generation Reform, web page of Center for International Private Enterprise, URL: http//www.cipe.org/
Some authors argue that state-owned factories often pollute more than privately owned factories. (Mary M. Shirley, "Getting Bureaucrats Out of Business: Obstacles to State Enterprise Reform", web page of Center for International Private Enterprise, URL: http://www.cipe.org/)

[87] Jack M. Mintz, Duanjie Chen and Evangelia Zorotheos, "Taxing Issues with Privatisation: A Checklist, International Tax Program", Institute of International Business, University of Toronto, p.2, URL: http://www.worldbank.org/; Legal Aspects of Privatization, p.26-28

[88] Mintz, Chen and Zorotheos, p.2

firm:[89] Issues of particular concern to investors and potential buyers are the overall fiscal pressure on enterprises and the predictability of tax administration and enforcement. Businesses should be able to determine what the applicable taxes are and estimate the amount of taxes that will be due.[90]

Tax laws need to be applied uniformly to private as well as public enterprises. Any tax benefits granted to SOEs in the competitive sector of the economy need to be removed.[91] Finally, some governments have granted special tax benefits to privatisation transactions, either pursuant to the country's investment code or to special provisions in the privatisation law.[92]

---

[89] Mintz, Chen and Zorotheos, p.2

[90] In former socialist countries one of the most substantial achievements of the economic reform process is the restructuring of the tax system. New market-oriented taxes have been introduced and some others are undergoing changes (the income, municipal and corporate taxes). [Alexander Stoyanov, "Economic Reform in Bulgaria", web page of Center for International Private Enterprise, URL: http://www.cipe.org/. According to Stoyanov: " The experience of the developed market economies support the necessity of equal and non-preferential treatment of the economic agents as opposed to generous tax allowances."]
Also see: Guislain, (The World Bank), p.29

[91] In reality, a state-owned company will lose its non-taxable privilege once being privatised. (Mintz, Chen and Zorotheos, p.2)

[92] Guislain, (The World Bank), p.29
Thus Turkish privatisation Law provides that: "...Transactions in respect to the privatisation process under the provisions of this law (including contracts) are exempt from all taxes, duties and fees with the exception of the Value Added Tax..." (Article 27) [Turkish Privatisation Law, web page of Turkish Privatisation Administration, URL: http://www.oib.gov.tr]
Some countries, like Russia, have been taking steps to reform their tax legislation in order to implement the privatisation process and create the legal environment for the market economy. [Alexander Chesnokov, "Transition of the State: Key Economic Issues, Speech in the conference Strategy for Reform: Seven Years After the Break-up, Moscow, September 14-16, 1998, web page of Center for International Private Enterprise, URL: http//www.cipe.org/; Alexander Chesnokov, "A Business View of Russia's Economy", an address to the Center for International Private Enterprise Board of Directors at the U.S. Chamber of Commerce in Washington, DC, on April 6, 1999, web page of Center for International Private Enterprise, URL: http//www.cipe.org/].
"...Russia must simplify its taxation rules and reduce the tax burden. Only then will we see real economic growth and more revenues..." ["Safeguarding Russian Investors: Securities Chief Speaks Out", interview with Dmitry Vasiliyev, (former) Chairman of the Federal Commission for the Securities Market in Russia], web page of Center for International Private Enterprise, URL: http//www.cipe.org/].
Furthermore, other former socialist countries like Albania should take further steps in its tax legislation to implement the privatisation programme and other economic reforms successfully. (Konstandin Kristo, "Economic Reform in Albania", web page of Center for International Private Enterprise, URL: http://www.cipe.org/).
For steps in other countries see: Maciej Grabowski, "Economic Reform in Poland", Economic Reform Today Working Papers, Number 4, web page of Center for International Private Enterprise, URL: http//www.cipe.org/; Ion Anton, Economic reform in Romania, Economic Reform Today, Working Papers, Number 1, web page of Center for International Private Enterprise, URL: http//www.cipe.org/

192

I. Currency and Foreign Exchange

A necessary element of foreign trade liberalisation is the free convertibility of the national currency and unrestricted private currency transactions.[93]

The currency and foreign exchange regime will affect the privatisation process, in particular when the selling government wants to attract foreign investors. By and large, restrictions on allocation, availability, convertibility, repatriation, registration, or other uses of foreign exchange will hamper efforts to attract foreign investors. In countries without stable convertible currency, restrictions on domestic payment in foreign exchange, in particular payment of expatriate staff, domestic suppliers and payments by clients, would be of some concern too.[94]

J. Dispute Settlement

Private investors would not only want to know which rules will be applicable to privatisation process but also want to learn the rules in case of a dispute occurs between them and the government. Privatisation legislation often provides rules on the procedure for the settlement of disputes.[95]

---

[93] Schrader, p.267
[94] Fischer and Sahay, p.7; Guislain, (The World Bank), p.30

Lithuanian Case: Currency reform began in May 1992 with the introduction of a transitional currency. This was replaced by a new currency, the Litas, which entered circulation on 25 June 1993. The Litas was made the country's sole legal tender on 20 July 1993, and settlement in convertible currency was prohibited as from 1 August 1993. In 1994 the Government sought to strengthen its stabilisation policies by creating an independent Currency Board with responsibility for monetary emission. Under a Currency Board system the amount of currency in circulation is strictly tied to the foreign currency and gold reserves. The objective was to insulate the monetary authorities from political pressure to relax monetary discipline and to reflate the economy. However, real appreciation of the exchange rate contributed to a rapidly worsening foreign trade deficit during 1996. As a result, the coalition Government formed after the parliamentary elections in November 1996 announced that it intended to abolish the Currency Board and allow the currency to float. During a transitional period the Litas will be pegged to a basket of currencies made up of the US Dollar and EURO. (Lithuanian Business Information Centre, URL: http://www.lbic.lt)

For other former socialist countries see: Maria Prohaska, "Privatization in Bulgaria: Pushing Forward", web page of Center for International Private Enterprise, URL: http//www.cipe.org/; Hrncir, p.168; Houbenova-Dellisivkova, p.219, 220

[95] According to Lithuanian Privatisation Law: "Disputes shall be settled according to the procedure established by laws of the Republic of Lithuania, international treaties of the Republic of Lithuania, and the

Litigation can very costly and time-consuming. The functioning of a country's court system is an essential, though often overlooked, part of any legal framework for business activity. Potential investors will be interested in the competence and independence of the court system, in its accessibility and efficiency, as well as in the possibility to settle out-of-court. Indeed, conflicts arising out of contracts with local labour, banks, suppliers and clients will typically be submitted to the jurisdiction of the local courts.[96]

IV. PRIVATISATION LAW

A. General

The legal and political situation and the specific characteristics of the enterprise to be privatised determines whether or not a country needs to enact a privatisation law; these elements including the goals of the privatisation programme also determine the structure of the privatisation legislation. In other words, a country's constitution, legislation or legal traditions in

---

privatisation transaction." [Article 23, Law on the Privatisation of State-Owned and Municipal Property, 4 November 1997 No. VIII-480, Vilnius, web page of Lithuanian State Property Fund, URL: http://www.vtf.lt/en/frame22.html]

For many reasons (unstable legislation system, slow judicial process etc) particularly foreign investors may require "private arbitration" instead of normal judicial view. In Turkey, constitution has been modified to allow foreign investors to ask for private arbitration in case there is a dispute with the government. (Web page of Turkish parliament, URL: http//www.tbbm.gov.tr/)

[96] Guislain, (The World Bank), p.30

In Turkey, the Turkish Parliament amended the Turkish Constitution in 1999 to provide for privatisation and international arbitration. It is hoped that these changes will positively affect energy (power), telecommunications and other infrastructure projects such as highways, bridges, tube tunnels, airport terminals, ports, etc. (Web page of US Commercial Service Turkey, URL: http://www.csturkey.com/)

In that context:

Article 47 of the Turkish Constitution was amended to provide for principles and methods of privatisation to be defined by law. The law will also determine which state enterprises will be privatised.

Article 125 of the Turkish Constitution was amended to allow for settling disputes by national or international arbitration. International arbitration will be applicable to disputes involving a foreign entity. ["...National or international arbitration may be suggested to settle the disagreements that arise from conditions and contracts under which concessions are granted concerning public services. International arbitration can only be applied in the case of the disagreements which involve foreign components..."(Article 125)]

Article 155 of the Turkish Constitution was amended to limit the participation of the Council of State (Danistay) in contracting. The new provisions give Danistay the right to review cases and draft regulations and give opinions. Danistay will also be able to settle administrative disputes. These powers are less than before the amendments.

Finally we should point out that the Turkish Parliament will have to pass separate enabling laws to specify which public services will be privatised. They will also need new laws on the application of the international arbitration provisions. (Web page of Turkish Parliament, URL: http//www.tbmm.gov.tr; web page of US Department of Energy, URL: http://www.fe.doe.gov)

effect may allow the government or other public bodies to divest without special recourse to the legislative branch. In this case, no enabling legislation is required from a legal point of view.[97] In other words, in some countries, the government does not need any special enabling legislation to privatise, either because constitutional principles do not require a law or because SOE (state owned enterprise) legislation or other laws provide the necessary legal framework to implement the privatisation transaction.[98]

However, in some other countries constitutions may require a "law" to implement the privatisation transactions. For example, article 47 of the Turkish constitution that was amended in 1999 states that:

"...The rules and regulations concerning privatisation of the assets and enterprises that are owned by the state, state economic enterprises or other public corporations are prescribed by law. Which of the investments or services that are carried out by the state, state economic enterprises or other public corporations may be performed by or delegated to real or corporate body through private law contracts are prescribed by law."[99]

Similarly article 34 of the French Constitution sets out exhaustively the subjects on which the parliament may pass legislation in the form of law. These include "the nationalisation of enterprises and transfers of the property of enterprises from the public to the private sector.[100]

---

[97] Guislain, (The World Bank), p.34
[98] Guislain, (The Privatization Challenge), p.111
Sometimes it is possible a country to implement its privatisation programme without any special law, either because the constitution and the legislation in force do not require such a law or because the government has been able to devise appropriate solutions that do not call for changes in existing legislation.
However, a law even it's not required legally required, may be useful or necessary to protect the government politically, to establish or cement a consensus between political forces, to impart a certain degree of stability to the new policy, or to render more difficult any reversal of approach by the future government. [Guislain, (The Privatization Challenge), p.145]
[99] For a full text of Turkish Constitution in English see the web page of Turkish Parliament at, URL: http://www.tbmm.gov.tr/
[100] Prosser, (Constitutions and Political Economy), p.306; Guislain, (The World Bank), p.34

Finally, in some cases, although (a) a law is not required by constitution or (b) there is already appropriate and sufficient legislation to cover the whole privatisation process a country may enact a separate privatisation law for various considerations (such as to clarify the privatisation process in terms of methods and relevant authorities, to show the high commitment of the government etc.). Finally privatisation law may prevent any confusion between privatisation authorities.

B. Scope and Structure of the Privatisation Law

1. General

The content of privatisation legislation may vary substantially. The core elements of privatisation legislation, namely, the enabling provisions authorising and organising the privatisation process, are handled very differently from one law to another. To determine which privatisation provisions should be left to the discretion of the parties involved and which should be included in the privatisation law, in implementing decrees or regulations, in decisions of the competent authority will depend partly on the country's constitutional, legal, and political system and traditions and partly on current political concerns, notably the degree of confidence parliament places in the government.[101]

Where privatisation legislation is required, it may be preferable to limit the provisions of the law to broad principles and leave the details and modalities of its application to subordinate instruments or decisions. In that case, there is no universal legal shape, however, to determine which privatisation provisions should be left to the discretion of the parties involved and which should be included in the privatisation law, in implementing decrees or regulations, in decisions

---

[101] For privatisation laws of different countries see: URL: http://www.privatizationlink.com/
Guislain, (The Privatization Challenge), p.111, 113, 114
For example, because the legal and political conditions vary from country to country, there is no generally accepted definition of an SOE.

of the competent authority (for example, the minister of finance or the chairman of the privatisation agency) or in general guidelines.[102]

When it comes to decide the structure and contest of the privatisation law, flexibility is an important issue. A flexible legal framework will allow the government and the responsible agencies to adjust their methods to chancing circumstances. A rigid framework, in contrast, would very probably slow the pace, impose ineffective methods, and compel the government to go back to parliament to obtain amendments to the law. However flexibility must not be confused with ambiguity. The privatisation law must be clearly worded, especially with the respect to delegation of powers, responsibilities of the various parties involved, scope of the mandate, minimum requirements for transparency and competitiveness of selling procedures, selection criteria, benefits accorded to specific categories of buyers, resources made available to the executing agencies, allocation of privatisation proceeds, and controls that will be applied to privatisation officials.[103]

Some aspects of the privatisation process, though essential from a strategic point of view- speed, timing, or the choice of a privatisation technique- should normally not be regulated by law in a detailed form.

Governments might impose certain conditions in the privatisation contract or they might require certain post privatisation commitments from the new investors such as a specific investment commitment or keeping the existing work force for a stated period.[104]

---

[102] Guislain, (The Privatization Challenge), p.112, 114
[103] Guislain, (The Privatization Challenge), p.146
The Privatisation Law often provides clear provisions for the terms and concept in the privatisation process. Some countries like Bulgaria had some difficulties since the Privatisation Law has not provided clear definition for some concepts like "small scale privatisation" and "potential buyer". (Maria Prohaska, "Bulgarian Privatisation Results", web page of Center for International Private Enterprise, URL: http//www.cipe.org/). Similar problems arised also in Lithuania. (Lithuanian Business Information Centre, URL: http//www.lbic.lt)
[104] For example according to Lithuanian Privatisation Law: "A privatisation transaction concluded in the manner prescribed by a public tender or direct negotiations may include the obligations of a buyer (buyers) to preserve the number of jobs, to invest in the enterprise controlled by the state (municipality) the shares whereof are being sold, or into other spheres of Lithuanian economy." [Article 21/4, Law on the Privatisation of State-Owned

The privatisation legislation must provide for sanctions against the buyer in proportion to the damage caused should he default on the obligations, including termination or annulment of the privatisation transaction in the event of non-compliance with the terms, obligations and/or guarantees (a guarantor who will pay damages to the state or municipality shall be indicated) set forth in the privatisation transaction; the contract must also provide for the liability of the holder of the privatisation object for default on the assumed obligations.[105]

2. Main Factors in the Privatisation Law

The content and structure of the privatisation law, the choice of the legal instrument including the methods of the privatisation process to be used will depend on several other factors, such as the objective to be promoted, customised and flexible approaches as opposed to be standardised and uniform ones, centralisation of the process. These choices and decisions will have to be made at the start of the process, as they will largely determine the design of the legal framework for privatisation. In other words, legal structure for privatisation legislation is influenced by various factors[106]:

(a) The *goals* of the privatisation process[107]: The chosen objectives have significant implications not only on the choice and structuring of legal instruments and modalities, but also on the pre-divestiture (privatisation) measures that need to be taken. In analysing the legal aspects of privatisation, one always has to go back to the objectives of privatisation.[108]

---

and Municipal Property, 4 November 1997 No. VIII-480, Vilnius, web page of Lithuanian State Property Fund, URL: http//www. http://www.vtf.lt/en/frame22.html]
[105] Article 21/4, Law on the Privatisation of State-Owned and Municipal Property, 4 November 1997 No. VIII-480, Vilnius, web page of Lithuanian State Property Fund, URL: http://www.vtf.lt/en/frame22.html
[106] Redwood, (A Consultant's Perspective), p.48; Guislain, (The Privatization Challenge), p.114
[107] Wright, p.40
[108] Guislain, (The World Bank), p.3, 5

(b) The *economic situation* and particularly the lack or the abundance of capital in the country concerned:[109] Legal and economic issues are closely intertwined in privatisation.[110]

(c) The *financial systems* through which the transfer of ownership to private investors is carried out.[111] For example, in countries with non-convertible currencies, it is in general easier to sell an SOE with the foreign exchange earnings than one with local currency revenue only.[112]

(d) The structure of the *existing legislation*[113] and legal system of the country, including whether a written constitution exists or not:[114]

In that context, the legal status of SOE to be divested varies greatly and affects the choice of techniques of privatisation.[115] In many cases, the SOE may need to be restructured (corporatised) if it is to be sold as a legal entity.

The specific laws and regulations affecting SOEs in general, and enterprises to be privatised in particular, also need to be checked, as some may need to be repealed or amended.

---

[109] The lack of capital has serious consequences on choosing legal instruments as it can be observed in Central and Eastern European countries. (Attila Harmathy, "General Report 2", Legal Aspects of Privatisation, XXIst Colloquy on European Law, Budapest, 15-17 October 1991, Council of Europe Press, 1993, p.212; Andic, p.35)
Market structures also affect the content of the privatisation law. This point makes differences particularly in ex-socialist countries.

[110] Guislain, (The World Bank), p.6

[111] Wright, p.40

[112] Guislain, (The World Bank), p.6

[113] The level of development and characteristic of other branches of law can have an influence on legal instruments of privatisation as well. So the low level of administrative and commercial law can be one of the reasons why a market-concentrated way of privatisation is accepted in some countries, while in other countries the high level of administrative law solutions and practice will mean at least a temptation for opting for an administrative law method.

[114] If a written constitution exists, the following points should be considered as well:
-the principles set by the constitution on the privatisation itself and/or economic activities,
-the structure of the constitution (whether it is flexible or non-flexible).
For example in the UK there is no written constitution. The British constitution is a mixture of legislation, case law, conventions and informal practices. The result of this system is that legal constraints on the government's privatisation programme have been minimal. (Graham, p.185-187)

[115] Some privatisation laws provide a definition for the state owned enterprises. For example, according to article 2 of Slovakian Privatisation Law: "For the purposes of this act, the property of the enterprise shall be defined as the sum of assets and financial means to which the enterprise has either management or ownership rights, as well as the sum of other relevant rights, proprietary valuables, and liabilities of the enterprise." (The Act No.92/1991, dated February 26, 1991 on the Conditions of Transfer of State Property to Other Persons, web page of Ministry for Administration and Privatisation of National Property of the Slovak Republic, URL: http://www.privatiz.gov.sk/anglicky/act92.htm)

Amendments to SOE legislation required for the purposes of divestiture may be broken down in two categories, namely those needed (i) to enable the divestiture, for example to give the government the power to sell the enterprise, or (ii) to put the SOE on a proper commercial footing prior to its privatisation.[116]

(e) *Traditions* (including political) of the country concerned. For example, in Britain, some laws had to be enacted to implement the privatisation process. However, since a written constitution does not exist, and legal traditions are important, from the constitutional point of view a privatisation law is not needed and required "to authorise" the government for privatisation transactions.

(f) *The political and institutional opportunity structures* in which the private companies operate, including the stability and structure of executive power, the nature of their respective party political systems, the degree of centralisation of political and industrial power, the structure of policy networks, and the prevailing styles of policy-making (political situation and system of the country);[117]

(g) *The technical ease* with which privatisation of the industry may be pursued;[118]

(h) *Size of the enterprise*: Legal issues vary great deal depending on whether the government is divesting a small restaurant or grocery store, the national telephone company or a major cement plant, for example.[119] All Eastern Europen privatisation programmes have special rules for the privatisation of small enterprises, such as retail stores, hotels, restaurants, gasoline

---

[116] Guislain, (The World Bank), p.36
[117] Wright, p.40
In the coalitions, the structure of the law is determined by all parties in the government.
Political scientists analysing privatisation practices of Western European countries have pointed out that political objectives have had important effects on the method of privatisation. Economic factors are obviously decisive in privatisation. (Wright, p.39)
[118] Wright, p.40
[119] Guislain, (The World Bank), p.8

stations, small service enterprises and accordingly, they have faced a strong domestic demand in all Eastern European countries.[120]

3. Analysis

Among the above-mentioned factors, political and economic elements are considered to be the most important, and some political scientists particularly emphasise the decisive role of politics in privatisation.[121]

Because of the reasons and factors set above, each country has its own measure in enacting laws about privatisation.[122]

---

[120] In other words, in former socialist procedure of privatisation varies depending on the size of the state owned enterprises. These countries adopted different provisions for (a) small and medium scale enterprises and (b) large-scale enterprises. In most cases, privatisation law provides different rules on these two groups of enterprises. For example Czech privatization has proceeded on several fronts. In this country, according to the size of the enterprises (small, medium, large) different measures have been taken. In the early years of the transition the small or medium scale enterprises have been privatised. (Jan Hanousek and Eugene A. Kroch, "A Model of Learning in Sequential Bidding: Voucher Privatization in the Czech Republic: Wave I", January 1995, URL: http//www.ssc.upenn.edu/~alexv/cast/february/jan.html)

Similarly, from the size of the enterprise point of view, privatisation in Latvia, Estonia and Lithuania may be divided in the two stages: Small privatisation and large privatisation. [For the case of these Baltic countries see: Niels Mygind, "Privatisation, Governance and Restructuring of Enterprises in the Baltics, Baltic Regional Programme," Organisation for Economic Co-operation and Development (OECD), Paris, April/May 2000]

In Albania, privatisation started with the privatisation of small and medium sized enterprises, and eventually the massive privatisation program for large enterprises was launched. (Web page of Economic Development Agency of Albanian Government, URL: http//www.aeda.gov.al/)

Finally according to article 11 of Law on Transformation of Socially Owned Enterprises of Macedonia "...the manner and the procedure of transformation shall depend on the size of the enterprise, i.e. small, medium or large. The large and medium scale enterprises shall be transformed into joint-stock companies. By exception, and by the agency's consent, medium scale enterprises may be transformed into limited liability companies. Small-scale enterprises shall be transformed into limited liability companies, and by a consent of the agency, into joint stock companies. A joint stock company or a limited liability company shall be considered incorporated as of the day of its entry into the corresponding registry".(Article 11). [Also see article: 41-73. (For the full text of Macedonian Privatisation law see the web page of Macedonian Privatisation Agency, URL: http//www.mpa.org.mk)

[121] Harmathy, (The Methods of Privatisation), p.40

[122] For example, in Sweden there is no special law on privatisation. Privatisation of state owned enterprises (SOEs) may occur as a consequence of a decision adopted by Parliament and implemented by the government. However, a reduction to a 34 per cent state shareholding can be made without parliamentary permission. (Willner, p.177) But at the same time, state ownership can be increased, though not extended to completely private companies, without a parliamentary decision.)

C. Case of Former Socialist Countries

Former socialist countries have a unique position in the case of legislation in privatisation. These countries had to enact several laws to convert their system to market economy.[123]

Privatisation is considered one of the significant ways of shifting the system to a market economy. In order to achieve a full transformation from a command economy to a free one, essential changes have to be introduced into various areas, particularly in the field of law.[124] Since, in these countries the legal and economic system was socialist; usually a law with other relevant laws are needed for the privatisation process.[125] Therefore the first step in the legal

---

[123] Legal Aspects of Privatization, p.13
In ex-socialist countries privatisation legislation and other relevant provisions should be designed to prevent the gaps that may occur during the transformation. For example one of the important issues is to prevent black economy and to register all new companies. (For example in Russia, many new companies operate in the informal economy. Only 1 million small businesses are officially registered. (Doran Doeh, "Special Report on Russia", Privatization, International Financial Law Review, Vol: 13, p.65-70, World Bank, URL: http//www.worldbank.org/)

[124] Ewa Baginska, "Legal Aspects of the Privatization Process in Poland", web page of Civic Education Project, URL: http//www.cep.org.hu/

[125] In other words former socialist countries often enact new laws or modify the existing laws to create a market a market friendly legal environment that is needed for the divestiture (privatisation) process. Massive number of laws might be enacted to convert all socialist type laws into market type legislation. For example, Federation of Bosnia and Herzegovina (BiH) enacted various laws to implement the privatisation process. [The following list shows the laws that have been enacted in this country to cover and implement the divestiture programme: (a) The Law on Privatization Agency ("Official Gazette of the Federation of Bosnia and Herzegovina", No 18/96), (b) The Law on Privatization of Enterprises ("Official Gazette of FB&H", No 27/97), (c) The Law on Determination and Realization of Citizens Claims in The Privatisation Process ("Official Gazette of FB&H" No. 27/97), (d) The Law on The Sale of Apartments with Existing Tenancy Rights ("Official Gazette of FB&H", No. 27/97) and The Law on Amendments and Changes to The Law on Sale of Apartments with Existing Tenancy Rights ("Official Gazette of FB&H", No. 11 /98), (e) The Law on Opening Balance Sheet of Enterprises and Banks ("Official Gazette of FB&H", No 12/98), (f) The Law on Privatization of Banks ("Official Gazette of FB&H", No 12/98), (g) Framework Law on Privatization of Enterprises and Banks in Bosnia and Herzegovina ("Official Gazette of FB&H", No 14/98), (h) The Law on Securities ("Official Gazette of FB&H", No 39/98), (i) The Law on Securities Register ("Official Gazette of FB&H", No 39/98), (j).The Law on Securities Commission ("Official Gazette of FB&H", No 39/98), (k) The Law on Fund Management Companies and Investment Funds ("Official Gazette of FB&H", No 41/98), (l) The Law on Claims in Privatization Process that are Based on Difference Between Pension Amounts Received and Pension Amounts to be Received by Beneficiaries of the Rights Stemming from Pension and Disability Plan ("Official Gazette of FB&H", No 41/98). For all these laws see: Web page of Agency for Privatisation of Federation of Bosnia and Herzegovina, URL: http://www.apf.com.ba/zakonie/index.htm/]

Also under heavy pressure from West Germany to privatise, East Germany's last socialist government adopted the first transformation laws in March 1990. These laws ruled that collective combines (Volkseigene kombinate) and VEBs (Volkseigene Betriebe, state-owned enterprises) adopt the legal form of either a public or a private company. They further established the Treuhandanstalt, a government-controlled public trust created to administer the shares of the new companies. Originally, the Treuhandanstalt was authorised, but not required, to sell

framework should be to amend, alter and convert the current socialist laws including the constitution. All former socialist countries have taken steps to adopt new law to implement their privatisation programs.[126]

In other words, one of the main issues facing post-communist countries is creating, restoring, or updating a systematic body of law governing the activities of a market economy. This requires restoring, updating or creating a framework of financial, commercial and civil law. The points that the post communist countries consider in order to apply the privatisation process can be summarised as follows:

(a) amending the constitution to repeal the ban on private property and re-establish private property rights;

---

the shares to private investors. It could also restore ownership, but only to the former owners of small businesses that had existed under the legal form of single-owner enterprises or partnerships prior to expropriation. In general, the creation of the Treuhandanstalt was intended to privatise firms in form but not in substance. The Treuhandanstalt was the legal agency that administered state-owned firms that had merely changed to a private legal form. (Raiser, p. 3, 4)
    The most important laws in East Germany were the Gesetz über den Verkauf volkseigener Gebaude vom 7.3.1990[Law on the sale of State-owned Real Estate and Buildings of March 7, 1990], Gesetzblatt DDR I Nr. 18 S. 137 (G.D.R); Gesetz uber die Ubertratung volkseigener landwirtschaftlicher Nutzflachen in das Eigentum von land wirtschaftlichen Produktionsgenossenschaften vom 6.3.1990 [Law Concerning the Transfer of State-owned Farmland in the Ownership of Private Producer Cooperatives of March 6, 1990]. Gesetzblatt DDR I Nr. 17 S. 135 (G.D.R.), Gesetz uber die Grundung und Tatigkeit privater Unternehmen und uber Unternehmensbeteiligungen vom 7.3.1990, [Law Concerning the Foundation and Activities of Private Enterprises of March 7, 1990], Gesetzblatt DDR I Nr. 17 S. 141 (G.D.R.); and Verordnung zur Umwandlung von volkseigenen Kombinaten, Betrieben und Einrichtungen in Kapitalgesellschaften vom 1.3.1990. [Regulation Concerning the Transformation of State-Owned Enterprises and Combines into Profit Corporations], Gesetzblatt DDR I Nr. 14 S. 107 (G.D.R.), [Raiser, footnote 1, p.1)]
    Furthermore in Poland different laws were enacted to implement and cover the privatisation process. In this country, regulation on privatisation is embraced by four legislative acts: (a) the State Enterprises Act of September 1981, (b) the Privatisation of State Enterprises Act of July 1990, (c) the Management of Agricultural Property of the State Treasury and Amendments to Certain Laws Act of 1990, (d) the National Investment Funds and the Privatisation Act of 30th April 1993. [Ewa Baginska, "Legal Aspects of the Privatisation Process in Poland", web page of Civic Education Project, URL: http//www.cep.org.hu/]
    For Hungarian case on this see: Gábor Papanek, "Legal Security in the Economy of Hungary", (Web page of Center for International Private Enterprise, URL: http//www.cipe.org/)
    For the legal and institutional aspects of privatisation in Estonia, Latvia and Lithuania see: Niels Mygind, "Privatisation, Governance and Restructuring of Enterprises in the Baltics, Baltic Regional Programme," Organisation for Economic Co-operation and Development (OECD), Paris, April/May 2000
    Also see: Cook and Kirkpatrick, "Privatisation Policy and Performance", p.4; Schrader, p.260.
    In Lithuania Private property was re-introduced under the Provisional Fundamental Law adopted on 11 March 1990. (Lithuanian Business Information Centre, URL: http//www.lbic.lt/)
    [126] Fischer, p.3

(b) subordinate legislation to re-establish property rights, rules governing ownership, registration of titles, transfers, succession, nationalisation and compensation;

(c) an up to date commercial code providing a framework for the law of contract, arbitration of civil disputes, patents and other intellectual property, business structures including public joint-stock and private limited liability companies, their registration, conduct, governance, and liability;

(d) bankruptcy legislation;

(e) competition laws to regulate monopolies, mergers and restrictive trade practices;

(f) an up-to-date labour code;

(g) legislation governing pensions and social security net;

(h) a market based tax system comprising personal income, corporate profits, value added, property and other taxes;

(i) laws regulating foreign investment, and foreign trade; central banking, commercial banking, banking supervision, securities trading, insurance, investment funds and laws covering other financial activities; and

(j) legislation to set standards of accounting, auditing, disclosure and financial reporting,[127]

---

[127] Jones, p.13; Ewa Baginska, "Legal Aspects of the Privatization Process in Poland", web page of Civic Education Project, URL: http//www.cep.org.hu/; Dabrowski, p. 26

D. Functions of Privatisation Law

1. General

A privatisation law offers advantages and disadvantages. In other words, in each country before enacting a privatisation law, legal, social, economic and political circumstances and conditions should be taken into account. And each country in question considers all these factors and develop its own measure.

Apart from stating the objectives and principles of privatisation, the rationale behind these privatisation laws is to set general framework rules for government on the conditions for sale, endow the executive with specific powers and create special provisions for employees. Certain laws also define the modalities of privatisation and valuation, and allow for the creation of special rights for the state after privatisation.

2. Advantages and Disadvantages

a. Advantages

Whether legally required or not, a law offers several advantages: It represents an immediate and concrete statement of explicit political support for and commitment to the privatisation process, increases the accountability of the executing agency, makes it more difficult to undo the reforms being implemented; provides an opportunity to change the existing business environment to facilitate privatisation; gives confidence to domestic and particularly foreign investors, prevents the uncertainty among the authorised bodies.[128]

---

[128] Guislain, (The Privatization Challenge), p.111
This will be a major advantage particularly in the countries where existing legislation is too complicated and does not provide certain rules for the bodies that will involve in the privatisation process. A privatisation law will provide confident to investors particularly in post-communist countries since it shows the high commitment and promise of the authorities.

b. Disadvantages

A law may have negative outcomes and disadvantages; delays in securing parliamentary approval, the possibility that the law provisions may be too restrictive or inflexible, and the risk of parliamentary micro-management; a law may state very complex and difficult bureaucratic proceedings and create major delays in the process.[129]

Because the economic conditions and other circumstances relevant to privatisation process change, and the law needed to be amended and modified this will take time and cause delays particularly where the government is based on weak coalitions or where there is a strong conflict in the parliament on the privatisation process itself.[130]

3. Analysis

Several countries have enacted general or specific (privatisation) laws to implement their privatisation process.

Various circumstances constitutional, economic, traditional and social system and circumstances of each country determines whether or not a privatisation law is needed; and these elements also effect and determine the structure and outcome of the privatisation law.

In developing countries including the ex-socialist ones, because of the market conditions and political environment privatisation law need to be modified several times, as seen in the case of Bulgaria. This can cause major delays and that are detrimental to the process.

[129] Web page of OECD, URL: http://www.oecd.org/

In some countries privatisation process faced some delays because of the modifications and amendments in the privatisation laws. Thus in Lithuania, privatisation has proceeded in two phases. The first phase followed the adoption on 28 February 1991 of the Law on Initial Privatisation of State Property that set out the basic principles and institutions for privatisation in Lithuania. In the first phase of privatisation, the law had to be amended several times. This factor was an important obstacle for government in the privatisation process. However, the new law governing the second phase of privatisation, the Law on Privatisation of State and Municipal Property was prepared under the experiences of the previous law, and came into force on 15 September 1995. (Lithuanian Business Information Centre, URL: http//www.lbic.lt)

[130] Guislain, (The Privatization Challenge), p.111

In the Netherlands whenever the government wants to create a legal entity, legislation by parliament is required. And in many cases, the implementation of privatisations have been delayed because legislation is a slow process in this country and the government has no control over the parliamentary timetable. (Andeweg, p.202)

E. General or Specific Privatisation Law

1. General

Most countries following a privatisation process have enacted laws, whether or not required to do so by the constitution. In the process they have had to choose between general legislation that is applicable to all SOEs to be privatised and a specific law that will cover and be applicable to a SOE or group of SOEs. In some cases the targeted SOEs are specially named; in others, the law addresses one or more categories of enterprises without naming them.[131]

2. General Legislation

a. General

Whether a country requires a general law governing privatisation depends on the existing constitutional order and political environment. Almost all former socialist countries and some other countries have enacted a "general law" to implement their privatisation programs. Countries with general privatisation legislation in Western Europe are Austria (enacted in 1993)[132], France (1986, modified in 1993, 1996)[133], Portugal (1990)[134] and Turkey (1984 and 1986)[135], Greece (1992).[136]

---

[131] Guislain, (The Privatization Challenge), p.115

[132] Information Technology in Austria, Privatization and Deregulation in Austria, web page of American University, Washington D.C., URL: http://www.american.edu; Karl Aiginger, The Privatization Experiment in Austria, Institute of Economic Research, URL: http://www.wifo.ac.at/; web page of Tradeport, URL: http://www.tradeport.org/

[133] Comparative Overview of Privatisation Policies and Institutions in Member OECD Countries, OECD Privatization and Enterprise Reform Unit (September 1998), p.3

[134] Web page of US State Department, URL: http://www.state.gov

[135] Web page of Turkish Privatisation Administration, URL: http://www.oib.gov.tr/

[136] Comparative Overview of Privatisation Policies and Institutions in Member OECD Countries, OECD Privatization and Enterprise Reform Unit (September 1998), p.3, web page of OECD, URL: http://www.oecd.org; web page of Croatian Government, URL: http://www.hfp.hr/privatization/privat.htm; Evangelia Antoniades, "Privatization in Greece: 1993 to the Present Its Impact on the Economy, the Society, and the Polity", web Page of Hellenic Resources Network, URL: http://www.hri.org/

b. Options in general legislation

The governments have options in determining the structure of a general law. A law that confers broad authorisation to privatise without specifying the enterprises in question will generally define its scope of application either by defining "privatisation" or other terms of prescribing inclusion or exclusion criteria. A law of general scope should be considered if common rules for all privatisation transactions are deemed important. Such a law may also confer a general mandate on the government or an agency to privatise SOEs.[137]

A general law may list the SOEs that are to be wholly or partially privatised. The government's authority to privatise is then usually limited to these listed SOEs. France (65 SOEs in 1986 and 21 in 1993) is an example for this case.[138]

To list the privatisable SOEs in the law is not necessarily a good solution. Because such a list limits the flexibility of the government since constantly changing domestic and world market conditions may dictate priorities other than those originally prescribed in the law. Moreover, designating specific enterprises can create uncertainty among the management and staff of the SOE. Long delays between the designation of an SOE to be privatised and the actual implementation of the transaction have indeed led to a deterioration of the condition of the SOE, and sometimes even to pilfering and misappropriation of SOE assets by workers and managers.[139]

Finally other way is to issue decrees pursuant to the privatisation law that lists the enterprises to be privatised. This method offers more flexibility than the designation of the SOEs in the law itself.[140]

---

[137] Guislain, (The Privatization Challenge), p.116
[138] Guislain, (The Privatization Challenge), p.116
[139] Andrej Juris, "Economic Reform in Slovakia" web page of Center for International Private Enterprise, URL: http//www.cipe.org; Fischer, p.2; Guislain, (The Privatisation Challenge), p.116, 117
[140] Guislain, (The Privatization Challenge), p.117

3. Specific Legislation

In this case, in every privatisation transaction a new law is enacted. This method seems to bring positive outcomes where the parliament is working fast and rapid enough to enact laws. Specific laws authorising the privatisation of one or more SOEs or of an entire sector have been enacted in a number of countries[141] including Belgium[142] and the United Kingdom[143]. This system of legislation tend to be used where the scope of the privatisation programme is limited or an SOE or group of SOEs poses special legal problems that cannot be resolved in a general enabling law.

Finally in some countries privatisation process has been implemented according to the provisions in some other acts. For example, in Spain budget law covers the privatisation process.[144]

---

[141] Guislain, (The Privatization Challenge), p.78-84
In Germany a general law does not exist. In certain cases, special laws have been voted in order to launch the privatisation of a SOE (e.g. Lufthansa). [Esser, p.109; Schwartz and Silva Lopes, p.44-47]

[142] Guislain, p.78-84

[143] Cosmo Graham and Tony Prosser, *Privatizing Public Enterprises, Constitutions, the State, and Regulation in Comparative Perspective, (Comparative Perspective)* Clarendon Press, Oxford University Press, Oxford, 1991, p.81, 82;

[144] Comparative Overview of Privatisation Policies and Institutions in Member OECD Countries, OECD Privatization and Enterprise Reform Unit (September 1998), p.3, the web page of OECD, URL: http://www.oecd.org

V. LEGAL STAGES in the PRIVATISATION PROCESS

A. General

1. Deciding the Stages in Privatisation

The privatisation process involves certain legal steps, starting from the selection of enterprises to be privatised and ending with the transfer of ownership from state to private hands.[145] And each legal stage has its own internal steps.

Furthermore privatisation process in former socialist countries, in many aspects, is different from western economies. In most ex socialist countries, privatisation process is divided into two processes. (a) Small-scale privatisation (small privatisation): Small privatisation generally refers to the privatisation of the retail trade, catering, some services, and small construction businesses. It can also include the privatisation of units or assets of larger enterprises.[146] (b) Large-scale privatisation (large privatisation or mass privatisation) refers the divestiture of large sized SOEs.[147]

---

[145] Different authors and governments may provide different list of steps in the privatisation transactions. For example the legal and organisational stage of privatisation in Poland is divided into nine stages: (Web Page of Polish Privatisation Agency, URL: http://www.mst.gov.pl/)
In (East) Germany the procedure of privatisation is divided into 5 steps: (i) selection of the enterprises to be privatised, (ii) estimation of its value, (iii) study of alternative ways of privatisation for the selected enterprise, (iv) decision on the method of privatisation, (v) transfer of the ownership. (Schwartz and Silva Lopes, p.44-47)

[146] "Trends and Policy in Privatisation-General Overview of Privatisation Developments", April 1995, URL: http://www.oecd.org/

[147] A number of countries are in the final stages of privatisation with three-quarters of their large enterprises in private hands. According to OECD estimates, the Czech Republic has privatised or liquidated over 81 per cent of its SOEs, Hungary 75 per cent, Estonia 74 per cent, Lithuania 57 per cent, the Russian Federation 55 per cent, Latvia 46 per cent, the Slovak Republic 44 per cent, Mongolia at 41 per cent, Poland 32 per cent, and Moldova 27 per cent. Large privatisation remains limited in Bulgaria at 10 per cent, Belarus at 11 per cent, Georgia at 2 per cent and Romania at 13 per cent. ("Trends and Policy in Privatisation-General Overview of Privatisation Developments", April 1995, URL: http://www.oecd.org)

2. Getting Ready for Privatisation

a. Initial Requirements and Considerations

Every government pursuing a privatisation programme often considers the following principles initially:

First of all, before embarking on a privatisation program, governments need to be sure that they have the necessary financial, human and administrative resources to carry it through. In addition to the staff and organisation costs, there are the enterprise-specific costs, such as redundancies, debt write-offs and capital improvements.[148]

The initiator of privatisation needs to decide what kinds of organisational, financial, and physical restructuring of an enterprise are necessary before divestiture and how they should be accomplished.[149]

Existing legislation, as well as the constitutional requirements and the legal status of the SOE(s) to be divested, must be analysed in order to determine whether they allow privatisation and are compatible with the government's objectives, or need to be amended. The constitution can be modified, altered or amended in order to launch the privatisation process. Privatisation legislation and sectoral regulation is either enacted, replaced or abolished where appropriate.[150] The same holds true for privatisation institutions.

In other words laws may need to be enacted to abolish a monopoly, regulate or deregulate the concerned sector, strengthen the country's capital markets, authorise the transfer of the

---

[148] S. Brian Samuel, "The Ten Commandments of African Privatization", International Finance Corporation (IFC), The World Bank, URL: http://www.ifc.org/ifc/publications/pubs/impact/impsm99/commandm/commandm.html

[149] Bornstein, p.238

[150] The Lessons of Experience, p.20; Comparative Overview of Privatisation Policies and Institutions in Member OECD Countries, OECD Privatization and Enterprise Reform Unit (September 1998), p.4, the web page of OECD, URL: http://www.oecd.org

concerned SOE(s) to the private sector, or organise the privatisation process itself.[151] Thus, if constitutional, political, economical, traditional or social circumstances require a privatisation law and/or any amendment or alteration in the current legislation, these legal activities should be ready in advance.[152]

Important issues may arise in the privatisation of the largest firms, such as the treatment of the firm's debt. Presumably the firms that are more heavily indebted are likely to be liquidated before being disposed of, though there must be certain rules how the creditors will be compensated.[153]

One of the critical issues arising is whether ownership in the SOE to be divested can be transferred without prior legal transformation (into a joint stock company, for example). Public law bodies are usually set up as such by or pursuant to acts of parliament and would normally require to be reorganised under company law prior to an ownership transfer to the private sector. If ownership of the enterprise in its current legal form cannot be transferred, sale of assets and prior corporatisation would constitute the two main approaches. The legal status of an SOE may have an incidence on the applicability of many other types of laws, such as labour, social security or tax laws.[154]

b. Legal Changes in the Company

A number of changes, other than the change in ownership, may occur during the process of privatisation. The enterprise may no longer be required to seek funds for investment from, or

---

Some SOEs may have a legal status that does not allow or facilitate divestiture, in which case a status change will be required. If the ownership of assets is disputed, the rights of contending parties must be clarified. All these elements need to be addressed before privatisation.

[151] The Lessons of Experience, p.20
[152] See: p. 193-208
[153] Fischer, p.9
[154] Guislain, (The World Bank), p.6

with the approval of, a Treasury or Ministry of Finance, with allocation being guided by political priorities and administrative procedures.[155]

In other words, once privatisation decision is given on an enterprise, its status might change and government may provide some restrictions on the activities of the enterprise. These restrictions may vary from prohibiting the enterprise from certain activities to requiring permission for some activities. If this is the case, (Privatisation Law or other laws) should provide clear rules on the status of the enterprise from the day of publishing of the object (enterprise shares) privatisation programme until the day of conclusion of privatisation transactions.

---

[155] John L. Williams, Privatisation of Large Publicly Owned Enterprises: A Public Choice Perspective, Department of Economics, Murdoch University, Working Paper No. 158, May 1997, p.3

Some privatisation laws provide provisions on that issue. Thus according to Lithuanian Privatisation Law during the privatisation transaction SOEs shall have no right to conclude the following contracts without the written consent of the State Property Fund:

(a) loan agreements, contracts of pledge, warranty, guarantee, lease, contracts of purchase, sale and any transfer of long-term tangible property, also to purchase securities of any other enterprise, issue debentures, increase or reduce the enterprise's authorised capital, where the value of the contract or several contracts (the total value per calendar year of the property which is the object of the contract) exceeds 5 per cent of the enterprise's authorised capital;

(b) contracts for the purchase and sale or any transfer of materials and raw materials where the value of the contract or several contracts (the total value per calendar year of the property which is the object of the contract) exceeds 10 per cent of the enterprise's authorised capital.

Furthermore, according to law, the contracts specified above concluded without the consent of the Property Fund shall be invalid except for the contracts concluded by third persons who did no know and could not know of the restrictions applied to the enterprise under the law. [Article 12/1-2-3, Law on the Privatisation of State-Owned and Municipal Property, 4 November 1997 No. VIII-480, Vilnius, web page of Lithuanian State Property Fund, URL: http//www. http://www.vtf.lt/en/frame22.html]

On the other hand according to Turkish Privatisation Law "...Organisations that are included directly in the privatisation program and organisations that are restructured for privatisation ... will be deemed to have been transferred to the (Privatisation) Administration as of the date of the Council's decision without any further transaction or payment of any consideration. Organisations included in the privatisation program and transferred to the (Privatisation) Administration will be deemed to have been disassociated from their related ministry or organisation and brought within the range of the (Privatisation) Administration, as of the date of the Council's decision. [(Article 17/B), Turkish Privatisation Law, web page of Turkish Privatisation Administration, URL: http://www.oib.gov.tr]

B. Stages

1. Decision to Privatise

a. General

This is the first stage of every privatisation program in each country.[156] The government need to decide who should have the responsibility for initiating the privatisation of an enterprise or the disposal of some of its assets.[157]

The authorisation body to decide and start the process can be parliament, the cabinet of ministers (government)[158], one minister, president, Prime Minister, or another public authority or in some cases the state owned enterprise itself.[159] This body or any other authority or association

---

[156] For this topic see: John D Donahue, *The Privatization Decision: Public Ends, Private Means*, Basic Books, New York, 1989
  We should point out that, the decision to privatise is political; political considerations play the major role in the privatisation decision. [For the same opinion: Richardson, p.57-82; Enrico C. Perotti, Pieter van Oijen, "Privatization, Political Risk and Stock Market Development in Emerging Economies", July 1999, http://www.oecd.org; Brown, p.96; Winiecki, p.71-96]
  Privatisation requires a political commitment from the decision-making and executive bodies. In some countries because of political obstacles there has been delays in the privatisation process. For example in Ukraine parliament, itself, has been an obstacle in moving toward mass privatisation. Privatisation activities were suspended by the Ukrainian parliament in July 1994. A presidential decree in November of that year introduced a voucher-based mass privatisation program. Parliament also voted to exclude more than 6,000 companies from privatisation. (State Property Fund of Ukraine, URL: http://www.ukrmassp.kiev.ua/Prgrm98-1.htm)
  Similarly, in Poland some political parties and unions remained hostile to privatisation, which caused privatisation to develop very slowly. In this country from 1994 to 1996, the new, left wing government was not in favour of privatisation and the process slowed. Therefore although Poland was one of the first socialist countries to pursue market reforms, it has been slow to convert to mass privatisation. [URL: http://www.worldbank.org/; Barbara Blaszczyk, Moving Ahead: Privatization in Poland ", web page of Center for International Private Enterprise, URL: http://www.cipe.org/; Henry Gibbon, Privatization in 1995 and Beyond, web page of Center for International Private Enterprise, URL: http:/www.cipe.org/]
  Hence, privatisation is a political process [Donaldson and Wagle, p.6; "Political and Organizational Strategies for Streamlining", Privatisation Database, URL: http://www.privatisation.org] In practice the design of privatisation programs in transition economies is largely dictated by political rather than economic conditions. (Havrylyshyn and McGettigan, p.5). Privatisation programs could achieve notable success if backed by a clear political agenda, executive action. ["International Perspectives on Privatisation of State Owned Enterprises", Narendar V. Rao, Northeastern, C. Bhaktavatsala Rao, Steve Dunphy, Small Business Advancement National Center, University of Central Arkansas, URL: http://www.sbaer.uca.edu/; General Accounting Office, p.4, 5]

[157] Bornstein, p.237

[158] For example in Slovakia, Privatisation Law, in principle, authorises government to get "privatisation decision". (Article 10, The Act No.92/1991, dated February 26, 1991 on the Conditions of Transfer of State Property to Other Persons, web page of Ministry for Administration and Privatisation of National Property of the Slovak Republic, URL: http://www.privatiz.gov.sk/anglicky/act92.htm)

[159] Article 13 of Law on Transformation of Socially Owned Enterprises of Macedonia states that small and medium scale enterprise may choose the manner and the procedures of the transformation independently, while a large scale enterprise shall do so in co-operation with the Agency. For small and medium scale enterprises the

appointed by this body may determine the details including the methods, valuation, pricing and financing and other vital aspects of the process.

b. Period between privatisation decision and actual privatisation

i. General

According to us there mustn't be a long period between the privatisation decision and actual privatisation of the state owned enterprise; privatisation transactions should be completed as fast as possible. A long period in business without effective decision-making has an adverse effect on the enterprise and its business. If the management of the SOE does not see any clear future and any perspective of its survival, short-term decisions prevail.[160] However, particularly in former socialist countries the period from corporatisation to full private ownership of firms that are to be privatised is generally expected to last several years, and in some instances up to a decade.[161]

---

decision on transformation shall be made by the board of directors of the enterprise, upon the recommendation made by the Managing Board of the enterprise. (Article 15/1) However, in large-scale enterprises, the managing body of a large-scale enterprise and the agency, shall constitute a board for transformation of the enterprise, on a parity basis. The large-scale enterprise shall make the decision on transformation, by the consent of the agency. (Article 69) [The law defines "small", "medium" and "large" scale enterprises. (Article 12) For the full text of Macedonian Privatisation law see the web page of Macedonian Privatisation Agency, URL: http://www.mpa.org.mk]

In literature, if privatisation is initiated by enterprise itself it refers to "spontaneous privatisation". However, this concept also refers to a particularly favourable deal that involved either the current management or other members of the old socialist bureaucrats (nomenclature). [Fischer, p17. Also see: Prosser, (Social Limits), p.230]

Finally in France Article L 432-1 of the 'Code du travail' [Labour Code] requires consultation of the works council on modifications in the economic or legal organisation of an enterprise, including mergers, cessions, and acquisitions and cessions of subsidiaries. The law would seem to require the consultation of staff on privatisation. But in two cases brought by the works council of enterprises being privatised, the courts refused to order the provision of the opportunity for the council to arrange a valuation of the enterprise, and to order consultation on the price of the enterprise and the choice of purchaser. The reason given by the Court was that the decision to privatise was a matter for decision by government, not by the enterprise itself. [Graham and Prosser, (Comparative Perspective), p.135, 136]

[160] Andrej Juris, "Economic Reform in Slovakia" web page of Center for International Private Enterprise, URL: http://www.cipe.org
[161] Fischer, p.2

ii. Transitional and Interim Provisions

Privatisation programs involve time-consuming and drawn out process, therefore interim measures are often adopted to manage assets while awaiting final divestiture. Such provisions typically address questions relating to: (i) the asset or the SOE being divested, transitional regime for SOE privileges, etc., (ii) the status of employees of former SOEs, including pre-privatisation lay-offs; (iii) the disposal of obligations remaining with the state; and (iv) the allocation of SOE revenues accruing during the interim period. They are commonly found in enterprise or sector specific legislation in situation requiring restructuring of the SOE(s) prior to privatisation.[162]

2. Identifying privatisation candidates

Identification and selection of privatisation candidates in the privatisation process will be the second stage.

Selection criteria depend on a country's privatisation objectives and legal framework. At a minimum, these criteria should include a policy test to establish what should be privatised and what should remain in government hands. If an enterprise does not pass this test, it becomes a candidate for privatisation or shutdown.[163] As we have discussed before, world-wide, many governments are narrowing their definition of what is considered a core government service and broadening the types of enterprises and services eligible for privatisation.[164]

Governments should consider all state enterprises in the initial analysis. Those that clearly perform core government functions (for example police force, border control, international relation etc.) will not be privatisation candidates once the analysis is complete. Moreover, governments should avoid making a list of "strategic" industries that are exempted

---
[162] Guislain, (The World Bank), p.58
[163] Welch and Frémond, p.4

from privatisation. Doing so only provides an opportunity for firms that are reluctant to privatise to lobby for inclusion on the list.[165]

3. Feasibility study

a. General

Once the government has compiled a list of candidates, it should decide which enterprises will proceed to the second step of the process. As it identifies candidates, the government will find that some state enterprises have excellent commercial potential, a number are attractive, and some will be difficult to privatise.[166]

b. Valuation of enterprises

i. General

One of the important steps in the privatisation process is the valuation of the SOEs to be privatised. Hence, all the methods of privatisation require a valuation of assets or company shares.[167]

Valuation is of paramount importance because it establishes a market price range for the enterprise. Valuations based on market principles are essential to stifle criticisms that the state is not receiving a fair price and to ensure that there is sufficient investor interest.[168] Furthermore proper valuation of state assets is important because privatisation sale will not be accomplished

---

[164] See: p. 114-165 on Limits of Privatisation
[165] Welch and Frémond, p.4
[166] Welch and Frémond, p.4
[167] Bornstein, p.238
As we will discuss in the following pages ownership of small shops, restaurants, or service facilities can be sold by auction, but the state would still want to specify a minimum price based on its valuation. Similarly, valuation of assets is needed for employee buyouts, competitive tenders, and public share offerings.
[168] As we discussed in the first chapter, because of their market conditions former socialist countries are facing problems in valuing the assets of the SOEs. In Eastern Europe, the value of enterprises is not well depicted in their financial statements. For example, balance sheets do not accurately represent assets, liabilities, and book values. In general, both assets and liabilities were recorded Land was not valued properly, because it was not traded. One the other hand the stock markets do not exist or very new (Morris Bornstein, p.238; Welch and Frémond, p.6)

at an unduly high price, whereas an unduly low price will reduce budget revenue.[169] Some countries have established valuation commissions or other special bodies responsible setting minimum prices.[170] For example, in France, valuation is to be carried out by a Privatisation Commission of seven members, nominated by a decree from those with experience of matters economic, financial, and legal.[171] On the other hand, in Turkey a special commission (Value Assessment Commission) is responsible for the valuation of the state owned enterprises.[172]

Different methods can be used in valuation of the SOEs. In Western market economies valuation is based on discounted cash-flow projections of future earnings and comparisons of similar firms' market prices or stock market valuations.[173] Furthermore, in developed capitalist

---

[169] Bornstein, p.238
[170] Guislain, (The Privatization Challenge), p.120
[171] Prosser, (Constitutions and Political Economy), p.314
In many ways valuation and pricing of the disposals in the French privatisation programme are similar to what has occurred in Britain. For example, private advisers play a major role. However, there are also important differences between the two nations. Firstly in France, issues are not underwritten, thus avoiding the payment of expensive fees to underwriters and the conflict of interests where underwriters are also advisers to the government. [Graham and Prosser, (Comparative Perspective), p.97]
[172] "... Value assessment of organisations in the scope of the privatisation program will be performed by Value Assessment Commission formed within the Administration pursuant to this Law...The Value Assessment Commission consists of five members chaired by the Head of the Project Group responsible for privatisation proceedings of the organisation in the scope of privatisation and having as members an expert of the project group responsible for the privatisation proceedings, Head of the Department of Project Evaluation and Preparation or an expert of this department, Head of the Department of Capital Markets or an expert of this department and Head of the Project Group responsible for Property Affairs Group Head or an expert of this group. The Commission resumes its duty upon proposal of the President of Administration and approval of the Prime Minister. Alternate members are appointed to the positions as described here above in the same number and method. [Article 18/B, 18/B-a, "Law Concerning Privatisation and Regulation of Implementations of Privatisation and Amendment to Certain Laws and Statutory decrees, Law Nr.4046, Date of Passage: 24 November 1994, Official Gazette Nr. 22124, Date of official Gazette: 27. 11. 1994. (Privatisation Law), web page of Turkish Privatisation Administration, URL: http://www.oib.gov.tr]
[173] Welch and Frémond, p.6, 7
"...The Commission [Value Assessment Commission], through the application of at least three of the internationally recognised methods as: discounted cash flow (net present value), book value, net asset value, depreciated replacement value, break-up (liquidation) value, price/profit ratio, market capitalisation value, market/book value, expertise value and price/cash flow ratio; shall undertake value assessments and tender method with regards to attribute, service distinction, potential future cash flow, sector and market specifications, industrial, commercial and social features, machinery, vehicles, equipment, goods and row materials, finished and unfinished material stocks, all movable and immovable properties owned by the organisation, virtues and current conditions, receivables and payable accounts and bills and all rights and obligations of those establishments within the scope of privatisation. The Administration will make public upon approval the tender outcome and value assessment results. Provided that the privatisation procedures of an establishment under the scope of privatisation is carried out based on ... this Law, value assessment shall be realised within the parameters as dictated in this paragraph under the guidance of a commission established through the judgement of the official decision making bodies and chaired by the exchequer of the establishment at hand..." [Article 18/B-c, "Law Concerning Privatisation and Regulation of Implementations of Privatisation and Amendment to Certain Laws and Statutory decrees, Law Nr.4046, Date of

market economies, with better accounting in enterprise financial statements than in former socialist countries, one may seek guidance in pricing shares in state enterprises by examining the stock market's price book value or price-earnings ratios for companies deemed similar important respects.[174]

Since valuation is an important aspect of the privatisation process, Privatisation Law or other acts often provide clear rules on valuation of the state owned enterprise that are going to be privatised. For example Article 7 of Law on Transformation of Socially Owned Enterprises of Macedonia states that: "...the value of the enterprise shall represent the difference between the value of the enterprise's assets and the other rights (total active capital) and the value of the enterprise's liabilities, including liabilities towards legal and physical entities, based on their fixed deposits in the enterprise."[175]

Passage: 24 November 1994, Official Gazette Nr. 22124, Date of Official Gazette: 27. 11. 1994, (Privatisation Law), web page of Turkish Privatisation Administration, URL: http://www.oib.gov.tr]
[174] Bornstein, p.238
[175] Furthermore according to Macedonian Privatisation Law: "The value of the enterprise shall be appraised, according to the methodology proposed by the Agency and approved by the Government...The appraising of the value of the enterprise... shall be carried out by legal and physical entities authorised by the Agency. The appraised value ... shall be expressed in Deutch Marks..." (Web page of Macedonian Privatisation Agency, URL: http://www.mpa.org.mk)
Finally Lithuanian Privatisation Law provides that the value of the privatisation object may be assessed by applying one of the following methods or a combination of these techniques: (a) Comparable price (analogous selling price) method, based on comparison, i.e. the market value is determined by comparing the contract prices of analogous objects upon taking into account minor differences between the object which is under valuation and analogous objects; (b) Replacement value (costs) method, based on the calculation of the cost of replacement of the objects in their current physical condition and with their current maintenance and utility properties according to the technologies and at the prices used at the time of valuation; (c) The yield method (income capitalisation or discounted cash flows method) where the asset is valued as a profit-yielding business rather than the sum total of separate assets. The method is based on future cash flows forecasts and the current cash value. Where less than 1/3 of the shares in the enterprise are offered for sale, a simplified variant of the method may be applied in the manner prescribed by the Government; (d) Special value method, applied for the valuation of unique objects of art and history, works of jewellery and antiques, also various collections (valued according to special valuation techniques, applicable to the above objects); (e) Other methods recognised as applicable in the European Union and approved by the Government [Article 9/2-(1),(2),(3),(4), (5), Law on the Privatisation of State-Owned and Municipal Property, 4 November 1997 No. VIII-480, Vilnius, web page of Lithuanian State Property Fund, URL: http://www.vtf.lt/en/frame22.html]

Finally we must point out that all too often, the enterprise in question has a negative value when viewed by every valuation methodology except future potential (after a heavy dose of new management, investment, technology, etc).[176]

ii. Principles in Valuation

When the valuation is done a careful pre-qualification of bidders should be also done. The valuation body should avoid over-valuation of the SOEs; because overvaluation and unrealistic expectations on the part of the government may create serious delays.[177] On the other hand, governments need to prevent under pricing of SOEs. It is argued that, selling SOEs would give an unfair advantage over citizens as a whole.[178]

Where a valuation is made, it should serve only as a guide to the selling agency. Legislation should *not* prevent this agency from concluding a sale at a price below the estimate if, following a competitive selection procedure, no acceptable bid has been received at or above the estimate.[179] On the other hand, prior valuation by independent professionals may, however, be useful by providing the sellers a reference price that can help them decide whether to accept

---

[176] S. Brian Samuel, "The Ten Commandments of African Privatization", International Finance Corporation (IFC), The World Bank, URL: http://www.ifc.org/ifc/publications/pubs/impact/impsm99/commandm/commandm.html

[177] The Lessons of Experience, p.34

[178] In France it was argued that, it would be unconstitutional to sell enterprises below their true value as this would breach constitutional principles of equality and would give purchasers an unfair advantage over citizens as a whole; indeed it was argued that the obligation to sell by 1991 could have precisely this effect, and could also lead to transfers to foreigners, threatening national independence. [Graham and Prosser, (Comparative Perspective), p.97-104]

In this country Constitutional Court (Conseil Constitutionnel) decided that selling SOEs below their true value would be unconstitutional. Therefore Conseil Constitutionnel imposed a form of a priori control over pricing. [Prosser, (Constitutions and Political Economy), p.311-316]

[179] As mentioned above, in some cases, governments may sale enterprises under the current market prices. This has three main reason:
-The first is simply to ensure that the disposal is successful and so to gain political capital from this.
-Secondly, by disposing of interests cheaply, a government can attempt to maximise the number of shareholders in a privatisation concern.
-Finally, to offset potential political and financial costs, some countries often discounts to small investors and ask higher prices, either fixed or by tender, from institutional investors. [The Lessons of Experience, p.35]

the bids received. Independent valuation may also reduce the risk of collusion between the buyer and the officials in charge of privatisation.[180]

In most cases, like in France, the members of the commission are prohibited from having interests in bodies buying capital in privatisation transactions.[181]

Government should use competition among investors to set the price for sale of state enterprises, and avoid complex valuations.[182]

c. Options for privatisation and timing

In most cases privatisation officials submit a privatisation proposal to the political authorities at the end of the feasibility study. Such proposals contain the valuation of the firm, the options for privatisation (trade sale, public offering of shares etc.), and the timing options (immediate sale, sale after restructuring). [183]

d. Minimising the risk of choosing poor candidates for privatisation

Governments are often concerned that the feasibility study will find that a state enterprise is not suited to privatisation, and that significant costs will have been incurred without identifying a viable privatisation candidate. [184]

This risk can be reduced by dividing valuation into two phases. In the first phase the financial adviser quickly evaluates a state enterprise's potential for privatisation. If the potential is low, the adviser can be terminated before valuing the enterprise and developing options for privatisation. [185]

---

[180] Guislain, (The Privatization Challenge), p.120
[181] Prosser, (Constitutions and Political Economy), p.314
[182] Routledge, p.3
[183] Welch and Frémond, p.7
[184] Welch and Frémond, p.7
[185] Welch and Frémond, p.7

4. Privatisation Plan

a. General

Once a government decides to privatise a state owned enterprise, it should prepare a privatisation plan with its advisers. This is the third stage. A privatisation plan of the enterprise is a set that consists of economic, technical, proprietary, time and other important points.[186] This plan often includes a communications plan (to build public support and attract investors); a plan to resolve the public policy issues surrounding the privatisation; a plan outlining the method of privatisation, the steps required to reach privatisation, and a timeline; and draft legislation or executive orders.[187]

As a summary, privatisation plan should particularly address the following issues: (i) payment conditions, (ii) employment plan, (iii) investment plan plus its financing, and (iv) ecological considerations.[188]

---

[186] For similar definition see: Article 6/1, The Act No.92/1991, dated February 26, 1991 on the Conditions of Transfer of State Property to Other Persons, (Web page of Ministry for Administration and Privatisation of National Property of the Slovak Republic, URL: http//www.privatiz.gov.sk/anglicky/act92.htm)

[187] Since every country has its own specific and unique circumstances and conditions, the structure and content of the privatisation plans may vary. For example, according to Privatisation Law of Federation of Bosnia and Herzegovina (BiH) the enterprise privatisation program (which is prepared by the enterprise and to be submitted for approval to the authorised Privatisation Agency) should include: (a) basic information on enterprise; (b) proposed method, or combination of privatisation methods; (c) anticipated methods of sale and payment; (d) size and structure of employment after privatisation; (e) initial enterprise value. [(Article 4), "Official Gazette of Federation BiH", No 27/97, Nov 28th, 1997. For the full text of the Law on Privatisation of Enterprises, Federation of Bosnia and Herzegovina (BiH) in word format see: Web page of Agency for Privatisation of Federation of Bosnia and Herzegovina, URL: http://www.apf.com.ba/zakonie/index.htm/]; Welch and Frémond, p.8

Finally according to article 12 of the Estonian Privatisation Agency privatisation programme shall include: (a) priorities of privatisation in different spheres of economy; (b) main ways of privatisation used in different spheres of economy; (c) general principles of transformation, merger, division, restructuring and stabilisation of enrolled enterprises; (d) the extent of usage of privatisation securities in privatisation of different objects; (e) the spheres of economy where the circle of entities entitled to participate in privatisation shall be restricted; (f) general principles of establishing additional conditions; (g) principles of privatisation of property to the co-operative societies of farmers. (Estonian Law on Privatisation, (unofficial translation), web page of Estonian Privatisation Agency, URL: http://www.eea.ee/)

[188] Maciej Grabowski, Economic Reform in Poland, Economic Reform Today Working Papers, Number 4, web page of Center for International Private Enterprise, URL: http://www.cipe.org/

b. Restructuring Discussions

i. General

One of the important questions and issues about privatisation is: what actions can or should the government take prior to the sale to raise the price? Or, alternatively, should the government sell as fast as it can without attempting to restructure the SOE?[189]

Generally, the word restructuring includes de-monopolisation, privatisation, and opening up the economy and enterprise rehabilitation.[190] Thus, restructuring before privatisation can take place at the company, industry, or country levels, requiring the intervention and co-ordination of other authorities beyond those in the office of privatisation. Specific areas of prior restructuring include: (a) Change in management and/or board of directors, (b) Labour cutbacks and worker contract renegotiations, (c) Absorption of either outsiders' debt, cross-liabilities among state owned enterprises (SOEs), or past-due fiscal debt, (d) Aid programs aimed at improving the firm's performance, (e) Investment measures in the form of rehabilitation plans, agreements on financial restructuring tied to operation improvements, or a temporary reopening of the plants, (f) Legal restructuring, including the legal disputes or the creation of patents and/or operation permits, (g) Changes in domestic regulation, trade barriers, or entry and exit rules, and (i) Asset restructuring in terms of spin-offs, break-ups, or even packaging of companies for sale.[191]

ii. Debate on restructuring

In the privatisation literature there is a debate over restructuring. The controversial issues are as follows:

---

[189] López-de-Silanes, p.7
[190] Dabrowski, p27
In this subtitle we will use restructuring as "enterprise rehabilitation".
[191] López-de-Silanes, p.7

(a) Should restructuring take place before privatisation or should it be left to the new investor(s)? (b) If government would prefer restructuring in what extend should it take place?, (c) The government and corporate boards will also have to decide how far to restructure firm balance sheets before privatisation. The firms' liabilities to banks, inter-enterprise credits, and the treatment of implicit or explicit pension liabilities, will be at issue.[192]

It has been argued that a privatisation program will evolve more rapidly if governments do not attempt to restructure their enterprises before they are put up for privatisation. The private investors will generally do a better job of making the business and financial decisions involved in restructuring. Delays in privatisation undermine governmental credibility and public support for privatisation. Delays also raise costs for the government, which may create or prolong macroeconomic imbalances.[193]

Furthermore in one World Bank study it is argued that, government should leave major enterprise restructuring to private investors and avoid major restructuring of state enterprises before privatisation.[194] Finally one study revealed that (a) direct costs of prior restructuring policies are quite substantial, amounting to an average of 30% of the sale price, (b) Additionally, restructuring measures such as efficiency and investment programs slow privatisation, (c) Delays in privatisation come at a substantial cost, particularly when subsidies poured on SOEs can quickly add up to outweigh privatisation revenues.[195]

---

[192] Fischer, p.12
[193] "Privatizing State-Owned Companies", The Prosperity Papers Series, Prosperity Paper Three, web page of Center for International Private Enterprise, URL: http://www.cipe.org/
[194] Rutledge, p.3
[195] López-de-Silanes, p.29. López-de-Silanes summarises the study as: "...do not do too much, simply sell."(p.29)

iii. Different Restructuring Implementations

i. Former Socialist Countries

Usually in former socialist economies, there has been a tendency to leave enterprise restructuring to those with the incentive to restructure efficiently— the new private owners. [196] For example in the Czech Republic in preparation for privatisation, firms were corporatised but only very limited restructuring was carried out.[197] Furthermore in Hungary no state restructuring is needed before selling the shares.[198]

ii. Western Economies

In Western Economies including Denmark, France, Finland, Germany, the Netherlands, Portugal, Spain and Sweden the general policy is to limit pre-privatisation restructuring to a minimum before privatisation, on certain occasions, (particularly if the SOE is large like in the case of Girobank in Denmark) the enterprises have been restructured before divestiture. [199]

iv. Analysis

According to us, governments need to limit pre-privatisation restructuring to legal, accounting (balance sheet), and organisational changes. However any major workforce reductions should take place before an enterprise is sold. Technology changes, capital investments, and major purchases should be left to the new owners. [200]

---

[196] Joseph Pernia and S. Ramachandran, "The Macedonian Gambit-Enterprise cum Bank Restructuring", Public Policy for the Private Sector, The World Bank, Note No. 62, November 1995, p.1; Fischer and Sahay, p.19

[197] Claessens, Djankov, and Pohl, p.2

[198] Eva Voszka, "Privatization in Hungary: Results and Open Issues", web page of Center for International Private Enterprise, URL: http//www.cipe.org/

[199] Comparative Overview of Privatisation Policies and Institutions in Member OECD Countries, OECD Privatization and Enterprise Reform Unit (September 1998), p. 23, web page of OECD, URL: http://www.oecd.org

[200] Rutledge, p.5

However, particularly in the cases of excess labour and excess debt, restructuring is needed; and this needs to be carried by the government.[201]

c. Privatisation Technique

The privatisation plan often states how the government and its financial advisers or sales agents will carry out the privatisation. The plan should contain the steps and timeline for the privatisation, covering the timing and method of privatisation, responsibilities of government officials and advisers, production of sale documents (for example, information memorandums prospectuses), legal tasks and timeline, and the composition and hierarchy of the placement syndicate and underwriting syndicate (if a public offering is being used).[202]

d. Selecting Buyers

i. General

The privatisation plan often also lays down the broad principles for the selection of buyers, typically by mandating a competitive and transparent process. This involves rules on advertising the sale, eligibility requirements, disclosure of information to investors, amount of time given investors to prepare bids, evaluation and selection, and so on.[203]

The choice of privatisation method may determine the selection of buyers. If a company is privatised by way of public flotation, the selection process will be anonymous; all investors can subscribe and be allocated shares. If mass privatisation (voucher system)[204] is chosen, like in ex-socialist countries in most cases, all eligible citizens will have the opportunity to buy or

---

[201] S. Brian Samuel, "The Ten Commandments of African Privatization", International Finance Corporation (IFC), The World Bank, URL: http://www.ifc.org/ifc/publications/pubs/impact/impsm99/commandm/commandm.html. (According to Samuel: "...The government can't expect the new owner to clean up its mess...")
[202] Welch and Frémond, p.8
[203] Guislain, (The Privatization Challenge), p.124
[204] See: p.256-265

receive shares or coupons. But even in that case, still rules are needed to govern these processes.[205]

The implementation body (government or privatisation agency) may have more discretion in the choice of buyers under other privatisation methods. This is the case, in particular, for the trade sales and for the selection of strategic or core investors, which are preferred privatisation method for many SOEs.

ii. Legal Restrictions on Buyer Selection

The privatisation law or the current legislation may have some restrictions on the selection of buyers.[206]

i. Restitution of Nationalised Enterprises

In some countries the privatisation law or a separate restitution law may contain provisions entitling former owners or their heirs to ask for the restitution of their assets. This is for sure, the ultimate restriction on the selection of buyers for enterprises to be privatised.[207]

ii. Exclusion of or Limitation on Public-Sector Participation

In order to implement the privatisation process effectively and purely and reduce the role of the public sector in the economy, many countries, including Bulgaria, Poland, and Russia have restricted the right of public sector entities to participate in the privatisation process by buying shares of other SOEs.[208]

---

[205] Guislain, (The Privatization Challenge), p.124
[206] However, the privatisation law should be free of unnecessary restrictions on the selection of buyers. Some restrictions, such as the exclusion of public agencies as buyers of privatised enterprises, may, however, be necessary to protect the objectives of the program. [Guislain, (The Privatisation Challenge), p.127]
[207] Guislain, (The Privatization Challenge), p.128
[208] Guislain, (The Privatization Challenge), p.128
It might be argued that if state own enterprises's own objectives are still obscured by non-commercial considerations and their incentive structures are distorted, they will not be very efficient agents of change in privatised companies. Moreover, they might prove to be formidable lobbyists in their efforts to limit competition, as

Moreover, some countries have inserted more restrictive rules under this head in their privatisation laws to further support the objectives and consistency of the privatisation programme by limiting the creation of new SOEs. [209]

iii. Restrictions on Foreign Participation in the Privatisation Process

Governments generally are reluctant to cede control over assets to foreign investors; behind this there are political and social concerns, particularly the ones considered "strategic" by them.[210]

iv. Restrictions on certain individuals

Certain employees working in the institutions (for example the Minister of Privatisation, the members of Privatisation Administration etc.) in charge of privatisation programme should not be allowed to participate in the process.

Thus privatisation legislation should provide provisions to restrict or ban certain individuals (members of Privatisation Agency, certain officers, members of evaluation

---

they are often backed directly by their government's diplomatic and political weight. In practice, however, these concerns might be overcome by the privatising government's resolve to resist capture. The questions to be asked, in addition to the ones that are put to all bidders, is whether these SOEs operate under investment constraints or other severe corporate finance handicaps in their home markets, in which case they might be unable or unwilling to contribute to the long term development of the privatised firm; and whether they have an experience in operating in competitive product and services markets. [Guislain, (The Privatization Challenge), p.55]

[209] Guislain, (The Privatization Challenge), p.128

[210] For example land is viewed sentimentally and often is seen as the national "soul," many governments that now allow for private land ownership still do not permit foreigners to own land. Thus most countries also bar foreign investors from owning land. They may lease land and, in some countries, land can be owned by locally incorporated which are 100 percent foreign owned. (Bruce A. Reznik, Property Rights in a Market Economy, web page of Center for International Private Enterprise, URL: http//www.cipe.org/; Welfens, p. 50; Jones, p.27)

See also p.330-348

In Latvia land may be owned by foreign-owned companies established in Latvia from countries with which Latvia has concluded investment protection agreements, companies with foreign participation established in Latvia in which at least 51% of statutory capital belongs to the citizens of Latvia, and foreign individuals who are citizens of Latvia. Land may be leased by foreigners or foreign-owned local companies. (Web page of Latvian Government, http://www.lpa.bkc.lv/Lpa02GB.htm)

Also see: The Lessons of Experience, p.36

commissions) to participate in the privatisation transactions; this will ensure the transparency in the divestiture program.[211]

v. Preferential Schemes

A common restriction is grant rights to SOE employees and management, particularly reserved share allocations and pre-emptive rights that may also constrain the selection process.[212] This restriction compare to other types of restrictions seems to have positive outcomes.

As a summary privatisation laws often allow or require the allocation of free or discounted shares in privatised companies to specific groups, including employees and small shareholders, as well as other special benefits. The reasons for such give-aways vary, but generally include the objective of winning the targeted groups over the privatisation cause. These benefits may, for instance, create worker support for privatisation or reduce their opposition and favourably impress citizens before an election.[213]

---

[211] According to Turkish Privatisation Law: "...(the members of the Privatisation Administration and Privatisation High Council) may not disclose any non-public information or dates they learn during their function on accounts, operations, and enterprises of their organisations. They are not allowed to use such information for their own benefit or for the benefit of third parties or to trade securities of such organisations on or off the stock exchange for pecuniary benefits or in such manner so as to disrupt the equality of opportunities among traders. They may not further be beneficiaries of transactions realised through methods of privatisation under this Law as or in the capacity of a buyer or a lessee. This prohibition shall be applicable also to the spouses and children of persons mentioned herein. (The members)... may not take office in privatised organisations for two years following their date of privatisation....Persons who violate these prohibitions will be sentenced to six month to two years' imprisonment and a fine equal to three times the unjust enrichment, jointly or separately, depending on the nature and importance of the act." [Article 7, "Law Concerning Privatisation and Regulation of Implementations of Privatisation and Amendment to Certain Laws and Statutory decrees, Law Nr.4046, Date of Passage: 24 November 1994, Official Gazette Nr. 22124, Date of Official Gazette: 27. 11. 1994, (Privatisation Law), web page of Turkish privatisation Administration, URL: http://www.oib.gov.tr]

[212] Guislain, (The Privatization Challenge), p.127

[213] Different countries have adopted different measures on preferential shares. For example, according to article 251 of Law on Transformation of Socially Owned Enterprises of Macedonia privileged right to purchase shall be given to: (a) Employees of the transformed enterprise, who have been employed for at least 2 years prior the decision on transformation was adopted; (b) Individuals whose employment in the enterprise was terminated, but who have been continuously employed by the enterprise for at least 2 years; and (c) Retired employees who were continuously employed by the transformed enterprise, being employed by the enterprise for at least 2 years. However, the article states that the right to privilege purchase shall be given once and refers to one enterprise only. [Web page of Macedonian Privatisation Agency, URL: http://www.mpa.org.mk]

Furthermore in Lithuania Employees may acquire up to 50 percent of the shares. (Lithuanian State Privatisation Agency and State Property Fund, URL: http//www.vtf.lb/)

Finally in Latvia employees who had worked a minimum of 5 years in the enterprise had a pre-emptive right to buy at the initial price. [Mygind, p.14]

vi. Retaining Shares

Particularly in former socialist countries in each privatisation transaction, the government retains a significant percentage of ownership, sufficient to make it the largest shareholder.[214] For example Slovak Privatisation Law provides that when certain enterprises (mainly in the energy sector) are privatised, a minimum capital share of 51 per cent of the State or the Fund at the enterprise must be retained.[215]

5. Costs (Expenses) in the Privatisation Process

Privatisation is not without cost. Transaction costs include the costs of legislation, legal advice, due diligence, brokerage and underwriting fees. In other words during privatisation transactions, in general the basic costs fall under a number of heads, namely underwriting and placing commissions, selling commissions, clearing bank costs, marketing and advertising costs and advisers' fees. The fees can easily reach 2-3 percent of the value of the enterprise and are not

---

On this topic also see: Guislain, (The Privatization Challenge), p. 132
[214] Fischer, p.22
[215] "When taking decisions on the privatisation of Slovak Gas Industry, State Company, Bratislava; Power Industry of Western Slovakia... a minimum capital share of 51 per cent of the State or the Fund at the enterprise must be retained." (Article 10/4, The Act No.92/1991, dated February 26, 1991 on the Conditions of Transfer of State Property to Other Persons, web page of Ministry for Administration and Privatisation of National Property of the Slovak Republic, URL: http://www.privatiz.gov.sk/anglicky/act92.htm)

Also in Russia, the state is retaining majority ownership of Gazprom, the natural gas monopoly and Russia's largest company by far. (Henry Gibbon, Privatization in 1995 and Beyond, web page of Center for International Private Enterprise, URL: http//www.cipe.org/). In Hungary, although privatisation of both large and small enterprises is nearly complete the state retains golden shares and long-term ownership stakes in some companies. 92 firms will remain in at least partial state ownership permanently, including all farming companies. [Chikán, p.23, 24]

Furthermore, in Lithuania the degree of privatisation should be such that after the privatisation of an enterprise the state would be a holder of at least 11 percent to 50 percent of the shares of the enterprise, i.e. more than 50 percent though not more than 89 percent of the shares should belong to the private sector after the privatisation of the enterprise. [Lithuanian State Privatisation Agency and State Property Fund, URL: http//www.vtf.lb/]

In Hungary approximately 50 companies are slated to remain fully government owned, including the railways and postal services. (Eva Voszka, "Privatization in Hungary: Results and Open Issues", web page of Center for International Private Enterprise, URL: http://www.cipe.org/; URL: http//www.worldbank.org/)

Finally, in the Czech Republic, the state has kept minority shares in many major financial and commercial entities through the National Property Fund. (The World Bank, http://www.worldbank.org/ecspf/final/html/czech_republic.htm)

irrelevant to the excitement privatisation generates among the legal and stock broking industries.[216]

In most developing countries and former socialist countries, the net financial balance of privatisation is likely to be negative; for example privatisation-related costs are likely to exceed privatisation proceeds. In these cases, the determination of priorities for the allocation of privatisation proceeds should be non-controversial, namely they should be used to cover the related costs. By and large, the allocation of such proceeds is a fiscal matter that should be governed by public finance regulations and be subject to parliamentary scrutiny. Many countries have rightly chosen to earmark privatisation proceeds to financing the costs associated with the privatisation program, including debt write-offs, payment of advisers and other privatisation related costs. To the extent total proceeds exceeds total costs and as these net proceeds tend to be one-time revenues, economists usually recommend that they be allocated to debt repayment or similar deficit-reduction expenditures.[217]

Some privatisation laws provide clear rules on the expenses of privatisation. For example according to article 10 of the Macedonian Privatisation Law, the expenses of the transformation procedure shall be covered by the enterprise, unless otherwise determined by the Privatisation Law or the sale agreement.[218]

Finally the introduction of competition in the choice of advisors and other outside agents in the privatisation process provides big savings to the government and helps to make the process much more efficient. The basic costs, (such as underwriting commissions, legal advice,

---

[216] Stampford, p.254; Privatization in the United Kingdom, Ernst & Young, 1994, p.11
Advertising costs in some privatisation transactions in Britain are as follows (£m): British Telecommunications (1984, 1991, 1993): 36.1, British Gas (1986): 21.4, Water Companies (1989): 17.3, National Power/PowerGen (1991, 1995): 16.1, Regional Electricity Companies (1990) :20.6, Scottish Electricity Companies (1991): 5.3, Northern Ireland Electricity (1993): 1.1, Railtrack (1996): 4.4, British Energy (1996): 4.1 [Source: Web page of UK Treasury, URL: http://www.hm-treasury.gov.uk/pep/advcosts.html]
[217] Guislain, (The World Bank), p.54
[218] For the full text of Macedonian Privatisation law see the web page of Macedonian Privatisation Agency, URL: http://www.mpa.org.mk

advertising and marketing costs) can be cut, in many cases, by more than half, if competitive open procedures are adopted for the procurement tenders.[219]

VI. LEGAL METHODS of PRIVATISATION[220]

A. Appropriate Method

1. General

It is important to choose the most appropriate method of privatisation. Every enterprise is different, and each country has its own unique culture and traditions, therefore no two acts of privatisation are ever identical.[221]

All too often, privatisation laws and regulations have restrictively determined the authorised methods and techniques of privatisation. From a legal point of view, one should first examine what techniques would be authorised in the absence of specific provisions in the privatisation legislation. If needed, provisions could then included in the legislation authorising additional techniques or restricting the use of some techniques, as the case may be. Implementing regulations will often provide further details on how such techniques may be used.[222]

Most privatisation techniques have been borrowed from private commercial practices, where mergers and acquisitions are common. Other methods, however, are specific to SOE privatisation and may have to be included in the privatisation law if the government intends to

---

[219] Web page of OECD, URL: http://www.oecd.org/
[220] The selection of an appropriate method of privatisation can be largely determined by the choice of buyer and the specific objectives of that privatisation. Who is to own the company after privatisation? Is it to be another national company, or a foreign investor? Is it to be the management and work force, or members of the public? The choice of buyer often points to the appropriate method that will best achieve the objectives.
[221] "...The (Privatisation High) Council shall determine which methods of privatisation described above will be used in each case depending on the particular requirements of the transaction. [Article 18/B, "Law Concerning Privatisation and Regulation of Implementations of Privatisation and Amendment to Certain Laws and Statutory decrees, Law Nr.4046, Date of Passage: 24 November 1994, Official Gazette Nr. 22124, Date of official Gazette: 27. 11. 1994, (Turkish Privatisation Law), web page of Turkish Privatisation Administration, URL: http://www.oib.gov.tr]

use them. Privatisation by free distribution of shares to the population, is a very appropriate example.[223]

The privatisation process in the ex-socialist countries has lent itself to the use of specialised techniques, which reflect the special circumstances faced by the countries of Central and Eastern Europe and the former Soviet Union.[224]

In other words, the privatisation methods that have been used in former socialist countries differ from the methods that have been applied in Western European countries. For example because of its character, one of the methods, restitution[225], has not been used in Western countries. On the other hand although there are some efforts to privatise SOEs via public offering, this method is not a common method for divestiture (privatisation) in the former socialist countries.[226]

---

[222] Guislain, (The World Bank), p.40, 49
[223] Guislain, (The Privatization Challenge), p.122
According to Turkish Privatisation Law privatisation methods are as follows:
"...(a) *Sales:* Transfer of the ownership of goods and services units in the assets of organisations in full or partially for consideration, or transfer of all or some of the shares of these organisations through domestic or international public offerings, block sales to actual persons and/or legal entities, block sales including deferred public offerings, sales to employees, sales on the stock exchange by standard or special orders, sales to securities investment funds and/or securities investment partnerships, or any combination thereof, by taking into consideration the prevailing conditions of the organisations,
 (b) *Lease:* Grant of the right of use of all or some of the assets of organisations for consideration and for a designated period of time,
 (c) *Grant of Operational Rights:* Grant of a right of operation of organisations as a whole or of their goods and services production units in their assets for consideration for a designated period of time, with retention of ownership rights,
 (d) *Establishment of Property Rights Other Than Ownership:* Restriction of the goods and services production units and assets of organisations with certain property rights, whereby the owner consents to dispositions of the assignee on the rights of facility thereon or the owner renounces from the use of these ownership rights, in the format and under the conditions specified in the Turkish Civil Code, with retention of ownership by the owner institution,
 (e) *Profit Sharing Model and other legal dispositions depending on the nature of the business:* ...methods defined in general provisions of law and/or special laws which are not included in the aforementioned privatisation methods and which take into account the particular characteristics and structures of the relevant organisations. [Article 18/A-a, b, c, d, e, "Law Concerning Privatisation and Regulation of Implementations of Privatisation and Amendment to Certain Laws and Statutory decrees, Law Nr.4046, Date of Passage: 24 November 1994, Official Gazette Nr. 22124, Date of official Gazette: 27. 11. 1994, (Privatisation Law), web page of Turkish privatisation Administration, URL: http://www.oib.gov.tr]
[224] "Privatizing State-Owned Companies", The Prosperity Papers Series, Prosperity Paper Three, web page of Center for International Private Enterprise, URL: http//www.cipe.org/; Bornstein, p.253, 254
[225] See: p.234-241
[226] After the collapse of European communism in 1989 the new governments of the region faced an excruciatingly difficult challenge: how to privatise SOEs in a politically acceptable way. The most straightforward

2. Legal Techniques

a. General

Different factors including the objectives of the privatisation programme, economic, social circumstances, constitutional and political differences of each country will determine the method of privatisation.[227]

In the broader understanding, privatisation covers both divestiture and non-divestiture options and measures.[228] In that context, a company can be privatised in various ways and more often each measure has its internal options.[229]

---

method-simply auctioning off the SOEs to the highest bidder—would surely have resulted in the wholesale transfer of the nation's most prized assets to foreign ownership, since only international corporations and investors had the necessary financial wealth and managerial expertise.
    While this was politically an unattractive option, waiting to determine the optimal method of privatisation was also an unattractive option during the early 1990s because many SOEs were either rapidly losing value in the managerial vacuum that followed communism's collapse or were being systematically looted by the former communist bureaucrats (nomenclature). [William L. Megginson, "The Impact of Privatization", web page of Center for International Private Enterprise, URL: http//www.cipe.org/]

[227] Kirkpatrick, p.236
    For a comparative analysis of British and French privatisation implementations: Prosser, (Constitutions and Political Economy), p.304-320

[228] See: p.24-32

[229] Some of the techniques (both divestiture and non-divestiture options) of privatisation are as follows:
  (a) Selling the whole by public share issue,
  (b) Selling a proportion of the whole operation,
  (c) Selling parts to private buyers,
  (d) Selling to workforce or management,
  (e) Giving it to workforce,
  (f) Contracting out the service to private business,
  (g) Diluting the public sector,
  (h) Buying out existing interest groups,
  (i) Charging for the interest,
  (j) Setting up counter-groups,
  (k) Deregulation via private associations,
  (l) Encouraging alternative institutions,
  (m) Making small-scale trials,
  (n) Repealing monopolies to let competition grow,
  (o) Encouraging exit from state provision,
  (p) Using vouchers,
  (q) Admitting demand pressures,
  (r) Curbing state powers,
  (s) Applying closure proceedings,
  (t) Withdrawal from the activity,
  (u) The right to private substitution. [Pirie, (Privatisation), 1988]

b. Scope of the Study

As we mentioned in the first chapter, -in principle- we will deal with the divestiture measures of privatisation. In other words, we focus on methods of privatisation leading to divestiture. Therefore, non-divestiture arrangements or broader definitions of privatisation such as contracting out, admitting demand pressures or applying closure proceedings will not be the focus of our study. As a result of this limitation, we will examine the following privatisation methods: (a) restitution, (b) public offering, (c) trade sale, (d) management-employee buy out, (e) mass privatisation [voucher system], and (f) liquidation.

B. Restitution

1. General

In the Central and Eastern Europe, the Communist regimes seized large amounts of private property. In that context restitution tries to return state assets to their former private owners in situations where the government's original acquisition is seen as unjust, such as uncompensated seizure. Redressing the worst examples of past injustices, it is argued, is essential on moral grounds. [230] Because of its characteristics this method has only been used in some former socialist countries.

Many countries, in particular those that went through large scale nationalisation programs, have established special commissions or bodies to examine claims on nationalised property by previous owners.[231]

---

[230] Havrylyshyn and McGettigan, p.3
[231] Guislain, (The World Bank), p.12, 13

2. Issues to be addressed in the restitution process

The determination of the rights of previous owners, whose property was confiscated, expropriated or nationalised in earlier decades, would require detailed analysis. The analysis would cover different branches of law including real estate law, land law, constitutional law, commercial law and international law. In that context there are important issues to be solved or to be addressed:

(a) Was the process carried out legally; do previous owners (or their heirs) still have legal rights on the assets to be divested? (b) Will restitution address expropriation only of real property or also of financial assets? In the case of real property, will it include agricultural land, urban residential and commercial real estate, and manufacturing, trade, service, and transportation facilities? Will restitution of financial assets comprise bank accounts, stocks and bounds; (c) How will the restitution programme allow for the deterioration, improvement, or transformation of physical assets since expropriation? How will it adjust the value of financial assets for inflation? (d) Are there different categories of previous owners, and have they been dealt with in the same way? (In East Germany, for example, some were expropriated by the Nazis, others between 1945 and 1949 under the Soviet military government, others yet by the East German communist regime. Furthermore, Jewish property was confiscated by nazi or local fascist regimes during World War II before the advent of communist regimes to power). In other words, what will be the cut-off date for expropriation?[232] (e) Must claimants be current citizens and residents of the country? (f) How soon must claims be filed, and how quickly will they be adjudicated? (g) Were they properly compensated or indemnified or do they still have financial

---

[232] In some countries legislation provides a certain date for restitution claims. Thus, Czech Republic adopted the "Law on Extrajudicial Rehabilitation" that promises natural persons with Czech citizenship the actual restitution of assets confiscated after the Communist take-over on February 25, 1948. Similarly, in Hungary the general law on restitution passed in April 1991. According to this law, former owners or their heirs will receive "property bonds" that can be used to reacquire assets expropriated prior to June 8, 1948, the date of convocation of the first Parliament control. (Boffito, 1993, p.53)

claims against state? [233], (h) Would claimants be allowed to take the case to the administrative courts if the decision of the public authorities on restitution claims is against of them? More importantly if a decision is made against a former owner, will the suit prevent the agency from transferring the property to the new investor?[234], (i) Will some properties be excluded from restitution claims?[235], (j) Who is to be the arbitrator for restitution claims? (government, privatisation agency, a court etc.)[236], (k) Against whom the claims lie? [237]

In the case of original owners would be given right to compensation there are some other issues: (a) Will the amount correspond to (i) the original value forty or more years ago, adjusted (how?) for inflation, (ii) present book value, perhaps revised for deficiencies in accounting, or (iii) the estimated sale price in privatisation; (b) Will payment be made (i) in cash, or (ii) in bonds (At what interest rate and with what restriction on sale?), (iii) or will payment be made as

---

[233] Bornstein, p.242, 243; Guislain, (The World Bank), p.12

[234] In Germany if a decision is made against a former owner, he or she may still challenge the Treuhandanstalt (the Privatisation Agency) in the administrative courts; however, the suit will not prevent the agency from transferring the property to the new investor. Usually, the administrative court's decision will be too late to stop the Treuhandanstalt's interim sale of the property or to bring about its return, and the former owner may prefer simply to accept financial compensation rather than pursue the suit. (Raiser, p.13)

[235] In the wake of the swift German unification a very significant question was initially left open: who should be able to own the property expropriated by the former regime, and under what conditions? Former owners and their heirs appealed to the principles ingrained in the property laws of the former West Germany in their claims that the socialist government had violated a fundamental human right to property by expropriating their property without adequate (or any) compensation.

The Unification Treaty between two Germany, in principle, gave the priority to reversion to the former owner, but excluded land and buildings when:
-a third person had purchased the land in good faith,
-considerable investment since expropriation had changed the purpose or use of the property,
-the property had been dedicated to public use,
-the property now part of a public housing project or,
-the property was now part of a commercial enterprise which reversion would severely impair. (Raiser, p.7, 9)

Furthermore in March 1991, the government amended the law. Specially, the amended law authorised the Treuhandanstalt to bypass former owners of certain properties when it deemed new investment proper, not necessary, to secure or create jobs, or to improve the competitiveness of the enterprise. For example, the agency can now sell an enterprise to new investors if the former owner cannot guarantee that they will manage the business successfully. Furthermore, to reduce the number of bureaucratic snags, the amended law also freed the Treuhandanstalt from having a rely on recorded claims for reversion. (Raiser, p. 13)

[236] Legal Aspects of Privatization, p.19

[237] Legal Aspects of Privatization, p.19

voucher coupons that can be used in auctions of state assets or purchases of shares in state enterprises to be privatised?[238]

3. Debate on restitution

a. Advocates' Points: Justifying the past

The advocates of this method stressed the legal aspect of the transaction, implying that property rights protection is the cornerstone of market economy and thus it should be imperative to restore the rights of the people disowned by the communist regime. It was argued that the communist injustice should be corrected if possible, and it was only a fair thing for a new democratic government to do. More sophisticated arguments included the creation of new entrepreneurial class and initial capital formation in the re-born private sector which would in turn give rise to a grateful constituency with pro-reform and pro-government attitudes. Finally, government officials considered restitution to be the fastest way to privatise the state property, de facto knowing the owners in advance.[239]

b. Opponents' Points: Detrimental to privatisation process

Opponents of restitution argued that by opening up the question of property rights, the government will only delay the privatisation transactions. The courts would be overburdened with legal complaints and the assets would linger in the state possession without any restructuring or market use for years. Also, even if the assets were restituted quickly, the fear remained that the new owners, receiving the property basically for free, would not undertake any serious effort at restructuring their newly acquired possession. This fear was especially pronounced with the restitution of land. Lastly, many opposed restitutions on the grounds that

---

[238] Bornstein, p.243
[239] Gabriel Sipos, Dual Transition in the Czech and Slovak Republics: Creating Support for Market and Democratic Reforms Through Restitutions, Dissertation for the Master's degree in Transition Central European

everybody suffered from communism and that no particular group deserved to be rehabilitated due to past injustice. [240]

Another argument is that why should former owners, who have been engaged in other activities for the past 40 years, receive a gift at the expense of the rest of society. There is also fear that restitution of property will limit the range of foreign investment and hamper the privatisation process.[241]

Finally, opponents of restitution counter that the process is necessarily selective, and therefore an unsatisfactory way of achieving justice retroactively. It is argued that as a practical matter, private claims can often be complicated and drawn out, bogging down privatisation unnecessarily. [242]

4. Approaches

A number of socialist countries have used restitution as a method of divestiture in their privatisation programmes.[243]

Thus, Slovakia[244], Germany, Bulgaria, Hungary,[245] Czech Republic, Estonia,[246] Latvia,[247] the Federation of Bosnia and Herzegovina,[248] Lithuania[249] all took legislative steps to return

---

University, Economics Department Budapest, Hungary, 15 June 1998, web page of Central European University, URL: http://www.ceu.hu/
[240] Gabriel Sipos, Dual Transition in the Czech and Slovak Republics: Creating Support for Market and Democratic Reforms Through Restitutions, Dissertation for the Master's degree in Transition Central European University, Economics Department Budapest, Hungary, 15 June 1998, web page of Central European University, URL: http://www.ceu.hu/
Thus, in Germany restoration of property also posed significant problems of procedure. About 1.3 million claims to approximately 2.6 million properties, mostly real estate, have been so far registered. The total number of claims for farms may add up to between ten thousand and twenty thousand, but the exact number is unknown. To handle these claims the Vermogensgesetz established 216 administrative boards (Vermogensamter) and six superior circuit boards (Landesvermogensamter). [Raiser, p. 10; Gesetz zur Regelung offener Vermogensfragen vom 3 Oktober 1990 (Law Concerning the Regulation of Open questions of Property of October 3, 1990) BGBI II at 1159 (1990), Raiser footnote 21, p.17]
[241] Boffito, p.51, 53, 54
[242] Havrylyshyn and McGettigan, p.3
[243] As mentioned above, because of certain characteristic, this method has only been applied and used in former socialist countries.
[244] Slovak Privatisation Law accepts "restitution" as a method of privatisation, however, it states that restitution procedure will be provided in a separate act. (Article, 3, The Act No.92/1991, dated February 26, 1991 on

property, including land, housing and enterprises, to their pre-Communist owners or their descendants.

5. Analysis

Although in some countries, restitution process slows down the privatisation programmes[250], we believe that, explicit legal treatment of the rights of former owners not only strengths the credibility of a country's commitment to the rights of private property, but also prevents the legal confusion over ownership that could arise if the issue were left to be settled later in the courts.[251]

---

the Conditions of Transfer of State Property to Other Persons, web page of Ministry for Administration and Privatisation of National Property of the Slovak Republic, URL: http//www.privatiz.gov.sk/anglicky/act92.htm)

[245] In Hungary in the restitution programme some compensation notes have been issued. The freely tradable compensation notes could be used in auctions for agricultural land, converted into shares of state firms listed on the stock exchange, or substituted for cash in purchasing privatised companies. (Eva Voszka, "Privatization in Hungary: Results and Open Issues", web page of Center for International Private Enterprise, URL: http//www.cipe.org/)

[246] Article 5 of the Estonian Privatisation Law provides rules on "privatisation of unlawfully expropriated property". According to this article: "Prior to announcing the sale the organiser of privatisation is under obligation to determine whether there is any unlawfully expropriated property in the composition of property to be privatised on which an application for compensation or return has been submitted and how this has been settled (paragraph 1). Furthermore article 5 states that unlawfully expropriated property on which the claimant has submitted an application to be returned or compensated may be privatised according to the following conditions: (a) the legally designated subject of Property Reform confirms in writing that he gives up his claim; (b) in accordance with legal acts, the decision not to return or compensate the unlawfully expropriated property has come into force; (c) the process of designating entitled entities or restitution of property has been terminated by law. (Paragraph 2) [Estonian Law on Privatisation, (unofficial translation), web page of Estonian Privatisation Agency, URL: http://www.eea.ee/; Privatisation in Estonia, web page of Estonia, URL: http//einst.ee/]

[247] Web page of Latvian Privatisation Agency, URL: http://www.lpa.bkc.lv/

[248] Web page of Agency of Privatisation of Federation of Bosnia and Herzegovina; URL: http://www.zpf.com.ba/

Law on Privatisation of Enterprises of Federation of Bosnia and Herzegovina (Privatisation Law) states that "certificates based on claims of physical entities towards the Federation" will be accepted as "payment" in the privatisation procedure. (Article 20/1, 25/1). However, the law provides in the restitution procedure, that in order to make a claim the person should bear the following criterias: (a) Be a citizen of Federation of Bosnia and Herzegovina on the date of March, 31, 1991, (b) 18 years old, (c) permanent residence on the territory of the Federation on the day the Privatisation Law comes into force. (1997) [Article 21, Web page of Agency for Privatisation of Federation of Bosnia and Herzegovina, URL: http://www.apf.com.ba/zakonie/index.htm/]

[249] In Lithuania, the legal basis for restitution is provided by the Law on Restoration of the Rights of Ownership to Existing Real Estate adopted on 1 July 1997. Real estate can be restored to former owners if they are citizens of the Republic of Lithuania (If the former owners are deceased, ownership can be restored to their children, parents or spouse and some other persons indicated in the Law provided they are citizens of the Republic of Lithuania). [Lithuanian Business Information Centre, URL: http://www.lbic.lt/]

[250] In Bulgaria implementing restitution laws proved slow and difficult, especially where scattered lands had been incorporated into large state agricultural complexes. In the Czech Republic some potential buyers of businesses backed down for fear of restitution claims. The Hungarian approach avoided such conflicts. (Chikán, p.25)

[251] Fischer, p.6

Restitution can be provided to former owners in a way that does not slow the privatisation process: to achieve this, the original owners would be given the right to compensation, by the state, rather than rights to the property itself. Thus new owners will find it difficult to get on with running their businesses if they face the possibility of claims for restitution by former owners.[252]

If enacted, restitution laws should definitely include a deadline for filing claims, past deadline, undisputed property could be privatised with a free and clear title, and previous owners' rights would either lapse or be subject to monetary compensation. This would limit post-privatisation claims against the new owners, which have occurred in Czech Republic and other countries and are very detrimental to the success of the privatisation program.[253]

---

[252] Fischer, p.6

In other words, compensation is in many instances not only more efficient but also more equitable that restitution. All affected parties can be treated in the same way, irrespective of their former property's fate. By dissociating the property to be privatised and the claims that may exist thereon, compensation schemes allow the state to divest previously nationalised property unencumbered. Buyers receive a clear title and residual claims are lodged against the state (or one of its agencies), rather than the new owner. [Guislain, (The World Bank), p.13]

For example, in Hungary, compensation coupons have been issued to 1.2 million residents as restitution for the nationalisation of property. Shares in some industries have been offered for coupon sales, but coupons have primarily been used for land purchases. Seventy-five percent of coupons worth almost Ft100 billion (US$650 million) had been used through 1996. (Web page of the World Bank, URL: http://www.worldbank.org)

However, Hungary is one of the few countries that did not return individuals' original property, opting instead for the distribution of compensation coupons that could be used to purchase privatised property, including land. Romania and Bulgaria had followed different paths. Thus, Romania returned agricultural land to private hands through restitution, resulting in the creation of 2.4 million private farms. (Chikán, p.25)

In Bulgaria the returning of farmland to its original owners prior to 1948 was initiated by the adoption of the Farm Land Law in 1991. The former state co-operative farms were closed down. Bulgaria is the only one of the reforming countries to reinstate farmland property within its former real boundaries. In the same time a restitution of small-scale urban property was effected. In 1992 several of the restitution laws were passed regulating the restitution of the nationalised urban property to its former owners within real boundaries, including apartment buildings, storehouses, workshops, enterprises and others. (Alexander Stoyanov, "Economic Reform in Bulgaria", web page of Center for International Private Enterprise, URL: http//www.cipe.org/)

In Germany the legislation provided that former owners receive financial compensation where a request was denied or the owner simply preferred compensation to ownership. The German government currently must confront a dilemma over how to calculate such compensation. (Raiser, p. 9)

Finally, in Lithuania restitution is achieved by transferring legal title to the property or, if this is not possible, to equivalent property. If neither option is possible, financial compensation will be paid. Individuals who do not qualify for restitution can apply to purchase agricultural land. The state retained the right to purchase property that would otherwise be restored to its previous owner if such property is deemed necessary for the state. (Lithuanian Business Information Centre, URL: http://www.lbic.lt/)

[253] Guislain, (The World Bank), p.12, 13

Finally once restitution is accepted in the legislation, and once restitution claims are in progress, government is obliged to exclude from its privatisation those assets that are objects of restitution claims.[254]

C. Public Offering

1. General

One of the methods of privatisation is to sell shares of SOEs (state owned enterprises) on the stock markets. Privatisation via public offering has been used in many countries to divestiture the assets of state owned enterprises.[255] For example, only in the United Kingdom between 1979 and 1993, this method have been used to divest assets of 41 state owned companies including British Airways, British Steel, British Gas.[256] In this method, shares can be offered on the domestic market as well as in international markets using American depository receipts or global depository receipts.[257]

---

[254] For example, according to Privatisation Law Federation of Bosnia and Herzegovina (BiH): "...(privatisation authority) is obliged to exclude from its privatisation (plan) those assets that are objects of restitution claims..." ["Official Gazette of Federation BiH", No 27/97, Nov 28th, 1997. For the full text of the Law on Privatisation of Enterprises, Federation of Bosnia and Herzegovina (BiH) in word format see: Web page of Agency for Privatisation of Federation of Bosnia and Herzegovina, URL: http://www.apf.com.ba/zakonie/index.htm/]

Furthermore Latvian Privatisation Law states that:" If a state asset unit designated for privatisation includes assets, on which restitution claims have been submitted by the former owner or his heir, and compensation according to the Law On Restitution of Ownership Rights for Enterprises and Other Asset Units has been declined by him, the Privatisation Agency, prior to adoption of the privatisation regulations for a particular state asset unit, completes operations stipulated in the said law.

If a state asset unit designated for privatisation includes residential building, on which restitution claims have been submitted in compliance with the Law... the Privatisation Agency, prior to the approval of privatisation regulations for a state asset unit, performs all the necessary activities to separate the said residential building from the unit in privatisation and to maintain it under the jurisdiction of the state until a decision on its restitution to its legal owner has been adopted. (Article 19, The Republic of Latvia Saeima Law On Privatization of State and Municipal Asset Units, passed on 17.02. 1994 effective from 18 March 1994, (Web page of Latvian Privatisation Agency, URL: http://www.lpa.bkc.lv/PrivatLawGB.htm#B001_)

[255] William L. Megginson, "The Impact of Privatization", web page of Center for International Private Enterprise, URL: http//www.cipe.org/

This method has also been used in Turkey in various privatisation transactions. (Web page of Turkish Privatisation Administration, URL: http://www.oib.gov.tr/)

[256] Privatisation in the United Kingdom, Ernst & Young, p.1

Because this method has widely been used in Britain, in our analysis in this subtitle, we will focus on UK implementations.

[257] Welch and Frémond, p.10

This method of divestiture can only be used if certain circumstances and conditions exist. Thus, state owned enterprises (SOEs) best suited for public offerings need to carry the following criteria:

(a) They should be legally formed as joint stock companies, (b) There should be no major financial weaknesses, planned restructuring, or imminent calls for more equity through rights issues, (c) The enterprise and the percentage of shares offered should not be so small that a flotation is uneconomic or not possible under local market conditions and stock exchange regulations. From a financial perspective public offerings are the only practical method of selling off the largest SOEs, (d) The size of the issue should be within the absorptive capacity of the local market, (e) Furthermore, to be successful, public offerings require a well-functioning and absorptive domestic capital market.[258]

2. Certain objectives in Public Offering

Privatisation via public offering has been widely used by many governments to achieve certain objectives. Thus in addition to transferring ownership, share offers often raise additional capital for an enterprise through the issue of new shares. Share offers can also meet a government's objective of broadening share ownership by allocating a portion of shares to small investors.[259] Therefore, public offerings of SOE shares have been used by many developing countries as a way to achieve widespread share ownership.[260]

---

[258] Stuart Bell, "Privatisation Through Broad-Based Ownership Strategies-A More Popular Option", Public Policy for the Private Sector, The World Bank, FPD note No. 33, January 1995, p.3

[259] Welch and Frémond, p.10

[260] Bell, p.3

For example in the United Kingdom public share offerings have been used to raise additional capital, as well as transferring ownership of the enterprise. It can also aid the objective of promoting transparency and widespread share-ownership through the allocation of a proportion of shares to small investors. (Cook, p.222)

Since 1979 over 60 national governments have raised almost $500 billion through about 600 separate public sales of stock in SOEs. These share-issue privatisations have almost always been the largest share issues in a nation's history. (William L. Megginson, "The Impact of Privatisation", web page of Center for International Private Enterprise, URL: http//www.cipe.org/)

Finally in some cases public offering is the most appropriate and easiest way of divestiture. Hence, large, profitable, relatively well-known state enterprises can only be privatised via public share offerings on stock markets.

3. Legal and organisational procedure

a. General

Shares are offered to retail and institutional investors, usually at a fixed price. In most cases stockbrokers overseen by government regulators sell shares.[261]

If domestic markets cannot absorb the entire share issue at once, governments often consider issuing shares in several trances.[262] However, if share prices are expected to go down, the treasury would be better off selling the enterprise in one shot.[263]

For example the normal method of floating a new issue on the UK stock exchange involves an invitation to the public to apply, for shares at a fixed price; in some cases it can be a tender offer.[264] The sale is underwritten by institutions that agree, in return for a fee, to buy any shares that are not taken up by the general public. If applications are received for more shares than are available, allotments are scaled down. A common procedure would be that if, for example, the issue were three times oversubscribed, applicants for substantial numbers of shares

---

[261] Welch and Frémond, p.10
Bishop and Kay, (Does Privatisation Work), p.31; Welch and Frémond, p.10
In the United Kingdom there has also been much criticism of the under pricing involved in many flotations. However, it is argued that under pricing was necessary in order to attract new shareholders, outside and inside the work force. (Foster, p.105). One important reason that was not been mentioned explicitly by the Conservative Party was political namely possible favourable effects on the size of the Conservative vote. (p.105).
Also see: Brown, p.80. [Brown states that: "To provide an incentive for investors, the issue price of shares in public floats is generally set at a level somewhat below the price at which thy are expected to trade when listed on the stock exchange."(p.80)]
[262] Welch and Frémond, p.10
[263] Galal, Jones, Tandon, and Vogelsang, p.569
[264] Small investors will prefer a fixed price rather than an auction, which they are likely to understand. (Bornstein, p.239)
The United Kingdom fixed the price of their initial public offerings. (Galal, Jones, Tandon, and Vogelsang, p.568)

would receive one third of those they had asked for, and small applicants would enter a ballot in which one in three would be successful.[265]

b. Financial advisers and sales agents

Governments often hire financial advisers or sales agents to underwrite (if required) and sell shares. The lead broker will lead the syndicate of brokers involved in the offer. For issues with a significant foreign component, governments often hire foreign brokers to co-lead the issue (or at least the foreign component). Brokers are often selected through competitive tender so that the comparative strengths of competing firms can be evaluated.[266]

For example in the United Kingdom each flotation is organised by a merchant bank. The preparation of a prospectus requires the services of solicitors and reporting accountants. Stockbrokers to the issue are appointed to smooth relations with potential investors. Advertising and public relations consultants are employed to promote interest in the shares. Most issues have been underwritten-the banks and brokers organise a group of investment institutions that agree to purchase any shares not subscribed by the general public, in return for a fee.[267]

c. Internal steps in public offerings

Officials involved in privatising an enterprise through an initial public offering often oversee a number of steps:

(a) Choosing sales agents (brokers or underwriters), lead brokers, and placement syndicate members.

---

[265] Bishop and Kay, (Does Privatisation Work?), p.28, 31; Richardson, p.67-69
[266] Welch and Frémond, p.11
[267] Bishop and Kay, (Does Privatisation Work?), p.62

(b) Drafting of the prospectus[268], which is done by the financial advisers or sales agents in co-operation with state enterprise managers and government officials.

(c) Selecting shares and the share instrument-for example, common or preference shares, instalment receipts convertible bonds, warrants, convertible preference shares, and so on,

(d) Resolving policy issues,

(e) Implementing the public sales campaign,

(f) Organising "road shows" where company officials and sales agents travel to key securities markets to showcase the company and share issue,

(g) Setting the subscription period (and book building, where appropriate),

(h) Determining pricing (retail and institutional) and distribution (domestic and foreign), with government approval,

(i) Closing, payment, and share delivery.[269]

d. Prospectus, share instrument, and timing.

The government often works closely with the lead broker on issues relating to the prospectus, its contents, and contributions from the enterprise being privatised. Of particular importance to the success of the issue will be the choice of share instrument (usually common shares) and the timing of sale and payment. Instalment receipts, for example, can spread payment over time.[270]

---

[268] The prospectus often addresses dividend policy, environmental issues, the regulatory regime, employee and management participation in the issue, management of government residual shareholdings (if any), and government intentions toward the firm and industry.
[269] Welch and Frémond, p.12
[270] Welch and Frémond, p.12
In the United Kingdom small investors have been permitted to pay by instalments, more commonly two but sometimes three. In such cases the total price was generally divided up into roughly instalments. The second method for inducing small investors to hold onto their shares was to offer a loyalty bonus at the end of a three year period,

246

4. Conclusions

The structure of privatisation share offerings varies tremendously over time and from country to country, depending on the political and economic circumstances of individual countries.

Public offering is one of the most effective ways of privatising SOEs. However, it requires developed domestic capital market. In other words, this method requires developed financial markets with a developed stock exchange. That is why, the use of stock exchanges to divestiture the assets of SOEs still remains limited in former socialist countries.[271]

---

invariably on the basis of one bonus share for every ten held continuously during that period to a stated maximum which varied between 150 shares and 500 shares. (Privatisation in the United Kingdom, Ernst & Young, p.2, 4)

[271] "Trends and Policy in Privatisation-General Overview of Privatisation Developments", April 1995, URL: http://www.oecd.org/

However, former socialist countries have been taking steps to create new stock markets or strength the existing ones. For example Latvia has established the new Riga Stock exchange, similarly Polish government has taken steps to strengths Warsaw Stock Exchange. (Henry Gibbon, Privatization in 1995 and Beyond, web page of Center for International Private Enterprise, URL: http//www.cipe.org/)

In Latvia, shares of the best-operated joint stock companies under privatisation were offered to the public within the Public Offering programme. This programme was launched in 1995, and by March 1, 1998, the number of companies whose shares were sold had reached 64. (Web page of Latvian Privatisation Agency, URL: http://www.lpa.bkc.lv/PriLatGB.htm#B004___)

In Estonia, the Tallinn Stock Exchange was opened in May 1996 but there has been no strong relation between the privatisation process and the development of the stock exchange. In Lithuania the National Stock Exchange of Lithuania was established in September 1993. Many of the enterprise involved in large privatisation were listed on the Lithuanian Stock Exchange, so the number of enterprises listed has been much higher than in the other Baltic countries. However, most of the companies have been relatively small compared to the average listed company in Estonia. [Mygind, p.27, 28]

Hungary has already instituted a stock market. (Fischer, p.18) In this country, public offering has been used in some major privatisations. (URL: http://worldbank.org/)

Other countries like Romania and Bulgaria are trying to create a stock exchange market. (Ion Anton, "Romania", News and Views, web page of Center for International Private Enterprise, URL: http//www.cipe.org/; Simona Iliescu Nastase, "La protection juridique de la propriété privée dans le nouveau contexte social et économique de la Roumanie", (Juridical Protection of Private Property in the New Social and Economic Context of Romania), Chapter 4, Individual Democratic Institutions Research Fellowships 1994-1996, web page of NATO, URL: http://www.nato.int/acad/fellow/94-96/iliescu/index.htm). In Bulgaria, Securities, Stock Exchanges and Investment Companies Law passed in July 1995. (Ivanka Petkova, "Bulgaria", News and Views, web page of Center for International Private Enterprise, URL: http//www.cipe.org/)

In Romania, a law has been passed to establish a stock exchange, but the institution is not yet operational. (Ion Anton, Economic Reform in Romania, Economic Reform Today, Working Papers, Number 1, web page of Center for International Private Enterprise, URL: http://www.cipe.org/)

Furthermore Poland's first stock exchange was opened in Warsaw in 1991. (Ewa Baginska, "Legal Aspects of the Privatization Process in Poland", web page of Civic Education Project, URL: http://www.cep.org.hu/)

Finally, we should point out that as well as in Hungary, Poland, Romania initial public offerings are also occurring in Latvia, and Slovenia. ("Trends and Policy in Privatisation-General Overview of Privatisation Developments", April 1995, URL: http//www.oecd.org/)

We should also point out that, public share offerings have seldom been used in other developing countries because capital markets are shallow and SOE conditions are so poor as to make them unfit for stock market flotations.[272]

Public offering has many advantages. For example it is a very effective and appropriate way of achieving wider share ownership among the society. At the same time this method is very transparent. Public share offers are generally transparent because of advertising (if permitted) and disclosure requirements. [273] Furthermore selling shares on the stock market is the most appropriate way of divesting the large sized enterprises.

However although it has many advantages selling the shares in the stock market does not guarantee the fiscal effect of privatisation. [274] Furthermore, because of its characteristics, as we have discussed above, privatisation via public offering cannot be implemented in every country and for every enterprise. Finally, this approach is especially suitable if the size of the sale justifies the costs involved. [275]

Finally one difficulty with placing a state owned enterprise in the stock market is that, with few exceptions, state owned enterprises are loss-making firms. As a result, it is unlikely that the stock market will place a positive price to those firms. A strategy that has been followed in some cases is for the government to restructure the state owned enterprise, and after a few profitable years launch a public offering. Such was the case of British Steel in the UK.[276]

---

[272] The Lessons of Experience, p.30
[273] Welch and Frémond, p.10
[274] Galal, Jones, Tandon and Vogelsang, p.569
[275] Welch and Frémond, p.10
[276] Tornell, p.28

248

D. Trade Sale

1. General

Trade sales are generally sales of enterprises to one or more specific investors through public tenders, closed tenders, direct sales and various forms of auctions.[277] In the trade sale method, the privatised company is acquired by another concern without a flotation.[278] There are two types of trade sale: (a) Auctions (open bidding) and (b) Negotiated sale

Many governments around the world including the United Kingdom, Turkey, (East) Germany, Estonia, Hungary, Poland, Bulgaria, Slovakia, Czech Republic have chosen trade sales to privatise the SOEs.[279] Thus since 1988 over 70 countries have used trade sales as a method of divesting state-owned firms. These sales have raised over $175 billion through more than 800 individual transactions.[280]

2. Certain Goals in Trade Sale Method

As we mentioned earlier, when governments determine the privatisation method they also consider the objectives of the privatisation programme.[281]

The initial goal in trade sales is to sell state assets to foreign investors in view of the underdeveloped state of domestic capital markets. Thus it is argued that governments expected three gains from privatisations via trade sales: revenue earnings for the state, the rapid infusion

---

[277] "Trends and Policy in Privatisation-General Overview of Privatisation Developments", April 1995, URL: http://www.oecd.org/
[278] Privatization in the United Kingdom, Ernst & Young, p. 27
[279] For example, the Treuhandanstalt (German Privatisation Agency) privatised some 80 per cent of the companies by this method. Furthermore in Hungary, over 60 per cent of the privatised companies were sold to investors through trade sales -- mainly tenders-- and Estonia has sold some 54 per cent of its companies to investors through internationally advertised tenders. ("Trends and Policy in Privatisation-General Overview of Privatisation Developments", April 1995, URL: http//www.oecd.org/; Havrylyshyn and McGettigan, p.3)
[280] William L. Megginson, "The Impact of Privatisation", web page of Center for International Private Enterprise, URL: http//www.cipe.org/
[281] See: p. 231-233

of foreign expertise, and the likelihood that management by foreign owners would be more effective.[282]

3. Procedure for Auction (Open Bidding)[283]

a. General

In this variation of trade sale, the financial advisers or sales working with state enterprise managers and government officials, prepare an information memorandum containing general information for potential investors. The memorandum is sent to potentially interested parties. In most cases the financial advisers or sales agents will have compiled a list of potential investors and will discuss it with the government prior to use.[284]

Then, non-binding expressions of interest are received from interested buyers. Based on these expressions of interest and a review of the financial capacity of potential bidders, a short list of potential buyers is selected. These bidders then move to the second stage of the process.[285]

During the second stage the government signs confidentiality agreements with the short-listed bidders and gives them much more detailed, commercially confidential information on the state enterprise, access to management, and a draft sales agreement. Bidders that wish to proceed then submit a binding offer (bid) and a deposit. Finally, the government and its advisers (tender

---

[282] Havrylyshyn and McGettigan, p.3
[283] In that context, Turkish Privatisation Law provides *detailed* rules on auctions. According to Article 18/C-c: "Proposals shall be received in written form. The proposal is sealed in an envelope ... The bidder must quote the offer price in letters and numbers, sign the proposal and state in writing that all specifications and appendices thereto have been read and understood. ...The proposal envelopes are delivered to the Administration ... All other matters are stated on the tender specifications. The submitted proposals may not be withdrawn for any reason whatsoever...all received proposals are listed in a memorandum... The envelopes are then opened in serial sequence, read aloud by the commission chairman or an assignee and recorded as a list which is later signed by the chairman and members...Should more than one bidder proposes the same price and all are determined to comply written second proposals are requested from those bidders, if present, and the process is continued until a higher price is proposed. If no proposals are submitted or the proposals are not deemed acceptable by the commission, a new a tender is opened under the same conditions or if deemed beneficiary by the commission, the tender is finalised by the bargaining or public auction method."
[284] Welch and Frémond, p.14, 15
[285] Welch and Frémond, p.15

commissions)[286] choose the best offer, and the sale closes with payment for the shares (or in special cases, assets) of the state enterprise. [287]

b. Two-Part Open Bidding Procedure

Some governments have used two-part open bidding procedures: a technical bid and a financial bid. The financial bid cannot be evaluated unless the technical bid meets the requirements of the tender. The terms of reference for the technical bid often require bidders to commit to investing capital in the enterprise over five years, and to describe their plans for the workforce. If the technical bid is satisfactory, a weighted average of the technical and financial bids of all retained bidders is calculated to determine the winning bid. [288]

Two part open bidding procedures have evolved in response to government concerns about the buyers of privatised assets. Governments often try to ensure that privatised enterprises

---

[286] Privatisation legislation often provides provisions on the foundation and structure of tender commissions. Thus Turkish Privatisation Law states that "...The Tender Commission consists of five members, chaired by the Vice President in charge of the project group responsible for the privatisation proceedings of the organisation in the privatisation portfolio and having as members the Head of the Project Group, an expert of the group, Head of the Department of Tender Services or an expert there from and a legal consultant or a lawyer from the Legal Consultancy Department. The Commission shall resume duties upon proposal of the President of the Administration and approval of the Prime Minister. Alternates are appointed to the positions in the Commission as described here above in the same number and method...The Commission convenes with the presence of all of members and sanctions decisions through an absolute majority. Abstentions are not allowed in decisions. Any member objecting to the decision must justify opposing views and record it beneath the decision with his / her endorsement..." [Article 18/C-a, b, Turkish Privatisation Law, web page of Turkish Privatisation Administration, URL: http://www.oib.gov.tr]

[287] Welch and Frémond, p.15
In Turkey the tender is concluded upon approval of the President of the Administration. Tender results are approved by the Council. [Article 18/C-g, Turkish Privatisation Law, web page of Turkish Privatisation Administration, URL: http://www.oib.gov.tr]

[288] Welch and Frémond, p.15; Michael Klein, "Designing Auctions for Concessions-Guessing the Right Value to Bid and the Winner's Curse", Public Policy for the private Sector, Note No: 160, The World Bank, November 1998, p.1
According to Klein the choice of auction method is affected by arguments about: (a) The political sustainability of the outcome, (b) The robustness of firms' bidding strategies, (c) The opportunities for collusion among firms. (p.1)
"...If the applied tender method do not give any positive result in at least two tenders and in cases where the organisation in the scope of privatization portfolio has contributions to the local and national economies, or it is deemed necessary for prevention of a probable monopoly, preservation or increase of employment possibilities, or partial or full commitment is given for technological innovations and investments, certain bidder or bidders qualified to enter into partnership in the form of a joint venture aiming at spreading the ownership and bearing the required technical or professional capability and financial standing or management responsibilities and powers shall be invited to bid by the close bidding method, with a prior consent of the Council. If only one proposal is received, the

will continue to be going concerns. They are wary of asset strippers, and concerned that new owners may lay off large numbers of employees. Thus governments seek buyers with sufficient resources to invest in the enterprise, transfer know-how, and increase employment.[289]

In choosing the best bidder, government might take different factors into account. The organiser of privatisation (government, privatisation agency etc.) shall determine the best bid taking into consideration the purchase price and all additional conditions. In some cases, the organiser of privatisation is also entitled to determine the second best bid. The contract of sale shall be concluded with the investor whose bid had been the best.[290]

4. Negotiated sales

a. General

Negotiated sales are a variant of the open bidding process. Once the government has chosen a buyer, it negotiates an agreement that is attractive, to a relative majority to the buyer and protects the government's interests.[291] Thus tender process may be commenced by inviting more than one bidder to submit their proposals in enclosed envelopes. More than one bargaining session may be held with the bidders and these are conducted separately with each bidder. At any stage of the bargaining, the privatisation commission or the authority may decide to hold joint bargaining with the bidders.[292]

---

tender shall be conducted by the bargaining method, whereas if more than one proposal is received, the public auction method shall be initiated". [Article 18/C-c, Turkish Privatisation Law, URL: http://www.oib.gov.tr]
[289] Welch and Frémond, p.15
[290] Article 21/8 of Estonian Privatisation Law, Estonian Law on Privatisation, (unofficial translation), web page of Estonian Privatisation Agency, URL: http//www.eea.ee/
Furthermore according to article 21 of the Estonian Privatisation Law: "Competing additional conditions may be: (a) guaranteeing of employment; (b) creating new jobs; (c) technical and financial plan which shall include technology used, amount of investments and sources of financing; (d) environmental commitment; (e) other conditions regulating the activities of an enterprise or a commercial undertaking." [Estonian Law on Privatisation, (unofficial translation), web page of Estonian Privatisation Agency, URL: http//www.eea.ee/]
[291] Welch and Frémond, p.15, 16
[292] Article 18/C-c, Turkish Privatisation Law, URL: http://www.oib.gov.tr

Different privatisation laws may state and design "negotiated sales" under different concepts. For example, Macedonian Privatisation Law (Law on Transformation of Socially Owned Enterprises of Macedonia, states this type of sale as "direct agreement". According to the law, an ideal part of the enterprise shall be sold through "direct agreement" (Article 86-a/1). The strategic investor, in terms of this Law, shall be the purchaser of the ideal part of the enterprise, assigned by the Government of the Republic of Macedonia, upon the proposal made by the Agency. (Article 86-a/3)[293]

Negotiated sales are used when there is only one bidder or a bidder has a marked advantage over in the government's eyes. It is difficult to get the highest price in such sales, however, and they are less transparent than open bidding.[294]

The organiser of privatisation is entitled not to allow the bidders, whose bids and warrants are considered insufficient, to participate in preliminary negotiations.[295]

b. Direct negotiation

There is a variation of negotiated sale that can be called sale by direct negotiation. In this case if only one bidder takes part in an auction or tender, or if no other bidders meet the conditions attached to a privatisation plan, the assets can be sold by direct negotiation between the privatisation agency and bidder (private investor).[296]

Finally some privatisation laws states that in case the bidder who had made the best bid shall not sign the contract of sale by the term fixed by the organiser of privatisation on the

---

[293] For the full text of Macedonian Privatisation law see the web page of Macedonian Privatisation Agency, URL: http//www.mpa.org.mk
[294] Welch and Frémond, p.16
[295] Article 21 of Estonian Privatisation Law. [Estonian Law on Privatisation, (unofficial translation), web page of Estonian Privatisation Agency, URL: http//www.eea.ee/]
[296] This method has been used in Lithuania. (Lithuanian Business Information Centre, URL: http://www.lbic.lt)

conditions offered by the bidder, the organiser of privatisation has the right to sign the contract of sale with the bidder whose bid had been the second best. [297]

E. Management-Employee Buyout

1. General

The alternative to mass privatisation in terms of speed and political acceptability has been the buy-out of enterprises by their managers and, more importantly, employees. In this method of privatisation the buyer is not the public or certain groups of investors but the manager or/and the employees of the state owned enterprises (SOEs).

Employees may involve in the privatisation process in different ways. However, there are essentially two forms of management and employee participation, those in which management and employees acquire (buy-out) the majority of a firm and become its owner/managers, and employee participation schemes, which include employees in the privatisation process under preferential terms, but do not put company control in their hands. [298]

Between these two approaches the most well known method is the Employee Stock Ownership Program, where a new firm is put together by employees pooling their resources and borrowing new funds. This new firm then buys the existing state-owned firm, thereby making it privately owned.[299]

---

[297] Article 21/8 of Estonian Privatisation Law, Estonian Law on Privatisation, (unofficial translation), web page of Estonian Privatisation Agency, URL: http//www.eea.ee/
[298] Mygind, p.33, 34; "Trends and Policy in Privatisation-General Overview of Privatisation Developments", April 1995, URL: http://www.oecd.org/; Henry Gibbon, "Privatization in 1995 and Beyond", web page of Center for International Private Enterprise, URL: http://www.cipe.org/; François Degeorge, Dirk Jenter, Alberto Moel and Peter Tufano, "Selling Company Shares to Reluctant Employees: France Telecom's Experience", NBER (National Bureau of Economic Research), Working Paper Series, Working Paper 7683, Cambridge, May 2000, p.1, URL: http://www.nber.org/papers/w7683
[299] "Privatizing State-Owned Companies", The Prosperity Papers Series, Prosperity Paper Three, web page of Center for International Private Enterprise, URL: http//www.cipe.org

Management and employee buy-outs have been used in several countries including England[300], Germany, Poland[301], Russia, Belarus, Latvia, Georgia, Romania[302], Bulgaria, Estonia, Czech Republic, Lithuania,[303] Hungary, [304] Croatia[305], the former Yugoslav Republic of Macedonia, Poland, Hungary, Romania, the Slovak Republic, Slovenia, and Russia.[306]

2. Criticisms on this method

There are criticisms on that method in the following points: (a) In regard to equity, concessional share prices for employees favour workers in some enterprises over the rest of the population. Why should industrial workers obtain larger claims on capital than workers in less capital-intensive industries, such as teaching?[307], (b) It is argued that budget revenue will be lost if shares are sold at discount prices, (c) With respect to efficiency it is questionable how much employee share ownership improves efficiency in larger firms where harder work by an individual cannot make such difference in total profits?[308] (d) Finally it is argued that management and employee buy-outs often mean large costs in inefficiency and poor management. They may grant excessive wage increases, maintain excessively high employment, and undertake insufficient investment. In the transitional economies, insiders may also lack

---

[300] Privatization in the United Kingdom, Ernst & Young, 1994, p. 28. Also see: Prosser, (Social Limits), p.229

[301] Bornstein, p.239

[302] Ion Anton, Economic reform in Romania, Economic Reform Today, Working Papers, Number 1, web page of Center for International Private Enterprise, URL: http://www.cipe.org/

[303] In Lithuania, employee ownership was an important element in the privatisation process, especially in large enterprises. [Mygind, p.22]

[304] "Trends and Policy in Privatisation-General Overview of Privatisation Developments", April 1995,
Finally we must point out that, this method has often been used in the United States because of special tax incentives. ("Privatizing State-Owned Companies", The Prosperity Papers Series, Prosperity Paper Three, web page of Center for International Private Enterprise, URL: http://www.cipe.org/)

[305] In Croatia, employees and management of the companies were entitled to subscribe up to DM 20,000 of nominal value of the shares with 20 percent discount plus 1 percent per every working year. (Web page of Croatian Government: URL: http://www.hfp.hr/privatization/privat.htm)

[306] Havrylyshyn and McGettigan, p.3; Fischer, p.6
In Lithuania, statistics revealed that employee owned enterprises are doing well compared to other groups of investors. [Mygind, p.41]

[307] Fischer, p.5, 6

[308] Bornstein, p.240

many of the skills necessary to function in a market-oriented economy.[309] In other words, employee ownership, are considered to have specific disadvantages because employees might have special objectives of stable jobs and high wages differing from profit maximisation. They might lack the necessary management skills and they have limited access to capital.[310]

3. Analysis on Management-Employee Buyouts

As we examined above, under management and employee buy-outs approach, shares of an enterprise are sold or given to some combination of managers and other employees.[311]

The powerful positions of employees-as, for example, in Poland, and of managers, as in Russia-give this approach the twin advantages of feasibility and political popularity. This method is also rapid and easy to implement. Furthermore, well-structured management-employee buyouts can sometimes lead to efficient results, since they align the incentives of workers and owners.[312]

---

[309] Havrylyshyn and McGettigan, p.3
[310] Mygind, p.43
[311] Havrylyshyn and McGettigan, p.3
[312] Havrylyshyn and McGettigan, p.3

F. Free Distribution of Shares-Mass Privatisation (Voucher System)[313]

1. General

a. Concept and structure

Free distribution of shares is another technique of privatisation; like restitution it has been used in former socialist countries. In the privatisation literature this method is also called "mass privatisation" or "voucher system". The concept of mass privatisation (voucher system) as an instrument to privatise post-communist economies was developed for the first time in Poland in 1988.[314] However, voucher system has been first used in Lithuania in 1991.[315]

Although there are different variants of free transfer of shares to the citizenry[316], mass privatisation usually involves the distribution of shares of state enterprises to the public, either

---

[313] There are three types of vouchers; therefore the different types of vouchers should be distinguished:
(a) Vouchers as means of free distribution of shares (voucher scheme privatisation), (b) Vouchers that have been issued to compensate original owners (or their heirs) whose property have been seized by the ex-communist regime (restitution vouchers), (c) Vouchers issued for other purposes. For example vouchers issued to the employers of the privatised enterprise when they have been working for a number of years.
We will deal with the first type of vouchers. However, the common point of all the type of vouchers is that they can be used interchangeably for the privatisation of housing and land, or for the purchase of shares of state owned enterprises or special funds.
Finally privatisation vouchers in USA refer to the government financial subsidies given to individuals for purchasing specific goods or services from the private or public sector. The government gives individuals redeemable certificates or vouchers to purchase the service in the open market. Under this approach, the government relies on the market competition for cost control and individual citizens to seek out quality goods or services. The government's financial obligation to the recipient is limited by the amount of the voucher. A form of vouchers are grants, which can be given to state and local governments that may use the funds to buy services from the private sector. (General Accounting Office, p.1, 47)
As mentioned above under this subtitle, we will deal with the vouchers as means of free distribution of shares. However, we must point out that, in former socialist countries different governments issued different type of vouchers. For example, in Estonia two types of vouchers have been distributed. Capital vouchers were distributed to all residents depending on years of work. Compensation vouchers were distributed to owners (or their heirs) of property nationalised in the early Soviet period if they did not want this property back, or if it was not possible to return this property. [Mygind, p.5]. Furthermore, Lithuanian government issued vouchers in the form of transfers of shares of leased enterprises to employees. (p.20)

[314] Jan Szomburg, " The Reasoning Behind the Polish Mass Privatization Program", web page of Center for International Private Enterprise, URL: http//www.cipe.org/

[315] Mygind, p.20

[316] There are different variants of free transfer of shares to the citizenry: (a) Voucher coupons to bid shares in operating companies, (b) Actual shares in operating companies, and (c) Shares in investment trusts like mutual funds or holding companies that in turn possess shares in operating companies. (Bornstein, p.244-246)

for free or for a minimal charge[317], generally through a voucher allocation scheme. Vouchers normally take the form of certificates or scrip distributed to the population and they are convertible into shares in state enterprises through an auction process.[318] The essence of mass privatisation is the distribution of privatisation vouchers to all adult citizens, free of charge and convertible into shares in privatised enterprises.[319]

Finally free transfer can involve personal entitlements (to former owners, employees, and the citizenry at large), endowments to institutions (like banks, and pension funds), or combinations of the two approaches, such as personal entitlements to shares in institutions like mutual funds and holding companies.[320]

b. Unique implementation

After the communist regime collapsed and Eastern and Central European countries started their privatisation programmes voucher system has been used almost in all former socialist countries, particularly in the Czech Republic[321], but also in Latvia[322], Lithuania[323],

---

[317] Governments often set a minimum acceptable bid price to deflect the inevitable criticism that they are "giving away the crown jewels" or in a misguided attempt to counter perceived collusion by bidders. However, almost in all cases, this price is too low. (S. Ramachandran, "The Veil of Vouchers", Public Policy for the Private Sector, The World Bank Group, Note No. 108, April 1997, p.3)

[318] W.Lieberman, Ewing, Mejstrik, Mukherjee and Fidler, p.3
Some privatisation laws provide a definition for privatisation vouchers. Thus, according to Albanian privatisation legislation: "Privatisation vouchers are privatisation money, privatisation bonds and vouchers issued by the Bank of Albania." (Article 1, Law No. 8306, dated 14.3.1998, On the Strategy for the privatisation of Strategic Sectors. Web page of Economic Development Agency of Albanian Government, URL: http://www.aeda.gov.al/)

[319] Jan Szomburg, " The Reasoning Behind the Polish Mass Privatization Program", web page of Center for International Private Enterprise, URL: http//www.cipe.org/

[320] Bornstein, p.242; Malle, p.84

[321] From 1991 through 1995, vouchers were used to privatise 1,849 companies, or 56% of the 3,278 businesses chosen for joint stock conversion. (The World Bank, URL: http://www.worldbank.org/ecspf/final/html/czech_republic.htm)
In this process citizens were given voucher points that they could use to bid for shares of designated firms in a series of price-administered bidding rounds. (Jan Hanousek and Eugene A. Kroch, "A Model of Learning in Sequential Bidding: Voucher Privatization in the Czech Republic: Wave I", January 1995, URL: http//www.ssc.upenn.edu/~alexv/cast/february/jan.html; Stijn Claessens, Simeon Djankov, and Gerhard Pohl, "Ownership and Corporate Governance—Evidence from the Czech Republic", Public Policy for the Private Sector, The World Bank Group, Note No: 111, May 1997, p.1)

[322] Mygind, p.17

[323] In Lithuania, vouchers system was used in the first phase of privatisation which covers mainly medium and large-sized enterprises and over two thirds of state property was scheduled for privatisation under a this system. The vouchers could be used to purchase shares at auctions, sold or otherwise transferred to other citizens. When

Albania[324], Poland,[325] Moldova,[326] Slovakia,[327] Romania,[328] Hungary,[329] Estonia[330] and Russia.[331] Furthermore mass privatisation programs in the Czech Republic, Russia and Lithuania are complete.[332]

2. Why Mass Privatisation?

The success of voucher programmes has gained a great deal of attention in several countries previously reticent to use the approach. [333] The following factors can be seen as the main reasons of this method of privatisation:

In much of Eastern Europe, the only politically feasible alternative to auctioning off SOEs was to effectively give the SOEs directly to the nation's citizens by giving them the exclusive right (and the means) to purchase shares. These voucher programs had the virtues of

---

bidding for shares, vouchers could be supplemented with cash up to their own value. (Lithuanian Business Information Centre, URL: http://www.lbic.lt/; Mygind, p.18, 24)

[324] Web page of Economic Development Agency of Albanian Government, URL: http://www.aeda.gov.al/
[325] Havrylyshyn and McGettigan, p.3; URL: http://www.worldbank.org/; Barbara Blaszczyk, "Moving Ahead: Privatization in Poland ", web page of Center for International Private Enterprise, URL: http://www.cipe.org/; Henry Gibbon, "Privatization in 1995 and Beyond", web page of Center for International Private Enterprise, URL: http//www.cipe.org/; Ewa Baginska, "Legal Aspects of the Privatization Process in Poland", web page of Civic Education Project, URL: http://www.cep.org.hu/
[326] In Moldova, most of the companies privatised have been through mass voucher privatisation, beginning with the distribution of National Patrimonial Bonds (NPBs) to 3.5 million people in 1995. By 1996 1,150 medium and large companies were partially privatised, and 1,400 small companies were fully privatised through NPBs. (Web page of the World Bank, URL: http//www.worldbank.org/)
[327] W.Lieberman, Ewing, Mejstrik, Mukherjee and Fidler, p.48
[328] Ion Anton, Economic reform in Romania, Economic Reform Today, Working Papers, Number 1, web page of Center for International Private Enterprise, URL: http://www.cipe.org/; Henry Gibbon, Privatization in 1995 and Beyond, web page of Center for International Private Enterprise, URL: http://www.cipe.org/
[329] Eva Voszka, "Privatization in Hungary: Results and Open Issues", web page of Center for International Private Enterprise, URL: http//www.cipe.org/
[330] "Privatisation in Estonia", web page of Estonia, URL: http://www.einst.ee/
[331] For example in Russia, more than 15,000 medium and large enterprises, employing more than 80% of the industrial labour force constituted the first voucher privatisation program which ended in 1994. [URL: http://www.worldbank.org/; Tornell, p.23, 24]
[332] Lieberman, Ewing, Mejstrik, Mukherjee and Fidler, p.48
In Slovakia, more than 1200 companies with property of almost $8 billion had been privatised by July 1994. (Andrej Juris, "Economic Reform in Slovakia" web page of Center for International Private Enterprise, URL: http//www.cipe.org/)
[333] For this point see: "Trends and Policy in Privatisation-General Overview of Privatisation Developments", April 1995, URL: http://www.oecd.org/
According to one study, mass privatisation schemes have three main objectives: (a) Political: Attempting to involve and commit the population at large to the economic transformation process, (b) Social: Seeking some form of distributive of shares to general public, (c) Economic: Quickly privatising a large number of firms to deepen market forces and competition within the economy. (W.Lieberman, Ewing, Mejstrik, Mukherjee and Fidler, p.3)

speed and perceived fairness: literally thousands of firms were privatised in five years or less, and the non-discriminatory nature of these voucher distribution programs ensured their popularity. This popularity had the added bonus of making privatisation politically irreversible because large percentages of the population in each country had effectively become capitalists.[334] From an economic point of view, the mass privatisation was justified by the difficulty of finding the necessary capital by selling assets on such a large scale, at the level of a whole economy.[335]

In former socialist countries lack of capital is a serious problem preventing many privatisation transactions. Vouchers system which involves free distribution of assets of SOEs is considered a solution to this issue. In other words, voucher privatisation helps to overcome the shortage of domestic capital.[336]

On the other hand, with voucher privatisation large amount of assets can easily be privatised. This makes the process fast.[337]

Voucher system supports the domestic ownership and from the political point of view it is a gain for the government. From that point of view it can be considered as a social compensatory scheme rather than a serious attempt at privatisation.[338]

Furthermore, voucher programmes have proven particularly successful in privatising the large number of hard-to-sell second tier firms for which trade sales are difficult to arrange.[339]

---

[334] William L. Megginson, "The Impact of Privatization", web page of Center for International Private Enterprise, URL: http//www.cipe.org/
[335] Simona Iliescu Nastase, "La protection juridique de la propriété privée dans le nouveau contexte social et économique de la Roumanie", (Juridical Protection of Private Property in the New Social and Economic Context of Romania), Chapter 4, Individual Democratic Institutions Research Fellowships 1994-1996, web page of NATO, URL: http://www.nato.int/acad/fellow/94-96/iliescu/index.htm
[336] Havrylyshyn and McGettigan, p.3
[337] However, in some countries like Hungary, Contrary to its original goal, for example, the free distribution of assets actually slowed down privatization due to the uncertainties surrounding both the beneficiaries and the assets. (Eva Voszka, "Privatization in Hungary: Results and Open Issues", web page of Center for International Private Enterprise, URL: http//www.cipe.org/)
[338] Fischer, p.17
[339] "Trends and Policy in Privatisation-General Overview of Privatisation Developments", April 1995, URL: http//www.oecd.org/

Finally the state may distribute free shares in enterprises that cannot be privatised by sales because of low profitability (or losses) and need for restructuring.[340]

3. Designing the voucher scheme

In order to design of a voucher system, the following points should be considered and different issues should be addressed: (a) Who is eligible to receive vouchers (all citizens, residents of a specific date, and all citizens above a certain age)?[341] (b) How are vouchers issued (one or a series of vouchers, tied to the auctioning of firms in a series of tranches)? (c) Should vouchers be assigned a monetary value (affects such issues as inflationary effects of vouchers, their tradability, and controls and security printing)? (d) Who issues the vouchers (for example voter registration system, saving banks, central bank, social security or pension system, government, a ministry)[342]? (e) Are vouchers immediately tradable[343] and transferable?[344] (f)

---

[340] Bornstein, p.244

[341] "All citizens of the Slovak Republic over 18 years old with permanent residence in the Slovak territory are entitled to obtain coupons." (Article 24/1, The Act No. 92/1991, dated February 26, 1991 on the Conditions of Transfer of State Property to Other Persons, web page of Ministry for Administration and Privatisation of National Property of the Slovak Republic, URL: http//www.privatiz.gov.sk/anglicky/act92.htm)
   In Lithuania the distribution of vouchers was dependent on the age of the citizens. [Mygind, p.21]
   In Czech Republic all citizens aged eighteen and over could buy vouchers for a nominal fee to use in bidding. (Stijn Claessens, Simeon Djankov, and Gerhard Pohl, Ownership and Corporate Governance-Evidence from the Czech Republic", Public Policy for the Private Sector, The World Bank Group, Note No:111, May 1997, p.2; Fischer, p.12)
   In Russia each Russian citizen born before 11 June 1992 has had a right to a voucher of 10.000 rubles. (Malle, p.84)
   Finally, in some cases, privatisation law states that (not all citizens) but certain group of people are entitled to get privatisation vouchers for free of charge. Thus, in Croatia, the Privatisation Law defines certain groups of people or entitled participants, who were either political prisoners before the declaration of independence of the Republic of Croatia, refugees from the fatherland war, invalids, widows or orphans. All in all it is estimated that around 300.000 individuals are entitled to receive vouchers, denominated in investment points and non - tradable, with which they can bid for shares in selected enterprises in a three round bidding procedure. According to the degrees of disability and other determining factors, the entitled participants will register and receive vouchers denominated in investment points, with which they can bid. (Web page of Croatian Privatisation Fund, URL: http://www.hfp.hr/privatization/privat.htm)

[342] "Coupons are issued by the Finance Ministry." (Article 23/2, The Act No. 92/1991, dated February 26, 1991 on the Conditions of Transfer of State Property to Other Persons, web page of Ministry for Administration and Privatisation of National Property of the Slovak Republic, URL: http//www.privatiz.gov.sk/anglicky/act92.htm)
   "Privatisation vouchers are...issued by the Bank of Albania." (Article 1, Law No. 8306, dated 14.3.1998, On the Strategy for the privatisation of Strategic Sectors. Web page of Economic Development Agency of Albanian Government, URL: http//www.aeda.gov.al/)
   In Russia vouchers were printed by Gosznak, the State Banknote production Association and then distributed to local areas. Vouchers were issued by branches of the Savings Banks to the citizens who had to reach the closest local branch and present some identification document. (Malle, p.85)

What are the roles of financial intermediates?[345] How they will be registered, regulated, and supervised? (g) How are vouchers converted into shares? (h) Can vouchers be used for anything other than state enterprises' shares (such as to buy land, small enterprises at auctions, or apartments)?[346] (i) How are vouchers and distribution of preference shares to employees linked?[347] (j) What is the content of a voucher?[348] (k) Is there a deadline to use the vouchers? When are they going to be expired?[349] (l) Do the voucher system includes free distribution of shares or do citizens need to pay a nominal fee?[350]

---

[343] In Estonia, vouchers were declared non-tradable from the start [Mygind, p.11]. On the other hand, in Latvia it is possible to trade the vouchers. (p.17)
In Russia vouchers could be used not only to buy shares of privatisable companies of shares in investment funds, but also sold for cash. (Malle, p.85)

[344] A coupon is untransferable and rights connected to it are subject of inheritance. A coupon cannot be redeemed. (Article 22/6, The Act No.92/1991, dated February 26, 1991 on the Conditions of Transfer of State Property to Other Persons, web page of Ministry for Administration and Privatisation of National Property of the Slovak Republic, URL: http//www.privatiz.gov.sk/anglicky/act92.htm)

[345] Investment funds play an important role in most voucher schemes. In Poland and Romania, government organised funds are supposed to function as the primary intermediaries in voucher sales. In both countries the population receives shares in funds rather than the underlying SOEs. In most other countries (including the Czech Republic, Slovak Republic, Georgia, Lithuania, Moldova, Russia, Slovenia and the Ukraine) funds were created by private agents. ("Trends and Policy in Privatisation-General Overview of Privatisation Developments", April 1995, URL: http://www.oecd.org/; Andrej Juris, "Economic Reform in Slovakia" web page of Center for International Private Enterprise, URL: http//www.cipe.org/)

[346] In Lithuania, the vouchers could be used both in the auctions for small enterprises, in share subscriptions for large enterprises, and in privatisation of housing. (Mygind, p.21)

[347] Lieberman, Ewing, Mejstrik, Mukherjee and Fidler, p.26

[348] "A coupon book must contain following mandatory items: (a) name, citizen's birth certificate number and his/her permanent residence; (b) identification of the body issuing the coupon; (c) acquisition price; (d) date of issuance and validity period; (e) registration date". [Article 23/1-a, b, c, d, e, The Act No.92/1991, dated February 26, 1991 on the Conditions of Transfer of State Property to Other Persons, (web page of Ministry for Administration and Privatisation of National Property of the Slovak Republic, URL: http//www.privatiz.gov.sk/anglicky/act92.htm]

[349] "Coupons shall be valid for ten months from the date of issuance. This period may, however, be extended by the decision of Finance Ministry." [Article 23a/1, The Act No. 92/1991, dated February 26, 1991 on the Conditions of Transfer of State Property to Other Persons, (web page of Ministry for Administration and Privatisation of National Property of the Slovak Republic, URL: http//www.privatiz.gov.sk/anglicky/act92.htm]
In Lithuania, the deadline for the vouchers was July 1995. [Mygind, p.21]

[350] In Russia 25 rubles were required for the collection of vouchers. These fees were supposed to cover the technical cost of printing the vouchers. (Malle, p.84)

4. Debate and Discussion on Voucher system

a. Criticisms

It is argued that in spite of the fact that voucher programs were probably the only feasible method of privatising Eastern European economies in the early 1990s, these programs have several serious weaknesses, and are unlikely to remain as important in future SOE divestitures.

A number of disadvantages and criticisms can be identified in the voucher system: (a) Voucher programs do not raise cash for the SOE or the government. In other words, insofar as the shares to be distributed free could instead be sold, budget revenue will be reduced. (b) In contrast to sales to foreign investors, free transfer of shares to the citizenry will not infuse new capital, technology, and management skills into enterprises. Therefore voucher privatisations do not result in an infusion of new technology or managerial expertise. (c) Vouchers do nothing to establish an effective monitoring mechanism for newly privatised firms, and the ownership structure that results from their exercise is usually highly flawed.[351] Dispersed ownership structure will lack the focus and power to direct effective corporate management. This, in turn, may scare off potential new sources of capital.[352] (d) Unlike sale of shares, free transfer of them does not absorb any of the monetary overhangs. Furthermore, inflationary pressure could increase if people with a higher propensity to consume sell their free shares to others with a lower prosperity to consume.[353] (e) Voucher privatisation cannot be seen as a distribution of

---

[351] William L. Megginson, "The Impact of Privatization", web page of Center for International Private Enterprise, URL: http:/www.cipe.org/; Fischer, p.12

[352] Havrylyshyn and McGettigan, p.3; Peter Young, "The Lessons of Privatisation", web page of Center for International Private Enterprise, URL: http://www.cipe.org/

One of the most frequent criticisms of voucher programs is that enterprises ownership can become so widely diffused that there will be no dominant owner to compel good management. It is argued that the best way to ensure effective corporate governance is to reserve a majority of shares for a core investor. (Bell, p.3; Marek Hessel, "How Corporate Governance Makes Privatization Succeed", web page of Center for International Private Enterprise, URL: http//www.cipe.org/)

According to one study: "...earlier hopes that voucher privatisation would create vast and liquid share markets in a short period of time seem to have been overly optimistic". ("Trends and Policy in Privatisation-General Overview of Privatisation Developments", April 1995, URL: http://www.oecd.org/)

[353] Bornstein, p.244

wealth to all citizens.[354] (f) Finally, it is argued that mass privatisation distributes ownership of an existing enterprise among many individuals who must entrust the responsibility for managing the enterprise to a professional manager. Those individuals need to make sure the manager operates the business in their interest.[355]

b. Advantages

Although free distribution of shares (voucher system) has some disadvantages there are certain advantages: (a) equal transfers to all citizens will reduce inequality in the distribution of wealth and of income from it, (b) Universal, or at least widespread, ownership of shares in firms promotes popular capitalism, (c) Furthermore free transfer of shares can avoid some of the valuation problems associated with sales of shares,[356] (d) Finally proponents of mass privatisation argued that the fast pace of voucher privatisation would add to the credibility of reform programs and bolster their chance of success. At times, the speed could prevent employees or other interests from mobilising opposition to privatisation. (e) Finally, the widespread participation of a country's citizens fosters a greater understanding of reform and creates a new owner class with a stake in the process.[357]

5. Analysis on Voucher System

Voucher-based programs (mass privatisation) involve the distribution of certificates, or coupons, to participants, who then exchange these vouchers for shares in individual SOEs or for shares in financial intermediaries (voucher funds). These intermediaries, in turn, bid their

---

[354] A person who receives a voucher may think that she is wealthier than before, but if everyone receives a voucher, she is not. Wealth represents her share of the economy's income, and everyone obviously cannot get a larger share...(furthermore)... state-owned assets are only part of such capital, so the potential wealth redistribution through vouchers is small..." [S. Ramachandran, "The Veil of Vouchers", Public Policy for the Private Sector, The World Bank Group, Note No. 108, April 1997, p.3, 4]
[355] Marek Hessel, "How Corporate Governance Makes Privatisation Succeed", web page of Center for International Private Enterprise, URL: http//www.cipe.org/
[356] Bornstein, p.244
[357] Havrylyshyn and McGettigan, p.3

accumulated vouchers for shares of SOEs. In most cases, vouchers can be freely traded for cash.[358]

As the name implies, mass privatisation is a quick, simple way of completing large, economy-wide privatisation programs--just what the transition economies (former socialist countries) needed.[359] Voucher programs are also attractive to policy-makers because they can simplify and accelerate the privatisation of large numbers of SOEs, many of which might be unattractive to strategic investors. Although vouchers started out as a tool for mass privatisation programs, they can also be used in other kinds of programs. For example, vouchers can be used where there are compelling social and political reasons to distribute ownership widely or to target the benefits of privatisation to disadvantaged segments of the population.[360]

Mass privatisation has proven to be an effective and popular means of accelerating the pace of privatisation.[361] For example in the Czech Republic some 39 per cent of all enterprises, (61 per cent of total book value of privatisations) was sold by the voucher method. In Lithuania and Moldova almost all state-owned enterprises privatised were sold for vouchers, accounting for 87 per cent and 94 per cent of total book value of privatisations in Lithuania and Moldova respectively.[362]

Vouchers will work best where voucher distribution and trading centres are easily accessible and where there is a competent administrative system capable of carrying out the distribution and registration. Weak institutional capacity makes implementation of a voucher-

---

[358] Bell, p.2
[359] Havrylyshyn and McGettigan, p.3
[360] Bell, p.2
[361] Voucher system, however, has not been very popular in some ex-socialist countries. In those countries one of the obstacles in the mass privatisation scheme was that, many people thought that there would be hidden costs in the voucher system. [This was the case for Bulgaria (Web page of Center for International Private Enterprise, URL: http//www.cipe.org/)]
[362] "Trends and Policy in Privatisation-General Overview of Privatisation Developments", April 1995, URL: http://www.oecd.org/; Privatization Update, web page of Center for International Private Enterprise, URL: http://www.cipe.org

based program difficult.[363] Finally despite the criticisms, using vouchers may seem a more equitable approach to the public, and it helps avoid claims that the government is selling assets "too cheaply"-thereby safeguarding the difficult transition to a market economy.[364]

G. Liquidation

Liquidation of state-owned enterprises (SOEs) is also of growing importance, particularly in the most advanced former socialist countries, as a means of privatising enterprises in poor condition and selling off residual state assets. Significant numbers of SOEs have been privatised through liquidation in the former German Democratic Republic, Hungary, Estonia[365] and Poland.[366]

H. Financing

Private investor would want to learn the payment details of the privatisation transaction.[367] Thus, privatisation legislation need to provide rules on the method of payment. Some privatisation laws provide clear measures on payment methods.[368]

---

[363] Bell, p.2
[364] S. Ramachandran, "The Veil of Vouchers", Public Policy for the Private Sector, The World Bank Group, Note No. 108, April 1997, p.3, 4
[365] From as early as September 1992 Estonia had implemented a rather tough law on bankruptcy. Most state-owned enterprises were cut off from subsidies and some of them were liquidated and their assets privatised. Fourty (medium to large) enterprises had been privatised through liquidation at the end of 1998, and a much larger number of small enterprises had been privatised in this way. [Mygind, p.11]
[366] "Trends and Policy in Privatisation-General Overview of Privatisation Developments", April 1995, URL: http//www.oecd.org/; "Privatizing State-Owned Companies", The Prosperity Papers Series, Prosperity Paper Three, web page of Center for International Private Enterprise, URL: http//www.cipe.org/
In Poland, there are 1165 are undergoing liquidation (according to bankruptcy law), with 225 cases were completed. (Maciej Grabowski, Economic Reform in Poland, Economic Reform Today Working Papers, Number 4, web page of Center for International Private Enterprise, URL: http://www.cipe.org/; Barbara Blaszczyk, Moving Ahead: Privatization in Poland", web page of Center for International Private Enterprise, URL: http://www.cipe.org/)
[367] Some of the details are as follows: (a) In which currency wills the payment be made? (b) Will government accept payment in instalments? (c) Does government require any security measures on payment, (d) Are there different rules on different investors in the payment method?
[368] According to Lithuanian Privatisation Law: "A potential buyer who makes the payment in Lithuania shall pay for the privatisation object only in the national currency of the Republic of Lithuania-the Litas, while a potential buyer who is registered and who makes the payment abroad shall also pay or shall pay in the foreign currency stipulated in the privatisation transaction. The procedure and the time limits for the payment shall be set forth in the privatisation transaction. The privatisation object (shares) may also be bought by instalments; the final purchase, however, may not be postponed for more than 5 years...When privatising the shares of an enterprise

Cash payment should be the rule. Special financing techniques have been included in many privatisation laws or programs. They include deferred payment (seller financing) and credit (bank financing). Where shares are payable in instalments, for example, the voting power of shareholders who have not paid the full amount of their shares can be limited and their shares may be held in escrow accounts until the last instalment is paid. [369]

I. Allocation of privatisation proceeds

The privatisation program or strategy should specify how privatisation proceeds are to be used. If the country's existing laws (including public finance and public enterprise laws) include no provisions to that effect, or if these provisions are not deemed appropriate for the use of privatisation proceeds, the privatisation legislation may need to include language on allocation proceeds. Issues include whether the proceeds should be (i) allocated to a special account or fund earmarked for specific expenditures, (ii) considered as general government revenue, (iii) a mix of both systems.[370] If special accounts or funds are established, the law or implementing regulations often determine how these should be set up, operated or monitored.[371]

---

controlled by the state (municipality) by a public tender or direct negotiations, the final payment for a shareholding of up to 5 per cent may be postponed for the employees of the enterprise for no longer than 5 years in the manner and method prescribed by the Government. [Article 20, Law on the Privatisation of State-Owned and Municipal Property, 4 November 1997 No. VIII-480, Vilnius, web page of Lithuanian State Property Fund, URL: http://www.vtf.lt/en/frame22.html]

In Lithuania, Lithuanian natural and legal persons must pay for the assets they acquire in Litas; foreign natural or legal persons can pay in Litas, US Dollars, Deutschmarks, French Francs or Sterling. Payments may be made in instalments but full payment must be made within five years and interest will be charged on the balance due. Fines or other sanctions (e.g. confiscation of shares) may be imposed if a purchaser fails to meet the conditions attached to a privatisation plan or otherwise fails to fulfil the terms of the privatisation agreement. (Lithuanian Business Information Centre, URL: http//www.lbic.lt)

Furthermore, article 20 of Law on Privatisation of Enterprises of Federation of Bosnia and Herzegovina states that: "...the means of payment in the privatisation procedure are: (a) certificates based on claims of physical entities towards the Federation, determined by this Law and separate regulations, (b) certificates based on claims of legal entities towards the Federation as compensation for property that is subject to restitution, (c) securities, (d) cash, (e) amounts from the Foreign Currency Military Books and certificates of the members of the BiH Armed Forces. (Web page of Agency for Privatisation of Federation of Bosnia and Herzegovina, URL: http://www.apf.com.ba/zakonie/index.htm/)

[369] Guislain, (The World Bank), p.52
[370] Guislain, (The World Bank), p.54, 55
[371] S. Brian Samuel, "The Ten Commandments of African Privatization", International Finance Corporation (IFC), The World Bank, URL:

Under most legal systems, privatisation proceeds would be considered a public revenue subject to public finance laws, rather than free revenue to be used by the government without constraints for any purpose it sees fit. In most cases, sales proceeds are used to fund the expenses involved in the process, redundancy payments, loan write-offs, etc. Expenditures financed out of these proceeds are thus normally subject to parliamentary authorisation and scrutiny.[372]

The case may be somewhat more complicated when SOEs sell part of their assets (e.g. a division, a factory or subsidiary) to private investors. Under normal company law (and many public enterprise laws) the proceeds would revert to the seller, for example the SOE. This may defeat the purpose of the privatisation program, in cases where the objective was to reduce the size the size of the public sector or obtain budgetary revenues. Of course, as sole or majority shareholder, the state should be in a position to recover the proceeds from such privatisations or part thereof through dividends or repayment of outstanding SOE debt. In practice, however, this may never happen due to poor oversight of SOEs, lack of clear dividends policy, fraud or collusion between board members and management. In a number of countries, privatisation provisions determine how the proceeds of such assets sales are to be allocated.[373]

---

http://www.ifc.org/ifc/publications/pubs/impact/impsm99/commandm/commandm.html; Guislain, (The World Bank), p.55

[372] S. Brian Samuel, "The Ten Commandments of African Privatization", International Finance Corporation (IFC), The World Bank, URL: http://www.ifc.org/ifc/publications/pubs/impact/impsm99/commandm/commandm.html; Guislain, (The World Bank), p.55

[373] Guislain, (The World Bank), p. 55

In France, government prohibited the use of privatisation receipts for the funding of current government expenditure. [Prosser, (Constitutions and Political Economy), p.310]

In Croatia, proceeds from the sale of shares in enterprises and possible profits have to be transferred to the Croatian Bank for Reconstruction that has to disburse these funds mainly to reconstruction and infrastructure projects. (Web page of Croatian Government: http://www.hfp.hr/privatization/privat.htm)

Some Privatisation Law states that payment for shares or assets of an enterprise that is being privatised cannot be financed, borrowed on or guaranteed by other assets of the same enterprise. [Article 16 Law on Privatisation of Enterprises, Federation of Bosnia and Herzegovina, "Official Gazette of Federation BiH", No 27/97, Nov 28th, 1997, web page of Agency for Privatisation of Federation of Bosnia and Herzegovina, URL: http://www.apf.com.ba/zakonie/index.htm/]

In Turkey, according to the law: "All proceeds obtained from the privatisation process...are credited to the Privatisation Fund..."(Article 9). "In utilisation of revenues accumulated in the Privatisation Fund priority shall be forwarded to redundancy payments, supply of other related services and for the payments to meet the administrative, financial and legal expenditures for preparatory work of organisations in the scope of privatisation" (Article 10) [Turkish Privatisation Law, web page of Turkish Privatisation Administration, URL: http://www.oib.gov.tr]

Finally Privatisation Law needs to specify how the agency in charge of privatisation should defray its costs, including the cost of operating the agency, prior restructuring (and in particular debt write-offs resulting from restructuring of SOE balance sheets), payment of advisers and other transaction costs. Funding for these expenditures is normally provided by the general budget, a special privatisation account set up as described above and/or the grant of borrowing authority.[374]

VII. CONCLUSIONS

(a) *Different Approaches:*

There are some general principles and rules that each government should follow in the privatisation progress. However, there is no simple, internationally applicable recipe for privatisation.[375] There is no single best way or single right way.[376] Many aspects of privatisation programs have to be country-specific and must be tailored to meet each country's domestic social, political and economic needs.[377] We should also point out that no two countries have taken an identical approach to privatisation.[378]

In some countries like Slovakia, revenues from privatisation were used to support the failing firms. (Andrej Juris, "Economic Reform in Slovakia", web page of Center for International Private Enterprise, URL: http://www.cipe.org/)
In Mexico and Latin American countries have allowed them continue macroeconomic stabilisation efforts and repay large portions of state debts. (Peter Young, "The Lessons of Privatisation", web page of Center for International Private Enterprise, URL: http//www.cipe.org/)
In Portugal the government has been using privatisation revenues primarily to reduce government debt. (URL: http://www.portugal.org/)
Also see: Guislain, (The World Bank), p.56
[374] Guislain, (The World Bank), p.52-55
[375] Galal, Jones, Tandon and Vogelsang, p.577
For example government of Bosnia and Herzegovina Federation states that while country's privatisation model is based on the experiences of other countries, it also has its own specifics. (Web page of agency of Privatisation of Federation of Bosnia and Herzegovina; URL: http://www.zpf.com.ba/)
Finally we must point out that even countries that have common points have followed different paths in privatisation. Thus, a study on the three Baltic countries (Latvia, Estonia, Lithuania) showed that although there are many similarities in the development of new ownership structures, but they have followed different paths of privatisation. [Mygind, p. 46]
[376] Stiglitz, (Some Theoretical Aspects), p.201
[377] For similar comments see: "International Perspectives on Privatisation of State Owned Enterprises", Narendar V. Rao, Northeastern, C. Bhaktavatsala Rao, Steve Dunphy, Small Business Advancement National Center, University of Central Arkansas, URL: http://www.sbaer.uca.edu/; S. Brian Samuel, "The Ten

Because of each method of privatisation has advantages and disadvantages, each country (particularly former socialist countries) have been employing more than one method, although not necessarily all of them. [379] Thus many countries including Turkey[380], Portugal[381], Croatia[382], Lithuania[383], Hungary[384], Federation of Bosnia and Herzegovina[385] Poland,[386] Slovakia,[387]

Commandments of African Privatization", International Finance Corporation (IFC), The World Bank, URL: http://www.ifc.org/ifc/publications/pubs/impact/impsm99/commandm/commandm.html
For example one of the important factor that has an influence on privatisation is the nature of the country's capital market. Where the capital market is small or relatively undeveloped and the enterprise being sold is relatively large, it may be deemed necessary to bring in foreign buyers. (Galal, Jones, Tandon and Vogelsang, p.548, 550). The sophistication of the stock market might also be a factor in determining whether it is possible to use stock market determined prices (p.549).
[378] Chikán, p.25
[379] We call this *mixed methods*. However, some authors name this "multi-track approach. (Maciej Grabowski, Economic Reform in Poland, Economic Reform Today Working Papers, Number 4, web page of Center for International Private Enterprise, URL: http//www.cipe.org/); Bornstein, p.250
[380] In Turkey privatisation methods (both divestiture and non-divestiture options) are as follows: (a) sale, (b) leasing, (c) granting rights of operation, (d) establishment of property rights other than ownership, (e) profit sharing model and other legal actions required by the nature of the business. (Article 18 of the Turkish Privatisation Law, web page of Turkish Privatisation Administration, URL: http://oib.gov.tr/. Also see: Ercüment Erdem, "Turkey", Privatisation-A Legal Perspective, A Supplement to the Euromoney Bank Register 1996, Published By: Euromoney Books, Euromoney Publications, London, July 1996, p.48)
[381] In Portugal privatisation was effected through public offerings, public tenders, private placements, and direct sales. (URL: http://www.portugal.org/)
[382] In Croatia, different methods including management and employees buyout, voucher system, public offering have been used in privatisation. Croatian government states that: "In order to improve speed and effectiveness the new Ministry of Privatisation was created..." (Web page of Croatian Government: http://www.hfp.hr/privatization/privat.htm)
[383] In Lithuania government used different methods, mostly different variations of sale. (Web page of Lithuanian State Privatisation Agency and State Property Fund, URL: http://www.vtf.lb/)
According to Lithuanian Privatisation Law privatisation methods shall be as follows: (a) public subscription for shares; (b) public auction; (c) public tender; (d) direct negotiations; (e) transfer of the state or municipal control at an enterprise controlled by the state or municipality; (f) lease with the option to purchase. [Article 13/1, Law on the Privatisation of State-Owned and Municipal Property, 4 November 1997 No. VIII-480, Vilnius, web page of Lithuanian State Property Fund, URL: http://www.vtf.lt/en/frame22.html]
In privatisation, Lithuania was one of the fastest in Eastern Europe. Vouchers and employee-ownership had a more important role, and direct sale and foreign investment had only a negligible role in this stage. (Mygind, p.18)
[384] In this country all methods of privatisation, including public share offerings on the stock exchange (public offering) have been used. Public offering has been used in Hungary's oil and gas company MOL. (Henry Gibbon, Privatization in 1995 and Beyond, web page of Center for International Private Enterprise, URL: http//www.cipe.org/)
[385] Web page of agency of Privatisation of Federation of Bosnia and Herzegovina; URL: http://www.apf.com.ba/zakonie/index.htm/
In this country, different variations of privatisation including restitution, sale (auctions, negotiated sale) have been tried. (Also see article 11-19 of Privatisation Law on privatisation methods in this country)
[386] Web page of the World Bank, URL: http://www.worldbank.org/; Fischer, p.9
In Poland mass privatisation, public offering, management and employee buy outs and public tender have been used in the privatisation process. (Maciej Grabowski, Economic Reform in Poland, Economic Reform Today Working Papers, Number 4, web page of Center for International Private Enterprise, URL: http://www.cipe.org/; Barbara Blaszczyk, Moving Ahead: Privatization in Poland ", web page of Center for International Private Enterprise, URL: http//www.cipe.org/)
According to one study: ""The case of Poland may be used as an example to illustrate the compartmentalisation of privatisation in Eastern Europe. The privatisation strategy of the Polish Ministry of Privatisation is based upon "a multi-track approach" comprising separate privatisation paths for the various

Latvia,[388] Czech Republic,[389] Estonia,[390] Romania,[391] Bulgaria,[392] Russia,[393] United Kingdom,[394] Georgia,[395] France,[396] Sweden[397] have combined different methods and techniques together.

(b) *Different Methods Together (Combinations of Methods)*: Several methods may be combined in the divestiture of a particular state enterprise. For instance, when a SOE (state owned enterprise) is privatised, some of SOEs shares may be sold to its employees and some to

---

categories of enterprise, often with a simultaneous use of different techniques of privatisation within a category enterprises are separated along the following lines (i) size; (ii) demand; (iii) perceived economic and financial viability; (iv) level of the state ownership and clarity of legal situation; and (v) quality of labour relations between management, workers, and unions within the enterprise. While the Polish case may be extreme in its degree of compartmentalisation of enterprises, it is not unlike the schemes operated by other countries. (Schwartz, p.37,38)

[387] In this country voucher system, management and employee buy outs, trade sales have been used. (Andrej Juris, "Economic Reform in Slovakia" web page of Center for International Private Enterprise, URL: http//www.cipe.org)

[388] Latvian Privatisation Agency utilises several approaches to privatisation, among which are: international tenders, direct sales or public auctions of enterprises, sale of the shares of enterprises to employees and pensioners, and the sale of shares by public offering. (Web page of Latvian Privatisation Agency, URL: http://www.lpa.bkc.lv/PriLatGB.htm#B004___; Mygind, p.16)

[389] In Czech Republic public auctions, voucher system and management and employee buy-outs have been used. (Henry Gibbon, Privatization in 1995 and Beyond, web page of Center for International Private Enterprise, URL: http//www.cipe.org/; Gabriel Sipos, "Dual transition in the Czech and Slovak Republics: Creating support for market and democratic reforms through restitutions", Dissertation for the Master's degree in Transition Central European University, Economics Department Budapest, Hungary, 15 June 1998, web page of Central European University, URL: http://www.ceu.hu/)

[390] According to article 20 Estonian Privatisation Law, ways of privatisation shall be: (a) sale of property in tender with preliminary negotiations; (b) sale of property on a public or restricted sale; (c) public sale of shares of commercial undertakings; (d) sale of property by way established by the organiser of privatisation in case no purchaser was found as specified in items 1 or 2. [Estonian Law on Privatisation, (unofficial translation), web page of Estonian Privatisation Agency, URL: http://www.eea.ee/]

However, in Estonia voucher system has played a secondary role in the privatisation process. Privatisation Agency has generally encouraged the privatisation of enterprises for cash from buyers who are able to inject effective management and capital. (Privatisation in Estonia, web page of Estonia, URL: http://einst.ee/)

[391] Simona Iliescu Nastase, "La protection juridique de la propriété privée dans le nouveau contexte social et économique de la Roumanie", (Juridical Protection of Private Property in the New Social and Economic Context of Romania), Chapter 4, Individual Democratic Institutions Research Fellowships 1994-1996, web page of NATO, URL: http://www.nato.int/acad/fellow/94-96/iliescu/index.htm

[392] In Bulgaria government plans to privatise major companies by direct sale were delayed throughout 1998 and early 1999 due to the limited administrative capacity of government agencies and the time taken for preparatory work by recently appointed government advisers. A second smaller round of voucher privatisation was launched in early 1999. [Chikán, p.35)]

[393] In Russia sale, voucher system, employee buy-outs have been used. (Malle, p.81)

[394] The United Kingdom combined various methods of sale, even for a single enterprise; these methods included stock market flotation, trade sales, employee-management buy outs, and other methods. (Galal, Jones, Tandon, and Vogelsang, p.568; Cook, p.222; Prosser, (Nationalised Industries), p.83-90; Graham and Prosser, (Privatising Nationalised Industries), p.21-30. The majority of privatisations have taken under the form of employee-management buyouts. Trade sales were the second common method. (Privatization in the United Kingdom, Ernst & Young, p. 28)

[395] In Georgia privatisation has been carried out using a number of established techniques, including tenders, auctions, long-term transfers of the right of management, direct sales and voucher privatisation. (Web page of Ministry of State Property Management of Georgia, URL: http://web.sanet.ge/mospm/)

other investors; or some shares may be sold by auction to domestic investors and others by sales negotiated with foreign investors.[398] Finally, some SOEs may be only partly, rather than fully, privatised by the combination of methods chosen.

(c) *Dominant Method*[399]: As we have discussed above in terms of privatisation methods, countries used a broad palette of techniques. Most countries tend to declare a preference for one method over another yet end up adopting a multi-track approach.

Voucher sales in combination with employee/management buy out are preferred in Russia, and Belarus.[400] In the United Kingdom[401], Romania, Georgia and Latvia the employment buy-outs are the dominant methods in the privatisation process.[402] Voucher sales tend to dominate in the Czech Republic and Lithuania.[403] The general trend in Latvia, Estonia and Lithuania is that management ownership is dominant for small enterprises;[404] while employee/management buy-outs are frequent in Romania and Poland.[405] In (former) East Germany and Hungary privatisation process was based mainly on trade sales.[406]

---

[396] Different techniques may also be combined, as was the case in many French privatisations where the government selected a stable core of large industrial or financial shareholders and sold the remaining shares to the public at large through public offerings. [Guislain, (The World Bank), p.50]

[397] Lane, p.188, 189, 195

[398] Bornstein, p.250
For example, in France, a public offering was typically combined with a separate sale of a core shareholding to a group of strategic or institutional investors. Also many governments have tried to combine the benefits of transferring management control to experienced international investors with national participation, particularly in the case of large high-profile companies. [Guislain, (The Privatization Challenge), p.123]

[399] Our analysis on dominant methods is based on the number of transactions, not the proceeds received in each privatisation transaction.

[400] "Trends and Policy in Privatisation-General Overview of Privatisation Developments", April 1995, URL: http://www.oecd.org/

[401] In the United Kingdom, in terms of number of privatisation transactions, the majority of privatisations have taken under the form of employee-management buyouts. Trade sales were the second common method. (Privatization in the United Kingdom, Ernst & Young, 1994)

[402] "Trends and Policy in Privatisation-General Overview of Privatisation Developments", April 1995, URL: http://www.oecd.org/

[403] "Trends and Policy in Privatisation-General Overview of Privatisation Developments", April 1995, URL: http://www.oecd.org/

[404] Mygind, p.42

[405] "Trends and Policy in Privatisation-General Overview of Privatisation Developments", April 1995, URL: http//www.oecd.org/

[406] Fischer, p.25; "Trends and Policy in Privatisation-General Overview of Privatisation Developments", April 1995, URL: http://www.oecd.org/

(d) *Method of privatisation and efficiency*: It is argued that that mass privatisation and employee-management buyouts would lead to weak pressures to restructure and that the preferred strategy should be trade sales and public offerings.[407] However some studies found different results. For example in Lithuania, statistics revealed that employee owned enterprises are more efficient compared to other groups of investors.[408]

Therefore we can conclude that, although there are some studies on that issue,[409] we believe that it is still early to draw some definite conclusions between the method of privatisation and efficiency. Different factors rather that the method may affect the efficiency of a company depending on different circumstances in each country. The governments need to decide most appropriate method according to its social, economic and political circumstances of the country.

(e) *Privatisation methods and transparency*: Transparency is an important factor that all governments often take into account.[410]

In comparing other privatisation methods for transparency, some argue that a public share offer is more transparent than trade sale. This might be true in the highly regulated and policed capital markets of developed economies. In those countries everyone has access to announcements of public offers in newspapers and by tens of thousands of stockbrokers. But it is not true in less developed countries, particularly where there is no formal stock market or

---

[407] Robert E. Anderson, Simeon Djankov, Gerhard Pohl, "Privatization and Restructuring in Central and Eastern Europe", Public Policy for the Private Sector, The World Bank, July 1997, Note no. 123, p.3
William L. Megginson, "The Impact of Privatization", web page of Center for International Private Enterprise, URL: http//www.cipe.org/. Megginson argues that: "Where politically feasible, direct sales are superior to voucher programs. In addition, they bring in significant revenue for the government; they frequently inject new technology and expertise into the SOE's operations; and they solve the monitoring problems that an atomistic ownership structure creates."
[408] Mygind, p.41
[409] See: Mygind, p.44. According to Mygind: ""...The general conclusions in most theoretical literature on the relation between ownership and economic performance is that (in Estonia, Latvia and Lithuania) private performs better than state, outsiders better than insiders, and within these groups: managers better than employees and foreigners better than domestic investors." (p.44)
[410] See: p.170-172

effective capital market regulation. In these cases, the most transparent method may be a well-publicised and well-run trade sales.[411]

(f) *Methods and the structure of the privatisation law:* The law should be broad, leaving the selection of the appropriate methods of privatisation to the discretion of the executing authority, or, at least, allowing the use of a wide range of privatisation techniques to fit the specific requirements of individual transactions. Liquidation should in any case not be precluded, as this tends to be the only or the best way to divest some SOEs.[412]

---

[411] "Building Transparency into the Privatization Process", Adam Smith Institute, web page of Center for International Private Enterprise, URL: http://www.cipe.org
[412] Guislain, (The World Bank), p.49

CHAPTER IV

LEGAL ISSUES ARISING DURING the PRIVATISATION TRANSACTIONS

I. COMPETITION LAW ISSUES

In this subtitle of the thesis, we will deal with the competition law issues arising in the privatisation process.
Competition can play an extremely useful role in ensuring cost efficiency and in curbing monopoly power in a newly privatised state monopoly. [1] *Competitive pressure ensures that a privately owned firm must produce efficiently if it is not to become bankrupt. Potential competition and the possibility that a rival could enter a monopolised industry also deter monopoly rents and create an incentive for cost efficiency on the part of an incumbent firm. Finally competition also furnishes the owners of the firm with information that enables them to evaluate the performance of the manager.* [2]
Effective competition offers many positive outcomes not only for the customers but for the actual or prospective competitors as well. It provides a major stimulus to management and staff alike, it clarifies the demands of the marketplace, and it could, ultimately, allow the replacement of a formal regulatory system by the natural regulation of the marketplace. [3]
In that context we will deal with the following issues:
a) What legislative and regulative measures can be taken if the state owned enterprise that is going to be privatised is a monopoly?
b) How can government introduce effective competition into each privatisation transaction?
c) Do consumers benefit from privatisation? What is the impact of privatisation on consumers?
d) In the context of privatisation, what might be the structure of the competition legislation or regulation?
e) What alternative or interim approaches can be adopted in case of privatisation legislation or anti-trust legislation is ineffective?
f) What specific competition law issues might arise in the privatisation process in former socialist countries?
g) How can some social or special groups be protected from the adverse effects of privatisation?
h) In the context of privatisation and competition law issues what conclusions can be drawn under the experience of current privatisation transactions?

A. Competition in the Context of Privatisation

Privatisation is, in many respects, a key component of the liberalisation and reform process of state owned enterprises, playing an important role in the transition from state

---

[1] Competition in relation to government activities is usually categorised in three ways: (a) public versus private, in which public-sector organisations compete with the private sector to conduct public-sector business; (b) public versus public, in which public-sector organisations compete among themselves to conduct public-sector business; and (c) private versus private, in which private-sector organisations compete among themselves to conduct public-sector business. (General Accounting Office, p.1, 44)

[2] Bhaskar, p.8; Vickers and Yarrow, (An Economic Analysis), p.51, 76, 77, 79; Michael J. Whincop and Stuart Rowland, "Plus ca Change....-The Effects of Markets and Corporate Law on the Governance of Privatised Enterprises", Who Benefits from Privatisation?, Edited by: Moazzem Hossain, Justin Malbon, Routledge Studies in the Modern World Economy, London and New York, 1998, p.58

[3] Robin Bomer, "The Privatisation of British Telecom", Privatisation in Practice, Edited By: Eamonn Butler, The Adam Smith Institute, Imediaprint Ltd., 1988, p.38; Bryan Carsberg, "The Role of the Regulator", (Regulator), Privatisation in Practice, Edited By: Eamonn Butler, The Adam Smith Institute, Imediaprint Ltd., 1988, p.43

monopolies to competitive markets. Particularly, in the sense of privatising the natural monopolies, introducing competition[4] to the market and breaking the monopolies will be one of the main concerns.

In this section of the thesis, we shall show that there is a need, if the benefits of competition are to be obtained for, the privatisation and competition legislation to provide appropriate provisions to ensure and obtain an effective level of competition.

In theory, privatisation with competition will benefit the economy. The steps are as follows: Privatisation introduces competition in the provision of a service previously provided by a public monopoly. This will have two effects. First, it will reduce public expenditure in that industry, the fall in the expenditure allows taxes to fall. A consequent fall in taxes will stimulate private spending. Secondly it will reduce costs to the private sector for the privatised good or service. The result of both effects can be more jobs in the private sector, and more output in the economy as a whole.[5]

In the context of privatisation, effective competition only occurs when new parties are introduced into industry to a rivalry to the incumbent firm by offering lower prices and thereby avoiding monopoly rents.

Failing to introduction of liberalisation it is necessary to use regulation and the anti-monopoly laws to place limits on incumbent firms.

---

[4] We will use the concept of competition as "the contest among the enterprises in the markets for goods and services, which enables them to take their economic decisions independently." (This definition was also adopted in the Turkish Competition Law, for this see article 3, Law No 4054, published in the Official Gazette no. 22140 dated 13 December 1994, for the full text of this law see the web page of the Turkish Government Competition Authority, http://www.rekabet.gov.tr/kanuneng.html)

[5] Patrick Minford, "Introduction", Patrick Minford, E S Savas, Iain Mays, Privatisation in Practice, Patrick Minford Selsdon Group, Viewpoint Series, p.1

B. Privatisation and Monopolies[6]

1. General

An industry is a natural monopoly if a single firm can produce more efficiently than two or more firms. Thus, natural monopoly is a concept that relates to technology-to costs of production.[7] Furthermore, legislation can create legal monopolies; the law may provide legal protection, incentives, and governmental subsidies, etc. for certain sectors or certain state owned enterprises.

Finally many existing state enterprises in the former socialist countries have the advantage of being in a monopolistic or near monopolistic position and hence have relatively little motivation to act efficiently. Therefore particularly in the ex socialist countries, anti-monopoly legislation has to be introduced.[8]

2. Breaking up Monopolies

a. General

One of the issues in privatisation is the problem of monopoly[9] Breaking up monopolies and creating more competition is an important motive for privatisation. [10] Sales by monopolies

---

[6] Price, p.77-98
[7] Vickers, and Yarrow, (Natural Monopolies), p.4; Paul J&J. Welfens and Piotr Jasinski, *Privatisation and Foreign Direct Investment in Transforming Economies*, Dartmouth Publishing Company, England & USA, 1994, p.67. (According to Welfensand and Jasinsk a natural monopoly is usually defined as an in which output can be produced most efficiently by single producer.)
[8] Ash, Hare and Canning, p.232
[9] An industry is a natural monopoly if a single firm can produce more efficiently than two or more firms. [Vickers and Yarrow, (Natural Monopolies), p.4]. In other words, natural monopoly is the case in which competition is neither feasible nor desirable. (John Kay and John Vickers, "Regulatory Reform-An Appraisal", Deregulation or Re-regulation-Regulatory Reform in Europe and the United States, Edited by: Giandomenico Majone, Pinter Publishers, London, 1990, p.227)
Natural monopoly must be distinguished from the question of how many firms happen to be active in a particular industry.
[10] Carsberg, (Competition and Private Ownership), p.26

normally generate more income and entail fewer transactions for overburdened bureaucrats.[11] A firm is more valuable when sold off with its monopoly powers left wholly or largely intact.[12] Nevertheless, when a state-owned monopoly is privatised; the governments have tended to introduce competition into the product market;[13] budgetary income has not been the sole concern and objective of governments.

One problem is thus a privatised monopoly will often attempt to use its money and political influence to stifle reforms; especially these that threaten to introduce greater competition. If they succeed, monopoly rents will be transferred from the public sector to the private sector, with little gain in efficiency, prices, or service.[14]

b. Some measures

Breaking-up the utility's assets in upstream or downstream competitive markets prior to its privatisation, allows competition to develop more rapidly, especially when entry into such markets (such as electricity generation) requires large scale fixed capital investments. Furthermore, when some of the utility's activities are characterised by natural monopoly conditions at the local level (such as in electricity distribution services), prior de-concentration is often undertaken in order to increase the number of possible independent sources of information for the regulator, and to facilitate the implementation of regulatory schemes based on the comparison of the individual companies' performance.[15]

---

[11] Voszka, Eva, "Privatization in Hungary: Results and Open Issues", web page of Center for International Private Enterprise, URL: http//www.cipe.org/
[12] Privatization in the United Kingdom, Ernst & Young, p. 24
[13] However some authors argue that there are advantages to privatising firms that are likely to remain monopolies relatively late, after a regulatory framework is in place. (Fischer, p.12)
[14] Joseph E. Stiglitz, Promoting Competition and Regulatory Policy: With Examples from Network Industries, (Promoting Competition and Regulatory Policy), The World Bank, Beijing, China, July 25, 1999, p.16
[15] Paolo Saba, Privatizing Network Industries, The Competition Policy Perspective, OECD, Competition Law and Policy Division, Helsinki, September 17-18, 1998

c. Anti-trust provisions and regulations

i. General

Public monopolies have historically not been subject to public regulation, precisely because they were thought to serve the public interest rather than to follow a profit motive. Privatising those monopolies calls for the establishment of a regulatory framework for those activities that cannot be allowed to be exposed to competition.[16]

In the presence of natural monopolies, regulation will often be indispensable to prevent the monopoly company from extracting monopoly rents by restricting supply of its services and selling them at high prices or otherwise abusing its exclusive market position.[17] For example post-privatisation regulation is a very important issue in industries with network externalities. Regulation must cover pricing, access to the network and entry to the industry.[18] Thus, it is important to have fair trading rules to make sure that any monopoly power is not used in a way that makes competition impossible by giving the monopoly operator an unmatchable advantage in other areas of activity.[19]

Some countries including the United Kingdom have taken measures to break the monopoly and introduce the appropriate regulation of competition in the privatisation process.[20]

---

[16] Guislain, (The Privatization Challenge), p.55
[17] Guislain, (The Privatization Challenge), p.55; Santos, p.143
[18] Tornell, p.28
[19] Those fair trading rules are contained in the licensing regime as well as in the general competition law of the United Kingdom. For this see: Carsberg, (Regulator), p.38, 43
[20] In the UK early stages of a national privatisation program, viable government enterprises in competitive sectors of industry are routinely transferred to the private sector in their existing form. In other cases, a break-up proves necessary in order to achieve a successful sale or the promotion of competition.
To take examples from the U.K. program:
(a) In 1982, the exploration and production assets of the state-owned oil company British National Oil Corporation were separated out and sold in the Britoil flotation, (b) In 1984, the telecommunications functions of the former General Post Office were separated out and sold as British Telecom, (c) The oil assets of British Gas were separated out and sold in 1984 as Enterprise Oil and Wytch Farm, (d) National Bus was split into over 60 separate businesses, prior to a program of sales in 1986-88, in order to stimulate competition among bus operators in a largely deregulated environment, (e) Under the restructuring plan for the industry in England and Wales, the Central Electricity Generating Board (CEGB) was split into three generating companies and a transmission company from April 1990. The power stations were divided between two fossil-fired generators, National Power and PowerGen,

and a nuclear generator, Nuclear Electric. National Power and PowerGen became private companies in 1992, while Nuclear Electric was privatised as part of British Energy in 1996. At that time the older nuclear stations were transferred to Magnox Electric, which has subsequently become part of BNFL (British Nuclear Fuels). The ownership and operation of the transmission system were transferred in 1990 to the newly- created National Grid Company, which was given a specific remit to facilitate competition.

Twelve Regional Electricity Companies (RECs) were created as the successors to the previous Area Boards and were privatised in December 1990.The major activities of the RECs are the distribution of electricity over the network, and supply of electricity to final customers. The supply market was opened up to competition in three phases, culminating in May 1999 when all consumers became eligible to choose their suppliers, (f) In the privatisation of British Rail, track and train operations were separated. Operation of passenger transport services is being transferred over time to the private sector through competitive franchising. Private-sector operators are able to introduce new services for both passenger and freight through open access. Railtrack-the rail infrastructure company-was sold in May 1996. [Henry Gibbon, (Guide), p.5; "Introduction", p.1, Web page of UK Electricity Industry, URL: http://www.electricity.org.uk/uk_inds/uksystem_intro.pdf, Web page of Railtrack, URL: http://www.railtrack.co.uk/]

According to British government the privatisation programme has two main aims; to promote efficiency, whether through competition or other means, and to widen and deepen share ownership. The British government states that "Most privatised companies operate in competitive areas of the economy. But the United Kingdom government has not confined the benefits of privatisation to such businesses. Privatisation has been extended to the natural monopolies-telecommunications, gas, water, and electricity. In these cases, to the extent that competition does not exist, regulatory arrangements take the place of the market in holding down prices and ensuring good service for the consumer." [Her Majesty's Treasury Guide to the United Kingdom Privatisation Programme, December 1993, p.4; Gerry Grimstone, "The Mechanics of Privatisation", (The Mechanics of Privatisation), Privatisation in Practice, Edited by: Eamonn Butler, The Adam Smith Institute, Imediaprint ltd., 1988, p.21; Littlechild, p.20; David Clementi, "Details for a Successful Share Issue", Privatisation in Practice, Edited by: Eamonn Butler, The Adam Smith Institute, Imediaprint ltd., 1988, p.12]

For telecommunications case in Britain see: Robin Bomer, "The Privatisation of British Telecom", Privatisation in Practice, Edited By: Eamonn Butler, The Adam Smith Institute, Imediaprint Ltd., 1988, p.37-41; Carsberg, (Regulator), p.42-47; Littlechild, p.21, 22; Colin Meek, "Privatisation Doesn't Necessarily Equal Competition-The UK Experience", Who Benefits from Privatisation, Edited by: Moazzem Hossain, Justin Malbon, Routledge Studies in the Modern World Economy, London and New York, 1998, p.102

For the competition law issues in the telecommunications privatisation world-wide see: Paolo Saba, Privatizing Network Industries, The Competition Policy Perspective, OECD, Competition Law and Policy Division, Helsinki, September 17-18, 1998; Ada Karina Izaguirre, Private Participation in Telecommunications-Recent Trends, Public Policy for the Private Sector, Note No. 204, December 1999; web page of OECD, http://www.oecd.org/; Stiglitz, (Promoting Competition and Regulatory Policy), p.11; Penepole Brook Cowen and Nicola Tynan, Reaching the Urban Poor with Private Infrastructure, Public Policy for the Private Sector, Note No.188, June 1999

For competition law problems in mobile phones see: Carlo Maria, Rossotto, Michel Kerf, and Jeffrey Rohlfs, Competition in Mobile Phones, Public Policy for the Private Sector, Note No.184, August 1999

For the competition law issues in gas sector in Britain see: Andrej Juris, "Natural Gas Markets in the U.K. - Competition, Industry Structure, and Market Power of the Incumbent", Public Policy for the Private Sector, Note No.138, March 1998; Meek, p.101, 102

For the competition law issues in electricity sector in Britain see: Odgers Olsen, "Privatizing Electricity", Privatisation in Practice, Edited By: Eamonn Butler, The Adam Smith Institute, Imediaprint Ltd., 1988, p.43; Eric Anstee, "Techniques for Privatising Utilities", Privatisation in Practice, Edited By: Eamonn Butler, The Adam Smith Institute, Imediaprint Ltd., 1988, p.68, 69; David M. Newbery and Michael G. Pollitt, The Restructuring and Privatization of the U.K. Electricity Supply—Was It Worth It?, Public Policy for the Private Sector, The World Bank Group, Note No.124, September 1997; Meek, p.103; Littlechild, p.29, 31

For the competition law issues in electricity sector worldwide see: Tornell, p.28; Michael Shames, "Preserving Consumer Protection and Education in a Deregulated Electric Services World-Challenges for the Post-Modern Regulator", Who Benefits from Privatisation, Edited by: Moazzem Hossain, Justin Malbon, Routledge Studies in the Modern World Economy, London and New York, 1998, p.155. [According to Shames instead of regulating energy monopolies, the regulator would need to preserve and referee the competitive market place (p.155)]

For the competition law issues in water sector worldwide see: Stuart Holder, "Privatisation and Competition: the Evidence from Utility and Infrastructure Privatisation in the United Kingdom"; Regulation, Competition and Privatisation; Organisation for Economic Co-operation and Development in co-operation with the Finnish Ministry of Trade and Industry; Helsinki (Finland); 17-18 September 1998; Twelfth Plenary Session of the

Hence in the telecommunication sector the United Kingdom created OFTEL (the Office of Telecommunications) and introduced the RPI-X regulation in telecommunications shortly before divestiture.[21]

ii. Appropriate Legislation

Putting a new regulatory framework in place before privatisation is one of the most important prerequisites of the successful privatisation of infrastructure industries. This is the case when natural monopolies are privatised, but it seems to be required also for industries that are potentially competitive. Thus, regulation is not only needed in place of competition but also in order to introduce competition.

To deter attempts to restrict competition, it is often necessary to enact laws applicable to public and private enterprises that would prohibit the establishment of cartels, trusts, monopolies, and other restrictive business practices. The introduction of such legislation can block certain privatisation transactions that would have otherwise proceeded. For example, the acquisition of an SOE or other state-owned asset by one of its competitors could result in excessive concentration.[22]

General competition policy usually consists of comprehensive anti-monopoly and anti-restrictive practice legislation, a competition office to police the rules, and often a specialist competition court- to enforce them. Most countries in east and central Europe, together with the

---

OECD Advisory Group on Privatisation (AGP); National Economic Research Associates (UK); p.3-8; Caroline van den Berg, Water Privatization and Regulation in England and Wales, Public Policy for the Private Sector, The World Bank Group, May 1997)

For competition law issues in other sectors see: Gisele F. Silva, "Private Participation in the Airport Sector-Recent Trends", Public Policy for the Private Sector, Note No.202, November 1999; Andrej Juris, "Competition in the Natural Gas Industry", The Emergence of Spot, Financial, and Pipeline Capacity Markets, Public Policy for the Private Sector, Note No. 202, November 1999; Michael Webb and David Ehrhardt, "Improving Water Services Through Competition", Public Policy for the Private Sector, Note No.164, December 1998; Gisele F. Silva, Private Participation in the Airport Sector-Recent Trends", Public Policy for the Private Sector, Note No.202, November 1999; Eduardo Engel, Ronald Fischer and Alexander Galetovic, "Privatising Roads-A New Method for Auctioning Highways", Public Policy for the Private Sector, The World Bank Group, May 1997

[21] Galal, Jones, Tandon and Vogelsang, p.557
[22] Guislain, (The Privatization Challenge), p.55

Russian Federation and the Ukraine have already or in the process of installing such systems. Substantial parts of the Hungarian, Czech and Slovak legislation have been based upon European Community legislation which, like Poland, they are required to adopt within a limited term of years by the terms of their treaties of association with the community. [23]

iii. The Importance of Appropriate Legislation

If sufficient and appropriate legislation is not enacted and concluded, the problem of monopoly can reduce the effectiveness of privatisation. As we have discussed above a monopoly transferred to the private sector without controls could easily fall into the hands of those who not only wish to perpetuate bad service and high prices but also to exploit the pricing power the monopoly enjoys to extract its monopoly rents from its customers. There is also a danger that the private monopolist will close and stop certain types of service that are unprofitable which the public utility has carried on running. [24]

iv. Structure of Legislation

Privatisation and competition legislation often provide rules to break legal monopolies. Legislation often includes the following elements:

- Removal of subsidies, including public loan guarantees,

- Removal of incentives that deter the competition,

- Harmonisation and modification of the tax legislation and system applied to SOEs and private enterprises,

---

[23] Jones, p.13
[24] Letwin, p.xv-xvi
Some governments were aware of the important of competition during the privatisation process and they emphasised it. Andreas Papandreou, former prime minister of Greece, said that he was not opposed to privatisation in principle, but rather to the creation of private monopolies and to any changes that would impair the quality of social provision. (International Financial Law Review, Special Issue on Privatisation, Volume 13, p.5)

- Removal of restrictions on buyer selection,

- Uniform application of environmental law, labour law and other branches of legislation that affect all economic entities.

The scope and the structure of competition legislation on privatisation are often based on the idea of "ensuring and protecting the competition, preventing abuse of dominant position."

As a summary:

Legislation is often needed to remove legal barriers to access to the relevant sector. Similarly, legislation often provides measures to allow companies if they wish, to exit from the relevant sector.

The more successful legislation is often flexible in its methods of selecting buyers and valuation methods; such legislation must strike a balance between the need to create a competitive sector or market after the privatisation process, and the desire to raise privatisation revenues.

In some sectors, because of the insufficiency of the relevant markets, there may be natural monopolies. In such cases, privatisation legislation often provides incentives for new investors.[25]

---

[25] Turkish Case
1. General
Turkish privatisation law and company law provide provisions on the protection of competition in the privatisation process. These provisions provide sufficient legal protection for the protection of competition.
2. Background of Competition Regulation
As a necessity of this Constitutional clause, in order to prevent agreements, decisions and practices which prevent, restrict or distort competition within the markets for goods and services markets in the territory or Republic of Turkey and the abuse of dominant position by those enterprises which are dominant in the market, the Law on The Protection of Competition no 4054 was enacted in the Turkish Parliament on 07.12.1994 and published in the Official Gazette and became effective on 13.12.1994. [For this see web page of the Turkish competition Authority (Turk Rekabet Kurumu), URL: http://www.rekabet.gov.tr]
3. Privatisation Process and Legislation on Competition
a. Provisions in the Privatisation Law
Article 16 of the Turkish Privatisation Law states some provisions on the protection of the competition in the privatisation process. The article 16 prohibits the following activities:

v. Alternative and Interim Approaches and Provisions

In some situations where general antitrust legislation or a specific privatisation law have been weak or ineffective, these have been supplemented by specific competition rules inserted in tender documents and privatisation contracts. Privatisation agreements therefore sometimes include provisions that prohibit or restrict the company's potential for horizontal or vertical integration through take-overs.[26]

Even where privatisation has not been launched, some countries have taken measures to introduce competition into the market. Many state companies already operate in a competitive environment. When launching a new private firm from the state sector, all that is needed is the removal of any advantages it used to enjoy from its privileged status. These include any tax advantages or first claim on government contracts. For industries that have enjoyed a state

---

(a) Dividing up of good and services markets and sharing and/or controlling every type of market resources and units, (b) Creation of barriers or limitations for the activities of competitors or the prevention of new players from entering into the market, (c) Applying different conditions on contestants with equivalent status for equal rights, obligations and liabilities, (d) Obliging buyers to purchase other goods and services in conjunction with certain goods and services, or to make compulsory the sale of certain goods and services demanded by wholesalers or intermediaries on display of other goods and services or to place forth conditions for the resale of certain goods and services already supplied.

Necessary precautions are taken by the Ministry of Industry and Commerce safeguarding against the existence of any type of legal operations and acts in the form of mergers or take-overs through certain agreements, applications and decisions in a manner directly or indirectly, seriously preventing, disrupting or restricting competition and causing creation of monopolies, are observed." (Article 16)

b. Provisions in the Law on the Protection of Competition [Law No 4054, published in the Official Gazette no. 22140 dated 13 December 1994, for the full text of this law see the web page of the Turkish Government Competition authority, http://www.rekabet.gov.tr/kanuneng.html]

Turkish Competition code also provides some provisions.

Article 4 of the Turkish Competition law provides that "Agreements and concerted practices of the enterprises and decisions and practices of the associations of enterprises the object or effect or the possible impact of which is, directly or indirectly, to prevent, distort or restrict competition in a certain market for goods and services, are unlawful and prohibited..." (Article 4)."

On the other hand, article 6 of the act provides provisions on the abuse of the dominant position. According to mentioned article "Any abuse, by one or more enterprises acting alone or by means of agreements or practices, of a dominant position in a market for goods and services within the whole or part of the territory of the State, is unlawful and prohibited." (Article 6)

[26] Guislain, (The Privatization Challenge), p.5

On the other hand there are many obstacles to the appropriate legislation and regulation:

(a) Since privatisation is usually a politically controversial policy, governments want to implement the privatisation process fast,

(b) The managers of the SOE that is to be privatised, often expect to continue after privatisation, because of that reason they are naturally not keen on any regulation that reduces their freedom of manoeuvre. (Bhaskar, p.80)

monopoly, various ingenious ways have been found to introduce competition in the private sector.

vi. Implementation bodies

Enforcement of antitrust or antimonopoly legislation is often entrusted to a specialised competition commission or office, such as the German Federal Cartel Office, Turkish Competition Authority[27] or the United Kingdom's Competition Commission.[28] Sector-specific competition rules, on the other hand, are often subject to special regulatory bodies.[29]

---

[27] In Turkey Competition Authority is the unique body responsible to apply the Law on the Protection of Competition no 4054. Article 20 of the same law states that while carrying out its duties, the Authority shall be independent and shall not receive any orders or directives from any organ, authority, entity or person. [For this see the web page of the Turkish Competition Authority (Turk Rekabet Kurumu): http//www.rekabet.gov.tr; Erdem, p.49]

[28] "The role of the Competition Commission, set by statute, is to investigate and report on matters referred to it by, among others, the Secretary of State for Trade and Industry, the Director General of Fair Trading and the regulators of the privatised utilities. The matters which may be referred include mergers, monopolies, anti-competitive practices, and the modification of conditions of licences granted under the various privatisation Acts. It will also hear appeals against decisions made under the prohibition provisions of the Competition Act 1998."(Web page of UK Competition Commission, URL: http://www.competition-commission.org.uk/code.htm; http://www.competition-commission.org.uk/ch1.htm)

[29] Guislain, (The Privatization Challenge), p.55

Furthermore see: Merger Cases in the Real World: A Study of Merger Control Procedures, OECD, Paris, 1994. (URL: http://www.oecd.org/). With respect to regulation, Italy established independent regulatory authorities (in particular for energy, telecommunications and transport). The aim is that they should be independent not only from the interests of the corporation but also from political influence. (Alessandro Goglio, "Sectoral Regulatory Reforms in Italy: Framework and Implications", OECD Economics Department Working Papers No.294, Unclassified, ECO/WKP(2001)20, 14 May 2001; "Antitrust & Trade Regulation Report", Volume 80, Number 2004, 20 April 2001, URL: http://corplawcenter.bna.com/corplawcenter/1,1103,2_858,00.html)

Under Italian and EU law, there is no automatic exemption from competition law for public utilities. These industries tend to comprise some activities which are essentially natural monopolies and others which are at least potentially competitive. In addition, the opening up of such activities to competitive performance is more likely to stimulate technical progress than regulation. There is a complementary role for both the regulatory bodies and for the competition authority in the treatment of these industries. (For this see web page of OECD, URL: http://www.oecd.org)

d. Non-discrimination against the Private Sector

i. General

In many cases, SOEs are protected from competition through government regulations that grant them monopoly power in key sectors. Protection is also achieved through high tariff barriers or other measures designed to restrict or eliminate foreign competition.[30]

ii. An essential policy

An essential component of competition policy in relation to privatisation are measures to ensure an absence of discrimination between the private and public sectors and to ensure that, the private sector should be allowed to compete with the public sector on an equal footing. This implies, among other things, (i) removal of subsidies, including public loan guarantees, at least in the case of SOEs (State Owned Enterprise) operating in competitive sectors (public finance and SOE legislation); (ii) harmonisation or alignment of the tax systems applied to SOEs and private enterprises (tax legislation); uniform application of environmental law, labour law, and other legislation affecting areas of economic life important to all enterprises; removal of entry barriers hampering the private sector (sector legislation); and equal access to public contracts (public procurement regulations). Legislation needs to establish and maintain a level playing field for private and public firms.[31]

The abolition of preferential treatment for SOEs in public procurement is to be a vital component of good competition policy.[32] The public contracting system is important not only from the standpoint of public finances and public ethics. In most countries, the state and the public sector in general, including municipalities, SOEs, and other public entities, are by far the

---

[30] "Privatizing State-Owned Companies", The Prosperity Papers Series, Prosperity Paper Three, web page of Center for International Private Enterprise, URL: http://www.cipe.org/
[31] Guislain, (The Privatization Challenge), p.54
[32] Guislain, (The Privatization Challenge), p.53

largest potential customers for goods and services. Retaining access to this market is of vital importance for an investor in a newly privatised company. A fair and transparent public procurement system, consistently applied, is the best guarantee.[33]

3. Is privatisation vital for competition?

Privatisation does not itself necessarily increase competition.[34] Furthermore, while it is possible to retain industries within the public sector and subject them to greater competition, there are limitations to this approach. First, some of the enterprises such as those operating in the water, electricity, gas, and transportation sectors, contain large elements of natural monopoly. Therefore, competition without implementation of privatisation is not a viable option. A second constraint is that, in order to ensure a successful privatisation, governments need the co-operation of the incumbent management; and management has naturally been hostile to increasing competition, particularly by splitting up an industry.[35]

4. Analysis

It can be argued that, it is easier and more profitable to privatise a state monopoly as a whole. Breaking up the monopoly might be difficult if the aim is to achieve an optimally effective firm. Moreover there are often difficulties in an evaluation of the different parts of a company as separate entities.[36]

Nevertheless particularly in the case of natural monopolies, if privatisation is to be effective it is essential to implement regulation and supervision mechanisms to prevent private monopolies acquiring excessive profits or reducing actual efficiency gains.[37]

---

[33] Guislain, (The Privatization Challenge), p.53
[34] Prosser, (Nationalised Industries), p.79
[35] Graham and Prosser, (Comparative Perspective), p.175
[36] Merger Cases in the Real World: A Study of Merger Control Procedures, OECD, Paris, 1994. (URL: http://www.oecd.org/).
[37] Braddon and Deborah, p.292

Monopolies, whether public or private, can result in inefficiency and higher costs.[38] As long as monopoly power persists, some form of economic oversight is needed to prevent imprudent expenditure, discriminatory service, or excessive earnings.[39] Without these measures, the regulation of monopolies cannot be effective in preventing exploitation of consumers.[40]

The experiences of many countries show that the transition from monopoly to competitive markets has followed different paths, both across individual countries and public utility industries, depending to a large extent on the specific economic, institutional, and social context.[41] One solution to the problem of monopoly power is to encourage competition by removing barriers to entry and countering monopolistic practices, such as entry deterrence on the part of incumbent firms, etc.

However, effective competition may not be possible in many industries where technology creates natural monopoly conditions. If there are economies of scale, technical efficiency requires large-scale production. There are two alternatives: to allow large-scale private production, but to use regulatory policy to curb the exploitation of monopoly power, or to keep the industry in the public sector. Thus any privatisation of a monopolistic industry must be accompanied by effective regulation.[42]

If a governmental service is a natural monopoly, competition must be introduced if the service or the activity is privatised. The criteria to be followed in privatising state-owned assets should not rest exclusively on the principle of maximising income, but on the analysis of what will be the final make-up of the companies and corporate groups privatisation gives rise to, and

---

[38] K. Lee, Chang, "Privatization and Co-operative Labour-Management Relations", Cornell University, Department of City and Planning, May 1998, URL: http://www.cce.cornell.edu/

[39] A. Beecher, Janice, "Twenty Myths About Privatisation", Alliance for Redesigning Government, National Academy of Public Administration, URL: http://www.alliance.napawash.org/

[40] Galal, Jones, Tandon and Vogelsang, p.544

[41] Saba, Paolo, Privatizing Network Industries, The Competition Policy Perspective, OECD, Competition Law and Policy Division, Helsinki, September 17-18, 1998

[42] Bhaskar, p.7

whether this process can contribute to improving competition by permitting the entry of new players The aim should be to defend competition, not competitors.[43]

Privatisation can in itself serve to strengthen competition policy if it is associated with steps to break up large state monopolies.[44] More generally, breaking up large enterprises prior to privatisation is desirable where it promotes competition and technologically feasible.[45]

Technological progress continues to reduce the number of natural monopoly activities and thereby increases competitive opportunities. Moreover, even under public ownership, corporations do not necessarily act in the public interest. In conclusion, the consensus appeared to be that it was not so much government ownership but the degree of rivalry that was significant.

Even if competition policy is taken to its maximum extent, it will remain necessary to continue to regulate the prices of some large divested enterprises.[46]

---

[43] Gan and Jan, p.213; Martin and Parker, p.7; Welfens, p.38
[44] Ash, Hare and Canning, p.219
[45] Galal, Jones, Tandon and Vogelsang, p.580
[46] Galal, Jones, Tandon and Vogelsang, p.580, 581

C. The Consumer Dimension[47]

1. General

It is argued that Privatisation, as a social and economic policy, provides benefits for customers and consumers.[48]

One of the important aspects of assessing a privatisation exercise is whether consumers and other customers receive any benefit.[49]

2. Impact of privatisation on consumers

a. General

It has been argued that, because they do not have to face competition. SOEs lack the incentive to provide products or services efficiently.[50] Therefore many authors believe that consumers will benefit when state-owned firms are privatised.

In the privatisation literature it is often concluded that a firm that is forced to compete (by losing monopoly privileges) and that receives new investment capital, management, technology, etc., will tend to provide better services at lower costs. For this competitive pressure to result, however, the privatisation process should be structured in ways to ensure that public monopolies are not replaced by private ones.[51]

Furthermore some authors argue that customers benefit when the greater efficiency that can be achieved through privatisation is passed on to them, for example, in the form of prices

---

[47] Hondius, p.149
[48] Robert Troedson, "Corporatisation and Privatisation; In Whose Interest?"-A Review of a Conference held by Griffith University Law School and Griffith University School of International Business in conjunction with RIPAA on March 1996", Who Benefits from Privatisation?, Edited by: Moazzem Hossain, Justin Malbon, Routledge Studies in the Modern World Economy, London and New York, 1998, p.266
[49] Minford, p.2
[50] "Privatizing State-Owned Companies", The Prosperity Papers Series, Prosperity Paper Three, web page of Center for International Private Enterprise, URL: http://www.cipe.org/
[51] "Privatizing State-Owned Companies", The Prosperity Papers Series, Prosperity Paper Three, web page of Center for International Private Enterprise, URL: http://www.cipe.org/; Peter Young, "The Lessons of Privatisation", web page of Center for International Private Enterprise, URL: http://www.cipe.org/

which are lower than they would otherwise have been, wider choice and better service. Privatised businesses are likely to be more responsive to changing customer demands, and more innovative in introducing new products to the market.[52]

b. Price Control

Some countries have taken measures to control price increases and thereby protect consumers from monopoly power. Thus in Britain in many sectors, like electricity, gas, water and airports a price control method called "RPI-X price cap" was adopted. The RPI-X price cap allows prices to increase (or requires prices to reduce) at X per cent below the Retail Price Index, which is a measure of inflation, for a specified number of years. This gives assurance to investors, managers and customers. It also gives greater efficiency incentives to companies in the short term. It is argued that the RPI-X formula can also protect consumers when a public monopoly is privatised as a private monopoly.[53] Customers benefit from the prospect of the resulting increased efficiency being passed them over time, when the price cap is reset.[54]

---

[52] Gibbon, (Guide), p.3
[53] Littlechild, p.21
[54] Littlechild, p.20; Galal, Jones, Tandon, and Vogelsang, p.580, 581
According to Littlechild, "...British privatisation policy, and the associated regulatory framework, have been oriented to securing efficiency by the use of price controls rather than profit controls and have explicitly required the promotion of competition"(p.25, also see: p.40).
In RPI-x the basic idea is that a regulated company's prices cannot rise faster than the retail price index minus a certain degree. (Graham, p. 207). In other words in this method a ceiling is put on the annual increase in the enterprise prices-the ceiling being established at x percentage points below the increase in the retail price index. X was fixed at 3 for telecom and 1 for airports. For British Gas a modified formula allows it to pass on changes in the cost of its energy supplies. If the enterprise is able to reduce its costs more rapidly during the five-year period than is implied by the formula, it is able to retain the benefits, in the form of higher profits. Conversely, if costs are reduced less rapidly, the enterprise suffers a poor profit record. Under RPI-x formula a profit maximising enterprise has direct incentives to achieve productive efficiency, and retains the benefits. [Bishop and Kay, (Does Privatisation Work), p.16, 17; Foster, p.205-212; Privatization in the United Kingdom, Ernst & Young, p. 40-45; Prosser, (Nationalised Industries), p.91]

3. Consumers in the former socialist countries

a. General

In post-communist countries, privatisation has created greater competition as the previous monopolistic structure of the economy has been dismantled and smaller privatised units have emerged from large agglomerations. In many cases however there has been no coherent strategy for introducing more competition, and little co-operation exists between the bodies responsible for competition and those responsible for privatisation. Greater gains from competition could therefore have been realised if the various decision-making entities had co-ordinated their efforts.[55]

b. Differences in consumer dimension

The impact of privatisation on consumers in post-communist countries is different from that in western economies. Prices have increased greatly since privatisation and liberalisation of those economies, but many more products are also available for the first time. The price increases are more attributable to the introduction of market economics as a whole rather than to privatisation in particular. There is evidence that privatised enterprises seek more aggressively to improve quality and introduce new products to meet consumer demand.[56]

According to one study the process of transition changed consumers in the former socialist countries from passive recipients of the output of state monopolies to people exercising the power of choice.[57]

---

[55] Peter Young, "The Lessons of Privatisation", web page of Center for International Private Enterprise, URL: http://www.cipe.org/
[56] Peter Young, "The Lessons of Privatisation", web page of Center for International Private Enterprise, URL: http://www.cipe.org/
[57] "Central and Eastern European Businesses Poised to Challenge Western Competitors", Recent Headlines, Andersen Consulting Study, URL: http://www.ac.com

There is some empirical evidence of consumer benefits from privatisation. For example in the UK in long distance buses, deregulation and the prospect of national Bus Company privatisation has brought prices down 40% and stimulated 700 new services.[58]

4. Analysis

One of main objectives of privatisation programmes of governments worldwide, has been to improve industrial efficiency, by freeing industries from government control and subjecting them to the disciplines of the market place.[59]

In this context, competition is considered the most important mechanism for maximising consumer benefits, and for limiting monopoly power by creating rivalry and freedom to enter markets.[60] Where competition is introduced, costs are normally expected to fall.[61] Consumers will usually benefit from competition because the goods and services desired by the customer are provided at the lowest economic cost.[62] Customers' freedom of choice enables market forces that provide sustained pressures on companies to increase efficiency.[63]

When there is no competition in the market, an appropriate regulation is needed in order to protect consumers and avoid the use of private firms' monopoly power as a barrier to entry of potential competitors into market segments.[64]

According to the British government:

"The consumer has continued to benefit from downward pressure on prices and from rising standards of service. ...at March 1993, British Gas prices to its industrial customers had fallen by about 28 per cent in real terms over the previous years. Large electricity customers are able to shop around and select another supplier offering

---

[58] Minford, p.3
[59] Graham and Prosser, (Comparative Perspective), p.175
[60] Beesley and Littlechild, p.15
[61] Kolderie, p.29
[62] Hondius, p.154
[63] Gibbon, (Guide), p.2
[64] Santos, p.140

better and/or cheaper service. BT's main prices had fallen by about 27 per cent in real terms since privatisation. In addition, by 1993 95 per cent of payphones were working compared to 77 per cent sixteen years previously and, since privatisation, BT provide nearly 45 per cent more of them. Privatisation has enabled the water industry to put in hand more quickly a £ 5 billion investment programme to meet EC standards for drinking and bathing water. Finally, all the privatised utilities now operate against published codes of practice providing for, for example, compensation for domestic customers if appointments are missed".[65]

However, in the UK there has also been some price increases in some sectors; for example, in the water sector. According to some authors in such sectors prices may rise in the course of privatisation because of the need to make substantial improvements in water systems.[66]

Some authors argue that in many ways consumers are probably better informed as a result of privatisation. For example, considerable information on the costs of nuclear power generation has now become available as a result of privatisation and break-up of the monopolies.[67]

In some cases state owned enterprises seem to be able to provide low prices for the same or similar products. However, it should be taken into account that subsidies from governments, for example, allow SOEs to charge below-market prices for, say, electricity, gasoline, or other goods and services.[68]

Furthermore in most cases a state enterprise does not pay corporate tax, and a government agency does not charge value-added tax (VAT) on its products and services.

---

[65] Her Majesty's Treasury Guide to the United Kingdom Privatisation Programme, December 1993, p.5
In one speech (former) financial secretary of United Kingdom states that: "...Consumers are empowered because privatisation can give them freedom to choose, bringing pressure to bear on companies to become efficient and to offer their customers choice... suffice it to say that those who persist in failing to acknowledge and encourage these sustained achievements are really seeking to mislead the consumer..." [George Young, the (former) Financial Secretary's speech to the World Privatisation Conference, 6 March 1995, web page of the Treasury, URL: http://www.hm-treasury.gov.uk/pub/html/speech95/fst/sp060395.html]

[66] Janice A. Beecher, "Twenty Myths About Privatisation", Alliance for Redesigning Government, National Academy of Public Administration, URL: http://www.alliance.napawash.org/

[67] J. Haskel, S. Szymanski, *Privatisation, Jobs and Wages, Department of Economics*, Queen Mary and Westfield College, University of London, Paper No: 252, February 1992, p. 1

[68] "Privatizing State-Owned Companies", The Prosperity Papers Series, Prosperity Paper Three, web page of Center for International Private Enterprise, URL: http://www.cipe.org/

Privatised companies have to pay these taxes, which is likely to force them to raise their prices and which makes privatisation a less attractive option.[69] This might also be the one of the reasons for price increases after privatisation.

Moreover in evaluating why in some cases consumers lose to higher prices after privatisation[70], it is important to determine whether those losses occurred because prices were raised to an exploitative level, or because prices rose to an economically efficient level.[71] Because a problem is that under public ownership the pricing policies of utility enterprises were not closely aligned to costs, instead involving large cross-subsidies, largely in order to avoid geographical variations in rates and often providing an element of subsidy to economically underprivileged groups, especially small domestic consumers.[72]

Governments should take consumer legislation into account when they design the structure and the content of privatisation legislation. In that context the privatisation laws may alter or modify the existing consumer laws.

Furthermore it can be argued that privatisation is not always an ideal solution to the problem of the monopoly, since private companies are likely to wish to concentrate on operating in the profitable parts of the industry and that in areas of less profitability consumers would be

---

[69] Rudy B. Andeweg, "Privatisation in the Netherlands: The Results of a Decade", Privatization in Western Europe-Pressures, Problems and Paradoxes, Edited By: Vincent Wright, Pinter Publishers, Great Britain, 1994, p.203

[70] Galal, Jones, Tandon and Vogelsang, p.530; Moazzem Hossain and Justin Malbon, "Preface", (Preface), Who Benefits from Privatisation?, Edited by: Moazzem Hossain, Justin Malbon, Routledge Studies in the Modern World Economy, London and New York, 1998, p.xii

In Britain OFTEL admitted that the prices paid by domestic BT consumers have dropped by just 1 percent in the period 1990/91 to 1994/95. Water bills in England and Wales have risen by 39 per cent in the period from 1989/90 to 1995/96. The electricity regulator has stated that electricity prices for the domestic consumers have dropped by around 7 per cent in real terms. Finally according to Ofgas, gas consumers have fared better with a cut in fuel costs of some 20 per cent since the industry was privatised, although much of this boils down to a sharp drop in the cost of natural gas. (Meek, p.110-113; Malbon, p.22-24)

[71] Galal, Jones, Tandon and Vogelsang, p.530

[72] Prosser, (Social Limits), p.236, 237

neglected. An answer to this is that where social responsibilities exist, there may need to be government subsidisation.[73]

Finally, different regulatory measures can be taken, for example special provisions can be imposed into the privatisation contract to protect certain groups. In other words by imposing certain provisions into the privatisation contract, private investors can be forced to provide services to certain social groups. If a government is not able to provide such regulatory arrangements privatisation is not likely to be an attractive option. Thus in Britain the proposal to privatise the Royal Mail was withdrawn by the government at an advanced stage, largely due to fears about the network of rural post offices and the geographically uniform letter rate[74]

---

[73] Prosser, (Social Limits), p.237
[74] Prosser, (Social Limits), p.238, 239

D. Conclusions

It is clear that promoting competition is a vital point in the privatisation process.[75]

Competition should be introduced wherever possible[76], as an essential part of the privatisation process. All the gains that a transfer to the private sector brings about, will be enhanced if competitive pressures accompany it. Although a monopoly can be sold and privatised at a higher price, without effective competition in its markets it has negative outcomes in the long term.[77]

In general, competitive privatisation proceedings produced better outcomes for the sectors concerned. Countries that have chosen to limit competition in the corporate control market for privatised companies by directly or indirectly preselecting the new private owners

---

[75] Andive, p.39; "The Opportunities and Challenges of Privatisation", Chapter I, US Department of Energy, US Department of Energy, URL: http://home.osti.gov/; Sheshinski and López-Calva, p.27; Privatization in the United Kingdom, Ernst & Young, p.25

In Spain, for example, the Spanish privatisation plan takes as a general principle the need to introduce competition into the markets. (Vicente Jose Montes Gan and Amedeo Petitbo Jan, "The Privatisation of State Enterprises in the Spanish Economy", Privatisation in the European Union, Theory and Policy Perspectives, Edited By: David Parker, London, 1998, p.212)

The evidence of British experience also proved that that the privatisation process and its policy can work very well and be very popular if and when sufficient competition is introduced. [Letwin, p.xvi, xviii; Ben Slay, "From Monopoly Socialism to Market Capitalism", (Socialism to Capitalism), De-Monopolisation and Competition Policy in Post-Communist Economies, Edited by: Ben Slay, Wetview Press, 1996, USA, p.13]

British government denies the claims that competition has not been introduced into the markets during the privatisation process. ("...competition has made huge strides...It is a process which continues. But the effects have long been clear to see...suffice it to say that those who persist in failing to acknowledge and encourage these sustained achievements are really seeking to mislead the consumer. " [George Young, the (former) Financial Secretary's speech to the World Privatisation Conference, 6 March 1995, web page of the Treasury, URL: http//www.hm-treasury.gov.uk/pub/html/speech95/fst/sp060395.html]

Increasing competition have been important reasons also for privatisations in Denmark and in Sweden. (Willner, p.182)

[76] In certain circumstances it is impossible to apply competition policies immediately. (Eileen Webb, "The Other Side of the National Competition Policy Debate-Perspective on the Public Interest and Community Services" Who Benefits from Privatisation?, Edited by: Moazzem Hossain, Justin Malbon, Routledge Studies in the Modern World Economy, London and New York, 1998, p.244)

[77] Privatization in the United Kingdom, Ernst & Young, 1994, p.24

However, it is argued that in former socialist countries, during the initial steps of privatisation it is better to run the risks of imperfect competition and markets, and to accelerate the process, than it is to delay and possibility derail privatisation. (W.Lieberman, Ewing, Mejstrik, Mukherjee and Fidler, p.47, 48). We do agree to this idea.

have very often found themselves troubled by political controversy and charges of low transparency.[78]

In other words, the successful privatisation programmes are the ones where considerable effort has been devoted to introducing competition into industries previously dominated by a government monopoly, and establishing a coherent and sustainable regulatory framework, in each case before a utility or other similar enterprise has been transferred to the private sector.[79]

If the process of privatisation brings about or is accompanied by the introduction of more competition, productivity gains are likely to be strengthened.[80] Competition improves the performance of SOEs, not only because competition forces all firms to improve their performance, but also because competition lays bare the costs of allowing state firms to operate inefficiently. Competition also provides a basis of comparison for management: policymakers can easily assess the level of managerial effort by comparing the efficiency of a state enterprise with that of its private-sector rivals.[81]

In many of the ex-socialist countries, where SOEs dominated the economy, privatisation has been carried out through fragmentation or other techniques that have broken up large SOEs into smaller firms to prevent their continued monopoly power. Similarly, high tariffs or other barriers that keep out competitors have also been reduced or eliminated.[82]

In order to introduce competition to a monopolistic sector, the company itself can be broken up, either vertically by separating the various stages of production, or horizontally into competing producers. The easiest way of gaining competition, however, lies in removing the

---

[78] Web page of OECD, URL: http://www.oecd.org
[79] Rich and Plapinger, p.11
[80] Galal, Jones, Tandon and Vogelsang, p.539
[81] Mary M. Shirley, "Getting Bureaucrats Out of Business: Obstacles to State Enterprise Reform", web page of Center for International Private Enterprise, URL: http://www.cipe.org/
[82] "Privatizing State-Owned Companies", The Prosperity Papers Series, Prosperity Paper Three, web page of Center for International Private Enterprise, URL: http://www.cipe.org/; Peter Young, "The Lessons of Privatisation", web page of Center for International Private Enterprise, URL: http://www.cipe.org/

298

protection of the state's monopoly, and allowing new entrants into the field. Even in cases where this cannot be done immediately, government can announce in advance its intention to introduce competition, or at least to review the situation on competition in a few years time.[83]

Furthermore, it may be easier to introduce competition by privatising only a part of the system. Especially promising are moves in some countries[84] to try to enhance competition by contracting for the purchase of commodity-like aspects of the system, e.g. lines.[85]

The result of the privatisation process depends largely on whether the change is only the substitution of a monopoly or involves also the introduction of competition among producers.[86] If the change is simply from one monopoly supplier to another, then neither cost nor performance is likely to change very much.[87] Furthermore, if the privatisation process just makes a shift from state monopoly to private monopoly, the outcomes of this transaction may be much worse, particularly in the customer aspect.

Liberalising the market by creating incentives and removing barriers to market entry is an absolutely essential step in the privatisation process.[88]

Regulation is an important task in the privatisation process. The primary duty of the utility regulators is to promote competition and protect consumers.[89]

---

[83] With the British Telecom privatisation, this was the case, a small competitor called Mercury Communications was permitted to compete with BT in voice telephony, and BT was required to provide access over its terminal lines into offices and homes. This duopoly held for seven years, after which a review opened the market to full competition.
When Britain privatised its electricity industry, it was thought impossible to have competing lines going into every home or business, so area distribution companies were set up to buy competitively on behalf of their own customers. It constituted a kind of "proxy competition," in addition to the full competition there was between generating companies. The lesson is that there are various ingenious ways in which competition can be introduced, and that even if it cannot be done at the time of privatisation, it can be done later after a review period. [Stiglitz, (Promoting Competition and Regulatory Policy), p.17]

[84] Stiglitz, (Promoting Competition and Regulatory Policy), p.17
[85] Stiglitz, (Promoting Competition and Regulatory Policy), p.17
[86] Kolderie, p.28
[87] Kolderie, p.28
[88] John D. Sullivan, "Privatization and Economic Reforms", web page of Center for International Private Enterprise, URL: http://www.cipe.org/
[89] Littlechild, p.35

In that context one of the important purposes of the Privatisation Law or the Competition Code or is to provide the protection of competition by ensuring necessary regulation, supervision and the prevention of abuse of dominant position by those enterprises which are dominant in the market and the agreements, decisions and practices which prevent, restrict or distort competition within the markets for goods and services.[90]

To deter attempts to restrict competition, it may be necessary to enact laws applicable to public and private enterprises that would prohibit the establishment of cartels, trusts, monopolies, and other restrictive business practices.

Where antitrust legislation does not exist or is ineffective, specific competition rules may also be inserted in tender documents and privatisation contracts. Privatisation agreements therefore sometimes include provisions that prohibit or restrict the company's potential for horizontal or vertical integration through take-overs.

Former socialist countries should take further steps in the sphere of anti-trust regulations and restricting the abuse of economic power.[91] These countries must, as quickly as possible, remove all existing remnants of the command system and of state paternalism.[92]

Legislation must also provide some protection to consumers. Privately owned monopolies require regulation to ensure that their market power is not deployed to take advantage of consumers. Such provisions might be attached to privatisation agreements. This will make these provisions more effective and transparent. For example without appropriate regulation economic development in rural areas and small towns would suffer, if postal services were privatised. Because private companies may not find "profitable" to provide first class mail

---

[90] This purpose is provided in the article 1 of the Turkish Competition Law and article 16 of the Privatisation Law.
[91] Schrader, p.263
[92] Dabrowski, p26

service or a phone box to a rural area.[93] Therefore privatisation legislation should provide special "universal service" provisions to protect certain social groups.

It is evident that a monopoly position, combined with protection from competition, can allow a public enterprise to make financial profits while its economic performance is poor.[94]

In general, competition and regulation are likely to be more important determinants of economic performance than ownership. The protection of competition and, more generally, the creation and enforcement of a level playing field in the marketplace are among the most important and complex functions of government, affecting many different areas of economic policy and law and calling for a high level of bureaucratic competence. Re-privatisation reforms and restructuring measures will often be required to create the requisite competitive environment.[95]

Even if competition cannot be introduced in the short term, governments can use measures, like RPI-X formula, to protect consumers.

The approach of governments should be "competition where possible, regulation where necessary". Moreover one of the main purposes of regulation should be to promote and maintain conditions for effective competition.[96]

---

[93] Starr, (The Limits of Privatization), p.122; Bishop and Kay, (Does Privatisation Work?), p.16
[94] Kirkpatrick, p.239, 240
[95] Guislain, (The Privatization Challenge), p.53
[96] Kay and Vickers, p.224; Ericson, p.23

II. LABOUR LAW ISSUES DURING in PRIVATISATION

In this subtitle of the thesis we will deal with labour law issues in the privatisation process.

Privatisation winners (private investors) not only buy the physical capital of the company; they also acquire a work force and labour contract.[97] One expected result of privatisation is often a trimming of the work force of the enterprise, a loss of welfare to workers, and a reason for opposition from the labour unions. The strength and effectiveness of this opposition could have a direct effect on the success of privatisation.[98] In many countries including Britain, there have been mixed results. In some cases there have been lay offs. In other privatisation transactions this did not happen.

Furthermore, different labour law issues may derive from privatisation implementations including legal issues about salaries, social rights and fringe benefits together with any and all kinds of personal rights of the employees.

Governments may face significance opposition and reaction from the employees; this may block the privatisation progress. The social consequences may also bring privatisation into dispute. The privatisation legislation or the labour code should provide appropriate solutions and approaches to the labour law issues. Another option might be to impose special and detailed provisions in the privatisation contract.

In other words, privatisation legislation can solve the labour law issues in a balance; and the legislation can protect the pension and other employee benefits of the workers in the privatisation process. If legal and social issues cannot be solved in an appropriate way, the costs of privatisation and restructuring can be considered as having been passed on ultimately to workers and society.

The economic situation of the country, goals and objectives of the privatisation program, power and the pressure of the trade unions, political situation and current legislation of the country in question can effect the structure legislation or the labour code. The legislation should address all main issues; secondary points can be drafted in the decrees or in the privatisation contracts.

Finally, we should point out that the privatisation legislation cannot satisfy all interest groups. The main concern and goal will be to find the "consensus points" and balance the consequences.

A. Impact of Privatisation on Labour

Labour law issues constitute one of the important categories of issues during privatisation transactions. However, despite the increased attention given to privatisation and the issues during the privatisation; relatively little analysis has been made of labour law and employment issues in the privatisation literature.

The type of the labour law problems varies, depending on the countries legal and economic situation and the aims of privatisation. Furthermore even in the same country different issues may arise in different privatisation transactions.

---

[97] López-de-Silanes, p.16
[98] Galal, Jones, Tandon and Vogelsang, p.546

Particularly in Eastern and Central European countries, labour law issues are significant, as because of the massive job cuts in those countries. In many former socialist countries, policies of privatisation have become associated clearly in the public mind with increased unemployment.[99] The speed of privatisation has been slowed because of the fear of its social and political consequences.[100] However, in other countries, e.g. in France, Italy[101], Britain[102], Greece[103] and Turkey labour issues have also been one of the main legal problems in privatisation programmes.[104]

In the following pages we will discuss the different labour law problems as well as the different legislative measures taken to resolve such problems during the privatisation process in a number of countries.

---

[99] Prosser, (Social Limits), p.225

[100] For example, in Poland some political parties and unions remained hostile to privatisation, which caused privatisation to develop very slowly. (URL: http://www.worldbank.org/; Demetra Smith Nightingale and Nancy Pindus, "Privatization of Public Social Services: A Background Paper", October 15, 1997, Urban Institute, URL: http://www.urban.org/; Barbara Blaszczyk, "Moving Ahead: Privatization in Poland ", web page of Center for International Private Enterprise, URL: http//www.cipe.org/)

[101] Sabino Cassese, " Italy: Privatizations Announced, Semi Privatizations and Pseudo-Privatizations", Privatization in Western Europe-Pressures, Problems and Paradoxes, Edited By: Vincent Wright, Pinter Publishers, Great Britain, 1994, p.131

[102] For example in Britain, in 1984, government decided to close some inefficient coalmines, the union launched a nation-wide strike that lasted almost a year. The strike ended after government offered severance payments and some other benefits. (Tornell, p.10; Privatization in the United Kingdom, Ernst & Young, 1994, p.20)

[103] The opposition of trade unions and employees through the privatisation program is one of the main issues in Greek privatisation program. (Nicholaos Haritakis and Christos Pitelis, "Privatisation in Greece", Privatisation in the European Union, Theory and Policy Perspectives, Edited by: David Parker, London and New York, p. 127)

[104] Sunita Kikeri, *Privatisation and Labour, What Happens to Workers When Governments Divest*, World Bank Technical Paper, The World Bank, Washington D.C., 1998, p.9; Guislain, (The Privatization Challenge), p.76, 77.

For the labour opposition in the British Airways case see: David Burnside, "Taking British Airways to Market", Privatisation in Practice, Edited By: Eamonn Butler, The Adam Smith Institute, Imediaprint Ltd., 1988, p.34

B. Privatisation and Labour Relations: Labour Market Consequences of Privatisation

1. Initial remarks

a. Our approach

In analysing labour law issues, much depends, on the time and the country that is being considered.[105] In most cases, the first issue to be clarified is whether we are examining the effects on workers in the enterprises to be privatised or the effects on workers in the rest of the economy. It is also important to be clear whether employment is being looked at from a static, short-term point of view or from a dynamic, long term one.

In this study, mainly, we will focus on the effects of privatisation on workers in the enterprises to be privatised; but in some aspects our analysis will comprise both long and short-term periods if sufficient data are available.

Finally we should point out that, even in the same enterprise and in the same privatisation transaction; different provisions might apply to different types of employees. For example, in many countries privatisation legislation or Labour Codes provide special provisions for disabled employees.

b. A key issue: Restructuring the labour force

In analysing labour issues related to privatisation a key strategic issue is whether governments should restructure the labour force before privatisation or leave it to the new private owners. In any case, private investors wish to have a clear picture of the labour issues in the privatised enterprise.

One finding that emerges from the research is that in companies with minimal to modest levels of overstaffing, restructuring can and should be left to the private investors. Large scale redundancies however, are usually best handled by governments prior to sale to minimise labour resistance, enhance the likelihood that a social safety net will be provided, and increase the value of the firm.[106]

On the other hand if laying off workers is difficult under existing laws, potential investors may insist that redundancies be carried out by the state or the state owned enterprises (SOE) prior to the divestiture.[107]

2. Labour Legislation

a. General

Laws applicable to private labour will be of greater concern in the context of divestiture, as they may affect investors' ability to set wages and benefits, hire and fire workers, and in general manage their work forces.[108] If laying off workers is difficult under existing laws, potential investors may insist that redundancies be carried out by the state or the SOE before the privatisation.[109]

b. Structure of legislation

Depending on the measures taken, a country may need to enact new laws or modify current legislation on privatisation and labour. In some cases the current legislation or the labour

---

[105] Eivind Smith, "Means For Protecting the Users and Former Employees of Privatised Companies", Legal Aspects of Privatisation, XXIst Colloquy on European Law, Budapest, 15-17 October 1991, Council of Europe Press, the Netherlands, 1993, p.145
[106] Kikeri, p.ix; S. Brian Samuel, "The Ten Commandments of African Privatization", International Finance Corporation (IFC), The World Bank, URL: http://www.ifc.org/ifc/publications/pubs/impact/impsm99/commandm/commandm.html
[107] Guislain, (The World Bank), p.28
[108] Guislain, (The World Bank), p.29
[109] Guislain, (The World Bank), p.28

code might provide sufficient and appropriate measures for labour law issues. Structure of labour legislation can vary.

Labour legislation must be drafted to address all main issues, for example in the case of severance payment the law should provide the details of the dismissal compensation including the calculation methods and eligible employees.[110]

C. Opposition and Reaction of Employees

1. Public Sector Employees

In many countries, employees in state-owned enterprises have conditions of service equal to or resembling those of civil servants, in job security, social protection and in terms of regulations relating to union membership and collective bargaining.[111] Since public sector employees often enjoy special civil service benefits;[112] fear of insecurity and being marginalised in terms of collective bargaining often makes public enterprise or public sector unions opposed to privatisation schemes, particularly when the unions have not been involved in initial discussions on privatisation.[113]

2. Impact of Privatisation on Levels of Employment: Lay offs

a. Expectations: Fear of Job Losses

The employees of state-owned enterprises often oppose privatisation because they fear a loss of job security and social protection as well as deterioration in the industrial relations system.[114]

---

[110] Legal Aspects of Privatization, p.29
[111] Rolph van der Hoeven and Gyorgy Sziraczki, p.13
[112] Guislain, (The Privatization Challenge), p.74
[113] Rolph van der Hoeven and Gyorgy Sziraczki, "Privatisation and Labour Issues", Lessons from Privatisation: Labour Issues in Developing and Transitional Countries, Edited By: Rolph van der Hoeven and Gyorgy Sziraczki, International Labour Organisation (ILO), Geneva, 1997, p.14
[114] Kikeri, p.3

The common expectation concerning the effects of privatisation on employment is that privatisation will involve immediate job losses. According to this expectation privatisation will be disadvantageous to the workforce; it will lead to a labour shake out and a deterioration in wages for those who retain their jobs.[115] Therefore, privatisation may decrease the public's respect for government employees, resulting in low morale, lack of motivation, and eventually poor performance.[116]

Furthermore, it has been argued that the communist system hid a huge under-utilisation of labour and therefore exposure to even a small dose of market discipline will force large-scale shedding of labour. Privatisation, unless it involves some appropriate solutions, will necessarily lead to large-scale closures and unemployment, particularly in heavy industry.[117]

b. Practice

The expectation of lay offs has proven to be accurate in Eastern European countries. Hence in most Eastern European countries privatisation accompanied by hard budget constraints on newly privatised enterprises has resulted in large-scale job losses. As redundancies have occurred on a massive scale in the wake of economic reform, this has created a pool of unemployed workers that often cannot be absorbed by other privatised firms or new firms.[118]

In Britain, the longest campaign that conducted against the privatisation of British Telecom. (Foster, p.103). The outstanding strike against the Thatcher government, the 1984-85 miners' strike, was within a nationalised industry for which intention to privatise had been announced.

[115] For this approach and opinion see: van der Hoeven and Sziraczki, p.8; Bonavoglia, p.108

[116] Chang K. Lee, "Privatization and Co-operative Labour-Management Relations", Cornell University, Department of City and Planning, May 1998, URL: http://www.cce.cornell.edu/

[117] Michael Moran and Tony Prosser, "Introduction: Politics, Privatisation and Constitutions", Edited by: Michael Moran and Tony Prosser, Privatisation and Regulatory Change in Europe, Edited by: Michael Moran and Tony Prosser, Open University Press, Buckingham & Philadelphia, 1994, p.11, 12

Huge sums were spent propping up unprofitable enterprises in order to maintain full employment, the hallmark of Communist economic systems. (Chikán, p.24)

[118] B. Martin, "The Social and Employment Consequences of Privatisation in Transition Economies: Evidence and Guidelines", Interdepartmental Action Programme on Privatisation, Restructuring and Economic Democracy-Working Paper, International Labour Organisation, web page of International Labour Organisation, URL: http://www.ilo.org

The following examples reveal the privatisation effects on employment in Central and Eastern European countries:

Moreover, this phenomenon has also occurred on a smaller scale in the Western European countries. For example in the United Kingdom British Gas, British Steel, Associated British Ports, British Coal Enterprises and British Telecom (BT) have posted large job cuts.[119] But in other organisations there seems to have been more marginal loss of jobs or even a rise in employment; and in fact both British Gas and British Steel began cutting their labour forces long before privatisation was mooted.[120] However when the whole economy is concern in Britain number of employees in nationalised industries has fallen from 1,849,000 to 302,000.[121]

On the other hand, in Greece a large number of job losses resulted from privatisation and the restructuring of state-owned enterprises[122] Furthermore in Turkey 70 percent of workers retired upon dismissal and did not attempt to re-enter the labour market in cement industry.[123]

In Bulgaria between 1989 and 1991, industrial employment fell by 31.3 per cent; employment in privatised firms fell from 4 million to 1 million people. [Charles Rock, "Privatisation and Employment in Bulgaria's Reform", Lessons from Privatisation: Labour Issues in Developing and Transitional Countries, Edited By: Rolph van der Hoeven and Gyorgy Sziraczki, International Labour Organisation (ILO), Geneva, 1997, p.93-115; URL: http://www.ilo.org/]

In the Czech Republic a government survey of 572 companies revealed a "significant decline in employment", with engineering (12 per cent) showing the sharpest drop, manufacturing and construction each cutting jobs by 10 per cent, and the food sector by 4 per cent. [Martin, p.12; Liba Paukert, "Privatization and Employment in the Czech Republic", Lessons from Privatisation: Labour Issues in Developing and Transitional Countries, Edited By: Rolph van der Hoeven and Gyorgy Sziraczki, International Labour Organisation (ILO), Geneva, 1997, p.145-162]

In Hungary from 1992 to 1993, employment in engineering dropped by 12 per cent, in manufacturing by 10 per cent, in construction by 10 per cent and in food processing by 4 per cent. [Martin, p.12; Laszlo Neumann, "Privatisation in Telecommunications in Hungary", Lessons from Privatisation: Labour Issues in Developing and Transitional Countries, Edited By: Rolph van der Hoeven and Gyorgy Sziraczki, International Labour Organisation (ILO), Geneva, 1997, p.165-191]

In Poland government research into 130 companies employing 285 each on average, showed that employment fell by 15 per cent in the first year and by 25 per cent over the first two years after privatisation, levelling off in the third year with a drop of a further approximately 2 per cent. A study of ten privatised Polish industrial and trade companies indicated decreases in employment averaging around 12.5 per cent. (Martin, p.13)

In Russian Federation there were massive job losses as well. For example, Uralmash, the heavy machinery manufacturer in the Urals, reduced employment from 70,000 people to 20,000, while at the Shatura Furniture Company introduction of an electronic data management system enabled nearly half the 3,700 jobs to be cut. (Martin, p.13)

[119] For example in British Steel, employment in 1979 was 186,000, falling to 54,000 at privatisation in 1988 and 40,200 in 1993. In the case of coal, the nationalised coal enterprise employed 232,410 people in 1979, a figure which dropped to 104,400 in 1988. Upon privatisation in 1994, it had an estimated 18,868. [Prosser, (Social Limits), p.226]

[120] Martin and Parker, p.167; Foster, p.103

According to some authors in the telecommunication sector privatisation will lead to "firing workers" from the old company. [Stiglitz, (Promoting Competition and Regulatory Policy), p.28]

[121] Web page of UK Treasury, URL: http://www.hm-treasury.gov.uk/pep/newpage21.html

[122] Haritakis and Pitelis, p. 132, 133

[123] Kikeri, p.7

Finally according to us in general, total employment does not decline after a firm is privatised unless an SOE has been clearly overstaffed.[124]

3. Other points

a. General

While in the private sector employees have full collective bargaining and a right to strike; in some countries labour legislation imposes constraints on the full collective bargaining rights and the right to strike of employees in state owned enterprises. Consequently, a shift from civil service to private employment is therefore not always viewed as detrimental. Furthermore in some countries after the privatisation process although employees lost their lifelong employment security, which had been guaranteed under public ownership, their wages and welfare benefits have increased and their promotion prospects have improved. Therefore the impact of privatisation on employment conditions is not necessarily straightforward: There may be some trade-off between the different effects. But it is still difficult to say whether the overall balance has been positive or negative, especially in the long term.[125] Furthermore according to some

---

[124] William L. Megginson & Jeffry M. Netter, "Equity to the People: The Record on Share Issue Privatization Programs", p.4, Web page of the World Bank, URL: http://www.worldbank.org. According to these authors: "...(the) findings suggest that the great fear of those opposing privatisation--that this will lead to large scale job losses--will not generally be true, unless a state-owned enterprise is clearly over-staffed to begin with. In effect, what happens is that a newly-privatised firm's output increases fast enough (due to increased efficiency and/or in response to new entrepreneurial opportunities) to fully utilise all existing workers, in spite of their higher individual productivity...(p.4, 5)

Furthermore in Poland, average wages and salaries fell by 27 per cent between 1989 and 1992, opening up inequalities in income. In Estonia, foreign owners have blocked pay increases. In this country a law on collective bargaining, which took effect in 1993, forbids new private owners from unilaterally scrapping collective agreements; it does, however, allow them to be renegotiated. In Hungary, while some privatisation contracts have committed foreign companies to retaining staff levels for a set period of time, there have been other adverse effects, such as cuts in staff training. The same country has also had the opposite experience, however. (Martin, 13, 14; Martin and Parker, p. 155, 156)

In Germany, ordinary labour law restricts the acceptable grounds for dismissal; but parliament has granted buyers of privatised enterprises temporary exemption from such restrictions, however, to facilitate implementation of the privatisation program. [Guislain, (The Privatization Challenge), p.75] The numbers in employment fell from 9 million before transition to 6.3 million by the end of 1992; the numbers employed in enterprises under the privatisation agency, the Treuhandanstalt, fell from 4.1 million to 1.2 million during that period. [Jurgen Kuhl, "Privatisation and its Labour Market Effects in Eastern Germany", Lessons from Privatisation: Labour Issues in Developing and Transitional Countries, Edited By: Rolph van der Hoeven and Gyorgy Sziraczki, International Labour Organisation (ILO), Geneva, 1997, p.119-143; Martin, p.13; Esser, p.119]

[125] Rolph van der Hoeven and Gyorgy Sziraczki, p.14

authors privatisation will increase the capacity of the economy to create employment by generating more resources for investment and growth.[126]

b. Pay and Social Conditions

It is also clear that the effects of privatisation upon employees are not limited to lay offs. Privatisation will have an impact up on workers' pay and social conditions. As in the case of lay-offs privatisation has mixed effects on workers pay and social conditions.[127]

Research on 15 British companies show that privatisation has led to large scale labour shedding as companies have become more market oriented. On the other hand, the remaining workers have been quite successful in maintaining their wages relative to comparable groups.[128]

Other more recent studies concluded that privatisation does not have to have negative results for labours. According to this study in most cases workers gain from the trend.[129] As one World Bank study points out "…In sum, labour has not been hurt because it generally had sufficient power to negotiate pre-divestiture agreements that made them no worse off…in some cases making them better off…"[130]

---

[126] V., Vuylsteke, Techniques of Privatisation of State-Owned Enterprises, Vol. I., World Bank Technical Paper No.88, the World Bank, Washington DC.

[127] In term of employment the record varies considerably between British Steel and associated British Ports (ABP), which recorded extensive job losses, and the other firms, where employment reductions were more modest or did not really begin until some years after privatisation. Looking at wage levels, it seems that in most of the organisations those retained their jobs may have maintained their relative wage position comparing the years immediately before privatisation with the most recent data. (Martin and Parker, p.186). For British case in the water industry see: Julia O'Connell Davidson, *Privatisation Employment Relations-The Case of the Water Industry, (Water Industry)*, Mansell Publishing Limited, New York, 1993) At Devonport soon after the introduction of the commercial management the programme of orders offered by the Ministry of Defence was cut, resulting in 2,000 redundancies, and in mid-1988 further losses of 3,300 jobs were announced, including some compulsory redundancies, the total reduction of 5, 300 jobs to take effect by April 1990. A further loss of 1,000 jobs was announced in September 1989 [Graham and Prosser, (Comparative Perspective), p.134]

[128] Haskel and Szymanski, p.9-10; Bishop and Kay, (Does Privatisation Work?), p.6, 7, 40

In, Britain, labour managed to obtain assurances that most of the corporations would not be split up and that pay and conditions would not deteriorate in an acceptable manner. (Privatization in the United Kingdom, Ernst & Young, p.20)

[129] Galal, Jones, Tandon and Vogelsang, p.529, 530, 546. According to these authors: "…In sum, labour has not been hurt because it generally had sufficient power to negotiate pre-divestiture agreements that made them no worse off…in some cases making them better off…"(p.548)

[130] Galal, Jones, Tandon and Vogelsang, p.548

D. Legal Measures and Approaches to Labour Issues[131]

As we have seen above, the privatisation process will inevitably cause some labour law problems; and privatisation legislation itself to be effective must address those problems.

The labour rules can either come into force with the new legislation or the current labour legislation or code can provide, appropriate provisions on those issues. These legal measures include severance pay for workers made redundant, dismissal with compensation, early retirement schemes, training, retraining and redeployment, and other measures such as reduced working hours and the hiring of young employees. Different classifications can be made. The law measures that need to be provided during the privatisation process can include the following groups:

1. Delaying and freezing employment reduction

a. General

The first approach is to delay or freeze employment reduction or spreading it over a longer period after privatisation. In many cases, privatisation transactions (contracts) include arrangements to protect employment in a privatised enterprise for a specific period after the change in ownership. This approach and solution has been used in (East) Germany, Lithuania and Estonia.[132]

---

[131] Guislain, (The Privatization Challenge), p.74
[132] Kuhl, p.119-143
 The Association of Estonian Trades Unions has managed to attach employment guarantees to contracts to ensure that jobs are maintained for a period after privatisation (originally three years, but pressure on the government is now shortening this to one year). [Martin, p.23]
 Furthermore in Lithuania, one of the restrictions and conditions that can be attached to privatisation contracts is that private investors are prohibited from reducing the work force by more than 30% for a certain period of time (at least three years). [Web page of Lithuanian Business Information Centre, URL: http://www.lbic.lt]

b. Analysis

The main disadvantages of such measures are that they tend to slow down employment adjustment and add to the financial burden up on the state and the employers concerned. On the other hand, increased unemployment benefits are avoided. Freezing of recruitment and early retirement has also been used to minimise the number of redundancies and ease the transition.[133]

2. Severance payment regulations and a system of early warning for mass lay-offs

a. General

The second approach and group of policy measures relates to severance payment regulations and a system of early warning for mass lay-offs.

Another form of compensatory measure involves bonuses for employees who resign voluntarily instead of severance pay for retrenched workers.[134]

Early retirement schemes have probably been one of the most common measures used to speed up departures and reduce the workforce in the process of privatisation and restructuring. Particularly in countries where the need to reward or placate labour is strong and social safety nets are lacking, as well as in countries where labour legislation prohibits outright layoffs, governments have resorted to voluntary departures by providing severance pay packages that have exceeded legally mandated requirements.[135]

---

[133] Rolph van der Hoeven and Gyorgy Sziraczki, p.12

[134] Rolph van der Hoeven and Gyorgy Sziraczki, p.12
In Hungary the lighting company Tungsram employed 35,000 people until that figure was halved to 17,640 in preparation for its sale to General Electric, which soon almost halved the workforce again to 9,500 by 1993. This was done mainly through early retirement and voluntary redundancy, alongside a freeze on recruitment. Many of the jobs were redundant as a result of administrative functions being centralised with the new owner's offices outside Hungary. As a result, non-manual grades were affected disproportionately by the Tungsram job losses. (Martin, p.12; Neumann, p.165-191)

[135] Kikeri, p.14

b. Analysis

In most cases, it seems that the schemes are implemented on a voluntary basis. But depending on the results of the voluntary programme, staff may still need to be made compulsorily redundant.[136]

Furthermore in many cases, there are quite generous arrangements for redundancy payments, depending on provisions in national labour laws and collective agreements and often based on years of service. Thus in the United Kingdom, redundancy packages were negotiated in the water, electricity and in coal industry with some being voluntary and others compulsory.[137] Furthermore in some cases (British Telecom, British Airways) employees were given compensation.[138] On the other hand in Ireland, a generous severance package is in place to address the downsizing process in the electricity sector.[139]

Where the SOE is not divested as a going concern and the buyers are taking over limited assets and obligations from the SOE, contracts with some workers may be part of the package. Under prevailing labour legislation, these workers may be entitled to severance pay from the SOE even though they are immediately rehired by the new company. This "double dipping" may

---

[136] Kikeri, p.19

[137] For example in the United Kingdom, despite the scale of job losses in the electricity sector, serious industrial action was avoided by providing generous voluntary redundancy and early-retirement packages, which included job placement facilities, retraining, seminars on assertiveness and self-employment, financial investment advice and general help lines. (Web page of International Labour Organisation, URL: http://www.ilo.org/). In the British Telecom privatisation the government has chosen "natural wastage and voluntary early retirement" method; and some 96% of the staff of the company became shareholders at privatisation. (Robin Bomer, "The Privatisation of British Telecom", Privatisation in Practice, Edited By: Eamonn Butler, The Adam Smith Institute, Imediaprint Ltd., 1988, p.41)

For the coal sector see: Prosser, (Social Limits), p.233

[138] Galal, Jones, Tandon and Vogelsang, p.547

[139] In some countries, however, little or no compensation is paid to dismissed workers. Workers made redundant in the water industry in the Czech Republic received two months' salary in compensation (higher than this cannot be negotiated by law). If the worker was two years or less away from retirement then the employer had to pay the difference so that the worker could receive the full pension. (Web page of International Labour Organisation, URL: http://www.ilo.org)

be prevented by special provisions to be included in the law or contractual arrangements with the workers concerned.[140]

This policy should be implemented carefully. Hence where a large company has been split into small firms, collective agreements and employment contracts have sometimes been modified in such a way that the workers have lost their seniority rights and severance pay entitlement.[141]

3. Reintegration of laid-off workers

a. General

The third group of policy measures aims to facilitate the reintegration of laid-off workers into other forms of employment. Such measures have included job search and mobility assistance, retraining or vocational training, and job creation schemes.[142]

b. Analysis

These measures are often implemented on a voluntary basis, but at times may be compulsory. These schemes are often negotiated between governments, companies and trade unions before and during a privatisation or restructuring process.[143]

Finally, the rights of laid-off workers, including severance pay and unemployment benefits, may vary significantly depending on whether they were laid off by the new private owners or by the SOE before privatisation; there will also be a difference depending on whether

---

[140] Guislain, (The World Bank), p.28
[141] Kikeri, p.ix; "Political and Organizational Strategies for Streamlining", Privatisation Database, URL: http://www.privatisation.org
[142] Rolph van der Hoeven and Gyorgy Sziraczki, p.12, 13, Report on Privatisation and Lessons Learned, GAO (General Accounting Office of USA), URL: http://www.privatisation.org/Collection/P...egies/GaoPrivReport--lessons-learned.html; "Political and Organizational Strategies for Streamlining", Privatisation Database, URL: http://www.privatisation.org
[143] Web page of International Labour Organisation, URL: http://www.ilo.org/

these workers were governed by general labour legislation or by special public sector legislation.[144]

4. Restrictions in the privatisation legislation

a. General

The fourth approach the countries adopt for the labour law issues is to impose restrictions in the privatisation legislation to prevent new investors from dismissing the current employees. Such a restriction may be imposed in the privatisation contract.

In such a case, legislation forces private investor to accept certain attached conditions in order to have the ownership and the control of the SOEs.

Another measure related to this scheme is for governments to negotiate with the potential buyers on the labour law issues and demand certain guarantees or consider certain factors (for example keeping the entire labour force for a stated period) as "advantages and competing points" in the selection of buyers. For example in Estonia, one of the methods of privatisation is sale of property in tender with preliminary negotiations (Article 20/1 of the Privatisation Law). However, article 21 which provides provision on the sale methods states that, in the selection of buyers "guaranteeing of employment and creating new jobs" may be competing additional conditions.[145]

Another variation is to insist upon an employment and wage guarantee for a certain period of time. This approach involves imposing restrictions in the privatisation contract upon new investors to refrain from dismissing workers for a certain time. Thus, German labour laws require the buyer of an enterprise to continue to employ the firm's entire work force (the change

---

[144] Guislain, (Privatization Challenge), p.75; Guislain, (The World Bank), p.28
[145] Estonian Law on Privatisation, web page of Estonian Privatisation Agency, URL: http://www.eea.ee/english/indexe.htm

in ownership itself not being sufficient justification for laying off employees).[Civil Code, art. 613 (a), (F.R.G.)] [146] but the German parliament granted buyers of privatised enterprises a temporary exemption from these restrictions in order to facilitate the country's privatisation program.

However, the Treuhand (German Privatisation Agency) has included in many privatisation contracts a binding undertaking whereby the buyer guarantees a specified level of employment in the privatised firm, subject to contractually determined penalties for failure to comply with such undertakings.[147]

b. Analysis

According to some authors the negotiated approach is better than the legislative approach to employment protection chosen by some other countries,[148] where new owners prohibited from firing workers for one or two years following divestiture. This uniform requirement makes the whole privatisation process unnecessarily rigid and difficult.[149]

Like in other approaches, governments may let unions to take an active role in the privatisation process. In other words, unions may be allowed to negotiate with the potential investors in the privatisation transactions.

5. Working with the Attrition Rate/Transfer of Employees to Other SOEs

a. General

Perhaps the easiest method to reduce the work force after privatisation is to limit the rate of reduction to the normal rate of attrition. Workers on a given function targeted for privatisation

---

[146] Raiser, p. 10; Gesetz zur Regelung offener Vermogensfragen vom 3 Oktober 1990 [Law Concerning the Regulation of Open Questions of Property of October 3, 1990] BGB1 II at 1159 (1990), Raiser footnote 21, p.17]
[147] Guislain, (The World Bank), p.28
[148] Such as Sri Lanka and Pakistan
[149] Guislain, (The World Bank), p.28

are simply shifted to other government work, with staff reductions occurring only as employees retire.[150] Some countries have adopted this scheme.

For example, in the Turkish Privatisation Law article 22 of the Privatisation Law states that the personnel subject to Law No: 657 on Civil Servants and personnel under contract whom are employed in the organisations under the scope of the privatisation program, that are privatised, downsized, closed or liquidated, or whose activities are ceased, shall be transferred to other public organisations and/or institutions.

b. Analysis

SOEs in centrally planned economies employed more personnel than they really needed because the government guaranteed jobs for all workers. This guarantee also meant that workers would be paid regardless of their performance.[151] State owned enterprises SOEs often had excess workers.[152]

6. Employee Participation in the Privatisation Process[153]

a. General

Some countries have reserved some shares in SOEs to be divested on preferential terms to their employees.[154] This approach has been designed to reduce the opposition of the employees and therefore provides a good solution.

---

[150] Political and Organizational Strategies for Streamlining, Privatisation Database, URL: http://www.privatisation.org; Demetra Smith Nightingale and Nancy Pindus, "Privatization of Public Social Services: A Background Paper", October 15, 1997, Urban Institute, URL: http://www.urban.org/

[151] "Privatizing State-Owned Companies", The Prosperity Papers Series, Prosperity Paper Three, web page of Center for International Private Enterprise, URL: http://www.cipe.org/

[152] López-de-Silanes, p.5

[153] Incentives for employees

[154] Guislain, (The World Bank), p.29

In Lithuania Employees may acquire up to 50 percent of the shares. (Lithuanian State Privatisation Agency and State Property Fund, URL: http://www.vtf.lb/)

This measure has widely been used both in many former socialist countries.[155] It has also been used, in some industrial countries. Thus in the UK, there have been several examples of employee buyouts, or management buyouts, in the privatisation programme.[156] Moreover employee participation in both trade sales and public offerings has been encouraged by long-term employee share ownership schemes (especially in the utilities industries), by promoting management and employee buy-outs in suitable cases (usually smaller enterprises) and by developing incentives to encourage employees to participate in major share offers. Special arrangements for employees include free shares, a discount on the offer price of shares, or priority in the allocation of shares. (British Airways, British Gas, British Telecom, National Freight, Enterprise Oil, Associated British Ports, Jaguar, Cable and Wireless).

In some cases, companies have introduced long-term, share-based profit-sharing schemes.[157] In this country, over half a million employees were transferred to the private sector, of whom around 90 percent acquired shares in their companies and the total number of private shareholders in Britain roughly trebled.[158]

---

[155] In Bulgaria, article 5 of the Bulgarian "Transformation and Privatization of State-Owned and Municipal-Owned Enterprises Act (Published in the Official Gazette issue No 38 of 1992, for the full text of this law this see the web page of the Bulgarian Privatisation Agency at http//www.privatisation.online.bg/laws/ZPPDOP.html) states that "All natural and juristic persons shall be eligible to participate in privatisation on equal terms, save as where otherwise expressly provided by this Act. (Article 5/10)
However, the following persons shall be entitled to participate on preferential terms:
-any member of the staff of the privatising enterprise who has been in continuous employment therewith for at least two years prior to the date of declaration of the decision on privatisation;
-any person whereof the labour relationship with the privatising enterprise has been terminated according to the procedure established by the Labour Code and pursuant to the provisions of the Act on Defence and the Armed Forces of the Republic of Bulgaria not earlier than fourteen years prior to the date of declaration of the decision on privatisation ...;
-any person who has retired on pension whilst in employment with the privatising enterprise not earlier than ten years prior to the date of declaration of the decision on privatisation..." (Article 5/2.1-2.2)
For Russian case see: Ash, Hare and Canning, p.225; Barberis, Boycko, Shleifer and Tsukanova, p.25
[156] Bryan Carsberg, (Regulator), p.62; Mitchell, p.22
For instance, in the National Freight Corporation (1982) privatisation took the form of buy-outs by the management and/or workers. (Mitchell, p.22)
[157] Comparative Overview of Privatisation Policies and Institutions in Member OECD Countries, OECD Privatization and Enterprise Reform Unit, September 1998, web page of OECD, URL: http://www.oecd.org; Bishop and Kay, (Does Privatisation Work?), p.35, 63
[158] Vickers and Yarrow, (An Economic Analysis), p.1
In France employees benefit from a priority within the following limits: 10 per cent of the total amount sold, for each operation; 5 times the annual ceiling of the social security contributions for each employee. A

Finally according to the Bulgarian Privatisation Law any person who has retired on pension whilst in employment with the privatising enterprise not earlier than ten years prior to the date of declaration of the decision on privatisation, should the said person have completed at least three years of service prior to his or her retirement from the said employment shall be entitled to participate on preferential terms. But the law puts no restriction to any employee who has been registered as totally or partially disabled by any injury suffered in the course of his or her employment with the said enterprise.[159]

b. Analysis

There are different comments on this method in the privatisation literature. For example, employee prefences raise questions of equity as well: Why should employees of some SOEs get a government hand-out and not those of other SOEs, or civil servants, farmers or the unemployed? Does employee participation in company capital and/or profits contribute to higher efficiency?[160]

In some cases, this approach would deter some investors, who may not want employee shareholding in their company or simply want full ownership. The constraint can be partly circumvented, for example through preferential employees shares without voting rights.[161]

In that case, if employees are transferred, then the issue arises of what kind of employment status they have. In most cases, transferred employees are subject to private sector

---

preferential treatment could be granted to the employees either in the form of a discount not exceeding 20 per cent of the price offered to other subscribers or in the form of a deferred payment. When prices are discounted, the shares cannot be transferred for two years.

The privatisation of two companies (BNP and Rhône Poulenc) arised a great deal of interest among the employees of both companies, and all of the shares set aside for them were sold: 90 per cent of the BNPs French employees became shareholders of their company, as did over 80 per cent of those at Rhône Poulenc. (Comparative Overview of Privatisation Policies and Institutions in Member OECD Countries, OECD Privatization and Enterprise Reform Unit, September 1998, URL: http://www.oecd.org)

[159] Transformation and Privatization of State-Owned and Municipal-Owned Enterprises Act; (Published in the Official Gazette issue No 38 of 1992; web page of the Bulgarian Privatisation Agency, URL: http://www.privatisation.online.bg/laws/ZPPDOP.html)

[160] Guislain, (The World Bank), p.51

[161] Guislain, (The World Bank), p.29

contractual arrangements, which may entail the loss of certain benefits granted to public sector workers, in particular job security. They may also face some other restrictions on the right of strike. But the change in the legal status may bring certain positive outcomes, depending on the legislation and company, and the industrial relations climate. As their legal status has changed they (workers) may be able to bargain collectively for higher wages or other conditions of work.[162]

7. Transfer of Employees to the new Company: The Acquire Rights Directive 77/187/EEC[163]

a. General

The Acquire Rights Directive 77/187/EEC is intended to safeguard the rights of workers on a transfer of the employing undertaking by ensuring that workers are entitled to continue working for the transferee employer on the same terms and conditions as those agreed with the transferor employer. Whenever a transfer is within the directive, contracts of employment run with the undertaking; the transferee cannot take the business without the employees and must take those employees subject to existing employment rights and obligations.[164]

The directive was amended on 29 June 1998 in an attempt to create greater clarity over when it applies and to permit member states to include pensions in its scope.[165] It is implemented

---

[162] In other situations, employees may retain their public sector status, as was the case in Japan when gas companies were privatised. (Web page of International Labour Organisation, URL: http://www.ilo.org/)

[163] Council Directive 98/50/EC of 29 June 1998 amended Directive 77/187/EEC and the title was replaced by the following: "Council Directive 77/187/EEC of 14 February 1977 on the approximation of the laws of the Member States relating to the safeguarding of employees' rights in the event of transfers of undertakings, businesses or parts of undertakings or businesses".

[164] Steve D Anderman, *Labour Law-Management Decisions and Workers' Rights*, Fourth Edition, Butterworths, London, Edinburgh, Dublin, 2000, p. 215; Memorandum on acquired rights of workers in case of transfers of undertakings, Web page of the European Union, URL: http://www.europa.eu.int/comm/employment_social/soc-dial/labour/memo/memo_en.htm; Web page of Web Journal of Current Legal Issues, URL: http://webjcli.ncl.ac.uk/1998/issue5/shrubsall5.html

[165] Web page of Confederation of British Industry, URL: http://www.cbi.org.uk/ndbs/IssueInfoSys.nsf/d6f6ea27cdb27b1d80256721003ba8a2/2311f6bbaade70da802565cd0053bc40?OpenDocument; Web page of The Federation of European Employers, URL: http://www.euen.co.uk/transund.html; "Acquired Rights Directive: Amendments", Web page of Practical Legal Information for Business Lawyers, URL: http://www.plcinfo.com/scripts/article.asp?Article_ID=9870

in the UK by the Transfer of Undertakings (Protection of Employment) Regulations, or "TUPE".[166]

According to Article 1 (a) (c) of the directive:

"This Directive shall apply to any transfer of an undertaking, business, or part of an undertaking or business to another employer as a result of a legal transfer or merger...This Directive shall apply to public and private undertakings engaged in economic activities whether or not they are operating for gain".

Furthermore article 3 (1) (2) states that:

"1. The transferor's rights and obligations arising from a contract of employment or from an employment relationship existing on the date of a transfer shall, by reason of such transfer, be transferred to the transferee. Member States may provide that, after the date of transfer, the transferor and the transferee shall be jointly and severally liable in respect of obligations which arose before the date of transfer from a contract of employment or an employment relationship existing on the date of the transfer.
2. Member States may adopt appropriate measures to ensure that the transferor notifies the transferee of all the rights and obligations which will be transferred to the transferee under this Article, so far as those rights and obligations are or ought to have been known to the transferor at the time of the transfer".

On the other hand article 7 states the directive shall not affect the right of member states to apply or introduce laws, regulations or administrative provisions which are more favourable to employees or to promote or permit collective agreements or agreements between social partners more favourable to employees. (Article 7) Also the directive shall be without prejudice to national law as regards the definition of contract of employment or employment relationship. [Article 2(2)]

Finally the directive requires member states to bring into force the laws, regulations and administrative provisions necessary to comply with this Directive by 17 July 2001. (Final provisions, article 2)

b. Analysis

When a business is taken over by a new employer, the directive provides protection for employees' existing rights. The intention of the regulation is to provide the safeguard to the employees of the transferor firm that they may enter into relationship with the transferee

---

[166] Anderman, p.220-224; "Guidelines on the Application of Acquire Rights Directive 77/187/EEC (TUPE)", Web page of Business Information Publications Limited (BiP), URL: http://www.bipcontracts.com/briefings/Brief12_98.html

employer with all or almost all their individual and collective rights, powers, duties and obligations vis-à-vis their former employer (in our case SOE), in place.[167]

The directive clearly states that it shall apply to any transfer of public and private undertakings, businesses to another employer as a result of a legal transfer or merger. Therefore the provisions of the directive will also apply when a SOE is privatised in the EC member states. In that case government's rights and obligations arising from a contract of employment or from an employment relationship existing on the date of a transfer shall, by reason of such transfer, be transferred to the private investor.

However member states may adopt appropriate measures to notify the private investor of all the rights and obligations that will be transferred to the private investor under this directive. [Article 3(2)]

On the other hand in privatisation transactions member states are free to apply or introduce laws, regulations or administrative provisions that are more favourable to employees. (Article 7). Member states are also free to decide the definition of contract of employment or employment relationship in their national law. [Article 2(2)]

8. Overall Analysis on Legal Approaches

a. General

These legal approaches and solutions can be applied alone or, like in Turkey[168], in a comprehensive package. Besides Turkey, some other countries including former Eastern

---

[167] Anderman, p.215
[168] Turkish Case
Turkish Privatisation Law (The official name of the law is "Law Concerning Privatisation and Regulation of Implementations of Privatisation and Amendment to Certain Laws and Statutory Decrees, Law Nr.4046, Date of Passage: 24 November 1994, Official Gazette Nr. 22124, Date of Official Gazette: 27. 11. 1994) provides mixed legal measures to the labour law issues. In order to understand which rules and articles will be applied, the workers should be divided into two main groups:
1. Workers Subject to Law No: 657 on Civil Servants
a. General
In that case the solution of the Turkish Privatisation Law is to transfer of personnel in the privatised organisation to other governmental associations. Thus Article 22 of the Privatisation Law states that the personnel

Germany[169], Hungary[170], the Czech Republic,[171] the Netherlands,[172] the UK and Bulgaria[173] have also introduced mixed approaches that involves comprehensive system of compensatory and proactive measures to deal with labour dislocation.[174]

---

subject to Law No: 657 on Civil Servants and personnel under contract whom are employed in the organisations under the scope of the privatisation program, that are privatised, downsized, closed or liquidated, or whose activities are ceased, shall be transferred to other public organisations and/or institutions. These transfers will be done in accordance with the provisions stipulated in paragraph (f) of article 8 of the Decree No.217 with the Force of Law.
    b. Legal Procedure
    Turkish privatisation Law provides detailed provisions on the legal procedure on the transfer of the civil servants to other public organisations and institutions. According to the law:
    "...The organisation concerned shall send the information on both the civil servants and contracted personnel to the State Personnel Department within 30 days following the date of notification...Within the 45 days at the latest following the notification to State Personnel Department the personnel concerned, upon the proposal of this department, shall be transferred to those appropriate posts and positions in keeping with their status vacant in the public organisations and institutions. In case no appropriate vacant position in line with their status exists in organisations...Council of Ministers is authorised to change the class, title and degree of the existing posts..." [Article 22, paragraph, 2-6].
    c. Rights of the Employees
    "...The posts and positions to become vacant due to transfers to other public organisations and institutions ...shall be deemed to have been cancelled as of the vacancy date. Salaries, social rights and fringe benefits together with any and all kinds of personal rights of the personnel appointed to other public organisations and/or institutions...shall be paid from the Privatisation Fund, and those who are enrolled in the Turkish Pension Fund shall continue to remain under the Fund during this period..." (Article 22, paragraph 7, 8)
    2. Workers Subject to General Labour Legislation
    Turkish Privatisation Law is a specific code and provides specific and certain rules about the effects of privatisation on labours. Therefore, on labour law issues in the privatisation process provisions in the Privatisation Law have priority to the provisions in the general labour code.
    Turkish Privatisation Law provides three different rules on these types of workers. (In some specific cases if any lay-off occurs, these articles may be applied to the workers subject to Law no 657).
    a. Dismissal Compensation (Redundancy Payments)
    i. General
    According to article 2 of the Privatisation Law one of the principles in implementation of privatisation is the payment of a "compensation for redundancy", in connection with a possible decrease in employment, in addition to any compensation prescribed in existing laws and/or collective labour agreements
    Article 21 of the Privatisation Law provides that dismissal compensation must be paid to the former employees, if dismissal happens in the first year after the privatisation of the company. According to this law the redundancy payment is the daily net pay of the employee to be calculated in the accordance with the principles and procedures regulated in articles 77 and 78 of the Law No: 506 on Social Security. (Paragraph, 1)
    ii. Priority of the Dismissal Compensation
    "...Privatisation proceeds collected in the Privatisation Fund for the purpose of the redundancy payments and other services mentioned in this Law, shall first be applied to meet redundancy compensation payments..." (Paragraph, 3)
    b. Priority in services for finding new employment opportunities, career development, vocational and apprenticeship training
    Furthermore, article 21 states that if lay offs happen, the employees will be given priority in services for finding new employment, vocational and apprenticeship training. All these expenses will be supported and financed by the Privatisation Fund.
    c. Encouragement to Retirement (Early Retirement)
    Article 24 of the Privatisation Law provides that, of the personnel subject to Law No: 5434 on Turkish Pension Fund at organisations under the scope of the privatisation program, those who are entitled to retirement as of the period of service under the Turkish Pension Fund Law, shall receive pension bonuses at a %30 increment if they ask to be retired within two months.
    For labour law issues in privatisation implementations in Turkey also see: Erdem, p.49
    [169] Kuhl, p.119-143
    [170] Neumann, p.165-191

323

For EC countries, provisions in The Acquire Rights Directive 77/187/EEC[175] will be applied when a SOE is privatised in the member states.

Each country has its own unique circumstances requiring governments to decide the appropriate mix measures.

---

[171] Paukert, p.145-162

[172] In the Netherlands the government and the privatised company signed a social charter. The government allowed privatised employees to stay in the Civil Service Pension Fund for a few years, after which the Civil Service Pension Fund pays a compensatory sum to a new pension fund. The government and trade unions have now jointly set up a Federative Pension Fund for workers in privatised companies. (Andeweg, p.205)

[173] Rock, p. 93-115; Web page of International Labour Organisation, URL: http://www.ilo.org/

[174] In France, when water concessions are granted, workers are reportedly given three options: to remain as municipal employees and be redeployed; to be put on detached duty with renewal of contract every five years; or to be transferred and completely integrated in the new enterprise. (Web page of International Labour Organisation, URL: http://www.ilo.org/). In France Article L 432-1 of the Code du travail (Labour Law) requires consultation of the works council on modifications in the economic or legal organisation of an enterprise, including mergers, cessions, and acquisitions and cessions of subsidiaries. The law would seem to require the consultation of staff on privatisation. But in two cases brought by the works council of enterprises being privatised, the courts refused to order the provision of the opportunity for the council to arrange a valuation of the enterprise, and to order consultation on the price of the enterprise and the choice of purchaser. The reason given by the Court was that the decision to privatise was a matter for decision by government, not by the enterprise itself. [Graham and Prosser, (Comparative Perspective), p.135, 136]

In Hungary, transfers to the private sector have been the normal practice in energy privatisation. The transfers, with protection, were agreed between trade unions and the Government and written into the contractual conditions of the sale of the enterprises. (Web page of International Labour Organisation, URL: http://www.ilo.org/)

In Spain, employment reductions in the utilities have been based on collective agreements providing for voluntary early retirements, redundancy pay and rejuvenation of the workforce through the hiring of young people. Reorganisation of plants was achieved without dismissals and accompanied by retraining and redeployment. In Sweden, after negotiation with trade unions in the electricity sector, pensions were offered to older redundant employees, lump-sum payments to those voluntarily resigning to start up on their own and skills development and training. (Web page of International Labour Organisation, URL: http://www.ilo.org/)

In Britain, during the privatisation process, the policy on labour issues has been constructed so as to leave no employee threatened with unemployment if it could be avoided. Early retirement was the main measure in that process; for example in British Airways, during the privatisation its workforce was trimmed from 59,000 down to 39,000 and this was achieved by generous terms for voluntary redundancy. Also where private contractors have taken over public service operations, contracts have usually specified that workers displaced from state operation can have the first offer of new jobs created by the private firm. In other words it is common for contracts to specify that the existing employees should be given the chance of any new jobs which are created, before the new labour is taken on. Other workers have been absorbed internally by other departments that would have otherwise taken in recruits outside. (Madsen Pirie, *Privatisation*, Wildwood House Limited, England, 1988, p.62, 81, 142, 143)

The recent studies found that privatisation or changed objectives led to large-scale labour shedding, as companies became more profit oriented. Those workers remaining with the firms have generally maintained their wages relative to comparable groups, but relative wages have fallen in cases where liberalisation has reduced the firm's market power. Average wages increased at similar rates to those in the rest of the economy and in manufacturing, until 1992/3 when a shake-out of labour led to an increase in average wages. [Holder, p.11]

[175] Council Directive 98/50/EC of 29 June 1998 amended Directive 77/187/EEC and the title shall be replaced by the following: "Council Directive 77/187/EEC of 14 February 1977 on the approximation of the laws of the Member States relating to the safeguarding of employees' rights in the event of transfers of undertakings, businesses or parts of undertakings or businesses".

b. Special Provisions for Disabled Employees

In many countries privatisation legislation or Labour Code provide special provisions for disabled employees. The purpose of such provisions is to create an equal social environment among workers in the society. The provisions on disabled employees may vary.

These provisions may bring some restrictions on the dismissal of these employees or they may provide additional benefits most likely in the financial aspect.[176]

---

[176] For example article 21 of the Turkish Privatisation Law states that disabled employees...may not be dismissed except from organisations which are being closed or liquidated. In the case of closing and liquidation, the disabled personnel...shall be offered a redundancy payment equal to twice the amount set forth herein. (Web page of Turkish Privatisation Administration, URL: http://www.oib.gov.tr/)

E. Conclusions

The knowledge on the impact of privatisation on labours is still limited[177]; it is because it requires a long run observation. [178] However, there are some initial findings therefore we can draw some interim conclusions and point out certain remarks.

The main expectation in relation to the effects of privatisation on employment is that privatisation will often involve immediate job losses or otherwise disadvantage the workforce by resulting in lower wages for those who retain their jobs.[179]

However actual effects of privatisation up on labour depend on the conditions prior to privatisation. Large-scale labour force reductions often occur when large, poorly performing state enterprises are prepared for privatisation and when privatised companies are exposed to greater competition. The more governments privatise such firms, and the greater the exposure to competition, the larger those reductions are likely to be. It seems that in the short term the employment effect will be either negative or to preserve the status quo. In the longer run however the position is less clear from the available studies.

It also must be recognised that privatisation is not a zero-sum equation. Although the number of public jobs may decrease, jobs also are created in the private sector from privatisation.[180]

---

[177] Cook, p. 236; Sheshinski and López-Calva, p.22, 29

[178] In USA, the most comprehensive evaluation of the effect of privatisation on government workers was conducted in 1989 by the National Commission on Employment Policy (NCEP), a research arm of the U.S. Labour Department. The study, titled "The Long-Term Employment Implications of Privatisation," examined 34 privatised city and county services in a variety of jurisdictions around the country. The report found that of the 2,213 government workers affected over a five-year period by the privatisations, only 7 percent were laid off. More than half the worker (58 percent) went to work for the private contractor; 24 percent of the workers were transferred to other government jobs, and 7 percent of workers retired. The study concluded that "in the majority of cases, cities and counties have done a commendable job of protecting the jobs of public employees." (Political and Organizational Strategies for Streamlining, Privatisation Database, URL: http://www.privatisation.org)

[179] van der Hoeven and Sziraczki, p.8; Rosario Bonavoglia, "Evolution and Design in Eastern European Transition: Comment, Privatisation Process in Eastern Europe, Edited by: Mario Baldassari, Luigi Paganetto, Edmund S. Phelps, St. Martin Press, 1993, p.108

In many cases, staff redundancies are not so much a consequence of privatisation as of poor SOE (state owned enterprise) management leading to overstaffing. These SOEs would have had to be restructed and streamlined sooner or later, even without a change of ownership.[181] Furthermore if there will be lay offs, the magnitude of the employment effect of privatisation is determined by the relative share of public enterprise employment in total employment, the number of lay-offs expected just before or after privatisation, and the potential of the economy to generate employment for those who have been laid off both immediately and in the longer run.[182]

The effects of privatisation on employees occur in different legal shapes. Privatisation can cause small or massive lay offs; but in some cases although workers keep their current positions, the privatisation process may affect particular labour conditions such as working hours, wages and social security.[183]

The separate issues should be distinguished. When state owned enterprises are privatised, there might be a reduction in the number of public employees, but there is not necessarily a reduction in total employment nor are workers always worse off.[184]

---

[180] "Political and Organizational Strategies for Streamlining", Privatisation Database, URL: http://www.privatisation.org

[181] Guislain, (The Privatization Challenge), p.80; Prosser, (Social Limits), p.227. [As Prosser points out: "...It would be possible to argue, at considerable length, above the extent to which these job losses would have occurred without privatisation, and the degree to which they represent a reallocation of labour to more efficient use elsewhere in the economy" (p.227)]

[182] Rolph van der Hoeven and Gyorgy Sziraczki, p.8

[183] According to some economists the pay of workers in privatised areas may well fall as competition is introduced. However, this fact cannot be seen as a negative outcome because "...it creates more jobs, as lower wages increase employment. Second it reveals that previously pay was above the competitive market rate, because of union pressure within a monopoly environment; monopoly gains in pay are no more legitimate than monopoly gains in price". (Minford, p.1, 2)

Some authors think that wages of the employees may be kept low initially. (Robert E. Anderson, Simeon Djankov, Gerhard Pohl, "Privatization and Restructuring in Central and Eastern Europe", Public Policy for the Private Sector, The World Bank, July 1997, Note no. 123, p.3). According to these authors: "... the workforce... (should not)... absorb all the productivity gains through higher wages. Firms must finance much of their investment with retained earnings from current cash flow especially when the financial system is weak..."(p.3)

Finally some studies found out that, in the United Kingdom one very clear consequence of privatisation has been an increase in the salaries of senior management in privatised industry. [Bishop and Kay, (Does Privatisation Work?), p.64, 65]

[184] Demetra Smith Nightingale and Nancy Pindus, "Privatization of Public Social Services: A Background Paper", October 15, 1997, Urban Institute, URL: http://www.urban.org/

Employment reductions and lay offs often occur in Central and Eastern European countries. It is because in most cases the enterprises have had a very high and artificial employment level. Lack of modern technology and insufficient management are other reasons.[185] We should point out that although employment levels in privatised enterprises have generally fallen wage levels have tended to increase after privatisation.[186]

It is not right to give enterprise management or employees the power of veto over privatisation of the enterprise.[187] Appropriate labour legislation can prevent or change the opposition of the labour unions through the privatisation. Thus in general, privatisation has in fact had a minimal effect on employment in countries that carried out labour reforms well before privatisation.[188]

Privatisation legislation should solve the labour law issues in a balance; and the legislation should protect the pension and other employee benefits of the workers in the privatisation process. In other words, the legislation should provide the appropriate measures to minimise the (possible bad) effects of privatisation on employees. Otherwise the costs of privatisation and restructuring could be considered as having been passed on ultimately to workers and society.

The economic situation of the country, aims of the privatisation program, power and the pressure of the trade unions, political situation and current legislation will determine the structure and the scope of the legislation.

---

[185] For example, most of the Polish companies were overstaffed and labour productivity was low. (Maciej Grabowski, Economic Reform in Poland, Economic Reform Today Working Papers, Number 4, web page of Center for International Private Enterprise, URL: http://www.cipe.org/)
An IMF study point outs that, privatised firms reduced their labour force by 20 percent in former socialist countries. (Havrylyshyn and McGettigan, p.4)
Also see: Prosser, (Social Limits), p.234. [According to Prosser: "In the situation facing the former socialist nations this may be unavoidable anyway given the scale of the transition which has to be faced."(p.234)]

[186] Peter Young, "The Lessons of Privatisation", web page of Center for International Private Enterprise, URL: http://www.cipe.org/

[187] Rutledge, p.3

[188] Kikeri, p.5

The co-operation of public workers is essential to a successful privatisation program[189], and public officials should communicate a commitment to fair treatment for current employees. One of the principal reasons public employees are hostile to privatisation is the perception that they will lose their jobs as a result of it.[190]

Privatisation may have positive outcomes for employees and the economy; particularly if the labour issues are solved in a balance. For example when privatisation involves growth and/or diversification, job opportunities may expand.[191] The increasing profitability of privatised utilities can spur economic growth and employment creation.[192] Increased profits can also be reinvested in infrastructure, maintaining adequate workforce levels and in the retraining and continuous training of the utilities workforce, thereby providing good quality services.

Furthermore privatisation may bring positive outcomes in the case of working conditions and health issues in the working environments since new investor might introduce new and better measures, social and working conditions.[193] Thus in some countries, particularly in foreign owned privatised enterprises, the wages rose up after privatisation.[194]

---

[189] "The Opportunities and Challenges of Privatisation", Chapter I, US Department of Energy, US Department of Energy, URL: http://home.osti.gov/

This was the case in the Netherlands. In this country the civil service unions opposed the privatisation programme. They saw privatisation as an excuse for restructuring an inefficient and ineffective civil service and feared a loss of jobs, income and pension rights. But when the outcome of the privatisation programme didn't support their ears, the public sector unions became more moderate and co-operative. If particular labour conditions such as job security, wages and social security are safeguarded in equilibrium. (Willem Hullsink and Hans Schenk, "Privatisation and Deregulation in the Netherlands, Privatisation in the European Union, Theory and Policy Perspectives, Edited By: David Parker, London and New York, p.246)

[190] "Political and Organizational Strategies for Streamlining", Privatisation Database, URL: http://www.privatisation.org

The representatives of the workforce play an important role in the preparation of the workforce towards the privatisation of the company. The main responsibility of the employee council is to define the objectives of the workforce within the framework of the privatisation plan and to mediate between the board of directors and the workforce itself throughout the process. (R. Schliwa, "Enterprise Privatisation and Employee Buy-Outs in Poland: An Analysis of the Process", Interdepartmental Action Programme on Privatization, Restructuring and Economic Democracy" Working Paper IPPRED-2, training. web page of International Labour Organisation, URL: http://www.ilo.org/)

[191] Janice A. Beecher, "Twenty Myths About Privatisation", Alliance for Redesigning Government, National Academy of Public Administration, URL: http://www.alliance.napawash.org/

[192] Kikeri, p.5, 8, 9

[193] In Poland in the General Electric take-over of Tungsram, for example, although jobs and pay were cut, the company quickly put in place a number of environmental and health and safety measures. These included

Although employment reduction may be necessary due to past overstaffing, retaining the maximum number of employees possible is important for engendering the trust, co-operation and loyalty of the workforce which are essential factors for introducing change and boosting labour productivity.[195]

Generous compensation on a voluntary basis have proven to be an effective measure to reduce tension in industrial relations and can help make redundancy less traumatic for the workers and their families. However, government should not rely on financial incentives alone to ensure employee or management support for privatisation.[196] Different measures should be taken together to minimise the adverse effect of privatisation on labours.

Labour legislative measures can be implemented alone or they can be adopted in a package together. Similarly, governments may implement different provisions for different transactions.

---

monitoring factory air and noise pollution levels, fixing the worst problems immediately and adopting plans to make further gradual improvements. New safety devices were installed and comprehensive workers training programmes introduced. As a result, the number of serious work-related injuries has been substantially reduced. (Martin, 13, 14)

[194] A study on Lithuania revealed that in the foreign owned enterprises labours have higher salaries. [Mygind, p.41]

[195] Burnside, p.34

[196] Rutledge, p.3

III. FOREIGN INVESTMENT LEGISLATION ISSUES: LEGAL RESTRICTIONS ON FOREIGN INVESTMENT in the PRIVATISATION TRANSACTIONS

> There is the problem of the people to whom the shares in the firm that has been privatised should be sold; the whole question of the sales to foreigners is highly controversial but an acute and an important issue.[197] Foreign ownership is considered to have the highest potential for efficient economic performance and restructuring because of the access to capital, management skills, including corporate governance abilities, and access to international business networks.[198]
>
> Privatisation has become an important means for countries to attract foreign investment. Particularly in post-communist countries privatisation accounts for a large proportion of total foreign investment; for example, 86% in Hungary and 64% in Poland.[199]
>
> Restrictions on buyer's nationality or other characteristics are found in a number of laws. Some laws, introduce restrictions reflecting "national interests" or other government objectives (including industry policy objectives), usually in the form of protective measures against foreign take-over or control of privatised enterprises.
>
> Foreign investors can support particularly countries in many aspects, but they might also impair them. In the medium term they are likely to contribute to higher imports tariffs which help to achieve a greater amount of profitable investment.[200]
>
> Legal restrictions consider the buyer's nationality or ethnic origin lead to lower sale prices; they may also scuttle the whole transaction.[201] Finally more or less privatisation laws or current legislation in the countries in question have some restriction on buyer selection. The restructuring of the economies and the international trade of Eastern European countries, require a massive injection of Western capital, technology, modern managerial skills, as well as access to Western markets for Eastern European manufactured products. Thus privatisation, foreign direct investments, and international trade based on market principles are all essential to the successful restructuring and privatisation of the economies of Eastern Europe.[202]

A. Foreign Investment in the Privatisation Process

1. General

Privatisation provides foreign investors with the opportunity to penetrate new markets in developing countries and regions. The long-term growth and earnings potential in many of these markets is higher than in the mature, highly saturated markets of the industrialised countries. An

---

[197] "Dimensions of Privatisation", US Energy Information Administration, URL: http//www.eia.doe.gov

[198] Mygind, p.44

[199] Peter Young, "The Lessons of Privatisation", web page of Center for International Private Enterprise, URL: http//www.cipe.org/

For example In Hungary, some foreign investors after the privatisation process demanded protection on Hungarian markets. For this see: Adam Torok, "Competition Policy and De-Monopolisation in Hungary After 1990, De-Monopolisation and Competition Policy in Post-Communist Economies, Edited By: Ben Slay, Wetview Press, 1996, USA, p.38, 39; Ben Slay, "Post Communist Competition Policy: Conclusion and Suggestions", (Post Communist Competition Policy), De-Monopolisation and Competition Policy in Post-Communist Economies, Edited By: Ben Slay, Wetview Press, 1996, USA, p.231, 232.

In the Czech Republic foreign investors which have bought into privatised firms include Volkswagen, Philip Morris and Nestlé. (Henry Gibbon, Privatization in 1995 and Beyond, web page of Center for International Private Enterprise, URL: http://www.cipe.org/)

[200] Welfens, p. 50

[201] Guislain, (The Privatization Challenge), p.127

[202] Salvatore, p. 241

inexpensive and plentiful supply of both skilled and unskilled workers in these countries may help foreign investors create export platforms that are a strategic necessity in today's increasingly competitive global economy.

The acquisition of state-owned firms and participating in the privatisation process can help foreign investors establish operations much more quickly than investing in a new plant from scratch; a process often referred to as a "greenfield" investment. Foreign investors may also capture a ready-made share of new markets through the purchase of state owned enterprises (SOEs).[203]

We should also point out that some companies of certain origin become more prominent among investors in a particular industry or geography. Historic ties, geographic proximity, size of emigrant community from the region, commercial links during the post-war period and being pre-eminent in a particular industry seem to be the main reasons.[204]

2. Debate on Foreign Investment

a. General

Foreign participation in the privatisation process offers many advantages including advanced technology, management and marketing skills.

---

[203] "Privatizing State-Owned Companies", The Prosperity Papers Series, Prosperity Paper Three, web page of Center for International Private Enterprise, URL: http//www.cipe.org/

[204] In general, investors ask three key questions:
(a). Is there a potential opportunity?
-lower factor costs,
-additional markets,
-under-utilised assets,
(b). Is the opportunity robust enough to outweigh the risks?
-economic,
-political,
-cultural,
-legal,
(c). Am I capable of assessing and managing the risks involved?
-industry experience,
-business development experience,
-cultural, linguistic affinity,

However, the potential role of foreigners has been a matter of concern in some Western economies[205] and in all former socialist countries. Countries want the benefits of foreign expertise and foreign finance. But they are concerned that, in the absence of domestic sources of finance, foreigners will acquire a large part of industry at fire-sale prices.[206]

Therefore in order to have a clear view of the issue we will set out both advantages and the disadvantages of the foreign participation. In that context, the case of Turkey provides a good example to this controversial issue. Furthermore the foreign investor might require certain demands (external protection, tariffs, quotas) from the government.

b. Benefits of Foreign Investment in the Privatisation Process: Advantages

The advantages of sales to foreign investors, rather than domestic buyers include: (a) an inflow of capital into the economy, with payment in convertible currency; (b) transfer of production technology and management and marketing skills, (c) links to the world economy,[207] (d) Furthermore opening up a country to foreign investment and foreign acquisition exposes it to outside influences, it also strengthens its links with the world-wide network of production and trade.[208]

c. Disadvantages

There may be some disadvantages of foreign participation in the privatisation process. Thus, sales to foreign investors may be opposed on various grounds: (a) There may be reluctance to sell part of the national patrimony, created by decades of collective saving and investment, to

---

-geographic proximity,
[204] Robert, p.29, 30
[205] For example in Portugal it was argued that (a) privatisation would "deportugalise" vital sectors of the economy and surrender the country's independence and national economy. The government stood accused by some sectors of press of "putting the country up for sale" or being prepared to sell the family silver for a quick killing. It ran the risk according to some critics, of replacing excessive state control by too much foreign control, (b) Secondly it was accepted that Portuguese capital would have problems competing with foreign capital. (Corkill, p.222, 223)
[206] Fischer, p.16
[207] Bornstein, p.26

333

outsiders, (b) Some sectors or specific branches of large enterprises may be deemed too "basic" or "strategic" to permit foreign control, (c) The consequences of under pricing may be considered more serious when foreigners gain at the expense of nationals. [209] (d) Foreigners can use their superior power to cherry pick the best buys. Too large or too rapid a foreign influx will raise xenophobic fears. National sovereignty is even more sensitive an issue in countries so long subjected to Soviet domination.[210]

d. A case: Turkish Dilemma

i. General

Many developing countries are facing with a dilemma. They require advanced technology, management and skills but on the other hand because they consider certain sectors or enterprises as strategic they tend to impose restrictions. In that context Turkey provides a good example of this dilemma.

ii. Constitutional Court's Decisions

Constitutional challenges to privatisation legislation have become a regular feature in Turkey. In July 1994 Turkey's constitutional court ruled that privatisation enabling Law no.3987, which authorised the government to privatise through the issuance of statutory decrees, was illegal because this power belonged exclusively to the parliament. As a result of this ruling, the statutory decrees already issued to execute this law also become null and void, and the whole privatisation program came to a new halt. The constitutional court had already struck down a

---

[208] Jones, p.26
[209] Bornstein, p.242
[210] Jones, p.27

previous privatisation law. On February 28, 1996, the constitutional court annulled parts of Law no.4000 authorising the sale of up to 39 percent of the shares of Turk Telekom.[211]

Thus, the Turkish Constitutional Court demanded that foreign investors could not participate in privatisation transactions in strategic areas or sectors.[212] In that context the court ruled that government could not allow foreign investors to participate in the privatisation of strategic industries such as telecommunications.[213] This idea is based on the opinion and approach that a strategic industry should not be controlled from abroad.

Similarly, the transfer to Société des Ciments Francais in 1989 of five state-owned cement companies and the transfer of a majority shareholding in the company USAS (in-flight catering services) to a subsidiary of the Scandinavian company SAS were blocked by an administrative tribunal in January 1990, because a lawsuit was instituted by the opposition parties against the decision of the privatisation agency. In a judgment handed down in March 1990, the Court declared the two privatisation agreements to be null and void on the ground that they contravened the provisions of a 1987 decree on privatisation that gave priority to Turkish buyers. Finally, in July 1990 the council of state rejected the government's appeal, thereby annulling the sales of the cement companies and USAS.[214]

---

[211] Guislain, (The Privatization Challenge), p.40; Bülent Serim, *Anayasa ve Anayasa Mahkemesi Kararları Isığında Özellestirme, (Privatisation Under the Scope of Constitutional Court Decisions)*, Izgi Yayinlari, Ankara, 1996

[212] Privatisation in Europe, Asia and Latin America, What Lessons can be Drawn?, Summary of the Presentations at the International Workshop on Privatisation Organised by the OECD in April 1994, Sao Paulo, URL: http://www.oecd.org; Guislain, (The Privatization Challenge), footnote 69, p.244; "Privatization Update", web page of Center for International Private Enterprise, URL: http//www.cipe.org
 According to the Turkish Constitutional Court telecommunication is a strategic sector; and privatisation cannot be accepted in this industry.

[213] For the decisions of the Turkish Constitutional Court about this issue see decisions: [Number: 1994/70, K.1994/62-2, Date: 22. 12. 1994, (Official Gazette, Date: 28. 1. 1995, Number: 22185); Number: E.1984/9, K.1985/4, Date: 18. 2. 1985, (Anayasa Mahkemesi Kararlari Dergisi-Journal of Constitutional Court, Number: 21, p.60); Number: E.1994/49, K.1994/45-2 (Official Gazette, Date: 10. 9. 1994, Number; 220470), Number: E.1994/43, K.1994/42-2, (Official Gazette, Date: 24. 1. 1995, Number:22181]

[214] URL: http://www.turkhuksitesi.com, a web page which has been designed for Turkish law professionals

iii. Amendment to the constitution

In September 1999, the constitution was amended, and the concept of the privatisation for the first time was mentioned. Article 47 of the Turkish Constitution concerning nationalisation and privatisation is as follows:

"...The rules and regulations concerning privatisation of the assets and enterprises that are owned by the state, state economic enterprises or other public corporations are prescribed by law ... the investments or services that are carried out by the state, state economic enterprises or other public corporations those that may be performed by or delegated to real or corporate body through private law contracts are prescribed by law."[215]

iv. Provisions Governing Foreign Participation in the Privatisation Process

According to article 13 of Turkish Privatisation Law privatisation high council is authorised (a) To determine the subjects and establishments considered as strategic; (b) To protect national interests concerning national economy and security; (a) to determine the amount and structure of preferred shares.

The final paragraph of article 13 also provides that if and when more than 49% of the capital shares of the organisations listed below are decided to be privatised, preference shares must be established in them.

- Türk Hava Yollari A.O., (Turkish Airlines)
- T.C. Ziraat Bankasi A.S., (Agriculture Bank of Republic of Turkey)
- Türkiye Halk Bankasi A S., (A Government Bank)
- T.M.O. Alkaloid Müessesesi, (Soil Products Office and Alkaloid)

---

[215] For the full text of Turkish Constitution in English see web page of the Turkish Parliament, URL: http://www.tbmm.gov.tr/

- Türkiye Petrolleri A.O. (Turkish Petroleum). [216]

On the other hand according to article 14 of Turkish Privatisation Law, general rules apply for the foreign participation during the privatisation implementations.[217] In that context, another important legal restriction on foreign investment and participation in the privatisation implementations is the first article of law no. 6224 on "Incentives for Foreign Capital" dated 18.1.1954. According to this article foreign capital to be imported to Turkey shall not be allowed to hold majority shares in companies which engage in activities of a monopolistic nature in Turkey.[218]

Although these restrictions exist, the Privatisation Administration actively encourages inquiries from individual investors or purchasing groups interested in acquiring or expanding their stake in Turkey's developing economy.[219]

---

[216] Turkish Privatisation Law, web page of Turkish Privatisation Administration, URL: http://www.oib.gov.tr

[217] For Turkish legislation on foreign investment see: Law on the Encouragement of Foreign Capital, Law Nr. 6224, Date of Passage; 18 January 1954, Official Gazette Nr. 8615, Date of Official Gazette: 23 January 1954, Framework Decree on Foreign Investment (Decree Nr. 95/6990, 23 July 1995), Communiqué Concerning the Framework Decree on Foreign Investment, (Nr.2, 24 August 1995)

[218] Turkish Privatisation Law, web page of Turkish Privatisation Administration, URL: http://www.oib.gov.tr

[219] Beginning from 1980, the Turkish Government embarked upon series of reforms which were designed to remove price controls and reduce subsidies, lessen the role of the public sector in the economy, emphasise growth in the industrial and service sectors, encourage private investments and savings, liberalise foreign trade, reduce tariffs and promote exports, ease capital transfer and exchange controls, encourage foreign investments, make the Central Bank more independent and reform the taxation system. Turkey moved towards full convertibility of the Turkish Lira by accepting the IMF agreement's related article in 1990.

Turkey's exchange and trade systems have been liberalised extensively since the 1980s as a part of the economic reforms mentioned previously. Turkey now follows an independently floating exchange rates policy under which the exchange rate is determined daily. Commercial banks, special financial institutions, change offices and the PTT are free to set their exchange rates according to existing market conditions. (Prime Ministry Undersecretariat for Foreign Trade, Export Promotion Centre Publication, Turkey 1996)

3. Other issues: Certain demands from investors

a. General

Another problem is that foreign investors may demand increased protection of domestic markets when particularly the investor has a strategic and valuable position in the privatisation process.[220]

In their negotiations with the state, investors often try to ensure that trade legislation is applied or modified to their advantage, which may conflict with the objective of an efficient and competitive economy. In this context, many investors have sought special protection from competing imports.

b. Some examples

Of the foreign investment that has been made thus far in Eastern Europe, it has frequently been the case that the Western companies have demanded a high price from the governments of the former socialist countries. Thus announcement by Mercedes Benz is a case point. Mercedes expressed a willingness to acquire 31 per cent and 20 per cent share respectively in the two of the Czech Republic's main manufacturers of trucks, Avia and Liaz, but only on the understanding that the Czech government provided the company with tax holidays, agreed to the removal of tariffs on the import of spare parts for the company, provided state subsidies for investment, and agreed to the introduction of a 40 per cent tariff on all imports of utility vehicles in to the country so as to protect Mercedes Benz's investment.[221]

---

[220] For example In Hungary, some foreign investors after the privatisation process demanded protection on Hungarian markets. [Adam Torok, "Competition Policy and De-Monopolisation in Hungary After 1990", De-Monopolisation and Competition Policy in Post-Communist Economies, Edited By: Ben Slay, Wetview Press, 1996, USA, p.38, 39; Slay, (Post Communist Competition Policy), p.231, 232]

[221] Ash, Hare and Canning, p.227, 228. According to Ash, Hare and Canning authors: "...Given the reluctance of many foreign investors to participate in the privatisation of even the best East European enterprises without being provided with incentives it seems highly unlikely that this will provide an option for ...mass privatisation."(p.228)

c. Analysis

If any exemption from the normal provisions of trade legislation is granted to a buyer, this should be done in a transparent fashion and factored into the evaluation of offers. An investor would clearly be willing to offer more for a company if it protected from import competition, but this higher price has to be weighed against the cost to the economy of such added protection. Trade-related issues of interest to investors would further include regulations on tariffs, quotas, export subsidies, import and export controls, shipping documentation, as well as the country's adhesion to bilateral, regional or multilateral trade agreements.[222]

B. Types of Legal Restrictions on Foreign, Ownership in the Privatisation Process

Stricter controls on foreign investments have usually been based on the need to ensure congruence of interests between enterprises and nations regarding long-term corporate strategies.

Restrictions on foreign investors may derive from various laws including constitutions, Privatisation Law and Foreign Investment Law. These restrictions can be applied alone or different restrictions might be imposed together.

Restrictions on foreign investment can be in different forms:

1. Requiring special permission or approval

This type of restriction is very common in many countries. In this scheme foreign investors wishing to participate to participate in the privatisation process might be required to

---

Fiat in Poland and Samsung in Hungary asked higher tariffs in host countries in order to raise profitability of local investments made. (Welfens, p. 50)

In Poland Fiat, General Motors and Volkswagen have pressurised the government into allowing these companies to import 10,000 vehicles apiece duty free in exchange for an agreement to invest $50 million in the Polish automobile industry. As a result of the Polish government's compliance Fiat has agreed to purchase a 51 per cent stake in the FSM factory in Bielsko-Biala and General Motors has expressed an interest in acquiring a 70 per cent stake in the Warsaw FSO factory. [Ash, Hare and Canning, p.227, 228]

[222] Guislain, (The World Bank), p.19

For Bulgarian case see: Houbenova-Dellisivkova, p.225-227. For the case of Russia, Belarus and Ukraine see: Schrader, p.259-283

obtain an approval or a special permit from the certain governmental associations such as ministries, privatisation agencies or commissions. This approval or permit might be required in all sectors or areas or it can be required in certain privatisation transactions.

For example, in Poland, foreign investments requires special approval by the Agency of Foreign Investment if the value of the shares bought by a foreign investor exceeds 10 per cent of the share capital of the enterprise.[223]

---

[223] Schwartz, p.39
Similarly in Latvia participation in privatisation permitted with approval of the government-established Privatisation Agency. (Official web page of Latvian Government, http://www.lpa.bkc.lv/Lpa02GB.htm)
In Latvia, the relevant laws on foreign participation in privatisation and in foreign investment are Privatisation Law and Law on Foreign Investment. These laws state that:
-Permission is needed if gaining control of company with capital greater than US $ 1 million. Few industries prohibited, many others require licences.
-There is no restriction on profit or capital repatriation
-Participation in privatisation permitted with approval of the government-established Privatisation Agency. (Official web page of Latvian Government, http://www.lpa.bkc.lv/Lpa02GB.htm)
On the other hand, in Turkey foreign investment is within the scope of the authority of the under secretariat for the Treasury and Foreign Trade, General Directorate of Foreign Investment (FID). All foreign investment applications pass through this governmental body and are subject to its approval. Any foreign investment coming into Turkey by means of a company formation, participation in an existing company, establishing a branch office of liaison office; granting licensing, know-how, technical assistance or royalty rights are all subject to the approval of the FID. The FID gives permission on condition that the business in which the investment will be made is useful for the economic development of the country, is in a field of activity open to Turkish private enterprise and does not entail any monopoly or any special concession. Once FID permission is granted and a foreign investor is active in Turkey in a company with foreign capital, as per the regulations, all rights, exemptions and privileges granted to local companies are available to foreign capital companies working in the same field in Turkey and the foreign shareholders may freely repatriate their profits, share transfer values and liquidation proceeds abroad. Except for, unlike in local companies, certain corporate actions of the foreign capital company such as capital increases, obtaining of medium and long term loans from abroad, share transfers from a local shareholder to a foreign shareholder and vice-versa, certain amendments to Articles of Association are all subject to the FID's approval. The obtaining of incentives are also subject to approvals in both local and foreign companies with the difference hat FID is responsible for reviewing applications made by foreign investment companies. (Web Page of Turkish Embassy in Washington, DC., URL: http//www.turkey.org/)
In Denmark there are no limitations on the number of shares each investor may acquire in a state-owned company; this is the general principle and the rule. (Christian Emmeluth and Peter Fogh, "Special Report on Denmark", Privatization, International Financial Law Review, 3 May 1994, Vol. 13, p.29)
In Czech Republic although the rules for foreigners who wish to invest through large-scale privatisation are not very different from the rules applying to other investors (except for the extra approval that they require). [Michael Mejstrik, "Economic Transformation, Privatisation, and Foreign Investments in The Czech Republic", Privatisation and Foreign Investments in Eastern Europe, Edited By: Iliana Zloch-Christy, USA, 1995, p.49]
In Finland, shares in Finnish companies can, in principle, be acquired by foreign investors without the approval of the authorities. [Lauri Peltola and Tarja Wist, "Special Report on Finland", Privatization, International Financial Law Review, 3 May 1994, Vol 13, p.37]
In Norway a foreign investor may not acquire more than 20% of the total share capital or voting rights in a Norwegian-registered company without government approval. But in practice participation is welcomed where it is clearly beneficial to the Norwegian company. ("Introduction", Privatization, International Financial Law Review, 3 May 1994, Vol 13, p.40)

In France, article 10 of the Privatisation Law of August 1986 limited the total amount of shares transferred by the state to foreign persons, directly or indirectly, to 20 percent of the SOE's capital. This provision was first amended by article 8 of the law of July 1993, which provides that this ceiling shall not apply to European Union investors an amendment of April 12, 1996, abolished the remaining restriction.[224]

The Privatisation Law specially provides that, in the case of the transfer to the private sector of companies with the activities falling within the reserved sectors of Articles 55, 56 and 223 of the Treaty of Rome (in particular defence, security and health), any acquisition by foreign (including EC) individuals or legal entities exceeding 5 per cent of share capital is subject to the prior authorisation of the Ministry of Economy.[225]

Finally in Russia allowing foreign investors to participate in the privatisation of fuel and energy complexes or specific mining enterprises requires a decision of the Government of the Russian Federation or republic within the Russian Federation once the principle of privatisation has been agreed.[226]

---

[224] Guislain, (The Privatization Challenge), p.130
[225] Jean-Yves Martin and Adrian P. Gonzalez-Maltes, "Special Report on France", Privatization, International Financial Law Review, 3 May 1994, Vol 13, p.40. (There were 300 foreign-owned financial institutions in France at the end of 1992, more than in any other EC country except United Kingdom).
[226] Butler and Gashi-Butler, p.14, 22, 23, 25

Bulgaria is among the countries offering the broadest variety of forms of investment. There are no restrictions regarding the forms of business activity that foreign legal persons may carry out. Foreign physical persons are required to have a permit for permanent residence in the country in order to register as sole proprietors and to become members of co-operatives or of a general partnership and members with limited liability of a limited partnership or a company limited by shares. The formalities involved in setting up a business are transparent and generally the same as those applying to domestic business. The only additional obligation is to register the investment at the Ministry of Finance. (Daniela Bobeva and Alexander Bozhkov, "Privatisation and Foreign Investments in Bulgaria, "Privatisation and Foreign Investments in Eastern Europe, Edited By: Iliana Zloch-Christy, USA, 1995, p.151; Alexander Stoyanov, "Economic Reform in Bulgaria", web page of Center for International Private Enterprise, Economic Reform Today, Working Papers, Number 3, URL: http//www.cipe.org)

Although in Bulgaria there are no regulations prohibiting foreign investment three cases are subject to authorisation and a special permit is required in these cases if foreign participation is sufficient to secure majority in decision making:
-Banking and insurance,
-Production and trade in arms, ammunitions, an military equipment,
-Development or extraction of natural resources from the territorial sea, the continental shelf, or the exclusive economic zone. (An important factor in attracting foreign investments is the relatively low tax level in the country and the uncomplicated procedures for buying foreign currency and for the repatriation of profits. The profit

2. Prohibition of Participation in Certain Sectors

Some sectors or enterprises are considered strategic; particularly the ones connected with national independence and nuclear power. Foreign investors may not be allowed in some certain areas, and certain sectors can be excluded or only certain enterprises are offered for foreign acquisition.

For example land is viewed sentimentally and often is seen as the national "soul," many governments that now allow for private land ownership still do not permit foreigners to own land.[227] They may lease land and, in some countries, land can be owned by locally incorporated which are 100 percent foreign owned.[228]

3. Requiring Extra or Additional Conditions

Some extra or different conditions can be determined if the investor is a foreign company or a certain person. For example in some countries a special exchange rate has been used by foreigners buying privatised enterprises.

4. Creating Special Rights (Special Arrangements)

Restrictions on the participation of foreign investors sometimes take the form of golden shares, which give governments the option of blocking hostile or unwelcome bids. Foreign investors may be allowed to participate in the privatisation process but certain amounts of the

---

tax is 40 percent. Profits made by foreign investors within the territory of the nine free trade zones are exempt from taxes during the first five years and thereafter are taxed at a 20 percent rate. There are some other forms of tax relief, but they are currently subject to parliamentary discussions). [Bobeva and Bozhkov, p.151; Alexander Stoyanov, "Economic Reform in Bulgaria", web page of Center for International Private Enterprise, Economic Reform Today, Working Papers, Number 3, URL: http://www.cipe.org]

[227] Bruce A. Reznik, "Property Rights in a Market Economy", web page of Center for International Private Enterprise, URL: http//www.cipe.org/; Welfens, p. 50

[228] Jones, p.27

In Latvia land may be owned by foreign-owned companies established in Latvia from countries with which Latvia has concluded investment protection agreements, companies with foreign participation established in Latvia in which at least 51% of statutory capital belongs to the citizens of Latvia, and foreign individuals who are citizens of Latvia. Land may be leased by foreigners or foreign-owned local companies. (Web page of Latvian Government, http://www.lpa.bkc.lv/Lpa02GB.htm)

stakes are kept in hand by creating "golden shares". In this manner, after the privatisation government will still be able to control the management of the state owned enterprise. For example in the UK, in some cases (British Aerospace, Rolls-Royce and British Airways) government created golden shares to limit foreign participation in the privatisation process[229]

---

[229] Prosser, (Social Limits), p.219
See also p. 119-127 on golden shares.

C. Conclusions

Governments around the world have shown their interest in negotiating or encouraging joint ventures and other means of foreign participation.[230]

Many countries have been faced with a dilemma. Both Western and Eastern European countries imposed restrictions on foreign investors in privatisation transactions. On the other hand, many countries, particularly former socialist countries, have established special committees or commissions to attract or supervise foreign investment in the privatisation process.[231]

Provisions applicable to foreign investors should be clear.[232] In order to attract foreign investment the legislation should avoid complex or long processes.[233]

---

[230] Fischer, p.16

[231] For instance institutions encouraging foreign investments in Russia are being developed. Thus, in 1991 the State Committee on Foreign Investments was founded; its duty is to register foreign investments and control their activity. In 1992, the Russian Agency for International Co-operation and Development was founded and given much larger functions, among which are, of particular importance, providing information for foreign businessmen and attracting them to investing in Russia. (Alexander Barski, "Problems of Foreign Investments in Russia and in the Former Soviet Union", Privatisation and Foreign Investments in Eastern Europe, Edited By: Iliana Zloch-Christy, USA, 1995, p.17, 18; Butler and Gashi-Butler, p.14, 22, 23, 25)

Furthermore, in Bulgaria special commission also was established in May 1993 at the Council of Ministries to promote foreign investment. The commission is a policy co-ordinating body. It provides information about the investment environment in the country and information on the various branches and sectors of the economy. (Bobeva and Bozhkov, p.151; Alexander Stoyanov, "Economic Reform in Bulgaria", web page of Center for International Private Enterprise, Economic Reform Today, Working Papers, Number 3, URL: http//www.cipe.org)

[232] Schwartz, p.39

In some privatisation laws there is a clear definition and explanation on foreign participation in the privatisation process. For example, Article 24/1 o Law on Transformation of Socially Owned Enterprises of Macedonia states that: "Domestic and foreign legal entities shall participate in the transformation, under equal conditions." (For the full text of Macedonian Privatisation law see the web page of Macedonian Privatisation Agency, URL: http://www.mpa.org.mk)

However, in some post communist countries like Russia, foreign investment legislation still cannot provide clear rules for foreign investors. (Pekka Sutela, "Russian Foreign Trade Between Liberalization and State Control", Privatization, Liberalization and Destruction-Recreating the Market in Central and Eastern Europe, Edited by: László Csaba, Dartmouth Publishing Company Limited, England & USA, 1994, p.131)

[233] In Czech republic the procedures for foreign investors are quite complex. Elaboration of a privatisation plan often involves interaction with management; then project submitters must negotiate with branch ministries, with the Ministry of Privatisation, and finally with the government's Economic Council. These four steps mean that potential foreign investors must undergo a long, torturous process before their privatisation plan is fully evaluated- and there is still no guarantee that the plan will be accepted. From the other side in the course of the approvals the companies` market situation can change and lead to the resignation of the foreign investors. (Mejstrik, p.49)

The restrictions on foreign investors are generally detrimental to successful privatisation operations.[234] This fact has been learned by France, among other countries after introducing restrictions on foreign investors in privatisation; they had to abolish them.[235]

The European Commission has exerted significant pressure on France and Portugal to lift such restrictions, which are contrary to EU law.[236]

The most stringent restrictions on foreign participation are found mostly in the legislation of countries whose privatisation programs have not been particularly successful.[237]

In general, foreign investors have strong resources of capital, management and technological skills, as well as access to international supplier and distribution networks.[238] The lack of capital requires former socialist countries to get new technologies and managerial skills and from abroad. By rejecting foreign investment these countries are facing a contradictory position. Thus overseas companies offer production management skills; marketing and technical support and capital for modernisation often needed by firms in developing countries.[239]

---

[234] Peter Young, "The Lessons of Privatisation", web page of Center for International Private Enterprise, URL: http//www.cipe.org/
However some authors argue that some limits may be necessary since large-scale foreign purchases at low prices could discredit the entire privatisation process. (Fischer, p.16). But Fischer states that constraints on foreign ownership can be relaxed once the privatisation process is well-established (p.16).

[235] Guislain, (The Privatization Challenge), p.129

[236] Guislain, (The Privatization Challenge), p.129
Articles 6, 52, 86, 221 of the EC Treaty are some rules on foreign investment in the Treaty. Article 6 of the EC Treaty provides that within the scope of application of this Treaty, and without prejudice to any special pervasions contained therein, any discrimination on grounds of nationality shall be prohibited. On the other hand, the efforts of the most member states to keep shares in privatised industries in the hands of their own citizens may be in breach of the freedom of establishment of article 52. Article 221 similarly prohibits discriminating against citizens of other member states in the area of shareholding. Finally, Article 86 of the EC Treaty, may prevent a state from selling off to a company which already has a dominant market position if the buyer does not seem to obey the conditions provided in the article 86 of the EC Treaty.

[237] Guislain, (The Privatization Challenge), p.129

[238] Mygind, p.5

[239] On the other hand, some major state-owned enterprises are not always attractive for foreign investors because of the obligations that go with them. For instance, steel companies or mining firms in emergent economies have to provide more than just production plant. Housing for the workforce, water supply and treatment facilities, local roads, docks and railways are needed too. While a foreign firm may be willing to take over an existing project, it may be reluctant to provide and maintain the social capital to go with the plant. (Beesley and Littlechild, p.133).

Restrictions on foreign ownership exclude countries from an important source of new capital, markets, management, and technology.[240] Thus, by limiting the number of the eligible buyers and excluding the potential buyers who typically possess the most resources, these provisions reduce the likelihood of completing the sale on good terms. The situation is particularly paradoxical for poor or heavily indebted countries, which most need to attract foreign capital and often enact generous investment codes to appeal to those same investors.[241]

In some cases (for example if the enterprise is too large for domestic markets) foreign capital might be required to complete the divestiture transactions. For example the United Kingdom allowed foreign participation in the public bids for their telecommunications enterprises, primarily because these enterprises were large relative to domestic capital markets. In addition, foreign participation, together with share dispersion, may have been intended to reduce the probability of re-nationalisation.[242]

Lack of appropriate legal framework[243], the lack of reliable economic information[244], restrictions, political and social uncertainties are the main obstacles on foreign investment in former socialist countries. So far those countries, in general, have failed to attract large-scale foreign investment.[245]

---

[240] The Lessons of Experience, p.36
[241] Guislain, (The Privatization Challenge), p.129
[242] Galal, Jones, Tandon and Vogelsang, p.568
[243] "...Like in most of the Eastern European countries the main problem of large-scale privatisation in Czech Republic and for the inflow of foreign investment has been the lack the legal framework. The effects of changes in regulations have been to make the rules of this process unclear for potential investors and other project submitters...".(Mejstrik, p.63)
[244] Eugen Jurzyca, "Transparency in the Slovak Economy", web page of Center for International Private Enterprise, URL: http//www.cipe.org/
[245] Thus Russia was not successful in attraction foreign investors in privatisation process. In this country the adoption of the first democratic constitution on 12 December 1993 is a landmark for the foreign investor and Russian citizens.
 The principles and rules on foreign investment in that document are: the unity of economic space, free movement of goods, services and financial assets, support of competition, and freedom of economic activity. Private and other forms of ownership are to be recognised and defended equally in the Russian Federation (Article 8). Land and other natural sources may be in private and other forms of ownership (Article 9). Ideological diversity is recognised, and no ideology may be recognised as a State or as an obligatory ideology (Article 13). And the rule of law is strengthened by placing the constitution unequivocally at the apex of the sources of law and requiring official publication of all laws. (Butler and Gashi-Butler, p.14, 22, 23, 25; Alexander Barski, "Problems of Foreign

346

Foreign direct investment has been increasing since the mid-1980s; but it accounts for only ten percent of all private investment in 40 developing countries. The statistics show that, the majority of SOEs will have to be sold to domestic investors.[246]

Generally, foreign investors perform well[247], particularly in former socialist countries.[248] However we should point out that, the results on economic performance suggests that not only foreign companies can implement restructuring, also management- and employee owned enterprises undertakes restructuring although often more defensive than is the case for foreign owned enterprises.[249]

Eliminating restrictions to foreign direct investment and trade barriers, and government controls on prices and quantities fuels the catch-up of firms to competitive standards.[250]

Investments in Russia and in the Former Soviet Union", Privatisation and Foreign Investments in Eastern Europe, Edited By: Iliana Zloch-Christy, USA, 1995, p.17; Stefan Y. Zhurek, "Emerging Market Structures in Russia: Developments in Commodity Markets", Privatisation and Foreign Investments in Eastern Europe, Edited By: Iliana Zloch-Christy, p.21-38)
    However, because of political and economic instability Russia could no attract sufficient foreign investment in the privatisation transactions. Hence in one interview (former) chairman of the Federal Commission for the Securities Market in Russia states that: "…The Russian economy faces serious consequences unless it can offer adequate safeguards. Not only are foreigners reluctant to invest in Russia, but also Russians do not trust it either. ["Safeguarding Russian Investors: Securities Chief Speaks Out", interview with Dmitry Vasiliyev, (former) Chairman of the Federal Commission for the Securities Market in Russia], web page of Center for International Private Enterprise, URL: http://www.cipe.org/]
    However, some countries like Hungary, in the region are successful in attracting foreign investors. (Euromoney, Privatisation Special Issue, 15 February 1996, Month 2, p.71; Eva Voszka, "Privatization in Hungary: Results and Open Issues", web page of Center for International Private Enterprise, URL: http://www.cipe.org/)
    On the other hand, foreign capital investment in Poland and Romania is at the level of, much lower than in Hungary. (Maciej Grabowski, Economic Reform in Poland, Economic Reform Today Working Papers, Number 4, web page of Center for International Private Enterprise, URL: http://www.cipe.org/; Ion Anton, Economic reform in Romania, Economic Reform Today, Working Papers, Number 1, web page of Center for International Private Enterprise, URL: http://www.cipe.org/)
    Finally, in Estonia, Latvia, and Lithuania, foreign investors played only a minor role in the privatisation of small enterprises. However, Estonia was the most successful country in the Baltic region for the promotion of foreign investment in relation to large privatisation. (Mygind, p.26)
    [246] The World Bank, p.37
    [247] Fischer and Sahay, p.19
    [248] Havrylyshyn and McGettigan, p.5
    For example, according to one study, the performance of foreign owned enterprises in Baltic countries have the following characteristics: (a) high capital-intensity from the start; (b) high sales per employee, and high growth rate of sales; (c) high export share, (d) high labour-productivity, measured as value added per employee, (e) high investment level; (f) relatively high level of debt and good access to bank loans (bank loans per employee much higher than for other owner groups). [Mygind, p.45]
    [249] Mygind, p. 47
    [250] Sheshinski and López-Calva, p.27

The restructuring of the economies and the international trade of Eastern European countries, require a massive injection of Western capital, technology, modern managerial skills, as well as access to Western markets for Eastern European manufactured products. Thus privatisation, foreign direct investments, and international trade based on market principles are all essential to the successful restructuring and privatisation of the economies of Eastern Europe.[251]

Privatisation offers important potential benefits for foreign investors. A privatisation program by itself may not be a sufficient condition for attracting foreign capital, as foreign investors evaluate many other factors, including the overall economic climate and political stability.[252]

Governments should design their privatisation programs to maximise foreign participation. In order to attract foreign investment countries should create a favourable legal environment. In that context certain incentives and guarantees can be applied for stated period.

Many countries, particularly former socialist countries, have taken steps to create a market friendly legal environment for foreign investors.[253]

---

[251] Salvatore, p. 241
[252] According to a poll, the following countries' privatisation programmes have offered the best value for the investors:
(a) United Kingdom
(b) Argentina
(c) France
(d) Austria, Poland, Russia
(e) Netherlands, Philippines, Sweden. (Euromoney, Privatisation Special Issue, 15 February 1996, Month 2, p.71)
[253] In Bulgaria on the 23rd of April 1992, the National Assembly passed the Law on the Transformation and Privatisation of State-Owned and Municipal Enterprises. With this act, privatisation opened for foreign investment. The main principles of the law of 23rd of April 1992 are as follows: All physical and legal Bulgarian and foreign persons have equal rights to take part in the privatisation process. Foreign investors may obtain up to almost 100 percent of each company. [Daniela Bobeva and Aexander Bozhkov, "Privatisation and Foreign Investments in Bulgaria", Privatisation and Foreign Investments in Eastern Europe, Edited By: Iliana Zloch-Christy, USA, 1995, p.146, 147]
See also p. 343, footnote 231
In Poland there are some tax incentives for foreign firms. (Ewa Baginska, "Legal Aspects of the Privatization Process in Poland", web page of Civic Education Project, URL: http//www.cep.org.hu/)

If special circumstances exist, (for example if a very large SOE serving the national interests) political concerns can be reduced in a manner consistent with social and political objectives by reserving a "golden share" for government.

Foreign ownership, even in so-called "sensitive" sectors might bring substantial benefits to the domestic economy, as experience in Hungary and Estonia plainly demonstrates. It is also uncertain and fuzzy that which sectors or areas are "strategic" or "sensitive". The technology can change and quick shifts in the international economy international co-operations brings national economies close to each other and makes them transparent and open to international competitiveness. [254]

In the privatisation process former socialist countries not only impose restrictions on western investors, they also impose restrictions on other investors coming from other ex-socialist countries.[255]

Finally we should point out that, restrictions are not limited to foreign participation. In some countries, the government excludes certain categories of citizens from the benefits of privatisation by reserving sales to indigenous populations.[256]

For the Greek legislation on foreign investment see: Development Law 1892/90, articles 1-23 (Chapter A) and articles 24-32 (Chapter B) and the amendments/supplements of law (Law 1892/90 was published in Government Gazette 101/A/31.7.90 and Law 2234/94 in Government Gazette 142/A/31.8.94 and Law 2234/94 on modernisation and development and other provisions amends and supplements the main development law 1892/90. [Athanassios Vamvoukos of Bahas Gramatidis & Associates, International Financial Law Review, 3 May 1994, Special Issue of Privatisation, Vol: 13, Part: 4//S1, p.50, 51]

[254] Web page of OECD, URL: http://www.oecd.org/
[255] Andreff, p.105
[256] Guislain, (The Privatization Challenge), p.129

IV. PRIVATISATION and the EUROPEAN UNION

> *It looks more as if the current drive for privatisation is more or less inherent in the transition process from an internal market towards an economic union dominated by the principle of an open market economy with the free competition, favouring an efficient allocation of sources.*
>
> *In that context privatisation issues in the European Union should also be analysed.*
>
> *The aim of this section is to provide basic guidelines for the privatisation issues; (a) Policy of the EU on privatisation, (b) Privatisation and provisions on state aid, (c) Certain developments and factors encouraging member states to privatise, (d) EU privatisation policies and candidate countries*

A. Introduction

In the privatisation process in addition to review of domestic laws and regulations, the relevant treaties and international agreements the country has adhered to should also be considered.[1]

In that context, the international treaties and agreements to which it is a party can also affect the conduct of privatisation transactions in a given country. Thus international legal texts have three kinds of rules on privatisation: the rules which promote free trade by ensuring non-discriminatory access to economic activities; the rules that promote undistorted trade by seeking to control or eliminate subsidies; and finally the rules which both aims, regulate public procurement.[2]

Many countries have entered into regional agreements on trade, customs control, or broader economic integration. The examples are the European Union (EU), Mercosur (Latin America), Caricom (Caribbean), NAFTA (North America), and ASEAN (Southeast Asia). Such

---

[1] Guislain, (The World Bank), p.31

[2] Daintith, p.53

These kind of rules can be found in myriad bilateral agreements, such as trade, commerce and navigation agreements or investment promotion and protection agreements, and in multilateral agreements such as The General Agreement on Tariffs and Trade (GATT) and the associated Tokyo Round Codes, or in regional instruments such as the Convention on Establishment of 1995 of the Council of Europe.

regional agreements often generate supranational law or foster harmonisation of legislation in their member countries.[3]

B. Privatisation and the EU

1. Privatisation Transactions in EU: The Scale

Almost all countries in the EU have taken steps to implement privatisation programmes. Among EU countries, in particular the UK has extended its privatisation programme to almost all sectors, areas and enterprises.

Table-3 Total privatisation receipts, 1985-95 (selected EU countries)

	US$m	as% of 1996 GDP
Austria	2.961	1.5
Denmark	3.563	2.5
Finland	1.925	2.0
France	34.102	2.5
Germany	2.807	0.1
Italy	16.971	1.5
Netherlands	9.250	2.7
Portugal	5.304	5.8
Spain	8.255	1.6
Sweden	8.000	3.9
United Kingdom*	96.692	9.0

United Kingdom figures are from 1997.
Source: Parker, p.12

---

[3] Guislain, (The Privatization Challenge), p.41

2. Policy of European Union on Privatisation

a. General

In order to understand the approach and policy of EU on privatisation various official documents, texts, statements and reports particularly the Treaty of Rome must be taken into account.

b. The Treaty of Rome: "Neutral Policy" on the Type of Ownership

Treaty of Rome is the basic legal document that has established today's European Union[4]. In that Treaty article 295 *[ex article 222]* can be considered as the direct provision on privatisation.

Article 295 of the Treaty of Rome states that *"This Treaty shall in no way prejudice the rules in member states governing the system of the property ownership".* Therefore in principle article clearly establishes that each member state is entitled to decide on the most appropriate form of property ownership; this can be state, private or mixed ownership.[5]

Thus in one document the European Commission itself underlines the neutral policy on type of ownership: *"...According to the principle of neutrality provided for in Article 222 [new article 295] of the EC Treaty in relation to the system of public or private property ownership in the Member States..."*[6]

c. Certain documents and reports

On the other hand the concept of privatisation has been promoted in different documents and reports within EU. The following documents are some examples.

---

[4] Signed in Rome on 25 March 1957
[5] W. Devroe, "Privatisation and Community Law: Neutrality Versus Policy", Common Market Law Review 34, 1997, p.267

(a) "...the Commission...(should) present to the relevant committee of the European Parliament a comprehensive overview of the implications of the liberalisation and *privatisation* process in the telecommunications and energy sectors in the different Member States for competition policy, with particular regard to ownership structures and the overweening influence of certain large players in decisions regarding future development of the two sectors..."[7]

(b) "...(The European Parliament) is concerned, in the light of the current process of *privatization*, at the increased control of certain financial and industrial entities which may affect free competition and consumers, and at the strategic alliances in the energy and telecommunications sectors, and calls on the Commission to adjust its statistics to include the European and world concentration ratio of certain multinational industrial and financial businesses and sectors..."[8]

(c) "...Notes that the liberalization of a sector neither necessarily entails nor prevents the *privatization* of the undertakings responsible for providing services of general interest; takes the view, however, that where the state retains part-ownership of an undertaking, the regulatory authority must be kept strictly separate from the authority responsible for the exercise of ownership rights, so as to forestall any undesirable consequences for competition..."[9]

d. Analysis

Although the EU has traditionally and legally adopted a neutral stance to state ownership, recent directives, reports and documents, particularly the ones on opening up to competition

---

[6] European Commissions, European Competition Policy 1996, p.15, web page of European Union, URL: http://europa.eu.int/comm/index_en.htm

[7] Report on the application of the competition rules in the European Union (Report prepared under the sole responsibility of DG IV in conjunction with the Twenty-eighth Report on Competition Policy 1998 Đ SEC (99)743 final), p. 384

[8] Report on the application of the competition rules in the European Union, Competition Report 1996, p.358

[9] Report on the application of the competition rules in the European Union, Competition Report 1996, p.359

markets previously dominated by state enterprises are requiring privatisation transactions a review of ownership and regulation in the EU.[10]

In other words, these official documents and statements reveal that European Union, as an organisation supports and encourages privatisation within the member states. Furthermore as we will discuss later on the EU furthermore encourages candidates and non-member states to adopt privatisation programmes.

---

[10] Parker, (Privatisation in the European Union), p.42
"...state monopolies of a commercial character, public undertakings and undertakings with special and exclusive rights also present a risk for free and open competition..." (European Commission, White Paper 1995, web page of European URL: http://europa.eu.int/comm/index_en.htm)
One case: The Case of Telecommunications
Telecommunications is one of the areas in which technology (e.g. digital transmission and fibre optics) is quickly removing the "natural monopolies" this fact is leading governments to favour privatisation of state utilities in telecommunication sector. [Between 1985 and 1995 telecomms privatisations in Europe totalled the equivalent of $40.5bn, putting this sector well ahead of oil and gas ($32.7bn), banking and insurance ($32bn) and electricity ($26bn) in terms of the total value of asset sales [Parker, (Privatisation in the European Union), p.27)]
Liberalisation of telecommunications has occurred in four stages. The first stage, in 1988, broke the telecom monopolies hold over the supply of terminal equipment such as phones, fax machines, office switchboards etc. In 1990, stage two liberalised the supply of value-added services, data communications (including on-line services), and voice and data services for corporate networks and closed groups of users. Stage three, in 1994, opened the market to competition in the provision of satellite services and equipment. The final area to be liberalised from monopoly supply by national telecommunications carriers is voice telephony. It has been agreed that on 1 January 1998 there will be full liberalisation (that is, opening to competition) of all voice telephony services for the public and of network infrastructure in the EU, subject to possible derogations of up to five years for Greece, Ireland, Portugal and Spain and two years for Luxembourg. (Green Paper on the Liberalisation of Telecommunications Infrastructure and Cable Television Networks, Part-II, A Common Approach to the Provision of Infrastructure for Telecommunications in the European Union, URL: http://europa.eu.int/ISPO/infosoc/legreg/docs/93c21301.html; Council Resolution of 22 July 1993 on the review of the situation in the telecommunications sector and the need for further development in that market (93/C 213/01), URL: http://europa.eu.int/ISPO/infosoc/legreg/docs/93c21301.html; Council Directive of 28 June 1990 on the establishment of the internal market for telecommunications services through the implementation of open network provision (90/387/EEC), URL: http://europa.eu.int/ISPO/infosoc/legreg/docs/90387eec.html; Council Directive of 28 June 1990 on competition in the markets for telecommunications services (90/388/EEC), URL: http://europa.eu.int/ISPO/infosoc/legreg/docs/90388eec.html). Furthermore the European Commission has proposed measures to open up a substantial share of the postal services market to competition by 2003. On the basis of new proposals to be tabled before the end of 2004, a further share of the market would be opened up by 2007. (Web page of the European Union, URL: http://europa.eu.int/comm/internal_market/en/postal/evolframe/news/posten.htm).
Some other documents reveal the fact that European Union supports privatisation. (An Evaluation of Phare-Financed Telecommunications and Posts Programmes, Final Report, April 2000; An Evaluation of Phare Restructuring and Privatisation Programmes, Final Report, November 1998)
European Union also encourages African countries to take steps in the privatisation process, see: Green Paper on Relations between the European union and the ACP Countries on the Eve of the 21st Century, Challenges and Options for a New Partnership, European Commission, Directorate- General VIII Development, Study Group-Partnership 2000 DG VIII/1, Brussels, 20 November 1996, p.28, 29)

3. Privatisation and State Aid

a. General

Privatisation policies in each member state and provisions on state aid in the Treaty of Rome are interrelated. In the privatisation process many governments have been taking steps to restructure state owned enterprises to ensure that they would attract more buyers. Common restructuring policies include financial aid in the form of a capital injection or debt write-offs etc. These policies however may breach the provisions on state aid in the Treaty of Rome since article 87-89, *[ex articles 92-94]* in principle forbids state aid to enterprises.

In particular, article 87 *[ex article 92]* forbids state aid that distorts competition between member countries, although in practice derogations have been granted under the commission guidelines that allow for the influence of other policy objectives, such as regional development, protection of the environment, industrial policy. For example, state aid is permitted for regional development provided that the benefits exceed adverse effects on the industrial sector as a whole and if rationalisation or innovation is stimulated.

Therefore privatisation should also be examined in the context of "state aid"; and provisions on state aid should be taken into account by all governments that have been implementing privatisation programs. In that context important issues may arise in the relation between privatisation and state aid.

355

b. European Commission's Approach

i. General

The European Commission has been using its powers under the Treaty of Rome relating to state aids, examines the financial arrangements for privatisation before giving its consent for sales to go ahead.[11]

According to the European Commission:"... principle of neutrality provided for in Article 222 *[new article 295]* of the EC Treaty in relation to the system of public or private property ownership in the Member States, privatization cannot justify the grant of aid or be imposed as a condition of compatibility. However, where firms in difficulty are concerned, privatization may make it more credible that a firm will return to long-term viability.[12]

In that context further statements, reports and decisions of the European Commission should be taken into account to understand the approach of the European Union (Commission) towards privatisation.[13]

Thus in one document the European Commission states that:

"...the Commission adopted a notice on the possible aid content of sales of publicly owned land to the private sector. A distinction is made between cases where the sale is the outcome of a bidding procedure, which must be open and sufficiently advertised, and cases where there was no such procedure. In the former case, if the successful bid was the best or only

---

[11] Prosser, (Constitutions and Political Economy), p.313; Prosser, (Social Limits), p.232
[12] European Commissions, European Competition Policy 1996, p.15, web page of European Union, URL: http://europa.eu.int/comm/index_en.htm
Thus, in the case of Head Tyrolia Mares (HTM), the Commission considered that the privatisation of the company following an injection of ECU 118 million by its public parent, and subsequent sale for ECU 0.7 million, contained state aid which it nevertheless approved owing, in particular, to the conditions imposed. (European Commissions, European Competition Policy 1996, p.15, web page of European Union, URL: http://europa.eu.int/comm/index_en.htm)
[13] "...The Commission continued...to impose strict discipline whilst maintaining a balance between, on the one hand, compliance with the rules and principles of state aid and, on the other, the contribution made by some aid

offer, the Commission will assume that no aid was contained in the sale, the latter necessarily having taken place at the market price. In the second case, the Commission will ask an independent expert to establish the minimum value of the land: if the land is subsequently sold at that price or a higher price, the sale will not normally be regarded as containing an element of aid. [14]

Therefore according to European Commission a privatisation transaction does not in principle breach the provisions on state aid:

(a) If the sale is the outcome of an open and sufficiently advertised bidding procedure, and (b) The enterprise is sold the best or highest bidder.[15]

Finally in another report the European Commission underlines some important points on the relationship between privatisation and state aid:

"...for a measure to be regarded as aid that is subject to the principle of incompatibility with the common market set out in Article 92(1) *[new article 87]* of the EC Treaty, it must satisfy four criteria: it must provide the firm with an advantage; it must be granted by the State or

---

to the objectives of other Community policies..."(European Commissions, European Competition Policy 1996, p.11, web page of European Union, URL: http://europa.eu.int/comm/index_en.htm)
[14] European Commissions, European Competition Policy 1996, p.14, web page of European Union, URL: http://europa.eu.int/comm/index_en.htm
[15] Furthermore in another document Commission states the same principle: "...As regards privatizations, the Commission continues to apply the principle that there is no aid when shares are sold to the highest bidder following an open and unconditional bidding procedure. In the absence of such a procedure, the case must be notified to enable the Commission to decide whether aid is present and, if so, whether it is compatible with the common market. The privatisation of Belgacom and British Energy, where the Member States concerned transferred to the new owners all the liabilities as well as the assets of the firm, was regarded as not containing aid..." (European Commissions, European Competition Policy 1996, p.14, 15, web page of European Union, URL: http://europa.eu.int/comm/index_en.htm)
Finally in another report the European Commission emphasises that:
"...The Commission continued to apply the new guidelines on rescuing and restructuring firms in economic difficulty. Without strict control, rescue and restructuring aid may be used by Member States to sustain ailing companies artificially, with the risk that necessary structural adjustments in the internal market will be frustrated or unduly delayed and the burdens of such adjustments shifted onto viable companies. However, rescue and restructuring aid may be warranted, for instance, on the basis of social or regional policy considerations, and the main objective of the guidelines is to strike a reasonable balance between such considerations and the creation of a common market with free and undistorted competition..." [XXVth REPORT on Competition Policy 1995, (Published in conjunction with the "General Report on the Activities of the European Union - 1995"), Brussels-Luxembourg, 1996, p.85]

through state resources; it must have particular characteristics, i.e. it must favour only "certain undertakings or the production of certain goods"; lastly, it must affect trade between Member States. The four conditions are cumulative, i.e. if one of them is not satisfied, Article 92 is not applicable..."[16]

ii. Decisions of the commission

The European Commission has many decisions on relation between privatisation and state aid. In some decisions the Commission concluded that no state element were involved in the privatisation transactions. However in certain cases the European Commission has reached the conclusion that certain governments have breached provisions on state aid.[17]

---

[16] European Commissions, European Competition Policy 1996, p.13, web page of European Union, URL: http://europa.eu.int/comm/index_en.htm
Furthermore European Commission emphasise that: "...Where state aids are granted to promote general objectives such as research and development, environmental protection or ensuring regional cohesion, they may be accepted to the extent that the investment undertaken generates a positive effect for society which cannot be appropriated by the company itself. However, other forms of aid that have the effect of distorting competition without accompanying benefits must be condemned. This justifies strict state aid monitoring in the internal market..." (European Commission, White paper 1995, web page of European URL: http://europa.eu.int/comm/index_en.htm)

[17] We prefer to classify these decisions according to the countries since the Commission has given different decisions for each privatisation transaction in each country.
(a) Spain: "...On 21 January the Commission decided that no state aid elements were involved in the privatisation of the Spanish aluminium group Industria EspanÄola de Aluminio (Inespal)..." [Report on the application of the competition rules in the European Union (Report prepared under the sole responsibility of DG IV in conjunction with the Twenty-eighth Report on Competition Policy 1998 Ð SEC (99)743 final), Part Two, p. 222]
(b) France: "...In the course of 1999 the Commission approved two cases of restructuring aid in the banking sector. The two ailing banks...had received State aid in the context of a restructuring operation carried out by their governments with a view to their future privatisation..." [European Community Competition Policy, XXIXth Report on Competition Policy (1999), European Commission, Directorate-General for Competition, Luxembourg: Office for Official Publications of the European Communities, Printed in Italy, 2000, p.85. Also see p.79 the decision on two German yards]
(c) Germany: "...the Commission decided not to object to the granting of rescue and restructuring aid for (an) engineering firm... Rostock, in connection with its privatisation... The Commission concluded that this aid was compatible with the common market pursuant to the guidelines on aid for rescuing and restructuring firms in difficulty and given that the new owners would from then on be responsible for funding the firm's activities..." [Report on the application of the competition rules in the European Union (Report prepared under the sole responsibility of DG IV in conjunction with the Twenty-eighth Report on Competition Policy 1998 Ð SEC (99)743 final), Part Two, p. 264]
_"... the Commission authorised restructuring aid ...The Commission adopted a positive final decision in respect of grants..."[Report on the application of the competition rules in the European Union (Report prepared under the sole responsibility of DG IV in conjunction with the Twenty-eighth Report on Competition Policy 1998 Ð SEC (99)743 final), Part Two, p. 263]
_"...The Commission... to approve the privatisation agreements for...yards and to raise no objections to a second instalment of aid..."[Report on the application of the competition rules in the European Union (Report

prepared under the sole responsibility of DG IV in conjunction with the Twenty-eighth Report on Competition Policy 1998 Ð SEC (99)743 final), Part Two, p. 224]

_ "...the Commission initiated Article 93(2) proceedings on the spillover of aid given for the restructuring of two former East German shipyards to other parts of the Bremer Vulkan group and the unauthorized payment of a loan... from the German privatization agency Treuhandanstalt.." (Report on the application of the competition rules in the European Union, Competition Report 1996, p.216)

_ "... Following its privatization in 1993, the company... has struggled with continual financial difficulties, which ultimately led to the initiation of insolvency proceedings... The Commission had serious doubts as to the compatibility of the successive amounts of aid with the Community guidelines on state aid for rescuing and restructuring firms in difficulty, under which rescue aid must be restricted to the period needed to examine ways of restoring the relevant firm's situation. (Report on the application of the competition rules in the European Union, Competition Report 1996, p.221)

_ "...the Commission authorized aid for restructuring a German inland waterway company privatized in 1993 by the Treuhandanstalt and established in the Land of Berlin, since the measure helped to develop the use of inland waterways in the transport market..."(Report on the application of the competition rules in the European Union, Competition Report 1996, p.231)

_ "...In July the Commission decided to extend the Article 93 proceedings initiated with respect to aid granted by (state to certain privatised firms)..." [Report on the application of the competition rules in the European Union, Competition Report 1996, p.239]

"... in order not to jeopardize ongoing development in east Germany while ensuring the normal application of Articles 92 and 93 to these cases, the Commission should take all necessary measures to provide a quick, flexible and pragmatic decision on the compatibility of the measures to be taken by the German Government..."(p.356)]

_ "...After the collapse of the Bremer Vulkan Verbund the yards had to be taken over by the State again in view of a re-privatisation which is currently at an early stage of preparation. For the continuation and completion of the restructuring programs new aid... is needed..."(Competition Policy Newsletter, Number 1, Volume 3, Spring 1997, p.26)

_ "... The Commission investigated several individual cases of aid for the privatization of companies in the new Länder... In November, the Commission took a final decision allowing aid... for the restructuring..."(XXVth REPORT on Competition Policy 1995, (Published in conjunction with the "General Report on the Activities of the European Union - 1995"), Brussels • Luxembourg, 1996, p.92)

(d) Italy: "... the Commission decided to terminate the proceedings it had initiated under Article 88(2) of the EC Treaty in respect of aid received between 1995 and 1997 by the civil engineering firms... The Commission therefore authorised the aid on condition..."[Report on the application of the competition rules in the European Union (Report prepared under the sole responsibility of DG IV in conjunction with the Twenty-eighth Report on Competition Policy 1998 Ð SEC (99)743 final), Part Two, p. 252]

_ "...On 29 July the Commission approved aid for the reform, restructuring and privatisation of Banco di Napoli provided for in Decree Law No 163 of 27 March 1996, converted into Law No 588 of 19 November 1996..."[Report on the application of the competition rules in the European Union (Report prepared under the sole responsibility of DG IV in conjunction with the Twenty-eighth Report on Competition Policy 1998 Ð SEC (99)743 final), Part Two, p. 232]

_ "...In September the Commission adopted a negative final decision regarding the... aid element contained in the capital contribution made by Patrimonio del Estado to the Spanish textile manufacturer Hilaturas y Tejidos Andaluces S.A. (HYTASA) in the framework of its privatization in 1990. The Spanish authorities were asked to recover the aid from the company, with the corresponding interest due for late payment..."(Report on the application of the competition rules in the European Union, Competition Report 1996, p.237)

_ "...In July 1993 the Commission had authorized aid measures for the public holding company EFIM. The authorization was subject to conditions, accepted by the Italian authorities, designed to gradually reduce, through privatisations..."(Report on the application of the competition rules in the European Union, Competition Report 1996, p.238)

_ "...In June, the Commission decided to close two Article 93 procedures by approving the aid granted to the Italian companies...wholly owned by the two Italian state holdings... The Commission approved both restructuring aid measures, subject to certain conditions. In light of these conditions the two aid measures fulfil the criteria of the Community guidelines on state aid for rescuing and restructuring firms in difficulty. They are therefore compatible with the common market under Article 92 (3)(c)...The conditions imposed upon the restructuring are:

(1) the restructuring and liquidation plan must be carried out in full; (2) the Italian Government must respect its commitment to finally privatize the two companies; (3) the total income obtained through the sale of the restructured companies must be used to reduce the costs and losses covered by the aid. It cannot be invested in such a way as to result in further aid to other companies or activities in the group that have not yet been sold; (4) the

privatization must be open, transparent and unconditional, and must not be financed by further state aid; (5) the carrying-out of the restructuring plan will be monitored by the Commission..."(Application of Competition Rules in the European Union, Competition Report, p.228, 229)

_ The principle of a private investor in a market economy is often used in order to determine the presence of state aid in cases where public authorities transfer funds to public or private companies on more favourable terms than the recipients would find on the market in normal circumstances. On the basis of this principle, the Commission considered that the repeated loans, capital injections and debt write-offs enjoyed by (a SOE)... would not have been available to a firm with private owners and therefore constituted state aid. As the aid was intended only to ensure the industrial survival of the firm, without any compensatory benefits, the Commission decided to prohibit it..." (European Commissions, European Competition Policy 1996, p.15, web page of European Union, URL: http://europa.eu.int/comm/index_en.htm)

(e) France: "... the Commission decided to terminate proceedings initiated under Article 88 and to approve... aid for the privatisation of..(a SOE). The aid was approved on condition that (the SOE) refocused its activities on its commercial banking network and that the restructuring plan presented by the private-sector purchaser... was implemented..."(Report on the application of the competition rules in the European Union (Report prepared under the sole responsibility of DG IV in conjunction with the Twenty-eighth Report on Competition Policy 1998 Ð SEC (99)743 final), Part Two, p. 231)

_ "...The French Government had committed itself to privatising CreÂdit Lyonnais by October 1999. After privatisation, the bank's expansion would remain limited to 3.2% per year up to 2001 and the bank would have to distribute 58% of its net surplus in the form of dividends until the year 2003..."[Report on the application of the competition rules in the European Union (Report prepared under the sole responsibility of DG IV in conjunction with the Twenty-eighth Report on Competition Policy 1998 Ð SEC (99)743 final), Part Two, p. 232]

_ "...On 14 October the Commission decided to terminate proceedings initiated under Article 88(2) and to approve... aid for the privatisation of SocieteÂ Marseillaise de CreÂdit (SMC)..." [Report on the application of the competition rules in the European Union (Report prepared under the sole responsibility of DG IV in conjunction with the Twenty-eighth Report on Competition Policy 1998 Ð SEC (99)743 final), Part Two, p. 231]

(f) Spain: "...On 21 January the Commission decided that no state aid elements were involved in the privatisation of the Spanish aluminium group..." [Report on the application of the competition rules in the European Union (Report prepared under the sole responsibility of DG IV in conjunction with the Twenty-eighth Report on Competition Policy 1998 Ð SEC (99)743 final), Part Two, p. 222]

(g) The United Kingdom: "... the Commission decided not to raise any objections to the aid proposal notified by the United Kingdom authorities for financing the construction, maintenance and management of the Channel Tunnel Rail Link (CTRL), the high-speed rail link between London and the Channel Tunnel; the financing is linked to the privatization of two companies having activities connected with the CTRL. The United Kingdom Government decided to involve the private sector in the project, choosing the operator through a transparent and non-discriminatory tender procedure. Consequently, the Commission took the view that the financing provided by the State did not constitute aid within the meaning of Article 92 of the Treaty..."[Report on the application of the competition rules in the European Union, Competition Report 1996, p.231]

(h) Greece: "...The privatisation of the "Hellenic Shipyard" was, however, only achieved in September 1995, when the State sold 49% of its shares to a co-operative of the yard's workers. Whilst the Commission had approved in 1992... aid for debts write-off linked to the privatisation of the yard, this amount has meanwhile increased due to interests and penalties..."(Competition Policy Newsletter, Number 1, Volume 3, Spring 1997, p.27)

_ "...Commission eventually decided to approve the aid to Crédit Lyonnais conditional...." [XXVth REPORT on Competition Policy 1995, (Published in conjunction with the "General Report on the Activities of the European Union - 1995"), Brussels • Luxembourg, 1996, p.85]

_ "...In July the Commission decided to adopt a final positive decision under Article 93 with regard to aid that the Greek Government decided in 1991 to grant to Neorion Shipyard in the form of a debt write-off... The aid was granted pursuant to Article 10 of the Seventh Directive on aid to shipbuilding on condition the yard was privatized. However, since the yard had not been privatized by February 1994 the Commission decided to initiate the Article 93 procedure. The Commission's decision of July recognizes that the Greek Government has fulfilled its obligation to privatize Neorion Shipyard... and the aid was found to be compatible with the Shipbuilding Directive..."(Application of Competition Rules in the European Union, Competition Report, p.207, 208)

c. Services of general economic interest

In order to provide a clear approach to the state aid and privatisation in the European Union we need to analyse the concept of "services of general economic interest" used in the Treaty.

Article 16 [ex Article 7d] of the Treaty of Rome provides that:

"Without prejudice to Articles 73, 86 and 87, and given the place occupied by services of general economic interest in the shared values of the Union as well as their role in promoting social and territorial cohesion, the Community and the Member States, each within their respective powers and within the scope of application of this Treaty, shall take care that such services operate on the basis of principles and conditions which enable them to fulfil their missions."

Furthermore article 86 [ex Article 90] states that:

"1. In the case of public undertakings and undertakings to which Member States grant special or exclusive rights, Member States shall neither enact nor maintain in force any measure contrary to the rules contained in this Treaty, in particular to those rules provided for in Article 12 and Articles 81 to 89.
2. Undertakings entrusted with the operation of services of general economic interest or having the character of a revenue‹producing monopoly shall be subject to the rules contained in this Treaty, in particular to the rules on competition, insofar as the application of such rules does not obstruct the performance, in law or in fact, of the particular tasks assigned to them. The development of trade must not be affected to such an extent as would be contrary to the interests of the Community.
3. The Commission shall ensure the application of the provisions of this Article and shall, where necessary, address appropriate directives or decisions to Member States."

Services of general economic interest used in Article 86 of the Treaty and refers to market services which the member states subject to specific public service obligations by virtue of a general interest criterion. This would tend to cover such things as transport networks, energy and communications.[18]

According to the European Commission:

"...To understand how these provisions affect the arrangements made by the public authorities to ensure that certain services are provided to the public, it is useful to articulate three principles that underlie the application of Article 86. They are: neutrality, freedom to define, and proportionality.

Neutrality as regards the public or private ownership of companies is guaranteed by Article 295 of the EC Treaty... the Commission does not... require privatisation of public undertakings. On the other hand, the rules of the Treaty and in particular competition and internal market rules apply regardless of the ownership of an undertaking (public or private).

---

[18] Communication from the Commission, Services of General Interest in Europe (2001/C 17/04), Official Journal of the European Communities, 19.1.2001, URL:http://europa.eu.int/comm/competition/oj_extracts/2001_c_017_01_19_0004_0023_en.pdf

Member States' freedom to define means that Member States are primarily responsible for defining what they regard as services of general economic interest on the basis of the specific features of the activities... They may grant special or exclusive rights that are necessary to the undertakings entrusted with their operation, regulate their activities and, where appropriate, fund them... Whether a service is to be regarded as a service of general interest and how it should be operated are issues that are first and foremost decided locally... However, in every case, for the exception provided for by Article 86(2) to apply, the public service mission needs to be clearly defined and must be explicitly entrusted through an act of public authority (including contracts)...

Proportionality under Article 86(2) implies that the means used to fulfil the general interest mission shall not create unnecessary distortions of trade. Specifically, it has to be ensured that any restrictions to the rules of the EC Treaty, and in particular, restrictions of competition and limitations of the freedoms of the internal market do not exceed what is necessary to guarantee effective fulfillment of the mission. The performance of the service of general economic interest must be ensured and the entrusted undertakings must be able to carry the specific burden and the net extra costs of the particular task assigned to them. "[19]

As a summary the competition rules of the EC Treaty apply to both public and private undertakings. Article 86(2) provides a limited exception.

C. Certain Factors and Developments Encouraging Member States to Privatise in the EU

1. General

At the EU level no explicit stance has been taken on ownership. Under article 295 *[ex article 222]*, the member states in principle totally free to take the decision to nationalise or to privatise, whereas the implementation of such decisions can be tested against the Treaty's non-discrimination, competition and state aid provisions.[20]

---

[19] Communication from the Commission, Services of General Interest in Europe (2001/C 17/04), Official Journal of the European Communities, 19.1.2001, URL:http://europa.eu.int/comm/competition/oj_extracts/2001_c_017_01_19_0004_0023_en.pdf

[20] Non-discrimination to EU Citizens

Article 221, states that within three years of the entry into force of this Treaty, Member States shall accord nationals of the other Member States the same treatment as their own nationals as regards participation in the capital of companies or firms within the meaning of Article 58, without prejudice to the application of the other provisions of this Treaty.

Restrictions on other EU nationals during the privatisation would seem to breach the Community Law. But there are a number of exceptions to the general principles. Likewise, article 55 exempts activities connected, even occasionally, with the exercise of official authority; and article 56 exempts provisions providing for special treatment of foreign nationals on grounds of public policy, public security, and public health. Also article 223 allows measures to protect essential interests of state security in connection with the production of or trade in arms, munitions, and war material. [Graham and Prosser, (Comparative Perspective), p.143, 144; Graham and Prosser, (Privatising Nationalised Industries), p.46, 47]

In the United Kingdom special provisions have been made in some cases of golden shares to restrict more specifically foreign ownership. In Britain such restrictions have been introduced for British Aerospace, Rollys Royce, and British Airways. [Graham and Prosser, (Comparative Perspective), p.143, 144]. However because of the EU law, this has had to be expressed as a general prohibition, with the exception of British Aerospace which falls

However, the following factors and developments encourage member states to privatise state owned enterprises:

2. Single European Act (SEA)

The Single European Act (SEA) 1986 has been significant in changing policy within the EU. This act entered into force on July 1, 1987.[21]

(SEA) aimed to remove the remaining non tariff barriers to free trade within the EU by the end of 1992 and had implications for public utilities (and therefore privatisation policies), that were generally protected from the competition both in terms of outputs and procurement policies. Utilities remain governed by national legislation and regulatory rules, but following the

---

under the exemption for military production contained in Article 223 of the Treaty of Rome. [Graham and Prosser, (Privatising Nationalised Industries), p.37]
But because of the warnings of the Commission of the Community British government increased the limits on foreign ownership. (Daintith, p.54). The commission told that the ban on foreign ownership would be unlawful and would breach the community law and principles. The European Commission investigated the 15 per cent limit on foreign share ownership after it had been used to force the sale of excess foreign shareholdings in Rolls Royce. After negotiations, the Department of Trade and Industry agreed to raise the ceiling for British aerospace and Rolls Royce to 29.5 per cent. [Graham and Prosser, (Comparative Perspective), p.143, 144. For similar problems in the France see: (Daintith, p.54)].
Furthermore, the acquisition of a controlling interest in a company would come under the provisions on the right of establishment [Graham and Prosser, (Comparative Perspective), p.143]. In particular, article 52 provides that restrictions on the freedom of establishment of nationals of a Member State in the territory of another member state shall be abolished by progressive stages in the course of the transitional period. In other words article 52 outlaws the discrimination in relation to the right of establishment, and would apply in relation to the acquisition of a controlling interest in such a company. These provisions are such as to constrain any attempt by member states to favour their own nationals in any privatisation by way of a public offering shares, or to restrict the degree of control obtainable by non-nationals, whether at the time of privatisation or later. (Daintith, p.54)
In June 1997, the Commission issued a document clarifying the scope of EU Treaty provisions on capital movements and the right of establishment. The Commission took this initiative because certain EU Member States had imposed limits on the number of voting shares that investors from other EU Member States could acquire in privatisation operations. The Commission specified that such restrictions are illegal and that capital movements in the form of intra-Community investments can only be restricted in cases explicitly established by the Treaty: public order, public security, public health and defence. (Country Commercial Guides, FY 1999, European Union, Chapter VII, EU Investment Climate Statement, Report prepared by the U.S. Mission to the European Union, Brussels, Belgium, released July 1998, Web page of US State Department, URL: http://www.state.gov/www/about_state/business/com_guides/1999/europe/eu99.html)
While the member states were compelled by the Treaty to grant national treatment to investors from other EU countries, they could erect and maintain barriers to investors from non-EU countries, consistent with their international obligations. (Country Commercial Guides, FY 1999: European Union, Chapter VII, EU Investment Climate Statement, Report prepared by the U.S. Mission to the European Union, Brussels, Belgium, released July 1998, Web page of US State Department, URL: http://www.state.gov/www/about_state/business/com_guides/1999/europe/eu99.html)

[21] Meinhard Hilf, The Single European Act and 1992: Legal Implications for Third Countries, European Journal of International Law, URL; http://www.ejil.org/journal/Vol1/No1/art5.html

Single Market agreement; the European Commission has applied pressure for the markets of the utilities in member states to be opened up to competition.[22]

In other words the Single European Act committed all member states to an integrated method of trading with no frontiers between countries by 31 December 1992. It was the first act to amend the principles of the Treaty of Rome. In practice, some of its terms on harmonisation, such as the insurance market, have taken considerably longer to implement. The main creation of the Single European Act is the Single Market for trading in goods and services within the EU.[23]

3. The Maastricht Treaty and European Monetary Union (EMU)

a. General

In December 1991, in Maastricht, the European Union (EU) established the Maastricht Treaty. The Treaty provides for a single European currency, common citizenship, common foreign and security policy, a more effective European Parliament, and a common labour policy. Each of these goals presents some challenges for the countries involved, such as setting a new monetary policy.[24]

The Maastricht Treaty on the economic and monetary union of the EU gives a foundation for a single currency unit, and common economic and monetary policy.[25]

---

[22] Country Commercial Guides, FY 1999: European Union, Chapter VII, EU Investment Climate Statement, Report prepared by the U.S. Mission to the European Union, Brussels, Belgium, released July 1998, Web page of US State Department, URL: http://www.state.gov/www/about_state/business/com_guides/1999/europe/eu99.html

[23] Dictionary of Law, Oxford University Press, Market House Books 1997, URL: http://www.xrefer.com/entry.jsp?xrefid=467361&secid=

[24] Johan Olsson, The European Union and the Maastrich Treaty, URL: http://www.geocities.com/TimesSquare/1848/eu.html

[25] Johan Olsson, The European Union and the Maastrich Treaty, URL: http://www.geocities.com/TimesSquare/1848/eu.html

b. European Monetary Union (EMU)

EMU is a European Community programme intended to work towards full economic unity in Europe based on the phased introduction of a common currency (the Euro). Announced in 1989, it was delayed by difficulties with the exchange rate mechanism, but under the terms of the Maastricht Treaty the second stage came into effect on 1 January 1994.[26]

The heads of the member states laid the foundation for the European monetary policy in 1992, when the Treaty on European Union (better known as the Maastricht Treaty) was signed. The Treaty established the two central principles for the European Central Bank and its monetary policy. These are the primary objective of price stability and the independence of the central bank. Price stability as the primary objective means that the overriding goal of the European Central Bank is to provide low and stable inflation.

The Economic and Monetary Union (EMU) or a *single monetary market,* was a very ambitious proposition that had all critics outside and inside the EU expressing great doubt that it will ever happen. For the EU members, it was the only way to prosperity in the future. In the EU there are fourteen currencies to deal with. Hindering the daily business transactions between members, this factor is considered to be an obstacle to economic growth. In the December 1995 meeting in Madrid, the European Council achieved further decisive progress by adopting the scenario of changeover to the single currency.[27]

The Maastricht criteria for sustainable economic convergence and eligibility to join the EMU consists of four strict conditions all of which to be met by the individual nation states in the European Union: -An inflation rate in the previous year of 1.5 per cent, at most, above the three member states with the lowest inflation; long term nominal interest rates in the previous

---

[26] The Oxford English Reference Dictionary, Oxford University Press URL: http://www.xrefer.com/entry.jsp?xrefid=393902

year not exceeding by more than 2 per cent the average rate in the three member states with the lowest rates-general government net borrowing and nominal gross debt below 3 per cent and 60 per cent of GDP respectively *(known as the fiscal convergence requirement);* and –a stable currency within the narrow band of the EMS without realignments or 'severe tensions' for at least two years.[28]

The standards developed in the Maastricht Treaty will insure that there is economic convergence within the member nations. Privatisation and divesting state owned enterprises or their assets was seen an effective way of controlling budget deficits and inflation and fulfilling the economic and financial requirements in the Maastricht Treaty for EMU.

Many countries have been implementing privatisation programmes to control the budget deficits and inflation.[29]

D. EU Privatisation Policies and Candidate Countries

The European Union has been underlining the significance of privatisation process to the countries wishing to be member,[30] particularly in former socialist countries.[31] In that context the

---

[27] Thanos Voudouris, ECONOMICS, XTMAN - Seminar One, Module III, Economics Paper in: European Union and Single Currency Market, 29 June, 1997, URL: http://www.GRinet.com/thanos/study03/europe.html

[28] Johan Olsson, The European Union and the Maastrich Treaty, URL: http://www.geocities.com/TimesSquare/1848/eu.html; Joachim Volz, The Spanish Economy in the Run-up to European Monetary Union, web page of German Institute for Economic Research, URL: http://smith.diw.de/diwwbe/eb97-04/n97apr_3.htm#HDR0; Bill Dixon, "Summary the Maastricht Treaty", web page of Democratic Socialists of America, URL: http://www.dsausa.org/archive/Lit/Maastricht.html; Stephen Bush and Gill Bush, "The Meaning of the Maastricht Treaty", web page of Critical European Group, University of Keele, URL: http//www.keele.ac.uk/; Parker, (Privatisation in the European Union), p.22; Thanos Voudouris, ECONOMICS, XTMAN - Seminar One, Module III, Economics Paper in: European Union and Single Currency Market, 29 June, 1997, URL: http://www.GRinet.com/thanos/study03/europe.html

[29] Guislain, (The Privatization Challenge), p.41; Fanjul and Mañas, p.158. [In this study Fanjul and Mañas states that: "...the fulfilment of stipulations arising from the Maastricht agreement...should lead (Spain) to a more aggressive action in the field of privatisations (p.158)].

[30] According to the European Committee in order to be a member state Slovakia should take further steps in its privatisation process. (Ivan Miklos, "Europe's Outcast? Slovakia and the European Union", web page of Center for International Private Enterprise, URL: http//www.cipe.org/). One of the main concerns of the EU was that in Slovakia, there is no clear, measurable and controlled criteria of buyers' selection and so there is no equal chance to acquire property in privatization process. (Ivan Miklos, "Slovakia", News and Views, Web page of Center for International Private Enterprise, URL: http//www.cipe.org/; Chikán, p.34)

We must point out that Slovakia not only received criticism from European Union (EU), but from other international organisations like the World Bank, International Monetary Fund European Bank for Reconstruction

European Union demands candidate countries to implement comprehensive privatisation programmes or to conclude the ongoing privatisation transactions.

Thus in one White Paper the European Commission states that:

"...Transition in Central and Eastern Europe to political and economic systems compatible with those in the European Union is a complex process. It involves the strengthening of democracy and civil society, the implementation of sound macro-economic policies, *privatisation* and industrial restructuring, legal and institutional changes, and trade liberalisation,

---

and Development (EBRD) and OECD. (Ivan Mikloš, "Privatization in 1996", Centre for Economic and Social Analysis of Slovak Republic, URL: http//www.mesa10.sk/. According to Mikloš: "An analysis of privatisation legislation shows that procedural changes are increasingly less likely to improve the process, and more likely to promote the interests of narrow groups aiming to concentrate political and economic power among themselves).")
On this issue also see: Salem M. Nsouli, Amer Bisat and Oussama Kanaan, "The European Union's New Meditterian Strategy", URL: http://www.oneworld.org/euforic/fandd/nso.htm

[31] Fischer and Sahay, p.12, URL: http://www.nber.org/papers/w7664. For many countries in eastern and central Europe, the prospect of joining the European Union has been a powerful spur to reform (p.22).
Also see: Jane Perlez, "European Union Names New Candidates for Membership", New York Times, July 17, 1997; Government of the Republic of Poland, European Commission Directorate General for Economic and Financial Affairs, Joint Assessment of Medium-Term Economic Policy Priorities of the Republic of Poland, Brussels, 10 February 2000; "Joint Assessment of Bulgaria's Medium-Term Economic Policy Priorities, 31 May 1999, web page of Bulgarian government, URL: http://www.govrn.bg/eng/oficial_docs/other/assessment/ja_final.html; Slawomir Pierzchalski, Polish Road to European Union, Evaluation by Experts of the European Communities, Published by the Commercial Counsellors Office Embassy of the Republic of Poland in the Hague, URL: http://users.bart.nl/~polamb/brhbiul/brhbiul.htm; Inese Voika, Latvian Papers Report on Privatisation, European Integration, and Corruption, Support for Improvement in Governance and Management in Central and Eastern European Countries, Public Management Forum, Vol. IV, No. 6, 1998, web page of OECD, URL: http://www.oecd.org/puma/sigmaweb/pmf/4pmf6/46pmf14.htm; Estonia and the European Union, web page of Estonian Ministry of Foreign Affairs, URL: http://www.vm.ee/euro/english/
In order to provide technical and financial assistance, European Union established a fund and an organisation called Phare. In that context, Phare is a European Union initiative that provides grant finance to assist economic and democratic reform in central and Eastern Europe. The common aim of Phare's partner countries-Albania, Bosnia and Herzegovina, Bulgaria, the Czech Republic, Estonia, the Former Yugoslav Republic of Macedonia, Hungary, Latvia, Lithuania, Poland, Romania, the Slovak Republic and Slovenia-is integration with the European Union. Phare, along with the Europe Agreements and the Structured Dialogue, is one of the three planks of the European Union's pre-accession strategy. In its first six years of operation until 1996, Phare has made ECU 6617 million available, making Phare the largest single assistance programme to operate in central and eastern Europe. Phare programmes are identified on the basis of the reform policies and priorities of the governments of the partner countries. Restructuring and privatisation of state enterprises is one of the important aim s and tasks of Phare. [ACE Quarterly Phare, The Journal of the European Union's ACE programme-Action for Co-operation in the field of Economics, Issue no 9, Autumn 1997, p.2; The Phare Programme-An Interim Evaluation, Published by the European Commission, (produced by the Evaluation Unit of the European Commission, Directorate General for External Relations: Europe and the New Independent States, Common Foreign and Security Policy, External Service (DG 1A F/5), in close collaboration with George Mergos and Andreas Tsantis as external consultants), p.10, 11]

aiming at free trade with the Union and with neighbouring countries. Although the situation varies from country to country, this process of transformation is now well underway..."[32]

---

[32] European Commission, White Paper 1995, web page of European URL: http://europa.eu.int/comm/index_en.htm

E. Conclusions

The Treaty of Rome itself does not provide an explicit provision on privatisation[33] and officially, the community adopts a neutral attitude towards privatisation.[34]

However, when different official documents and reports are analysed it can be concluded that "privatisation as a policy" has been encouraged by the EU in the member states and in candidate countries.

Moreover, from time to time there has been recognition that privatisation may be beneficial.

In other words although the EU has traditionally adopted a neutral stance to state ownership, recent directives, reports and documents, particularly the ones on opening up to competition markets previously dominated by state enterprises are necessitating privatisation transactions a review of ownership and regulation in the EU.

In the EU the abolition of customs barriers, the liberalisation of formerly monopolistic markets, and the imposition of common competition rules on private as well as public enterprises all foster the privatisation process and the entry of private operators.[35]

At the Treaty of Maastricht, it was decided that there are certain economic and monetary conditions (requirements) that have to be fulfilled before a member state is allowed to join the European Monetary Union.[36] Low and certain inflation rate and budget deficit are among the requirements that member states should fulfil in order to join the European Monetary Union (EMU).

---

[33] The reason might be that privatisation is a quiet new concept and a current issue.
[34] Daintith, p.53
[35] Guislain, (The Privatization Challenge), p.41
[36] Thanos Voudouris, ECONOMICS, XTMAN - Seminar One, Module III, Economics Paper in: European Union and Single Currency Market, 29 June, 1997, URL: http://www.GRinet.com/thanos/study03/europe.html

In times of economic hardship, the EU member states are forced to limit expenditure and look for now resources, especially if they intend to join the third phase of the EMU (European Monetary Union). Since the selling of government assets makes it possible to generate new resources relatively "painlessly", certainly compared with raising taxes, it should come as no surprise that national governments frequently resort to privatise. Privatisation has proved to be one of the favoured options taken by governments to reduce public sector debt and deficits and meet the macroeconomic criteria set by the Maastricht Treaty for joining the new European currency.[37]

The European Union has been underlining the significance of privatisation process to the countries wishing to be member, particularly in former socialist countries. In that context European Union demands candidate countries to implement comprehensive privatisation programmes or to conclude the ongoing privatisation transactions.

---

[37] Guislain, (The Privatization Challenge), p.41; Fanjul and Mañas, p.158

GENERAL CONCLUSIONS for the THESIS

> *This section of the thesis not only aims to underline the core conclusions of the whole work but it also aims provide the final analysis of the whole work and set out the final points that have not been discussed in individual chapters. Lastly it represents the final remarks for the study.*

As we presented in the first chapter privatisation is often used as an umbrella concept that covers a broad range of methods and models of social and economic policies or reforms. From the legal point of view, however, it refers to the divestiture and transfer of state owned enterprises or their assets from government or its agencies to private bodies, which results in private body control over the company.

Privatisation represents a reversal of the process of nationalisation begun early in the 20th century. It is a withdraw of state from many economic activities or services. The trend historically started in the United Kingdom and the Thatcher government which held the office for eleven years after the election of 1979, has been associated with privatisation efforts. Since the launch of the United Kingdom privatisation program in the early 1980s, the privatisation wave touched almost every country and every industry. The question "What should be privatised?" has changed into "What else can be privatised"? Today there are even discussions on how to privatise the privatisation process.

State-led policies for economic growth were popular for many decades. Lack of capital and experience in the private sector to finance large-scale projects and services left the government the only player in the field. State owned enterprises were seen as a way to create jobs, enhance regional development and prevent control of the economy by foreign firms. The performance of state owned enterprises, however, has been unsatisfactory. In most cases public enterprises failed to generate even sufficient revenue to cover their current costs. Low quality service appeared to have been a consequence of poor organisation and management, interferences in day-to-day operation, and non-commercial objectives that they have to fulfil.

The private sector gained important momentum after the Second World War. The lack of capital and resources was not an obstacle in many cases anymore. In that context, the decision for privatisation came from a combination of disillusionment with the result of state ownership and from a belief that private ownership would bring substantial economic benefits. This belief is the direct result of the consensus that state owned enterprises are typically inefficient and require substantial subsidies to operate, acting as a drain on the government treasury and the economy as a whole.

Privatisation is a pragmatic solution to specific administrative and economic problems. Financial crises faced by many countries around the world, forced governments to divest it assets of state owned enterprises. Revenue from privatisation transactions offered a tempting source of state funding at a time when economic policy was geared to reducing the public sector-borrowing requirement for many governments. Finally politicians found it easy to sell and get rid of SOEs instead of raising taxes.

Privatisation policies are not unique in all countries; hence in post communist countries the case was different. In the privatisation exercise, there are important differences between western economies and former socialist countries. Privatisation, in ex-socialist countries has been regarded as a vital element on the way to a market economy. Unique circumstances forced those countries to follow different paths and adopt different policies in the privatisation exercise. Because of unique circumstances formerly socialist economies; need to privatise in all possible ways and with all available methods. Finally because of various differences in economic, social, politic and legislative structure western economies such as the United Kingdom cannot be the model for privatisation in former socialist countries. The former socialist countries often develop their own unique model and tailor it according to their circumstances. Post communist countries, however, may benefit from some privatisation experiences of western countries.

In most cases government spending has been full of incompetence, waste and fraud and many criticisms about the state owned enterprises are true. In many countries politicians have often intervened in state owned enterprises and in many cases decisions have been taken according to political considerations instead of market conditions.

Even though, privatisation programmes around the world have, so far, fallen short of expectations technically it is not always possible to measure and compare the performance of the firms before and after privatisation. Furthermore it is, in some cases, still early to draw some definitive conclusions on privatisation and privatisation related problems.

The second chapter set up the limits of privatisation. In that context the core issue was: What services should or should not be privatised? The chapter tried to find a dividing line or an accurate answer to that issue and presented a detailed and comprehensive analysis on the boundaries of privatisation.

There is no definitive solution or answer to the question of what services should a government finance or what services should be privatised. The set of services a government should finance or provide may differ both among nations and over time and will depend importantly on the social, economic, legal circumstances of each country. Privatisation is also a political transformation, that is, a change in the government's role in the economy and in society as a whole. The decision to privatise and how to privatise is political. While Turkey imposed restrictions on privatisation of Turkish Agriculture Bank considering it "strategic", the United Kingdom has taken steps to privatise certain services in naval bases for nuclear submarines.

Therefore the boundaries and limits of privatisation are driven by political considerations and by politicians. The United Kingdom experience shows quite clearly that there is no core of governmental activity which *cannot* be privatised.

Privatisation is an essential but insufficient element for structural economic reform in the economy and society. Privatisation is not a panacea, it is not the solution to every economic and administrative problem; selling an enterprise to the private sector does not mean an end to all problems. Also privatisation is not an overnight process or a magic touch; it will be a lengthy process. Furthermore, there is no single best way or single right way. Moreover a decision that something can be privatised does not mean that it should be privatised. In each case government should analyse the costs and benefits of public versus private provision of a given service, including the associated transaction costs, as well as economic, financial, political, social, and other aspects.

In that context, privatisation is not good or bad; it is an economic and social instrument. If it is well designed it may bring substantial benefits to the economy and society.

This is also not to say that a government should not own any enterprises. Public enterprises are often expected to fulfil at least some social objectives. Moreover, the sector in many developing countries includes loss-making companies that government acquires for non-commercial reasons, and these are often located in slow-growing basic industries. Finally private investors and corporate leaders may be involved in corruption and misuse their positions.

In other words, state owned enterprises are not, always useless nor do they always have adverse effect on the society and economy. It is important to note that almost all countries have at least some state owned enterprises (SOEs) that are necessary in areas or sectors to promote social goals and objectives.

The third chapter has presented a detailed analysis on the legal and institutional framework of privatisation. This chapter aimed to provide and set out the basic legislative and institutional requirements for a successful privatisation programme.

Privatisation process often requires new institutions and laws and governments need to establish an organisational and analytical structure to implement the privatisation effort. A privatisation law may be needed or required to implement a privatisation programme. Various circumstances including constitutional, economic, traditional and social system and circumstances of each country determines whether or not a privatisation law is needed; and these elements also effect and determine the structure and outcome of the privatisation law.

There is no simple, internationally applicable recipe for privatisation; various legal methods and techniques can be used to divest state owned enterprises. Because each country has different circumstances, it is impossible to provide a unique model for privatisation; every country should design its own model according to its needs and circumstances.

Different techniques could be used in each country and even in the same privatisation transaction. Thus almost all countries have been employing more than one privatisation method, although not necessarily all of them. Each method of divestiture of state assets has advantages and disadvantages. For example public offering is one of the most effective ways of privatising state owned enterprises. It cannot, however, be carried out for smaller enterprises. Mass privatisation (voucher system) is a quick, simple way of completing large, economy-wide privatisation programs. It, conversely, does not raise revenue for government. Lastly in the ex-socialist countries, different economic and political circumstances have dictated unique privatisation methods that have not been implemented in western European countries-such as restitution or voucher privatisation (free distribution of shares).

There are important elements that governments need to take into account in each privatisation transaction. For example speed is an important factor for success. Particularly small enterprises can be privatised by sale immediately and simply. If it is needed, larger state owned enterprises can be corporatised as soon as possible. On the other hand, transparency, in every aspect of privatisation process, is critical for the economic and political success of the privatisation process. The legal reform strategy needs to be pragmatic and built on the removal of existing bottlenecks and restrictions. It is important to enact a privatisation law free from restrictions hence the more constraints, objectives or restrictions are introduced in the law, the harder the privatisation will be.

Finally, restructuring prior to privatisation may be needed in certain privatisation operations and it is better to leave restructuring to the new investor. In the cases of excess labour and excess debt, however, restructuring needs to be carried out by the government.[1]

The fourth chapter provided a detailed analysis on the issues surrounding privatisation transactions and it presented appropriate legal solutions to each legal issue in the privatisation transactions.

Competition Law Issues

Privatisation, without competition measures can be ineffective; therefore legislation often prevents private monopolies and it often provides appropriate rules to break the state monopolies in the privatisation process.

Governments need to introduce a effective competition wherever possible, as an essential aspect of the privatisation process. Furthermore in the case of natural monopolies, it is essential

---

[1] S. Brian Samuel, "The Ten Commandments of African Privatization", International Finance Corporation (IFC), The World Bank, URL: http://www.ifc.org/ifc/publications/pubs/impact/impsm99/commandm/commandm.html. (According to Samuel: "...The government can't expect the new owner to clean up its mess...")

to implement regulation and supervision mechanisms to prevent private monopolies acquiring excessive profits, measures that may reduce an effective privatisation. The approach of the government needs to be "competition where possible and regulation where necessary".

Finally, a very important dimension of the privatisation policy is the customer aspect. In some cases consumers lose and in some cases they gain. Privatisation may make certain social groups economically worse off. For example after privatisation new companies may not be willing to deliver first class mail to remote areas or it may raise prices. Therefore special provisions need to be imposed into the privatisation contract to protect certain social groups and private investors can be forced to provide services to certain social groups.

Labour Law Issues

Labour law problems constitute an important dimension of privatisation policies. It is important because opposition of employees can block privatisation transactions. In analysing labour law issues, various factors [level of overstaffing (if any), financial situation of state owned enterprise prior to privatisation, new investors future investment plan] are important factors. In some cases employees gain and in some cases they lose. In most cases staff redundancies are not, however, so much a consequence of privatisation as of poor state owned enterprise management leading to overstaffing. Even though privatisation policies have not been launched, many state owned enterprises would have to dismiss workers or closed down.

Finally privatisation is not a zero-sum equation; although the number of public jobs may decrease, jobs also are created in the private sector from privatisation.

Foreign Investment Legislation Issues

Privatisation offers a good opportunity to investors around the world; it is an important opportunity for world-wide trade and globalisation. Many countries, however, impose restrictions or barriers on foreign investors and investment. Governments around the world state various factors or reasons (strategic/vital enterprises, national sovereignty, national interest etc.) as the reason for restrictions. Whatever the reason is, limitations on foreign investors are generally detrimental to successful privatisation operations. Therefore privatisation legislation needs to be designed free from restrictions on foreign investors.

Privatisation and the European Union

Although, at the European Union level no explicit stance has been taken on ownership, certain developments and factors have been encouraging member states or candidate countries to privatise. In other words, the EU has encouraging privatisation as a policy in the member states and in candidate countries. For example one of the economic criteria that the EU is requiring from Turkey is to continue the privatisation of state owned enterprises.[2]

Future of Privatisation

There are important reasons to conclude that the most challenging privatisations have not yet been attempted. Most governments have chosen to privatise the "easy" enterprises (the healthiest, both economically and operationally) first, and have not yet attempted controversial privatisations of companies that are obviously over-staffed and excessively indebted. Given that these state owned enterprises will require painful financial restructuring and massive layoffs before they can attract private buyers, it seems clear that the most politically difficult privatisations lie in the future. This finding revealed that the privatisation process will be in the political and economic agenda for at least two more decades.

---

[2] "Turkish Accession Partnership", Document prepared by EU Commission, November 8, 2000, web page of Turkish Ministry of Foreign Affairs, URL: http://www.mfa.gov.tr/EU/explanatory.htm

Will Public Administration Disappear?

It is quite clear that privatisation does not mean the end of governmental influence on enterprises.[3] Thus privatisation is not self-implementing. With the possible exception of the total transfer of a system from the public to the private sector, privatisation arrangements generally cause governments to incur additional administrative responsibilities in the areas of contract development, competitive bidding, and performance monitoring.[4]

Privatisation does not mean public administration will disappear. As privatisation requires new techniques of regulation, civil servants will need to be trained to be familiar with different techniques of economic regulation and to make choices between the new alternatives that are available.[5]

But privatisation does not mean the state's withdrawal from the management of the economy. Indeed, its role may even increase in years to come in response to the major challenges posed by the far-reaching upheavals in the structure of the world economy. But its role will be more subtle: to offer a stable, predictable framework for the proper development of economic activities, with the maximum respect for market forces.[6]

---

[3] Prosser, (Constitutions and Political Economy), p.316
[4] Janice A. Beecher, Twenty Myths About Privatisation, Alliance for Redesigning Government, National Academy of Public Administration, URL: http//www.alliance.napawash.org/
[5] de Ru and Wettenhall, p.10
[6] Privatisation in Europe, Asia and Latin America, What Lessons can be Drawn?, Summary of the Presentations at the International Workshop on Privatisation Organised by the OECD in April 1994, Sao Paulo, URL: http://www.oecd.org/

BIBLIOGRAPHY

BOOKS

- Anderman D Steve, *Labour Law-Management Decisions and Workers' Rights*, Fourth Edition, Butterworths, London, Edinburgh, Dublin, 2000

- Aristotle, *Aristotle's Politics and Athenian Constitution*, Edited and Translated by: John Warrington, J. M. Dent & Sons Ltd., London, 1959

- Ascher, Kate, *The Politics of Privatisation-Contracting out Public Services*, Macmillian Education Limited, Hong Kong, 1987

- Beesley, Michael and Littlechild, Stephen, *Privatisation: Principles, Problems and Priorities*, Lloyds Bank Annual Review, Volume I, Edited By: Christopher Johnson, Pinter Publishers, London and New York, 1988

- Bishop, Matthew and Kay, John, *Does Privatisation Work?-Lessons from the United Kingdom, (Does Privatisation Work?)*, Centre for Business Strategy Report Series, Centre for Business Strategy, London Business School, Hobbs the Printers of Southampton, 1988

- Black, John, *A Dictionary of Economics*, Oxford Paperback Reference, Oxford University Press, New York, 1997

- Bös, Dieter, *Privatization-A Theoretical Treatment*, Clarendon Press, Oxford, 1991

- Carsberg, Bryan, *Competition and Private Ownership: The New Orthodoxy, (Competition and Private Ownership)*, The Stamp Memorial Lecture, University of London, 29 November 1993

- *Comparative Experiences with Privatization-Policy Insights and Lessons Learned, United Nations Conference on Trade and Development*, United Nations, New York and Geneva, 1995

- D. Donahue, John, *The Privatization Decision: Public Ends, Private Means*, Basic Books, New York, 1989

- Fukuyama, Francis, *The End of History and the Last Man*, Penguin Books, England, 1992

- Galal, Ahmed, Jones, Leroy, Tandon, Vogelsang and Pankaj, Ingo, *Welfare Consequences of Selling Public Enterprises-An Empirical Analysis*, The International Bank for Reconstruction and Development, The World Bank, Published for the World Bank, Oxford University Press, New York, 1994

- Graham, Cosmo and Prosser, Tony, *Privatizing Public Enterprises, Constitutions, the State, and Regulation in Comparative Perspective*, (*Comparative Perspective*), Clarendon Press, Oxford University Press, Oxford, 1991

- Guislain, Pierre, *Divestiture of State Enterprises-An Overview of the Legal Framework*, *(The World Bank)*, The World Bank Technical Paper, Number 186, The World Bank, Washington, D.C., 1992

- Guislain, Pierre, *The Privatisation Challenge: A Strategic, Legal, and Institutional Analysis of International Experience*, *(The Privatization Challenge)*, The World Bank, Washington DC, 1997

- Haskel, J., Szymanski, S., *Privatisation, Jobs and Wages*, Department of Economics, Queen Mary and Westfield College, University of London, Paper No: 252, February 1992

- Hayek, F. A., *Law Legislation and Liberty-Volume-3-the Political Order of a Free People*, Routledge & Kegan Paul, 1979

- Hayek, F. A., Law, *Legislation, and Liberty-Volume-2-The Mirage of Social Justice*, Routledge & Kegan Paul, London and Henley, 1976

- Hayek, F. A., *The Road to Serfdom*, George Routledge & Sons Ltd., Frome and London, 1944

- Hayek, F.A., *The Constitution of Liberty*, Routledge & Kegan Paul, London, 1960

- *Her Majesty's Treasury Guide to the United Kingdom Privatisation Programme*, December 1993

- Jänicke, Martin, *State Failure-The Impotence of Politics in Industrial Society*, Translated by: Alan Braley, Polity Press, Cambridge & Oxford, 1990

- Jones, Colin, *Privatisation in East Europe and the Former Soviet Union*, A Financial Times Management Report Published and Distributed, London, 1986

- Khan, Khalid, *Privatisation and its Legal Aspects in Developing Countries with Special Reference to Pakistan*, Lahore, February 1998

- Kikeri, Sunita, *Privatisation and Labour, What Happens to Workers When Governments Divest*, World Bank Technical Paper, The World Bank, Washington D.C., 1998

- *Legal Aspects of Privatization in Industry, (Legal Aspects of Privatization)*, United Nations Publications, Geneva, January 1992

- Major, Iván, *Privatization in Eastern Europe-A Critical Approach*, Edward Elgar Publishing Limited, England & USA, 1993

- Martin, Stephen and Parker, David, *The Impact of Privatisation-Ownership and Corporate Performance in the UK*, London and New York 1997

- O'Connell Davidson, Julia, *Privatisation Employment Relations-The Case of the Water Industry, (Water Industry)*, Mansell Publishing Limited, New York, 1993

- Pirie, Madsen, *Privatisation*, Wildwood House Limited, England, 1988

- Plato, *The Republic*, Edited by: G. R. F Ferrari, Translated by: Tom Griffith, Cambridge University Press, Cambridge, UK, 2000

- *Privatisation in the UK and Turkey with Particular Reference to the Coal Sector, (Privatisation in the UK and Turkey)*, University of Marmara, European Community Institute, Istanbul, 1996

- *Privatization: The Lessons of Experience, (The Lessons of Experience)*, Country Economics Department, The World Bank, (no date)

- Prosser, Tony and Moran, Michael, *Privatization and Regulatory Change in Europe*, Edited By: Michael Moran and Tony Prosser, Open University Press, Buckingham-Philadelphia, 1994

- Prosser, Tony, *Law and Regulators, (Law and Regulators)*, Clarendon Press, Oxford, 1997

- Prosser, Tony, *Nationalised Industries and Public Control-Legal, Constitutional and Political Issues, (Nationalised Industries)*, Basil Blackwell Ltd., 1986, UK & USA

- Serim, Bülent, *Anayasa ve Anayasa Mahkemesi Kararlari Isiginda Ozellestirme, (Privatisation under the Scope of Constitutional Court Decisions)*, Izgi Yayinlari, Ankara, 1996

- Smith, Adam, *An Inquiry into the Nature and Causes of the The Wealth of Nations*, John Lubbock's Hundred Books, Gorge Routledge and Sons Limited, London and New York, (no date)

- Vickers, John and Yarrow, George, *Privatisation and the Natural Monopolies, (Natural Monopolies)*, Public Policy Center, London, 1985

- Vickers, John and Yarrow, George, *Privatization: An Economic Analysis*, The MIT Press, England, 1988

- W.Lieberman, Ira, Ewing, Andrew, Mejstrik, Michael, Mukherjee, Joyita and Fidler, Peter, *Mass Privatisation in Central and Eastern Europe and the Former Soviet Union, A Comparative Analysis, Studies of Economies in Transformation*, The World Bank, Washington, D.C., 1995

- Welfens, Paul and Jasinski, Piotr, *Privatisation and Foreign Direct Investment in Transforming Economies*, Dartmouth Publishing Company, England & USA, 1994

ARTICLES, PAPERS, REPORTS, SPEECHES and INTERVIEWS

❏ "A History of Libertarian", URL: http://www.daft.com/~rab/liberty/history/

❏ "Acquired Rights Directive: Amendments", Web page of Practical Legal Information for Business Lawyers, URL: http://www.plcinfo.com/scripts/article.asp?Article_ID=9870

❏ "Antitrust & Trade Regulation Report", Volume 80, Number 2004, 20 April 2001, URL: http://corplawcenter.bna.com/corplawcenter/1,1103,2_858,00.html

❏ "Background Information on the OECD`s Privatisation Activities", URL: http://www.oecd.org:80/daf/peru/CONTENT/backpriv.htm#The RAGP

❏ "Banks and Privatisation,"OECD Advisory Group on Privatization- Synthesis Note (September 1998), URL: http://www.privatizationlink.com

❏ "Building Transparency into the Privatization Process", Adam Smith Institute, web page of Center for International Private Enterprise, URL: http://www.cipe.org

❏ "Central and Eastern European Businesses Poised to Challenge Western Competitors", Recent Headlines, Andersen Consulting Study, URL: http://www.ac.com

❏ "Dimensions of Privatization", US Energy Information Administration, URL: http://www.eia.doe.gov

❏ "Estonia and the European Union", web page of Estonian Ministry of Foreign Affairs, URL: http://www.vm.ee/euro/english/

❏ "Finding Real Owners-Lessons from Estonia's Privatisation Program", Public Policy for the Private Sector, The World Bank, Note no: 66, January 1996

- "Gauging the Results of State Enterprise Reform", web page of Center for International Private Enterprise, URL: http://www.cipe.org/

- "Institutional Reforms: Privatisation", U.S. Agency for International Development, URL: http://www.info.usaid.gov/

- "Introduction-Privatisation", International Financial Law Review, 3 May 1994, Vol 13

- "Is Privatization Succeeding in Central and Eastern Europe?", An Interview with Roman Frydman, by the Centre for International Private Enterprise, Centre for International Private Enterprise, web page of the World Bank, URL: http:/www.worldbank.org

- "Political and Organizational Strategies for Streamlining", Privatisation Database, URL: http://www.privatisation.org

- "Privatisation as a Global Phenomenon", Chapter I, URL: http://www.eia.doe.gov

- "Privatisation in Estonia", web page of Estonia, URL: http://www.einst.ee/

- "Privatization Policy", web page of the Fraser Institute, URL: http://www.fraserinstitute.ca/

- "Privatizing State-Owned Companies", The Prosperity Papers Series, Prosperity Paper Three, web page of Center for International Private Enterprise, URL: http://www.cipe.org/

- "Report on Privatisation and Lessons Learned", GAO (General Accounting Office of USA), URL: http://www.privatisation.org/Collection/P...egies/GaoPrivReport-lessons-learned.html

- "Russia", US Energy Information Administration, URL: http://www.eia.doe.gov

- "Skoda's Receipe for Success", web page of Center for International Private Enterprise, URL: http://www.cipe.org/

- "State Owned Enterprises, Privatisation, and Corporate Governance in OECD Countries," web page of OECD, URL: http://www.oecd.org:80/daf/peru?CONTENT/agpsoes.htm

- "Systemic Change and Privatisation Law, (Summary)", The Hungarian Academy of Sciences, URL: http://www.mta.hu/strat/angol/kot4.html

- "Terms Related to Privatization Activities and Processes", July 1997 GAO (General Accounting Office of USA), URL: http://www.privatisation.org/

- "The Evolution of Privatisation", Privatisation: Motives and Methods, US Energy Information Administration, URL: http://www.eia.doe.gov

- "The Legal and Political Environment of Privatisation", US Energy Information Administration, URL: http://www.eia.doe.gov

- "The United Kingdom", Chapter V, General Accounting Office of USA, URL: http://eia.doe.gov

- "Trends and Policy in Privatisation-General Overview of Privatisation Developments", April 1995, URL: http://www.oecd.org/

- "What is Privatisation", Privatisation Database, URL: http://privatisation.org

- "World Labour Report 1995-Privatisation-the Human Impact", URL: http://www.ilo.org

- "Cautious Privatisation in China", web page of Le Monde Diplomatique, URL: http://www.monde-diplomatique.fr/en/1997/11/china

- "Conclusions", Privatization in Central and Eastern Europe-Perspectives and Approaches, Edited by: Demetrius S. Iatridis and June Gary Hopps, Praeger Publishers, USA, 1998

- "Consultation on Reporting Side Procedures and Practices", 5 July 1999, web page of UK Competition Commission, URL: http://www.competition-commission.org.uk/trancon.htm; Consultation on Steps to Increase Openness and Transparency, web page of UK Competition Commission, URL: http://www.competition-commission.org.uk/trancon.htm

- "Consultation on Steps to Increase Openness and Transparency", web page of UK Competition Commission, URL: http://www.competitioncommission.org.uk/trancon.htm

- "Guidelines on the Application of Acquire Rights Directive 77/187/EEC (TUPE)", Web page of Business Information Publications Limited (BiP), URL: http://www.bipcontracts.com/briefings/Brief12_98.html

- "Harnessing the Market: The Opportunities and Challenges of Privatisation", Department of Energy of USA-Privatisation Home Page, URL: http://www.osti.gov

- "Historical Roots of Libertarianism", web page of Libertarian Organisation, URL: http://www.libertarian.org/history.html

- "Joint Assessment of Bulgaria's Medium-Term Economic Policy Priorities", 31 May 1999, web page of Bulgarian government, URL: http://www.govrn.bg/eng/oficial_docs/other/assessment/ja_final.html

- "Management and Sale of Residual State Shareholdings", web page of OECD, URL: http://www.oecd.org:80/daf/peru/CONTENT/agpresi.htm

- "Mass Privatisation: An initial Assessment", web page of OECD, URL: http://www.oecd.org

- "Privatisation in Estonia", web page of Estonia, URL: http//www.einst.ee/

- "Privatization Update", web page of Center for International Private Enterprise, URL: http://www.cipe.org/

- "Safeguarding Russian Investors: Securities Chief Speaks Out", [interview with Dmitry Vasiliyev, (former) Chairman of the Federal Commission for the Securities Market in Russia], web page of Center for International Private Enterprise, URL: http://www.cipe.org/

- "Special Rights Shares", web page of UK Treasury, URL: http://www.hmtreasury.gov.uk/pep/specialg.pdf

- "The Privatization Revolution, Adapted from Remarks by Lawrence W. Reed", Mackinac Center for Public Policy for The Future of American Business, A Shavano Institute for National Leadership Seminar, Indianapolis, Indiana, May 21, 1997, URL: http://www.privatisation.org

- "Theoretical Roots of Libertarianism", web page of Libertarian Organisation, URL: http://www.sbe.csuhayward.edu/~sbesc/frlect.html

- "Types and Techniques of Privatization", Privatization Database, URL: http://www.privatization.org

- 1998 Privatisation Trends, "Introduction and Summary", URL: http://www.oecd.org//daf/peru/no_frames/privatisation/priv_trends98.htm

- ACE Quarterly Phare, The Journal of the European Union's ACE Programme- Action for Co-operation in the field of Economics, Issue no 9, Autumn 1997, web page of the European Union, URL: http://europa.eu.int/

- Adhikari, Ramesh and Kirkpatrick, Colin, "Public Enterprise in Less Developed Countries: An Empirical Review", Public Enterprise at the Crossroads-Essays in Honour of V.V. Ramanadham, Edited By: John Heath, London and New York, Routledge, 1990

- Aharoni, Yair, "Managerial Discretion", State-Owned Enterprise in the Western Economies, Edited By: Raymond Vernon and Yair Aharoni, Croom Helm Ltd., 1981

- Ahrens, John, "The Classical Liberal Tradition in Contemporary US Politics", University of Hartford, September 1990, web page of John Ahrens, URL: http://ahrens.hanover.edu/ahrens/vita_mss/lib-con.html

- Aizenman, Joshua, "Privatisation in Emerging Markets", Working Paper Series, National Bureau of Economic Research (NBER), Working Paper 6524, Cambridge, April 1998, URL: http://www.nber.org/papers/w6524

- Ajmone Marsan, V., "Public Enterprise Holding Companies and Privatisation: The Case of IRI, Italy", Public Enterprise at the Crossroads-Essays in Honour of V.V. Ramanadham, Edited by: John Heath, London and New York, Routledge, 1990

- An Evaluation of Phare-Financed Telecommunications and Posts Programmes, Final Report, April 2000; An Evaluation of Phare Restructuring and Privatisation Programmes, Final Report, November 1998, web page of the European Union, URL: http://europa.eu.int/

- Anastassopoulos, Jean-Pierre C., "The French Experience: Conflicts with Government", State-Owned Enterprise in the Western Economies, Edited By: Raymond Vernon and Yair Aharoni, Croom Helm Ltd., 1981

- Anderson, Robert, Djankov, Simeon; Pohl, Gerhard, "Privatization and Restructuring in Central and Eastern Europe", Public Policy for the Private Sector, The World Bank, July 1997, Note no. 123

- Andeweg, Rudy, "Privatisation in the Netherlands: The Results of a Decade", Privatization in Western Europe-Pressures, Problems and Paradoxes, Edited By: Vincent Wright, Pinter Publishers, Great Britain, 1994

- Andreff, Wladimir, "Economic Disintegration and Privatization in Central and Eastern Europe", Privatization, Liberalization and Destruction-Recreating the Market in Central and Eastern Europe, Edited by: László Csaba, Dartmouth Publishing Company Limited, England & USA, 1994

- Anstee, Eric, "Techniques for Privatising Utilities", Privatisation in Practice, Edited By: Eamonn Butler, The Adam Smith Institute, Imediaprint Ltd., 1988

- Anton, Ion, "Romania, News and Views", web page of Center for International Private Enterprise, URL: http//www.cipe.org/

- Anton, Ion, Economic Reform in Romania, Economic Reform Today, Working Papers, Number 1, web page of Center for International Private Enterprise, URL: http//www.cipe.org/

- Antoniades, Evangelia, "Privatization in Greece: 1993 to the Present Its Impact on the Economy, the Society, and the Polity", web Page of Hellenic Resources Network, URL: http://www.hri.org

- Arrow, Kenneth, "On Finance and Decision Making", State-Owned Enterprise in the Western Economies, Edited By: Raymond Vernon and Yair Aharoni, Croom Helm Ltd., 1981

- Ash, Timothy; Hare, Paul and Canning, Anna, "Privatisation in the Former Centrally Planned Economies", Privatisation and Regulation-A Review of the Issues, Edited By: Peter M Jackson and Catherine M Price, Long, London & New York, 1994

- Babic, Mate, "Privatization and Restructuring in Croatia", Privatization in Central and Eastern Europe-Perspectives and Approaches, Edited by: Demetrius S. Iatridis and June Gary Hopps, Praeger Publishers, USA, 1998

- Baginska, Ewa, "Legal Aspects of the Privatization Process in Poland", web page of Civic Education Project, URL: http//www.cep.org.hu/

- Baker, Bill and Trémolet, Sophie, "Utility Reform, "Regulating Quality Standards to Improve Access for the Poor", Public Policy for the Private Sector, September 2000, The World Bank, p.17-21

- Barberis, Nicholas, Boycko, Maxim; Shleifer, Andrei; Tsukanova, Natalia, How Does Privatization Work? Evidence from the Russian Shops, National Bureau of Economic Research, NBER Working Paper Series, Working Paper No: 5136, Cambridge, MA, May 1995

- Barski, Alexander, "Problems of Foreign Investments in Russia and in the Former Soviet Union", Privatisation and Foreign Investments in Eastern Europe, Edited By: Iliana Zloch-Christy, USA, 1995

- Bartell, Ernest, Privatization: The Role of Domestic Business, The Helen Kellogg Institute for International Studies, University of Notre Dame, Working Paper Series, Number 198, June 1993

- Beecher, Janice, "Twenty Myths About Privatisation", Alliance for Redesigning Government, National Academy of Public Administration, URL: http://www.alliance.napawash.org/

- Beesley, Michael and Avans, Tom, "The British Experience: The Case of British Rail", State-Owned Enterprise in the Western Economies, Edited By: Raymond Vernon and Yair Aharoni, Croom Helm Ltd., 1981

- Bell, Stuart, "Privatisation Through Broad-Based Ownership Strategies-A More Popular Option", Public Policy for the Private Sector, The World Bank, FPD note No. 33, January 1995

- Bengtsson, Maria, Marell, Agneta and Baldwin, Andrew, "Business-Induced Barriers in Explaining the Effects of Deregulation-Two Swedish Case Studies", Who Benefits from Privatisation?, Edited by: Moazzem Hossain, Justin Malbon, Routledge Studies in the Modern World Economy, London and New York, 1998

- Bernstein, Ann, "The State and the Market in Developing Countries", web page of Center for International Private Enterprise, URL: http://www.cipe.org/

- Beyer, Hans-Joachim, Dziobek, Claudia, and R. Garrett, John, Economic and Legal Considerations of Optimal Privatisation: Case Studies of Mortgage Firms (DePfa Group and Fannie Mae), IMF, Monetary and Exchange Affairs, Working Papers 99/69, May 1999

- Bhaskar, V., Privatisation and Developing Countries: The Issues and the Evidence", United Nations Publications, No.47, August 1992

- Bisák, Peter, "Goals and Policies of the Privatisation Process", Minister of Privatisation & Administration of National Property, Slovak Republic, http://www.kenpubs.co.uk/investguide/slovakia/bisak.html

- Bishop, Matthew and Kay, John, "Privatisation in Western Economies", Privatisation-Symposium in Honor of Herbert Giersch, Edited By: Horst Siebert, Institut fur Weltwirtschaft an der Universitat Kiel, J.C.B. Mohr (Paul Siebeck), Tubingen, 1992

- Blaszczyk, Barbara, "Moving Ahead: Privatization in Poland", web page of Center for International Private Enterprise, URL: http://www.cipe.org/

- Bobeva, Daniela and Bozhkov, Aexander, "Privatisation and Foreign Investments in Bulgaria", Privatisation and Foreign Investments in Eastern Europe, Edited By: Iliana Zloch-Christy, USA, 1995

- Boffito, Carlo, "Privatisation in Central Europe and the Soviet Union", Privatisation Process in Eastern Europe- Theoretical Foundations and Empirical Results, Edited by: Maria Baldassarri, Luigi Paganetto, Edmund S. Phelps, St. Martin`s Press, 1993

- Bomer, Robin, "The Privatisation of British Telecom", Privatisation in Practice, Edited By: Eamonn Butler, The Adam Smith Institute, Imediaprint Ltd., 1988

- Bonavoglia, Rosario, " Evolution and Design in Eastern European Transition; Comment", Privatisation Process in Eastern Europe-Theoretical Foundations and Empirical Results, Edited by: Maria Baldassarri, Luigi Paganetto, Edmund S. Phelps, St. Martin`s Press, 1993

- Bornstein, Morris, "Privatisation in Central and Eastern Europe: Techniques, Policy Options and Economic Consequences", Privatisation Liberalisation and Destruction-Recreating the Market in Central and Eastern Europe, Edited By: László Csaba, Dartmouth Publishing Company Limited, England & USA, 1994

- Bös, Dieter, "Theoretical Perspectives on Privatisation: Some Outstanding Issues", Privatisation in the European Union, Theory and Policy Perspectives, Edited By: David Parker, London and New York, 1998

- Bouin, Olivier, "The Privatisation in Developing Countries: Reflections on a Panacea", Policy Brief No. 3, OECD Development Centre, OECD 1992

- Bouton, Lawrence and A. Sumlinski, Mariusz, IFC Discussion Paper Number 31- Trends in Private Investment in Developing Countries, Statistics for 1970-95, December 1996, February 1997 (revised)

- Braddon, Derek and Foster, Deborah, "An Inter-disciplinary Approach to the Analysis of Privatization and Marketization", Privatization: Social Science Themes and Perspectives, Edited By: Derek Braddon and Deborah Foster, Centre for Social and Economic Research, Faculty of Economics and Social Science, University of West England, Ashgate Publishing Limited, England & USA, 1996

- Bradley, Jonathan, "Privatisation in Central and Eastern Europe: Models and Ideologies", Privatisation: Social Science Themes and Perspectives, Edited by: Derek Braddon and Deborah Foster, Centre for Social and Economic Research, Faculty of Economics and Social Science, University of West England, Ashgate Publishing Limited, England & USA, 1996

- Brook Cowen Penelope and Tynan, Nicola, "Reaching the Urban Poor with Private Infrastructure", Public Policy for the Private Sector, Note No: 188, The World Bank, June 1999

- Brown, Allan, "The Economics of Privatisation-Case Study of Australian Telecommunications", Who Benefits from Privatisation?, Edited by: Moazzem Hossain, Justin Malbon, Routledge Studies in the Modern World Economy, London and New York, 1998

- Burke, Melvin, "Private versus Public Construction in Honduras: Issues of Economics and Ideology", Privatization and Deregulation in Global Perspective, Edited by: Dennis J. Gayle and Jonathan N. Goodrich, Pinter Publishers, London, 1990

- Burnside, David, "Taking British Airways to Market", Privatisation in Practice, Edited By: Eamonn Butler, The Adam Smith Institute, Imediaprint Ltd., 1988

- Bush, Stephen and Bush, Gill, "The Meaning of the Maastricht Treaty", web page of Critical European Group, University of Keele, URL: http//www.keele.ac.uk/

- Butler, Stuart, "Privatisation for Public Purposes", Privatisation and its Alternatives, Edited By: William T. Gormley, The University of Wisconsin Press, USA, 1991

- Butler, W.E. and E. Gashi-Butler, Maryann, "Foreign Investment in Russia: The New Legal Environment", Privatisation and Economic Development in Eastern Europe and the CIS, Investment, Acquisition and Managerial Issues, Edited By: Haydn Shaughnessy, John and Wiley & Sons, England, 1994

- Buttle, Nicholas, "Privatisation and Ethichs", Privatization: Social Science Themes and Perspectives, Edited By: Derek Braddon and Deborah Foster, Centre for Social and Economic Research, Faculty of Economics and Social Science, University of West England, Ashgate Publishing Limited, England & USA, 1996

- C. Daintith, Terence, "Legal Forms and Techniques of Privatisation", Legal Aspects of Privatisation, XXIst Colloquy on European Law, Budapest, 15-17 October 1991, Council of Europe Press, the Netherlands, 1993

- C. Werlau, María, "Update on Foreign Investment in Cuba:1996-97", web page of University of Texas, URL:http://lanic.utexas.edu/

- Carsberg, Bryan, "The Role of the Regulator", (Regulator), Privatisation in Practice, Edited By: Eamonn Butler, The Adam Smith Institute, Imediaprint Ltd., 1988

- Cassese, Sabino, "Public Control and Corporate Efficiency", State-Owned Enterprise in the Western Economies, Edited By: Raymond Vernon and Yair Aharoni, Croom Helm Ltd., 1981

- Cassese, Sabino, "Italy: Privatizations Announced, Semi Privatizations and Pseudo-Privatizations", Privatization in Western Europe-Pressures, Problems and Paradoxes, Edited By: Vincent Wright, Pinter Publishers, Great Britain, 1994

- Chesnokov, Alexander, "A business View of Russia's Economy", an address given by Alexander Chesnokov to the Center for International Private Enterprise Board of Directors at the U.S. Chamber of Commerce in Washington, DC, on April 6 1999, web page of Center for International Private Enterprise, URL: http://www.cipe.org/

- Chikán, Attila, "The Revolution in Ownership", Reconnecting Europe, URL: http://www.ac.com

- Claessens, Stijn, Djankov, Simeon, and Pohl, Gerhard, "Ownership and Corporate Governance-Evidence from the Czech Republic", Public Policy for the Private Sector, The World Bank Group, Note No: 111, May 1997

- Clementi, David, "Details for a Successful Share Issue", Privatisation in Practice, Edited by: Eamonn Butler, The Adam Smith Institute, Imediaprint ltd., 1988

- Colin Meek, "Privatisation Doesn't Necessarily Equal Competition-The UK Experience", Who Benefits from Privatisation?, Edited by: Moazzem Hossain, Justin Malbon, Routledge Studies in the Modern World Economy, London and New York, 1998

- Comparative Overview of Privatisation Policies and Institutions in Member OECD Countries, OECD Privatization and Enterprise Reform Unit, September 1998

- Competition Policy Newsletter, Number 1, Volume 3, Spring 1997

- Constantinescu, Emil, President of Romania, the President of Romania, speech at CIPE's Regional Conference, "Generating Investment through Economic Reform," on May 5,

1997, Bucharest, Romania, web page of Center for International Private Enterprise, URL: http://www.cipe.org/

- Cook, Paul and Kirkpatrick, Colin, "Privatisation Policy and Performance", Privatisation Policy and Performance-International Perspective, Edited By: Paul Cook, Colin Kirkpatrick, Prentice Hall, Harvester Wheatsheaf, Great Britain, 1995

- Cook, Paul, "Privatisation in the United Kingdom-Policy and Performance", Privatisation in the European Union-Theory and Policy Perspectives, Edited By: David Parker, London and New York, 1998

- Cooray, L.J.M., "The Australian Achievement: From Bondage To Freedom", URL: http://www.ourcivilisation.com/cooray/btof/chap162.htm

- Corkill, David, "Privatisation in Portugal", Privatization in Western Europe-Pressures, Problems and Paradoxes, Edited By: Vincent Wright, Pinter Publishers, Great Britain, 1994

- Country Commercial Guides, FY 1999: European Union, Chapter VII, EU Investment Climate Statement, Report prepared by the U.S. Mission to the European Union, Brussels, Belgium, released July 1998, web page of US State Department, URL: http://www.state.gov/www/about_state/business/com_guides/1999/europe/eu99.html

- Dabrowski, Marek, "The Role of the Government in Postcommunist Countries", Privatization, Liberalization and Destruction-Recreating the Market in Central and Eastern Europe, Edited by László Csaba, Dartmouth Publishing Company Limited, England & USA, 1994

- Daianu, Daniel, "The Changing Mix of Disequilibra during Transition: A Romanian Perspective", Privatisation, Liberalization and Destruction-Recreating the Market in

Central and Eastern Europe, Edited By: László Csaba, Dartmouth Publishing Company Limited, England & USA, 1994

- Daintith, Terence, "Legal Forms and Techniques of Privatisation", Legal Aspects of Privatisation, XXIst Colloquy on European Law, Budapest, 15-17 October 1991, Council of Europe Press, the Netherlands, 1993

- David Satter, "Russia's Deepening Crisis", web Page of Houston Institute, URL: http://www.hudson.org

- de Alessi, Louis, "Property Rights and Privatization", Prospects for Privatization, Edited by: Steve H. Hanke, APS (Proceedings of The Academy of Political Science), Volume 36, Number 3, New York, 1987, p.24-35

- de Brandt, Jacques, "Privatisation in an Industrial Policy Perspective-The Case of France", Privatisation in the European Union, Theory and Policy Perspectives, London and New York, 1998

- Degeorge, François; Jenter, Dirk; Moel, Alberto; Tufano, Peter, "Selling Company Shares to Reluctant Employees: France Telecom's Experience", NBER (National Bureau of Economic Research), Working Paper Series, Working Paper 7683, Cambridge, May 2000, p.1, URL: http://www.nber.org/papers/w7683

- Devroe, W., "Privatisation and Community Law: Neutrality Versus Policy", Common Market Law Review 34, 1997

- Dini, Lamberto, "Privatisation Processes in Eastern Europe: Theoretical Foundations and Empirical Results", Privatisation Process in Eastern Europe- Theoretical Foundations and Empirical Results, Edited by: Maria Baldassarri, Luigi Paganetto, Edmund S. Phelps, St. Martin's Press, 1993

- Dixon, Bill, "Summary the Maastricht Treaty", web page of Democratic Socialists of America, URL: http://www.dsausa.org/archive/Lit/Maastricht.html

- Doeh, Doran, "Special Report on Russia", Privatization, International Financial Law Review, Vol: 13, p.65-70

- Domanski, Grzegorz, "Legal Concepts of Privatisation: Privatisation of State-Owned Enterprises Through Transformation into Corporate Entities", Privatisation in Eastern Europe: Legal, Economic, and Social Aspects, Edited By: Hans Smit, Vratislav Pechota, Parker School of Foreign and Comparative Law Columbia University, New York, 1993

- Donaldson, David and Wagle, Dileep, "Privatization: Principles and Practice", (Executive Summary), International Finance Corporation, 1995

- Dumez, Hervé and Jeunemaitre, Alain, "Privatization in France: 1983-1993", Privatization in Western Europe-Pressures, Problems and Paradoxes, Edited By: Vincent Wright, Pinter Publishers, Great Britain, 1994

- E.Van Horn, Carl, "The Myths and Realities of Privatisation", Privatisation and Its Alternatives, Edited By: William T. Gormley, The University of Wisconsin Press, Wisconsin, USA, 1991

- Edwards, Sebastian, "Public Sector Deficits and Macroeconomic Stability in Developing Countries", Working Paper Series, National Bureau of Economic Research (NBER), Working Paper 5407, Cambridge, January 1996

- Emmeluth, Christian and Fogh, Peter, "Special Report on Denmark", Privatization, International Financial Law Review, 3 May 1994, Vol 13

- Engel, Eduardo, Fischer, Ronald and Galetovic, Alexander, "Privatising Roads-A New Method for Auctioning Highways", Public Policy for the Private Sector, The World Bank Group, May 1997

- Erdem, Ercüment, "Turkey", Privatisation-A Legal Perspective, A Supplement to the Euromoney Bank Register 1996, Published By: Euromoney Books, Euromoney Publications, London, July 1996

- Ericson, Richard, "The Concept and Objectives of Privatisation", Privatisation in Eastern Europe: Legal, Economic, and Social Aspects, Parker School of Foreign and Comparative Law, Edited By: Hans Smit and Vratislav Pechota, the Netherlands, 1993

- Esser, Josef, "Germany: Symbolic Privatizations in a Social Market Economy", Privatization in Western Europe-Pressures, Problems and Paradoxes, Edited By: Vincent Wright, Pinter Publishers, Great Britain, 1994

- Estrin, Saul, "Economic Transition and Privatisation: The Issues", Privatisation in Central and Eastern Europe, Edited By: Saul Estrin, Longman Group Limited, 1994, London and New York

- Euromoney, Privatisation Special Issue, Month 2, 15 February 1996

- European Commission, White Paper 1995, web page of European Union, URL: http://europa.eu.int/comm/index_en.htm

- European Commissions, European Competition Policy 1996, web page of European Union, URL: http://europa.eu.int/comm/index_en.htm

- European Community Competition Policy, XXIXth Report on Competition Policy (1999), European Commission, Directorate-General for Competition, Luxembourg: Office for Official Publications of the European Communities, Printed in Italy, 2000

- Ewing, Andrew and Goldmark, Susan, "Privatization by Capitalization The Case of Bolivia: A Popular Participation Recipe for Cash-Starved SOEs", Public Policy for Private Sector, The World Bank, FPD Note No.31, November 1994

- Fanjul, Oscar and Mañas, Luis "Privatization in Spain: The Absence of a Policy", Privatization in Western Europe-Pressures, Problems and Paradoxes, Edited By: Vincent Wright, Pinter Publishers, Great Britain, 1994

- Fischer, Stanley and Sahay, Ratna, "The Transition Economies after Ten Years", IMF (International Monetary Fund), Working Paper 7664, Cambridge, February 2000, URL: http://www.nber.org/papers/w7664

- Fischer, Stanley, "Privatisation in East European Transformation", National Bureau of Economic Research (NBER), Working Paper Series, No: 3703, Cambridge, May 1991

- Foster, C., "Privatisation, Public Ownership and the Regulation of Natural Monopolies", Blackwell Publishers, Oxford (UK) & Cambridge, (USA), 1992

- Frederic Robert, Jacques, "Law and Privatisations-A General Presentation of Issues", Legal Aspects of Privatisation, XXIst Colloquy on European Law, Budapest, 15-17 October 1991, Council of Europe Press, the Netherlands, 1993

- Frei, Eduardo, "The Chilean Perspective", President of Chile, web page of Center for International Private Enterprise, URL: http://www.cipe.org/

- Friedman, Milton, "Economic Freedom, Human Freedom, Political Freedom", Delivered November 1, 1991, web page of The California State University, Hayward, School of Business & Economics, URL: http://www.sbe.csuhayward.edu/~sbesc/frlect.html

- Frydman, Roman and Rapaczynski, Andrzej, "Evolution and Design in the East European Transition", Privatisation Process in Eastern Europe- Theoretical Foundations and Empirical Results, Edited by: Maria Baldassarri, Luigi Paganetto, Edmund S. Phelps, St. Martin's Press, 1993

- Gayle P. W. Jackson, "Government for Modern Markets", web page of Center for International Private Enterprise, URL: http//www.cipe.org/

- Gibbon, Henry, "Privatization in 1995 and Beyond", web page of Center for International Private Enterprise, URL: http//www.cipe.org/

- Gibbon, Henry, "Guide for Divesting Government-Owned Enterprises", (Guide), How-To Guide No: 15, Reason Public Policy Institute, URL: http://www.privatization.org

- Gillen, David and Cooper, Douglas, "Public Versus Private Ownership and Operation of Airports and Seaports in Canada", The Fraser Institute, URL: http//www.fraserinstitute.ca

- Global Equity Markets, A joint conference of the SBF Bourse de Paris and the New York Stock Exchange, Le Gran Hotel Inter-Continental, Paris, France, December 10-11, 1998, Current Draft: February 9, 1999

- Goglio, Alessandro, "Sectoral Regulatory Reforms in Italy: Framework and Implications", OECD Economics Department Working Papers No.294, Unclassified, ECO/WKP(2001)20, 14 May 2001

- Goh, Winnie and Sundram, Jomo, "Privatisation in Malaysia-A Social and Economic Paradox", Who Benefits from Privatisation?, Edited by: Moazzem Hossain, Justin Malbon, Routledge Studies in the Modern World Economy, London and New York, 1998

- Government of the Republic of Poland, European Commission Directorate General for Economic and Financial Affairs, Joint Assessment of Medium-Term Economic Policy Priorities of the Republic of Poland, Brussels, 10 February 2000

- Grabowski, Maciej, "Economic Reform in Poland", Economic Reform Today, Working Papers, Number 4, web page of Center for International Private Enterprise, URL: http//www.cipe.org/

- Graham, Cosmo and Prosser, Tony, "Golden Shares: Industrial Policy by Stealth", (Golden Shares), Public Law, Autumn, 1988, p.413-431

- Graham, Cosmo and Prosser, Tony, "Privatising Nationalised Industries: Constitutional Issues and New Legal Techniques", (Privatising Nationalised Industries), Modern Law Review, Volume: 50, January 1987, p. 16-51

- Graham, Cosmo, "Privatization-The United Kingdom Experience", Brooklyn Journal of International Law, Volume XXI, 1995, Number 1, p.185-211

- Grassini, Franco, "The Italian Enterprises: The Political Constraints", State-Owned Enterprise in the Western Economies, Edited By: Raymond Vernon and Yair Aharoni, Croom Helm Ltd., 1981

- Green Paper on the Liberalisation of Telecommunications Infrastructure and Cable Television Networks, web page of the European Union, URL: http://europa.eu.int

- Green Paper, on Relations Between the European Union and the ACP Countries on the Eve of the 21st Century, Challenges and Options for a New Partnership, European Commission, Directorate- General VIII Development, Study Group-Partnership 2000 DG VIII/1, Brussels, 20 November 1996

- Green, Richard, "Utility Regulation-A Critical Path for Revising Price Controls", Public Policy for the Private Sector, Note No; 185, The World Bank, May 1999

- Grimstone, Gerry, "The British Privatisation Programme", (British Privatisation), Privatisation and Deregulation in Canada and Britain-Proceedings of a Canada/United Kingdom Colloquium, Gleneagles, Scotland, Edited by: Jeremy Richardson, The Institute for Research on Public Policy, Dartmouth Publishing Company Limited, England, Canada, 1990

- Grimstone, Gerry, "The Mechanics of Privatisation", (The Mechanics of Privatisation), Privatisation in Practice, Edited by: Eamonn Butler, The Adam Smith Institute, Imediaprint ltd., 1988

- Grunewald, Donald, "Privatization at the State and Local Level", URL: http://www.self-gov.org

- Guislain, Pierre and Kerf, Michel, "Concessions-The Way to Privatise Infrastructure Sector Monopolies", Public Policy for the Private Sector, The World Bank, Note no 59, October 1995

- H. Sturgis, Amy, "The Rise, Decline, and Reemergence of Classical Liberalism", The Locke Smith Institute, 1994, web page of Belmont University, URL: http://www.belmont.edu/lockesmith/essay.html

- Hanousek, Jan and A. Kroch, Eugene, "A Model of Learning in Sequential Bidding: Voucher Privatization in the Czech Republic: Wave I", January 1995, URL: http://www.ssc.upenn.edu/~alexv/cast/february/jan.html

- Haritakis, Nicholaos and Pitelis, Christos, "Privatisation in Greece", Privatisation in the European Union, Theory and Policy Perspectives, Edited By: David Parker, London and New York, 1998

- Harmathy, Attila, "General Report", (General Report), Legal Aspects of Privatisation, XXIst Colloquy on European Law, Budapest, 15-17 October 1991, Council of Europe Press, 1993

- Harmathy, Attila, "General Report 2", (General Report 2), Legal Aspects of Privatisation, XXIst Colloquy on European Law, Budapest, 15-17 October 1991, Council of Europe Press, 1993

- Harmathy, Attila, "The Methods of Privatisation", (Methods), Privatisation in Eastern Europe: Legal, Economic, and Social Aspects, Parker School of Foreign and Comparative Law, Edited By: Hans Smit and Vratislav Pechota, the Netherlands, 1993

- Hart, Oliver; Shleifer, Andrei; W. Vishny, Robert, "The Proper Scope of Government: Theory and an Application to Prisons", National Bureau of Economic Research (NBER), Working Paper Series, No: 5744, Cambridge, September 1996

- Hartley, Keith, "Contracting-out in Britain- Achievements and Problems", Privatisation and Deregulation in Canada and Britain-Proceedings of a Canada/United Kingdom Colloquium, Gleneagles, Scotland, Edited by: Jeremy Richardson, The Institute for Research on Public Policy, Dartmouth Publishing Company Limited, England, Canada, 1990

- Havrylyshyn, Oleh and McGettigan, Donal, "Privatization in Transition Countries: Lessons of the First Decade", IMF, Economic Issues No.18, Washington DC, August, 1999

- Heath, John, "Survey of Contributions", Public Enterprise at the Crossroads- Essays in Honour of V.V. Ramanadham, Edited By: John Heath, London and New York, Routledge, 1990

- Hessel, Marek, "How Corporate Governance Makes Privatization Succeed", web page of Center for International Private Enterprise, URL: http//www.cipe.org/

- Hilf, Meinhard, "The Single European Act and 1992: Legal Implications for Third Countries, European Journal of International Law", web page of European Journal of International Law, URL: http://www.ejil.org/journal/Vol1/No1/art5.html

- HM Treasury Departmental Report for 1995, web page of UK Treasury, URL: http://www.hm-treasury.gov.uk/drep/1995/index.html

- Holder, Stuart, "Privatisation and Competition: the Evidence from Utility and Infrastructure Privatisation in the United Kingdom", Regulation, Competition and Privatisation; Organisation for Economic Co-operation and Development in co-operation with the Finnish Ministry of Trade and Industry; Helsinki (Finland), 17-18 September 1998, Twelfth Plenary Session of the OECD Advisory Group on Privatisation (AGP); National Economic Research Associates (UK)

- Hondius, Ewoud, "Privatisation and Consumer Protection", Legal Aspects of Privatisation, XXIst Colloquy on European Law, Budapest, 15-17 October 1991, Council of Europe Press, the Netherlands, 1993

- Hossain, Moazzem and Malbon, Justin, "Introduction", (Introduction), Who Benefits from Privatisation?, Edited by: Moazzem Hossain, Justin Malbon, Routledge Studies in the Modern World Economy, London and New York, 1998

- Hossain, Moazzem and Malbon, Justin, "Preface", (Preface), Who Benefits from Privatisation, Edited by: Moazzem Hossain, Justin Malbon, Routledge Studies in the Modern World Economy, London and New York, 1998

- Hossain, Moazzem, "Liberalisation and Privatisation-India's Telecommunications Reforms", Who Benefits from Privatisation?, Edited by: Moazzem Hossain, Justin Malbon, Routledge Studies in the Modern World Economy, London and New York, 1998

- Houbenova-Dellisivkova, Tatiana, "Liberalization and Transformation in Bulgaria", Privatization, Liberalization and Destruction-Recreating the Market in Central and Eastern Europe, Edited by: László Csaba, Dartmouth Publishing Company Limited, England & USA, 1994

- Hrncír, Miroslav, "Financial Intermediation in ex-Czechoslovakia: An Assessment", Privatisation, Liberalization and Destruction-Recreating the Market in Central and Eastern Europe, Edited By: László Csaba, Dartmouth Publishing company Limited, England & USA, 1994

- Hullsink, Willem and Schenk, Hans, "Privatisation and Deregulation in the Netherlands", Privatisation in the European Union, Theory and Policy Perspectives, Edited By: David Parker, London and New York, 1998

- Iatridis, Demetrius, "A Global Approach to Privatization", Privatization in Central and Eastern Europe-Perspectives and Approaches, Edited by: Demetrius S. Iatridis and June Gary Hopps, Praeger Publishers, USA, 1998

- Iliescu Nastase, Simona, "La protection juridique de la propriété privée dans le nouveau contexte social et économique de la Roumanie", (Juridical Protection of Private Property in the New Social and Economic Context of Romania), Chapter 4, Individual Democratic Institutions Research Fellowships 1994-1996, web page of NATO, URL: http://www.nato.int/acad/fellow/94-96/iliescu/index.htm

- Implementing Privatisation: The UK Experience, web page of UK Treasury, URL: http://www.hm-treasury.gov.uk

- Inotai, András, "Experience with Privatisation in East Central Europe", Privatisation-Symposium in Honor of Herbert Giersch, Edited By: Horst Siebert, Institut fur Weltwirtschaft an der Universitat Kiel, J.C.B. Mohr (Paul Siebeck), Tubingen, 1992

- J. Arrow, Kenneth and S. Phelps, Edmund, "Proposed Reforms of the Economic System of Information and Decision in the USSR: Commentary and Advice", Privatisation Process in Eastern Europe- Theoretical Foundations and Empirical Results, Edited by: Maria Baldassarri, Luigi Paganetto, Edmund S. Phelps, St. Martin's Press, 1993

- J. Arrow, Kenneth, "On Finance and Decision Making", State-Owned Enterprise in the Western Economies, Edited By: Raymond Vernon and Yair Aharoni, Croom Helm Ltd., 1981

- J. Callebaut, John, "Reforms are Key to China's Global Integration", web page of Center for International Private Enterprise, URL: http//www.cipe.org/

- J. Dannin, Ellen, "White Paper on Privatisation", web page of California Western School of Law, URL: http//www.cwls.edu/

- J. de Ru, Hendrik and Wettenhall, Roger, "Progress, Benefits and Costs of Privatisation: An Introduction", National Review of Administrative Sciences, Volume 56, Number 1, March 1990

- J. Gayle Dennis, and Seaton, Bruce, "New Zealand: A Welfare State through Corporatization?", Privatization and Deregulation in Global Perspective, Edited by: Dennis J. Gayle and Jonathan N. Goodrich, Pinter Publishers, London, 1990

- J. Gayle, Dennis and N.Goodrich, Jonathan, "Exploring the Implications of Privatisation and Deregulation", Privatisation and Deregulation in Global Perspective, Edited By: Dennis J. Gayle and Jonathan N. Goodrich, Pinter Publishers, London, 1990

- J. Juan, Ellis, "Privatising Airports-Options and Case Studies", Public Policy for the Private Sector, The World Bank, Note No. 82, June 1996

- J. Whincop, Michael and Rowland, Stuart, "Plus ca Change...-The Effects of Markets and Corporate Law on the Governance of Privatised Enterprises", Who Benefits from Privatisation?, Edited by: Moazzem Hossain, Justin Malbon, Routledge Studies in the Modern World Economy, London and New York, 1998

- J. Wiarda, Howard, "Modernizing the State in Latin America", web page of Center for International Private Enterprise, URL: http//www.cipe.org/

- J.J. Welfens, Paul, "Privatization and Foreign Direct Investment in the East European Transformation: Theory, Options and Strategies", Privatization, Liberalization and Destruction-Recreating the Market in Central and Eastern Europe, Edited By: László Csaba, Dartmouth Publishing Company Limited, England & USA, 1994

- Jackson, Peter and Price, Catherine, "Privatisation and Regulation: A Review of the Issues", Privatisation and Regulation-A Review of the Issues, Edited by: Peter M. Jackson and Catherine Price, Longman Group Limited, 1994

- Jose Montes Gan, Vicente and Petitbo Jan, Amedeo, "The Privatisation of State Enterprises in the Spanish Economy", Privatisation in the European Union, Theory and Policy Perspectives, Edited By: David Parker, London, 1998

- Jossa, Bruno, "Is There an Option to the Denationalization of Eastern European Enterprises", Privatization Process in Eastern Europe-Theoretical Foundations and Empirical Results, Edited by: Maria Baldassarri, Luigi Paganetto, Edmund S. Phelps, St. Martin's Press, 1993

- Juris, Andrej, "Competition in the Natural Gas Industry, The Emergence of Spot, Financial, and Pipeline Capacity Markets", Public Policy for the Private Sector, Note No. 202, November 1999

- Juris, Andrej, "Economic Reform in Slovakia" web page of Center for International Private Enterprise, URL: http//www.cipe.org/

- Juris, Andrej, "Natural Gas Markets in the U.K.-Competition, Industry Structure, and Market Power of the Incumbent", Public Policy for the Private Sector, Note No.138, March 1998

- Jurzyca, Eugen, "Transparency in the Slovak Economy", web page of Center for International Private Enterprise, URL: http//www.cipe.org/

- K. Lee, Chang, "Privatization and Cooperative Labor-Management Relations", Cornell University, Department of City and Planning, May 1998, URL: http://www.cce.cornell.edu/

❏ K. Lioukas, Spyros and B. Papoulias, Demetrios, "The Effectiveness of Public Enterprises in Greece", Public Enterprise at the Crossroads-Essays in Honour of V.V. Ramanadham, Edited By: John Heath, London and New York, Routledge, 1990

❏ Karasapan, Ömer, "The World Bank Contribution to Private Participation in Infrastructure", Public Policy for the Private Sector, The World Bank, Note No: 55, October 1995

❏ Karina Izaguirre, Ada, Private Participation in Telecommunications-Recent Trends, Public Policy for the Private Sector, Note No. 204, December 1999

❏ Kay, John and Vickers, John, "Regulatory Reform-An Appraisal", Deregulation or Re-regulation-Regulatory Reform in Europe and the United States, Edited by: Giandomenico Majone, Pinter Publishers, London, 1990

❏ Keefer, Philip, "Contracting out-An Opportunity for Public Sector Reform and Private Sector Development in Transition Economies", The World Bank, July 1998

❏ Kikeri, Sunita; Nellis, John; Shirley, Mary, Outreach Number: 3, Policy Views from the Country Economics Department, The World Bank, July 1992

❏ Kirkpatrick, Colin, "The United Kingdom Privatisation Model: Is it Transferable to Developing Countries", Privatisation in the United Kingdom, Edited By: V.V. Ramanadham, Routledge, London and New York, 1988

❏ Klein, Michael and Roger, Neil, Back to the Future, "The Potential in Infrastructure Privatisation", Public Policy for the Private Sector, The World Bank, FPD Note No: 30, November 1994

- Klein, Michael, "Designing Auctions for Concessions-Guessing the Right Value to Bid and the Winner's Curse", Public Policy for the Private Sector, Note No: 160, The World Bank, November 1998

- Klein, Michael, "Infrastructure Concessions-To Auction or Not to Auction?", Public Policy for the Private Sector, Note No: 159, The World Bank, November 1998

- Klein, Michael, "Rebidding for Concessions", Public Policy for the Private Sector, Note No: 161, The World Bank, November 1998

- Koen, Vincent, "Poland-Privatisation as the Key to Efficiency", web page of OECD, URL: http://www.oecd.org/publications/observer/213/spotlight.htm

- Kolderie, Ted, "The Two Different Concepts of Privatisation", Privatisation and Deregulation in Global Perspective, Edited By: Dennis J. Gayle and Jonathan N.Goodrich, Pinter Publishers, London, 1990

- Kristo, Konstandin, "Economic Reform in Albania", web page of Center for International Private Enterprise, URL: http//www.cipe.org/

- Kuhl, Jurgen, "Privatisation and its Labour Market Effects in Eastern Germany", Lessons from Privatisation: Labour Issues in Developing and Transitional Countries, Edited By: Rolph van der Hoeven and Gyorgy Sziraczki, International Labour Organisation (ILO), Geneva, 1997

- L. Benson, Bruce "Crime Control Through Private Enterprise", The Independent Review, Volume: II, Number: 3, Winter 1998

- L. Megginson, William and M. Netter, Jeffry, "Equity to the People: The Record on Share Issue Privatization Programs", the World Bank, URL: http://www.worldbank.org

- L. Megginson, William and M. Netter, Jeffry, "From State to Market: A Survey of Empirical Studies on Privatization", for presentation at: Global Equity Markets, A Joint Conference of the SBF Bourse de Paris and the New York Stock Exchange, Paris, France, December 10-11, 1998, Current Draft, February 9, 1999

- L. Megginson, William, "The Impact of Privatisation", web page of Center for International Private Enterprise, URL: http//www.cipe.org/

- L. Megginson, William; C. Nash, Robert; and van Randenborgh, Matthias, "The Privatization Dividend, A Worldwide Analysis of the Financial and Operating Performance of Newly Privatized Firms", Public Policy for the Private Sector, The World Bank, February 1996, Note No. 68

- L. Rutledge, "Susan, Selling State Companies to Strategic Investors-Trade Sale Privatizations in Poland, Hungary, the Czech Republic, and the Slovak Republic", Volume One, Analysis of Issues, The World Bank, January 1995, URL: http://www.privatizationlink.com

- L. Williams, John, Privatisation of Large Publicly Owned Enterprises: A Public Choice Perspective, Department of Economics, Murdoch University, Working Paper No. 158, May 1997

- La Porta, Rafael and López-de-Silanes, Florencio, "The Benefits of Privatisation: Evidence from Mexico", Public Policy for the Private Sector, The World Bank Group, Note No: 117, June 1997

- Laffan, Brigid, The European Union: A Distinctive Model of Internationalisation?, European Integration Online Papers (EIoP) Vol. 1 (1997) N° 18; URL: http://eiop.or.at/eiop/texte/1997-018a.htm

- Lancaster, Thomas, "Deregulating the French Banking System", Privatization and Deregulation in Global Perspective, Edited by: Dennis J. Gayle and Jonathan N. Goodrich, Pinter Publishers, London, 1990

- Lane, Jan-Erik, "Sweden: Privatization and Deregulation", Privatization in Western Europe-Pressures, Problems and Paradoxes, Edited By: Vincent Wright, Pinter Publishers, Great Britain, 1994

- Langseth, Petter, "How to Fight Corruption on the Ground", Web page of the Center for International Enterprise", URL: http//www.cipe.org/

- Lesher, Richard, "Democracy's Promise: Building a Modern Economy", web page of Center for International Private Enterprise, URL: http//www.cipe.org/

- Letwin, Oliver, "Privatising the World-A Study of International Privatisation in Theory and Practice", London, 1988

- Lintner, John, "Economic Theory and Financial Management", State-Owned Enterprise in the Western Economies, Edited By: Raymond Vernon and Yair Aharoni, Croom Helm Ltd., 1981

- Littlechild, Stephen, Privatisation, Competition and Regulation, The Institute of Economic Affairs, Occasional Paper 10, London, 2000

- López-de-Silanes, Florencio, "Determinants of Privatisation Prices", NBER (National Bureau of Economic Research) Working Paper Series, Working Paper 5494, URL: http://papers.nber.org/papers/w5494, Cambridge, March 1996

❏ López-de-Silanes, Florencio, Andrei Shleifer, Robert W. Vishny, "Privatisation in the United States", National Bureau of Economic Research (NBER), Working Paper #5113, May 1995

❏ M. A. Gronbacher, Gregory, "The Philosophy of Classical Liberalism", web page of Acton Institute, URL: http://www.acton.org/cep/papers/classicallib.html

❏ M. Andic, Fuat, "The Case for Privatisation: Some Methodological Issues", Privatisation and Deregulation in Global Perspective, Edited By: Dennis J. Gayle and Jonathan N.Goodrich, Pinter Publishers, USA, 1990

❏ M. Buchanan, James, "Notes on the Liberal Constitution", the Cato Journal, Vol.14, No1, web page of Cato Institute, URL: http://www.cato.org/pubs/journal/cj14n1-1.html

❏ M. Hanke, Steve, "Privatization versus Nationalization", Prospects for Privatization, Edited by: Steve H. Hanke, APS (Proceedings of The Academy of Political Science), Volume 36, Number 3, New York, 1987, p.1-3

❏ M. Mintz, Jack; Chen, Duanjie and Zorotheos, Evangelia, "Taxing Issues with Privatisation: A Checklist, International Tax Program", Institute of International Business, University of Toronto, URL: http://www.worldbank.org/

❏ M. Newbery, David and G. Pollitt, Michael, The Restructuring and Privatization of the U.K. Electricity Supply-Was It Worth It?, Public Policy for the Private Sector, The World Bank Group, Note No.124, September 1997

❏ M. Nsouli, Salem, Bisat, Amer and Kanaan, Oussama, "The European Union's New Meditterian Strategy", URL: http://www.oneworld.org/euforic/fandd/nso.htm

- M. Shirley, Mary, "Getting Bureaucrats Out of Business: Obstacles to State Enterprise Reform", web page of Center for International Private Enterprise, URL: http//www.cipe.org/

- MacGregor, Laura, Prosser, Tony and Villiers, Charlotte, "Introduction", Regulation and Markets Beyond 2000, Edited By: Laura MacGregor, Tony Prosser and Charlotte Villiers, Dartmouth and Ashgate Publishing Companies, UK & USA, 2000

- MacGregor, Laura, Prosser, Tony and Villiers, Charlotte, "Regulation and Markets Beyond 2000: Conclusion", Regulation and Markets Beyond 2000, Edited By: Laura MacGregor, Tony Prosser and Charlotte Villiers, Dartmouth and Ashgate Publishing Companies, UK & USA, 2000

- Malbon, Justin, "Gaining Balance on the Regulatory Tightrope", Who Benefits from Privatisation? Edited by: Moazzem Hossain, Justin Malbon, Routledge Studies in the Modern World Economy, London and New York, 1998

- Malle, Silvana, "Privatisation in Russia: A Comparative Study in Institutional Change", Privatisation, Liberalisation and Destruction-Recreating the Market in Central and Eastern Europe, Edited by: László Csaba, Dartmouth Publishing Company, England &USA 1994

- Maria Rossotto, Carlo, Kerf, Michel and Rohlfs, Jeffrey, Competition in Mobile Phones, Public Policy for the Private Sector, Note No.184, August 1999

- Martin B., The Social and Employment Consequences of Privatisation in Transition Economies: Evidence and Guidelines, Interdepartmental Action Programme on Privatisation, Restructuring and Economic Democracy-Working Paper, International Labour Organisation, URL: http://www.ilo.org/

- Martin, Jean-Yves and Gonzalez-Maltes, Adrian P., "Special Report on France", Privatization, International Financial Law Review, 3 May 1994, Vol 13

- Martin, Will, "China's Economic Policies and World Trade Reforming China's Trading System", web page of Center for International Private Enterprise, URL: http//www.cipe.org/

- Martinelli, Alberto, "The Italian Experience: A Historical Perspective", State-Owned Enterprise in the Western Economies, Edited By: Raymond Vernon and Yair Aharoni, Croom Helm Ltd., 1981

- Martinez, Elizabeth and Garcia, Arnoldo, "What is "Neo-Liberalism"?, web page of Corporate Watch, URL: http://www.corpwatch.org/trac/corner/glob/neolib.html

- Meek, Colin, "Privatisation Doesn't Necessarily Equal Competition-The UK Experience", Who Benefits from Privatisation?, Edited by: Moazzem Hossain, Justin Malbon, Routledge Studies in the Modern World Economy, London and New York, 1998

- Mencinger, Joze, "Privatization Dilemmas in Slovenia", Privatization, Liberalization and Destruction-Recreating the Market in Central and Eastern Europe, Edited by: László Csaba, Dartmouth Publishing Company Limited, England & USA, 1994

- Merger Cases in the Real World: A Study of Merger Control Procedures, OECD, Paris, 1994, web page of OECD, URL: http://www.oecd.org/

- Meth-Cohn, Delia and C. Müller, Wolfgang, "Looking Reality in the Eye: The Politics of Privatization in Austria", Privatization in Western Europe-Pressures, Problems and Paradoxes, Edited By: Vincent Wright, Pinter Publishers, Great Britain, 1994

- Miklos, Ivan, "Corruption Risks in the Privatisation Process-A Study of Privatisation Developments in the Slovak Republic, Focusing on the Causes and Implications of Corruption Risks", Bratislava, May 1995, URL: http://privatizationlink.com.

- Miklos, Ivan, "Europe's Outcast? Slovakia and the European Union", web page of Center for International Private Enterprise, URL: http://www.cipe.org

- Mikloš, Ivan, "Privatization in 1996", Centre for Economic and Social Analysis of Slovak Republic, URL: http//www.mesa10.sk/

- Miklos, Ivan, "Slovakia", News and Views, Web page of Center for International Private Enterprise, URL: http//www.cipe.org/

- Miljan, Mait and Turk, Kuino, "Privatization in Estonia", Privatization in Central and Eastern Europe-Perspectives and Approaches, Edited by: Demetrius S. Iatridis and June Gary Hopps, Praeger Publishers, USA, 1998

- Minford, Patrick, "Introduction", Edited by: Patrick Minford, E S Savas, Iain Mays, Privatisation in Practice, Patrick Minford Selsdon Group, Viewpoint Series

- Mitchell, James, "Britain: Privatisation as Myth", Privatisation and Deregulation in Canada and Britain-Proceedings of a Canada/United Kingdom Colloquium, Gleneagles, Scotland, Edited by: Jeremy Richardson, The Institute for Research on Public Policy, Dartmouth Publishing Company Limited, England, Canada, 1990

- Mizsei, Kalman, Eleventh Plenary Session of the OECD Advisory Group on Privatisation (AGP) on Banks and Privatisation, Privatisation of Individual Banks or of the Banking System?, Rome, 18 and 19 September 1997

- Moran, Michael and Prosser, Tony, "Introduction: Politics, Privatisation and Constitutions", Privatisation and Regulatory Change in Europe, Edited by: Michael Moran and Tony Prosser, Open University Press, Buckingham & Philadelphia, 1994

- Mygind, Niels, "Privatisation, Governance and Restructuring of Enterprises in the Baltics, Baltic Regional Programme," Organisation for Economic Co-operation and Development (OECD), Paris, April/May 2000

- Narendar V. Rao, Northeastern, C. Bhaktavatsala Rao and Dunphy, Steve, "International Perspectives on Privatisation of State Owned Enterprises", Small Business Advancement National Center, University of Central Arkansas, URL: http://www.sbaer.uca.edu/

- Nellis, John, "Is Privatisation Necessary", Public Policy for the Private Sector, The World Bank, FPD Note No. 7, May 1994

- Nellis, John, "Time to Rethink Privatisation in Transition Economies", IFC-International Finance Corporation, Discussion Paper Number 38, The World Bank, Washington, D.C.

- Nestor, Stilpon and Mahboobi, Ladan, Privatisation of Public Utilities; The OECD Experience, Rio, 23 April 1999

- Neumann, Laszlo, "Privatisation in Telecommunications in Hungary", Lessons from Privatisation: Labour Issues in Developing and Transitional Countries, Edited By: Rolph van der Hoeven and Gyorgy Sziraczki, International Labour Organisation (ILO), Geneva, 1997

- Niskanen, William, "Guidelines for Delineating the Private and the Government Sector", Privatisation-Symposium in Honor of Herbert Giersch, Edited By: Horst Siebert, Institut fur Weltwirtschaft an der Universitat Kiel, J.C.B. Mohr (Paul Siebeck), Tubingen, 1992

- Nogueira Pinto, Jaime, "The Crisis of the Sovereign State and the Privatisation of Defence and Foreign Affairs", Heritage Foundation Lecture, No 649, Lectures and Educational Programs, The Heritage Foundation, URL: http//www.heritage.org/, November 19, 1999

- Noreng, Øystein, "State-Owned Oil Companies: Western Europe", State-Owned Enterprise in the Western Economies, Edited By: Raymond Vernon and Yair Aharoni, Croom Helm Ltd., 1981

- Normanton, E. Leslie, "Accountability and Audit", State-Owned Enterprise in the Western Economies, Edited By: Raymond Vernon and Yair Aharoni, Croom Helm Ltd., 1981

- O. Krueger, Anne, "Comment on Wiliam A. Niskanen, Guidelines Delineating the Private and the Government Sector", Privatisation-Symposium in Honor of Herbert Giersch, Edited By: Horst Siebert, Institut fur Weltwirtschaft an der Universitat Kiel, J.C.B. Mohr (Paul Siebeck), Tubingen, 1992

- O'Connell Davidson, Julia, "Metamorphosis? Privatisation and the Restrucuring of Management and Labour", (Metamorphosis), Privatisation and Regulation-A Review of the Issues, Edited by: Peter M. Jackson and Catherine Price, Longman Group Limited, 1994

- Oleh Havrylyshyn, Donal McGettigan, "Privatization in Transition Countries: Lessons of the First Decade", IMF, Economic Issues No.18, Washington DC, August, 1999

- Olsen, Odgers, "Privatizing Electricity", Privatisation in Practice, Edited By: Eamonn Butler, The Adam Smith Institute, Imediaprint Ltd., 1988

- Olsson, Johan, The European Union and the Maastrich Treaty, URL: http://www.geocities.com/TimesSquare/1848/eu.html

- Öniş, Ziya, "The Evolution of Privatisation in Turkey: The Institutional Context of Public-Enterprise Reform", Int. J. Middle East Studies 23, 1991, USA

- P. Glade, William, "Privatisation in Chile", Public Enterprise at the Crossroads-Essays in Honour of V.V. Ramanadham, Edited By: John Heath, London and New York, Routledge, 1990

- Paganetto, Luigi and Lucio Scandizzo, Pasquale, "Privatisation and Competitive Behaviour: Endogenous Objectives, Efficiency and Growth (Comment)", Privatisation Process in Eastern Europe-Theoretical Foundations and Empirical Results, Edited by: Maria Baldassarri, Luigi Paganetto, Edmund S. Phelps, St. Martin's Press, 1993

- Papanek, Gábor, "Legal Security in the Economy of Hungary", web page of Center for International Private Enterprise, URL: http//www.cipe.org/

- Parker, David, "Nationalisation, Privatisation, and Agency Status within Government: Testing for the Importance of Ownership", (Nationalisation, Privatisation, and Agency), Privatisation and Regulation-A Review of the Issues, Edited by: Peter M. Jackson and Catherine Price, Longman Group Limited, 1994

- Parker, David, "Privatisation in the European Union, An Overview", (Privatisation in the European Union), Privatisation in the European Union, Theory and Policy Perspectives, Edited By: David Parker, London, 1998

- Paukert, Liba, "Privatization and Employment in the Czech Republic", Lessons from Privatisation: Labour Issues in Developing and Transitional Countries, Edited By: Rolph van der Hoeven and Gyorgy Sziraczki, International Labour Organisation (ILO), Geneva, 1997

- Peltola, Lauri and Wist, Tarja, "Special Report on Finland", Privatization, International Financial Law Review, 3 May 1994, Vol: 13

- Perlez, Jane, "European Union Names New Candidates for Membership", New York Times, July 17, 1997

- Pernia, Joseph and Ramachandran, S., "The Macedonian Gambit-Enterprise cum Bank Restructuring", Public Policy for the Private Sector, The World Bank, Note No. 62, November 1995

- Perotti, Enrico and van Oijen, Pieter, "Privatization, Political Risk and Stock Market Development in Emerging Economies", July 1999, URL: http://oecd.org

- Petkova, Ivanka, "Bulgaria", News and Views, web page of Center for International Private Enterprise, URL: http//www.cipe.org/

- Piasecki, Matthew, "Looking for Fresh Investment Opportunities in Central Europe and Russia: A Path Finding Guide", Privatisation and Economic Development an Eastern Europe and the CIS-Investment, Acquisition and Managerial Issues, Edited By: Haydn Shaughnessy: John Wiley & Sons, England, 1994

- Pidluska, Inna, "Corruption Versus Clean Business in Ukraine", web page of the Center for International Enterprise", URL: http//www.cipe.org/

- Pierzchalski, Slawomir, "Polish Road to European Union, Evaluation by Experts of the European Communities", Published by the Commercial Counsellors Office Embassy of the Republic of Poland in the Hague, URL: http://users.bart.nl/~polamb/brhbiul/brhbiul.htm

- Pirie, Madsen, "Privatisation: 10 Lessons of Experience", President of the Adam Smith Institute, http://privatizationlink.com

- Price, Catherine, "Economic Regulation of Privatised Monopolies", Privatisation and Regulation-A Review of the Issues, Edited by: Peter M. Jackson and Catherine Price, Longman Group Limited, 1994

- Prime Ministry Undersecretariat for Foreign Trade, Export Promotion Centre Publication, 1996, Turkey

- Privatisation in Europe, Asia and Latin America, What Lessons can be Drawn?, Summary of the Presentations at the International Workshop on Privatisation Organised by the OECD in April 1994, Sao Paulo, URL: http://www.oecd.org

- Privatisation in the United Kingdom, The Facts and Figures, (Compiled by Peter Curwen), [Privatisation in the United Kingdom, Ernst & Young], Ernst & Young, 1994

- Privatisation Trends in OECD Countries-June 1996, URL: http://www.oecd.org

- Privatisation: Lessons Learned by State and Local Governments United States General Accounting Office (GAO) Report to the Chairman, [General Accounting Office], House Republican Task Force on Privatisation, March 1997, United States General Accounting Office Washington, D.C. 20548 General Government Division, March 14, 1997, URL: htpp//www.privatisation.org/

- Prögler, Yusuf, "Economic Neo-Liberalism: The Target of Popular Protests against Global Capitalism", web page of Muslimedia International, URL: http://www.muslimedia.com/archives/features00/capitalism.htm

- Prohaska, Maria, "Bulgarian Privatisation Results", web page of Center for International Private Enterprise, URL: http://www.cipe.org/

- Prohaska, Maria, "Privatization in Bulgaria: Pushing Forward", web page of Center for International Private Enterprise, URL: http://www.cipe.org/

- Prosser, Tony, "Constitutions and Political Economy: The Privatisation of Public Enterprises in France and Great Britain", (Constitutions and Political Economy), Modern Law Review, Volume 53, May 1990, p.304-320

- Prosser, Tony, "Social Limits to Privatization", (Social Limits), Brooklyn Journal of International Law, Volume XXI, 1995, Number 1, p.213-242

- Public Private Partnerships-The Government's Approach, London: The Stationery Office, Published with the permission of HM Treasury on behalf of the Controller of Her Majesty's Stationery Office, 2000

- R. Garner, Maurice, "Has Public Enterprise Failed?" Privatisation in the United Kingdom, Edited by: V.V. Ramanadham, Routledge, London and New York, 1988

- R. Hunter, David, "Putting Government Reform on a Firmer Foundation", Andersen Consulting Company, URL: http://www.ac.com

- Raiffa, Howard, "Decision Making in the State-Owned Enterprise", State-Owned Enterprise in the Western Economies, Edited By: Raymond Vernon and Yair Aharoni, Croom Helm Ltd., 1981

- Raiser, Thomas, "The Challenge of Privatization in the Former East Germany: Reconciling the Conflict Between Individual Rights and Social Needs", A Fourth Way?- Privatization, Property, and the Emergence of New Market Economies, Edited By: Gregory S. Alexander and Grazyna Skapska, Routledge, 1994

- Ramachandran S., "The Veil of Vouchers", Public Policy for the Private Sector, The World Bank Group, Note No. 108, April 1997

- Redwood, John, "Foreword", (Foreword), Oliver Letwin, "Privatising the World- A Study of International Privatisation in Theory and Practice", London, 1988

- Redwood, John, "Privatisation: A Consultant's Perspective", (Consultant's Perspective), Privatisation and Deregulation in Global Perspective, Edited By: Dennis J. Gayle and Jonathan N.Goodrich, Pinter Publishers, USA, 1990

- Rees, Ray, "Economic Aspects of Privatization in Britain", Privatization in Western Europe-Pressures, Problems and Paradoxes, Edited By: Vincent Wright, Social Change in Western Europe Series, Pinter Publishers, Great Britain, 1994

- Report on the Application of the Competition Rules in the European Union [Report prepared under the sole responsibility of DG IV in conjunction with the Twenty-eighth Report on Competition Policy 1998 Ð SEC (99)743 final], Part Two, web page of the European Union, URL: http://europa.eu.int/

- Report on the Application of the Competition Rules in the European Union, Competition Report 1996, web page of the European Union, URL: http://europa.eu.int/

- Reznik, Bruce, "Property Rights in a Market Economy", web page of Center for International Private Enterprise, URL: http//www.cipe.org/

- Rich, Frederic and A. Plapinger, William, "Getting It Right in Privatisation", International Financial Law Review, Special Issue on Privatisation, Volume 13

- Richardson, Jeremy, "The Politics and Practice of Privatisation in Britain", Privatization in Western Europe-Pressures, Problems and Paradoxes, Edited By: Vincent Wright, Pinter Publishers, Great Britain, 1994

- Robinson, Neil, "Corporate Interests and the Politics of Transition in Russia: 1991-1994" Privatization in Central and Eastern Europe-Perspectives and Approaches, Edited by: Demetrius S. Iatridis and June Gary Hopps, Praeger Publishers, USA, 1998

- Robinson, Ray, "Markets in Health Care", Privatisation and Regulation-A Review of the Issues, Edited by: Peter M. Jackson and Catherine Price, Longman Group Limited, 1994

- Rock, Charles, "Privatisation and Employment in Bulgaria's Reform", Lessons from Privatisation: Labour Issues in Developing and Transitional Countries, Edited By: Rolph van der Hoeven and Gyorgy Sziraczki, International Labour Organisation (ILO), Geneva, 1997

- Roger, Neil, "Recent Trends in Private Participation in Infrastructure", Public Policy for the Private Sector, The World Bank, Note No: 196, September 1999

- Rosa, Jean-Jacques, "Comment on Jan Winiecki (The Political Economy of Privatization)", Privatisation-Symposium in Honor of Herbert Giersch, Edited By: Horst Siebert, Institut für Weltwirtschaft an der Universitat Kiel, J.C.B. Mohr (Paul Siebeck), Tubingen, 1992

- Rose-Ackerman, Susan, "The Political Economy of Corruption-Causes and Consequences", Public Policy for the Private Sector, The World Bank, Note No: 74, April 1996

- Rothenberg Pack, Janet, "The Opportunities and Constraints of Privatisation," Privatisation and Its Alternatives, Edited By: William T. Gormley, The University of Wisconsin Press, Wisconsin, USA, 1991

- Russell, Dean, "Who is a Libertarian?", URL: http://www.daft.com/~rab/liberty/history/whois-1955.html

- S. Earle, John, "Privatization in Russia Offers Lessons for Others", web page of Center for International Private Enterprise, URL: http//www.cipe.org

- Saba, Paolo, Privatizing Network Industries, The Competition Policy Perspective, OECD, Competition Law and Policy Division, Helsinki, September 17-18, 1998

- Salvatore, Dominick, "Foreign Trade, Foreign Direct Investments and Privatisation in Eastern Europe", Privatization Process in Eastern Europe-Theoretical Foundations and Empirical Results, Edited by: Maria Baldassarri, Luigi Paganetto, Edmund S. Phelps, St. Martin's Press, 1993

- Samuel, S. Brian, "A New Look at African Privatization", IFC Corporate Finance Services Department, The World Bank, 1999, URL: www.http://www.ifc.org/ifc/publications/pubs/impact/impsm99/privatization/privatization.html

- Samuel, S. Brian, "The Ten Commandments of African Privatization", International Finance Corporation (IFC), The World Bank, URL: http://www.ifc.org/ifc/publications/pubs/impact/impsm99/commandm/commandm.html

- Santos, Anibal, "Privatisation and State Intervention-(An Economic Approach)", Deregulation or Re-regulation-Regulatory Reform in Europe and the United States, Edited by: Giandomenico Majone, Pinter Publishers, London, 1990

- Schliwa, R., "Enterprise Privatisation and Employee Buy-Outs in Poland: An Analysis of the Process, Interdepartmental Action Programme on Privatization, Restructuring and Economic Democracy" Working Paper IPPRED-2, URL: http//www.ilo.org/

- Schmieding, Holger, "Alternative Approaches to Privatisation: Some Notes on the Debate", Privatisation-Symposium in Honor of Herbert Giersch, Edited By: Horst Siebert, Institut für Weltwirtschaft an der Universitat Kiel, J.C.B. Mohr (Paul Siebeck), Tubingen, 1992

- Schrader, Klaus, "In Research of the Market: A Comparison of Post-Soviet Reform Policies", Privatisation Liberalization and Destruction-Recreating the Market in Central and Eastern Europe, Edited By: Laszló Csaba, England, 1994

- Schwartz, Gerd and Silva Lopes, Paulo, "Privatization and Reform of Public Enterprises: An Overview of Policy Trade-offs, Experiences, and Outcomes", Privatization in Central and Eastern Europe-Perspectives and Approaches, Edited by: Demetrius S. Iatridis and June Gary Hopps, Praeger Publishers, USA, 1998

- Schwartz, Gerd, "Privatisation in Eastern Europe, Experience and Preliminary Policy Lessons", Privatisation Policy and Performance-International Perspective, Edited By: Paul Cook, Colin Kirkpatrick, Prentice Hall, Harvester Wheatsheaf, Great Britain, 1995

- Shames, Michael, "Preserving Consumer Protection and Education in a Deregulated Electric Services World-Challenges for the Post-Modern Regulator", Who Benefits from Privatisation?, Edited by: Moazzem Hossain, Justin Malbon, Routledge Studies in the Modern World Economy, London and New York, 1998

- Sheng, Hua and Haiyan, Du, "State-Owned Enterprise Reform in China", Public Enterprise at the Crossroads-Essays in Honour of V.V. Ramanadham, Edited By: John Heath, London and New York, Routledge, 1990

- Sheshinski Eytan and López-Calva, Luis Felipe, Privatisation and its Benefits: Theory and Practice, Development Discussion Paper No: 698, Harvard Institute for International Development, Harvard University, April 1999

- Silva, Gisele, "Private Participation in the Airport Sector-Recent Trends", Public Policy for the Private Sector, Note No.202, November 1999

- Sipos, Gabriel, Dual Transition in the Czech and Slovak Republics: Creating Support for Market and Democratic Reforms through Restitutions, Dissertation for the Master's Degree in Transition Central European University, Economics Department Budapest, Hungary, 15 June 1998, web page of Central European University, URL: http://www.ceu.hu/

- Slay, Ben, "From Monopoly Socialism to Market Capitalism", (Socialism to Capitalism), De-Monopolisation and Competition Policy in Post-Communist Economies, Edited by Ben Slay, Wetview Press, 1996, USA

- Slay, Ben, "Post Communist Competition Policy: Conclusion and Suggestions", (Post Communist Competition Policy), De-Monopolisation and Competition Policy in Post-Communist Economies, Edited By: Ben Slay, Wetview Press, 1996, USA

- Smith Nightingale, Demetra, and Pindus, Nancy, "Privatization of Public Social Services: A Background Paper", October 15, 1997, Urban Institute, URL: http://www.urban.org/

- Smith, Eivind, "Means For Protecting the Users and Former Employees of Privatised Companies", Legal Aspects of Privatisation, XXIst Colloquy on European Law, Budapest, 15-17 October 1991, Council of Europe Press, the Netherlands, 1993

- Snell, Lisa, "Getting Greens in the Black: Golf-course Privatization Trends and Practices", Policy Study No. 260, Reason Public Policy Institute, URL: http://www.rppi.org/

- Soltwedel, Rudiger, "Comment on Holger Schmieding, (Alternative approaches to Privatisation: Some Notes on the Debate)", Privatisation-Symposium in Honor of Herbert Giersch, Edited By: Horst Siebert, Institut für Weltwirtschaft an der Universitat Kiel, J.C.B. Mohr (Paul Siebeck), Tubingen, 1992

- Spechler, Martin, "Privatization, Competition, and Structural Change in Eastern Europe", Edited by: Demetrius S. Iatridis and June Gary Hopps, Praeger Publishers, USA, 1998

- Stampford, Charles, "Cautionary Reflections on the Privatisation Push", Edited by: Moazzem Hossain, Justin Malbon, Routledge Studies in the Modern World Economy, London and New York, 1998

- Starr, Paul, "The New Life of the Liberal State: Privatisation and the Restructuring of State-Society Relations", http://www.princeton.edu/~starr/newstate.html

- Starr, Paul, "The Limits of Privatization", (The Limits of Privatization), Privatization and Deregulation in Global Perspective, Edited by: Dennis J. Gayle and Jonathan N. Goodrich, Pinter Publishers, London, 1990

- Starr, Paul, "The Meaning of Privatisation", web page of University of Princeton, http://princeton.edu/~starr/meaning.html

- State-Owned Enterprise (SOE) Reform in China, Senior Experts Meeting organised by the OECD and the Development Research Centre (DRC) of the State Council of the People's Republic of China, Synthesis Note, by the OECD Secretariat Beijing (China), 20-21 July 1998, URL: http://www.oecd.org/

- Stiglitz, Joseph, "Some Theoretical Aspects of the Privatization: Applications to Eastern Europe", (Some Theoretical Aspects), Privatization Process in Eastern Europe-Theoretical Foundations and Empirical Results, Edited by: Maria Baldassarri, Luigi Paganetto, Edmund S. Phelps, St. Martin's Press, 1993

- Stiglitz, Joseph, Promoting Competition and Regulatory Policy: With Examples from Network Industries, (Promoting Competition and Regulatory Policy), The World Bank, Beijing, China, July 25, 1999

❑ Stoyanov, Alexander, "Economic Reform in Bulgaria", web page of Center for International Private Enterprise, Economic Reform Today, Working Papers, Number 3, URL: http//www.cipe.org

❑ Sullivan, John, "Privatization and Economic Reforms", web page of Center for International Private Enterprise, URL: http//www.cipe.org/

❑ Sullivan, John, "Market Institutions and Democracy", web page of Center for International Private Enterprise, URL: http//www.cipe.org/

❑ Susan Rose-Ackerman, "Redesigning the State to Fight Corruption-Transparency, Competition, and Privatization", Public Policy for the Private Sector, The World Bank, Note No.75, April 1996

❑ Sutela, Pekka, "Russian Foreign Trade Between Liberalization and State Control", Privatization, Liberalization and Destruction-Recreating the Market in Central and Eastern Europe, Edited By: László Csaba, Dartmouth Publishing Company Limited, England & USA, 1994

❑ Szomburg, Jan, " The Reasoning Behind the Polish Mass Privatization Program", web page of Center for International Private Enterprise, URL: http//www.cipe.org/

❑ T. Gormley, William, "The Privatisation Controversy", Privatisation and Its Alternatives, Edited By: William T. Gormley, The University of Wisconsin Press, USA, 1991

❑ Ter-Minassian, Teresa, "Decentralization and Macroeconomic Management", Western Hemisphere Department, International Monetary Fund (IMF) Working Paper, IMF, November 1997

- The Opportunities and Challenges of Privatisation Chapter I, US Department of Energy, US Department of Energy, URL: http://home.osti.gov/

- The Oxford English Reference Dictionary, Oxford University Press URL: http://www.xrefer.com/entry.jsp?xrefid=393902

- The Phare Programme-An interim Evaluation, Published by the European Commission, (produced by the Evaluation Unit of the European Commission, Directorate General for External Relations: Europe and the New Independent States, Common Foreign and Security Policy, External Service (DG 1A F/5), in close collaboration with George Mergos and Andreas Tsantis as external consultants), web page of the European Union, URL: http://europa.eu.int/

- Thomas, Ceri, "Contracting-Out: Managerial Strategy or Political Dogma", Privatisation in the United Kingdom, Edited By: V.V. Ramanadham, Routledge, London and New York, 1988

- Tornell, Aaron, "Privatizing the Privatised", NBER (National Bureau of Economic Research) Working Paper Series, Working Paper 7206, URL: http://www.nber.org/papers/w7206, Cambridge, July 1999

- Torok, Adam, "Competition Policy and De-Monopolisation in Hungary After 1990", De-Monopolisation and Competition Policy in Post-Communist Economies, Edited By: Ben Slay, Wetview Press, 1996, USA

- Troedson, Robert, "Corporatisation and Privatisation; In whose Interest-A Review of a Conference held by Griffith University Law School and Griffith University School of International Business in Conjuction with RIPAA on March 1996" Who Benefits from

Privatisation?, Edited by: Moazzem Hossain, Justin Malbon, Routledge Studies in the Modern World Economy, London and New York, 1998

- Trujillo, Lourdes and Nombele, Gustavo, "Multiservice Infrastructure: Privatizing Port Services", Public Policy for the Private Sector, September 2000, The World Bank, p.43-46

- V. Ramanadham, V., "A Concluding Review", Privatisation in the United Kingdom, Edited By: V.V. Ramanadham, Routledge, London and New York, 1988

- Valdez, José, "Capitalization: Privatizing Bolivian Style", web page of the Center for International Enterprise", URL: http//www.cipe.org/

- Vamvoukos, Athanassios, Bahas Gramatidis & Associates, International Financial Law Review, 3 May 1994, Special Issue of Privatisation, Vol: 13, Part: 4//S1

- van Brabant, Jozef M., "Industrial Policy in Eastern Europe-Governing the Transition", (Industrial Policy in Eastern Europe), International Studies in Economies and Econometrics, Volume 31, Kluwer Academic Publishers, Dordrecht, The Netherlands, 1993

- van Brabant, Jozef M., "On the Economics of Property Rights and Privatisation in Transitional Economies", (Property Rights, Privatisation, Transitional Economies), Privatisation Policy and Performance-International Perspective, Edited By: Paul Cook, Colin Kirkpatrick, Prentice Hall, Harvester Wheatsheaf, Great Britain, 1995

- van den Berg, Caroline, "Water Privatization and Regulation in England and Wales", Public Policy for the Private Sector, The World Bank Group, May 1997

- van der Hoeven, Rolph and Sziraczki, Gyorgy, "Privatisation and Labour Issues", Lessons from Privatisation: Labour Issues in Developing and Transitional Countries, Edited By:

Rolph van der Hoeven and Gyorgy Sziraczki, International Labour Organisation (ILO), Geneva, 1997

- Veljanovski, Cento, "Privatisation: Progress, Issues, and Problems", Privatisation and Deregulation in Global Perspective, Edited By: Dennis J.Gayle and Jonathan N.Goodrich, Pinter Publishers, USA, 1990

- Vernon, Raymond, "Introduction", State-Owned Enterprise in the Western Economies, Edited By: Raymond Vernon and Yair Aharoni, Croom Helm Ltd., 1981

- Vidos, Tibor, "The Role Of Transparency In Political Decision Making and Its Effect on The Economy" web page of Center for International Private Enterprise, URL: http://www.cipe.org

- Voika, Inese, Latvian Papers Report on Privatisation, European Integration, and Corruption, Support for Improvement in Governance and Management in Central and Eastern European Countries, Public Management Forum, Vol. IV, No. 6, 1998, web page of OECD, URL: http://www.oecd.org/puma/sigmaweb/pmf/4pmf6/46pmf14.htm

- Volz, Joachim, "The Spanish Economy in the Run-up to European Monetary Union", web page of German Institute for Economic Research, URL: http://smith.diw.de/diwwbe/eb97-04/n97apr_3.htm#HDR0

- Voszka, Eva, "Privatization in Hungary: Results and Open Issues", web page of Center for International Private Enterprise, URL: http://www.cipe.org/

- Voudouris, Thanos, ECONOMICS, XTMAN-Seminar One, Module III Economics Paper in: European Union and Single Currency Market, 29 June, 1997, URL http://www.GRinet.com/thanos/study03/europe.html

- Vuylsteke, V., Techniques of Privatisation of State-Owned Enterprises, Vol. I., World Bank Technical Paper No.88, the World Bank, Washington DC.

- W. Bailey, Robert, "Uses and Misuses of Privatization", Prospects for Privatization, Edited by: Steve H. Hanke, APS (Proceedings of The Academy of Political Science), Volume 36, Number 3, New York, 1987, p.138-152

- W. Dnes, Antony, "Franchising and Privatisation", Public Policy for the Private Sector, The World Bank, Note No: 40, March 1995

- W. Lieberman, Ira, "Privatisation: The Theme of the 1990s-An Overview", Columbia Journal of World Business, Focus Issue: Privatisation, Spring 1993, Volume XXVIII, No.1

- W. Poole, Robert, "The Limits of Privatization", (Limits), Progress, Benefits and Costs of Privatisation: An Introduction", National Review of Administrative Sciences, Volume 56, number 1, March 1990

- W. Poole, Robert, "Privatization: Providing Better Services with Lower Taxes", web page of Reason Magazine, URL: http://www.reason.com

- Waterbury, John, "Deregulating the Economy: A Key Second Generation Reform", web page of Center for International Private Enterprise, URL: http//www.cipe.org/

- Webb, Eileen, "The Other Side of the National Competition Policy Debate-Perspective on the Public Interest and Community Services", Who Benefits from Privatisation?, Edited by: Moazzem Hossain, Justin Malbon, Routledge Studies in the Modern World Economy, London and New York, 1998

- Webb, Michael and Ehrhardt, David, "Improving Water Services Through Competition", Public Policy for the Private Sector, Note No.164, December 1998

- Weisskopf, Thomas, "Economic Perspectives on Privatization in Russia: 1990-1994", Privatization in Central and Eastern Europe-Perspectives and Approaches, Edited by: Demetrius S. Iatridis and June Gary Hopps, Praeger Publishers, USA, 1998

- Welch, Dick and Frémond, Olivier, The Case-by-Case Approach to Privatisation-Techniques and Examples, World Bank Technical Paper No. 403, The World Bank, Washington, D.C.

- Welfens, Paul, "Privatization and Foreign Direct Investment in the East European Transformation: Theory, Options and Strategies", Privatisation Liberalization and Destruction-Recreating the Market in Central and Eastern Europe, Edited By: Laszló Csaba, England, 1994

- Weyman-Jones, Tom, "Deregulation", Privatisation and Regulation-A Review of the Issues, Edited by: Peter M. Jackson and Catherine Price, Longman Group Limited, 1994

- Williams, Susan, "Globalization, Privatisation, and a Feminist Public", web page of Indiana University, USA, URL: http://www.law.indiana.edu/glsj/vol4/no1/wilpgp.htm

- Willner, Johan, "Privatisation in Finland, Sweden and Denmark-Fashion or Necessity", Privatisation in the European Union-Theory and Policy Perspectives, Edited By: David Parker, London and New York, 1998

- Winiecki, Jan, "The Political Economy of Privatization", Privatisation-Symposium in Honor of Herbert Giersch, Edited By: Horst Siebert, Institut fur Weltwirtschaft an der Universitat Kiel, J.C.B. Mohr (Paul Siebeck), Tubingen, 1992

- Woodward, Nick, "Public Enterprise, Privatization, and Cultural Adaption", Public Enterprise at the Crossroads-Essays in Honour of V.V. Ramanadham, Edited By: John Heath, London and New York, Routledge, 1990

- Wright, Mike and Thompson, Steve, "Divestiture of Public Sector Assets", Privatisation and Regulation-A Review of the Issues, Edited by: Peter M. Jackson and Catherine Price, Longman Group Limited, 1994

- Wright, Vincent, "Industrial Privatization in Western Europe: Pressures, Problems and Paradoxes", Privatization in Western Europe-Pressures, Problems and Paradoxes, Edited By: Vincent Wright, Social Change in Western Europe Series, Pinter Publishers, Great Britain, 1994

- XXVth REPORT on Competition Policy 1995, (Published in conjunction with the 'General Report on the Activities of the European Union-1995'), Brussels-Luxembourg, 1996, web page of the European Union, URL: http://europa.eu.int/

- Y. Zhurek, Stefan, "Emerging Market Structures in Russia: Developments in Commodity Markets", Privatisation and Foreign Investments in Eastern Europe, Edited By: Iliana Zloch-Christy, USA, 1995

- Yifu Lin, Justin, Cai, Fang and Li, Zhou, "The Lessons of China's Transition to a Market Economy", The Cato Journal, Volume 16, No: 2, web page of Cato Institute, URL:http://www.cato.org/pubs/journal/cj16n2-3.html

- Young, George, the (former) Financial Secretary's speech to the World Privatisation Conference, 6 March 1995, web page of the Treasury, URL: http://www.hm-treasury.gov.uk/pub/html/speech95/fst/sp060395.html

- Young, Peter, "The Lessons of Privatisation", web page of Center for International Private Enterprise, URL: http://www.cipe.org/

❏ Young, Peter, "Privatization Around the World", (Privatization Around the World), Prospects for Privatization, Edited by: Steve H. Hanke, APS (Proceedings of The Academy of Political Science), Volume 36, Number 3, New York, 1987, p.190-205

❏ Zucker Boswell, Nancy, "New Tools to Fight Corruption", web page of the Center for International Enterprise", URL: http://www.cipe.org/

INTERNET SOURCES

- URL: http//www.turkhuksitesi.com, (A web page which has been designed for Turkish law professionals)

- URL: http://www.portugal.org/, (A web page for the global Portuguese culture and community)

- URL: http://www.privatization.org/, (A Web page that has been provided by Reason Foundation)

- URL: http://www.privatizationlink.com, (A service of the World Bank Group to deliver information on privatisation in developing countries and transition economies to privatisation professionals worldwide)

- Web page of Adam Smith Institute, URL: http://www.adamsmith.org.uk/

- Web Page of Agency for Privatisation in the Federation of Bosnia and Herzegovina, URL: http://www.apf.com.ba/

- Web page of Bulgarian Foreign Investment Agency, URL: http://www.bfia.org/privat.htm

- Web page of Bulgarian Privatisation Agency, URL: http://www.privatisation.online.bg

- Web page of Canadian Department of Foreign Affairs and International Trade, URL: http://www.dfait-maeci.gc.ca/english/geo/europe/84679-e.htm

- Web page of Center for International Private Enterprise, URL: http://www.cipe.org/

- Web page of CNN, URL: http://www.cnn.com

- Web page of Confederation of British Industry, URL: http://www.cbi.org.uk/
- Web page of Connecticut University, URL: http://www.uconn.edu/
- Web page of Croatian Government, URL: http://www.hfp.hr/privatization/privat.htm
- Web page of Economic Development Agency of Albanian Government, URL: http://www.aeda.gov.al
- Web page of Estonian Privatisation Agency, URL: http://www.eea.ee/
- Web page of International Labour Organisation, URL: http://www.ilo.org/
- Web page of International Monetary Fund, URL: http://www.imf.org
- Web page of Latvian Government, URL: http://www.lpa.bkc.lv/Lpa02GB.htm
- Web page of Latvian Privatisation Agency, URL: http://www.lpa.bkc.lv
- Web page of Lithuanian State Privatisation Agency and State Property Fund, URL: http://www.vtf.lb/
- Web page of M2 PressWIRE, URL: http://www.presswire.net (An electronic press release distribution service)
- Web page of Macedonian Privatisation Agency, URL: http//www.mpa.org.mk/
- Web page of Ministry for Administration and Privatisation of National Property of the Slovak Republic, URL: http://www.privatiz.gov.sk/anglicky/act92.htm
- Web page of OECD, URL: http://www.oecd.org/
- Web Page of Polish Privatisation Agency, URL: http://www.mst.gov.pl/
- Web page of Railtrack, URL: http://www.railtrack.co.uk/

- Web page of Republic of Macedonia Ministry of Transport and Communications, URL: http:/www.mpt.com.mk

- Web page of State Property Fund of Ukraine, URL: http://www.ukrmassp.kiev.ua/Prgrm98-1.htm

- Web page of the European Union, URL: http://europa.eu.int

- Web page of The Federation of European Employers, URL: http://www.euen.co.uk/

- Web page of the Turkish Government Competition Authority (Türk Rekabet Kurumu), URL: http://www.rekabet.gov.tr

- Web page of the Turkish Parliament, URL: http://www.tbmm.gov.tr/

- Web page of the United Kingdom Treasury, URL: http://www.hm-treasury.gov.uk/

- Web page of the World Bank, URL: http://www.worldbank.org/

- Web Page of Turkish Embassy in Washington, DC, URL: http://www.turkey.org/

- Web page of Turkish Ministry of Trade, URL: http://www.sanayi.gov.tr/

- Web page of Turkish Privatisation Administration, URL: http://www.oib.gov.tr/

- Web page of UK Competition Commission, URL: http://www.competition-commission.org.uk/

- Web page of UK Electricity Industry, URL: http://www.electricity.org.uk/

- Web page of Web Journal of Current Legal Issues, URL: http://webjcli.ncl.ac.uk

- Web page of, Lithuanian Business Information Centre, URL: http://www.lbic.lt/

Printed in the United Kingdom
by Lightning Source UK Ltd.
101255UKS00001B/39